Corporate Governance and Its Implications on Accounting and Finance

Ahmad Alqatan
University of Portsmouth, UK

Khaled Hussainey
University of Portsmouth, UK

Hichem Khlif
University of Sfax, Tunisia

A volume in the Advances in Finance, Accounting, and Economics (AFAE) Book Series

IGI Global
PUBLISHER of TIMELY KNOWLEDGE

Published in the United States of America by
IGI Global
Business Science Reference (an imprint of IGI Global)
701 E. Chocolate Avenue
Hershey PA, USA 17033
Tel: 717-533-8845
Fax: 717-533-8661
E-mail: cust@igi-global.com
Web site: http://www.igi-global.com

Library of Congress Cataloging-in-Publication Data

Names: Alqatan, Ahmad J., 1988- editor. | Hussainey, Khaled, 1972- editor. | Khlif, Hichem, 1982- editor.
Title: Corporate governance and its implications on accounting and finance / Ahmad J. Alqatan, Khaled Hussainey, Hichem Khlif.
Description: Hershey : Business Science Reference, 2020. | Includes bibliographical references and index. | Summary: "This book explores the implications of a good corporate governance system after global financial crises. Corporate governance mechanisms may include board and audit committee characteristics, ownership structure, and internal and external auditing"-- Provided by publisher.
Identifiers: LCCN 2020005765 (print) | LCCN 2020005766 (ebook) | ISBN 9781799848523 (hardcover) | ISBN 9781799854463 (paperback) | ISBN 9781799848530 (ebook)
Subjects: LCSH: Corporate governance. | Social responsibility of business. | Accounting,
Classification: LCC HD2741 .C77481772 2020 (print) | LCC HD2741 (ebook) | DDC 338.6--dc23
LC record available at https://lccn.loc.gov/2020005765
LC ebook record available at https://lccn.loc.gov/2020005766

This book is published in the IGI Global book series Advances in Finance, Accounting, and Economics (AFAE) (ISSN: 2327-5677; eISSN: 2327-5685)

British Cataloguing in Publication Data
A Cataloguing in Publication record for this book is available from the British Library.

Advances in Finance, Accounting, and Economics (AFAE) Book Series

Ahmed Driouchi
Al Akhawayn University, Morocco

ISSN:2327-5677
EISSN:2327-5685

Mission

In our changing economic and business environment, it is important to consider the financial changes occurring internationally as well as within individual organizations and business environments. Understanding these changes as well as the factors that influence them is crucial in preparing for our financial future and ensuring economic sustainability and growth.

The **Advances in Finance, Accounting, and Economics (AFAE)** book series aims to publish comprehensive and informative titles in all areas of economics and economic theory, finance, and accounting to assist in advancing the available knowledge and providing for further research development in these dynamic fields.

Coverage

- Microeconomics
- Applied Accounting
- Finance
- Economics of Agriculture and Biotechnology
- Macroeconomics
- Statistical Analysis
- Comparative Accounting Systems
- Economic Downturn
- Ethics in Accounting and Finance
- Investments and Derivatives

IGI Global is currently accepting manuscripts for publication within this series. To submit a proposal for a volume in this series, please contact our Acquisition Editors at Acquisitions@igi-global.com or visit: http://www.igi-global.com/publish/.

The Advances in Finance, Accounting, and Economics (AFAE) Book Series (ISSN 2327-5677) is published by IGI Global, 701 E. Chocolate Avenue, Hershey, PA 17033-1240, USA, www.igi-global.com. This series is composed of titles available for purchase individually; each title is edited to be contextually exclusive from any other title within the series. For pricing and ordering information please visit http://www.igi-global.com/book-series/advances-finance-accounting-economics/73685. Postmaster: Send all address changes to above address.

Titles in this Series

For a list of additional titles in this series, please visit:
https://www.igi-global.com/book-series/advances-finance-accounting-economics/73685

Handbook of Research on Emerging Theories, Models, and Applications of Financial Econometrics
Burcu Adıgüzel Mercangöz (Istanbul University, Turkey)
Business Science Reference • © 2020 • 300pp • H/C (ISBN: 9781799831969) • US $275.00

Circular Economy and Re-Commerce in the Fashion Industry
Archana Shrivastava (Jaypee Business School, JIIT, Noida, India) Geetika Jain (FMS, Amity University, Noida, India) and Justin Paul (University of Puerto Rico, Puerto Rico)
Business Science Reference • © 2020 • 204pp • H/C (ISBN: 9781799827283) • US $195.00

Mapping, Managing, and Crafting Sustainable Business Strategies for the Circular Economy
Susana Serrano Rodrigues (Polytechnic Institute of Leiria, Portugal) Paulo Jorge Almeida (Polytechnic Institute of Leiria, Portugal) and Nuno Miguel Castaheira Almeida (Polytechnic Institute of Leiria, Portugal)
Business Science Reference • © 2020 • 401pp • H/C (ISBN: 9781522598855) • US $195.00

Applied Econometric Analysis Emerging Research and Opportunities
Brian W. Sloboda (University of Phoenix, USA) and Yaya Sissoko (Indiana University of Pennsylvania, USA)
Business Science Reference • © 2020 • 264pp • H/C (ISBN: 9781799810933) • US $195.00

Handbook of Research on Accounting and Financial Studies
Luís Farinha (University of Beira Interior, Portugal) Ana Baltazar Cruz (School of Management, Polytechnic Institute of Castelo Branco, Portugal) and João Renato Sebastião (Polytechnic Institute of Castelo Branco, Portugal)
Business Science Reference • © 2020 • 487pp • H/C (ISBN: 9781799821366) • US $295.00

Emerging Tools and Strategies for Financial Management
Begoña Álvarez-García (Universidade da Coruña, Spain) and José-Pablo Abeal-Vázquez (Universidade da Coruña, Spain)
Business Science Reference • © 2020 • 357pp • H/C (ISBN: 9781799824404) • US $225.00

Recent Advances and Applications in Alternative Investments
Constantin Zopounidis (Technical University of Crete, Greece & Audencia Business School, France) Dimitris Kenourgios (National and Kapodistrian University of Athens, Greece) and George Dotsis (National and Kapodistrian University of Athens, Greece)
Business Science Reference • © 2020 • 385pp • H/C (ISBN: 9781799824367) • US $205.00

IGI Global
PUBLISHER of TIMELY KNOWLEDGE

701 East Chocolate Avenue, Hershey, PA 17033, USA
Tel: 717-533-8845 x100 • Fax: 717-533-8661
E-Mail: cust@igi-global.com • www.igi-global.com

Table of Contents

Detailed Table of Contents

Previous research studies have used multiple theories, such as resource dependence, human capital, social capital, busyness, signalling, behavioural, and agency theories in order to investigate the association between board diversity and earnings management and the association between board diversity and firm performance. This chapter surveys 75 research studies and used 37 theories. Most of the studies focused on agency and resource dependent theories. Also, this study used social capital theory as a contribution of the chapter, which was rarely used and which examined the relationship between board diversity and earnings management in addition to firm performance.

High earnings quality (EQ) is one of the company's pillars of long-term success in building investor confidence. This study investigates whether or not corporate governance (CG) affects the EQ of non-financial companies listed on the Saudi Arabian Stock Exchange known as Tadawul. This research study uses data from a sample of 482 firm-year observations of these companies in the period from 2009 to 2013. The author adopts the Generalized Method of Moments (GMM) regression model. This research study contributes to the current literature by providing new evidence of the effect of CG on the EQ of the Saudi Arabian non-financial companies listed on the Tadawul. Specifically, not all CG attributes affect each company's EQ in the same way. This study's findings show that important CG attributes, which enhance the company's EQ, are the number of the company's independent directors, the separation of the dual role between the company's CEO and chairperson, and the financial or accounting expertise of the members of the company's audit committee members.

The aim of the research is to clarify the role and importance of corporate governance (CG) mechanisms in mitigating earnings management (EM) practices. To achieve this objective, reference was made to previous studies and relevant research. An analysis was mentioned in accounting about the relationship between agency theory and earnings management clarifying the theoretical framework for earnings management from where the concept, motives, techniques of earnings management, methods of disclosure of earnings management, the risks resulting from earnings management, as well as know corporate governance, in terms of concept, goals, importance, principles, characteristics, and mechanisms of corporate governance, and finally, the role of corporate governance in limiting earnings management practices.

Information technology (IT) has become a vital function, and almost all organizations depend on IT. The IT dependency causes the executives to use IT governance practices for the IT investment decision-making process. Organizations spend more on IT investments even those that are over budget, come under pressure, behind schedule, and are generating fewer paybacks than anticipated. Hence, business organizations are continuously examined and believed to be answerable for their IT investment more than ever. This chapter focuses on various IT governance and business-IT alignment frameworks, models, and best practices to discuss in this context.

Although the multifaceted effects of managing or governing IT have been taken into consideration in both practice and theoretical debate, the mechanism through which these bring firm performance is yet unclear and limited. Drawing on the resource-based theory and the process theory, this chapter aims to systematically review the antecedents of business-IT alignment on the firm performance context. The findings of this study show that the business-IT alignment is derived from IT governance practices and managing IT investment to achieve firm performance. This study proposes that the firm performance cannot be attained by merely investing in IT; instead, firms should focus on effective management of IT practices and strategically align their business and IT strategies.

Ceyda Yerdelen Kaygın, Kafkas University, Turkey

The aim of this study is to measure the 2018 financial performance of 49 businesses that are registered in the Istanbul Stock Exchange Corporate Governance Index. Therefore, the financial performances of 49 businesses were compared to the ROA, ROE, ROS, and MV performance indicators that were determined for the measurement of financial performance. For comparison, first, the significance levels of the indicators were determined by the AHP method, and MV was determined to be the most important indicator. The PROMETHEE method was used to be able to financially compare the businesses, and Tüpraş Türkiye Petrol Rafinerileri A.Ş. (Tüpraş Turkey Petroleum Refineries Inc.) was the most successful corporate governance business within the specified time period. The least successful business is Pınar Su ve İçecek Sanayi ve Ticaret A.Ş. (Pınar Water and Drink Industry and Trade Inc).

Chapter 7
Effect of Ownership Structure on Firm Performance Evidence From Non-Financial Listed Firms: Ownership Structure and Performance 143
Muhammad Arslan, KIMEP University, Kazakhstan

In modern organizations, there is a separation between ownership and control of the firm. On the lenses of agency theory, this study statistically examines the relationship between ownership structure (i.e., ownership concentration and owner identity) and firm performance of non-financial listed firms of Pakistan by taking firm-level control variables of size, age, liquidity, financial leverage, and growth of the firm. Secondary data is collected from annual reports of 65 non-financial listed firms for the year 2008 to 2012. The least-square dummy variable model followed by the random effect model has been employed to statistically determining the impact of ownership structure on firm performance. The results of the least square dummy variable model reveal that the ownership concentration has a significant positive impact on firm performance. The owner identity (such as dispersed, family, institutional, and government ownership) has a significant causal effect on firm performance as indicated from t and p values.

Chapter 8
The Effect of the Mandatory IFRS Adoption on Audit Fees in Malaysia 171
Yosra Makni Makni Fourati, Faculté des Sciences Economiques et de Gestion, Université de Sfax, Tunisia
Dorra Bougacha, Faculté des Sciences Economiques et de Gestion, Université de Sfax, Tunisia

This study examines the effect of the mandatory IFRS adoption on audit fees in an emergent context, such as the case of Malaysia. Using a comprehensive dataset of all publicly-traded Malaysians companies, the authors quantify an economy-wide increase in the mean level of audit costs after the IFRS transition. The final sample consists of 204 companies listed on the stock exchange of Malaysia, and publishes their information on audit fees in their annual reports allowed on the site of the Malaysian scholarship (Boursa Malaysia). Empirical results suggest that there has been some increase in audit fees in Malaysia after the mandatory adoption of IFRS in 2012. But this increase is considered more or less significant because Malaysia adopted the IFRS voluntarily in 2006. To discuss this meaning, the authors added an additional test that makes the results more robust.

Chapter 9
The Audit Committee as Component of Corporate Governance: The Case of the Netherlands 188
Sana Masmoudi Mardessi, Ecole Supérieure de Commerce, Université de Sfax, Tunisia

Recently, numerous financial scandals (WorldCom, Enron, Parmalat, eToys) have shown that plentiful companies produce manipulated financial information. Consequently, regulators have prescribed corporate governance structures to protect investors and to avoid fraudulent financial reporting which are likely to control managers and limit their opportunistic behavior. Thus, there has been much debate over the extent to which corporate governance is playing a crucial role in increasing financial reporting quality from the theoretical perspective of agency theory, signaling theory, and stakeholder theory. This chapter aims at scrutinizing the internal and external mechanisms of corporate governance mainly the audit committee in the Dutch context. Firstly, the authors expose the numerous corporate governance mechanisms. Secondly, they focus on the audit committee as the main component of corporate governance, and they present the theoretical background, the role, and the characteristics of audit committee. Eventually, they exhibit the regulatory background of the Dutch context of the audit committee.

The purpose of this chapter is to study the role of the internal audit function in detecting and preventing fraud. First, this chapter will determine the notion and types of fraud on the one hand and the fraud triangle that companies face and that internal auditors try to detect and address on the other hand. Second, a description of the notion of internal audit will be provided, along with the specificities of this function at the heart of companies. The procedure of internal control and the fundamental principles leading to its effectiveness will be identified. In this regard, the authors analysed the profile of internal auditor. Therefore, an internal audit function with competent staff would generate a good system of internal control and is able to maintain the internal audit's ability to detect fraud. Finally, the role of the internal auditor in preventing fraud is analysed with reference to three dimensions: The first dimension is preemptive. The second dimension is social and ethical. The third dimension is the practical dimension.

Family-owned businesses (FOBs) play an important role in the economy of a country through the creation of jobs. However, most FOBs lack strategies regarding succession planning in both developed and developing economies. This study explores the strategies that are used by FOBs to prepare future leaders. Drawing on qualitative research design, this study employed a multiple case study approach and selected 13 cases by employing a purposive sampling technique from the FOBs of Pakistan. Semi-structured interviews were conducted with the successors of FOBs. The findings reveal that succession planning is pivotal for the development of business and the successful transition of FOB from one generation to another. Most of the respondents fully understand the importance of succession planning for the sustainability of the business. However, in some cases, socioemotional aspects of generational succession planning require strategies that concurrently focus on successor suitability, the consensus of the family, mode of transition, leadership, and challenges faced by the FOBs.

The importance of information disclosure is increasing for stakeholders, mainly the non-financial disclosure, and the primary objective of the current study is to investigate the impact of a set of governance attributes on the level of corporate social responsibility disclosure in the Jordanian context. The study sample consisted of 51 industrial companies listed during 2012 to 2017; a set of statistical analyzes were used, such as descriptive statistics and multiple regression. Empirical evidence shows that the board size and audit committee play a crucial role in the social responsibility disclosure, while other factors (board activity, board compensation, non-executive directors, and audit company type) have no effect on disclosure. The findings are expected to have potential effects on the capital market in Jordan in terms of focusing on the strengths that support the social responsibility disclosure and the development of guidelines that contribute to promoting a disclosure culture between the listed companies, which support government plans in achieving sustainability.

This chapter investigates the impact of board structure on the voluntary disclosure level in a Tunisian context. It aims to analyse the relationship between the different boards of directors characteristics of 51 companies listed on the Tunisian Stock Exchange for the year 2010. The empirical results affirm that the board independence and the presence of institutional shareholders in the board have a positive and significant influence on the voluntary disclosure in the Tunisian annual reports. However, the other characteristics presented in the chapter do not have significant impact on voluntary disclosure. This study could be considered as an important extension of prior research investigating the impact of governance mechanisms on voluntary disclosure, particularly those related to the impact of the board directors. It should be noted that, contrary to prior research, this chapter considers both financial and non-financial firms. Also, few studies examined the ownership structure within the board. The findings have potential implications for countries' regulators.

Corporate cash induces the opportunistic behavior of corporate managers that can create an agency problem. A corporate governance system controls the opportunistic behavior of managers and can affect the firm's policy on holding cash. This study explains how the aspects of corporate governance, country-level and firm-level governance, can affect the corporate policy on holding cash. First, the study provides the nature, definition, and importance of corporate cash holdings. Second, it outlines various motivations and theories behind holding corporate cash. Third, it explains the relation between firm-level governance and corporate cash holdings. Fourth, it focuses on the impact of firm-specific governance attributes on the level of corporate cash holdings. Fifth, it presents the relation between country-level governance and corporate cash holdings.

Preface

OVERVIEW

Corporate governance has been gaining momentum over the past decades after several corporate financial scandals in both sides of Atlantic (e.g., Enron, Parmalat). Corporate governance represents a set of processes that help an organization balance conflicting interests between diverse stakeholders (Khlif, Ahmed, & Souissi, 2017). These processes include various internal and external mechanisms such board of directors, audit committee, internal auditing, ownership structure and external auditing.

CHALLENGES

Due to the critical role played by corporate governance in promoting corporate transparency and performance, it becomes crucial for policy makers to establish regulations that fit legal and institutional infrastructure prevailing in their country. The optimal way to manage company may also depend on industry characteristics (e.g., banking and insurance sectors) and the size of the company. Accordingly, different legal and institutional characteristics, industry features and company size may represent challenging factors that may constrain the adoption of a unique corporate governance style, and this goes in line with the general wisdom in management pointing out that no governance style model fits all business structures (Samaha, Khlif, & Hussainey, 2015). This is particularly true in emerging and developing countries where there is a weak legal enforcement and companies are suffering from the lack of resources and they are in dire need of external finance to extend their activities (Barako, Hancock, & Izan, 2006).

SEARCHING FOR SOLUTIONS

Given the diversity observed in corporate governance styles worldwide, it become critical for researchers in management, accounting and finance fields to identify the implications of corporate governance characteristics on accounting and finance. By doing so, they will assist professional bodies and regulators in adopting or adapting governance rules to increase transparency and reduce discretionary power of top management.

ORGANISATION OF THE BOOK

This book is dedicated to the presentation of several studies related to governance and their effects in various emerging countries located in Asian, African, and European settings. Authors contributing to this book have conducted empirical enquiries to examine how ownership structure, board and audit committee characteristics may influence corporate performance, earnings quality, disclosure policy, corporate social responsibility, and cash holdings. Aside from these topics, the remaining chapters have focused on the efficiency of the Shariah supervisory board within Islamic banking industry, the effect of International Financial Reporting Standards (IFRS) adoption on audit fees and Information Technology (IT) corporate governance.

The results reported in the chapters included in this book may be useful to diverse types of readers, with academic or professional background, who are interested in accounting, finance and management fields. For instance, chapters' findings demonstrate that the quality of internal or external governance mechanisms is the cornerstone to increase performance, improve transparency and reduce earnings management. Furthermore, studies included in this book deal with different settings with varying levels of investor protection and diverse qualities of accounting and auditing infrastructure highlighting the importance of institutional setting in shaping corporate governance effects.

Our intent is that this book will impact future accounting and finance empirical enquiries related to corporate governance attributes, on the one hand. On the other hand, the results reported across different chapters may alert policy makers and professionals, worldwide, about the necessity of adopting good governance practices to increase the credibility of accounting numbers reported in financial statements, especially after the economic instability caused by Covid-19 pandemic.

REFERENCES

Barako, D. G., Hancock, P., & Izan, H. Y. (2006). Factors influencing voluntary corporate disclosure by Kenyan companies. *Corporate Governance*, *14*(2), 107–125. doi:10.1111/j.1467-8683.2006.00491.x

Khlif, H., Ahmed, K., & Souissi, M. (2017). Ownership structure and voluntary disclosure: A synthesis of empirical studies. *Australian Journal of Management*, *42*(3), 376–403. doi:10.1177/0312896216641475

Samaha, K., Khlif, H., & Hussainey, K. (2015). The impact of board and audit committee characteristics on voluntary disclosure: A meta-analysis. *Journal of International Accounting, Auditing & Taxation*, *24*(1), 13–28. doi:10.1016/j.intaccaudtax.2014.11.001

Chapter 1
Theories Related to the Relationship Between Board Diversity, Earnings Management, and Firm Performance

Ahmad Alqatan
https://orcid.org/0000-0001-5699-7602
University of Portsmouth, UK

Imad Chbib
University of Portsmouth, UK

Khaled Hussainey
https://orcid.org/0000-0003-3641-1031
University of Portsmouth, UK

ABSTRACT

Previous research studies have used multiple theories, such as resource dependence, human capital, social capital, busyness, signalling, behavioural, and agency theories in order to investigate the association between board diversity and earnings management and the association between board diversity and firm performance. This chapter surveys 75 research studies and used 37 theories. Most of the studies focused on agency and resource dependent theories. Also, this study used social capital theory as a contribution of the chapter, which was rarely used and which examined the relationship between board diversity and earnings management in addition to firm performance.

DOI: 10.4018/978-1-7998-4852-3.ch001

INTRODUCTION

Previous research studies have used multiple theories, such as resource dependence, human capital, social capital, busyness, signalling, behavioural and agency theories, in order to investigate the association between BD and earnings management and the association between BD and firm performance (FP). These studies have additionally investigated the impact of corporate governance codes (CGCs). As shown in Table 1, 75 research studies have used 37 theories. Moreover, as displayed in the chart below, 30 studies have used agency theory and 17 have used resource dependence theory. However, as shown in Table 1 and the chart below, 21 studies did not use any theory. This study contribution is used social capital theory to study the relationship between board diversity and earnings management, besides firm performance.

This research study uses agency and resource dependence theories, which are also those most commonly used in the literature (see Figure 6). Darmadi's (2011) used social capital theory to explain the relationship between BD and FP, while Kim and Lim (2010) used it to study the relationship between the diversity of independent outside directors and company valuation. Nevertheless, few other studies have used this theory in Kuwait. This study uses social capital theory due to its relevance in explaining the relationship between BD and EM as well as the relationship between BD and FP.

Consequently, social capital theory makes several contributions to this research study. The operations of a business firm increase both corporation and conflict. Conflict can occur between the owners and the managers of an organisation when it comes to the division of the value that the firm has created as well as among the BOD while struggling for power and control of rights within the firm. Thus, agency theory, resource dependence theory and social capital theory have been selected to analyse conflict and diversification, from three different perspectives. From the agency theory perspective, conflict among the directors of a company exists when managers at the headquarters are connected in an agency relationship with those in the operating division. However, while there is the incorporation of autonomous decision-making subsidiary managers, their decision-making autonomy may be categorised as discretion (Barroso-Castro et al., 2016). On the other hand, resource dependence theory posits that power is based on ruling over the resources that are considered to be strategic within an organisation and in most instances will be presented in terms of budget and the allocation of resources (Chisholm & Nielsen, 2010). The theory is externally focused and survival in a competitive environment will call for diversification in the BOD. Social capital theory seeks to create a connection between the internal and external environments of an organisation through diversifying the board by hiring females, young people and foreign directors. Thus, the three theories selected in the study provide a complementary framework within which we can understand the decision-making processes of diverse organisations based on gender, age, ND, those with resources and even the establishment of external connections.

There is an integrated relationship between social capital theory and resource dependence theory. Resource dependence theory aims to hire directors who are powerful and have a connection and a good resource better than letting other companies hire him or her. On the other hand, social capital theory focuses on the situation whereby a company needs to hire female, young and foreign directors who have good connections so that the firm can these for its own interests. Thus, we can stipulate that both theories focus on establishing a connection as the main aim for the firm to be competitive (Johnson et al., 2013). In resource dependence theory, the firm is seen as a pool of resources, including intangible resources, which are vital to creating a competitive advantage (Chisholm & Nielsen, 2010). Hence, social capital theory will figure prominently among the intangible resources in strengthening the analytical powers of

Figure 1. Theoretical framework
Source: Kostopoulos et al. (2002)

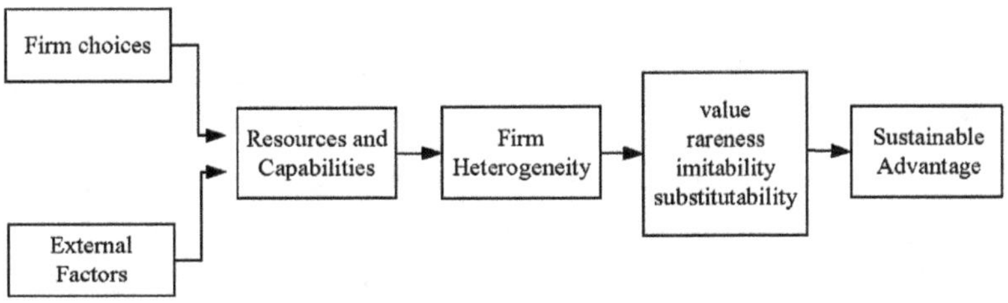

the view of resource dependence theory in relation to several issues. Some of these issues include the relative merits of the firm and markets as the organisational form and the interfirm networks for connections.

As shown in Figure 4, firm choices are guided by the perspectives offered by resource dependence theory and social capital theory. The two theories seek to create good connections with the external environment so that a firm can use these to its competitive advantage. These connections are developed through hiring powerful directors and/or female, young and foreign directors (Barroso-Castro et al., 2016). The resultant development of resources and capabilities will lead to the greater heterogeneity of the organisation and the creation of values within the management, in turn leading to sustainable growth (Kostopoulos et al., 2002).

THEORIES

1. Agency Theory

Agency theory is one of the main theories. At this point, it is essential to explain this theory in order to gain an understanding of the context in which the present study is examining CG practices. According to Jensen and Meckling (1976), agency theory is a contract that describes the relationship between a firm's shareholders and its BOD. This means that the first party (the shareholders) has an agreement with the second party (the BOD) whereby the second party manages the firm's resources (both financial and human) and looks after the first party's interests. Hence, agency theory differentiates between ownership and control, whereby the shareholders own the firm while the BOD is responsible for managing the firm and therefore the shareholders' assets. Bhagat and Black (2002) explain how in an agency theory context, the managers-shareholders relationship presents a significant challenge, because it is linked with agency problems such as conflicts of interest and information asymmetry.

Consequently, agency theory problems arise from the separation between a firm's shareholders and its managers. The BOD, which sits between the shareholders and the managers, is responsible for solving problems and working on behalf of the former to protect their interests and wealth (Donaldson & Davis, 1991; Hermalin & Weisbach, 2003; Rowley, Shipilov, & Greve, 2017). Given that the shareholders are a mixture of men and women, the BOD should also consist of a mix of men and women to provide 'board diversity' and solve the agency theory problem. Furthermore, Das (2019) agrees that it is necessary to use agency theory through BD for firms' CG practices. Similarly, as supported by agency theory, GD has a negative relationship with EM. This means that GD reduces a firm's EM (Hoffmann et al., 2018). Furthermore, Pucheta-Martínez and Gallego-Álvarez (2019) use agency theory to test the relationship between board characteristics, including GD and FP.

Figure 2. Theories used by previous research studies
Created by the author using Excel and Table 1

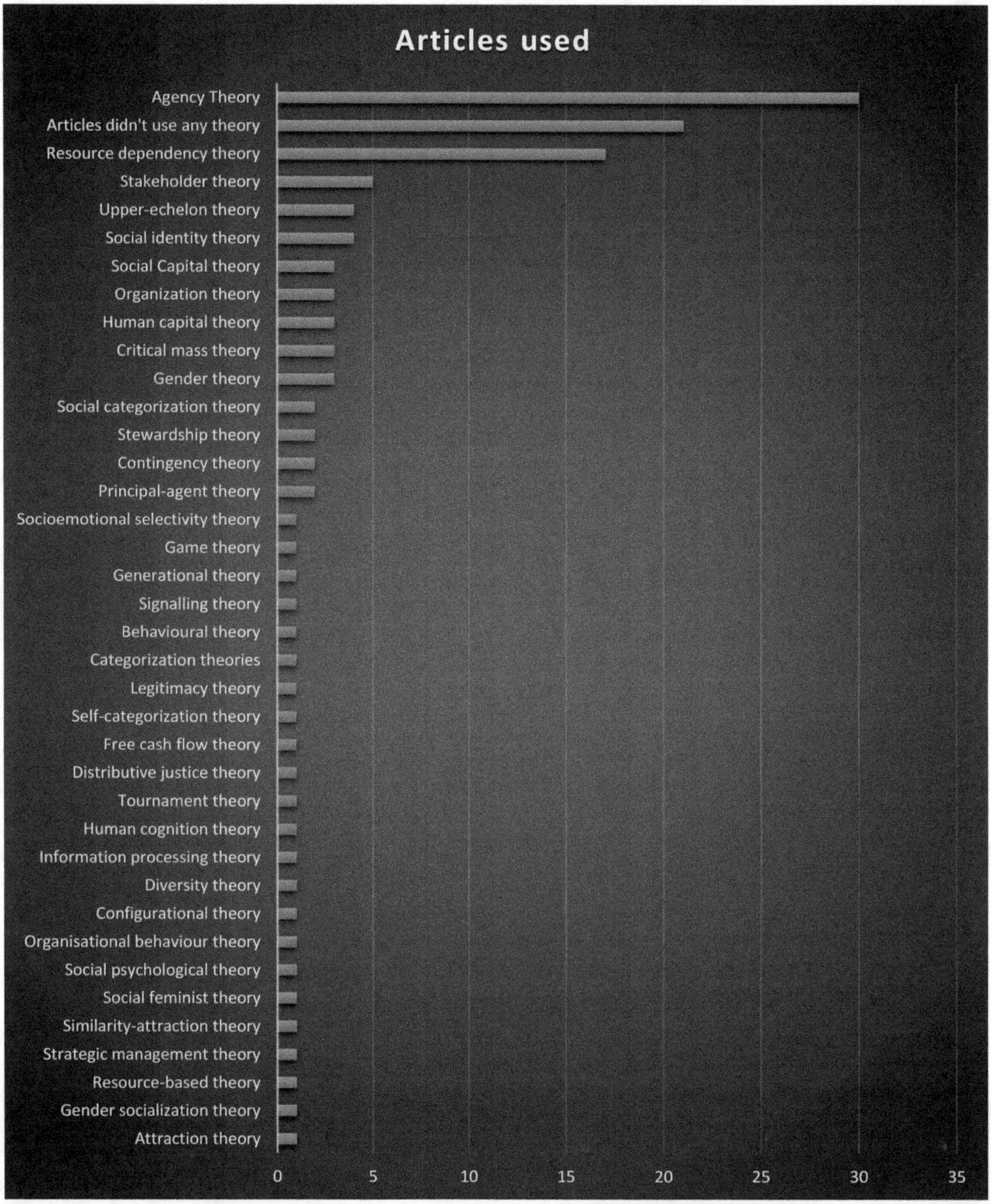

Table 1. Theories used by previous research studies

Theories	Authors
Agency theory	Alshammari & Alsaidi (2014), Arioglu (2018), Carter et al. (2003, 2010), Diepen (2015), Enofe et al. (2017), Erhardt et al. (2003), Eulerich, Velte, & Van (2014), Guedes et al. (2018), Gull et al. (2018), Hoffmann et al. (2018), Jiraporn et al. (2008), Jurkus et al. (2011), Labelle et al. (2010), Lakhal et al. (2015), Low et al. (2015), Lückerath-Rovers (2013), Pucheta-Martínez & Gallego-Álvarez (2019), Rahman et al. (2015), Ramaswamy et al. (2001), Rauf et al. (2012), Robbiano (2019), Rose (2007), Sanda et al. (2008), Shehata et al. (2017), Susanto (2016), Triki Damak (2018), Zalata et al. (2018).
Resource dependency theory	Abdullah et al. (2017), Alesina & La Ferrara (2005) ; Ali & Kulik (2014), Arioglu (2018), Choi & Rainey (2010), Darmadi (2011), Diepen (2015), Eulerich et al. (2014), Gull et al. (2018), Kaplan et al. (2009), Kunze et al. (2011), Low et al. (2015), Lückerath-Rovers (2013), Martín-Ugedo & Minguez-Vera (2014), Pucheta-Martínez & Gallego-Álvarez (2019), Robbiano (2019).
Social identity theory	Al-Mamun et al. (2013), Arioglu (2018), Shehata et al. (2017), Wegge et al. (2008).
Human capital theory	Arioglu (2018), Darmadi (2011); Gull et al. (2018).
Attraction theory	Choi & Rainey (2010).
Social categorisation theory	Choi and Rainey (2010), Tanikawa et al. (2017).
Gender socialisation theory	Clikeman, Geiger, & O'Connell (2001).
Gender theory	Gavious, Segev, & Yosef (2012), Guedes et al. (2018), Triki Damak (2018).
Resource-based theory	Guedes et al. (2018).
Critical mass theory	Joecks et al. (2013), Lakhal et al. (2015), Lückerath-Rovers (2013).
Principal-agent theory	Eulerich et al. (2014), Lausten (2002).
Strategic management theory	Ramaswamy et al. (2001).
Organisation theory	Adams & Ferreira (2009), Ramaswamy et al. (2001), Srinidhi et al. (2011).
Stakeholder theory	Abdullah et al. (2017), Harjoto et al. (2015), Lückerath-Rovers (2013), Sanda et al. (2008), Shehata et al. (2017).
Similarity-attraction theory	Wegge et al. (2008).
Social feminist theory	Alowaihan (2004).
Social capital theory	Darmadi (2011), Johnson et al. (2013), Kim & Lim (2010).
Social psychological theory	Darmadi (2011).
Organisational behaviour theory	Darmadi (2011).
Upper echelons theory	Darmadi (2013), Dwyer et al. (2003), Ferrero-Ferrero et al. (2015), Tanikawa et al. (2017).
Contingency theory	Dwyer et al. (2003), Shehata et al. (2017).
Configurational theory	Dwyer et al. (2003).
Stewardship theory	Eulerich et al. (2014), Low et al. (2015).
Diversity theory	Ferrero-Ferrero et al. (2015).
Information processing theory	Ferrero-Ferrero et al. (2015).
Human cognition theory	Ferrero-Ferrero et al. (2015).
Tournament theory	Ferrero-Ferrero et al. (2015).
Distributive justice theory	Ferrero-Ferrero et al. (2015).
Free cash flow theory	Jurkus et al. (2011).
Self-categorisation theory	Kunze et al. (2011).
Categorisation theories	Martín-Ugedo & Minguez-Vera (2014).
Behavioural theory	Miller et al. (2009).

continues on following page

Table 1. Continued

Theories	Authors
Signalling theory	Miller et al. (2009).
Generational theory	Petersson & Wallin (2017).
Game theory	Rose (2007).
Socioemotional selectivity theory	Tanikawa et al. (2017).
None	Algharaballi & Albuloushi (2008), Arun et al. (2015), Betz et al. (1989), Carter et al. (2007), Croson & Gneezy (2009), Ferreira (2015), Gordini & Rancati (2017), Hart (2004, 2014), Julizaerma & Sori (2012), Krishnan & Parsons (2008), Kunze et al. (2013), Kyaw et al. (2015), Liu et al. (2014), Na & Hong (2017), Omoye et al. (2014), Peni & Vahamaa (2010), Pitts (2005), Powell & Ansic (1997), Strobl, Rama, & Mishra (2016), Wahid (2018).
Total of the theories: 37	Studies: 75

Agency Theory (Managers-Shareholders)

Bhagat and Black (2002) explain how in an agency theory context, the managers-shareholders relationship constitutes a significant challenge because it is linked with agency problems. These problems range from information asymmetry to differentiating between ownership and control. According to Berle and Means (1930), when executive directors have a stake in the firm and the shareholders are inactive in monitoring those executives, there is a high risk that the former will direct the firm's assets towards their interests rather than those of the shareholders. Thus, the issue of conflicts of interest, which are derived from the separation between ownership and control, represent one of the major problems of the agency theory. Therefore, it is argued that an effective mechanism that can mitigate the problem of conflicts of interest is the alignment of shareholders' interests with the BOD's interests.

By using negative or positive mechanisms, a firm's shareholders can fix the issues arising from conflicts of interest in the differentiation of control and ownership (Guest, 2019). For instance, negative actions are portrayed by the dismissal of underperforming managers, shareholders' activism, a hostile takeover, or rejecting and challenging the BOD's proposals. Conversely, positive mechanisms involve the provision of directors' incentives as an approach to motivating them and integrating their interests with shareholders' interests. This is achieved through the provision of long- and short-term financial rewards as a way of linking the BOD's interests to shareholders' concerns. The provision of share ownership to managers mitigates the problem of conflicts of interest and therefore aligns managers' interests with shareholders' interests.

An additional problem that arises from the separation of ownership and control is the issue of information asymmetry. In such circumstances, one party (the directors) has an advantage over the other (shareholders), as they have more private information that they can use to benefit their interests. Information asymmetry is a sensitive concern to shareholders because it is prone to manipulation by the BOD for their gains: manipulation results in shareholders lacking information, thereby translating to poor economic decisions. Depken et al. (2005) argue that the agency problem can be reduced through external mechanisms such as regulation and legislation. This may be achieved through compulsory disclosures in financial reports and standardised reporting formats.

Moral hazard is another problem that arises from the separation of a firm's ownership and management. This arises when the management works in good faith on behalf of the firm's owners but makes some of its actions unobservable by the owners. Consequently, the owners come to be tied into contractual obligations such as risky projects/investments (Kolbjørnsrud, 2017). In such circumstances, the managers use their skills and knowledge in risky investments of which the owners are unaware. However, in the end they are the providers of capital to be invested and the ultimate bearers of the total risk. The probability of the success or failure of such projects/investments is dependent on the management's hidden actions. Therefore, it becomes very difficult for owners to measure the project's progressive performance.

Shareholders can address the management's moral hazard malpractices through the introduction of risk incentives, such as taking some proportion of ownership in all the firm's investments/projects. According to Ratnawati, Abdul-Hamid and Popoola (2016), through such a mechanism, the management is compelled to disclose all information concerning potential firm investment decisions to ensure that all key decision makers are well informed. Therefore, by imposing some risk on the management, the owners' concerns are secured in most if not all of the firm's projects.

The separation of ownership and management additionally brings about the agency problem of the time horizon. The owners have no definite time within which they will own the business and have a long-term view regarding the firm's plans (Kim & Yi, 2006). They are the bearers of the firm's vision and mission statement, which defines why the company exists and how its existence will be maintained. On the other hand, the managers are the firm's employees' company and their stay is defined by the contractual agreement between them and the firm. In addition to contractual obligations, they have their own interests and ambitions, such as climbing the corporate ladder or increasing their bargaining power for the next job opportunity. These two-timing perspectives bring about a severe conflict of interest between the firm's owners and the managers. Consequently, there is a justifiable need to create a mechanism that harmonises the timing of these two perspectives (Kolbjørnsrud, 2017).

The time horizon problem also arises in terms of when cash flows are expected from an investment. The management is concerned with projects that will generate cash flows in the short term and, more especially, within the period when performance appraisals will be carried out. In this regard, the firm's management prefers projects that affect its remuneration in the shortest possible time. Nevertheless, Kim and Yi (2006) state that owners are more concerned with projects that result in long-term, sustainable cash flows. Most projects with such cash flows are long-term in nature and therefore require long-term capital commitments. These exert less pressure on owners and are hence preferable to them.

Similar to any other agency problem, the time horizon requires carefully considered mechanisms in order to ensure that it does not hinder the firm's vision and mission statement. One way to achieve this aim is to align contractual management obligations, such as employment contracts, to the firm's long-term plans (Panda & Leepsa, 2017). Another approach is to give the management shares in the firm and thereby turn them into the firm's owners. Accordingly, the two groups' interests are harmonised and thus the conflict between them is minimised. Moreover, the firm's value is increased because all decisions are aimed at maximising the owners' wealth.

BD, particularly in the form of gender, age and nationality, has a significant impact on FP. Terjesen, Couto and Francisco's (2016) multi-country study of BD has examined the effects of female BODs on FP. Their findings suggest that firms with more female directors report higher performance in terms of market and accounting measures. Moreover, their results suggest that, unless the board is gender-diversified, a non-diverse board is less likely to contribute towards improving the firm's performance. Consequently, their study rejects the hypothesis by confirming that there is a positive association between GD and FP.

Agency theory helps to highlight the inherent conflicts between the management's needs and the owner's interests. Terjesen et al. (2016) are among the authors to have used agency theory to explore whether or not the presence of female BODs affects FP. Their multi-country study of BD notes that the agency theoretical perspective suggests that board directors are less likely to have conflicts of interest with the firm. In turn, this ensures that they offer impartial judgments and provide greater integrity. However, although BODs both value and strive towards preserving their reputations, they are often required to represent the shareholders' interests and potentially take a stand against the firm's management (Adams et al. 2010). Adams et al. (2010) have also used agency theory to examine BODs' role in firms' CG. These authors have developed a conceptual framework and survey showing that board of members' concerns for their reputations are more likely to cause them (agents) to act more in their principal's interests than standard approaches. For example, a strong as opposed to weak reputation presumably helps agents to obtain more seats on the board or retain existing ones. Consequently, diverse BODs bring their previous experience with them, enabling them to reinforce their firms' FP.

Agency theory is concerned with mitigating the problems within agency relationships caused by unaligned goals. Consequently, the theory can help address the challenges associated with the relationship between board and monitoring committees concerned with EM. According to Osma and Noguer (2007), board composition plays a significant role in determining the manipulation practices that should be enforced in EM. Further, Thiruvadi and Huang (2011) state that the presence of female on the audit committee increases negative discretionary accruals that reduce the firm's income. In turn, this constrains EM.

Thiruvadi and Huang's (2011) study contributes four aspects to the existing literature on GD and EM. First, their study leverages agency theory to highlight the effects of unaligned goals on agency relationships within an audit committee. For example, the authors provide new evidence that suggests that, when compared to men, women are more risk-averse and ethical. As a result, female directors on the audit committee are more likely to exhibit caution when determining EM (Huang, 2011). Second, Thiruvadi and Huang's (2011) findings highlight how sex-linked characteristics are transmitted and maintained across boards and organisational cultures. Third, their findings are crucial to developing a better understanding of BODs' contemporary CG practices and their impact on EM and FP. Fourth, this study highlights the importance of BD in reinforcing FP.

2. Resource Dependence Theory

Resource dependence theory refers to the impact of resource acquisition on a firm's behaviour (Hillman et al., 2009). The theory is based on the principle that, in order to acquire resources, a firm must engage in transactions with other actors and firms in its environment (Pfeffer, 1982). In this regard, as explained by Pfeffer and Salancik (1978), through co-selecting the assets expected to survive, a firm's BOD serves as the link between the firm and its external factors. Therefore, the board serves as an essential instrument in bringing necessary components of ecological vulnerability into the firm. With regard to the board, resource dependence theory addresses how it facilitates access to valuable resources. As Rondoy et al. (2006) have explained, the theory emphasises a firm's ability to form links in order to secure access to critical resources, including capital, customers, suppliers and cooperative partners. Given that it is likely to have different insights, a more diverse board is deemed to have a greater ability to understand customers' needs. According to Thomsen and Conyon (2012) with respect to nationality, education, experience and background, BD means that the BOD has a considerable range of knowledge and skills. Accordingly, its members can offer more significant insights into markets, customers, employees and business opportunities. This is likely to lead to a better understanding of business conditions and hence better FP (Hillman et al., 2000). For instance, given that women offer more insights, a more gender-diverse BOD is better able to understand the needs of the entire market. Therefore, female representatives on the board are better able to understand women's requirements; the same is true of male representatives (Drees & Heugens, 2013; Hillman et al., 2007). The same can be said of AD, where having board members of different ages is essential for the firm being able to meet the needs of all ages within the market. In addition, ND on the BOD brings different insights with regard to different nationalities. This is important in ensuring the firm's ability to acquire various resources that are vital to its success (Carter et al., 2010). Based on resource dependence theory, Pucheta-Martínez and Gallego-Álvarez (2019) claim that an effective CG system attracts aptitude and investment and thereby increases the firm's confidence.

Resource dependence theory is significant to this study because it has implications regarding the recruitment of a firm's board members and the optimal divisional structure of its EM and FP. Unlike the other theories, resource dependence theory helps in responding to all the research questions as well as testing this study's hypotheses. In this way, it facilitates the development of an in-depth understanding of how a board's GD, AD and ND affect both EM and FP. Resource dependence theory assumes that the BOD is an essential part of the firm and its environment. It provides the resources and information necessary to mitigate risks, which help to cushion the firm against any uncertainties within both its external and internal environments. Hessels and Terjesen (2010) argue that resource dependence theory reinforces the fact that, based on their respective backgrounds, board members bring information and resources to the firm. Therefore, resource dependency theory may be the most effective model in examining the consequences of BD. The theory accepts that there is a negative association between GD and EM in Kuwaiti non-financial firms listed on Boursa Kuwait because it assumes that these firms are contingent on multidimensional resources. Consequently, a board's gender quota does not play a central role in developing countervailing initiatives aimed at managing all the earnings generated through the firm's multiple resources. As a result, these firms should put greater emphasis on the principles of scarcity and criticality rather than focusing on the effects of their boards' GD on EM.

Singh (2007) draws on resource dependency theory to examine the human and social capital of ethnic minority directors. The theory helps Singh to explore how a firm's external resources affect its tactical and strategic management. According to this author, the BOD has more social capital than its ethnic majority counterpart, rendering it a key driver in improving FP.

In addition to linking ND with increased FP, resource dependence theory supports the hypothesis that, in the case of Kuwaiti non-financial firms listed on Boursa Kuwait, there is a positive association between AD and FP. One of the theory's primary assumptions is that board members perform an internal control function and that they can influence their firm's efficiency through administrative efforts. Thus, the board's AD can play a central role in determining FP because people often adopt policies that reflect their age groups. According to Makhlouf, Laili, Basah and Siam (2015), older directors are more likely to avoid making risky decisions, whereas their younger counterparts are more inclined towards developing and implementing riskier strategies. Therefore, firms with younger directors may experience higher rates of growth than those with older directors. In turn, this confirms that in the case of Kuwaiti non-financial firms listed on Boursa Kuwait, there exists a positive association between AD and FP.

However, unlike FP, there is a negative association between AD and EM in such firms. For example, older directors have significant impacts on certain performance measures, such as cumulative returns and abnormal returns (Ararat, Aksu, & Tansel Cetin, 2010). According to Nakano and Nguyen (2011), while there is a significant negative relationship between a board's AD and EM, it becomes even more significant after using ROA as the controlling variable. These research findings are also consistent with agency theory, whereby in strongly performing firms, older directors are more likely to retain their board positions. Thus, the proportion of young board members is more likely to relate positively to the firm's overall performance rather than its EM (Darmadi, 2011).

Julizaerma and Sori (2012) consider GD an emerging issue in the corporate world. Omar and Davidson (2001) add that, despite the dramatic increase in the number of women seeking managerial careers, their representation on BODs remains low. Carter, Simkinsand and Simpson's (2003) study provides evidence that, in the case of Kuwaiti non-financial firms listed on Boursa Kuwait, there is a positive association between GD and FP. The authors argue that BD is essential to increasing a board's independence as women are more likely to ask questions that their male counterparts avoid. Moreover, due to the collaborative skills that women often bring with them, the presence of female directors on a firm's board makes a significant contribution to the firm's bottom line. Adams and Ferreira's (2009) study on the impact of women in the boardroom with regard to CG and FP has found a significant positive relationship between a firm's GD and ROA. This is consistent with hypothesis H4, which states that in the case of Kuwaiti non-financial firms listed on Boursa Kuwait, there is a positive association between GD and FP. Moreover, resource dependency theory supports the hypotheses because it is more concerned with the humane resources that often originate in the firm's environment, namely the board. Consequently, a gender-diverse board is more likely to be positively associated with higher levels of FP.

While resource dependence theory helps to examine the consequences of BD, it has several problems that undermine its efficiency in measuring the impact of BD on both EM and FP. Resource dependence theory is less expansive than institutional and behavioural theories. Indeed, behavioural theories leverage a wider perspective and are more open to scholars interested in one of their central concepts (Ferreira, 2009). Its lack of open approach makes it difficult for resource dependence theory to evolve quickly from explaining the rationalisation of the firm to a broader theory related to its macro-cultural environment. Consequently, resource dependence theory is less flexible, hence most management scholars shy away from it, not least when seeking non-economic explanations for a specific firm phenomenon. This is because behavioural and institutional theories are often perceived as being more flexible from a theoretical perspective. Consequently, these theories have become a formidable competitor to resource dependence theory. The various problems associated with resource dependence theory indicate that it may no longer be an effective theoretical model. However, this study uses resource dependence theory because it can inspire necessary insights and interpretations to appraise the impact of BD on EM and FP. Moreover, resource dependence theory provides this study with a window into understanding what makes a theoretical programme successful.

In addition, resource dependence theory is one of the most influential economic models of workplace diversity because it sets the framework of a firm's policies, especially when determining EM and FP. One of the primary strategies in determining a firm's economic performance involves employing a conception of board members as human capital and different economic metaphors such as innovation, technological change, productivity and competitiveness.

The theoretical perspectives developed in strategic management focus on establishing why some boards consistently outperform others in the same industry (Barney & Clark, 2007). From a wider perspective, the resource dependence school of thought focuses on determining how a board is able to reinforce a firm's competitive advantage from within its own resources. Resource dependence theory model assumes that if a board uses its resources effectively to utilise opportunities and neutralise threats, the firm's competences and resources will serve as a source of competitive advantage. Thus, the resource dependency paradigm is likely to dominate in the board's decision-making processes. Barney and Clark (2007) note that board members are not expected to agree with every decision and instead are supposed to leverage their diverse backgrounds, opinions and inputs to achieve a holistic perspective of the issues at hand. Consequently, resource dependency theory supports BD and supports the hypothesis that, in the case of Kuwaiti non-financial firms listed on Boursa Kuwait, there is a positive association between GD and FP.

In conclusion, resource dependence theory helps to show that, in the case of Kuwaiti non-financial firms listed on Boursa Kuwait, there is a negative association between GD and AD and between ND and EM. The theoretical perspectives developed for the resource dependence model indicate that a more diverse board is better positioned to make superior decisions through brainstorming to improve FP. Moreover, the theory helps to highlight the negative association between ND and EM in the case of Kuwaiti non-financial firms listed on Boursa Kuwait. The resource dependence model agrees with the theoretical assumption that, when compared with a non-diverse board, a diverse board uses more information and makes better contributions to discussions. Consequently, resource dependence theory shows that in the case of Kuwaiti non-financial firms listed on Boursa Kuwait, there is a positive association between GD and FP, between AD and FP and between ND and FP. Moreover, the theoretical perspectives indicate that firms with more GD, AD and ND on their boards perform better and have superior financial returns. Thus, the theory supports the hypothesis that in the case of Kuwaiti non-financial firms listed on Boursa Kuwait, there is a positive association between BD and FP.

3. Social Capital Theory

Social capital can be defined as all the resources – whether real or implicit – that a person or group accrues through possessing a long-lasting network of institutionalised relationships of shared contact and respect (Hernández-Carrión et al., 2020; Sealy & Vinnicombe, 2007). It has also been defined as "the ability of actors to secure benefits by virtue of membership in social networks or social structures" (Portes, 1998, p. 6). Social capital encompasses the advantages that individuals or collective actors possess owing to their location in the social network structure. Age diversification assists in the utilisation of natural resources and threats that an organisation may encounter while establishing links with its external environment. Consequently, the theory advocates diversity given that a diverse BOD is able to bring in various types of social capital from its members (Niu & Chen, 2017). For instance, given that both genders differ considerably in terms of social capital, a gender-diverse board is likely to have more social capital than a single-gender board. The same case applies to ND boards (Adams & Ferreira, 2009). This is because different nationalities present significant variations that are likely to result in substantially diverse social capital (Luckerath-Rovers, 2013). In addition, AD on a BOD brings with it a wealth of social capital. This is because different age groups offer different insights and the inclusion of every age group on a board brings different forms of social capital. Therefore, a board with various aspects is likely to possess more social capital and hence it is likely to perform better than a board that has no diversity (Carter et al., 2010).

Social capital on the board encompasses two types of relationships, namely internal and external connections. Internal social capital can be measured through the experiences of co-workers on the board (Barroso-Castro et al., 2016). By contrast, external social capital can be determined through the links that the board has with outside organisations from the interlocking directorates (Sealy & Vinnicombe, 2007). From the theory, we can stipulate that when organisations reconsider members of their boards, they should aim to increase internal connections, in addition to considering the primary role played by internal social capital. In order to increase external connections and use them to their advantage, organisations must hire female, young and foreign directors who have already established good connections externally (Barroso-Castro et al., 2016).

Social capital theory is significant in this study because it encourages BD. The theory holds that diverse boards are better positioned to leverage various forms of social capital from their members. The concept of social capital helps to describe the board's participation in EM and FP. This viewpoint tends to reinforce the hypothesis that, in the case of Kuwaiti non-financial firms listed on Boursa Kuwait, there is a negative association between EM and ND and the average age of the directors. The theory suggests that directors on less diverse boards possess significant social capital, which strengthens the firm's ability to monitor earnings. Ooi et al.'s (2017) findings support the theory's viewpoint by providing evidence that BD – especially in terms of human and social capital – does not significantly improve FP, but rather mitigates the negative impacts of crises that undermine it. Johnson et al. (2013) further support this perspective by stating that a board's composition is crucial in contributing to its ability to determine an organisation's outcome. While most of the arguments presented in different articles have focused on the size and the independence of the board, Johnson et al. (2013) emphasise the composition of the board based on demography. They suggest that there is no correlation between various demographic traits such as gender, age, race and ethnicity with the level of performance of the organisation (Johnson et al., 2013). However, social capital has a significant influence on the advice and counsel that the directors will provide; moreover, it will also affect the decision-making process. Tasheva and Hillman (2019) have presented an argument as to the benefits of diversification for team effectiveness. They suggest that diversity is multifaceted, as it entails different sources, including demographic, human capital and social capital, all of which operate at different levels. Hence, the diversity that takes place at both the individual and the team level is not independent, as there should be a link ensuring the effectiveness of the performance of the directors of an organisation (Tasheva & Hillman, 2019). Social capital is the conduit from the flow of resources and information in both the internal and external environment of an organisation.

Unlike cultural and physical capital, social capital is contingent on the BOD being a part of the connections that they keep and the extent to which they engage with the firm's management (Stevenson & Radin, 2009). For example, in a large multinational corporation, the chairman of the board possesses a significant amount of social capital because he or she maintains a large and influential social network developed throughout his or her career. The chairman enjoys even more social capital if the board is more diverse and this leads to more positive outcomes for the firm (Mabogunje & Kates, 2020; Stevenson & Radin, 2009). Consequently, social capital theory accepts the hypothesis that, in the case of Kuwaiti non-financial firms listed on Boursa Kuwait, there is a positive association between a firm's performance and gender, age and ND. The approach establishes how social capital at the individual level will affect the choice of directors as well as the effectiveness of the board selected. At the personal level, social capital largely depends on the interpersonal linkages that each of the directors has both in the internal and the external environment of the organisation (Kim & Cannella, 2008). However, at the group level, social capital will represent an asset that incorporates both the relationships of the directors and other potential resources resulting from the link. Hence, theoretically, social capital can be divided into internal and external types based on locus and function. Chisholm and Nielsen (2010) support the argument by stipulating that both internal and external social capital are in a position to generate unique resources that will prove relevant to the level of effectiveness of the BOD.

The benefits of BD in terms of AD and ND can be categorised into five distinct business rationales: market rationale, talent rationale, employee relations rationale, litigation rationale and governance rationale (Booth-Bell, 2018). In this regard, Booth-Bell (2018) argues that, if social capital theory's viewpoint regarding a director's ability to secure crucial human resources for his or her firm is taken into consideration, the social capital rationale becomes one of the primary benefits associated with BD. First, the market rationale suggests that boards with both younger and older directors are more likely to maximise their market share by leveraging the innovative and risk-oriented mindset of the younger directors while taking into account the risk factors (which have the potential to undermine the firm's success) often highlighted by the older directors. Second, diverse boards with directors from different age groups are more likely to have varying talents, a key driver in making successful strategic decisions. For example, younger directors may offer crucial insights about fostering innovations. Older directors may share their views but also know how to maintain such innovations sustainably, in turn improving overall FP. Moreover, talent has become the primary competitive advantage for firms (Booth-Bell, 2018). Third, BD in ND helps to improve overall employee relations, especially in multinational companies (Dore, 1973). Successful employee relations strategies leverage diversity and inclusion programmes in the workplace. However, a firm cannot have a comprehensive employee relations programme if the board itself does not lead by example. Therefore, diverse boards are more likely to motivate employees by reducing the risks of racial or ethnic segregation. Finally, diverse boards with directors from different age groups and nationalities are more likely to report better outcomes when addressing their litigation and governance issues.

Giannetti, Liao and Yu (2015) present an argument on the implication of the foreign experiences of foreign directors regarding the level of FP in the upcoming market. They suggest that foreign directors transmit knowledge to the organisation concerning various management practices and corporate governance. Oxelheim and Randoy (2003) offer a similar argument, as they try to establish the effects that the board membership of foreigners has for the level of corporate performance of an organisation. Their argument suggests that superior performance is an indication that a company has completely broken from the partially segmented domestic capital market. Other than the market rationale and different age groups, Kim (2005) suggests the need to consider the network characteristics of the BOD. The two main network characteristics are the board network density and the board's external social capital. Density will determine the extensiveness and the cohesiveness of interaction between members. External social capital, on the other hand, will establish the level to which the members of the board have connections with the outside world. Having a moderate level of board network density is crucial to enhancing a firm's value, as an excess will lead to destruction (Kim, 2005). Corporate boards are the focal point for the strategic and investment decisions of a firm. Boards that are more diverse and that include individuals with different nationalities perform positively, and in most instances they are connected with stakeholders' heterogeneity and the various international market operations available (Estélyi & Nisar, 2016).

Seibert, Kraimer and Liden (2001) note that firms can improve their social capital irrespective of their financial situation, age or future plans by appointing more educated directors, exploring beyond their industry, being more versatile and gaining more experience. While the debate continues on whether or not certain levels of education among directors are worth the investment, often the return on investment in social capital is contingent on the quality of the human resources. Thus, a firm's return on an educational investment has far-reaching implications and has the potential to improve its overall outcomes (Seibert, Kraimer & Liden, 2001). However, older directors are often more educated than younger counterparts. Consequently, it is necessary to maintain a diverse board to ensure sustainability in EM and FP. Gaining more experience opens up a firm to more opportunities for advancement (Seibert et al. 2001). In this way, different groups of people bring with them varying experiences. Consequently, maintaining a diverse board may be one of the most effective ways of increasing a firm's overall social capital. Finally, a versatile board is more likely to explore opportunities for growth beyond the firm's industry. A board comprising directors from diverse genders, ages and nationalities means that it is valuable in more than one area. Therefore, diversity plays a central role in helping a firm to excel at multiple facets even beyond its industry. In turn, this results in better earnings quality and FP. There is a clear connection between the valuation of an organisation and the proportion of the outside BD who are independent (Kim & Lim, 2010). The diversification of the outside directors focuses on the academic degree and age, which is believed to have a positive effect on the valuation process of the firm. Not only will the quantity be implicated, but also the quality of the outside independent directors will affect the valuation process of the organisation. Peck-Ling, Nai-Chiek and Chee-Seong (2016) support this opinion by suggesting that an increase in the number of foreign directors sitting on a board plays a key role in increasing the ROE. However, only when foreign investors dominate the voting rights will the ROE increase. Polovina and Peasnell (2015) provide an outcome that strongly supports the need for having foreign directors as board members. The presence of foreign board directors has a positive impact on the profitability level of the majority of foreign-acquired banks and an increase in income creates on the interest operations. Foreign directors have a significant positive impact on a firm's performance, measured by ROA, ROE and market value (Rahman, 2018). However, in line with many people's expectations, foreign directors have created negative implications for the monitoring role of boards due to their different languages and backgrounds.

Social capital theory can help to develop a better understanding of the consequences of BD (Aguilera, 2005). The theory highlights the importance of diversity in increasing a firm's ability to recognise and value the differences that each director brings to the board (Lin, 2002). Although the primary aspects of workplace diversity revolve around obvious traits such as gender, age and nationality, there are other less noticeable aspects. These include employees' thinking and working styles (Gul et al., 2011; Reguera-Alvarado et al., 2017). One of social capital theory's primary arguments is that firms should leverage these differences to drive FP (Van der Walt & Ingley, 2003). For example, a highly diverse board is more likely to remain open-minded, progressive and unbiased when making critical decisions. In turn, these qualities reinforce innovation and the level of employee engagement and motivation (Adler & Kwon, 2002; Lin et al., 1981). Highly engaged employees play a central role in providing a firm with a competitive edge over its rivals. Moreover, especially in the short term, a board's decisions become easier to implement (Cyert & March, 1963; Hambrick & Mason, 1984; Haynes & Hillman, 2010).

The need for boardroom diversity has grown over the past three decades with firms today seeking directors with diverse skills and perspectives. Miller and del Carmen Triana (2009) note that the broad acceptance of the need for BD has been fuelled primarily by strong evidence from theoretical studies showing a strong correlation globally between BD and FP. The importance of increased BD has been further reinforced by the need to mitigate growing schisms, especially for firms in polarised societies. Parker's (2016) findings into the ethnic diversity of UK boards show that boards must now earn a licence to operate. This makes it necessary to align the board's composition more broadly with its customer base and the local community. Parker (2016) adds that firms that have made use of diverse multi-ethnic and multicultural boards have not only successfully increased their overall FP but also managed workplace conflicts.

The analysis conducted on the consequences of BD suggest that public companies have taken the lead in championing the advantages of BD. This is partly because public companies are expected to be more socially responsible than private ones. Moreover, public companies have a larger social capital that makes it necessary to encourage diversity, especially among the top management. State Street Global Advisors is one of the companies taking the lead in promoting BD. One of the implications of firms advocating boardroom diversity is that now other firms have publicly joined the movement, stimulating investors to seek to conduct business with firms that are inclusive in terms of gender, age and nationality. Most of these firms utilise the concepts advocated by social capital theory, which views social capital as an essential component in improving FP.

Diverse boards in terms of age and nationality exhibit higher levels of expertise and experience. Thus, some firms have made it mandatory to have highly diverse boards, especially with respect to GD. Although social capital theory remained a vague concept in the mid-19th century, it is now the driving concept behind the networks of relationships between people who live and work within a society (Lin et al., 1981; Portes, 1998). Haynes and Hillman (2010) argue that social capital plays a central role in enabling firms to function effectively. Thus, the theory holds that a person's position within a particular group provides unique benefits that work to their advantage as well as that of the firm (Miller & Triana, 2009). For example, when choosing to hire between two directors with identical levels of experience and qualifications, shareholders choose the one who is either better known within the company or serves on more committees, this being essential to the company's income (Hitt et al., 2002; Khoury et al., 2013; Palmer & Barber, 2001; Sundaramurthy et al., 2014). Consequently, the job should be awarded on the basis of social capital. In this case, the director is awarded the job based on his/her level of association with other directors as well as with the firm, the extent to which he/she participates and, occasionally, his/her popularity within the group (Fondas & Sassalos, 2000, p. 172). Social capital theory holds that because it works to their advantage, people are more likely to participate in improving firm outcomes and in bonding with those around them (Reguera-Alvarado et al., 2017). Therefore, one of social capital's potential benefits is that directors will focus on participating towards the well-being of the firm while seeking to create and maintain stronger social bonds with those around them, helping the company to survive and improve its networking (Terjesen et al., 2009).

Although social capital theory helps to highlight the positive association between GD, AD and ND on FP, there are some limitations that undermine its effectiveness in examining the consequences of BD. Erhardt et al. (2003) argue that social capital theory's characteristics, which highlight the productive benefits of leveraging diversity, also result in negative externalities. One of the potential downsides of the theory is its potential to foster behaviours within boards that exacerbate rather than improve EM. Carroll and Stanfield (2003) argue that social capital can undermine a firm's economic performance because it often acts as a barrier to social mobility and inclusion. Moreover, social capital is more likely to divide rather than unite members of a board along the lines of age groups, ethnicity and gender.

Social capital is often defined as the outcome of social relationships. Thus, it not only comprises the financial benefits accrued by a firm but, also the expected benefits often derived from cooperation between individuals and various groups. The primary difference between social capital and financial capital is that the former promotes positive relationships that in turn enhance the confidence and fulfilment of board members. However, despite its numerous benefits, social capital also results in unwanted outcomes. Portes and Landolt (2000) have identified some of the negative effects of social capital, including restrictions on individual freedoms, the exclusion of outsiders and excessive claims on board members. Moreover, the social capital model emphasises the importance of bridging the gap between GD, AD and ND rather than focusing on creating and maintaining the inherent bonds between different people. Consequently, social capital may further widen the gap between people, especially those experiencing reduced social mobility.

Portes and Landolt (2000) state further that directors who work in social enterprises should abide by the set rules and regulations and carry out only the assigned tasks. Thus, new ideas and personal views are not welcome in most cases. Consequently, social capital may be regarded as a liability, especially when the board consists of younger directors who are likely to propose different ways of doing things. Although social capital plays a central role in bridging the gap between the BOD and the firm's CEO, the individuals who benefit the most from social capital tend to lose their mobility. Portes and Landolt (2000) note that the resultant change from social capital is negligible in relation to the mobility trade-off. This often leaves them stuck in the same employment or board position for most of their career.

Another limitation of social capital theory is that, unlike in the case of the firm's employees, it takes no consideration of the impact of outsiders on FP. For example, only a particular section of the top management tends to avail itself of the benefits of social capital and this in turn discourages other employees from actively participating in the firm's decision-making processes. According to Kostova and Roth (2003), most firms' democratic and administrative arrangements are frequently overwhelmed by particular social groups, resulting in adverse outcomes. The situation is regularly exacerbated by workplace diversity, whereby people are more likely to form social groups based on their GD, AD and ND.

From the literature, it can be concluded that both internal and external social capital exist in connection with the composition of the board through direct selection, despite the casual logic differing entirely. Furthermore, the influence of social capital on direct selection varies based on the context of the application (Johnson et al., 2013). Both internal and external social capital create resources that are unique and necessary to a board's effectiveness. However, social capital does not only contribute positively to a board, as there are negative implications such as restrictions on freedom and outside members. Board diversification is necessary as it increases the level of performance and operational efficiency within an organisation (Kim & Lim, 2010).

SUMMARY

In conclusion, the literature review has shown that BD, particularly in the form of GD, AD and ND, has a significant impact on FP. The present study uses agency theory, resource dependence theory and social capital theory to measure the impact of BD on EM and FP. First, agency theory has helped to explain and resolve issues in the relationship between firm principals and their agents. Most commonly, the relationship refers to that between the firm's executive as the agent and the shareholders as the firm's principals. The agency theory has helped to confirm arguing that embedding gender quotas on the membership of a firm's BOD and on its top management may help to increase the values of Kuwaiti non-financial firms listed on Boursa Kuwait. Second, resource dependence theory studies have shown how a firm's external resources affect its behaviour. Resource dependence theory has demonstrated that in the case of Kuwaiti non-financial firms listed on Boursa Kuwait, there is a negative association between AD and EM. Thus, the proportion of young board members is more likely to be positively related to a firm's overall FP rather than its EM. Third, social capital theory has proved equally important in encouraging BD by arguing that diverse boards are better positioned to leverage various forms of social capital from their members. Social capital theory has shown that BD, particularly in the form of GD, AD and ND, has a significant impact on FP. Fourth, the results from using agency theory, resource dependence theory and social capital theory have shown that GD is essential to increasing a board's independence, as women are more likely to ask questions that their male counterparts avoid. Moreover, due to the collaborative skills that women often bring with them, the presence of women directors on a firm's board contribute significantly to its bottom line. On the other hand, this paper suffers from several limitations. For example, this research paper is limited to 75 studies. Also, it explained three theories only. For future research, we will study it systematically and use other factors that may affect earnings management and firm performance. Also, we will add other measurements of board diversity.

REFERENCES

Abdallah, A. A. N., & Ismail, A. K. (2017). Corporate governance practices, ownership structure, and corporate performance in the GCC countries. *Journal of International Financial Markets, Institutions and Money*, *46*, 98–115. doi:10.1016/j.intfin.2016.08.004

Adams, R. B., & Ferreira, D. (2009). Women in the boardroom and their impact on governance and performance. *Journal of Financial Economics*, *94*(2), 291–309. doi:10.1016/j.jfineco.2008.10.007

Adams, R. B., Hermalin, B. E., & Weisbach, M. S. (2010). The role of boards of directors in corporate governance: A conceptual framework and survey. *Journal of Economic Literature*, *48*(1), 58–107. doi:10.1257/jel.48.1.58

Aguilera, R. (2005). Corporate governance and director accountability: An institutional comparative perspective. *British Journal of Management*, *16*(s1), S39–S53. doi:10.1111/j.1467-8551.2005.00446.x

Al-Mamun, A., Yasser, Q. R., Entebang, H., & Nathan, T. M. (2013). Gender diversity and economic performance of firms: Evidences from emerging market. *Journal of Economic Development, Management, IT. Finance and Marketing*, *5*(2), 100–110.

Al-Shammari, B., & Al-Saidi, M. (2014). Kuwaiti women and firm performance. *International Journal of Business and Management*, *9*(8), 51. doi:10.5539/ijbm.v9n8p51

Alesina, A., & Ferrara, E. L. (2005). Ethnic diversity and economic performance. *Journal of Economic Literature*, *43*(3), 762–800. doi:10.1257/002205105774431243

Algharaballi, E., & Albuloushi, S. (2008). Evaluating the specification and power of discretionary accruals models in Kuwait. *Journal of Derivatives & Hedge Funds*, *14*(3-4), 251–264. doi:10.1057/jdhf.2008.23

Ali, M., Ng, Y. L., & Kulik, C. T. (2014). Board age and gender diversity: A test of competing linear and curvilinear predictions. *Journal of Business Ethics*, *125*(3), 497–512. doi:10.100710551-013-1930-9

Alowaihan, A. K. (2004). Gender and business performance of Kuwait small firms: A comparative approach. *International Journal of Commerce and Management*, *14*(3/4), 69–82. doi:10.1108/10569210480000185

Ararat, M., Aksu, M. H., & Tansel Cetin, A. (2010). *The impact of board diversity on boards' monitoring intensity and firm performance: evidence from the Istanbul Stock Exchange*. Working paper, 1-33.

Arıoglu, E. (2018). *Female Directors and Earnings Management: Director Characteristics*. Retractive from https://www.researchgate.net/publication/329443984_Female_Directors_and_Earnings_Management_Director_Characteristics/stats

Arun, T. G., Almahrog, Y. E., & Aribi, Z. A. (2015). Female directors and earnings management: Evidence from UK companies. *International Review of Financial Analysis*, *39*, 137–146. doi:10.1016/j.irfa.2015.03.002

Barney, J.B., & Clark, D.N. (2007). *Resource-based theory: Creating and sustaining competitive advantage*. Oxford University Press.

Barroso-Castro, C., Villegas-Periñan, M. D. M., & Casillas-Bueno, J. C. (2016). How boards' internal and external social capital interact to affect firm performance. *Strategic Organization*, *14*(1), 6–31. doi:10.1177/1476127015604799

Berle, A. A. Jr, & Means, G. C. (1930). Corporations and the public investor. *The American Economic Review*, 54–71.

Betz, M., O'Connell, L., & Shepard, J. M. (1989). Gender differences in proclivity for unethical behavior. *Journal of Business Ethics*, *8*(5), 321–324. doi:10.1007/BF00381722

Bhagat, S., & Black, B. S. (2002). *The Non-Correlation Between Board Independence*. Academic Press.

Booth-Bell, D. (2018). Social capital as a new board diversity rationale for enhanced corporate governance. Corporate Governance. *The International Journal of Business in Society*, *18*(3), 425–439.

Carroll, M. C., & Stanfield, J. R. (2003). Social capital, Karl Polanyi, and American social and institutional economics. *Journal of Economic Issues*, *37*(2), 397–404. doi:10.1080/00213624.2003.11506587

Carter, D., D'Souza, F., Simkins, B., & Simpson, W. (2010). The Gender and Ethnic Diversity of US Boards and Board Committees and Firm Financial Performance. *Corporate Governance*, *18*(5), 396–414. doi:10.1111/j.1467-8683.2010.00809.x

Carter, D. A., D'souza, F., Simkins, B. J., & Simpson, W. G. (2010). The diversity of corporate board committees and firm financial performance. *Corporate Governance*, *18*, 396–414. doi:10.1111/j.1467-8683.2010.00809.x

Carter, D. A., Simkins, B. J., & Simpson, W. G. (2003). Corporate governance, board diversity, and firm value. *Financial Review*, *38*(1), 33–53. doi:10.1111/1540-6288.00034

Carter, S., Shaw, E., Lam, W., & Wilson, F. (2007). Gender, entrepreneurship, and bank lending: The criteria and processes used by bank loan officers in assessing applications. *Entrepreneurship Theory and Practice*, *31*(3), 427–444. doi:10.1111/j.1540-6520.2007.00181.x

Chisholm, A., & Nielsen, K. (2010). Social Capital and the Resource Based View of the Firm. *International Studies of Management & Organization*, *39*(2), 7–32. doi:10.2753/IMO0020-8825390201

Choi, S., & Rainey, H. G. (2010). Managing diversity in U.S. federal agencies: Effects of diversity and diversity management on employee perceptions of organizational performance. *Public Administration Review*, *70*(1), 109–121. doi:10.1111/j.1540-6210.2009.02115.x

Clikeman, P. M., Geiger, M. A., & O'Connell, B. T. (2001). Student perceptions of earnings management: The effects of national origin and gender. *Teaching Business Ethics*, *5*(4), 389–410. doi:10.1023/A:1012252922571

Croson, R., & Gneezy, U. (2009). Gender differences in preferences. *Journal of Economic Literature, 47*(2), 448–474. doi:10.1257/jel.47.2.448

Cyert, R. M., & March, J. G. (1963). A Behavioral Theory of the Firm (2nd ed.). Prentice Hall.

Darmadi, S. (2011). Board diversity and firm performance: The Indonesian evidence. *Corporate Ownership and Control., 9*(1), 524–539. doi:10.22495/cocv8i2c4p4

Darmadi, S. (2013). Board members' education and firm performance: Evidence from a developing economy. *International Journal of Commerce and Management, 23*(2), 113–135. doi:10.1108/10569211311324911

Das, P. K. (2019). Impact of Women Directors on Corporate Financial Performance- Indian Context. *American Journal of Humanities and Social Sciences Research, 3*(2), 29–36. doi:10.22158/wjssr.v6n3p320

Depken, C. A. II, & Sonora, R. J. (2005). Asymmetric effects of economic freedom on international trade flows. *International Journal of Business and Economics, 4*(2), 141.

Donaldson, L., & Davis, J. H. (1991). Stewardship theory or agency theory: CEO governance and shareholder returns. *Australian Journal of Management, 16*(1), 49–64. doi:10.1177/031289629101600103

Dore, R. (1973). *British Factory–Japanese Factory: The Origins of National Diversity in Industrial Relations*. University of California Press.

Drees, J., & Heugens, P. (2013). Synthesizing and extending resource dependence theory: A meta-analysis. *Journal of Management, 39*(6), 1666–1698. doi:10.1177/0149206312471391

Dwyer, S., Richard, O. C., & Chadwick, K. (2003). Gender diversity in management and firm performance: The influence of growth orientation and organizational culture. *Journal of Business Research, 56*(12), 1009–1019. doi:10.1016/S0148-2963(01)00329-0

Enofe, A. O., Iyafekhe, C., & Eniola, J. O. (2017). Board ethnicity, gender diversity and earnings management: Evidence from quoted firms in Nigeria. *International Journal of Economics. Commerce and Management, 6*, 78–90.

Erhardt, N. L., Werbel, J. D., & Shrader, C. B. (2003). Board of director diversity and firm financial performance. *Corporate Governance, 11*(2), 102–111. doi:10.1111/1467-8683.00011

Estélyi, K. S., & Nisar, T. M. (2016). Diverse boards: Why do firms get foreign nationals on their boards? *Journal of Corporate Finance, 39*, 174–192. doi:10.1016/j.jcorpfin.2016.02.006

Eulerich, M., Velte, P., & van Uum, C. (2014). The impact of management board diversity on corporate performance. An empirical analysis for the German two-tier system. An Empirical Analysis for the German Two-Tier System (November 8, 2013). *Problems and Perspectives in Management, 12*, 25–39.

Ferreira, D. (2015). Board diversity: Should we trust research to inform policy? *Corporate Governance, 23*(2), 108–111. doi:10.1111/corg.12092

Ferrero-Ferrero, I., Fernández-Izquierdo, M. Á., & Muñoz-Torres, M. J. (2015). Age diversity: An empirical study in the board of directors. *Cybernetics and Systems, 46*(3-4), 249–270. doi:10.1080/01969722.2015.1012894

Fondas, N., & Sassalos, S. (2000). A different voice in the boardroom: How the presence of women directors affects board influence over management. *Global Focus*, *12*(1), 13–22.

Gavious, I., Segev, E., & Yosef, R. (2012). Female directors and earnings management in high-technology firms. *Pacific Accounting Review*, *24*(1), 4–32. doi:10.1108/01140581211221533

Giannetti, M., Liao, G., & Yu, X. (2015). The Brain Gain of Corporate Boards: Evidence from China. *The Journal of Finance*, *70*(4), 1629–1682. doi:10.1111/jofi.12198

Gordini, N., & Rancati, E. (2017). Gender diversity in the Italian boardroom and firm financial performance. *Management Research Review*, *40*(1), 75–94. doi:10.1108/MRR-02-2016-0039

Guedes, M. J., Gaio, C., & Soares, N. (2018). Exploring the Relationship Between Gender Diversity and Earnings Management: Does Critical Mass Matter? In *International Conference on Gender Research*, (pp. 181-188). Academic Conferences and Publishing Limited.

Guest, P. M. (2019). Does Board Ethnic Diversity Impact Board Monitoring Outcomes? *British Journal of Management*, *30*(1), 53–74. doi:10.1111/1467-8551.12299

Gul, F., Srinidhi, B., & Ng, A. (2011). Does board gender diversity improve the in formativeness of stock prices? *Journal of Accounting and Economics*, *51*(3), 314–338. doi:10.1016/j.jacceco.2011.01.005

Gull, A. A., Nekhili, M., Nagati, H., & Chtioui, T. (2018). Beyond gender diversity: How specific attributes of female directors affect earnings management. *The British Accounting Review*, *50*(3), 255–274. doi:10.1016/j.bar.2017.09.001

Hambrick, D. C., & Mason, P. A. (1984). Upper echelons: The organization as a reflection of its top managers. *Academy of Management Journal*, *9*(2), 193–206.

Harjoto, M., Laksmana, I., & Lee, R. (2015). Board diversity and corporate social responsibility. *Journal of Business Ethics*, *132*(4), 641–660. doi:10.100710551-014-2343-0

Hart, D. M. (2014). Founder nativity, founding team formation, and firm performance in the U.S. high-tech sector. *The International Entrepreneurship and Management Journal*, *10*(1), 1–22. doi:10.100711365-011-0188-x

Haynes, K. T., & Hillman, A. (2010). The effect of board capital and CEO power on strategic change. *Strategic Management Journal*, *31*(11), 1145–1163. doi:10.1002mj.859

Hermalin, B. E., & Weisbach, M. S. (2003). Boards of directors as an endogenously determined institution: A survey of the economic literature. *FRBNY Economic Policy Review*, *9*, 7–26.

Hernández-Carrión, C., Camarero-Izquierdo, C., & Gutiérrez-Cillán, J. (2020). The internal mechanisms of entrepreneurs' social capital: A multi-network analysis. *BRQ Business Research Quarterly*, *23*(1), 1–19. doi:10.1177/2340944420901047

Hessels, J., & Terjesen, S. (2010). Resource dependency and institutional theory perspectives on direct and indirect export choices. *Small Business Economics*, *34*(2), 203–220. doi:10.100711187-008-9156-4

Hillman, A., Cannella, J., & Paetzold, R. (2000). The resource dependent role of corporate directors: Strategic adoption of board composition in response to environmental change. *Journal of Management Studies*, *37*(2), 235–255. doi:10.1111/1467-6486.00179

Hillman, A., Withers, M., & Collins, B. (2009). Resource dependence theory: A review. *Journal of Management*, *35*(6), 1404–1427. doi:10.1177/0149206309343469

Hillman, A. J., Shropshire, C., & Cannella, A. A. Jr. (2007). Organizational predictors of women on corporate boards. *Academy of Management Journal*, *50*(4), 941–952. doi:10.5465/amj.2007.26279222

Hitt, L. M., Wu, D. J., & Zhou, X. G. (2002). Investment in enterprise resource planning: Business impact and productivity measures. *Journal of Management Information Systems*, *19*(1), 71–98. doi:10.1080/07421222.2002.11045716

Hoffmann, S., & Rodrigo, P. (2018). *Board of Director Gender Diversity and Its Impact on Earnings Management: An Empirical Analysis for Selected European Firms*. Academic Press.

Jensen, M. C., & Meckling, W. H. (1976). Agency Costs and the Theory of the Firm. *Journal of Financial Economics*, *3*(4), 305–360. doi:10.1016/0304-405X(76)90026-X

Jiraporn, P., Miller, G. A., Yoon, S. S., & Kim, Y. S. (2008). Is earnings management opportunistic or beneficial? An agency theory perspective. *International Review of Financial Analysis*, *17*(3), 622–634. doi:10.1016/j.irfa.2006.10.005

Joecks, J., Pull, K., & Vetter, K. (2013). Gender diversity in the boardroom and firm performance: What exactly constitutes a "critical mass?" *Journal of Business Ethics*, *118*(1), 61–72. doi:10.100710551-012-1553-6

Johnson, S. G., Schnatterly, K., & Hill, A. D. (2013). Board composition beyond independence: Social capital, human capital, and demographics. *Journal of Management*, *39*(1), 232–262. doi:10.1177/0149206312463938

Julizaerma, M. K., & Sori, Z. M. (2012). Gender diversity in the boardroom and firm performance of Malaysian public listed companies. *Procedia: Social and Behavioral Sciences*, *65*, 1077–1085. doi:10.1016/j.sbspro.2012.11.374

Jurkus, A. F., Park, J. C., & Woodard, L. S. (2011). Women in top management and agency costs. *Journal of Business Research*, *64*(2), 180–186. doi:10.1016/j.jbusres.2009.12.010

Kaplan, S., Pany, K., Samuels, J., & Zhang, J. (2009). An examination of the association between gender and reporting intentions for fraudulent financial reporting. *Journal of Business Ethics, 87*(1), 15-30.

Khoury, T., Junkunc, M., & Deeds, D. (2013). The social construction of legitimacy through signaling social capital: Exploring the conditional value of alliances and underwriters at IPO. *Entrepreneurship Theory and Practice*, *37*(3), 569–601. doi:10.1111/etap.12030

Kim, H., & Lim, C. (2010). Diversity, outsider directors' and firm valuation: Korean evidence. *Journal of Business Research*, *63*(3), 284–291. doi:10.1016/j.jbusres.2009.01.013

Kim, N. B., & Yi, C. H. (2006). Ownership structure, business group affiliation, listing status, and earnings management: Evidence from Korea. *Contemporary Accounting Research*, *23*(2), 427–464. doi:10.1506/7T5B-72FV-MHJV-E697

Kim, Y. (2005). Board network characteristics and firm performance in Korea. *Corporate Governance*, *13*(6), 800–808. doi:10.1111/j.1467-8683.2005.00471.x

Kim, Y., & Cannella, A. A. Jr. (2008). Toward a social capital theory of director selection. *Corporate Governance*, *16*(4), 282–293. doi:10.1111/j.1467-8683.2008.00693.x

Kolbjørnsrud, V. (2017). Agency problems and governance mechanisms in collaborative communities. *Strategic Organization*, *15*(2), 141–173. doi:10.1177/1476127016653727

Kostopoulos, K. C., Spanos, Y. E., & Prastacos, G. P. (2002). The resource-based view of the firm and innovation: identification of critical linkages. *The 2nd European Academy of Management Conference*, 1-19.

Kostova, T., & Roth, K. (2003). Social capital in multinational corporations and a micro-macro model of its formation. *Academy of Management Review*, *28*(2), 297–317. doi:10.5465/amr.2003.9416356

Krishnan, G. V., & Parsons, L. M. (2008). Getting to the bottom line: An exploration of gender and earnings quality. *Journal of Business Ethics*, *78*(1-2), 65–76. doi:10.100710551-006-9314-z

Kunze, F., Boehm, S., & Bruch, H. (2013). Age, resistance to change, and job performance. *Journal of Managerial Psychology*, *28*(7/8), 741–760. doi:10.1108/JMP-06-2013-0194

Kunze, F., Boehm, S. A., & Bruch, H. (2011). Age diversity, age discrimination climate and performance consequences—A cross organizational study. *Journal of Organizational Behavior*, *32*(2), 264–290. doi:10.1002/job.698

Kyaw, K., Olugbode, M., & Petracci, B. (2015). Does gender diverse board mean less earnings management? *Finance Research Letters*, *14*, 135–141. doi:10.1016/j.frl.2015.05.006

Labelle, R., Gargouri, R. M., & Francoeur, C. (2010). Ethics, diversity management, and financial reporting quality. *Journal of Business Ethics*, *93*(2), 335–353. doi:10.100710551-009-0225-7

Lakhal, F., Aguir, A., Lakhal, N., & Malek, A. (2015). Do women on boards and in top management reduce earnings management? Evidence in France. *Journal of Applied Business Research*, *31*(3), 1107. doi:10.19030/jabr.v31i3.9236

Lausten, M. (2002). CEO turnover, firm performance and corporate governance: Empirical evidence on Danish firms. *International Journal of Industrial Organization*, *20*(3), 391–414. doi:10.1016/S0167-7187(00)00083-7

Lin, N. (2002). *Social capital: A theory of social structure and action*. Cambridge university press.

Lin, N., Vaughn, J. C., & Ensel, W. (1981). Social resources and occupational status attainment. *Social Forces*, *59*(4), 1163–1181. doi:10.2307/2577987

Liu, J., Shively, G. E., & Binkley, J. K. (2014). Access to variety contributes to dietary diversity in China. *Food Policy*, *49*, 323–331. doi:10.1016/j.foodpol.2014.09.007

Low, D. C. M., Roberts, H., & Whiting, R. H. (2015). Board gender diversity and firm performance: Empirical evidence from Hong Kong, South Korea, Malaysia and Singapore. *Pacific-Basin Finance Journal, 35*, 381–401. doi:10.1016/j.pacfin.2015.02.008

Lückerath-Rovers, M. (2013). Women on boards and firm performance. *The Journal of Management and Governance, 17*(2), 491–509. doi:10.100710997-011-9186-1

Mabogunje, A. L., & Kates, R. W. (2020). *Sustainable development in Ijebu-Ode, Nigeria: The role of social capital, participation, and science and technology.* CID Working Paper Series.

Makhlouf, M. H., Laili, N. H. B., Basah, M. Y. A., & Siam, Y. I. S. A. (2015). *Board Members' age, Gender Diversity and Firm Performance, Proposing Conceptual Framework.* Kuala Lumpur International Business, Economics and Law Conference (KLIBEL6), Kuala Lumpur.

Martín-Ugedo, J. F., & Mínguez-Vera, A. (2014). Firm performance and women on the board: Evidence from Spanish small and medium-sized enterprises. *Feminist Economics, 20*(3), 136–162. doi:10.1080/13545701.2014.895404

Miller, T., & del Carmen Triana, M. (2009). Demographic diversity in the boardroom: Mediators of the board diversity–firm performance relationship. *Journal of Management Studies, 46*(5), 755–786. doi:10.1111/j.1467-6486.2009.00839.x

Na, K., & Hong, J. (2017). CEO gender and earnings management. *Journal of Applied Business Research, 33*(2), 297–308. doi:10.19030/jabr.v33i2.9902

Nakano, M., & Nguyen, P. (2011). *Do older boards affect firm performance? An empirical analysis based on Japanese firms.* Working paper. Retrieved from http://ssrn.com/abstract=1879825

Omar, A., & Davidson, M. J. (2001). Women in management: A comparative cross-cultural overview. *Cross Cultural Management, 8*(3/4), 35–67. doi:10.1108/13527600110797272

Omoye, A. S., & Eriki, P. O. (2014). Corporate governance Determinants of earnings management: Evidence from Nigerian quoted companies. *Mediterranean Journal of Social Sciences, 5*(23), 553.

Ooi, C. A., Hooy, C. W., & Mat Som, A. P. (2017). The influence of board diversity in human capital and social capital in crisis. *Managerial Finance, 43*(6), 700–719. doi:10.1108/MF-08-2016-0226

Osma, B. G., & Noguer, B. G. D. A. (2007). The effect of the board composition and its monitoring committees on earnings management: Evidence from Spain. *Corporate Governance, 15*(6), 1413–1428. doi:10.1111/j.1467-8683.2007.00654.x

Oxelheim, L., & Randoy, T. (2003). The impact of foreign board membership on firm value. *Journal of Banking & Finance, 27*(12), 2369–2392. doi:10.1016/S0378-4266(02)00395-3

Palmer, D., & Barber, B. M. (2001). Challengers, elites, and owning families: A social class theory of corporate acquisitions in the 1960s. *Administrative Science Quarterly, 46*(87), 120. doi:10.2307/2667126

Panda, B., & Leepsa, N. M. (2017). Agency theory: Review of Theory and Evidence on Problems and Perspectives. *Indian Journal of Corporate Governance, 10*(1), 74–95. doi:10.1177/0974686217701467

Parker, J. (2016). A Report into the Ethnic Diversity of UK Boards. The Parker Review Committee, 56.

Peck-Ling, T., Nai-Chiek, A., & Chee-Seong, L. (2016). Foreign ownership, foreign directors and profitability of Malaysian listed companies. *Procedia: Social and Behavioral Sciences*, *219*, 580–588. doi:10.1016/j.sbspro.2016.05.037

Peni, E., & Vähämaa, S. (2010). Female executives and earnings management. *Managerial Finance*, *36*(7), 629–645. doi:10.1108/03074351011050343

Petersson, C., & Wallin, F. (2017). *Three Types of Age Diversity in Boards of Directors and the Relationship to Firm Performance.* Uppsala University. Available at: https://uu.diva-portal.org/smash/get/diva2:1111350/FULLTEXT01.pdf

Pfeffer, J. (1982). *Organizations and organization theory*. Pitman.

Pfeffer, J., & Salancik, G. (1978). *The external control of organizations: A resource dependence perspective*. Herper & Row.

Pitts, D. W. (2005). Diversity, Representation, and Performance: Evidence about Race and Ethnicity in Public Organizations. *Journal of Public Administration: Research and Theory*, *15*(4), 615–631. doi:10.1093/jopart/mui033

Polovina, N., & Peasnell, K. (2015). The Effects of Foreign Management and Board Membership on the Performance of Foreign Acquired Turkish Banks. *International Journal of Managerial Finance*, *17*(43), 32–40. doi:10.1108/IJMF-06-2014-0086

Portes, A. (1998). Social capital: Its origins and applications in modern sociology. *Annual Review of Sociology*, *24*(1), 1–24. doi:10.1146/annurev.soc.24.1.1

Portes, A., & Landolt, P. (2000). Social capital: Promise and pitfalls of its role in development. *Journal of Latin American Studies*, *32*(2), 529–547. doi:10.1017/S0022216X00005836

Powell, M., & Ansic, D. (1997). Gender differences in risk behaviour in financial decision-making: An experimental analysis. *Journal of Economic Psychology, 18*(6), 605-628.

Pucheta-Martínez, M. C., & Gallego-Álvarez, I. (2019). Do board characteristics drive firm performance? An international perspective. *Review of Managerial Science*, 1–47. doi:10.100711846-019-00330-x

Rahman, H. (2018). The Impact of Boardroom National Diversity on Firms Performance and Boards Monitoring in Emerging Markets: A Case of Malaysia. *International Journal of Managerial Science*, *8*(6), 13–18.

Rahman, H. U., Ibrahim, M. Y., & Ahmad, A. C. (2015). Corporate governance, firm financial performance, and shareholder's confidence: A proposed analysis of MCCG 2012. *Global Business and Management Research*, *7*(1), 139–147.

Ramaswamy, K., & Li, M. (2001). Foreign investors, foreign directors and corporate diversification: An empirical examination of large manufacturing companies in India. *Asia Pacific Journal of Management*, *18*(2), 207–222. doi:10.1023/A:1010620008101

Ratnawati, V., Abdul-Hamid, M. A., & Popoola, O. M. J. (2016). The Influence of Agency Conflict Types I and II on Earnings Management. *International Journal of Economics and Financial Issues*, *6*(S4), 126–131.

Rauf, F. H. A., Johari, N. H., Buniamin, S., & Rahman, N. R. A. (2012). The impact of company and board characteristics on earnings management: Evidence from Malaysia. *Global Review of Accounting and Finance*, *3*(2), 114–127.

Reguera-Alvarado, N., de Fuentes, P., & Laffarga, J. (2017). Does Board Gender Diversity Influence Financial Performance? Evidence from Spain. *Journal of Business Ethics*, *141*(2), 337–350. doi:10.100710551-015-2735-9

Robbiano, M. (2019). *Different approaches toward gender diversity in European boards: a comparison between Germany, Italy and United Kingdom* (Doctoral dissertation).

Rose, C. (2007). Does female board representation influence firm performance? The Danish evidence. *Corporate Governance*, *15*(2), 404–413. doi:10.1111/j.1467-8683.2007.00570.x

Rowley, T. J., Shipilov, A. V., & Greve, H. R. (2017). Board reform versus profits: The impact of ratings on the adoption of governance practices. *Strategic Management Journal*, *38*(4), 815–833. doi:10.1002mj.2545

Sanda, A. U., Garba, T., & Mikailu, A. S. (2008). *Board independence and financial performance: evidence from Nigeria.* Paper presented at the Centre for the Study of African Economics at St Catherine's College, University of Oxford. Retrieved from https://www.africaportal.org/publications/board-independence-and-firm-financial-performance-evidence-from-nigeria

Sealy, R. & Vinnicombe. (2007). *The female FTSE report 2007.* Cranfield University.

Seibert, S. E., Kraimer, M. L., & Liden, R. C. (2001). A social capital theory of career success. *Academy of Management Journal*, *44*(2), 219–237.

Shehata, N., Salhin, A., & El-Helaly, M. (2017). Board diversity and firm performance: Evidence from the UK SMEs. *Applied Economics*, *49*(48), 4817–4832. doi:10.1080/00036846.2017.1293796

Singh, V. (2007). Ethnic diversity on top corporate boards: A resource dependency perspective. *International Journal of Human Resource Management*, *18*(12), 2128–2146. doi:10.1080/09585190701695275

Srinidhi, B., Gul, F. A., & Tsui, J. (2011). Female directors and earnings quality. *Contemporary Accounting Research*, *28*(5), 1610–1644. doi:10.1111/j.1911-3846.2011.01071.x

Stevenson, W. B., & Radin, R. F. (2009). Social capital and social influence on the board of directors. *Journal of Management Studies*, *46*(1), 16–44. doi:10.1111/j.1467-6486.2008.00800.x

Strobl, S., Rama, D. V., & Mishra, S. (2016). Gender diversity in compensation committees. *Journal of Accounting, Auditing & Finance*, *31*(4), 415–427. doi:10.1177/0148558X16655704

Sundaramurthy, C., Pukthuanthong, K., & Kor, Y. (2014). Positive and negative synergies between the CEO's and the corporate board's human and social capital: A study of biotechnology firms. *Strategic Management Journal*, *35*(6), 845–868. doi:10.1002mj.2137

Susanto, Y. K. (2016). The effect of audit committees and corporate governance on earnings management: Evidence from Indonesia manufacturing industry. *International Journal of Business. Economics and Law*, *10*(1), 32–37.

Tanikawa, T., Kim, S., & Jung, Y. (2017). Top management team diversity and firm performance: Exploring a function of age. *Team Performance Management*, *23*(3/4), 156–170. doi:10.1108/TPM-06-2016-0027

Tasheva, S., & Hillman, J. (2019). Integrating Diversity at Different Levels: Multileval Human Capital, and Demographic Diversity and Their Implications for Team Effectivness. *Academy of Management Review*, *44*(4), 12–22. doi:10.5465/amr.2015.0396

Terjesen, S., Couto, E. B., & Francisco, P. M. (2016). Does the presence of independent and female directors impact firm performance? A multi-country study of board diversity. *The Journal of Management and Governance*, *20*(3), 447–483. doi:10.100710997-014-9307-8

Terjesen, S., Sealy, R., & Singh, V. (2009). Women directors on corporate boards: A review and research agenda. *Corporate Governance*, *17*(3), 320–337. doi:10.1111/j.1467-8683.2009.00742.x

Thiruvadi, S., & Huang, H. W. (2011). Audit committee gender differences and earnings management. *Gender in Management*, *26*(7), 483–498. doi:10.1108/17542411111175469

Thomsen, S., & Conyon, M. (2012). *Corporate governance: Mechanisms and systems*. McGraw-Hill.

Triki Damak, S. (2018). Gender diverse board and earnings management: Evidence from French listed companies. *Sustainability Accounting. Management and Policy Journal*, *9*(3), 289–312.

Van der Walt, N., & Ingley, C. (2003). Board dynamics and the influence of professional background, gender and ethnic diversity of directors. *Corporate Governance*, *1*(3), 218–234. doi:10.1111/1467-8683.00320

van Diepen, N. (2015). *The effect of gender, age and nationality diversity on company performance – Evidence from the Netherlands Supervisors: Evidence From Indonesian Publicly- Listed Financial Firms* (PhD thesis). University of Canberra.

Wahid, A. (2018). The Effects and the Mechanisms of Board Gender Diversity: Evidence from Financial Manipulation. *Journal of Business Ethics*, 1–21. doi:10.100710551-018-3785-6

Wegge, J., Roth, C., Neubach, B., Schmidt, K. H., & Kanfer, R. (2008). Age and gender diversity as determinants of performance and health in a public organization: The role of task complexity and group size. *The Journal of Applied Psychology*, *93*(6), 1301–1313. doi:10.1037/a0012680 PMID:19025249

Zalata, A. M., Tauringana, V., & Tingbani, I. (2018). Audit committee financial expertise, gender, and earnings management: Does gender of the financial expert matter? *International Review of Financial Analysis*, *55*, 170–183. doi:10.1016/j.irfa.2017.11.002

Chapter 2
The Effects of Corporate Governance (CG) on Saudi Arabian Companies' Earnings Quality

Zahra Al Nasser
Department of Banking and Finance, College of Business, Dar Uloom University, Saudi Arabia

ABSTRACT

High earnings quality (EQ) is one of the company's pillars of long-term success in building investor confidence. This study investigates whether or not corporate governance (CG) affects the EQ of non-financial companies listed on the Saudi Arabian Stock Exchange known as Tadawul. This research study uses data from a sample of 482 firm-year observations of these companies in the period from 2009 to 2013. The author adopts the Generalized Method of Moments (GMM) regression model. This research study contributes to the current literature by providing new evidence of the effect of CG on the EQ of the Saudi Arabian non-financial companies listed on the Tadawul. Specifically, not all CG attributes affect each company's EQ in the same way. This study's findings show that important CG attributes, which enhance the company's EQ, are the number of the company's independent directors, the separation of the dual role between the company's CEO and chairperson, and the financial or accounting expertise of the members of the company's audit committee members.

INTRODUCTION

The company managers' efficient use of Corporate Governance (CG) practices allow the Board of Directors (BoD) to evaluate its monitoring role and help, also, to develop favourable perceptions among the shareholders of the quality of the company's available financial information. The availability of reliable and accurate information enables the shareholders to make effective decisions about the company's financial performance (Afzal and Habib, 2018; Masulis and Mobbs, 2014). Despite the worldwide revision

DOI: 10.4018/978-1-7998-4852-3.ch002

and enhancement of Corporate Governance Codes (CGCs) and regulations, investors have experienced in previous years large numbers of CG violations through scams and financial frauds. More especially in emerging markets, policy makers and regulators try to achieve the global CG standards. However, the high number of financial fraud cases demonstrate the poor implementation of CG standards in emerging economies. This study attempts to examine empirically the effectiveness of CG standards on the EQ of Saudi Arabian non –financial companies listed on the Tadawul.

Earnings are one of the important factors used by shareholders when deciding whether or not to invest in a company (Masulis and Mobbs, 2017). Additionally, the company's earnings are more likely to be the basis of the salaries paid to its managers (Masulis and Mobbs (2016). Therefore, managers may be incentivised to use different accounting techniques in order to manipulate the company's earnings; this is known as Earnings Management (EM)[1] (Masulis and Mobbs,2017;Healy and Wahlen, 1998). Consequently, in order to protect and enhance the confidence of the existing and potential investors, it is important to detect and prevent EM. Therefore, in the context of Saudi Arabia, there is a need for companies to have effective CG standards in order to maximise their shareholders' wealth and to increase both their growth and stability and the long term success of the Saudi Arabian economy. Consequently, in the light of financial crises and corporate scandals, much worldwide attention has been paid recently to CG standards. In other words, weak CG structures may provide companies' managers to engage in behaviours that would result in poorer quality of the companies' reported earnings. Such behaviours are a strong indicator of a serious break-down in business ethics and CG (Gonzalez and Garcia-Meca, 2014).

Therefore, in this study, the author investigates the effects of CG standards on the EQ of non-financial companies listed on Saudi Arabia's Tadawul. The author used data from a sample of 482 firm-year observations of these companies in the period from 2009 to 2013. The findings provide four contributions. First, they add to the limited number of previous studies on CG and EQ in emerging markets and, more especially, in GCC countries. Consequently, this study's findings present a more comprehensive picture of the relationship between CG and EQ. Second, in the context of Saudi Arabia, the findings evidence provide useful reference points for investors and corporations from other regions and, more especially, from developed countries. Third, the findings show that in emerging economies, while CG attributes are important, not all of them have a positive effect on companies' EQ. Consequently, policymakers should customise CGC standards to match their market and cultural needs. Fourth, to the best of the author's knowledge, this is the first Saudi Arabian research study that has used GMM regression analysis to eliminate from regular and tradition regression analysis shortcomings such as eteroskedasticity, serial (auto) correlation and endogeneity. This study's results show that, in order to enhance the company's EQ, the important CG attributes, are: the number of independent directors; the separation of the dual role between CEO and chairperson; and the financial or accounting expertise of the members of the company's audit committee. However, the findings show that the company's board meetings do not play an effective role in improving the management of the company's EQ. In summary, this study's findings demonstrate that efficient CG practices increase investor confidence and their faith in the transparency, accountability and integrity of the companies' financial reporting. Also, in the context of emerging economies, this study's findings should expand the existing literature by improving understanding of the CG attributes on companies' EQ.

Institutional Setting of Saudi Arabia (SA)

Having regard to its geographical area and population, Saudi Arabia is the largest Middle Eastern Gulf Co-operation Council (GCC) country. Riyadh is the capital of Saudi Arabia and the Saudi Riyal is its currency. King Salman bin Abdulaziz AL-Saud rules Saudi Arabia which has at around 25% one of the largest oil reserves in the world (Held and Ulrichsen, 2013). Therefore, Saudi Arabia is one of the world's largest exporters of oil and, consequently, the country's economy depends heavily on oil revenues. For instance, oil represents 85% of Saudi Arabia's exports, 75% of government revenues and 35% of the country's Gross Domestic Product (GDP) (AlNasser, 2018). Among Arab countries, Saudi Arabia has the largest GDP, economy and capital market and it is part of the significant G20[2] economy. The capitalisation of the *"Tadawul"* stock exchange market accounts for 40% of the MENA region and more than two-thirds of the Tadawul's traded value (Alsaeed, 2006; Algamdi,2012). Many investors in the *"Tadawul"* seek a short-term return (Henry and Springborg, 2010). However, the Tadawul lags behind other emerging stock markets such as those in BRICS[3] countries. Saudi Arabia's economy is relatively open since the *"Tadawul"* is based on a free market system and encourages Foreign Direct Investment (FDI) (Algamdi,2012).

Saudi Arabia reflects the "market model" which emphasises the importance of maximising shareholder wealth and value (Eulaiwi *et al.,* 2016). This model is characterised by having one tier whereby the company's shareholders select the most significant governance body, namely, a board of directors. Although individual shareholders do not interfere with the work undertaken by the company's Board of Directors (BOD) (Keasey and Wright, 1993), this means, also, that the controlling shareholders can influence the company's activities and, correspondingly, the work undertaken by the company's BOD (Eulaiwi *et al.,* 2016). Consequently, while individual shareholders exert no influence, the controlling shareholders exert collectively substantial powers over the company's affairs. Among other factors and particularly when it comes to monitoring management behaviour, the most significant aspects of CG are the structure of the company's ownership and the role of the independent directors on the BOD.

Also, Saudi Arabia has separate CG Codes (CGCs) for banks and financial institutions. In this regard, Table 1 provides information on Saudi Arabia's CGC in terms of the date of issue, the code enforcement status and other codes or guidelines that have been issued. On the other hand, Table 2 provides an overview of Saudi Arabia's CG attributes.

Table 1. Corporate Governance

Country	Date of Issue	Legal Status	Name of Code	Other Codes and Guidelines
Saudi Arabia	2006 Amended in 2009	Mandatory	CG regulations in the Kingdom of SA	Guidelines for banks

Table 2. Corporate Governance Code

Items	SA
Non- executive	Majority
Board independence	One third or minimum 2
CEO duality	Must be separate
Board meeting	Not stipulated
Board size	Between 3 to 11 members
Board committees	2 committees, audit committee, remuneration and nomination committee
Audit Committee Characteristics	
Composition	At least 3 members
Independence	Not stipulated
Committee chair	Not stipulated
Financial expertise	At least one member has financial expertise
Meeting	Not stipulated
Independence of Board Members	
Items	**SA**
Being former employees or senior executives	Within the preceding two years
Material business relationship	Employee or holder of controlling interests in the preceding two years at an affiliated (auditor or supplier)
Has received or receives additional remuneration	Not stipulated
Has close family ties with any of the company's advisers, directors or senior employees	First degree relative of a senior executive of the company or in group company related to the company within the preceding two years
Represent a significant shareholder	Controlling interest in the company or in a group company
Holds cross directorship	Board membership in any group company
Board tenure	Not stipulated

THEORETICAL FRAMEWORK

Agency Theory

Agency theory focuses on the relationship between the principals (owners) and the agents (managers). Agency theory's justification for its existence is to establish appropriate and adequate incentives in order to eliminate opportunistic behaviours by the company's management and to ensure that they pursue and maximise not only the company's wealth and interests but, also, work on behalf of the company's shareholders (Jensen and Meckling, 1976). From agency theory's perspective, a reduced agency problem leads to maximising the company's value and the returns on investments to its shareholders. Furthermore, agency theory suggests ways of reducing agency costs in order to increase the company's EQ. These are: namely, monitoring costs; bonding costs; and residual losses which stem from the company's internal CG structure (Eisenhardt, 1989; Shabbir and Padget, 2005). Monitoring costs are borne by the principals and are the basis of the company's monitoring mechanisms, such as internal CG mechanisms, which are used to monitor management behaviour. Bonding costs relate to the financial or non-financial mechanisms which are used to ensure the agents make an effort to maximise the principals' wealth. Residual losses happen despite the involvement of monitoring cost and bonding cost because either these can fail or be insufficiently effective to align the principals' (owners) interests with those of the agents (management). Consequently, the owners can reduce the incentives to look after themselves by using some tools such as monitoring managers' behaviours and by introducing a contract which provides an incentive to align their interests with those of the company's management (Eisenhardt, 1989; Jebran *et al.,* 2019).

Stewardship Theory

Another theory of corporate governance is stewardship theory. This theory is rooted in psychology and sociology (Donaldson and Davis,, 1990). Under stewardship theory, managers are the company's stewards and have the main responsibility of extending and maximising the company's performance. Therefore, due to the relationship of trust, they act in the shareholders' best interests (Donaldson and Davis, 1991). This theory predicts that there is a strong association between the company's success and the principal's level of satisfaction (Davis *et al.,* 1997; Donaldson, 1990). This theory claims, also, that there is no conflict of interest between the company's management and principals since they cooperate with each other to achieve a "goal alignment." However, this theory assumes that, if the conflict of interest exists and the managers cannot solve it, they would favour the solution to meet the owners' interests because managers are aware of their special obligations to ensure that the shareholders receive fair returns on their investments. Therefore, stewardship theory depends more on creating a structure that facilitates and empowers rather than one of monitoring and control (Davis *et al.,* 1997). Stewardship theory proposes that increasing the number of the company executive directors leads to better firm performance because they provide more effective and efficient decision- making and contribute to maximising profits for the shareholders (Kiel and Nicholson, 2003).

LITERATURE REVIEW AND DEVELOPMENT OF HYPOTHESES

Board of Directors (BOD)

The Board of Directors (BOD) is an important part of the company's CG structure since the BOD has a fiduciary obligation to the company's shareholders (Monks and Minow, 1995; Jebran *et al.,* 2019). Consequently, by monitoring the performance of the company's management, the BOD should discharge their responsibilities and perform their duties in order to ensure that the company's management acts in the best interests of the company's shareholders (Masulis and Mobbs, 2017). In addition, a number of previous studies have confirmed that the BOD's effectiveness in the performance of CG activities helps to align the managerial interests with the shareholders' interest and, by reducing agency costs, helps to protects the latter's interests (Jensen and Meckling, 1976; Fama, 1980; Jensen, 1993; Linck *et al.,* 2009). In turn, this leads to an improvement in the company's EQ. Previous studies have considered already some aspects of an effective BOD. These are such as its size, the number of independent directors, CEO duality and the frequency of BOD meetings (Masulis and Mobbs, 2016).

Board Size

Agency theory describes the importance of the board size to control the management. In addition, best CG practices and most CGCs mention the importance of board size. The Saudi Arabian CGC suggests both a minimum board size of 3 members and a maximum board size of 11 members. There is no universal agreement on the optimal size of a BOD (Alagha, 2016; Alqatan *et al.,* 2019). In addition, previous studies have documented mixed findings in relation to the optimal size of the BOD. For instance, Klin (2002), Yu (2008) and Khan *et al.,* (2019) posit that, because of the members' diverse expertise and skills, a large board size is more capable of acting in the shareholders' best interests. Nonetheless, the side effects of a large board is a slow decision-making process which may not encourage innovation (Ismail *et al.,* 2010). Some other researchers, such as Jensen (1993), Vafeas (2000) and Alonso *et al.,* (2000) have concluded that a small board size is more effective in increasing the company's market value through monitoring the CEO and reporting more informative earnings (Lipton and Lorsch, 1992; Karamanou and Vafeas, 2005). These findings support the view that, compared to a large board, a small board has better communication skills which are good for controlling and monitoring the management's activities. Certo (2003) argues that the role of a large BOD is more symbolic and that, in terms of communication and coordination, its members may not be a dynamic group. They may be involved as advisors rather than simply monitoring the management. In addition, a large BOD may experience more difficulties in terms of coordination and may be controlled more easily controlled by a dominant CEO (Jensen, 1993). Based on agency theory and the above mentioned argument, this study's first hypothesis is as follows:

H_1: A small board size increases the company's earnings quality.

Independent Directors

The appointment of independent directors to the BOD is considered to be one of most important decisions made by modern companies in terms of their internal CG mechanisms in order to reduce agency cost and information asymmetry problems (Fama, 1980; Lipton and Lorsch 1992; Jensen, 1993). However, there are two theoretical views about the appointment of independent directors to the BOD. One view supports more independent directors while the other view favours more executive directors on the BOD .

Those, who support the first view, base their argument on Agency theory. They claim that, when compared to executive directors, independent directors can be more accountable because they make independent judgements when considering the decisions to be taken by the BOD (Fama, 1980; Cadbury Report,1992;Chhaochharia and Grinstein, 2009). This is because independent directors are not financially dependent on the company and, in accordance with the best practice CGC, they should not have close family ties to the company. Independent directors should not receive fees, which are unrelated to the company's performance, and they should not serve on the BOD for more than nine years. They should not hold directorships in other companies and they should not represent specific groups of shareholders. If these characteristics are met, independent directors are thought to be able to monitor the company's management more effectively and be able, also, to overcome any pressure to accept earnings manipulation. For instance, the findings of studies by Byrd and Hickman (1992), Brickley *et al.,* (1994), Sila *et al.,* (2017) and Khan *et al.,* (2019) show that companies, which have more independent directors, are more effective in monitoring the management's activities.

The opponents of more independent directors on the BOD based on the stewardship theory argue that they have less knowledge about the company (Weir and Laing, 2000) and this has the potential for the BOD to make poorer decisions (Haniffa and Hudiab, 2006). Independent directors are part- timers who are normally present on other companies' BODs (Jiraporn *et al.,* 2009). Therefore, they have little time to understand and offer effective monitoring on the complexities of the company's activities. Accordingly, this has a negative influence on the company's performance (Baysinger and Hoskisson, 1990; Weir and Laing, 2000). On the contrary, Kiel and Nicholson (2003) claim that, due to their having a greater knowledge of the company's activities, a larger number of executive directors on the BOD can provide better decision- making and can lead to better firm performance. Al-Haddad and Whittington's (2019) findings show that, in relation to Jordanian companies, board independence is significant and relates positively to real earnings management and accrual- based earning management. They conclude that Jordanian firms follow an overall EM strategy in order to achieve the desired impact on EQ.

In addition, some scholars claim that, in emerging countries, independent directors have a ceremonial role on the BOD and are more likely to follow the lead taken by the executive directors (Mahadeo *et al.,* 2012). Consequently, the independent directors are involved less in the BOD's decision –making process because it is more than likely that their selection neither meets the recommendations of worldwide CGCs nor copys those adopted by Western countries (Ferrarini and Filoppelli, 2014). Therefore, based on stewardship theory and the above -mentioned argument, this study's second hypothesis is as follows:

H_2: A high proportion of independent directors reduces the company's earnings quality.

CEO Duality

CEO duality is when the company's CEO is, also, the chairman of the BOD board of directors. It is another feature of the BOD that has been investigated. The role of chairman of the BOD and the CEO are supposed to be different. On one hand, the chairman's responsibility is to nominate new board members; review the performance of the company's senior management; and to set the agenda for BOD meetings. The chairman is responsible, also, for settling conflicts that arise within the BOD (Weir and Laing, 2000). On the other hand, the CEO's role is to run and manage the company's day to day operations.

CEO duality is regsrded as a "double edged sword" (Finkelstein and D' Aveni., 1994). There are two different viewpoints within the literature which either support or oppose CEO duality. The proponents of CEO duality, which support the stewardship theory, claim that the CEO's knowledge, understanding and experience of the company can help to improve the BOD's decision-making and can provide the company with an efficient strategy. This is because the CEO has often a greater knowledge of the company than the chairman (Weir *et al.,* 2002; Anderson *et al.,* 2004) and focuses more on the company's objectives which leads to better company performance (Haniffa and Cooke, 2002).

The opponents of CEO duality argue that this role has a negative influence on the company's performance which in turn reduce EQ (Lipton and Lorsch, 1992; Jensen, 1993). The agency theory highlights that the power of the BOD is concentrated in the hands of the CEO when he holds, also, the position of chairman. Therefore, the CEO can control the availability of information provided to the BOD and shareholders and this can lead to a reduction in the effectiveness of the BOD's monitoring of the company's management (Jensen, 1993; Ullah *et al.,* 2019; Masulis and Mobbs, 2016). The GCC countries' CGCs recommend against CEO duality since the chairman's role is to monitor and to evaluate the effectiveness of the CEO. Hence, the existence of CEO duality may compromise the BOD's effectiveness in monitoring CEO performance and, in turn, this increases the agency problem (Jensen, 1993; Khan *et al.,* 2019).

Based on the Agency theory and the argument discussed above, this study's third hypothesis is as follows:

H_3: The presence of CEO duality reduces the company's earnings quality.

Board of Directors (BOD) Meetings

Based on Agency theory, the frequency of BOD meetings can play an important role in monitoring and tackling more effectively the issues within a company. The worldwide CG best practices and the Saudi Arabian CGC code recommend that the BOD holds regular meetings to carry out their duties efficiently. The findings of some previous studies support this recommendation. However, the findings of some other studies show that BOD meetings are not necessarily beneficial because they take up too much time and, thereby, they constrain routine tasks.

The existing literature documents, also, the importance of the BOD meeting frequently in order to measure the board operations and the company's activeness (Vafeas, 2000). Therefore, a higher number of meetings reflects that the BOD is active and is able to resolve problems and monitor the company's management (Managena and Tauringana, 2008; Adam and Ferrira, 2009; Khan *et al.,* 2019).

However, the findings of other studies argue that most of the problems in a publicly traded company are due to the members of the BOD having insufficient time to attend meetings in order to discharge their duties and to monitor the company's management effectively (Lipton and Lorsch, 1992; Afzal and Habib, 2018). Therefore, due to time constraints, the BOD meetings may not reflect truly the exchange of information and ideas between board members and the company's management. This is particularly true based on stewardship theory. In addition, Jensen (1993) argues that the BOD is inactive unless it is required to deal with a problem. Based on Agency theory and the argument discussed above, this study's fourth hypothesis is as follows:

H4: A higher frequency of board of directors' meetings increases the company's Earnings Quality.

METHODOLOGY

Sample and Data

The sample comprises non- financial companies listed on the Saudi Stock Exchange "*Tadawul*" during the period from 2009 to 2013. The author selected these years due to the sufficient number of available observations. The author obtained the sample from the Tadawul website. Also, the author obtained the accounting data from the Tomson Reuters DataStream while the author collected by hand the CG data from the companies' CG and annual reports. In total in the period from 2009 to 2013, the author obtained information about 97 firms and a total of 482 observations (firm- year).

Measurement of Earnings Quality (EQ)

Dechow *et al.,* (2010) highlight that EQ reflects the company's fundamental performance and that the company's performance is contingent on the decisions made by the BOD. The literature defines EQ as a faithful representation of the company's financial performance in the current period (Wahlen *et al.,* 2012; Nelson and Skinner, 2013). By doing so, this enables users of the company's financial reports to develop reasonable expectations of its future performance (Wahlen *et al.,* 2012). This study adopts this definition of EQ to reflect the focus of the study. This definition indicates that high EQ is free from opportunistic Earnings Management (EM) and, thereby, allows investors to make accurate decisions. Also, it is observed that EM, which most companies practice, is the dominant aspect investigated by previous studies (Graham *et al.,* 2005). In addition, Meek and Thomas (2004) recommend that there should be many more worldwide investigations of EM in order to discover if EM is simply an American phenomenon and if it is, also, present elsewhere. Therefore, based on argument above, this study's research question attempts to measure EQ through opportunistic EM. In addition, the vast majority of previous studies have employed discretionary accruals as a proxy of EQ (Dechow *et al.,* 1995; Dechow and Dichev, 2002; Dechow *et al.,* 2010; Eliwa *et al.,* 2019). It is apparent from the findings of previous studies that the Chief Financial Officers (CFO) of most companies agrees that high EQ should be sustainable and repeatable (Dichev *et al.,* 2013; Dechow *et al.,* 1996). However, the previous studies list a number of measurements of EQ which include earnings persistence, predictability, asymmetric loss recognition, income increasing accrual and the absolute value of accrual (Nelson and Skinner, 2013).

Eliwa *et al.,* (2019) state that accrual accounting is more flexible than cash accounting and, therefore, leads to the finding that the accrual component of revenues is more credible and reliable than the cash flow component of earnings. Moreover, accrual accounting alleviates the problem of a mismatch from using cash flow as a short-term performance measure. Furthermore, accrual accounting is better able to reflect the company's current performance and, when compared to cash flow, has the ability to predict and generate future cash flows. However, due to the flexibility of accrual accounting, which allows for judgements and estimations, managers may use accrual accounting to hide or delay some crucial information about the company's performance. Consequently, this may have an adverse influence on the decisions made by the BOD may result in the company having a lower EQ (Dechow *et al.,* 1995). Nevertheless, there has been a lot of criticism of the limitations of abnormal accrual models, they are still considered to be the most acceptable proxy measures of EQ. Furthermore, these models have undergone some developments and improvements and are relevant in terms of developing a more rigorous proxy of EQ (Dechow *et al.,* 1995; Dechow *et al.,* 2010; Defond, 2010).

Abnormal Working Capital Accrual (AWCA) Based on the Defond and Park Model (2002)

Based on argument above about accrual accounting, this study employed the Defond and Park (2001) model. This model estimates the Abnormal (discretionary) Working Capital Accrual model (AWCA). According to Becker *et al.,* (1998), Defond and Park (2001) and Ashbaugh *et al.,* (2003), managers have the greatest discretion over AWCA. Additionally, Defond and Jiambalvo (1994) and Teoh *et al.,* (1998a and1998b) claim that, when compared to non-working capital, working capital is more sensitive and is easier to manipulate. The author's rational for selecting this model is that it estimates only the firm- specific accounting information rather than the average information per industry (Defond and Jiambalvo, 1994). Also, in deducting EM, the Defond and Park (2001) model is more potent than total accrual. In order to avoid the above mentioned problem and since this research question focuses on a small emerging stock market as compared to the USA (Defond and Park, 2001; Francis *et al.,* 2009), the author decided that, when it came to detecting EM, the Defond and Park (2001) model was the best one for this study. In literature, previous European and other international studies by Defond and Park (2001), Carey and Simentt (2006), Francis and Wang (2008), Prencipe and Bar- Yosef (2011), and Eliwa *et al.,* (2019) employed abnormal working capital accrual to detect EM.

As a proxy of EM, AWCA calculates abnormal (unexpected) working capital accrual as the difference between the actual (realised) working capital accrual and the expected working capital accrual. The following equation and Table 3 show the calculations of AWCA.

Table 3. Defond and Park (AWCA)

Symbol	Variable	Definition
$AWCA_{t-1}$	Abnormal working capital accrual	The absolute value of abnormal working capital accruals for firm i in year t calculated from equation (2)
WC $_{t}$	Current working capital	Non-cash working capital accrual at the end of year t computed as (current assets – cash and short-term investment) – (current liabilities – short-term debt) in year t.
WCt-1	Previous working capital	Working capital at the end of year t-1
St	Current total annual sales	total annual sales at the end of year t
St-1	Previous total annual sales	Total annual sales at the end of year t-1

In the primary analysis, AWCA is considered in its absolute value. The purpose of this study is to investigate EM per se, rather than income- increasing and income decreasing policies. The author prefers this approach since there is no expectation on the direction of EM (Defond and Park, 1997; Francis *et al.,* 1999; Prencipe and Bar-Yosef, 2011).

CONTROL VARIABLES

Family Ownership (FAMC) and EQ

Two theories have emerged to explain the conflict between the controlling families and the minority shareholders on FOC. There are, on the one hand, alignment effect theory and, on the other hand, entrenchment effect theory. Through their use of these theories, the controlling families act differently. When using alignment effect theory, the controlling family's interests aligns with those of the minority shareholders and this alignment results in the controlling family monitoring its company effectively (Gomes, 2000). On the other hand, when using entrenchment effect theory, the controlling family attempts to protect their interests even at the expense of the minority shareholders (Stulz and Williamson, 2003; La Porta *et al.,* 1999). The findings of many studies relating to developing countries reveal that, due to the poorly protected environments for both shareholders and emerging markets, such countries make greater use of entrenchment effect theory in relation to family ownership (Choi *et al.,* 2007; Machuga and Teitel, 2009; Anwar and Buvanendra, 2019). Al Nasser, (2018) also highlighted that entrenchment theory is more applicable in emerging countries and controlling shareholders more likely abuse their position for their own interest. Therefore, based on entrenchment theory and the argument discussed above, this study expects that FMC has a negative impact on EQ.

State Ownership (STATC) and EQ

From reviewing the literature, there are two schools of thought. According to the first school of thought, there is a potential conflict of interest between the government as the major shareholder and minority shareholders. The government's political incentive may outweigh economic incentives and, therefore, lead to poor EQ. Therefore, the government may have different interests or goals to pursue and prefer to benefit themselves. Accordingly, the findings of many previous studies (Alghamdi, 2012; AL-Janadi *et al.,* 2016; Anwar and Buvanendra, 2019; Khan *et al.,* 2019) show that government ownership has a negative influence on EQ. According to the second school of thought, these companies are crucial for the market because the government provides proper monitoring to the management and, in challenging times attempts to solve such issues. Therefore, the government protects investors, markets, contractors and suppliers (AL-Janadi *et al.,* 2016). Ding et al.'s (2007) and Wang and Yung's (2011) findings show a positive association between state ownership and EQ. Based on the first school of thought this study expects that STATC has a negative influence on EQ.

Institutional Ownership (INSTITIC) and EQ

The existing literature's findings are inconsistent in relation to the effect of institutional ownership on EQ. Scholars argue that institutional investors may have either effective objectives or they may destroy the company's efficiency. The first group argues that, because they are active and aim to increase the value of their equity investment (Batta *et al.,* 2014), this enhances the company's EQ. The findings of previous studies (Pucheta-Martinez and Garcia-Meca, 2014; Khan *et al.,* 2019) agree that institutional ownership has a positive influence on EQ. The second group of scholars suggest that institutional investors may exert an entrenchment effect in order to exploit the minority shareholders (Afzal and Habib, 2018). This reflects their focus on short-term gains and their lack of interest in maintaining control over the company's management. Batta *et al.,* (2014) pointed out that in emerging market institutional ownership more likely to incentive to increase the efficiency of the company compared to family ownership and state ownership. Based on the above-mentioned argument, this study expects that ISTITIC has a positive influence on EQ.

Audit Committee Expertise (AUDITEX) and EQ

The previous studies' findings are inconsistent because each side uses a different argument. However, agency theory supports the importance of the company's audit committee with its financial expertise for efficient and effective monitoring (Xie *et al.,* 2003; Al-Hadi *et al.,* 2016). In addition, the best practice of worldwide CGCs support and encourage the company's audit committee to have directors with financial expertise. In addition, the findings of the majority of previous studies (Abernathy *et al.,* 2015; Yeung and Lento, 2018; Anwar and Buvanendra, 2019; Hasan, 2020) agree that EQ increases when there is a higher number of audit committee members with financial expertise. This study follows agency theory and expects that AUDITEX has a positive influence on EQ.

Growth and EQ

This study includes company growth as a control variable due to likelihood of differences in the extent of information asymmetry at different points in the company's life cycle (Aljifri and Moustafa, 2007). The findings of studies by Abdul Rahman and Ali, (2006), Dimitropoulos and Asterious, (2010) and Khan *et al.* (2019) document the negative association between company growth and EQ. Based on the above-mentioned argument, this study expects a correlation between growth and AWCA because both make a significant change to the sales component. Therefore, the study expects that company growth has a negative influence on EQ.

Leverage and EQ

Leverage reflects the company's debt structure. In addition, many previous studies have used leverage either as a control variable or as a proxy of debt violation (Jelinek, 2007; Jiang *et al.,* 2008; Dimitropulos and Asterious, 2010). Leverage captures the risk which is associated with high debt and which influences, also, EQ (Elayan *et al.,* 2008; Khan *et al.,* 2019). Leverage has a positive association with EM as a means to avoid a debt covenant being violated (Defond and Jiambalvo, 1994; Efendi *et al.,* 2007; Jiang *et al.,* 2008). On the other hand, some studies (Becker *et al.,* 1998; Ismail and Weelman, 2008) show a negative relationship between leverage and EM. Based on the above-mentioned argument, this study expects that leverage has a negative influence on EQ.

Company Size (SIZE) and EQ

According to agency theory, Jensen and Meckling (1976) argue that the larger the company, the higher the agency cost. This is due to the increased opportunities for managerial discretions. Rajgopal *et al.,* (2002) note that large companies place more pressure on managers to report more predictable earnings. Consequently, managers are incentivised to alter the company's earnings figures by taking advantage of the complexity of the company's operations and the difficulty in understanding them (Afzal and Habib,

2018). Moreover, large companies are more likely to manage earnings downwards (Bartov *et al.,* 2001) in order to reduce political attention from such as the government and the unions (Watts and Zimmerman, 1990; Gore *et al.,* 2001; Khan *et al.,* 2019). However, other scholars argue that the large companies care more about their reputations; earn higher profits; and have more resources. Therefore, large companies avoid EM. The findings of some previous studies (Klein, 2002; and Abdul Rahman and Ali, 2006) document a negative association between SIZE and EM. Based on agency theory and the above-mentioned argument, this study expects that SIZE has a negative influence on EQ.

Big4 Auditing Firms (BIG4) and EQ

There are two standpoints in relation to the effect of the Big4 auditing firms on a company's EQ. On the one hand, the literature provide evidence that investors have more confidence in reported earnings audited by Big4 auditing firms (Francis and Krishnan,1999, 2002). There is a mandatory argument of the need for the Big4 auditing firms to improve financial reporting in the country which displays poor disclosure (Hail, 2002; Al-Hadi *et al.,* 2016). As expressed by Lennox (1999) and Colbert and Murray (1999), the difference between the Big4 auditing firms and other auditing firms is the Big4's reputation, resources, specialisation and expertise. In environments, which have weak investor protection, companies, which hire one of the Big 4 auditing firms, have a better performance record (Niskanen *et al.,* 2011; Rodriguez and Alegria, 2012; Khan *et al.,* 2019).

Some scholars (Francis and Wang, 2008; Chen and Zhang, 2010) argue that, due to the institutional setting and legal and cultural environment, it is unnecessary for the Big 4 auditing firms to provide better EQ and, similar to developed markets, to reduce EM in emerging markets. Based on the above-mentioned argument, this study expects that Big4 auditing firms have a negative influence on EQ.

REGRESSION MODEL

GMM Estimations

Generalized Method of Moment (GMM) estimations differ from OLS in sense that the fixed effects can be included to account for unobservable heterogeneity. GMM differs, also, from traditional fixed effect since it permit current CG practices to be effected by previous performance. In addition, under this dynamic panel GMM estimator, instruments are internal and, due to the dynamic nature of the relationship, it is for the panel itself to solve the problem of simultaneity. GMM dynamic panel has been used in the financial and non-financial sector and in the economy when there is an apparent dynamic relationship between dependent and independent variables (Wintoki *et al.,* 2012; Naguyen *et al.,* 2014).

Following Naguyen *et al.,* (2014), in the multivariate regression model, this study uses one-year legged AWCA as the explanatory variable in order to capture the dynamic nature of the relationship. This reflects that, as suggested among others by Wintoki *et al.,* (2012), CG is a function of past and other company characteristics. Following Wintoki *et al.,* (2012) and Naguyen *et al.,* (2014). This study considers that the exogenous variables are company age, industry dummies and year dummies.

However, this study uses *reg* (pooled OLS with the robust standard error), *xtreg* (panel data with random effect and the robust standard error), *xtivreg* (2sls) two stage least squares regression and *xtbound* (GMM) command in STATA to ensure the validity of the statistical results. These commands are valid for balanced and unbalanced panels. Nevertheless, this study's reported GMM regression results are the primary results in terms of answering the research question. GMM is better than other methods since it is more robust as regards heteroskedasticity, serial (auto) correlation, sample gaps in unbalanced panels non-normality and measurement error. Also, the use of these instruments allows the researcher to control the problems of endogeneity (Wintoki *et al.*, 2012).

As shown in the Equation below and Table 4, the author tested this study's hypotheses by using the absolute value of AWCA regress on individual CG attributes and STATA analysis software in relation to the quantitative data on the different controlled variables.

$$AWCA = \alpha + \beta_1 BSIZE_{it} + \beta_2 IND_{it} + \beta_3 CEOD_{it} + \beta_4 BMEET_{it} + \beta_5 FAMC_{it} + \beta_6 STATC_{it} + \beta_7 INSTITC_{it} + \beta_8 AUDITEX_{it} + \beta_9 BIG4_{it} + \beta_{10} GROWTH_{it} + \beta_{11} LEVERAGE_{it} + \beta_{12} SIZE_{it} + INDUSTRY\ DUMM + YEAR\ DUMMY + \varepsilon_{it}$$

Table 4. Variables Definition

Symbol / Dependent Variable	Name of Variable	Predicted Sign[4]
Y	LAWCA- the abnormal working capital accrual	
Independent Variables		
BSIZE	The natural logarithm of Board size	-
IND	Independent directors on the board	+
CEOD	CEO Duality	+
BMEET	Board of directors meetings	-
Control Variables		
FAMC	Percentage of Family ownership	+
STATC	Percentage of State ownership	+
INSTITC	Percentage of Institutional ownership	-
AUDITEX	The expertise of audit committee members	-
GROWTH	The natural logarithm of Firm growth	+
LEVERAGE	The natural logarithm of Leverage	+
SIZE	The natural logarithm of the Firm size	+
BIG 4	Big 4 audit firms dummy	+
INDUSTRY	Industry dummy	?
YEAR	Year dummy	?

The coefficients of the model predicted that β_1 would has a negative value while β_2 would has a positive value and that β_3 would have a positive value. The expectations were that β_4 would have a negative influence on EM and that β_5 and β_6 would have a positive value while β_7 and β_8 would have a negative value. Turning to the control variables, it was expected that the signs of β_9, $\beta_{10,}$ β_{11}, and β_{12} would have positive values.

ROBUSTNESS TEST

Abnormal Accrual Accounting (AAA) Based on Modified Jones Model (1995)

Modified Jones model (1995) is similar to the original Jones model (1991). However, under Jones model (1991), the revenue is assumed to be free from management discretion, considered as normal accrual. Dechow *et al.,* (1995) who developed the modified Jones model, rejected this assumption and argued that it is easier for management to alter the recognition of revenues or credit sales than cash sales. Therefore, Dechow *et al.,* (1995) considered two variables (income to adjust for the change in receivable and gross plant, property and equipment) to enhance the power of detecting EM. The managerial discretion is free from change in revenue less than a change in receivable (Dechow *et al.,* 1995). Modified Jones model (1995) has received some criticisms. For instance, McNichols (2000) argues that time series of modified Jones model requires at least ten years of data (observation). However, Bernard and Skinner (1996) believe that this problem is noticeable in most models. Dechow *et al.,* (1995) examined the applicability of four models, namely Healy model (1985), Deangelo model (1986), Jones model (1991) and modified Jones model (1995) to detect EM. They concluded that modified Jones model (1995) is one of the most powerful model among them. Despite the limitation of modified Jones model, it is the most commonly used in literature since it was introduced up to now. Klein, (2002), Xie *et al.,* (2003), Peasnell *et al.,* (2005), used the cross-sectional and panel approach instead, along with the modified Jones model and asserted that it was more potent in detecting EM than the original one. The advantage of using the panel data approach of modified Jones model (1995) is to increase the sample size and control for industry and year specific influence (Peasnell *et al.,* 2005).

Following Dechow *et al.,* (1995) model, the research first regresses total accruals on different variables expected to vary with normal accruals. Table 5 defines all variables.

$$TA_{it} = \beta_0 + \beta_1 \left(\Delta AR_{it} - \Delta AR_{it}\right) + \beta_2 GPPE_{it} + \varepsilon_{it} \tag{1}$$

Second, the research estimates the coefficients from equation (1) and the study uses them to assess the normal accrual in a specific industry.

$$TA_{it} = \widehat{\beta_0} + \widehat{\beta_1} \left(\Delta AR_{it} - \Delta AR_{it}\right) + \widehat{\beta_2} GPPE_{it} + \varepsilon_{it} \tag{2}$$

Third, the research estimates abnormal accruals by subtracting total accruals from normal accruals.

$$AAA_{it} = TA_{it} - NA_{it}$$

Table 5. Variables definition: CG and EQ- Modified Jones model

Symbol	Variable	Definition
TA_{it}	The total accruals	Net income before extraordinary items – operating cash flow in year t scaled by average total assets using assets from the start and end of the fiscal year.
ΔREV_{it}	The change in revenues	The change in revenues for firm i in year t in comparison with previous year scaled by average total assets.
ΔAR_{it}	The change in account receivable	The change in account receivable for firm i in year t in comparison with previous year scaled by average total assets.
$GPPE_{it}$	The gross property, plant and equipment	The gross property, plant and equipment for firm i in year t scaled by average total assets.
ε_{it}	Error term	Error term for firm i in year t.
NA_{it}	The normal accruals	The normal accruals for firm i in year t calculated from equation (2)
AAA_{it}	The abnormal accruals accounting	The abnormal accruals for firm i in year t calculated from equation (3)

EMPIRICAL FINDINGS

Descriptive Statistics

Table 6 provides descriptive statistics for the predicted, predictor and control variables used in the research question. On average, BOD Size (BSIZE) is composed of eight members. Among these members, 50% are independent directors (IND). Only 10% of the sampled companies have CEO duality (CEOD). Furthermore, the BOD meets five times (BMEET). Turning to the control variables, the average family ownership (FAMC) is approximately 14% and state ownership (STATC) is 11%. Institutional ownership (INSTITC) represents about 10%. On average, 30% of the audit committees have at least one member who possesses financial or accounting expertise (AUDITEX). On average, the company growth (GROWTH) is about 4.3%. The means of leverage (LEVERAGE) is approximately 37%. The average of firm size (SIZE) is USD 13. 186 million. More than half of the companies hire one of the Big 4 auditing firms (BIG4).

Table 7 shows a correlation matrix for predicted, predictor and control variables. BOD Size (BSIZE) is negative when correlated with AWCA. CEO duality (CEOD) appears to show a positive and significant association with AWCA. Turning to the control variables, there is a significant positive correlation between Family ownership (FAMC), State ownership (STATC) and Institutional ownership (INSTITIC) and AWCA. Firm size (SIZE) and leverage (LEVERAGE), both show a positive correlation with AWCA. All other correlations are relatively low and all Variance Inflation Factors (VIF) are below 10; this indicates that multicollinearity is not problematic. Therefore, these results verify the validity of the data (Bowerman and O' Connell, 1990; Tabachnick and Fidell, 2001).

Multivariate Analysis

Table 8 presents the results of the multivariate model of the total sampled companies. As mentioned previously, AWCA, which is the absolute value of abnormal working capital, is the predicted variable (a proxy of EQ). Also, in the context of Saudi Arabia, the CG attributes and control variables are the predictor variables used to examine the effectiveness of the CG variables on EQ.

Table 6. Descriptive statistics

Variable	Mean	Medium	Std. Dev.	Min	Max
AWCA	0.047	0.031	0.051	0.002	0.201
BSIZE	8.298	9	1.495	4	12
IND	0.509	0.444	0.196	0	1
CEOD	0.101	0	0.302	0	1
BMEET	5.301	5	2.238	1	17
FAMC	0.139	0.074	0.181	0	0.708
STATC	0.111	0	0.212	0	0.836
INSTITC	0.103	0	0.169	0	0.75
AUDITEX	0.305	0.333	0.058	0	0.5
BIG4	0.593	1	0.491	0	1
GROWTH	0.043	0.026	0.1045	-0.186	0.336
LEVERAGE	0.373	0.336	0.219	0.071	0.856
SIZE	13.186	13.102	1.481	9.896	16.004

N= 482

Note: BSIZE is the natural logarithm of Board size. IND is independent directors on the board. CEOD is a dummy variable of CEO Duality. BMEET is board of directors meeting. FMAC is percentage of Family ownership. STATC is percentage of State ownership. INSTITC is percentage of institutional ownership. AUDITEX is the expertise of audit committee members. BIG4 is Big 4 audit firms. GROWTH is the natural logarithm of firm growth. LEVERAGE is the natural logarithm of Leverage. SIZE is the natural logarithm of the firm size

Table 7. Correlation Matrix

	AWCA	BSIZE	IND	CEOD	BMEET	FAMC	STATC	INSTITC	AUDITEX	BIG4	GROWTH	LEVERAGE	SIZE
AWCA	1												
BSIZE	-0.074	1											
IND	0.015	-0.203*	1										
CEOD	0.061*	-0.056	-0.082	1									
BMEET	-0.017	0.050	-0.058	0.046	1								
FAMC	-0.098*	-0.032	-0.166*	-0.001	-0.054	1							
STATC	-0.112*	0.112*	-0.123*	-0.107*	0.322*	-0.268*	1						
INSTITC	0.112*	0.174*	-0.254*	0.0348	-0.171*	-0.189*	-0.213*	1					
AUDITEX	-0.005	-0.216*	-0.033	-0.044	-0.115*	0.061	-0.212*	-0.049	1				
BIG4	0.045	0.079	-0.309*	-0.029	-0.096*	0.134*	0.026	0.170*	-0.039	1			
GROWTH	0.078	-0.010	-0.115*	-0.107*	-0.081	0.152*	-0.097*	0.113*	0.059	0.200*	1		
LEVERAGE	0.127*	0.074	-0.209*	-0.112*	0.058	0.128*	0.091*	0.102*	-0.117*	0.359*	0.239*	1	
SIZE	-0.112*	0.470*	-0.232*	-0.189*	0.135*	-0.156*	0.505*	0.1535*	-0.330*	0.172*	0.026	0.467*	1

Notes: this table presents the results for the Spearman rank correlation matrix. Please refer to the Appendix for detailed definition. *, **, *** indicate significance at the, 10,5, and 1 present level, respectively.

BSIZE is the natural logarithm of Board size. IND is independent directors on the board. CEOD is a dummy variable of CEO Duality. BMEET is board of directors meeting. FMAC is percentage of Family ownership. STATC is percentage of State ownership. INSTITC is percentage of institutional ownership. AUDITEX is the expertise of audit committee members. BIG4 is Big 4 audit firms. GROWTH is the natural logarithm of firm growth. LEVERAGE is the natural logarithm of Leverage. SIZE is the natural logarithm of the firm size.

Independent directors have a negative and significant association with AWCA (coefficient= -0.009, P-value <5). This result is not in line with the study hypothesis but is in line with the theoretical claim (agency theory) and most of the empirical evidence. The findings of previous studies by such as Byrd and Hickman (1992), Brickley *et al.,* (1994) and Khan et al., (2019), show that companies, which have more independent directors, have more effective monitoring arrangements.

CEO duality (CEOD) has a positive association with AWCA (coefficient= 0.026, P-value <10%). This result is in line with the study hypothesis, the theoretical claim (agency theory) and most of the empirical evidence. Agency theory argues that the separation of power is important for an effective balance of power to be distributed among the members of the BOD and, more especially, CEO duality. This may impair the BOD's ability and, more specifically the non-executive and independent directors, to monitor the company's management (Jensen, 1993). Consequently, agency theory recommends strongly that the two roles of leadership be separated in order to emphasize the effective checks and balances required in CG mechanisms (Jensen, 1993; Ullah *et al.,* 2019, Khan *et al.,* 2019).

Turning to the control variables, there is a statistically negative association between STATC and AWCA. The result is in line not only with this study's expectation and the theoretical claim (agency theory) but, also, with some previous empirical findings. The existing literature highlights the benefit of STATC on EQ. For instance, from studying the impact of private versus state ownership on EQ in China, Ding *et al.*'s (2007) and Wang and Yung's (2011) findings show that companies, which are owned by the Chinese Government, have higher EQ.

There is a statistically negative association between AUDITEX and AWCA. The result is in line with this study's expectation, the theoretical claim (agency theory) and with previous empirical findings. The findings of studies by Lin and Hwang (2010), Abernathy et al. (2015), Yeung and Lento, (2018), Anwar and Buvanendra, (2019) and Hasan, (2020) show a positive association between AUDITEX and EQ.

Additionally, a company, which has a higher level of growth (GROWTH), has a positive and statistical association with AWCA. This result meets this study's expectation and is consistent with the findings of previous studies by Abdula Rahman and Ali (2006), Huang *et al.,* (2008), Dimitropoulos and Asterious (2010) and Khan *et al.,* (2019). These studies' findings conclude that the management of a fast-growing company is incentivised to manage the earnings in order to meet its targets.

There is a significantly negative relationship between LEVERAGE and AWCA is significantly negative. This result does not meet this study's expectation but is in line with the results of some previous studies. For instance, the findings of Becker *et al.*'s (1998) and Ismail and Weelman's (2008) studies show a negative association between leverage and EM.

Robustness Tests

In order to check the robustness of its results, this study conducted an additional test. The study re-ran regression by using a different measurement of EM as a proxy of EQ. This study employed the absolute value of abnormal total accrual based on the Modified Jones Model (1995). The results in Table 9 support the findings of Defond and Park's (2001) study.

Table 8. Main test- (AWCA) Regression

AWCA	1	2	3	4
	reg (Pooled OLS)	**xtreg[5] (Panel Data)**	**xtivreg (2sls)[6]**	**xi: xtabond GMM**
BSIZE	0.002	0.004	0.014	-0.020
	(0.014)	(0.015)	(0.022)	(0.045)
IND	-0.001*	-0.000***	-0.003**	-0.009**
	(0.013)	(0.012)	(0.016)	(0.028)
CEOD	0.006*	0.003*	0.004*	0.026*
	(0.007)	(0.007)	(0.009)	(0.015)
BMEET	0.000	0.000	0.002	0.001
	(0.001)	(0.001)	(0.001)	(0.001)
FAMC	-0.047	-0.045	-0.028	-0.045
	(0.0142)	(0.017)	(0.022)	(0.068)
STATC	-0.008***	-0.006**	-0.026*	-0.082*
	(0.0146)	(0.017)	(0.023)	(0.153)
INSTITC	0.024	0.023	0.018	0.104
	(0.015)	(0.019)	(0.029)	(0.134)
AUDITEX	-0.047*	-0.038*	-0.000*	-0.150*
	(0.041)	(0.048)	(0.060)	(0.081)
BIG4	-0.000	-0.000	-0.005	-0.016
	(0.005)	(0.005)	(0.006)	(0.010)
GROWTH	0.022	0.042	0.041	0.072**
	(0.022)	(0.027)	(0.040)	(0.033)
LEVERAGE	0.059***	0.056***	0.025	0.011*
	(0.013)	(0.014)	(0.024)	(0.079)
SIZE	0.009***	0.009***	0.005	0.019
	(0.002)	(0.003)	(0.005)	(0.030)
AWCA L				-0.0480
				(0.095)
Constant	0.158***	0.153***	0.074	-0.234
	(0.039)	(0.049)	(0.065)	(0.374)

Notes: Panels A and B of this table present the results for ordinary least squares (OLS), random effect regression analysis, the second and first stages of the two least squares analysis, and the generalized method of moments dynamic panel analysis, respectively. AWCA is proxy for earning management.

Please refer to the Appendix for detailed control variable definitions. Standard errors are located in the parentheses. *, **, *** indicates significance at the 10, 5, and 1 percent level, respectively.

BSIZE is the natural logarithm of Board size. IND is independent directors on the board. CEOD is a dummy variable of CEO Duality. BMEET is board of directors meeting. FMAC is percentage of Family ownership. STATC is percentage of State ownership. INSTITC is percentage of institutional ownership. AUDITEX is the expertise of audit committee members. BIG4 is Big 4 audit firms. GROWTH is the natural logarithm of firm growth. LEVERAGE is the natural logarithm of Leverage. SIZE is the natural logarithm of the firm size

Table 9. Robusness test- (AAA)- GMM Regression

AAA	Expected Sign	xi: xtabond GMM
BSIZE	-	-0.066
		(0.05)
IND	+	-0.017**
		(0.01)
CEOD	+	0.012**
		(0.02)
BMEET	-	0.005
		(0.02)
FAMC	+	0.018
		(0.02)
STATC	+	0.122
		(0.4)
INSTITC	-	0.101
		(0.23)
AUDITEX	-	-0.001*
		(0.06)
BIG4	-	-0.005
		(0.02)
GROWTH	+	-0.045
		(0.03)
LEVERAGE	+	0.001
		(0.04)
SIZE	+	0.006**
		(0.005)
AAA L		0.006
		(0.122)
Constant		0.122
		(0.33)

Notes: *,** and *** denote significant at10%, 5% and 1% levels respectively

BSIZE is the natural logarithm of Board size. IND is independent directors on the board. CEOD is a dummy variable of CEO Duality. BMEET is board of directors meeting. FMAC is percentage of Family ownership. STATC is percentage of State ownership. INSTITC is percentage of institutional ownership. AUDITEX is the expertise of audit committee members. BIG4 is Big 4 audit firms. GROWTH is the natural logarithm of firm growth. LEVERAGE is the natural logarithm of Leverage. SIZE is the natural logarithm of the firm size

DISCUSSION

The study has analysed the effect of CG on EQ measured by abnormal working capital for a sample of non-financial companies listed on Tadawul, the Saudi Arabian Stock Exchange. In order to have a clear and fuller understanding of this study's findings, this section discusses them.

In relation to independent directors, this study's result shows that there is a nonlinear relationship between independent directors and EM (increases EQ). This result rejects the second hypothesis and stewardship theory but is line with agency theory. This result suggests that, despite the observation in GCC countries that independent directors are ineffective in an emerging market, they enhance the company's EQ by providing oversight of management decisions and mitigating the agency conflict in saudi non-financial listed companies. This supports the claim that independent directors restrict the use of discretionary accruals; monitor the managers; and controlling majority shareholders in order to protect the minority shareholders' interests. Arising from the fact that they care more about their reputations, independent directors play a significant role in monitoring the company's managers (Khan *et al.,* 2019). Consequently, this result is consistent with the findings of Byrd and Hickman, (1992); Brickley *et al.,* (1994), Sila *et al.,* (2017) and Khan *et al.,* (2019). In the context of Saudi Arabia, companies, which have more independent directors, have higher EQ.

As regards the influence of CEO duality, this study's results confirm hypothesis three and agency theory by suggesting that CEO duality has a positive effect on a company's EM (reduces EQ). A possible explanation is that the separate structure between the CEO and the chairman is the best for companies. The previous studies' findings support the fact that a unity of leadership reduces a company's ability to grow. These findings claim, also, that the unity of leadership reduces the focus on flexible leadership that helps a company to become more effective. Other studies Jensen, (1993), Ullah *et al.,* (2019), Masulis and Mobbs (2016) and Khan *et al.,* (2019) have produced similar results. Therefore, in the context of Saudi Arabia, companies, which follow the best CG practices and the country's CGC in relation to CEO duality, have a higher EQ .

As regards State ownership, this study's result suggests that, when the State controls a high percentage of the company, its EQ increases due to the efficient monitoring indicated by agency theory (Jensen and Meckling, 1979). It is noteworthy, also, that other studies' findings show that the State's ownership of the company has a positive potential to monitor and constrain the managers' opportunistic behaviours, which, in turn, affect earnings informativeness. This result indicates that, when compared to non-governmental owned companies, the Saudi Arabian Government's ownership of non-financial listed companies is more likely to have higher EQ.

As expected, the quality of financial reporting depends, also, on the financial and accounting expertise of the members of the company's audit committee. As a consequence of their knowledge and expertise, they can be involved in specific strategic interests and responsibilities (Abernathy *et al.,* 2015). This study's results, which are consistent with agency theory and previous findings, show that an audit committee reduces the probability of financial fraud. These results demonstrate, also that, when compared to companies whose audit committees members have no financial and accounting expertise, those companies, whose audit committee members have financial and accounting expertise, are more likely to have higher EQ.

As expected, companies with high levels of growth are more likely to have higher EM (lower EQ). It is notewothy, also, that mamagers of fast-growing companies are more likely to alter the earnings figures. Moreover, growth influences working capital accrual, which, in turn, influences EQ. Some previous studies, such Matsumoto (2002), Abdul Rahman and Ali (2006), Huang *et al.,* (2008) and Dimitropoulos and Asteriou, (2010) document the positive association between company growth and EM.

This study's findings show, also, that higher leveraged companies are more likely to have higher EM (lower EQ). These findings confirm that leverage captures the risk associated with high debt and which, in turn, influences EQ (Elayan *et al.,* 2008; Khan *et al.,* 2019). Leverage has a positive association with EM as a means to avoid the violation of the debt covenant (Efendi *et al.,* 2007; Jiang *et al.,* 2008).

Empirically, it is important to account for econometric problems such as endogeneity as the control of endogeity issues is a matter for further analysis. Finally, these findings have provided a number of practical recommendations. The policymakers should encourage companies to have independent directors on the BOD in order to improve the company's EQ. Accordingly, the policymakers should foster the requirement of companies nominating independent directors to their BODs. In addition, policymaker should encourage the separation of combined leadership in order to reduce the concentration of power in the hands of the company's CEO.

Based on this study's finding in the context of Saudi Arabia, companies, which have high EQ, are more likely to have independent directors on their BODs; are more likely to separate the roles of CEO and chairman; are more likely to have state ownership; are more likely to have audit committee members with finance and accounting backgrounds; and are less likely to be leveraged and fast growing.

This study's findings are subject to several limitations, first, this study's focus on Saudi Arabia may not reflect the effects on other countries in the region that have similar cultures. This study may be extended to other GCC countries in order to gain further understanding of the effect of CG on the EQ of other companies in the region. This would result in more interesting stories and robust analysis. Second, this study does not include one of most important variables in an institutional setting which is, namely, members of the Royal Family on the BOD. Consequently, it would be interesting to study in such circumstances, the effect of CG practices on a company's EQ .

CONCLUSION

This study aimed to investigate the effect of CG practices on the EQ of Saudi Arabian non-financial companies listed on *"Tadawul",* the Saudi Arabian Stock Exchange. The author divided this research paper into sections. Section 1 detailed the introduction, institutional setting, theoretical framework, literature review, and the development of this study's hypotheses. Section 2 detailed the methodology used in this research study. Section 3a presented the descriptive statistics and the correlation matrix which was the starting point in understanding the data and in answering the research question. Section 3b described the regression results and explained the results of the robustness tests in order to confirm these results in the context of Saudi Arabia. Section 3c provided the discussion and the conclusions arising from these results.

This research study used data from a sample of 482 firm-year observations of Saudi Arabian non-financial companies listed on *"Tadawul"* in the period from 2009 to 2013. The author adopted the Generalized Method of Moments (GMM) regression model to analyse the data set.

This study's main findings were that the important CG attributes that enhanced Saudi Arabian companies' EQ were: the number of independent directors; the separation of the dual role between the company's CEO and chairman; and the members of the company's audit committee having financial or accounting expertise. However, this study's results demonstrated that the meetings of the company's BOD did not prove to play an effective role in mitigating the management's influence on the company's EM. Therefore, investors should be aware of the benefit of imbedding Saudi Arabia's CGC in the company's capital structure when it comes to these companies investing in emerging markets. In the other words, this study's findings expand the understanding of CG attributes in the context of an emerging economy such as Saudi Arabia. As explained previously, the use of different robustness tests did not alter this study's results.

This study's findings are consistent with extant literature and CGCs. Thus, this study's findings provide the following contribute to the existing literature. First, they add to the limited number of previous studies on CG and EQ in emerging markets and, more especially, in GCC countries. Consequently, this study's findings present a more comprehensive picture of the relationship between CG and EQ. Second, in the context of Saudi Arabia, the findings evidence provide useful reference points for investors and corporations from other regions and, more especially, from developed countries. Third, the findings show that in emerging economies, while CG attributes are important, not all of them have a positive effect on companies' EQ. For example, this study's findings show that there is a negative association between company BOD meetings and EQ. Similarly, the negative relationship between the size of the BOD and EQ indicates that insufficient importance is being given to this matter. Consequently, policymakers should customise CGC standards to match their market and cultural needs. Fourth, to the best of the author's knowledge, this is the first Saudi Arabian research study that has used GMM regression analysis to eliminate from regular and tradition regression analysis shortcomings such as eteroskedasticity, serial (auto) correlation and endogeneity.

In summary, in answering the research question, this study's findings reinforce the view that a good number of corporate governance mechanisms help to increase a company's EQ. Therefore, in the context of Saudi Arabia, policymakers and regulators should place greater emphasis on these CG attributes.

REFERENCES

Abdul Rahman, R., & Ali, F. H. (2006). Board, Audit Committee, Culture and Earnings Management: Malaysian Evidence. *Managerial Auditing Journal*, *21*(7), 783–804. doi:10.1108/02686900610680549

Abernathy, J. L., Beyer, B., Masli, A., & Stefaniak, C. M. (2015). How the source of audit committee accounting expertise influences financial reporting timeliness. *Current Issues in Auditing*, *9*(1), 1–P9. doi:10.2308/ciia-51030

Afzal, M., & Habib, M. D. (2018). Corporate Governance and Earnings Management: A Model and Empirical Investigation from Karachi Stock Exchange. *Journal of Finance and Economics Research*, *3*(2), 51–67. doi:10.20547/jfer1803204

Al-Haddad, L., & Whittington, M. (2019). The impact of corporate governance mechanisms on real and accrual earnings management practices: evidence from Jordan. *Corporate Governance: The International Journal of Business in Society*, *19*(6), 1167-1186.

Al-Hadi, A., Hasan, M. M., & Habib, A. (2016). Risk committee, firm life cycle, and market risk disclosures. *Corporate Governance*, *24*(2), 145–170. doi:10.1111/corg.12115

Al-Janadi, Y., Al-Janadi, Y., Abdul Rahman, R., Abdul Rahman, R., Alazzani, A., & Alazzani, A. (2016). Does government ownership affect corporate governance and corporate disclosure? Evidence from Saudi Arabia. *Managerial Auditing Journal*, *31*(8/9), 871–890. doi:10.1108/MAJ-12-2015-1287

Alagha, H. S. (2016). *Corporate governance practices and firm performance of listed companies including Islamic financial institutions in the United Arab Emirates* (Doctoral dissertation). Victoria University.

Alghamdi, S. A. (2012). *Investigation into Earnings Management Practices and the Role of Corporate Governance and External Audit in Emerging Markets!* Empirical Evidence from Saudi Listed Companies.

Aljifri, K., & Moustafa, M. (2007). The impact of corporate governance mechanisms on the performance of UAE firms: An empirical analysis. *Journal of Economic and Administrative Sciences*, *23*(2), 71–93. doi:10.1108/10264116200700008

AlNasser, Z. (2018). *The effect of internal corporate governance on earning quality in GCC country* (Unpublished thesis). Trinity College University.

Alonso, P., Palenzuela, V., & Iturriaga, F. (2000). *Managers' Discretionary Behavior, Earnings Management and Corporate Governance: An Empirical International Analysis*. Working Paper, Universidad de Valladolid.

Alqatan, A., Chbib, I., & Hussainey, K. (2019). How does board structure impact on firm performance in the UK? *Corporate Board: Role, Duties and Composition, 15*(2).

Alsaeed, K. (2006). The association between firm-specific characteristics and disclosure: The case of Saudi Arabia. *Managerial Auditing Journal*, *21*(5), 476–496. doi:10.1108/02686900610667256

Anderson, R. C., Mansi, S., & Reeb, D. M. (2004). Board characteristics, accounting report integrity, and the cost of debt. *Journal of Accounting and Economics*, *37*(3), 315–342. doi:10.1016/j.jacceco.2004.01.004

Anwar, H., & Buvanendra, S. (2019). *Earnings Management and Ownership Structure: Evidence from Sri Lanka*. Academic Press.

Ashbaugh, H., LaFond, R., & Mayhew, B. W. (2003). Do nonaudit services compromise auditor independence? Further evidence. *The Accounting Review*, *78*(3), 611–639. doi:10.2308/accr.2003.78.3.611

Bartov, E., Gul, F. A., & Tsui, J. S. L. (2001). Discretionary-accruals models and audit qualifications. *Journal of Accounting and Economics*, *30*(3), 421–452. doi:10.1016/S0165-4101(01)00015-5

Batta, G., Sucre Heredia, R., & Weidenmier, M. (2014). Political connections and accounting quality under high expropriation risk. *European Accounting Review*, *23*(4), 485–517. doi:10.1080/09638180.2014.906316

Baysinger, B., & Hoskisson, R. E. (1990). The composition of boards of directors and strategic control: Effects on corporate strategy. *Academy of Management Review*, *15*(1), 72–87. doi:10.5465/amr.1990.4308231

Becker, C., DeFond, M., Jiambalvo, J., & Subramanyan, K. R. (1998). The effect of audit quality on earnings management. *Contemporary Accounting Research*, *15*(1), 1–24. doi:10.1111/j.1911-3846.1998.tb00547.x

Bernard, V. L., & Skinner, D. J. (1996). What motivates managers' choice of discretionary accruals? *Journal of Accounting and Economics*, *22*(1-3), 313–325. doi:10.1016/S0165-4101(96)00431-4

Bowerman, B. L., & O'Connell, R. T. (1990). *Linear statistical models: An applied approach*. Duxbury.

Brickley, J. A., Coles, J. L., & Terry, R. L. (1994). Outside directors and the adoption of poison pills. *Journal of Financial Economics*, *35*(3), 371–390. doi:10.1016/0304-405X(94)90038-8

Byrd, J. W., & Hickman, K. A. (1992). Do outside directors monitor managers?: Evidence from tender offer bids. *Journal of Financial Economics*, *32*(2), 195–221. doi:10.1016/0304-405X(92)90018-S

Cadbury Committee. (1992). Report of the committee on the financial aspects of corporate governance. Gee.

Carey, P., & Simnett, R. (2006). Audit partner tenure and audit quality. *The Accounting Review*, *81*(3), 653–676. doi:10.2308/accr.2006.81.3.653

Certo, S. T. (2003). Influencing initial public offering investors with prestige: Signaling with board structures. *Academy of Management Review*, *28*(3), 432–446. doi:10.5465/amr.2003.10196754

Chen, J. J., & Zhang, H. (2010). The impact of regulatory enforcement and audit upon IFRS compliance–Evidence from China. *European Accounting Review*, *19*(4), 665–692. doi:10.1080/09638180903384684

Chhaochharia, V., & Grinstein, Y. (2009). CEO Compensation and Board Structure. *The Journal of Finance*, *64*(1), 231–261. doi:10.1111/j.1540-6261.2008.01433.x

Choi, J. J., Park, S. W., & Yoo, S. S. (2007). The value of outside directors: Evidence from corporate governance reform in Korea. *Journal of Financial and Quantitative Analysis*, *42*(4), 941–962. doi:10.1017/S0022109000003458

Colbert, G., & Murray, D. (1999). The Association between Auditor Quality and Auditor Size: an Analysis of Small CPA Firms. *Journal of Accounting & Auditing &Finance-Control*, 976-983.

Davis, J. H., Schoorman, F. D., & Donaldson, L. (1997). *Davis, Schoorman, and Donaldson reply: The distinctiveness of agency theory and stewardship theory*. Academic Press.

Dechow, P., Ge, W., & Schrand, C. (2010). Understanding earnings quality: A review of the proxies, their determinants and their consequences. *Journal of Accounting and Economics*, *50*(2), 344–401. doi:10.1016/j.jacceco.2010.09.001

Dechow, P. M., & Dichev, I. D. (2002). The quality of accruals and earnings: The role of accrual estimation errors. *The Accounting Review*, *77*(s-1), 35–59. doi:10.2308/accr.2002.77.s-1.35

Dechow, P. M., Sloan, R. G., & Sweeney, A. P. (1995). Detecting Earnings Management. *The Accounting Review*, *70*, 193–225.

Dechow, P. M., Sloan, R. G., & Sweeney, A. P. (1996). Causes and consequences of earnings manipulation: An analysis of firms subject to enforcement actions by the SEC. *Contemporary Accounting Research*, *13*(1), 1–36. doi:10.1111/j.1911-3846.1996.tb00489.x

DeFond, M. L., & Jiambalvo, J. (1994, January). Debt covenant violation and manipulation of accruals. Accounting choices in troubles companies. *Journal of Accounting and Economics*, *17*(1-2), 145–176. doi:10.1016/0165-4101(94)90008-6

DeFond, M. L., & Park, C. W. (2001). The reversal of abnormal accruals and the market valuation of earnings surprises. *The Accounting Review*, *76*(3), 375–404. doi:10.2308/accr.2001.76.3.375

Dichev, I. D., Graham, J. R., Harvey, C. R., & Rajgopal, S. (2013). Earnings quality: Evidence from the field. *Journal of Accounting and Economics*, *56*(2-3), 1–33. doi:10.1016/j.jacceco.2013.05.004

Dimitropoulos, P. E., & Asteriou, D. (2010). The effect of board composition on the informativeness and quality of annual earnings: Empirical evidence from Greece. *Research in International Business and Finance*, *24*(2), 190–205. doi:10.1016/j.ribaf.2009.12.001

Ding, Y., Zhang, H., & Zhang, J. (2007). Private versus state ownership and earnings management: Evidence from Chinese listed companies. *Corporate Governance*, *15*(2), 223–238. doi:10.1111/j.1467-8683.2007.00556.x

Donaldson, L., & Davis, J. H. (1990). *CEO governance and shareholder returns: Agency theory or stewardship theory*. Australian Graduate School of Management, University of New South Wales.

Donaldson, L., & Davis, J. H. (1991). Stewardship theory or agency theory: CEO governance and shareholder returns. *Australian Journal of Management*, *16*(1), 49–64. doi:10.1177/031289629101600103

Efendi, J., Srivastava, A., & Swanson, E. P. (2007). Why do corporate managers misstate financial statements? The role of option compensation and other factors. *Journal of Financial Economics*, *85*(3), 667–708. doi:10.1016/j.jfineco.2006.05.009

Eisenhardt, M. (1986). Agency Theory! And Assessment Review. *Accounting Management Review*, *14*(1), 57–74.

Eliwa, Y., Gregoriou, A., & Paterson, A. (2019). Accruals quality and the cost of debt: The European evidence. *International Journal of Accounting & Information Management*, *27*(2), 333–351. doi:10.1108/IJAIM-01-2018-0008

Eulaiwi, B., Al-Hadi, A., Taylor, G., Al-Yahyaee, K. H., & Evans, J. (2016). Multiple directorships, family ownership and the board nomination committee: International evidence from the GCC. *Emerging Markets Review*, *28*, 61–88. doi:10.1016/j.ememar.2016.06.004

Fama, E. F. (1980). Agency Problems and the Theory of the Firm. *Journal of Political Economy*, *88*(2), 288–307. doi:10.1086/260866

Ferrarini, G., & Filippelli, M. (2014). *Independent directors and controlling shareholders around the world*. Academic Press.

Finkelstein, S., & D'aveni, R. A. (1994). CEO duality as a double-edged sword: How boards of directors balance entrenchment avoidance and unity of command. *Academy of Management Journal*, *37*(5), 1079–1108.

Francis, B. B., Hasan, I., & Sun, X. (2009). Political connections and the process of going public: Evidence from China. *Journal of International Money and Finance*, *28*(4), 696–719. doi:10.1016/j.jimonfin.2009.01.002

Francis, J. R., & Krishnan, J. (1999). Accounting accruals and auditor reporting conservatism. *Contemporary Accounting Research*, *16*(1), 135–165. doi:10.1111/j.1911-3846.1999.tb00577.x

Francis, J. R., & Krishnan, J. (2002). Evidence on auditor risk-management strategies before and after the Private Securities Litigation Reform Act of 1995. *Asia-Pacific Journal of Accounting & Economics*, *9*(2), 135–157. doi:10.1080/16081625.2002.10510607

Francis, J. R., & Wang, D. (2008). The joint effect of investor protection and Big-4 audits on earnings quality around the world. *Contemporary Accounting Research, 25*(1), 157–191. doi:10.1506/car.25.1.6

Gomes, A. (2000). Going Public without Gover- nance: Managerial reputation effects. *The Journal of Finance, 55*(2), 615–646. doi:10.1111/0022-1082.00221

Gonzalez, J. S., & Garcia-Meca, E. (2014). Does corporate governance influence earnings management in Latin American markets? *Journal of Business Ethics, 121*(3), 419–440.

Gore, P., Pope, P., & Singh, A. (2001). *Non-audit services, auditor independence and earnings management.* Working Paper, Lancaster University.

Graham, J. R., Harvey, C. R., & Rajgopal, S. (2005). The economic implications of corporate financial reporting. *Journal of Accounting and Economics, 40*(1-3), 3–73. doi:10.1016/j.jacceco.2005.01.002

Hail, L. (2002). *The Impact of Voluntary Corporate Disclosures on the Ex Ante Cost of Capital for Swiss Firms.* Working Paper, University of Zurich.

Haniffa, R., & Hudaib, M. (2006). *Corporate Governance Structure and Performance of Malaysian Listed Companies.* Academic Press.

Haniffa, R. M., & Cooke, T. E. (2002). Culture, corporate governance and disclosure in Malaysian corporations. *Abacus, 38*(3), 317-349. 10.1111/1467-6281.00112

Hasan, S. (2020). Audit Committee Effectiveness towards Financial Reporting Quality in Malaysia. In *Postgraduate Research Symposium-January 2020* (*Vol. 1*, No. 1, pp. 1-1). Academic Press.

Healy, P. M., & Wahlen, J. M. (1998). A review of the earnings management literature and its implications for standard setting. Boston. *Accounting Horizons*, 365–383.

Held, D., & Ulrichsen, K. (Eds.). (2013). *The transformation of the Gulf: politics, economics and the global order.* Routledge. doi:10.4324/9780203813218

Henry, C. M., & Springborg, R. (2010). *Globalization and the Politics of Development in the Middle East* (Vol. 1). Cambridge University Press. doi:10.1017/CBO9780511778162

Huang, P., Louwers, T., Moffitt, J., & Zhang, Y. (2008). Ethical Management, Corporate Governance, and Abnormal Accruals. *Journal of Business Ethics, 83*(3), 469–487. doi:10.100710551-007-9632-9

Ismail, W., Adibah, W., Van Zijl, T., & Dunstan, K. (2010). *Earnings quality and the adoption of IFRS-based accounting standards: Evidence from an emerging market.* Available at SSRN 1566634

Jebran, K., Chen, S., & Tauni, M. Z. (2019). Principal-principal conflicts and corporate cash holdings: Evidence from China. *Research in International Business and Finance, 49*, 55–70. doi:10.1016/j.ribaf.2019.02.010

Jelinek, K. (2007). The effect of leverage increases on earnings management. Journal of Business and. *Economic Studies., 13*(2), 24–46.

Jensen, M. (1993). The modern industrial revolution, exit, and the failure of internal control systems. *The Journal of Finance, 48*(3), 831–880. doi:10.1111/j.1540-6261.1993.tb04022.x

Jensen, M. C., & Meckling, W. H. (1976). Theory of the firm: Managerial behavior, agency costs and ownership structure. *Journal of Financial Economics*, *3*(4), 305–360. doi:10.1016/0304-405X(76)90026-X

Jiang, W., Lee, P., & Anandarajan, A. (2008). The association between corporate governance and earnings quality: Further evidence using the GOV-score. *Advances in International Accounting*, *24*(2), 191–201. doi:10.1016/j.adiac.2008.08.011

Jiraporn, P., Singh, M., & Lee, C. I. (2009). Ineffective corporate governance: Director busyness. *Journal of Business Finance & Accounting*, *26*, 797–805.

Karamanou, I., & Vafeas, N. (2005). The Association between Corporate Boards, Audit Committees, and Management Earnings Forecasts: An Empirical Analysis. *Journal of Accounting Research*, *43*(3), 453–486. doi:10.1111/j.1475-679X.2005.00177.x

Keasey, K. & Wright, M. (1993) Issues in corporate accountability and governance: An editorial. *Accounting and Business Research, 23*(91A), 291-303.

Khan, M. A., Khidmat, W. B., Ullah, F., & Khan, N. U. (2019). Corporate governance and earnings management: The role of the board of director. *Sarhad Journal of Management Sciences*, *5*(2), 317–342.

Kiel, G. C., & Nicholson, G. J. (2003). Board Composition and Corporate Performance: How the Australian Experience Informs Contrasting Theories of Corporate Governance. *Corporate Governance*, *11*(3), 189–205. doi:10.1111/1467-8683.00318

Klein, A. (2002). Audit committee, board of director characteristics, and earnings management. *Journal of Accounting and Economics*, *33*(3), 375–400. doi:10.1016/S0165-4101(02)00059-9

La Porta, R., Lopez-De-Silanes, F., & Shleifer, A. (1999). Corporate ownership around the world. *The Journal of Finance*, *54*(2), 471–51. doi:10.1111/0022-1082.00115

Lennox, C., (1990). *Audit Quality and Auditor Size: an Evaluation of Reputation and Deep Pockets Hypotheses*. Academic Press.

Lin, J., & Hwang, M. (2010). Audit Quality, Corporate Governance, and Earnings Management: A Meta-Analysis. *International Journal of Auditing, 10*, 1099-1123.

Linck, J. S., Netter, J. M., & Yang, T. (2009). The effects and unintended consequences of the Sarbanes-Oxley Act on the supply and demand for directors. *Review of Financial Studies*, *22*(8), 3287–3328. doi:10.1093/rfs/hhn084

Lipton, L., & Lorsch, J. (1992). A modest proposal for improved corporate governance. *Business Lawyer*, *48*(1), 59–77.

Machuga, S. M., & Teitel, K. (2009). Board of director characteristics and earnings quality surrounding implementation of a corporate governance code in Mexico. *Journal of International Accounting, Auditing & Taxation*, *18*(1), 1–13. doi:10.1016/j.intaccaudtax.2008.12.002

Mahadeo, J. D., Soobaroyen, T., & Hanuman, V. O. (2012). Board composition and financial performance:Uncovering the effects of diversity in an emerging economy. *Journal of Business Ethics*, *105*(3), 375–388. doi:10.100710551-011-0973-z

Masulis, R. W., & Mobbs, S. (2014). Independent director incentives: Where do talented directors spend their limited time and energy? *Journal of Financial Economics*, *111*(2), 406–429. doi:10.1016/j.jfineco.2013.10.011

Masulis, R. W., & Mobbs, S. (2016). *Independent Director Reputation Incentives: CEO Compensation Contracting and Financial Accounting Quality*. Available at SSRN 2832549.

Masulis, R. W., & Mobbs, S. (2017). *Independent Director Reputation Incentives: The Supply of Monitoring Services*. ECGI-Finance Working Paper, (353).

Matsumoto, D. (2002). Managements incentives to avoid negative earnings surprises. *The Accounting Review*, *77*(3), 483–514. doi:10.2308/accr.2002.77.3.483

McNichols, M. F. (2000). Research design issues in earnings management studies. *Journal of Accounting and Public Policy*, *19*(4-5), 313–345. doi:10.1016/S0278-4254(00)00018-1

Meek, G. K., & Thomas, W. B. (2004). A review of markets-based international accounting research. *Journal of International Accounting Research*, *3*(1), 21–41. doi:10.2308/jiar.2004.3.1.21

Monks, R. A. G., & Minow, N. (1995). *Corporate Governance*. Blackwell.

Nelson, M. W., & Skinner, D. J. (2013). How should we think about earnings quality? A discussion of "Earnings quality: Evidence from the field". *Journal of Accounting and Economics*, *56*(2-3), 34–41. doi:10.1016/j.jacceco.2013.10.003

Niskanen, J., Karjalainen, J., Niskanen, M., & Karjalainen, J. (2011). Auditor gender and corporate earnings management behavior in private Finnish firms. *Managerial Auditing Journal*, *26*(9), 778–793. doi:10.1108/02686901111171448

Peasnell, K. V., Pope, P. F., & Young, S. (2005). Board monitoring and earnings management: do outside directors influence abnormal accruals? *Journal of Business Finance & Accounting, 32*(7S8), 1311-1346.

Prencipe, A., & Bar-Yosef, S. (2011). Corporate Governance and Earnings Management in Family-Controlled Companies. *Journal of Accounting, Auditing & Finance*, *26*(2), 199–227. doi:10.1177/0148558X11401212

Pucheta-Martínez, M. C., & García-Meca, E. (2014). Institutional investors on boards and audit committees and their effects on financial reporting quality. *Corporate Governance*, *22*(4), 347–363. doi:10.1111/corg.12070

Rajgopal, S., Venkatachalam, M., & Kotha, S. (2002). Managerial Actions, Stock Returns, and Earnings: The Case of Business-to-Business Internet Firms. *Journal of Accounting Research*, *40*(2), 529–556. doi:10.1111/1475-679X.00060

Rodríguez, M. C., & Alegría, S. S. (2012). The value of audit quality in public and private companies: Evidence from Spain. *The Journal of Management and Governance*, *16*(4), 683–706. doi:10.100710997-011-9183-4

Shabbir, A., & Padgett, C. (2005). *The UK Code of Corporate Governance: Link between Compliance and Firm Performance*. Working Paper, ICMA Centre. Available at: http://ssrn.com/abstract=934313

Sila, V., Gonzalez, A., & Hagendorff, J. (2017). Independent director reputation incentives and stock price informativeness. *Journal of Corporate Finance*, *47*, 219–235. doi:10.1016/j.jcorpfin.2017.09.018

Stulz, R. M., & Williamson, R. (2003). Culture, openness, and finance. *Journal of Financial Economics*, *70*(3), 313–349. doi:10.1016/S0304-405X(03)00173-9

Tabachnick, B., & Fidell, L. (2001). *Using Multivari- ate Statistics* (3rd ed.). Harper Collins College.

Teoh, S. H., Welch, I., & Wong, T. J. (1998b). Earnings management and the underperformance of seasoned equity offerings. *Journal of Financial Economics*, *50*(1), 63–99. doi:10.1016/S0304-405X(98)00032-4

Teoh, S. H., Wong, T. J., & Rao, G. R. (1998a). Are accruals during initial public offerings opportunistic? *Review of Accounting Studies*, *3*(1/2), 175–208. doi:10.1023/A:1009688619882

Ullah, F., Jiang, P., Shahab, Y., Li, H. X., & Xu, L. (2019). Block ownership and CEO compensation: Does board gender diversity matter? *Applied Economics*, 1–15.

Vafeas, N. (2000). Board structure and the informativeness of earnings. *Journal of Accounting and Public Policy*, *19*(2), 139–160. doi:10.1016/S0278-4254(00)00006-5

Wahlen, J. M., Jones, J. P., & Pagach, D. P. (2012). *Intermediate Accounting: Reporting and Analysis*. South-Western Pub.

Wang, L., & Yung, K. (2011). Do State Enterprises Manage Earnings More than Privately Owned Firms? The Case of China. *Journal of Business Finance & Accounting*, *38*(7–8), 794–812. doi:10.1111/j.1468-5957.2011.02254.x

Watts, R., & Zimmerman, J. (1990). Positive accounting theory: A ten year perspective. *The Accounting Review*, *65*, 131–156.

Weir, C., & Laing, D. (2000). The performance-governance relationship: The effects of Cadbury compliance on UK quoted companies. *The Journal of Management and Governance*, *4*(4), 265–281. doi:10.1023/A:1009950903720

Weir, C., Laing, D., & McKnight, P. J. (2002). Internal and External Governance Mechanisms: Their Impact on the Performance of Large UK Public Companies. *Journal of Business Finance & Accounting*, *29*(5), 579–611. doi:10.1111/1468-5957.00444

Wintoki, M. B., Linck, J. S., & Netter, J. M. (2012). Endogeneity and the dynamics of internal corporate governance. *Journal of Financial Economics*, *105*(3), 581–606. doi:10.1016/j.jfineco.2012.03.005

Xie, B., Davidson, W. III, & DaDalt, P. (2003). Earning management and corporate governance: The role of the board and the audit committee. *Journal of Corporate Finance*, *9*(3), 295–316. doi:10.1016/S0929-1199(02)00006-8

Yeung, W. H., & Lento, C. (2018). Ownership structure, audit quality, board structure, and stock price crash risk: Evidence from China. *Global Finance Journal*, *37*, 1–24. doi:10.1016/j.gfj.2018.04.002

Yu, F. (2008). Corporate Governance and Earnings Management. *Journal of Financial Economics*, *88*(2), 245–271. doi:10.1016/j.jfineco.2007.05.008

ENDNOTES

1. Earnings management (EM) occurs "when managers use judgment in financial reporting and in structuring transactions to alter financial reports to either mislead some stakeholders about the underlying economic performance of the company, or to influence contractual outcomes that depend on reported accounting numbers (Healy and Wahlen, 1998).
2. Group of 20 (G20) is an international forum of 20 major economies; this accounts for 85% of the global economy.
3. BRICS is an acronym for five major emerging economies namely Brazil, Russia, India, China and South Africa.
4. The expected sign based on the relation between individual CG or control variables and AWCA, which is a proxy of EQ. For instance, CEOD is expected to have a positive association with AWCA, which means (lower EQ) and so on.
5. xtreg (panel data with random effect and the robust standard error)
6. xtivreg (2sls) two stage least squares regression

APPENDIX

Variables Used in the Multivariable Analysis

Dependent Variables

AWCA: is the absolute value of abnormal working capital accrual based on Defond and Park, (2001) model scaled by beginning total assets.

Independent Variables

BSIZE: board size is natural logarithm of the board size.
IND: independent director is the ratio of independent director to the total directors
CEOD: CEO duality is a dummy variable that takes the value of one if the CEO also serve as chairman of the board and zero otherwise.
BMEET: Board meetings is the number of board meetings held per year.

Control Variables

FAMC: is the percentage of family ownership,
STATC: is the percentage of state ownership
INSTATIC: is the percentage of institutional ownership
AUDITEX: audit committee expertise is the ration of member with financial or accounting expertise to the total directors.
GROWTH: firm growth is the natural logarithm of the annual change in net sales divided by total assets.
LEVERAGE: leverage is the natural logarithm of total liabilities divided by total assets
SIZE: firm size is the natural logarithm of total assets
BIG4: big 4-audit firm is a dummy variable that takes the value of one if the company is audited by one of the BIG4 and zero otherwise.

Chapter 3
The Role of Corporate Governance in Mitigating Earnings Management Practices:
A Review Study

Nagat Mohamed Marie Younis
Faculty of Business, University of Jeddah, Saudi Arabia

ABSTRACT

The aim of the research is to clarify the role and importance of corporate governance (CG) mechanisms in mitigating earnings management (EM) practices. To achieve this objective, reference was made to previous studies and relevant research. An analysis was mentioned in accounting about the relationship between agency theory and earnings management clarifying the theoretical framework for earnings management from where the concept, motives, techniques of earnings management, methods of disclosure of earnings management, the risks resulting from earnings management, as well as know corporate governance, in terms of concept, goals, importance, principles, characteristics, and mechanisms of corporate governance, and finally, the role of corporate governance in limiting earnings management practices.

INTRODUCTION

The separation of ownership from corporate management results in an attempt to maximize the economic benefits for each party in company as the shareholders (owners/ principal) seek to preserve the company's assets to maximize the wealth of the owners, while the managers (corporate management/ agent) seek to maximize the rewards by achieving the largest level of profits for the companies that they manage. The agency theory is considered one of the most important theories that explain the behaviors resulting from the shareholders 'relationship with managers, and the accounting and financial information is the most important link between them, as the shareholders seek to review the financial statements to know the financial position of the company, while the management tries to influence the content of the financial

DOI: 10.4018/978-1-7998-4852-3.ch003

statements in order to direct decisions to guarantees the realization of personal benefits for them, and this opportunistic behavior is called "Earnings Management".

As a result of conflicts of interests between the owners and management and the rest of the stakeholders in the company, and according to the principle of rational choice, each party tries to maximize its own benefits over the interests of other, this a problem called the "agency problem", so "agency theory" came as an attempt to solve that problem and limit management behavior by preferring their personal interests over the interests of other parties (Rodriguez, et al., 2016).

Earnings management has known that it a tool for satisfying the self-interest of the managers, it can be used for the welfare of the stakeholders if it is ethically used. To get the optimum benefit of earnings management, steps should be taken to improve corporate governance. Accounting standards should be revised to there remain no for manipulating earnings and auditors should be more careful in detecting earnings manipulation and their independence should be ensured (Alvarado, et al., 2019). Earnings management involves the manipulation of company earnings towards a pre-determined target. This target can be motivated by a preference for more stable earnings, in which case management is said to be carrying out income smoothing. Opportunistic income smoothing can, in turn, signal lower risk and increase a firm's market value. Other possible motivations for earnings management include the need to maintain the levels of certain accounting ratios due to debt covenants, and the pressure to maintain increasing earnings and to beat analyst targets. (Wikipedia, 2019)

The successful techniques in earnings management are categorized into several sub-categories as follow: Big Bath Techniques, Cookie Jar Reserve Techniques, "Big Bet on the Future" and "Flushing" the Investment Portfolio, Write-off of Long-Term Operating Assets, Sale/Lease Back, Shrink the Ship, Introducing new standard, Operating versus non-operating Income, Early Retirement of Debt, Use of Derivatives. (Nia, et al., 2015) The companies practice earnings management through a set of methods and techniques, the most important of which are the following: the nature of accounting estimates, flexibility in accounting principles, changing the disclosure pattern used in the financial statements, structuring operations associated with inelastic accounting standards. Rigorous accounting standards, awareness of audit committee, corporate governance and the morality of the stakeholders play a necessary role to control earnings management.

To avoid the agency's problem, the importance of applying the rules of governance came, especially after the Asian financial crises and the Enron scandal, which was the reason behind the discovery of manipulation of profits by management, which affected the reliability of the published financial statements (Palmer, et al., 2019), the changes in the global markets and the increasing intensity of competition between economic units, globalization and privatization programs that led to the implementation of governance, Therefore, many studies have urged to apply corporate governance mechanisms to provide reliability, honesty, and fairness in the information contained in financial statements, which would enhance financial reports quality, It control cases of fraud and manipulation with the financial statements, and in addition to the insufficient role of accounting standards in facing management practices in manipulating profits, It was necessary to search for ways to facing the earnings management phenomenon, and the solution was what is known as "corporate governance". (Asogwa, et al., 2019)

Previous studies confirmed that recently there has been increased interest in corporate governance as a result of the transition to market economies, the transfer of capital across borders, the expansion of projects, the separation of ownership from management, and the weakness of internal control systems, especially on the practices of corporate managers, and the resulting collapse of some large economic units, such as Enron, WorldCom, and others, which led to mistrust of investors and stakeholders in the honesty and fairness of the published accounting information, accordingly, the countries have taken many laws and procedures such as "Sarbanes-Oxley Act, 2002" which was imposed on companies listed on the United States Stock Exchange to implement the rules of governance in order to eliminate financial and administrative corruption of companies by activating the role of non-executive members on boards of directors. Also, this law has a major impact in formulating the concept of corporate governance, and activating its mechanisms to ensure the quality of accounting information and providing more transparency and at the appropriate time, as well as protecting stakeholders. (Hmeidat & Al-Rifai, 2019)

The researcher believes that Some companies may practice earnings management by influencing the accounting measurement and disclosure processes for serves their interests as a result of flexibility in international accounting standards by choosing between methods and alternative accounting policies, although In the short term, earnings Management practice brings benefits to the organization, but it may lead to serious problems in the long term, which are reflected in the weak operational and economic efficiency of the companies, and given the seriousness of this phenomenon, the importance of this study emerged, and the issue of obtaining honest and reliable information has become urgent and important for investors because they need such information to assist them in making their correct investment decisions. Therefore, the current study focuses on clarifying the role of corporate governance in reducing earnings management practices. The study is divided into three points: (1) the relationship between agency theory and earnings management, while clarifying the theoretical framework for earnings management. (2) the conceptual framework of corporate governance. (3) The Role of Corporate Governance in Limiting Earnings Management Practices.

THE RELATIONSHIP BETWEEN AGENCY THEORY AND EARNINGS MANAGEMENT, WITH CLARIFYING THE THEORETICAL FRAMEWORK FOR EARNINGS MANAGEMENT

The Relationship Between Agency Theory and Earnings Management

The agency theory is one of the most important theories that explain the behaviors resulting from the relationship of shareholders and managers, and was defined as "a contract whereby the client appoints an agent in order to perform some business and services on his behalf" (Kopp, 2019). The agency theory depends on a set of assumptions that may affect the relationship between managers and shareholder, and the most important of these assumptions are: the hypothesis of market efficiency, the hypothesis of rational behavior, the hypothesis of different preferences, the assumption of risk, the hypothesis of asymmetry of information. And agency theory includes some costs that are categorized into supervision and follow-up costs and the costs prohibited by the agent. According to the agency's theory, management behavior arises in influencing the accounting numbers mentioned in the financial statements as a result of the contractual relationships between the parties involved (Andrijasevic, 2018). It is noted that the of freedom enjoyed by the management when preparing and presenting the financial statements, makes the process of choosing between accounting policies will be influenced by its own goals at the expense of honesty of expression of the events and operations that the company carried out during a specific period.

Thus, earnings management has emerged, as it is done through the practices that the administration produces and results from its selection among the accounting policies of the company to achieve its own goals in order to mislead the shareholders, and thus it is the set of activities and measures taken by the management of the company aiming to maximize management benefits regardless of their legitimacy, and that by utilizing flexibility in accounting principles and standards. Recently, interest in earnings management has increased as a result of the financial collapses that occurred for large companies, which are due to administrative and financial corruption and the administration's lack of proper exercise in supervision and control, lack of transparency and weak interest in applying accounting standards correctly, and the lack of accurate accounting information. This has resulted in increased interest in adopting the concepts of quality of auditing in the audit work and applying corporate governance and benefiting from it in developing accounting and administrative practices to limiting earnings management practices (Matteo & Paolone, 2018).

The Theoretical Framework for Earnings Management

Concept

Earnings management has attracted the interests of many researchers in accounting thought, and there are many definitions for this term, it has been defined as a deliberate intervention in the financial reporting for the purpose of achieving some of the special gains. And so, it is the use of accounting techniques to produce financial statements that present an overly positive view of a company's business activities and financial position. Many accounting rules and principles require that a company's management make judgments in following these principles. Earnings management takes advantage of how accounting rules are applied and creates financial statements that inflate or "smooth" earnings (Tuovila, 2019). In accounting, earnings management is a method of manipulating financial records to improve the appearance of the company's financial position, and also, it defined as manipulating the accounting results and the administration's attempt to influence the number of profits announced in the short term with the aim of creating a different perception of the company's true performance to achieve special gains. It is clear from the above that earnings management is carried out by managers with the aim of influencing accounting numbers by utilizing flexibility in accounting policies and practicing personal estimates in order to achieve the personal benefits or to mislead users of financial statements with regard to the financial performance of the company. In many articles, it is called creative accounting, it includes utilizing flexibility inside accounting to convey a predetermined benefit, the expression "Creative Accounting" describes the methods that directors utilize for controlling the figures that are detailed in Company Financial Statements, it is conceivable by the flexibility and unclearness of accounting rules and of the Law of the Company. (Yaseen, et al., 2018)

The accounting literature defines earnings management as "distorting the application of generally accepted accounting principles" (GAAP), many in the financial community assume that GAAP prevents earnings management, so, it results from a distortion of the application of GAAP. Ali (2013) defined earnings management as the accounting policies or the accruals control, chosen by the management of enterprises to make the earnings reach the expected level under the pressure from the relevant stakeholders and the constraints of GAAP. In addition to the choice of accounting policy and the control of accruals, the means of earnings management have also included lobbying for the regulatory organization to modify the accounting principles and the manipulation of profit figures in the fiscal report, earnings management differs from financial fraud if the former is covered by GAAP. There are a set of restrictions that control management behavior when exercising earnings management, including Company size, debt ratio, profitability, ownership structure, quality of the audit process, type of sector to which the company belongs.

Motives

There are different categories of incentives, Freihat (2014) stated stock market incentives, Hiding private information, political costs, personal Incentives, internal motives, management compensation contract motivations, lending contract motivations, regulatory motivations, and income-smoothing incentives, and also Nia et al. (2015) showed different categories of incentives, such as management compensation, contract motivations, income-smoothing motivation, meeting or beating the earnings expectations of analysts, avoiding debt covenant violation, regulatory incentives, and earnings management performed to avoid financial distress. We will explain the incentives in some detail as follows:

1. **Stock Market Incentives:** Managers are encouraged to manipulate profits if the pre-managed earnings are lower than analysts' expectations in the market, in order to influence the stock price performance in the short term. It is noted that companies that show an increase in profits are less likely to manage profits to align shareholder goals with the goals of managers and give less space to agency disputes. Finally, companies must meet or exceed analyst profit expectations to maintain, enhance, and enhance their financial position, so companies may tend to use profit management to achieve this goal.
2. **Personal Incentives:** There might be other than financial motives for the CEO to manage earnings. A new CEO can be tending to downwards earnings management in the year of change and upwards earnings management in the following years. Retiring CEO's use upwards earnings management to leave performance in good.
3. **Hiding Private Information:** Failing firms engage in earnings management and change their annual accounts to conceal their financial without measuring the consequences on stock price or CEO compensation.
4. **Management Compensation Contract Motivations:** Management compensation theory confirms that managers are motivated to use earnings management to improve compensation because management bonuses are often tied to firm earnings. Opportunist theory assumes that managers act with short-term self-interest motivation and use loopholes such as the flexibility of accounting standards to manage earnings. So, earnings management is used to increase income and managers are keen on maintaining earnings growth because of their effects on stock prices and because their compensations are often tied to firm earnings, or decrease research and development expenditure to increase earnings and thus their payout over leaving the company.
5. **Political Costs:** Political costs are a strong incentive for firms to manage their earnings. It can be important for companies to seem more/less profitable to escape from governmental interference when accounting numbers are the basis for tax calculation, there might be large tax avoidance incentives for earnings management.
6. **Internal Motives:** There are internal motives for earnings management that are not linked to external stakeholders but are intra-company, such as the change financial reports or structuring transactions in a way that avoids increasing the budget or performance standards.
7. **Lending Contracts Motivations:** Certain contracts between the company and other parties depend on the accounting numbers, this is an incentive for managers to manage profits to complete these

contracts in a manner that achieves the goals of the managers. such as lending contracts, as creditors impose restrictions on the payment of dividends, share buybacks and the issuing of additional debt in order to ensure the repayment of the firm's borrowings. So, firms who have a lot of debt have strong incentive to manage earnings.

8. **Regulatory Motivations:** They are called organizational or political motives, and they aim to reduce organizational or political costs, it is used to manage earnings which may help managers influence the actions of regulators or government officials, for example, some industries as insurance, banking, and utility industries, that are monitored for compliance with regulations linked to accounting figures and ratios. These industries are often subject to requirements for ensuring that they have sufficient assets or capital to meet their financial obligations. These regulations may motivate managers to use earnings management to meet the requirements, from earnings management techniques: overstating loan loss provisions, reduce loan write-offs and recognizing unrealized gains.
9. **Income-Smoothing Incentives:** It is a technique in accounting to overcome net income fluctuations from one period to the next. Managers make discretionary accounting choices in an attempt to smooth reported earnings around the expected target, there are several reasons for earnings smoothing. First, poor performance may result in management ejection. Thus, managers shift current earnings to the future and vice versa. Second, managers smooth earnings to reduce the earnings volatility of a firm and to present sustainable earnings that may lead to high stock prices.
10. **Avoiding Financial:** When companies face financial distress, executives will hide the actual financial in the financial statement, as managers of distressed firms have low morale and high stress caused by increased chances of bankruptcy, which will motivate them to engage in earnings management to ensure that their reported earnings meet targets and thereby postpone bankruptcy.

Techniques of Earnings Management

Managers can achieve earnings from accounting choices or operating decisions and also managers can manage earnings by they have flexibility in making accounting or operating choices. The most widely used earnings management techniques can be classified as follows: (Rahman, et al., 2013)

1. **"Big Bath" Techniques:** It is an earnings management technique whereby a one-time charge is taken against income in order to reduce assets, which results in lower expenses in the future, such as the write-off or reduces the asset from the financial books and results in lower net income for that year. The objective is to 'take one big bath' in a single year so future years will show increased net income.
2. **"Cookie Jar Reserve" Technique:** It deals with estimations of future events according to GAAP; management has to estimate and record obligations that will be paid in the future as a result of events or transactions in the current fiscal year based on an accrual basis. But there is always uncertainty surrounding the estimation process because the future is not always certain. There is no correct answer, management has to select a single amount according to GAAP so there is a chance of taking advantage of earnings management. Under the cookie-jar technique, the corporation will try to overestimate expenses during the current period to manage earnings. If and when actual expenses turn out lower than estimates, the difference can be put into the "cookie jar" to be used later when the company needs a boost in earnings to meet predictions. Some examples of estima-

tion to manage earnings are sales returns and allowances, estimates of bad debt and write-downs; estimating inventory write-downs; warranty costs; pension expenses; terminating pension plans and estimating the percentage of completion for long term contracts, etc.

3. **"Big Bet on the Future" Technique:** When an acquisition occurs, the corporation acquiring the other is said to have made a big bet on the future. Under GAAP regulations, an acquisition must be reported as a purchase. This leaves two doors open for earnings management. In the first instance, a company can write off continuing R&D costs against current earnings in the acquisition year, protecting future earnings from these charges. This means that when the costs are actually incurred in the future, they will not have to be reported and thus future earnings will receive a boost. The second method is to claim the earnings of the recently acquired corporation. When the acquired corporation consolidated with parent company earnings, then immediately receive a boost in the current year's earnings. By acquiring another company, the parent company buys a guaranteed boost in current or future earnings through big bet technique.
4. **"Flushing" the Investment Portfolio:** To achieve strategic pact and invest excess funds, a company buys the shares of another company. Two forms of investment are trading securities and available for sale securities. Actual gains or losses from sales or any changes in the market value of trading securities are reported as operating income whereas any change in the market value of available for sale securities in "other comprehensive income components" at the bottom of the income statement. When available for sale securities are sold, any loss or gain is reported in operating income. A manager can manage its earnings through various techniques which are: (1) The company can sell portfolio security that has an unrealized gain and can report the gain as operating earnings if it is required. (2) If the manager wants to show lower earnings then he can sell the security that has an unrealized loss and report the loss in operating earnings. (3) Management can manage earnings through the change of its holdings from available to sale securities to trading securities and vice versa. This would have the effect of moving any unrealized gain or loss on the security to or from the income statement, (4) Write-down "impaired securities, so securities that have a long-term decline in fair market value can be written down reduced value regardless of their portfolio classification.
5. **Introducing New Standard:** New rules and regulations are introduced in GAAP due to the changing demand of the business environment. Accounting principles can be modified in a way that will not change the earnings. When a new accounting standard is adopted it takes two to three years. Voluntary early adoption may provide an opportunity to manage the earnings. A company can take advantage of manage earnings by changing the time an accrual basis rather than cash basis those are recorded as an expense on a cash basis. Moreover, the timely adoption of a better revenue recognition rule will provide a new window to manage the earnings.
6. **Write-off of Long-Term Operating Assets:** A company can increase its earnings by selling long-term assets with unrealized gain or loss. When the real earnings of a company cannot meet analyst expectations, managers would likely attempt to boost reported earnings to the expected level by selling assets. Conversely, when the real earnings of a company are higher than expectations, the company would attempt to drop reported earnings to the expected level by selling loss-making assets, so the manipulation of earnings occurs by selling assets.
7. **"Throw Out" a Problem Child:** To increase profits for a future period, the company can manage the earnings by selling subsidiaries with poor performance, and the profit or loss is recorded in the statement of the current period when selling a subsidiary. Shareholders become the owner of the problem by distributing or exchanging the shares of a subsidiary with the existing shareholders.

So, no gain or loss is reported in the sub-offer. It is possible to "exchange" shares in a company affiliated with the equity method without having any recordable profit or loss.

8. **Early Retirement of Debt:** Management can manage the earnings by selecting the fiscal period of early retirement of debt. A gain or loss has occurred when the company makes the early payment of cash which is different from the book value of long-term debt such as bonds. This gain or loss is recorded as an extraordinary item at the bottom of the income statement which boosts the earnings of that period.
9. **Operating Versus Non-Operating Income:** Earnings are two types: operating and non-operating. Non-operating earnings will not affect future earnings whereas operating earnings are expected to continue in the near future. Non-operating income includes discontinued operations, extraordinary gains or losses, the cumulative effect of change in accounting principles. The manager can manage its earnings when making decisions about items that fall into those areas.
10. **Sale/ Lease Back:** It is another management strategy that may lead to earnings management. In a sale-leaseback transaction, a company sells an asset to a buyer and immediately leases the asset back from the buyer. Companies often enter sale-leaseback transactions to obtain cash financing, and the company can manage its earnings by recording the gain or loss. According to IAS 17, losses occurring in a sale/leaseback transaction are recognized on the seller's book immediately and gain is amortized over the period if it is capital lease or proportion of the payment is operating lease.
11. **Use of Derivatives:** Derivatives offer a lot of opportunities for a manager to manage earnings. It can be used to protect against some types of business risk, such as interest rate changes; commodity price change; oil price changes; changes in foreign currency exchange rates. Derivates should be reported as assets and liabilities in the balance sheet and measured at fair value. Gains and losses from derivate transactions are recognized immediately in regular income. For example, suppose a company had a large issue of bonds outstanding at a fixed interest rate. The company could enter into an interest rate swap that would convert the fixed-rate bonds into variable-rate bonds. When the interest rate increases, the company would record an increase in interest expense and a decrease if the rate has decreased. Since, when the company enters into the swap, the timing option provides an opportunity to manage earnings.
12. **Shrink the Ship:** Companies sometimes decide to repurchase their own share, it uses this technique for manage earnings to meet or beat the EPS forecast of analysts, build credibility and maintain their reputation with capital markets and increase stock prices. Firms buy back their own stocks to improve their financial ratios because share repurchase reduces the number of shares outstanding. Thus, ratios tied to this measure, such as earnings per share and price-to-earnings ratio, can be temporarily boosted. The stock buyback also increases firms' return on assets and return on equity because of less outstanding equity and assets in repurchasing.

The Risks Resulting from Earnings Management

Earnings management practice leads to inaccuracy of accounting information, and a loss of confidence and credibility in the published accounting information, and thus negatively affects investor decisions, lack of transparency and disclosure in financial statements, and the lack of clarity of the financial position which affects negatively on the movement of the stock market, and thus affects the economic performance of society (Younis, 2019). Alkababji (2019) stated for hiding operational management problems, management resorted to earnings management practice to obtain promotions and bonuses, which leads to keeping the errors because of unresolved, with exposure to severe economic sanctions as The American Stock Exchange imposed severe penalties on companies that exercised earnings management and asked them to recalculate their profits and announce them clearly because the company reduced its profits. earnings management practice conflicts with ethical performance standards, leading to material errors of the financial statements. Also, Sanad (2019) indicated earnings management practices may result in a lower quality of reported earnings that do not reflect the true financial performance of the company. Consequently, it reduces investor confidence in financial reports. Therefore, companies use different monitoring systems to eliminate the opportunistic behavior of managers to increase Financial reporting transparency and reliability. so, that corporate governance mechanisms can limit a manager's ability to manage earnings.

THE CONCEPTUAL FRAMEWORK OF CORPORATE GOVERNANCE

The Concept of Corporate Governance

To avoid the agency's problem, companies implement corporate governance practices that control, direct, and monitor the actions of managers and direct their concerns towards maximizing the wealth of shareholders. (Cruz & Vargas-Hernández, 2018), so corporate governance refers to the system of rules, practices, and processes by which a firm is directed and controlled. Corporate governance essentially involves balancing the interests of a company's many stakeholders, such as shareholders, senior management executives, customers, suppliers, financiers, the government, and the community. Since corporate governance also provides the framework for attaining a company's objectives, it includes every field of management, from action plans and internal controls to performance measurement and corporate disclosure. (Chen, 2019)

Also, governance is defined as the system by which rights and responsibilities are distributed to various parties in the company, including the board of directors and managers, shareholders and other stakeholders, and it also sets rules and procedures for making decisions related to the company. (IOG, 2019) Corporate Governance deals with determining ways to take effective strategic decisions, which gives authority and complete responsibility to the Board of Directors, the need for corporate governance arises in today's market-oriented economy, also efficiency, as well as globalization, are significant factors urging corporate governance. It is an essential tool to develop added value to the stakeholders, achieve transparency, ensures strong, balanced economic development, interests of all shareholders are safeguarded, and also it ensures that all shareholders fully exercise their rights and that the organization fully recognizes their rights. So, Corporate Governance has a broad scope, it includes both social and institutional aspects and encourages a trustworthy as well as the ethical environment. (MSG, 2019)

The Importance and Goals of Corporate Governance

Rathod (2018) explained that good corporate governance ensures corporate success, economic growth, minimizes wastages, corruption, control of risks, and mismanagement, efficient processes because procedures are streamlined and consistent, visibility of errors and reduced costs. Strong corporate governance maintains investors' confidence, as a result of which, the company can raise capital efficiently and effectively. It lowers the capital cost, it has a positive impact on the share price, Maximizing the company value and achieving stability in the financial markets, it provides a proper inducement to the owners and managers to achieve objectives that are in interests of the shareholders and the organization. Also, goals of Corporate Governance include protecting the interest of the investing public, maintaining confidence in companies and enhancing global reputation as a trusted financial center, promote transparency and accountability, allow flexibility in the enforcement of the rights and duties of the different corporate, empower the board of directors and its members but at the same time acknowledging the need for independence of directors. Alignment of reward with long-term interest and transparency, Growing importance on the role of the board regarding risk management. (Lan, 2012)

Tsoi (2017) seen that Corporate governance makes companies more accountable and transparent to investors, gives them the tools to respond to stakeholder concerns such as sustainable environmental and social development. It contributes to the development and increased access to capital, encourages new investments, boosts economic growth, and provides employment opportunities, limit risk. A lack of corporate governance can lead to profit loss, corruption not only to the corporation but to society. Poor corporate governance can create potential conflicts of interests, expropriation and unfair of minority shareholders, small shareholders with little impact on the stock price are ignore for the interests of majority shareholders and the executive board and this can weak public confidence.

The study confirmed (OECD, 2019) that good corporate governance helps to build an environment of trust, transparency, and accountability necessary for fostering long-term investment, financial stability, and business integrity, thereby supporting stronger growth and more inclusive societies. Governance also contributes to improving the company's management by helping directors and boards for developing the right strategies for the company, ensuring make decisions are on sound foundations, and thus determining rewards fair. (Paine and Srinivasan, 2019) So, the importance of governance is due to the fact that it helps to protect the rights of shareholders and stakeholders and organize the relationship between the company's executive management and board of directors and audit committees, and it is a tool to motivate workers and management to perform business efficiently and effectively, and this leads to a reduction in the company's risks and raising the value of its shares in the market, The governance system also improves the quality and efficiency of leadership in the company and improves of production quality, and helps to improve efficiency in the use of the company's assets, and to work to reduce the cost of capital, and also helps to achieve the wishes and goals of society. Good corporate governance helps attract investment, which reflects positively on the financial position of companies by emphasizing transparency in corporate dealings and in the auditing and accounting procedures.

Corporate Governance Principles

Rathod (2019) confirmed good corporate governance has come to have an extended vision of organizations for achieving the best possible results, organizations are expected to take actions that have a beneficial effect on all stakeholders, and that includes employees, stakeholders and OECD registered this change when it revised its "Principles of Corporate Governance" in 2015. as following "Corporate governance involves a set of relationships between a company's management, its board, its shareholders and other stakeholders. Corporate governance also provides the structure through which the objectives of the company are set, and the means of attaining those objectives and monitoring performance are determined". The six Organization for Economic Cooperation and Development (OECD) Principles includes the following an effective corporate governance framework, protecting rights of shareholders, the equitable treatment of shareholders, protecting the role of stakeholders in corporate governance, full disclosure, and transparency, and achieving fair responsibilities of the board. (OECD, 2015)

But Ali (2019) mentioned that there are 10 Principles of corporate governance as follows: lay solid foundations for management and oversight, promote ethical and responsible decision-making, safeguard integrity in financial reporting, make timely and balanced disclosure, respect the rights of shareholders, recognize and manage risk, encourage enhanced performance, remunerate fairly and responsibly, recognize the legitimate interests of stakeholders. In addition to its obligation to its stakeholders, there are other obligations to non-shareholders such as employees, customers and the community. The Board has a responsibility to set the tone and standards with respect to corporate social responsibility.

Effective implementation of the G20/OECD Principles requires a good understanding of economic realities and adaption to changes in corporate and market developments. The G20/OECD Principles, therefore, state that policymakers have a responsibility to put in place a framework that is flexible enough to meet the needs of corporations that are operating in widely different circumstances, facilitating their development of new opportunities. The builds the 2018 OECD report Flexibility and Proportionality in Corporate Governance. The report finds that a vast majority of countries have criteria that allow for flexibility and proportionality at company level in each of the seven areas of regulation that were reviewed: 1) board composition, board committees, and board qualifications; 2) remuneration; 3) related party transactions; 4) disclosure of periodic financial information; 5) disclosure of major shareholdings; 6) takeovers; and 7) pre-emptive rights. The report also contains case studies of six countries, which provide a more detailed picture of how flexibility and proportionality are being used in practice (OECD, 2019).

Characteristics of Corporate Governance

There are seven Characteristics of Good Corporate Governance, we mention it as follows: (Mack, 2019; VComply, 2018; Hossain, et al., 2011)

- **Discipline and Commitment:** It is an obligation by the company's senior management to internationally recognized and accepted behavior, and this means the company understands the principles of good governance, especially at the senior management level. Therefore, all parties involved will be committed to the procedures, processes and power structures of the company, and good corporate governance requires ownership of discipline and commitment to implementing policies, decisions, and strategies.
- **Transparency and Information Sharing:** Transparency is a measure of the extent to which the necessary, accurate and timely information is provided and represents the key to corporate success. It reflects whether investors get a true picture of what is happening inside the company, and transparency helps employees in the company understand their roles well, understand management strategies and allow monitoring of the company's financial performance. Transparency is also important for an audience that has no confidence in secret companies. The corporate governance framework must ensure that all matters related to financial position, performance and ownership are disclosed in a timely and accurate manner.
- **Social Responsibility:** Responsibility means the behavior that allows corrective action and punishment for mismanagement, responsible management will take steps to put the company on the right path, and the board of directors is responsible towards the company and must act responsibly in front of all stakeholders, and social responsibility at the company level is an important topic,

and consumers expect companies to be Effective members of the community such as efforts of recycling, waste minimization, and pollution, and good corporate governance outlines ways to improve company practices by reinvesting in the local community.

- **Fairness to Employees and Customers:** There should be fair and equal attention to all stakeholders and considering their rights and opinions, the systems within the company must be balanced. For example, managers must motivate employees to do their best, recognizing that a heavy workload can have negative impacts such as low morale and a high turnover rate. Also, companies must deal with clients fairly for moral reasons and public relations because unfair treatment can bring benefits in the short term, but it will harm in the long-term.
- **Well defined roles:** Everyone has a role in the company and be sure to give the right people selected roles such as managers and employees. Since everyone plays their part and there is no room for confusion.
- **Accountability:** Individuals or groups within the organization must be responsible for their decisions and actions such as boards of directors taking action on specific issues, the mechanisms of governance must be effective to allow accountability and provides investors with the means to query and assess the actions of the board and its committees.
- **Regular Self-Evaluation:** Self-evaluation represents the best type of evaluation of the company's management by surveying the opinions of clients and employees, where self-assessments are conducted to identify problems and shortcomings in order to correct and improve. An example of this is assessing your current company policies, and outside consultants can be used to analyze your operations to determine ways to improve your company's performance and efficiency.
- **Independence:** It means setting up mechanisms to avoid conflicts of interest through the formation of the company's board of directors independent of shareholders and management, as well as the lack of control by the members of the board on the executive authority for ensuring that independent members are able to play the role of oversight and follow-up to executive management in a way that serves the interests of shareholders.
- **Risk management:** The company must exercise risk management effectively in order to protect it from potential risks.
- **Balanced objectives:** The goals of all concerned must be balanced, to match other goals, and be synchronized.

Dewey (2019) noted that there are four characteristics of good governance: managing the organization's strategic risks to avoid unforeseen risks to the company, having a clear strategy that fits with the organization's mission, transparency, and disclosure that unifies public organization and trust, as well as annual self-assessment by the board of directors In order to improve the corporate governance model, managers are assured that they have left a stronger board of directors than the current one.

Mechanisms of Corporate Governance

Governance rules and regulations aim to achieve transparency and fairness, granting the right to accountability of the company's management, achieving protection for shareholders, and limiting the exploitation of power in a non-public interest, thus the development of investment and savings, maximizing profitability, and providing new job opportunities, and these rules emphasize the importance of commitment With the law, and to ensure a review of financial performance, with the formation of an audit committee that will have many tasks to achieve independent oversight. Commitment to corporate governance mechanisms reduces financial and administrative corruption, increases the efficiency of performance, investor confidence, and thus increases the state's ability to attract investment and develop the country's economy (Mustafa, 2010). There is an agreement that a good application of corporate governance depends on the level of quality of internal and external mechanisms. Study (Wimelda & Chandra, 2018) indicated Corporate governance mechanisms can be divided into two ways: internal corporate governance mechanisms and external corporate governance mechanisms. External corporate governance mechanisms are determined by external factors and aim to govern firms in shareholders' interests, such as legal protection and takeover rules. Internal corporate governance is decided by internal factors, such as board structure, board composition, board meetings, audit committees, compensation committee, ownership structure, and institutional shareholders.

Internal Corporate Governance Mechanisms

Internal corporate governance controls monitor activities and then take corrective actions to accomplish organizational goals. So, the internal governance mechanisms focus on the company's activities and take the necessary measures to achieve the company's goals. the internal governance mechanisms can be categorized into the following: (Hossain, 2017; Hamidat & Al-Rifai, 2019)

1. **Board of Directors:** The corporate governance framework should ensure the strategic guidance of the company, the effective monitoring of management by the board, and the board's accountability to the company and the shareholders. It is the best tool for monitoring management behavior, as it protects the capital invested in the company from misuse, through its legal authority to hire, fire and compensate top management, the strong board of directors participates in setting the company's strategy, provides appropriate incentives for management, monitors its behavior and continuous supervision of the company's performance, and removing individuals who don't improve the company's overall financial performance, thereby maximizing the value of the company. For these boards to be effective, they must work to achieve the company's interests and social goals. And Shareholders often elect board members at the corporation's annual shareholder meeting or conference, board Structure is consisting of different disciplines and sectors which surely support the good corporate governance. If the board is structured in such a way that there is the representation of all-important stakeholder that exists, this will positively impact corporate governance.
2. **Internal Audit:** it is review of a company's business and financial operations, the internal audit plays an important role in the governance process and increases the shareholders 'ability to hold the company accountable, where the internal auditors within an organization who test the design and implementation of the entity's internal control procedures and the reliability of its financial reporting. And carry out many of the activities which increase credibility, fairness, improve employee behavior, and reduce the risks of administrative and financial corruption, Audits also can improve an organization's standing in the business environment. The internal and external audit is an important monitoring mechanism within the governance framework structure because it ensures the accuracy and integrity of financial reports and the prevention and detection of fraud and counterfeiting cases. Professional and regulatory bodies have recognized the importance of the internal audit function in the governance process.

3. **Balance of Power:** Balancing power ensures no one can increase resources, segregating duties between board members, managers, and other individuals to ensure that everyone's responsibility is well and within scope of the organization. Corporate governance can separate the number of functions that one division or department completes within an organization and creating well-defined roles for keeping the organization flexible, ensuring that operational changes or new hires can be made without interrupting current operations, and also there is a separation of ownership and management as one of the main pillars of corporate governance.
4. **Remuneration:** Performance-based remuneration is designed to relate some proportion of salary to individual performance in the form of cash or non-cash payments such as shares and share options, or other benefits such as incentive schemes, so it is reactive in the sense that they provide no mechanism for preventing mistakes or opportunistic behavior.
5. **Monitoring by large shareholders and/or banks and other large creditors:** Given their large investment in the firm, these stakeholders have the incentives, the right degree of control and power to monitor the management.

External Corporate Governance Mechanisms

External corporate governance controls the external stakeholders' exercise over the organization, and the pressure exerted by international organizations interested in this matter, and it indicates the general climate for investment in the state. Examples of these mechanisms include the following: (Vitez, 2017; Hai, et al., 2019)

1. **External Auditing:** The external auditor plays an important role in helping to improve the quality of financial deviations, and to achieve this he must discuss the audit committee in the quality of those deviations, and the external audit represents the cornerstone of corporate governance, as the external auditors help to achieve accountability and integrity and improve operations in the company, and establish trust between Stakeholders and citizens in general. The definition of the audit committee's independence is the non-executive director must have no relation with the company, the independence of the audit committee can assist the external auditor to preserve the tasks entrusted to him without influence from any directors.
2. **Competition in the Market for Products or Services and the Administrative labor Market:** Competition in the market for products or services is considered one of the important mechanisms for corporate governance, as this competition refines the behavior of management, and this means that the management of the company that is in bankruptcy will have a negative impact on the future of the director and members of the board of directors, as it often determines the appropriate tests for appointment and the exclusion of members A board or executives who previously led their companies to bankruptcy or liquidation.
3. **Legislation, laws and standards:** Regulators have to play a role to establish the corporate governance practice and culture. For example, the Securities and Exchange Commission (SEC) and Registrar of the corporations, Stock Exchanges can issue regulatory directives and guidelines that corporations under their regulations will be bound to adhere to. Side by side regulators, different professional bodies issue "Best Practice" and/or Standards like International Accounting Standards (IAS). Corporations would voluntarily adopt those Best Practice or Standards in their corporate practice and sometimes regulators tag those with the regulations. The importance of external

mechanisms is due to ensuring the implementation of laws and regulations that guarantee the good management of the company, reduce administrative and financial corruption, and reduce conflict between social and private returns.

4. **Corporate Culture:** There must be a culture of compliance in the company and the commitment of the owners and the Board of Directors, and commitment must be exercised in the daily values of the company with a view to ensuring good corporate governance, as well as from the controls of external corporate governance; debt contracts, media pressure, acquisitions, and agent companies.

The importance of external governance is because its presence guarantees the implementation of laws and regulations that lead to good management of the company, which reduces the conflict between social and private returns. Corporate governance mechanisms and controls are designed to reduce the inefficiencies that arise from moral risk and adverse selection. There are both internal and external monitoring systems, an ideal monitoring and control system should regulate both motivation and ability while providing incentive alignment toward corporate goals. We care should be taken that incentives are not so strong that some individuals are tempted to cross ethical behavior such as manipulating profit figures to increase the share price of the company. (Wikipedia, 2019)

THE ROLE OF CORPORATE GOVERNANCE IN LIMITING EARNINGS MANAGEMENT PRACTICES

Several studies concluded that there found a relationship between corporate governance mechanisms and earnings management, as corporate governance affects earnings management practices, Riyadh (2012) found that there is an inverse relationship between corporate governance and earnings management in the Egyptian pharmaceutical companies, so the higher the level of corporate governance in the company, the more this will contribute to limiting earnings management. Wang and Men (2012) confirmed that the application of corporate governance mechanisms has an important role in earnings management, as the effective application improves the level of transparency in accounting information, and this is then reflected in the reduction of earnings management practices. It also found a negative correlation between corporate governance and earnings management.

With regard to agency theory, internal governance mechanisms are more appropriate, as the governance literature revealed three mechanisms that can be used to maximize the benefits both managers and shareholders, reduce opportunistic management practices and limit earnings management, represented by the board of directors, internal audit, and audit committee.

1. **Board of Directors:** The board of directors is one of the important mechanisms governing the performance of managers in companies, as its task is to monitor the performance of managers to reduce their undesirable behavior and lay down the strategies of the company that aims to maximize profits. For the board to fully perform its duties, there are two characteristics that must be available: the first: the size of the board, and the second: the degree of independence of the board. With regard to the first feature: the size of the board, the studies that tested the effect of the size of the board on the earnings management practices varied, Some researchers see a direct correlation between the size and earnings management practices, as the large size of the board is better because it provides a benefit to the company through the diversity of experiences, While others believe that the large

board are characterized by difficulty in communication, low speed in accomplishing tasks, and low effectiveness of decisions, so they prefer that the size of the board of directors be small. With regard to the second feature: independence, researchers have demonstrated that independence is important to influence the effectiveness of the supervisory to limit managers 'ability to act in the interests of their own interests, independence is that the board includes non-executive and external members, as the importance of the board's independence, has been proven in controlling opportunistic practices for management. Also, separating the main roles between the chairman and the general manager, as it has proven to be an effective way to reduce agency costs and improve performance because the performance of managers is subject to the supervision of the chairman and members of the board, which leads managers to improve their performance and achieve the goals of shareholders in order to ensure their stay in the job and get rewards Agreed (Man, et al. 2018).

Adegbie, et al. (2019) examined the effect of corporate governance on the earnings quality of quoted financial and nonfinancial firms in Nigeria. Findings revealed that corporate governance (board size, board independence, board meetings, audit committee size, audit committee independence, and audit committee meetings) has a significant effect on earnings quality, as the earnings of financial firms are significantly and positively influenced by board size and negatively influenced by board meetings; therefore, good corporate governance affects the financial practices of firms which boost the corporate images, growth and market value of companies. And also, the study Asogwa, et al. (2019) showed the effect of corporate governance mechanisms on firms' earnings quality using evidence from Nigerian firms, it focused on the impact of board leadership structures and leaders' attributes on the corporations' income quality such as financial expertise and legal skills. It was found that when board leadership is separated such that CEOs and board chairpersons have equal accounting and financial skills, the firms' earnings quality significantly improves, also found that the legal skill of board chairperson plays a significant constraining role in accrual manipulation that negatively impacts earnings quality. Thus, lawyers in the boards mitigate earnings manipulation that could reduce the persistence of earnings. And audit quality, board sizes and the frequency audit committee meeting all positively affect earnings quality. So, investors should target firms where CEOs and board chairpersons have strong accounting and financial skills.

Study (Al-Kabbaji, 2019) found that there is a direct correlation relationship of significant between both the size of the board of directors, the duplication of executives, the size of the company, financial leverage ratio and earnings management, the existence of an inverse correlation relationship between the meetings of the board of directors and the type of the audit company and earnings management and there is no relationship between the independence of the board of directors and the independence of the audit committee and earnings management. Alareeni (2018) concluded that corporate governance influences earnings management in listed companies in Bahrain bourse, as earnings management is negatively correlated with board size, board independence is positively correlated with earnings management, as the larger the number of independent directors, the higher the level of earnings management practices and also internal ownership is positively related to earnings management, confirming that a higher level of internal ownership increases earnings management practices. Study (Ramachandran, et al., 2015) see there is the influence of corporate governance practices on earnings management, as the board of directors and key committees influence earnings management through discretionary accruals, so, board independence, segregation of duties between the CEO and chairman, audit committee size and nomination committee size has a significant positive influence on board size, as the nomination committee influences the remuneration committee directly implying that the motivation for recording discretionary accruals is higher leading to higher earnings management, and we sure that segregation of responsibilities between the remuneration committee and the nomination committee when the Board size is big, will reduce earnings management and increase transparency of information. So, governance practices will reduce the agony of stakeholders.

Al-Fad & Hamad (2015) examined the relationship between corporate governance and its role to control earnings management practices- a Case study in Iraq, its findings that there is a significant role by the board of directors to control earnings management practices. The more efficient the board of directors is in terms of its small size and increased external members, the less the earnings management practices will be, and vice versa, there is no significant role by the audit committee to control earnings management practices, the more quality the Internal Review Section is in the company, the more the earnings management practices will be. That means the Board of Directors employs the company's Internal Review Section towards earnings management practices. Study (Kassar, F. M., 2018) aims to identify the impact of complying with corporate governance rules in reducing earnings management practices through a sample of companies listed in the Damascus Securities Exchange Market. The researcher concluded several results; the most important is that there is no significant impact between compliance with the rules of corporate governance and earnings management practices in the Syrian environment. There is a significant effect of company size on earnings management, and there is no significant effect on the debt ratio and management efficiency in limiting earnings management practices. Salman (2016) showed the relationship between good practices of corporate governance and the ownership structure in reducing and mitigating manipulation of the company's earnings by management, as companies that have good governance are less in manipulating earnings management and financial statements, and the study found that there is a direct relationship between the size of the board of directors and earnings management, in When the study did not find a relationship between the size of the audit office, the tasks of the CEO and the chairman of the board, and manipulation of earnings by management, and also a positive relationship between ownership structure and earnings management, where increased ownership of investment institutions, government ownership, and ownership of board members in capitals, which helps reduce the earnings management in Saudi companies.

2. **Internal Audit:** The internal audit function has an important and effective role in corporate governance, and for this function to be a powerful tool it must be characterized by a high level of quality, as the companies that have a good internal audit activity usually have low earnings management practices, and to ensure the quality of corporate governance for all stakeholders, The internal audit function must be integrated with the Board and the Audit Committee, and there are three criteria for the quality of internal audit activities that are professional ability, objective, and quality in the performance of duties. The results of the study (Abu Jibril & Al-Thunaibat, 2016) showed that there is a positive impact with statistically significant effect of the independence of the internal audit, the efficiency of the employees in the internal audit department, the scope of the internal audit work, and the professional care of the employees in the internal audit department on earnings management of industrial companies in the Oman Financial Market and that these independent variables perform to reduce the practice of corporate earnings management. Other research suggests that Big 4 auditors are more able to curb earnings management than non-Big auditors, the ability of Big 4 auditors in curtailing a client's earnings management is affected by the type of accounting standards used for financial reporting and it indicated the superiority of Big 4 auditors in audit quality because auditor competency, reporting tendency, big 4 auditors have revenues more than

four times the revenue of other firms and more resources to devote to improving audit effectiveness (Vann, 2018).

3. **Audit Committee:** The audit committee is a corporate governance mechanism aimed at controlling opportunistic practices for management through monitoring and evaluation of the internal audit system and the work of the external auditor and overseeing the preparation of financial statements. The audit committees play a vital role in ensuring the quality of financial reports and achieving confidence in accounting information. For this committee to perform its duties, two elements are necessary: the independence and professional experience of the members. Regarding the importance of the independence of the members of the audit committee, he found a positive relationship between independence and the quality of financial reports. As for the professional experience of members of the audit committee, we find that companies in which members of the audit committee have enough experience and professional competence, it has a low probability of manipulating in financial reports, and lowest earnings management practices and vice versa. Chen and Zhang (2014) showed the impact of Corporate Governance on earnings manipulations. it concluded that Corporate Governance positive effect limit earnings management through the introduction of independent non-executive directors to the board of directors and the audit committee, audit committee plays an important role in deterring the use of earnings management.

Study (Lin & Hwang, 2010) confirmed that negative relationships exist between earnings management and the audit committee's independence, its size, expertise, and the number of meetings, and audit quality, auditor tenure, auditor size, and specialization. Auditor independence measured by ratio or total of fee, which is also a deterrent to earnings management and the audit committee's share ownership has a positive effect on earnings management, and also the independence of the board of directors and its expertise has a negative relationship with earnings management.

Study (Slaheddine, 2015) noted the impact of new UK corporate governance code on earnings quality and it showed the impact of audit rotation on earnings quality, so earnings quality is measured by the investors' ability to predict future earnings for public and private firms. it used a sample consist of 4,117 firms for the period 2004-2013. the study concluded that investors can better anticipate future earnings when the company regularly changes the auditor. However, the findings are not applicable to private firms, and auditor rotation is a good proxy for the actual and perceived audit quality. Therefore, firms need to pay attention to who audit their financial statements because this type of information is important to their stakeholders i.e. investors and financial analysts in making their investment decisions. Study Diria, et al. (2020) confirmed that corporate governance is more effective in mitigating earnings management in non-concentrated markets, regulators and auditors have role in preventing real earnings management in concentrated markets because of its negative impact on firm value, stakeholders, and the whole economy, so, it potentially useful to regulators in enhancing the legitimacy of corporate governance in concentrated markets. This can be achieved by emphasizing the role of the independent members of the board of directors in evaluating management accrual accounting choices and real economic decisions, and results might be of interest to potential investors to evaluate their investment chances in concentrated markets.

Al-Wakeel (2019) indicated the impact of the mandatory periodic change of the external auditor on the reduction of earnings management practices in the Egyptian business environment, a field study was carried out to study the justifications for demanding the application of the mandatory periodic change of the external auditor. An applied study was also carried out on sample data of the financial reports on some of the listed companies in the Egyptian Stock Exchange during the period from 2011 to 2017 to study the relationship between the mandatory periodic change of the external auditor and the practices of earnings management. The field study concluded that there is many justifications that call for the application of the mandatory periodic change of the external auditor in the Egyptian business environment, the most important of which are: providing a new vision for the audit process, increasing the ability to detect on deficiencies in internal control systems, Reduction of the closeness and familiarity between the auditor and its own client, Enhancing auditor independence, Improving audit quality, Reduction of earnings management practices and increasing the quality and confidence of financial reports, Increasing confidence in the audit profession.

There are other studies that deal with the relationship between corporate governance and earnings management, including study (Elghuweel, et al., 2017) examines the impact of corporate and Islamic governance mechanisms on corporate earnings management behavior in Oman, it reached the following results: better-governed corporations tend to engage significantly less in earnings management than their poorly-governed counterparts, companies that have a greater commitment towards incorporating Islamic religious beliefs and values into their operations through the establishment of an Islamic governance committee tend to engage significantly less in earnings management, and by contrast, we do not find any evidence that board size, audit firm size, the presence of a corporate governance committee and board gender diversity have relationship with earnings management. Another study (Mersni and Othman, 2016) is showing the impact of corporate governance mechanisms on earnings management in Islamic banks in the Middle East region, results report a positive relationship between sharia board size and discretionary loan loss provisions. This indicates that small sharia supervisory boards are more effective than larger ones, which could be due to the higher costs and negative effects of large groups on decision-making, the existence of scholars with accounting knowledge sitting on the sharia board reduces discretionary behavior, results provide evidence that an external sharia audit committee to reduce discretion in Islamic banks. Regulators could use the findings to focus on corporate governance mechanisms that restrain earnings management practices in Islamic banks and implement regulations to strengthen them. Additionally, this study gives shareholders further insight which enables them to better monitor the actions of managers and thus increases their control over their investments. But the study (Wimelda & Chandra, 2018) concluded that motivational bonuses, leverage, firm size, and free cash flow have an influence on earnings management practices, as motivational bonuses and free cash flow as opportunistic behavior influence earnings management. In addition, leverage and firm size as external monitoring mechanisms influence earnings management practices. Also, Audit committee size, the proportion of independent commissioners, institutional ownership and managerial ownership as corporate governance practices has no significant effect on earnings management practices, it is concluded that corporate governance has no effect on earnings management practices in Indonesia.

Azzoz et al., (2016) examined the impact of corporate governance characteristics on earnings quality and earnings management, the study used the board size, CEO duality, board composition, audit committee size, audit committee composition, and audit committee activity to measure the corporate governance characteristics. The results indicated that the relation between audit committee size and earnings management was positive, companies must reduce the number of board members in order to increase of monitoring and to assess the company performance which in turn increases the quality of earnings and capability in discovering earnings management, these results illustrated that the meeting of the audit committee is effective in the discussion between members and in discovering potential errors in the financial reporting, which in turn is reflected in the level of earnings quality and discovering earnings management. Further, the study recommends adjusting the proportion of the external directors and non-executive in each of the board of directors and the audit committee to reduce the agency conflict, we noted firms have good corporate governance tend to conduct fewer earnings management, there is a size effect for earnings smoothing, that is, large size firms are prone to conduct earnings smoothing, but good corporate governance can mitigate the effect (Hua and Chih, 2007).

Moss (2016) examined the influence of earnings management and corporate governance on the cost of equity capital in listed companies in Thailand to restore investor confidence. Earnings management is measured from the absolute value of discretionary accruals. Corporate governance variables include board interlocking, board independence, the board size, CEO-Chair duality, audit committee financial expertise, audit opinion, managerial ownership, and institutional shareholders, the results revealed that companies with higher earnings management, a higher proportion of managerial ownership, institutional ownership, CEO-Chair duality and which receive modified audit opinions are likely to have a higher cost of equity capital. In contrast, the companies that have a higher proportion of board independence, audit committee financial expertise, and board interlocking are likely to have a lower cost of equity capital. Another study noted, board independence constrains earnings manipulation in companies, but in family-controlled companies characterized lower board independence and a higher risk of collusion, so, to reduce board effectiveness in limiting the earnings management (Prencipe & Bar-Yosef, 2011).

Gonzalez & Meca (2014) indicated the relationship between the internal mechanisms of corporate governance and earnings management behavior, it found that the role of external directors is limited and that Boards that meet more take a more active position in the monitoring of insiders, so leads a lower manipulative practice, the study concluded board size, Family ownership positively affects earnings management, the existence of a concentration of power increases earnings management. On the contrast, board independence, Institutional investors, Insider shareholding, ownership concentration, the number of board meetings negatively affect earnings management. Finally, the study sees the company which implements corporate governance will reducing corruption, improving the effectiveness of government, this leads to a reduction in earnings management. Another study confirmed that managers may use earnings management to meet voluntary earnings forecasts, companies with better corporate governance systems are less likely to use earnings management to achieve their earnings forecasts (Cormier, et al., 2014).

There is a large negative relationship between Corporate Social Responsibility (CSR) and earnings management, Corporate Social Responsibility oriented firms are less engaging in earnings management practices. but other evidence of a positive relationship between CSR and earnings management was also provided and concluded that CSR is used by managers to mask their earnings management practice. A firm with good corporate governance is more successful in preventing managers from exploiting its assets by monitoring the manager's business decisions and since corporate governance is a monitoring mechanism that can control the decisions made by managers and restrict the managers' opportunism. so, corporate governance plays an important role in constraining earnings management by monitoring managers' opportunistic behavior. So, there is a definite relationship between CSR and earnings management, the firm's commitment to CSR should monitor through earnings management to monitor the social purpose of the firm, and the study showed the positive or negative mixed role of various attributes of ownership structure on CSR and earnings management (Ehsan, et al., 2018). Another study finds that after controlling for corporate governance characteristics, earnings management is positively related to the volume of trade and there is the joint impact of corporate governance mechanisms and earnings management on market liquidity in a setting of high noninstitutional ownership concentration (Bar-Yosef & Prencipe, 2013).

CONCLUSION AND RECOMMENDATIONS

We summarize from the above, The agency theory is one of the most important theories that explain the behaviors resulting from the relationship of shareholders and managers, the separation of ownership from management has resulted in the management of some companies exercising the profit management policy to achieve private benefits, but in light of the application of good corporate governance and the limitation of management authority and provides the opportunity for other parties to protect their rights, we find that earnings management becomes non-existent. Awareness of corporate management of the risks involved in earnings management practices and their negative implications for long-term performance, and that corporate governance effectively affects earnings management practices, as the application of corporate governance mechanisms, increases the level of disclosure and transparency of the financial information issued by firms, improving ethical behavior of their managers, reducing corruption, strengthen the rule of law or improving the effectiveness of government, which in turn is reflected in reducing information asymmetry, reduction of discretionary accruals and reducing the company's practice of earnings management operations. The study showed that corporate governance helps protect the rights of shareholders and stakeholders and regulate the relationship between the company's executive management, the board of directors and audit committees, and is a tool to motivate workers and management to perform business efficiently and effectively. It helps to build an environment of trust, transparency, and accountability necessary for fostering long-term investment, achieve financial stability, thereby supporting stronger growth and more inclusive societies. ;

This study recommends the necessity of disclosure and transparency of the accounting information related to the financial and operating performance, and its provision in a timely manner, as well as the disclosure of all data related to corporate governance that serves profit management practices. The necessity of reformulating the accounting policies, principles, and standards in a way that ensures that companies do not use the flexibility in manipulating their profits. The necessity of maintaining the independence of the members of the board of directors, the audit committees and the efficiency and expertise of its members, as one of the dimensions of governance, and that its composition is from members outside the company in order to increase the effectiveness of the process of supervising the preparation of financial statements. Non-duplication of executives and limiting their negative practices for earnings management. The policymakers and regulators to introduce binding policies to apply effectively the corporate governance principles and impose penalties on companies that do not comply with corporate governance principles and implement additional corporate governance reforms for protecting stakeholders and investors.

REFERENCES

Abu Jibril, A. Y., & Al-Thunaibat, A. (2016). The Effect of Internal Audit on Limiting Earnings Management for Industrial Companies Listed on The Oman Financial Market. *The Jordanian Journal of Business Administration*, *12*(4), 789–811.

Adegbie, F., Salawu, R. O., & Shiyanbola, A. (2019). Effect of Corporate Governance on Earnings Quality of Quoted Financial and Non-Financial Firms in Nigeria. *Journal of Research in Business and Management*, *7*(3), 40–51.

Al-Fad, M. A., & Hamad, M. A. (2015). Corporate Governance and its Role in Limiting Earnings Management A Test Study of the Iraq Case. Al-Qadisiyah. *Journal of Administrative and Economic Sciences*, *17*(3), 192–221.

Al-Kabbaji, M. (2019). The Role of Corporate Governance in Controlling Earnings Management Practices in Palestinian Public Shareholding Industrial Companies - A Field Study. *The Arab Journal of Management*, *39*(2), 99–124.

Al-Wakeel, H. A. (2019). The effect of the mandatory periodic change of the external auditor on reducing earnings management practices in the Egyptian Business Environment - An Applied Study. *ATASU*, *23*(4), 1–48.

Alareeni, B. (2018). Does Corporate Governance Influence Earnings Management in Listed Companies in Bahrain Bourse? *Journal of Asia Business Studies*, *12*(4), 551–570. doi:10.1108/JABS-06-2017-0082

Ali, K. E. (2019). *10 Principles of corporate governance*. Available at https://ethicalboardroom.com

Ali, M. (2013). *Corporate Governance and its Role in Reducing Earnings Practices - An Analytical Field Study on Khartoum Stock Exchange* (Master Thesis). Al-Neelain University, College of Graduate Studies, Sudan.

Alkababji, M. W. (2019). The Role of Corporate Governance in Controlling the Earnings Management Practices of Palestinian Shareholding Industrial Companies: A Field Study. *Arab Journal of Management*, *39*, 99–124.

Alvarado, N. R., Fuentes, P., & Laffarga, J. (2019). Do Auditors Mitigate Earnings Management During Economic Crisis? *Revista de Contabilidad*, *22*(1), 6–20.

Andrijasevic, M. (2018). *Theoretical Assumptions of Agency Problem*. https://www.researchgate.net

Asogwa, C. I., Grace, N., Nnam, J. I., & Chukwunwike, O. D. (2019). Effect of Corporate Governance Board Leadership Models and Attributes on Earnings Quality of Quoted Nigerian Companies. *Cogent Business & Management*, *6*(1), 2–24. doi:10.1080/23311975.2019.1683124

Azzoz, A., & Khamees, B. (2016). The Impact of Corporate Governance Characteristics on Earnings Quality and Earnings Management: Evidence from Jordan. *Jordan Journal of Business Administration*, *12*(1), 187–207. doi:10.12816/0030061

Bar-Yosef, M. S., & Prencipe, A. (2013). The Impact of Corporate Governance and Earnings Management on Stock Market Liquidity in a Highly Concentrated Ownership Capital. *Journal of Accounting, Auditing & Finance*, *28*(3), 292–316. doi:10.1177/0148558X13492591

Chen, J. (2019). *Corporate Governance Definition*. Available at https://www.investopedia.com

Chen, J., & Zhang, H. (2014). The Impact of the Corporate Governance Code on Earnings Management – Evidence from Chinese Listed Companies. *European Financial Management*, *20*(3), 596–632. doi:10.1111/j.1468-036X.2012.00648.x

Cormier, D., Antunes, P., & Mc-Conomy, B. (2014). Forecasts in IPO Prospectuses: The Effect of Corporate Governance on Earnings Management. *Journal of Business Finance & Accounting*, *41*(1,2), 100–127.

Cruz, M. E., & Vargas-Hernández, J. G. (2018). Corporate Governance and Agency Theory: Megacable Case. *Corporate Governance and Sustainability Review*, *2*(1), 59–70. doi:10.22495/cgsrv2i1p5

Dewey, K. (2019). *What are Four Characteristics of Good Corporate Governance?* Available at https://www.quora.com

Diria, M., Lambrinoudakis, C., & Alhadab, M. (2020). Corporate Governance and Earnings Management in Concentrated Markets. *Journal of Business Research*, *108*, 291–306. doi:10.1016/j.jbusres.2019.11.013

Ehsan, S., Abbas, Q., & Nawaz, A. (2018). An Inquiry into the Relationship between Earnings' Management. Corporate Social Responsibility and Corporate Governance. *Abasyn Journal of Social Sciences*, *11*(1), 104–116.

Elghuweel, M., Ntim, C., Opong, K., & Avison, L. (2017). Corporate Governance, Islamic Governance and Earnings Management in Oman: A new Empirical Insights from a Behavioral Theoretical Framework. *Journal of Accounting in Emerging Economies*, *7*(2), 190–224. doi:10.1108/JAEE-09-2015-0064

Freihat, M. A. J. (2014). The Role of Disclosure of Other Elements of Comprehensive Income on the Practice of Earnings Management: A study Applied to the Saudi Banking and Financial Services Sector. *Journal of Scientific Research. Assiut University*, *57*, 125–140.

Goncharov, I., & Hodgson, A. (2011). Measuring and Reporting Income in Europe. *Journal of International Accounting*, *10*(1), 30–31.

Gonzalez, J., & Meca, E. (2014). Does Corporate Governance Influence Earnings Management in Latin American Markets? *Journal of Business Ethics*, *121*(3), 419–440. doi:10.100710551-013-1700-8

Hai, P., & Toan, L. D.c & Quy, N. (2019). Effect of Audit Rotation, Audit Fee and Auditor Competence to Motivation Auditor and Audit Quality: Empirical Evidence in Vietnam. *Academy of Accounting and Financial Studies Journal*, *23*(2), 1–14.

Hamidat, M., & Al-Rifai, K. (2019). Commitment to the Requirements of Corporate Governance and Its Impact on the Quality of Financial Reports (From the Point of View of the Internal Auditors in the Jordanian Public Shareholding Industrial Companies). *Ramah Research and Studies*, *31*, 12–44.

Hossain, K. K. (2017). *The primary drivers and mechanisms of corporate governance.* https://www.quora.com

Hossain, M., Mitra, S., Rezaee, Z., & Sarath, B. (2011). Corporate Governance and Earnings Management in the Pre– and Post–Sarbanes-Oxley Act Regimes: Evidence from Implicated Option Backdating Firms. *Journal of Accounting, Auditing & Finance*, *26*(2), 279–315. doi:10.1177/0148558X11401218

Institute on Governance (IOG). (2019). *What is Governance*. Available at https://iog.ca/what-is-governance

Kassar, F. M. (2018). The Impact of Compliance with Corporate Governance Rules in Reducing Earnings Management Practices -An Empirical Study on Private Banks and Insurance Companies Listed in Damascus Stock Exchange Market. *Al-Quds Open University Journal for Administrative and Economic Research*, *3*(10), 97–122.

Kopp, M. (2019). *Agency Theory*. Available at https://www.investopedia.com

Lan, L. (2012). *Goals of Corporate Governance - A Singapore Perspective.* EU-Asia Corporate Governance Dialogue, Faculty of Law & NUS Business School, The National University of Singapore. Available at https://www.fsa.go.jp

Lin, J., & Hwang, M. (2010). Audit Quality, Corporate Governance, and Earnings Management: A Meta-Analysis. *International Journal of Auditing, 14*(1), 57–77. doi:10.1111/j.1099-1123.2009.00403.x

Mack, S. (2019). *Seven Characteristics of Good Corporate Governance.* Available at https://smallbusiness.chron.com

Man, Y. (2018). *Earnings Management and Agency Costs: Evidence from China.* Available at https://www.researchgate.net/publication/323983941

Matteo, P., & Paolone, Fr. (2018). *The Case of Brazilian Real Estate Industry.* Available at https://www.abacademies.org

Mersni, H., & Othman, H. (2016). The impact of corporate governance mechanisms on earnings management in Islamic banks in the Middle East region. *Journal of Islamic Accounting and Business Research, 7*(4), 318–348. doi:10.1108/JIABR-11-2014-0039

Moss, S. (2016). The Impact of Corporate Governance and Earnings Management Practices on Cost of Equity Capital: Evidence from Thai Listed Companies. *ACRN Oxford Journal of Finance and Risk Perspectives, 5*(1), 163–185.

MSG. (2019). *Corporate Governance - Definition, Scope and Benefits.* Available at https://www.managementstudyguide.com

Mustafa, M. B. (2010). *Impact of corporate governance on earnings management practices - An applied study on industrial companies listed on the Amman Financial Market* (Master Thesis). Faculty of Economics and Administrative Sciences, Al-Yarmouk University, Jordan.

Nia, M. S., Huang, C. C., & Abidin, Z. (2015). A Review of Motives and Techniques and their Consequences in Earnings Management. *Malaysian Accounting Review, 14*(2), 1–28.

OECD. (2015). *G20/OECD Principles of Corporate Governance.* OECD Publishing. doi:10.1787/9789264236882-

OECD. (2019). *OECD Corporate Governance Factbook 2019.* Available at www.oecd.org/corporate/corporate-governance-factbook.htm

OECD. (2019). *OECD Corporate Governance Factbook 2019.* OECD Publishing. Available at https://www.oecd.org/corporate/corporate-governance-factbook.htm

Paine, L. S., & Srinivasan, S. (2019). A Guide to the Big Ideas and Debates in Corporate Governance. *Harvard Business Review*, Available at https://hbr.org/2019

Palmer, J., Rae, C., & Sykes, G. (2019). *Corporate Governance: Chambers and Partners.* Available at racticeguides.chambers.com

Prencipe, A., & Bar-Yosef, S. (2011). Corporate Governance and Earnings Management in Family-Controlled Companies. *Journal of Accounting, Auditing & Finance, 26*(2), 199–227. doi:10.1177/0148558X11401212

Rahman, M., Moniruzzaman, M., & Sharif, J. (2013). Techniques, Motives and Controls of Earnings Management. *International Journal of Information Technology and Business Management, 11*(1), 22–34.

Ramachandran, J., Nget, Z. A., Subramanian, R., & Sambasivan, M. (2015). Does Corporate Governance Influence Earnings Management? Evidence from Singapore. *Journal of Developing Areas, 49*(3), 264–274. doi:10.1353/jda.2015.0169

Rathod, L. (2018). *Why Is Corporate Governance Important?* Available at https://diligent.com/en-gb

Rathod, L. (2019). *What Are the Principles of Good Corporate Governance?* Available at https://diligent.com/en-gb

Riyadh, S. M. R. (2012). The Role of Corporate Governance in Limiting Earnings Management: An Applied Study on Egyptian Pharmaceutical Companies. *The Arab Journal of Accounting, 15*(8), 1–51.

Rodriguez, R., Salter, S. B., & Smith, M. (2016). An Examination of the Agency Theory Problem of Earnings Management: Is it an Anglo-Saxon Cultural Phenomenon? *International Journal of Critical Accounting, 7*(5/6), 487–511.

Salman, A. (2016). Corporate Governance and Concentration of Property and Its Impact on Earnings Management in Emerging Markets: The Case of Saudi Joint Stock Companies. *Journal of Administrative and Economic Sciences, 10*(1), 1–48.

Sanad, Z., Shiwakoti, R., & Kukreja, G. (2019). *The Role of Corporate Governance in Mitigating Real Earnings Management: Literature Review*. Conference Paper, PwR Symposium, Annual PwR Doctral Symposium.

Shen, C., & Chih, H. (2007). Earnings Management and Corporate Governance in Asia's Emerging Markets. *Corporate Governance, 15*(5), 999–1021. doi:10.1111/j.1467-8683.2007.00624.x

Slaheddine, T. (2015). Impact of New UK Corporate Governance Code on Earnings Quality- Evidences from UK FTSE 350 Companies. *Business and Economics Journal, 6*(2), 1–5. doi:10.4172/2151-6219.1000142

Slaheddine, T. (2015). Impact of New UK Corporate Governance Code on Earnings Quality- Evidence from UK FTSE 350 Companies. *Business and Economics Journal, 6*(2), 1–5. doi:10.4172/2151-6219.1000142

Tsoi, P. (2017). *The Importance of Corporate Governance*. Available at https://www.linkedin.com/pulse

Tuovila, A. (2019). *What is Earnings Management*. Available at https://www.investopedia.com

Vann, C. (2018). Big 4 Auditors, Corporate Governance, and Earnings Management under Principles- and Rules-Based Reporting Regimes: Cross-Country Empirical Evidence. *Journal of Managerial Issues, 3*(3), 279–302.

VComply. (2018). *9 characteristics to look out for, for good corporate governance*. Available at https://blog.v-comply.com/good-cg

Vitez, O. (2017). *Three Types of Corporate Governance Mechanisms*. Available at https://bizfluent.com/

Wang, L., & Men, R. (2012). Impacts of other comprehensive income disclosure on earnings management. *Business Review International, 3*(1), 93–101.

Wikipedia. (2019). *Earnings management*. Available at https://en.wikipedia.org

Wimelda & Chandra, A. (2018). Opportunistic Behavior, External Monitoring Mechanisms, Corporate Governance, and Earnings Management. *Accounting Financial Review*, *3*(1), 49–57.

Yaseen, A. T., Adam, A. K., & Fashakh, M. J. (2018). Creative Accounting Standards and its Techniques. *Opción*, *34*(86), 1611–1642. https://www.researchgate.net/publication/331687350

Younis, N. M. (2019). The Impact of Disclosure of Other Comprehensive Income on Earnings Management: An Applied Study on the Banking Sector in the Egyptian Stock Exchange. *Scientific Journal Economics and Commerce*, Faculty of Commerce. *Ain Shams University*, *49*(1), 169–214.

Chapter 4
IT Governance and Business–IT Alignment Frameworks, Models, and the Best Practices

Aboobucker Ilmudeen
https://orcid.org/0000-0002-9450-6816
Department of Management and Information Technology, Faculty of Management and Commerce, South Eastern University of Sri Lanka, Sri Lanka

ABSTRACT

Information technology (IT) has become a vital function, and almost all organizations depend on IT. The IT dependency causes the executives to use IT governance practices for the IT investment decision-making process. Organizations spend more on IT investments even those that are over budget, come under pressure, behind schedule, and are generating fewer paybacks than anticipated. Hence, business organizations are continuously examined and believed to be answerable for their IT investment more than ever. This chapter focuses on various IT governance and business-IT alignment frameworks, models, and best practices to discuss in this context.

1. INTRODUCTION

IT is the key enabler for all organizations, and it has confronted the traditional way of doing business (Abdulrasool and Turnbull 2020). Though, the businesses have invested a huge amount of money in IT investment; the payoff from IT is always a major concern for executives and managers. Despite the growing amount of IT investment, managing IT and IT governance decisions have ever more become complicated due to vague cost relationships, uncertain payoffs, rapid technological changes, and uncertain business environments. Similarly, the traditional view of IT governance may not sufficiently address today's strategic, managerial, and technological complexity and it no longer resembles with what is trendy in the real world business phenomenon. Nowadays, IT governance made to a growing clock speed of enterprises, imposing firms to govern their IT investment (Turel et al. 2017). The IT governance has

DOI: 10.4018/978-1-7998-4852-3.ch004

a direct impact on how IT is managed within the organization and includes the implementation of IT management techniques and procedures in conformity with well-known IT governance practices and policies (Bowen et al. 2007).

As IT governance is a vital part of enterprise governance, it imposes a set of IT governance practices to implement more efficiently as to stimulate the analogy with the corporate mission, strategy, culture, value, norm, and business processes (Ali and Green 2012; Dong 2012; Van Grembergen and De Haes 2009; Wu et al. 2015). IT can have a positive effect, no effect, or even a negative effect on performance, in relation to how well IT is managed and governed (Turel et al. 2017). IT is recognized as a vital part of business processes, and IT covers all business functions consequently, firm designs and recombines IT resources in the direction of alignment between business and IT functions (Turel et al. 2017). Hence, the objective of this chapter is to discuss existing various IT governance and business-IT alignment frameworks, models and best practices in detail in this context. This chapter contribute to the literature that to discuss the existing IT governance and business-IT alignment frameworks, models and best practices to manage IT investments in an organization.

2. EXISTING MODELS AND FRAMEWORKS IN IT GOVERNANCE

IT governance is defined as "the organizational capacity exercised by the board, executive management and IT management to control the formulation and implementation of IT strategy and in this way ensure the fusion of business and IT''(Van Grembergen and De Haes 2009). Whereas the enterprise governance of IT addresses the definition and implementation of processes, structures, and relational mechanisms that enable both business and IT stakeholders to execute their responsibilities in support of business-IT alignment and the creation and protection of IT business value (De Haes et al. 2020). IT governance is a subset of overall governance responsibilities of the Boards and denotes the decisions about key IT activities and investments in the organizations (Parent and Reich 2009). The effective IT governance is an active means to decrease risk, lessen the impact of IT-related failures, reduce the cost of capital, and make lasting shareholder value (Parent and Reich 2009). With the effective IT governance framework, IT-enabled business investments are well managed and generate value, whereas the weak IT governance provides the same chance to destroy the value (Centre 2005).

The industry cases make shock stories for value destruction example, Nike lost over US$ 200m failure in implementing its supply chain software, failures in IT-enabled logistics systems at MFI and Sainsbury vanished to multi-million pound (Centre 2005). Today, IT serve a vital function, and almost all organizations depend on IT. This IT dependency causes executives to use IT governance practices in the decision-making process. There are reasons why IT governance has evolved as a field and exists on its own. Because, most of the organizations' IT investment account for a larger portion of their budget, IT always referred to as a technical field which cannot easily be understood, and investment in IT and its value generation not visible for non- technical executives. Furthermore, IT investments are not able to create the apparent value unlike the business case, and IT itself is a complex, and it require governance to make transparency. Figure 1 and Table 1 illustrates IT governance frameworks and standard with their primary IT-related functions.

Figure 1. Frameworks and standard and their primary IT-related functions
Adopted from: Cater-Steel et al. 2006 and Wilkin et al. 2016

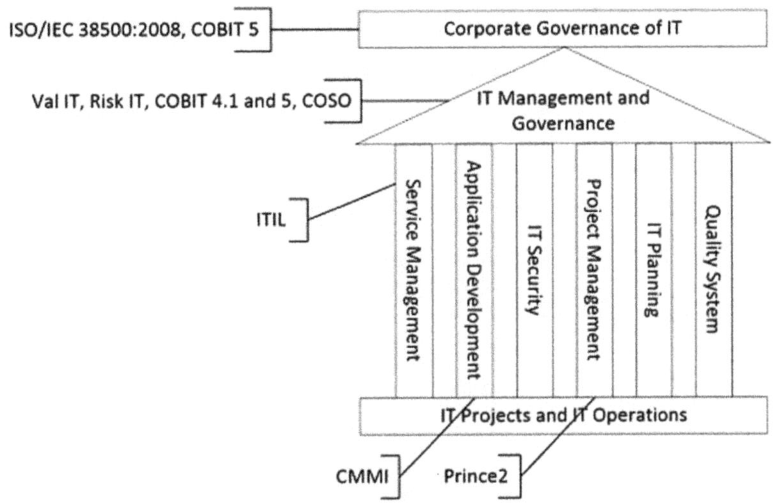

In the literature, the term IT governance tends to be used to refer the organizational competencies to manage, govern and control the formulation and implementation of IT strategy and shows the direction for achieving organizational goals. De Haes and Van Grembergen (2015) argued that IT governance mainly stayed within IT area, while it is obvious the business value from IT investments cannot be realized IT itself, but which will always be created by the business side. The reasons why IT governance has evolved as a field and exists on its own due to the followings. Most of the organizations' IT investment account for a larger portion of their budget, IT always referred as a technical field which cannot easily be understandable, and investment on IT and its value generation not visible for non- technical executives. Moreover, IT investment not able to create the apparent value that IT provides unlike the business case and IT itself is complex and need governance to make clarity and simplicity.

Table 1. IT governance frameworks, standard, and methodologies (as related to figure 1)

Framework Origin	Definition and Focus	Coverage
IT governance and management frameworks **COBIT 5** (Control Objectives for Information and related Technologies) developed by the IT Governance Institute for Information Systems Audit and Control Association - ISACA	A "comprehensive framework that assists enterprises in achieving their objectives for the governance and management of enterprise IT… [to]… create optimal value … by maintaining a balance between realistic benefits and optimizing risk levels and resource use …considering the IT-related interests of internal and external stakeholders."	COBIT 5, combines and incorporates COBIT 4.1, Val IT 2.0 and Risk IT, and draws from ISACA's IT Assurance Framework and the Business Model for Information Security. It lines up with frameworks and standards such as ITIL, International Organization for Standardization (ISO), Project Management Body of Knowledge (PMBOK), PRINCE 2 and The Open Group Architecture Framework (TOGAF). It is framed with 5 principles and 7 organizational resources called enablers

continues on following page

Table 1. Continued

Framework Origin	Definition and Focus	Coverage
COBIT 4.1	Offers an internal control framework for IT by demanding firm to define their motivation for IT investment, the stakeholders and the desired outcomes	By linking business goals to IT goals, it recognizes the associated responsibilities of business and IT process owners, and through metrics and maturity models, measures the success of goals
Val IT *Information Systems Audit and Control Association (ISACA)*	Val IT assists in creating business value from IT investments. It links management of the IT portfolio to the firm's strategic objectives	It comprises of a set of guiding principles and processes with suggested key management practices domains such as value governance, portfolio management and investment management
Risk IT	Complete view of all risks in the use of IT and their treatment via risk management practices	It covers 3 domains (risk governance, risk evaluation and risk response), which are detailed by process components, management practice, inputs and outputs, RACI charts, goals and metrics
COSO Committee of Sponsoring Organizations of the Treadway Commission	A combined framework aimed to Enterprise Risk Management (ERM) and related Internal Control. It views Internal Control as a process effected by an entity's board, management and others to manage risk	A cube with 4 organizational objectives, 8 risk management components and 4 organizational units
AS 8015 (2005) *Australian Standard for Corporate Governance of Information & Communication Technology*	The world's first national standard for governing ICTs, introduced in March 2003 and subsequently revised in 2005.	Prescribes 3-sequential step approach governing ICT projects and operations: *evaluate*-uses of ICT, *direct*-preparation, and implementation of ICT plans and policies to best support the organization, *monitor*-conformance to policies and performance against the plans.
Standard **ISO/IEC 38500:2008**	A structure of principles that directors can use to evaluate, direct and monitor IT use in their organization	Offers direction on CGIT via 6 "good practice" principles (responsibility, strategy, acquisition, performance, conformance and human behaviour), each with its own set of suggested practices structured under 3 task areas (evaluation, direction, and monitoring)
ISO/IEC 20000	International Organization for Standardization/ International Electro technical Commission Standard 20000	Terms and Code of Practice for IT Service Management. It is the first international standard for IT service management and is aligned with ITIL best practices.
Methodologies for IT projects and IT operations **ITIL - IT Infrastructure Library**	Guiding framework of best practices for service and asset management. In its 3rd version, it presently has 5 best practice volumes focused around the service lifecycle and continuous service upgrading.	IT service management and operations through IT as a whole-of-organization engagement
CMM /CMMI – Capability Maturity Model Integration -Software Engineering Institute at Carnegie - Mellon University	To help in managing large software development projects. Focuses on product and service development, managing services & acquiring related products and services	A program for process improvement, training, and Appraisal. It suggests 5 maturity levels. CMM was replaced by CMMI, which is broader in scope to take in most business processes
Prince 2 Developed by the UK government for project managers	A project management methodology that includes high-level management, control, and organization in a project	A project management and control methodology. It defines project management along 8 broad processes, with 45 sub-processes

Adopted from Parent and Reich (2009; Wilkin et al. (2016 and modified

The above table 1 lists the existing IT governance frameworks, standard, and methodologies which are matching with the layers shown in the figure 1. Accordingly, for the corporate governance of IT, COBIT 5 and ISO/IEC 38500:2008 are discussed. COBIT 5 is the latest version of IT governance framework developed by IT Governance Institute. It focuses the governance and management of enterprise IT to generate maximum value by retaining a balance between realistic benefits and optimizing risk levels while considering internal and external stakeholders. Similary, the ISO/IEC 38500:2008 is also a corporate governance of IT framework that focuses the structure and principles the directors use to evaluate, direct and monitor IT use in their organization. These two namely, COBIT 5 and ISO/IEC 38500:2008 are the corporate level IT governance frameworks used by directors and superior business leaders for corporate level decision making for their IT investment.

In the second layer, IT management and governance frameworks such as Val IT, Risk IT, COBIT 4.1, and COSO are included. The *Val IT* is the IT governance framework consist of value governance, portfolio management and investment management that are aims to create business value from IT investment. The *Risk IT* offers a complete overview of all risks by including risk governance, risk evaluation and risk response to treat IT investment risks via risk management practices. The COBIT 4.1is another IT governance framework that gives an internal control mechanism for IT investment by emphasizing the firm to define their rational for IT investment, the stakeholders and the expected outcomes from the IT investment. Finally, the COSO is also another IT governance framework that targets the enterprise risk management and related internal control for efficient risk management. Accordingly, these IT governance and management frameworks are exercised by the middle level / executive management of an organization to govern, manage, and supervise IT investment and to mitigate IT investment related risks.

In the bottom layer, there are two IT governance and management frameworks namely Capability Maturity Model Integration (CMMI) and Prince 2. The capability maturity model integration aims to manage large software development projects by looking product and service development, managing services, and getting connected products and services. Similarly, the prince 2 is a project management methodology that comprises of high-level management, control, and organization in a project. These two governance frameworks are exercised by the operational level managers to oversee the IT investment effectively at the bottom level of an organization.

3. CURRENT AND EMERGING BUSINESS/IT ALIGNMENT MODELS, FRAMEWORKS AND STANDARDS

In the past, the relationship between business strategies and IT strategies clearly described by Henderson and Venkatraman in their well-known Strategic Alignment Model or SAM (see Fig. 3). Later many information systems scholars grounded this model for further research. The idea behind this SAM is based on two building blocks: "strategic fit" and "functional integration." The strategic fit identifies that the IT strategy should be expressed in terms of an external domain (how the firm is positioned in the IT marketplace) and an internal domain (how the IT infrastructure should be configured and managed). Strategic fit is of course equally relevant in the business domain. Two types of functional integration exist: strategic integration and operational integration. Strategic integration is the link between business strategy and IT strategy reflecting the external components which are important for many companies as IT emerged as a source of strategic advantage. Operational integration covers the internal domain and deals with the link between organizational infrastructure and processes and IT infrastructure and processes.

Business - IT alignment highlights the improved rapport between IT and business to accomplish a better harmony in the organization. According to (Luftman 2004) alignment refers the function of IT and business to adapt their strategies together and addresses how IT is in harmony with the business, and how the business should, or could, be in harmony with IT. According to Sethibe et al. (2007) holds the view that strategic alignment is a driving force to achieve business value through IT investments by ensuring IT contributes to the achievement of business objectives. *There is no commonly accepted approach exist to measure business - IT alignment. Researchers developed their own models or approaches which have its own way, hence it is very difficult to distinguish them. Each approach has its own strengths and weaknesses and it is extremely important to select the suitable approach that fits the context.* Some of the well-known Business - IT alignment approaches are discussed as follows.

1. Strategic Alignment Model (SAM)

It was developed by Henderson and Venkatraman in 1993 to conceptualize strategic management of IT (see Figure 03). SAM contains four domains namely business strategy, IT strategy, organizational infrastructure and processes, and IT infrastructure and processes each with its principal dimensions. This model is based on two building blocks such as s*trategic fit* - inter-relationships between external and internal components (how the firm is placed in the IT marketplace) and *functional integration* - integration between business and functional domains. This strategic fit distinguishes between external focus, directed towards the business environment, and internal focus, directed towards administrative structures. The functional integration further divided into two types such as *Strategic integration* - the link between business strategy and IT strategy reflecting the external components. *Operational integration* - linked with internal domain and deals with the link between organizational infrastructure and processes and IT infrastructure and processes. Some researchers claimed that the strategic alignment can only take place when three of the four domains are in alignment. According to (Leonard 2008) SAM model merely describes what needs to be aligned and there has been far less consent regarding how alignment is to be achieved.

2. Generic Framework

The generic framework broadens the Strategic Alignment Model by adding an additional row and column. The row represents the structural components and variables, particularly the deeply rooted competencies and infrastructures of the organization. The column represents the connection between business and IT: information and communication. The newly introduced column and row, i.e. the architecture of the information/communication/knowledge infrastructure is at the heart of any modern organization. The business-IT relationship appears to be much more complex than can be derived from the SAM; it involves amongst others cultural, political and financial aspects.

The strategies are worthless unless they are adopted by the tactical and operational level. The tactical level needs to outline which projects are needed to really execute the strategy. And on an operational level, the projects need to be implemented and included in daily operations. The tactical level translates goals and preconditions of the strategic domain into concrete, realizable objectives, responsibilities, authorizations, frameworks, and guidelines for the operational domain. Hence, even if on a strategic level, business and IT appear to be aligned, this doesn't guarantee that it will lead to success. In fact, one should be concentrating on the way the different cells are connected. To make it even more realistic, we should add more cells. Most larger enterprises are organized in different units. This can be functional or divisional. This will lead to additional 9-cells connected. In the following figure 2.3, the 3 x 3 x 3 cube is constructed, which is the Generic Alignment Framework.

Figure 2. Strategic Alignment Model
Adopted from: (Henderson and Venkatraman 1993)

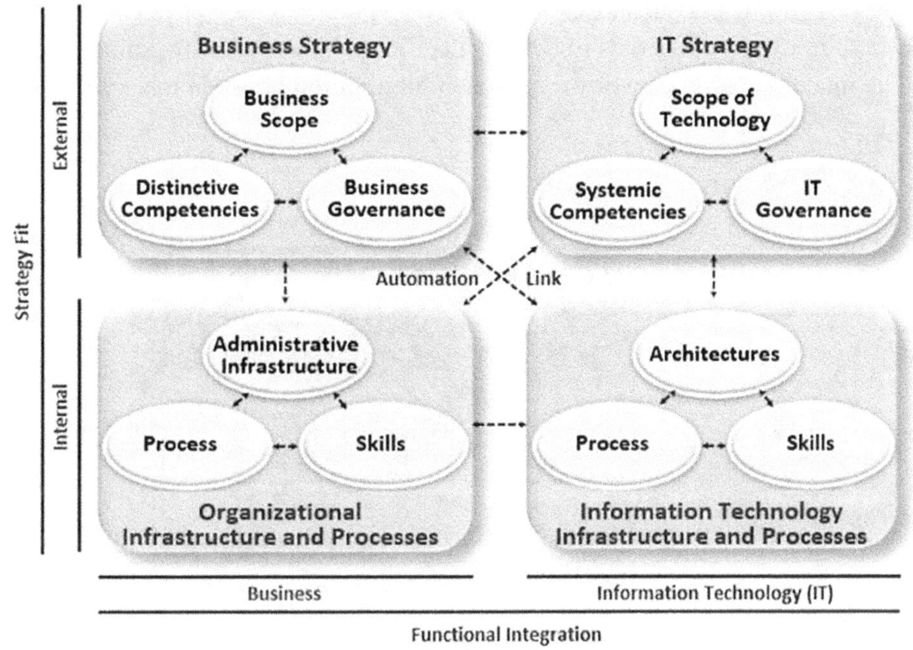

Figure 3. Generic Alignment Framework.

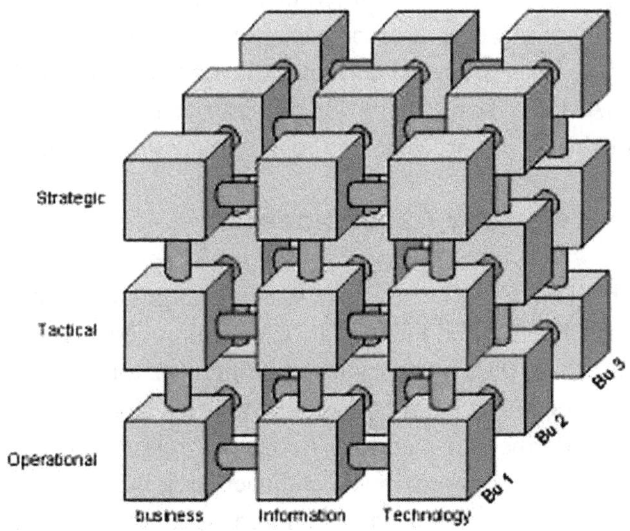

3. Integrated Architecture Framework

The framework lies on architectural design and used to bring together the business vision and IT vision of the firm to create an IT-enabled organization. As the name depicts, it resembles mainly to supporting the integrated architectural design of business and IT hence, it advocates architectural design as a catalyst in aligning business and IT. It defines four major architecture areas: business, information, information systems and technology infrastructure. A second dimension defines the different phases in the architectural design process such as contextual, conceptual, logical, physical and transformational phase. Finally, a third dimension exists to define specific architectural viewpoints, such as security or governance. The model follows a top down approach for aligning between main architecture areas.

Figure 4. Integrated Architecture Framework.

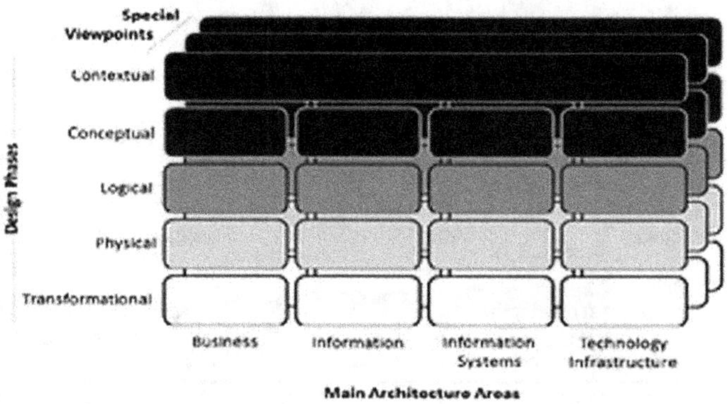

4. Strategic Alignment Maturity Model (SAMM)

The SAMM describes six IT - business alignment criteria determining different alignment maturity levels. These criteria are communications, competency/value measures, governance, partnership, scope and architecture, skills. These set of criteria determines the maturity level of the organization in terms of strategic alignment. The SAMM defines five levels of maturity for strategic alignment: initial process, committed process, established focus process, imp roved process and optimized process.

5. Strategic Alignment Maturity Assessment

Developed by Luftman which includes five levels of strategic alignment maturity such as Initial/Ad Hoc Process, Committed Process, Established Focused Process, Improved/Managed Process, and Optimized Process (see Figure 04). Each of the five levels of alignment maturity focuses in turn on a set of six IT-business alignment criteria such as Communications Maturity, Competency/Value Measurement Maturity, Governance Maturity, Partnership Maturity, Scope & Architecture Maturity and Skills Maturity. These six alignment areas have various attributes and each area is clearly defined the maturity levels. Whereas (Luftman 2000) points out that all areas should be given attention to mature the alignment between business and IT.

Figure 5. Strategic Alignment Maturity Model (SAMM)

The alignment maturity assessment is essential to identify whether IT is in the right place and function as projected in accordance with business unit needs. Further to measure the business/IT Alignment the book titled "*Enterprise Governance of Information Technology*" by De Haes and Van Grembergen (2015) explained many approaches such as matching and moderation approach, profile deviation approach, scoring approach and maturity model approach.

6. Reich & Benbasat Model (RBM)

This model lay down factors connected to the social dimension that can potentially capture alignment between business and IT objectives. The four factors involved; shared domain knowledge, IT implementation success, communication between business and IT executives, and connections between business and IT planning. The Model follows a top- down approach by centering on the antecedents along with the current practices that directly influence alignment. There are two dimensions of strategy creation, namely intellectual and social, but the authors of RBM have selected the social domain as it would more examine people involved in the creation and maturity of alignment.

Figure 6. Strategic Alignment Maturity Assessment
Source: Luftman (2000)

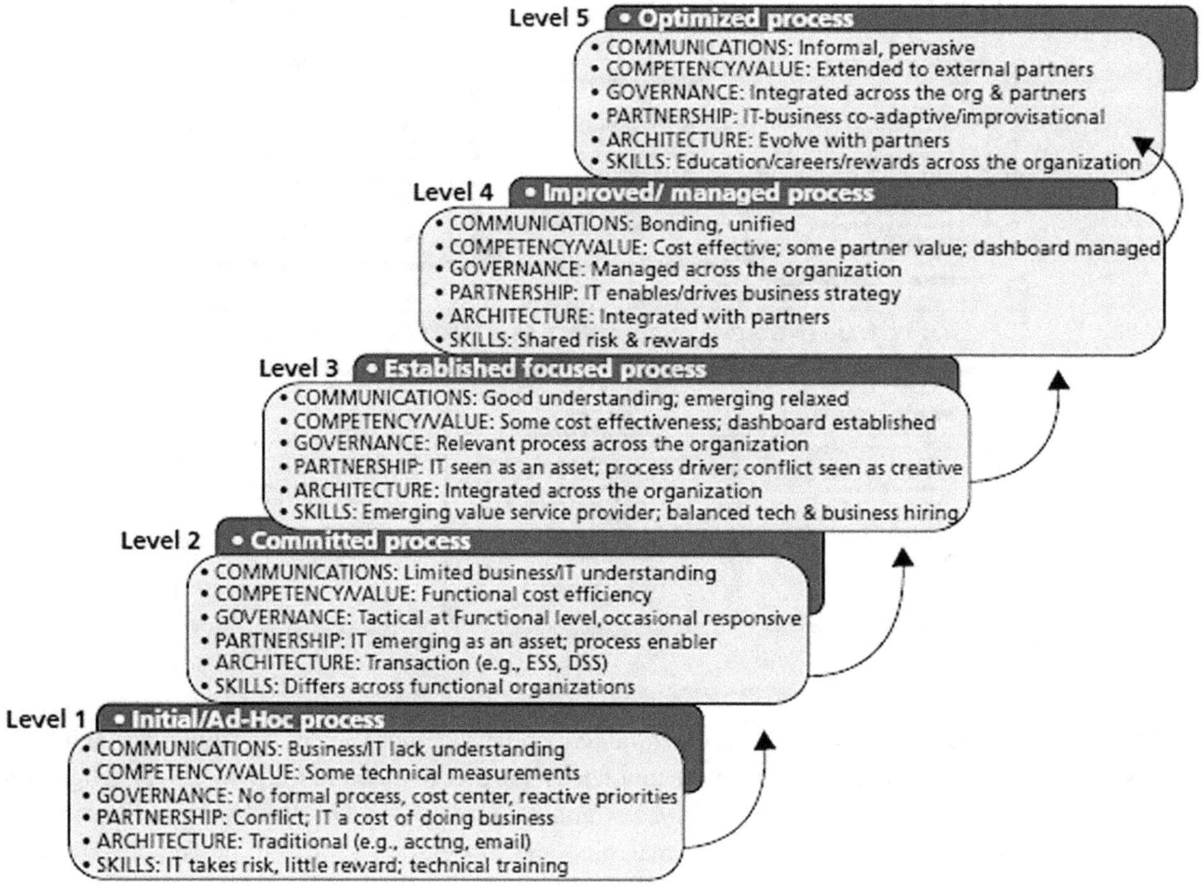

Figure 7. Reich & Benbasat Model

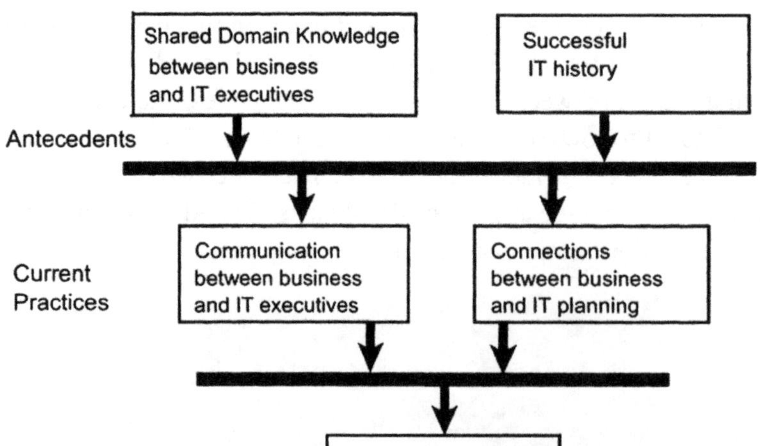

4. THE RELATIONSHIP BETWEEN IT GOVERNANCE AND BUSINESS/IT ALIGNMENT

Scholars define the business/IT alignment in numerous ways. For instance, Van Grembergen and De Haes (2009) define business/IT alignment as "the fit and integration among business strategy, IT strategy, business structures and IT structures". As the term denotes it includes two major questions: How is IT aligned with the business? And How is the business aligned with IT? In the past, business leaders and managers could get rid of IT decisions, but this is now impossible due to its vitality in any sector. IT governance has become a great importance for IT alignment and value delivery for organizations. When IT has become vital to generate value to the organization, IT governance has to turn out to be the forefront as an important enabler to create and capture value for the organizations. The purpose of IT governance is to accomplish a link between the business and IT thus, the applied processes, structures and relational mechanisms facilitate to realize business/IT alignment. In addition, an organization must have a successful IT governance and IT alignment in practice, in order to realize a superior return on IT investments.

The key to successful IT business alignment is the creation of value at each step of the value chain of the organizations' internal and external processes. IT is used by many organizations to automate, integrate, assimilate, and deliver real time information in the business processes. IT is used to expand into newer geographical and virtual market segments as automating and using IT often results in an anywhere, anytime, everywhere, every time experience for the end users. For all these to happen, the IT and the business functions must work together as a team and in a synergistic manner. As a result, organisations started with the execution of IT governance in order to realize a better alignment between business and IT.

5. COBIT AS A FRAMEWORK

CobiT framework exhibits how IT practices deliver information to the businesses to realize its objectives. CobiT editions were released in different years with their scope such as, 1st edition scope *audit* in 1996, 2nd edition scope *control* in 1998, 3rd edition scope *management* in 2000, 4th edition scope *IT governance* in 2005 with revised version 4.1 in 2007 with Val IT 2.0 in 2008 and Risk IT 2009 and 5th edition scope *governance of enterprise IT* in 2012. The latest CobiT 5 built on by integrating other major frameworks, standards, and resources, including ISACA's Val IT, Risk IT, ITIL and other related ISO. According to (Van Grembergen et al. 2004) CobiT offers 34 IT processes with their high-level control objectives and management guidelines, together with their maturity models and their scorecards in the form of key goal indicators and key performance indicators.

COBIT is a globally recognized framework, developed by ISACA, to support organizations that govern and manage IT efficiently. It helps organizations to meet business challenges in the areas of regulatory compliance, risk management and aligning IT strategy with organizational goals. COBIT 5, the latest iteration of the framework, was released in 2012. The COBIT 5 has been designed with amalgamation at its heart. It is aligned with numerous best-practice frameworks and standards, such as ITIL, ISO 20000 and ISO 27001. It may be best to take an integrated approach when implementing an IT governance framework, using parts of several different frameworks and standards to deliver the results for the organizations.

Figure 8. CobiT4.1 framework
Source: ISACA

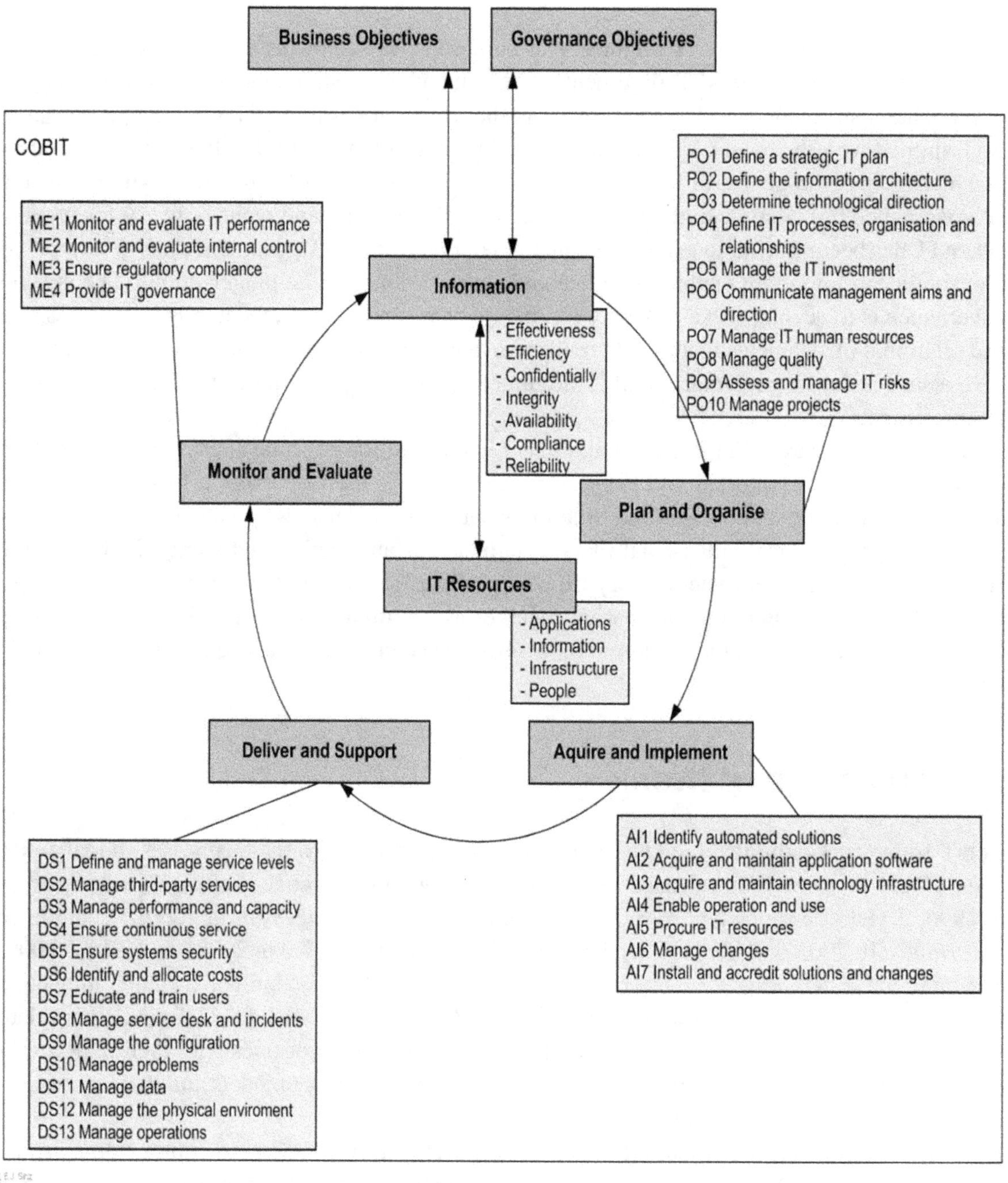

6. Val - IT AS A FRAMEWORK

Val IT is introduced by the IT Governance Institute; and it presents a set of IT-related business processes and associated key management practices, management guidelines and maturity models to help managers directing that the value creation out of IT Investments (Van Grembergen and De Haes 2009). It covers a set of practical governance principles and practices that help the board and executive management to enhance the value from IT investments (Val 2008a; Van Grembergen and De Haes 2009). Val-IT consists of a set of principles, processes and management practices for managing IT-enabled business investments from the inception to its realization of benefits from a project (Merhout and Havelka 2008). The three domains of Val-IT are a) *value governance* - enables the enterprise to be safe, optimal value from its IT-enabled investments during their full economic life cycle, b) *portfolio management* - confirms an enterprise obtains optimal value across its portfolio of IT-enabled investments, and c) *investment management* - makes sure that enterprise's individual IT-enabled investments produce optimum value (Val 2008a; Wilkin et al. 2012). The study 1 is adopted the Val-IT 2.0 framework to examine the management of IT investment.

The Val-IT framework is strongly connected with COBIT[1] in terms of business and financial perspective but offers value to the firm in its own right (Lombardi et al. 2016; Merhout and Havelka 2008; Wilkin et al. 2012). The Val-IT framework looks at IT governance with an upper lens of abstraction[2] that allows how to manage IT from a business point of view (Simonsson et al. 2010). Moreover, the Val- IT framework based on value creation out of IT investments is a business responsibility to support business people. It suggests a set of IT-related business processes, and link key management practices and maturity models (Van Grembergen and De Haes 2009). According to Van Grembergen and De Haes (2009), IT is in a unique position to direct the business in adopting Val-IT practices, which in turn craft more value by levering IT to the firm. Hence, the Val-IT framework in this study is a panacea and applicable as the frame of references. In addition, as this study 1 focuses on management of IT investment, the resource-based theory and process theory offer a more salient and insightful theoretical foundation.

1. Val IT Processes and Their Key Practices

To realize the value delivery from IT investment Val IT includes processes such as *Value governance* - optimize value by establishing control mechanism, provide strategic direction and portfolio characteristics for IT investment. *Portfolio management* - makes sure IT investment is aligned with and contributing best possible value to the firm's strategic objectives. *Investment management*- make sure the IT investment deliver most favorable value at a reasonable cost and tolerable level of risk. Each process has its own set of practices which support the management for the optimal value delivery. Figure 08 shows three Val IT Processes.

7. IT BALANCED SCORECARD AS A FRAMEWORK

Balanced Scorecard (BS) was introduced by Kaplan and Norton (1992, 1993, 1996a, 1996b) at the enterprise level (Van Grembergen 2000). The BS initial idea was the assessment of an organization concerning customer satisfaction, internal processes, and innovation. On the other hand, the traditional financial evaluation measures which is a comprehensive tool to evaluate an organization while maintaining all perspectives in balance. The BS can be applied to the IT function of an organization to evaluate

Figure 9. Key Management Practices Supporting 03 Val IT Processes
Adopted (Val 2008b): IT governance Institute

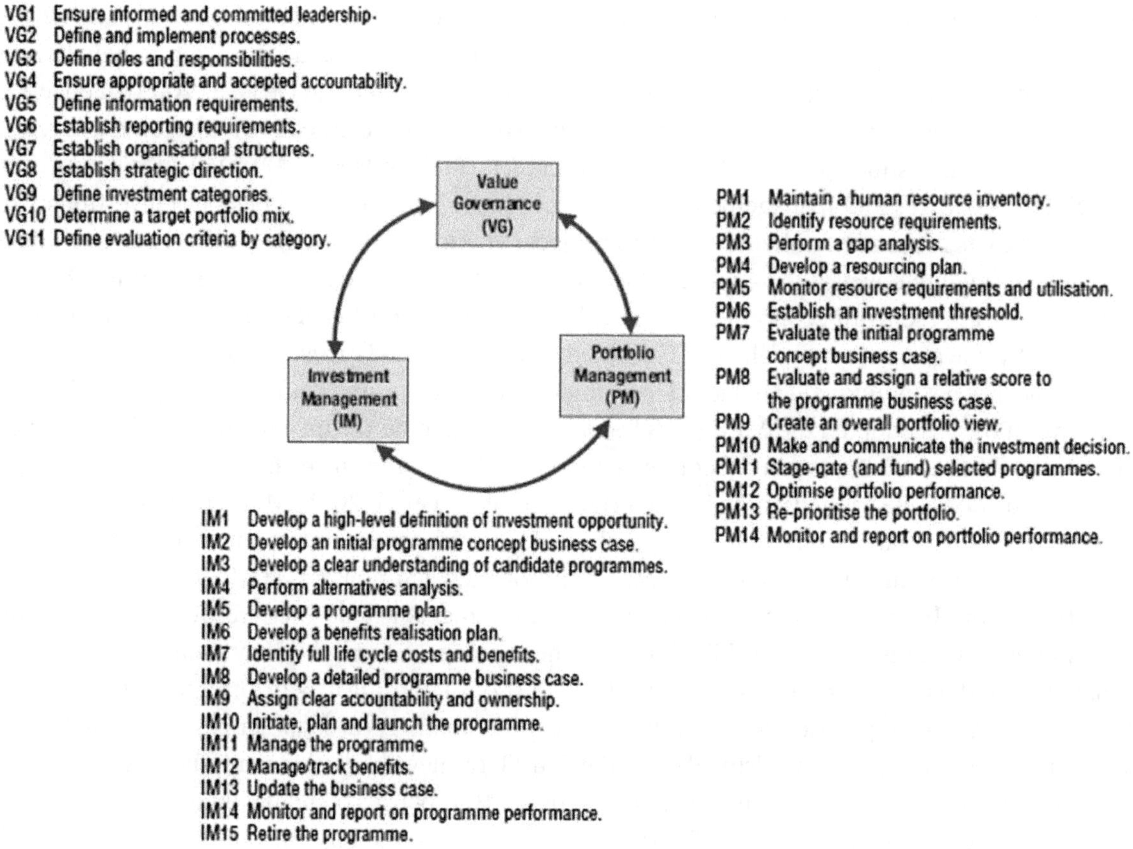

its processes. Many IT executives realized that the integration of IT strategy with business strategy is a timely need and the comprehensive tool is IT balanced scorecard. The business balanced scorecard focuses performance and progress in achieving strategic goals while IT balanced scorecard includes inter-related perspectives of business scorecard such as *User Orientation* - how users see the IT function, *Operational Excellence* - Evaluate effectiveness of the IT function, *Business Contribution* - management's view of the IT function and *Future Orientation/Innovation* - how well IT is positioned to meet future needs. BSC can be a tool for aligning the organization's vision and strategy as well as improving both the internal and external communications and monitoring performance against goals.

In the typical organizations, the success of performance measurement plan depends on the mutual integration of business and IT objectives. It covers strategic, customer, financial, quality, process innovation, and operational effectiveness which support firm's vision, mission, plan, and objectives. It is significant to have reporting system based on critical success factors and key performance indicators. Moreover, in executing these plans and objectives it should be monitored and measured with the combination of balanced scorecard key performance indicators (KPI) and formal and informal status review meetings and reports (Selig 2008). Further, the result should connect with critical success factors to KPIs that are measurable and linked to a governance component. IT scorecard should not be developed in isolation and Key Performance Indicators (KPIs) can be applied to measure the success of strategic objectives.

Figure 10. IT Balanced Scorecard
Adopted: (Shahid 2008)

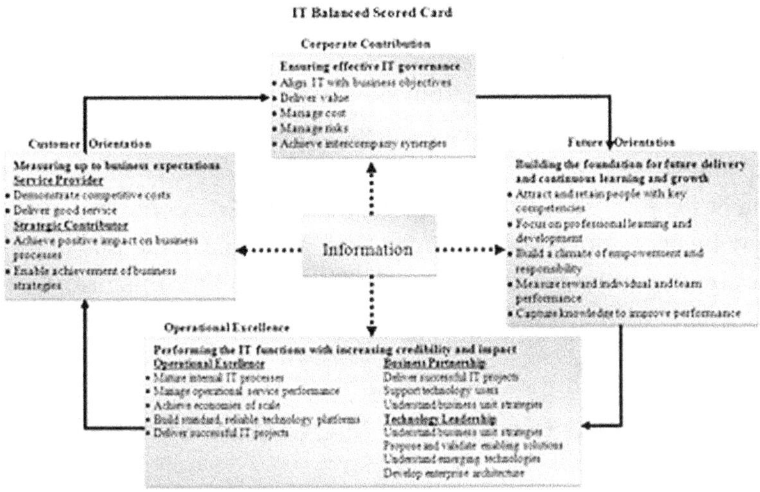

8. SETTING A DIRECTION FOR IMPROVING BUSINESS/ IT ALIGNMENT AND STRATEGIC IT INVESTMENT

Business-IT Alignment aims to match the IT strategy with business strategy with the goal of exploiting value generated by the enterprise. An enterprise has reached business-IT alignment when all its IT initiatives are entirely in line with the requirements set by its business functions. This means that every IT-related investment, activity, service or project must play a role in generating or enhancing business value. Aligning an IT strategy and a business strategy symbolize that every aspect of the IT strategy should support the business goals of an organization. As a result, IT should work towards attaining business-related metrics, not IT, so that advance alignment.

Conversely, the business-IT alignment is not the sole responsibility of IT department / unit. Similarly, business-IT alignment gap is the degree to which IT initiatives deviate from business requirements. Hence, the significant to achieve an aligned IT and business strategy is shared leadership and accountability. IT. An organization must have the correct IT leaders working with the people in the business make the strategy become a reality. The IT strategy that drives and enables business goals is a vital component of any firm, however it only will not result in alignment. The idea behind strategic alignment is very widespread, but the question is how firms can achieve this vital goal. To be truly aligned, the organization must use the corporate strategy to regulate resources and processes it can most effectively employ to reach its goals.

Strategic IT Investment

Today IT becomes more powerful and pervasive, particularly with the growing evolution of the industrial revolution and digital economy. The new technologies and technology-driven business opportunities are being developed and presented to managers at an ever-accelerating rate. Hence, investment in IT systems remains to increase and measuring IT investment is becoming riskier and complex. Consequently, business leaders are looking not only wise investments in IT but also ways of generating more value through strategic IT investment. Industry leaders are attracted by the business opportunities for strategic impact, but struggle with the enormous expenditures and uncertainties involved.

The IT strategy emphases on how IT will support the business to succeed, and an IT strategic investment plan is a roadmap that assist the businesses to implement those strategies. This strategic investment plan summaries areas where IT can generate business value and where an organization can gain competitive advantage by making the best use of IT resources. The key idea of an organization's strategic IT investment focus is to align the organization's goals and mission, but are flexible enough to accommodate new business priorities and technologies that have the potential for driving business growth. Hence, it is significant for an organization's IT team to know its priorities and identify the IT projects that the business should invest in.

9. IT INVESTMENT RISK ASSESSMENT, MANAGEMENT AND MITIGATION

IT plays a key role for enabling business operation in the digital economy. For every organization, it is vital to pinpoint risks to their IT systems and data, to reduce or manage those risks, and to develop a response plan in the event of an IT crisis. Similarly, the business firms have the legal obligations in relation to privacy, electronic transactions, and staff training that influence IT risk management strategies. IT risks can be in different forms such as hardware and software failure, human error, spam, viruses and malicious attacks, as well as natural disasters such as fires, cyclones or floods. Today organizations are under ever growing pressure to comply with the regulatory requirements, preserve strong operational performance, and maintain shareholder value. In this hyper-competitive environment enterprises can no longer afford ad-hoc risk assessment measures. Protecting intellectual property, sensitive customer information, and other business-critical information involves a complete risk management and mitigation that thoroughly matches with the business objectives.

There are five key components to IT risk management:

1. **Identify risk.** An effective IT risk management's first step is to evaluate the unique weaknesses and vulnerabilities of the organization as well as the theoretical effectiveness of the organization's existing security measures.
2. **Measure risk.** Once the threats and vulnerabilities are identified, decide the possibility of their occurrence and measure their influence on the organization's operations.
3. **Rank risk**. After evaluating the risks to determine which risks pose the biggest threat to the operation of the firm, and rank those risks in a top priority.
4. **Mitigate risk.** In this step organization assess their highest ranked risks and set out a plan to treat or modify these risks to achieve acceptable risk levels."
5. **Monitor risk.** At last, the effective risk management program is to track and monitor risks through complete data to avoid future risks that require workable reactions.

Figure 11. Risk Management Fundamental Steps

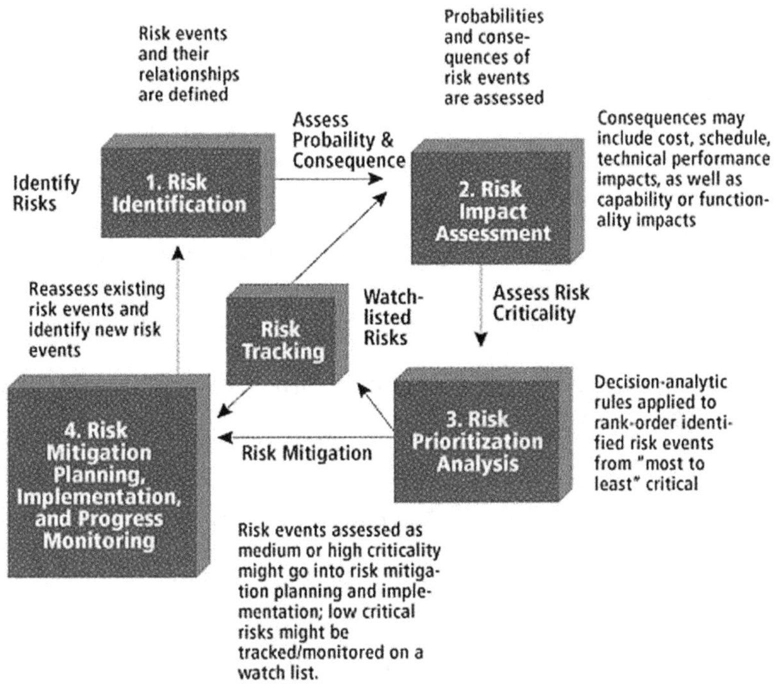

SUMMARY

In today's competitive business setting the IT has become a key component of an organization and almost all functions of the organization depend on this IT. Firms are continuously investing large amount of money on IT investment for their operation. Hence, the management and governance on this IT investment has received considerable attention among the practitioners and academic community. IT governance is a subset of corporate governance and offer mechanisms for IT councils, Steering committee and board in the organizations. IT governance is crucial for successful IT management that addresses issues like alignment, planning, leadership, execution, accountability, and metrics. The successful execution of best practice or model depends on how the organizations evaluate its current state and realize its business value to the organization's growth and sustainability. This chapter discussed some of the useful industry best practices and models in IT governance and IT alignment context.

REFERENCES

Abdulrasool, F., & Turnbull, S. (2020). The Role of It Governance in Enhancing the Performance of Smart Universities. *Joint European-US Workshop on Applications of Invariance in Computer Vision*, 708-720. 10.1007/978-3-030-44289-7_66

Ali, S., & Green, P. (2012). Effective Information Technology (It) Governance Mechanisms: An It Outsourcing Perspective. *Information Systems Frontiers*, *14*(2), 179-193.

Bowen, P. L., Cheung, M.-Y. D., & Rohde, F. H. (2007). Enhancing It Governance Practices: A Model and Case Study of an Organization's Efforts. *International Journal of Accounting Information Systems*, *8*(3), 191-221.

Centre, N. C. (2005). *It Governance Developing a Successful Governance Strategy. Oxford House.*

De Haes, S., & Van Grembergen, W. (2015). *Enterprise Governance of Information Technology*. Springer. doi:10.1007/978-3-319-14547-1

De Haes, S., Van Grembergen, W., Joshi, A., & Huygh, T. (2020). Enterprise Governance of It, Alignment, and Value. In *Enterprise Governance of Information Technology* (pp. 1–13). Springer. doi:10.1007/978-3-030-25918-1_1

Dong, S. (2012). Decision Execution Mechanisms of It Governance: The Crm Case. *International Journal of Information Management*, *32*(2), 147-157.

Henderson, J. C., & Venkatraman, N. (1993). Strategic Alignment: Leveraging Information Technology for Transforming Organizations. *IBM Systems Journal*, *32*(1), 4-16.

Leonard, J. (2008). What Are We Aligning? Implications of a Dynamic Approach to Alignment. ACIS 2008 Proceedings, 76.

Lombardi, R., Del Giudice, M., Caputo, A., Evangelista, F., & Russo, G. (2016). Governance and Assessment Insights in Information Technology: The Val It Model. *Journal of the Knowledge Economy*, *7*(1), 292-308.

Luftman, J. (2000). Assessing Business-It Alignment Maturity. *Communications of the Association for Information Systems*, *4*(1), 14.

Luftman, J. (2004). *Assessing Business-It Alignment Maturity*. Strategies for Information Technology Governance.

Merhout, J. W., & Havelka, D. (2008). Information Technology Auditing: A Value-Added It Governance Partnership between It Management and Audit. *Communications of the Association for Information Systems*, *23*(1), 26.

Parent, M., & Reich, B. H. (2009). Governing Information Technology Risk. *California Management Review*, *51*(3), 134-152.

Selig, G. J. (2008). *Implementing It Governance-a Practical Guide to Global Best Practices in It Management*. Van Haren.

Sethibe, T., Campbell, J., & McDonald, C. (2007). It Governance in Public and Private Sector Organisations: Examining the Differences and Defining Future Research Directions. ACIS 2007 Proceedings, 118.

Shahid, S. (2008). *A Business-Driven Evaluation of Distributed-Computing Models*. Academic Press.

Simonsson, M., Johnson, P., & Ekstedt, M. (2010). The Effect of It Governance Maturity on It Governance Performance. *Information Systems Management*, *27*(1), 10-24.

Turel, O., Liu, P., & Bart, C. (2017). Board-Level Information Technology Governance Effects on Organizational Performance: The Roles of Strategic Alignment and Authoritarian Governance Style. *Information Systems Management*, *34*(2), 117-136.

Val, I. (2008a). Enterprise Value: Governance of It Investments. *The Val IT Framework,* (2).

Val, I. (2008b). *Enterprise Value: Governance of It Investments. The Val It Framework 2.0*. IT Governance Institute.

Van Grembergen, W. (2000). The Balanced Scorecard and It Governance. *IRMA Conference*, 1123-1124.

Van Grembergen, W., & De Haes, S. (2009). *Enterprise Governance of Information Technology: Achieving Strategic Alignment and Value*. Springer Science & Business Media.

Van Grembergen, W., De Haes, S., & Guldentops, E. (2004). Structures, Processes and Relational Mechanisms for It Governance. *Strategies for Information Technology Governance*, *2*(4), 1-36.

Wilkin, C., Campbell, J., Moore, S., & Van Grembergen, W. (2012). Co-Creating Value from It in a Contracted Public Sector Service Environment: Perspectives on Cobit and Val It. *Journal of Information Systems*, *27*(1), 283-306.

Wilkin, C. L., Couchman, P. K., Sohal, A., & Zutshi, A. (2016). Exploring Differences between Smaller and Large Organizations' Corporate Governance of Information Technology. *International Journal of Accounting Information Systems*, *22*, 6–25. doi:10.1016/j.accinf.2016.07.002

Wu, S. P.-J., Straub, D. W., & Liang, T.-P. (2015). How Information Technology Governance Mechanisms and Strategic Alignment Influence Organizational Performance: Insights from a Matched Survey of Business and It Managers. *MIS Quarterly*, *39*(2), 497-518.

ENDNOTES

1 The Control Objectives for Information and related Technology (COBIT) is the most renowned framework for IT governance maturity assessments by the IT Governance Institute. The framework offers a definition of IT governance as consisting of four domains and 34 processes. Each process contains a number of IT governance maturity indicators, such as activities, documents, metrics, and support for role and responsibility assignment (Simonsson et al. 2010; Wilkin et al. 2012).

2 Val IT views IT governance onto a higher level of abstraction by offering general directions on how to manage IT from a business point of view. Val IT clearly focuses on the interface between IT and the business. Val IT takes on where COBIT ends, and the two frameworks complement each other well (Simonsson et al. 2010).

Chapter 5
The Role of IT Governance and Managing IT Investment on Firm Performance

Aboobucker Ilmudeen
https://orcid.org/0000-0002-9450-6816
Department of Management and Information Technology, Faculty of Management and Commerce, South Eastern University of Sri Lanka, Sri Lanka

ABSTRACT

Although the multifaceted effects of managing or governing IT have been taken into consideration in both practice and theoretical debate, the mechanism through which these bring firm performance is yet unclear and limited. Drawing on the resource-based theory and the process theory, this chapter aims to systematically review the antecedents of business-IT alignment on the firm performance context. The findings of this study show that the business-IT alignment is derived from IT governance practices and managing IT investment to achieve firm performance. This study proposes that the firm performance cannot be attained by merely investing in IT; instead, firms should focus on effective management of IT practices and strategically align their business and IT strategies.

1. INTRODUCTION

An enormous growing body of IS literature has examined the relationship such as IT investment - firm performance (Ali, Green, & Robb, 2015; Kim, Xiang, & Lee, 2009; Peppard, Ward, & Daniel, 2007), IT spending - firm performance (e.g., Melville, Kraemer, & Gurbaxani, 2004; Paul P Tallon, 2007), and business-IT alignment - firm performance (Bergeron, Raymond, & Rivard, 2004; Cragg, King, & Hussin, 2002; Ilmudeen, Bao, & Alharbi, 2019; Preston & Karahanna, 2009; Sabherwal & Chan, 2001), leading to a key conclusion that firms with superior IT management and alignment commonly achieve greater firm performance. Drawing on the above studies, we cogitate to understand that the unavoidability of management of IT investment and IT governance to attain superior firm performance. Nevertheless,

DOI: 10.4018/978-1-7998-4852-3.ch005

the examination of how the management of IT investment and IT governance derive firm performance is still inadequate.

The IT governance has a direct impact on how IT is managed within the organization and includes the implementation of IT management techniques and procedures in conformity with well-known IT strategies and policies (Bowen, Cheung, & Rohde, 2007). It is obvious that IT-enabled investments can bring enormous rewards, but only with the right governance and management processes and full commitment from all management levels. The business value of IT resources makes IT Governance a significant concern for both IS researchers and practitioners (Bergeron, Croteau, Uwizeyemungu, & Raymond, 2020). In particular, how the various management levels like board members, executive management, and operational management will be involved in this process. the effective IT governance helps to ensure that IT supports business goals, optimizes business investment in IT, and manage IT-related risks and opportunities (Williams, 2012). The limited views on IT governance no longer resemble with what is happening in the real world, where firms are executing a portfolio of different governance mechanisms (Boh & Yellin, 2006).

In prior studies, the notion how the performance outcomes and the significance of managing IT's impact on firm performance have been called for further studies in numerous ways (Ilmudeen & Yukun, 2018; Turel, Liu, & Bart, 2017; S. P.-J. Wu, Straub, & Liang, 2015). Example, it warrants empirical studies with either mediation or moderator model to elucidate whether IT generates business value directly or indirectly with firm factors (Cao, Wiengarten, & Humphreys, 2011). Likewise, the managing IT and business-IT alignment can be understood as complementary and deeply embedded concepts (Tiwana & Konsynski, 2010; S. P.-J. Wu et al., 2015). However, realizing and fostering business-IT alignment has continued a pervasive management concern (Luftman, Lyytinen, & ben Zvi, 2015); that warrants researchers to consider alignment in a fresh approach (Coltman, Tallon, Sharma, & Queiroz, 2015). The prior studies evidence that the business-IT alignment is crucial to allow firms to maximize the benefit of IS investments and derive the value to the firm performance (Chan, Huff, Barclay, & Copeland, 1997; Papp, 1999; Sabherwal & Chan, 2001). Despite of its significance, the business-IT alignment has stayed elusive for many firms (Luftman et al., 2015; Preston & Karahanna, 2009; Paul P Tallon, 2007). Nevertheless, it is not well understood if and how some contextual factors shape to drive business – IT alignment on firm performance context.

Realizing and nurturing business-IT alignment has received a significant management concern, that permits scholars to think alignment in a fresh approach (Coltman et al., 2015). However, the literature absences to prove that how the management of IT investment together with business-IT alignment derive firm performance yet vague. IT governance is worried with both governing of IT and governing through IT (C. L. Wilkin & Chenhall, 2019). Similarly, prior studies proved that the business-IT alignment is vital to allow firms to exploit the benefit of IS investments and derive the value to the firm performance (Chan et al., 1997; Papp, 1999; Sabherwal & Chan, 2001). The past studies (e.g., Ilmudeen & Yukun, 2018; Turel et al., 2017; S. P.-J. Wu et al., 2015) have called for additional investigations on the importance of managing IT investment and business-IT alignment on firm performance context. These drawbacks motivated to conduct a compressive review investigation for this chapter organization. This chapter is drawn on the below theories that elucidates the utmost necessity of managing IT and business-IT alignment to realize superior firm performance.

2. THEORETICAL BACKGROUND

2.1 Managing IT and Firm Performance

It is quite true that IT investment can increase firm performance (Turel et al., 2017). However, investments in IT are not adequate by themselves to improve firm performance (Y. Wang, Shi, Nevo, Li, & Chen, 2015). Hence, it necessitates the practice of managing IT to generate its superior performance outcomes. The managing IT involves the activities e.g., planning, organizing, controlling, and directing the use of IT within an organization (Boynton & Zmud, 1987; Van Der Zee & De Jong, 1999; Y. Wang et al., 2015); that reached a significant concern among IS scholars, and executives (Ilmudeen & Yukun, 2018; Lowry & Wilson, 2016; Mithas, Tafti, Bardhan, & Goh, 2012; Paul P Tallon, Kraemer, & Gurbaxani, 2000; Xu, Zhang, & Li, 2016). The managing IT investment include processes like developing, operating, implementing and maintaining financial controls over IT investments and expenses in line with IT strategic plans (Centre, 2005). The effective use of IT significantly depends on managing IT and governance practices which are highly important to its value creation from IT investment (Ali et al., 2015; Prasad, Heales, & Green, 2010; S. P.-J. Wu et al., 2015). In this belief, IT can have a positive effect, no effect, or even a negative effect on performance, in relation to how well IT is managed and governed (Turel et al., 2017). Firms can contribute to its performance having strong managing IT by orchestrating various business units activities, streamlining operation processes, reducing production cost, synchronizing IT and business units, regular checking of IT priorities, and timely allocation of IT assets (Y. Wang et al., 2015).

The traditional performance measures (see figure 2.2) like ROI, net present value, internal rate of return, and payback method require monetary values. When they applied to IS the problem arises as IS regularly create intangible outcomes for IT investment like improved customer service, technical and managerial skills, unique or competitive advantage, knowledge-based assets that are challenging to quantify (C. L. Wilkin & Chenhall, 2010). Besides, the value of IT is perceived differently by various levels of management and users (De Haes & Van Grembergen, 2015). Accordingly, identifying how IT delivers value can be challenging as the benefits become absorbed into business processes, hard to measure IT at the business unit level, and less obvious at the level of financial reporting (C. L. Wilkin & Chenhall, 2010).

2.2 IT Governance Practices in the Context of Managing IT Investment

IT governance is defined as "the organizational capacity exercised by the board, executive management and IT management to control the formulation and implementation of IT strategy and in this way ensure the fusion of business and IT''(Van Grembergen & De Haes, 2009). IT governance is a subset of overall governance responsibilities of the Boards and denotes the decisions about key IT activities and investments in the organizations (Parent & Reich, 2009). The effective IT governance is an active means to decrease risk, lessen the impact of IT-related failures, reduce the cost of capital, and make lasting shareholder value (Parent & Reich, 2009). With the effective IT governance framework, IT-enabled business investments are well managed and generate value, whereas the weak IT governance provides the same chance to destroy the value (Centre, 2005). The industry cases make shock stories for value destruction example, Nike lost over US$ 200m failure in implementing its supply chain software, failures in IT-enabled logistics systems at MFI and Sainsbury vanished to multi-million pound (Centre, 2005).

Today, IT serve a vital function, and almost all organizations depend on IT. This IT dependency causes executives to use IT governance practices in the decision-making process. There are reasons why IT governance has evolved as a field and exists on its own. Because, most of the organizations' IT investment account for a larger portion of their budget, IT always referred to as a technical field which cannot easily be understood, and investment in IT and its value generation not visible for non- technical executives. Furthermore, IT investments are not able to create the apparent value unlike the business case, and IT itself is a complex, and it require governance to make transparency. Figure 1 and Table 1 illustrates IT governance frameworks and standard with their primary IT-related functions.

Figure 1. Frameworks and standard and their primary IT-related functions

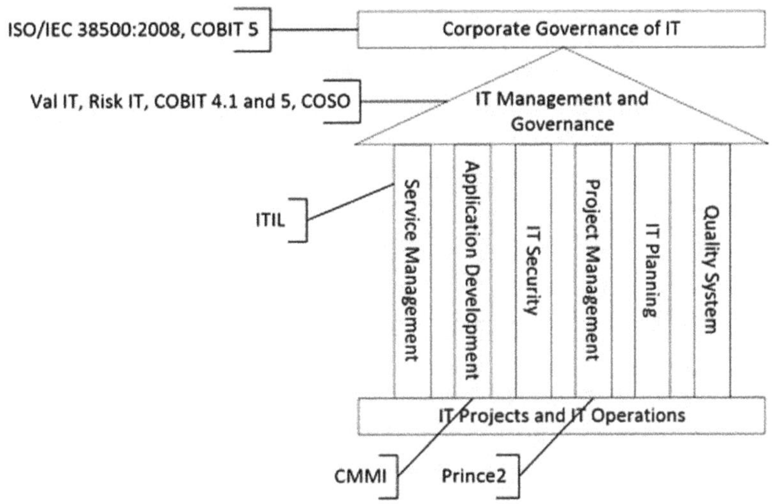

2.3 Underlying Theories

2.3.1 Val-IT in Management of IT Investment

Val IT is introduced by the IT Governance Institute; and it presents a set of IT-related business processes and associated key management practices, management guidelines and maturity models to help managers directing that the value creation out of IT Investments (Van Grembergen & De Haes, 2009). It covers a set of practical governance principles and practices that help the board and executive management to enhance the value from IT investments (Val, 2008; Van Grembergen & De Haes, 2009). Val-IT consists of a set of principles, processes and management practices for managing IT-enabled business investments from the inception to its realization of benefits from a project (Merhout & Havelka, 2008). The three domains of Val-IT are a) *value governance* - enables the enterprise to be safe, optimal value from its IT-enabled investments during their full economic life cycle, b) *portfolio management* - confirms an enterprise obtains optimal value across its portfolio of IT-enabled investments, and c) *investment management* - makes sure that enterprise's individual IT-enabled investments produce optimum value (Val, 2008; C. Wilkin, Campbell, Moore, & Van Grembergen, 2012). The study 1 is adopted the Val-IT 2.0 framework to examine the management of IT investment.

Table 1. IT governance frameworks, standard, and methodologies (as related to figure 1)

Framework Origin	Definition and Focus	Coverage
IT governance and management frameworks **COBIT 5** (Control Objectives for Information and related Technologies) developed by the IT Governance Institute for Information Systems Audit and Control Association - ISACA	A "comprehensive framework that assists enterprises in achieving their objectives for the governance and management of enterprise IT… [to]… create optimal value …by maintaining a balance between realistic benefits and optimizing risk levels and resource use …considering the IT-related interests of internal and external stakeholders."	COBIT 5, combines and incorporates COBIT 4.1, Val IT 2.0 and Risk IT, and draws from ISACA's IT Assurance Framework and the Business Model for Information Security. It lines up with frameworks and standards such as ITIL, International Organization for Standardization (ISO), Project Management Body of Knowledge (PMBOK), PRINCE 2 and The Open Group Architecture Framework (TOGAF). It is framed with 5 principles and 7 organizational resources called enablers
COBIT 4.1	Offers an internal control framework for IT by demanding firm to define their motivation for IT investment, the stakeholders and the desired outcomes	By linking business goals to IT goals, it recognizes the associated responsibilities of business and IT process owners, and through metrics and maturity models, measures the success of goals
Val IT *Information Systems Audit and Control Association (ISACA)*	Val IT assists in creating business value from IT investments. It links management of the IT portfolio to the firm's strategic objectives	It comprises of a set of guiding principles and processes with suggested key management practices domains such as value governance, portfolio management and investment management
Risk IT	Complete view of all risks in the use of IT and their treatment via risk management practices	It covers 3 domains (risk governance, risk evaluation and risk response), which are detailed by process components, management practice, inputs and outputs, RACI charts, goals and metrics
COSO Committee of Sponsoring Organizations of the Treadway Commission	A combined framework aimed to Enterprise Risk Management (ERM) and related Internal Control. It views Internal Control as a process effected by an entity's board, management and others to manage risk	A cube with 4 organizational objectives, 8 risk management components and 4 organizational units
AS 8015 (2005) *Australian Standard for Corporate Governance of Information & Communication Technology*	The world's first national standard for governing ICTs, introduced in March 2003 and subsequently revised in 2005.	Prescribes 3-sequential step approach governing ICT projects and operations: *evaluate*-uses of ICT, *direct*-preparation, and implementation of ICT plans and policies to best support the organization, *monitor*-conformance to policies and performance against the plans.
Standard **ISO/IEC 38500:2008**	A structure of principles that directors can use to evaluate, direct and monitor IT use in their organization	Offers direction on CGIT via 6 "good practice" principles (responsibility, strategy, acquisition, performance, conformance and human behavior), each with its own set of suggested practices structured under 3 task areas (evaluation, direction, and monitoring)
ISO/IEC 20000	International Organization for Standardization / International Electro technical Commission Standard 20000	Terms and Code of Practice for IT Service Management. It is the first international standard for IT service management and is aligned with ITIL best practices.
Methodologies for IT projects and IT operations **ITIL - IT Infrastructure Library**	Guiding framework of best practices for service and asset management. In its 3rd version, it presently has 5 best practice volumes focused around the service lifecycle and continuous service upgrading.	IT service management and operations through IT as a whole-of-organization engagement

continues on following page

Table 1. Continued

Framework Origin	Definition and Focus	Coverage
CMM /CMMI – Capability Maturity Model Integration -Software Engineering Institute at Carnegie - Mellon University	To help in managing large software development projects. Focuses on product and service development, managing services & acquiring related products and services	A program for process improvement, training, and Appraisal. It suggests 5 maturity levels. CMM was replaced by CMMI, which is broader in scope to take in most business processes
Prince 2 Developed by the UK government for project managers	A project management methodology that includes high-level management, control, and organization in a project	A project management and control methodology. It defines project management along 8 broad processes, with 45 sub-processes

The Val-IT framework is strongly connected with COBIT[1] in terms of business and financial perspective but offers value to the firm in its own right (Lombardi, Del Giudice, Caputo, Evangelista, & Russo, 2016; Merhout & Havelka, 2008; C. Wilkin et al., 2012). The Val-IT framework looks at IT governance with an upper lens of abstraction[2] that allows how to manage IT from a business point of view (Simonsson et al., 2010). Moreover, the Val- IT framework based on value creation out of IT investments is a business responsibility to support business people. It suggests a set of IT-related business processes, and link key management practices and maturity models (Van Grembergen & De Haes, 2009). According to Van Grembergen and De Haes (2009)), IT is in a unique position to direct the business in adopting Val-IT practices, which in turn craft more value by levering IT to the firm. Hence, the Val-IT framework in this study is a panacea and applicable as the frame of references. In addition, as this study 1 focuses on management of IT investment, the resource-based theory and process theory offer a more salient and insightful theoretical foundation.

2.3.2 Resource-based View (RBV) of Managing IT and Firm Performance

The Resource-Based Theory is broadly accepted as one of the foremost leading theories for describing, explaining, and predicting IT-firm relationship (J. B. Barney, Ketchen, & Wright, 2011; Rivard, Raymond, & Verreault, 2006; Son, Lee, Lee, & Chang, 2014). The RBV specifies that firm has a bundle of heterogeneous resources that are rare, immobile and hard to replicate, and these resources have the potential to offer a foundation for superior firm performance (J. B. Barney et al., 2011; Kearns & Lederer, 2003; Paul P Tallon, 2007; Turel et al., 2017). Firm resources consist of all assets, capabilities, firm processes, firm attributes, knowledge, information, etc. (J. Barney, 1991, p.101; Rivard et al., 2006). Similarly, a firm's resources and capabilities contain tangible and intangible factors, such as physical assets, human capital, and organizational routines and procedures (Hwang, Yang, & Hong, 2015). In IS literature, scholars have identified different types of resources that are valuable for firm performance such as human, technological, and relationship resources (Ravichandran, Lertwongsatien, & LERTWONGSATIEN, 2005); IT-related resources such as infrastructure, human-IT resources, and IT-enabled intangibles (Huang, Ou, Chen, & Lin, 2006). Controlling over these limited resources, firms can become more profitable than their competitors and gain a competitive advantage (J. B. Barney et al., 2011; Ravichandran et al., 2005; Seddon, 2014; Turel et al., 2017; N. Wang, Liang, Zhong, Xue, & Xiao, 2012; Xu et al., 2016). The growing body of IS literature is used RBV as the main theoretical background to elucidate why IT can be a source of competitive advantage (Kearns & Lederer, 2003; Melville et al., 2004; Rivard et al., 2006; Wade & Hulland, 2004; F. Wu, Yeniyurt, Kim, & Cavusgil, 2006).

Under RBV, the notion of managing IT has articulated in numerous lens, For example; effective IT governance (C. L. Wilkin, Couchman, Sohal, & Zutshi, 2016; S. P.-J. Wu et al., 2015), IT capabilities (e.g., IT management and IT technical skills)(Y. Chen, Wang, Nevo, Benitez, & Kou, 2017), IT practices (Turel et al., 2017) and IS resources (e.g., IS planning and change management, and IS-business partnerships) (Wade & Hulland, 2004). In this belief, IT is presumed as a crucial part of business processes, and IT covers all business functions consequently, firm designs and recombines IT resources in the direction of alignment between business and IT functions that allows internal fit under RBV (Turel et al., 2017). Therefore, RBV emphasizes the managing IT empowers effective execution of IT and business strategies to grasp superior alignment that subsequently offers firm performance. Under RBV, the notion of managing IT investment has been articulated in various lenses such as effective IT governance (C. L. Wilkin et al., 2016; S. P.-J. Wu et al., 2015), IT capabilities (e.g., IT management and IT technical skills) (Y. Chen et al., 2017), IT practices (Turel et al., 2017) and IS resources (e.g., IS planning and change management, and IS-business partnerships) (Wade & Hulland, 2004).

Drawing on RBV studies suggested that firms' IT resources are complementary resources enlarging the value of other firm resources and capabilities subsequently increase firm performance (Cao et al., 2011; Ghobakhloo & Hong, 2014; Melville et al., 2004; C. L. Wilkin et al., 2016). In the same way, RBV emphasizes that the value of IT may depend on how IT is managed in relation to other firm factors (Mittal & Nault, 2009). The RBV highlights the managing IT allows effective execution of IT and business strategies to realize superior alignment, and then achieves superior firm performance. In particular to IT, firm leverages from IT to generate value on the resources it depends on are unique, rare, valuable, and costly to replicate under RBV (Prasad et al., 2010; Z. Wang, Huo, Qi, & Zhao, 2016). According to Xu et al. (2016)), the more unique and dissimilar resources a firm holds, the more chance of competitive advantage it gains and sustains. It is noteworthy that the various IT resources assumed by the RBV and IT capabilities make durable firm performance and preserve their impacts ahead for their future. Managing IT is the firm's IT capability to produce value from IT investment and IT as a firm's resource can be managed thoroughly to realize firm performance (Ilmudeen & Yukun, 2018).

Further, there is a less agreement that IT resources solely can create business value (Peng, Quan, Zhang, & Dubinsky, 2016). In this similar view, yet many studies adopted the RBV's positive IT contribution to firm performance (e.g. Ravichandran et al., 2005; Rivard et al., 2006), some research limit this opinion. For example; Powell and Dent-Micallef (1997)) stated that IT merely has not made sustainable performance benefits in their retail industry study. Likewise, the RBV of IT resources are only insufficient to produce a superior firm performance due to many theoretical limitations[3] (Nevo & Wade, 2011; Paul Patrick Tallon, 2008). Owing to the limitation in the RBV, researchers proposed other theories which support IT's contribution to firm performance. For instance, the contingency view suggests fresh insights to explain IT's role in contributing towards firm performance. Under the view of contingency RBV, Cao et al. (2011)) claimed that IT is a fundamental part of a system of interconnected firm factors where the level of IT business value rest on the degree of systems fit (or misfit), with numerous moderators and mediators. Further, IT functioning as alone may not accomplish the RBV criteria (F. Wu et al., 2006), and IT resources proposed in the traditional RBV merely cannot generate value in a vacuum (Y. Chen et al., 2014). Hence, IT needs to be combined with other organizational factors to produce business value (Cao et al., 2011). According to Mao, Liu, Zhang, and Deng (2016)), a contingent resource perspective covers the traditional RBV and supports the exogenous context and endogenous variables, including management intervention, business strategies, and other industry-level and firm-level variables (Y. Chen et al., 2014; Xu et al., 2016).

2.3.3 Process Theory Supports IT Business Value and Alignment

Despite the current theoretical models that highlight some common aspects especially cause-effect argument, Soh and Markus (1995)) demonstrated how IT creates value in view of process theory (Figure 2.3). The process-based view renowned as one of the most common theories to explain how business value of IT contributes to realize firm performance (Peng et al., 2016; Soh & Markus, 1995; Paul P Tallon, 2007). In this way, the process view of IT value cogitates IT investments as a necessary but not necessary condition for superior firm performance (Hu, 2005). Hence, the main idea suggested in process theory is that the IT investment improve firm performance subject to interaction among three processes. These processes are a) *IT conversion process* - IT expenditure becomes IT assets, b) *IT use process* - IT assets generate IT impacts, and c) *the competitive process* - IT impacts are transformed into firm performance (Soh & Markus, 1995). Prior studies on the process-based theory advocate that IT investment creates a positive impact on performance by enhancing operational efficiency, facilitating intermediary business processes, and creating new business capabilities (Hu, 2005; Peng et al., 2016). In addition, the process based view claims that IT creates value by enlightening individual business processes, or inter-process relations, or both for the organization (Paul P Tallon et al., 2000).

Figure 2. How IT creates value model
Adopted form Soh and Markus (1995, p. 37)

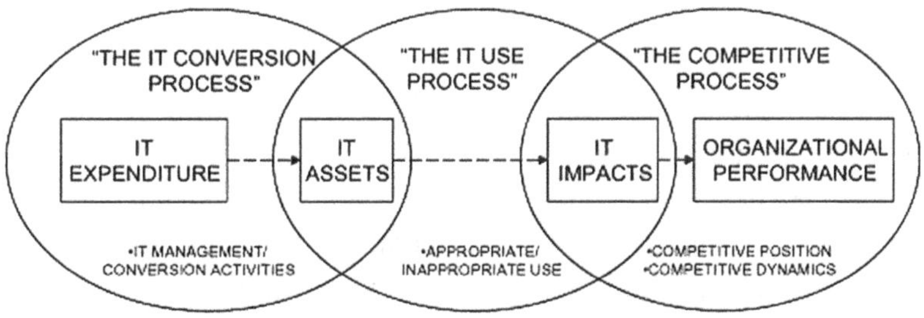

Source: Soh and Markus (1995:37)

The process theory is abstracted in two aspects in prior studies. (1) *alignment* – is the fit between business activities and IT strategy that in turn enhance IT business value, and that could support a deeper and meaningful understanding of how alignment affects firm performance (Paul P Tallon, 2007). (2) *Intermediate business processes* - firms derive business value from IT when IT and firm processes support each other. Thereby, greater synergy will be created; that in turn have a positive effect on intermediate process performance and firm performance (Cao et al., 2011; Mooney, Gurbaxani, & Kraemer, 1996). For example in prior study, the intermediate capabilities such as business process management capability and supply-chain management capability fully mediate the impact of IT on company performance (Peng et al., 2016). In this study 1, we theorize and adapt the process-based view for two reasons. First, it allows IT investment to create superior value through managing IT practices to effect alignment, and its subsequent impact will influence on firm performance. Second, it facilitates the business and IT strategies to create an alignment that seems to be the intermediate process to transform the effect of management of IT investment on firm performance.

3. RESULTS AND FINDINGS

Prior studies that have been focused on managing IT and business-IT alignment on firm performance context. When it comes to managing IT investment there are various factors and aspects that drive managing IT to achieve firm performance. Accordingly, some studies necessitated that for the better management of IT investment the best practices, guidelines and policies should be practiced by the managers and business leaders. For instance, value governance, portfolio management, investment management, IT investment governance (ITIG), IT management capability, and enterprise architecture (EA) standards, investment decisions, Val-IT framework, benefits-driven execution plans have been identified in the prior studies (e.g., Ali et al., 2015; Boh & Yellin, 2006; Ilmudeen & Yukun, 2018; Lombardi et al., 2016; Peppard et al., 2007; Y. Wang et al., 2015). Similarly, some studies proved that firm level strategies would enable for the better management of IT investment. For instance, business-process and supply-chain management capability, IT strategies, (e.g.,Mithas & Rust, 2016; Peng et al., 2016). Some of the prior studies identified that the managerial capability or management skills would enable for the better management of IT investment. For instance IT management duties, managerial IT knowledge, and IT planning (e.g.,Boynton, Zmud, & Jacobs, 1994; Masli, Richardson, Watson, & Zmud, 2016; Van Der Zee & De Jong, 1999).

In prior studies the managing IT has been focused in various themes. For instance, many studies focused IT investment under governance or managerial perspective (e.g., Ali et al., 2015; Ilmudeen & Yukun, 2018; Peppard et al., 2007). Some studies focused the IT investment management purely on the firm performance context (Peng et al., 2016; Y. Wang et al., 2015). In addition, there are studies which focused the managing IT investment on the theme of value creation or IT pay-off context (Lombardi et al., 2016; Mithas & Rust, 2016; Peppard et al., 2007; Van Der Zee & De Jong, 1999). Some studies focused the managing IT investment by connecting with the enterprise architecture (Boh & Yellin, 2006).

Similarly, in order to get alignment more effectively there are various factors and aspects that drive business-IT alignment to achieve firm performance. Accordingly, prior studies highlighted the alignment into various dimensions such as intellectual alignment, social alignment, operational alignment, cross-domain alignment, alignment maturity dimensions (e.g.,L. Chen, 2010; Gerow, Grover, & Thatcher, 2016; Gerow, Grover, Thatcher, & Roth, 2014; Liang, Wang, Xue, & Ge, 2017). Some of the prior studies proved that the alignment is the output of managerial skills such as Shared domain knowledge, shared language, and structural systems of knowing (e.g., Preston & Karahanna, 2009). Moreover, in some studies highlight that the alignment is the linkage between the IT plan and the business plan, synergistic connection between IT and business strategies, business structure, IT structure (e.g., Bergeron et al., 2004; Byrd, Lewis, & Bryan, 2006; Kearns & Lederer, 2003). In addition, scholars have classified the alignment into different types such as prospectors, analyzers and defenders (e.g.,Sabherwal & Chan, 2001).

When it comes to the theme of the studies in the context of business-IT alignment there are various aspects have been addressed in prior studies. For instance, some studies focused the dimension of alignments such as intellectual alignment, and social alignment (Liang et al., 2017). Further, alignment has been focused on review or meta-analysis view (Coltman et al., 2015; Gerow et al., 2014). Alignment has been identified as the fit between business strategy and IT strategy (Byrd et al., 2006; Cragg et al., 2002; Sabherwal & Chan, 2001). Alignment has been tested as a nomological network for instance (Gerow et al., 2016; Preston & Karahanna, 2009). Though the business-IT alignment has focused on various theme, the scholars long been agreed that alignment is the fit or harmony between the business strategy and IT strategy for an organization.

4. DISCUSSION

Businesses have invested a massive amount of money in IT; however, the payoff from IT is always a major concern for managers and executives. In spite of the growing amount of IT investment, managing IT and IT governance decisions have ever more become complicated due to vague cost relationships, uncertain payoffs, rapid technological changes, and uncertain business environments. Business-IT alignment is higher when firms are applying a mix of mature IT governance practices (De Haes & Van Grembergen, 2009), and adopting IT management practices that ensure the closer alignment between IT and firm's business goals (Paul P Tallon et al., 2000). The IT investment cannot realize its desired outcomes if a firm does not manage its IT assets thoroughly and the effect of IT on firm performance is subject to relations between IT and business processes (Soh & Markus, 1995). Hence, we posited in this study that management of IT investment is the firm's management capability that enable to align the firm's business and IT strategies to achieve superior firm performance.

The business-IT alignment drives firm performance when realizing the alignment (Preston & Karahanna, 2009; Sabherwal & Chan, 2001; Paul P Tallon et al., 2000), and fit between IT and business strategies (Bergeron et al., 2004; L. Chen, 2010; Cragg et al., 2002). Further, a firm with well aligned IT and business strategies can invest in extra IT resources with the guarantee that they will be leveraged significantly (Byrd et al., 2006). Moreover, the study of Paul P Tallon et al. (2000)) found that firms whose IT was closely aligned with the business strategy had higher perceived payoffs from IT, in contrary when firms' strategic alignment is weak the perceived IT payoffs were significantly lower. Over time, prior studies have also documented numerous antecedents that impact alignment, for example, shared understanding between business and IT (Preston & Karahanna, 2009), strategic direction (Sabherwal & Chan, 2001), and IT governance mechanisms (S. P.-J. Wu et al., 2015). Likewise, this study proves that management of IT investment is the antecedents of business-IT alignment, that in turn directs to achieve firm performance.

5. CONCLUSION

Regardless of the increasing amount of IT investment, through what mechanisms the impact of IT governance and management of IT investment drives firm performance is still not clear. Drawing on the RBV and the process theory, this chapter systematically reviews on the antecedents of business-IT alignment on the firm performance context. This review study revealed that the business-IT alignment derived by the IT governance and managing IT investment practices to achieve firm performance. This study suggests that firms cannot simply attain performance by merely investing in IT instead firms should focus on effective management of IT practices and strategically align their business and IT strategies. This chapter greatly contributes to the IS literature with the richer view on IT governance, management of IT investment, business-IT alignment, and firm performance while extending on the theories used in this chapter.

REFERENCES

Ali, S., Green, P., & Robb, A. (2015). Information technology investment governance: What is it and does it matter? *International Journal of Accounting Information Systems, 18*, 1–25. doi:10.1016/j.accinf.2015.04.002

Barney, J. (1991). Firm resources and sustained competitive advantage. *Journal of Management, 17*(1), 99–120. doi:10.1177/014920639101700108

Barney, J. B., Ketchen, D. J. Jr, & Wright, M. (2011). The future of resource-based theory revitalization or decline? *Journal of Management, 37*(5), 1299–1315. doi:10.1177/0149206310391805

Bergeron, F., Croteau, A.-M., Uwizeyemungu, S., & Raymond, L. (2020). *A framework for research on information technology governance in SMEs. In Start-Ups and SMEs: Concepts, Methodologies, Tools, and Applications*. IGI Global.

Bergeron, F., Raymond, L., & Rivard, S. (2004). Ideal patterns of strategic alignment and business performance. *Information & Management, 41*(8), 1003–1020. doi:10.1016/j.im.2003.10.004

Boh, W. F., & Yellin, D. (2006). Using enterprise architecture standards in managing information technology. *Journal of Management Information Systems, 23*(3), 163–207. doi:10.2753/MIS0742-1222230307

Bowen, P. L., Cheung, M.-Y. D., & Rohde, F. H. (2007). Enhancing IT governance practices: A model and case study of an organization's efforts. *International Journal of Accounting Information Systems, 8*(3), 191–221. doi:10.1016/j.accinf.2007.07.002

Boynton, A. C., & Zmud, R. W. (1987). Information technology planning in the 1990's: Directions for practice and research. *Management Information Systems Quarterly, 11*(1), 59–71. doi:10.2307/248826

Boynton, A. C., Zmud, R. W., & Jacobs, G. C. (1994). The influence of IT management practice on IT use in large organizations. *Management Information Systems Quarterly, 18*(3), 299–318. doi:10.2307/249620

Byrd, T. A., Lewis, B. R., & Bryan, R. W. (2006). The leveraging influence of strategic alignment on IT investment: An empirical examination. *Information & Management, 43*(3), 308–321. doi:10.1016/j.im.2005.07.002

Cao, G., Wiengarten, F., & Humphreys, P. (2011). Towards a contingency resource-based view of IT business value. *Systemic Practice and Action Research, 24*(1), 85–106. doi:10.100711213-010-9178-0

Centre, N. C. (2005). *IT Governance Developing a successful governance strategy. Oxford House, Manchester M1 7ED*. National Computing Centre.

Chan, Y. E., Huff, S. L., Barclay, D. W., & Copeland, D. G. (1997). Business strategic orientation, information systems strategic orientation, and strategic alignment. *Information Systems Research, 8*(2), 125–150. doi:10.1287/isre.8.2.125

Chen, L. (2010). Business–IT alignment maturity of companies in China. *Information & Management, 47*(1), 9–16. doi:10.1016/j.im.2009.09.003

Chen, Y., Wang, Y., Nevo, S., Benitez, J., & Kou, G. (2017). Improving strategic flexibility with information technologies: Insights for firm performance in an emerging economy. *Journal of Information Technology*, *32*(1), 10–25. doi:10.1057/jit.2015.26

Chen, Y., Wang, Y., Nevo, S., Jin, J., Wang, L., & Chow, W. S. (2014). IT capability and organizational performance: The roles of business process agility and environmental factors. *European Journal of Information Systems*, *23*(3), 326–342. doi:10.1057/ejis.2013.4

Coltman, T., Tallon, P., Sharma, R., & Queiroz, M. (2015). Strategic IT alignment: Twenty-five years on. *Journal of Information Technology*, *30*(2), 91–100. doi:10.1057/jit.2014.35

Cragg, P., King, M., & Hussin, H. (2002). IT alignment and firm performance in small manufacturing firms. *The Journal of Strategic Information Systems*, *11*(2), 109–132. doi:10.1016/S0963-8687(02)00007-0

De Haes, S., & Van Grembergen, W. (2009). An exploratory study into IT governance implementations and its impact on business/IT alignment. *Information Systems Management*, *26*(2), 123–137. doi:10.1080/10580530902794786

De Haes, S., & Van Grembergen, W. (2015). *Enterprise Governance of Information Technology: Achieving Alignment and Value, Featuring COBIT 5*. Springer. doi:10.1007/978-3-319-14547-1

Gerow, J. E., Grover, V., & Thatcher, J. (2016). Alignment's nomological network: Theory and evaluation. *Information & Management*, *53*(5), 541–553. doi:10.1016/j.im.2015.12.006

Gerow, J. E., Grover, V., Thatcher, J. B., & Roth, P. L. (2014). Looking toward the future of IT-business strategic alignment through the past: A meta-analysis. *Management Information Systems Quarterly*, *38*(4), 1059–1085. doi:10.25300/MISQ/2014/38.4.10

Ghobakhloo, M., & Hong, T. S. (2014). IT investments and business performance improvement: The mediating role of lean manufacturing implementation. *International Journal of Production Research*, *52*(18), 5367–5384. doi:10.1080/00207543.2014.906761

Hu, Q., & Quan, J. J. (2005). Evaluating the impact of IT investments on productivity: A causal analysis at industry level. *International Journal of Information Management*, *25*(1), 39–53. doi:10.1016/j.ijinfomgt.2004.10.006

Huang, S.-M., Ou, C.-S., Chen, C.-M., & Lin, B. (2006). An empirical study of relationship between IT investment and firm performance: A resource-based perspective. *European Journal of Operational Research*, *173*(3), 984–999. doi:10.1016/j.ejor.2005.06.013

Hwang, D., Yang, M. G. M., & Hong, P. (2015). Mediating effect of IT-enabled capabilities on competitive performance outcomes: An empirical investigation of ERP implementation. *Journal of Engineering and Technology Management*, *36*, 1–23. doi:10.1016/j.jengtecman.2015.03.001

Ilmudeen, A., Bao, Y., & Alharbi, I. M. (2019). How does business-IT strategic alignment dimension impact on organizational performance measures: Conjecture and empirical analysis. *Journal of Enterprise Information Management*, *32*(3), 457–476. doi:10.1108/JEIM-09-2018-0197

Ilmudeen, A., & Yukun, B. (2018). Mediating role of managing information technology and its impact on firm performance: Insight from China. *Industrial Management & Data Systems, 118*(4), 912–929. doi:10.1108/IMDS-06-2017-0252

Kearns, G. S., & Lederer, A. L. (2003). A resource-based view of strategic IT alignment: How knowledge sharing creates competitive advantage. *Decision Sciences, 34*(1), 1–29. doi:10.1111/1540-5915.02289

Kim, J. K., Xiang, J. Y., & Lee, S. (2009). The impact of IT investment on firm performance in China: An empirical investigation of the Chinese electronics industry. *Technological Forecasting and Social Change, 76*(5), 678–687. doi:10.1016/j.techfore.2008.03.008

Liang, H., Wang, N., Xue, Y., & Ge, S. (2017). Unraveling the Alignment Paradox: How Does Business—IT Alignment Shape Organizational Agility? *Information Systems Research, 28*(4), 863–879. doi:10.1287/isre.2017.0711

Lombardi, R., Del Giudice, M., Caputo, A., Evangelista, F., & Russo, G. (2016). Governance and assessment insights in information technology: The Val IT model. *Journal of the Knowledge Economy, 7*(1), 292–308. doi:10.100713132-015-0328-6

Lowry, P. B., & Wilson, D. (2016). Creating agile organizations through IT: The influence of internal IT service perceptions on IT service quality and IT agility. *The Journal of Strategic Information Systems, 25*(3), 211–226. doi:10.1016/j.jsis.2016.05.002

Luftman, J., & Lyytinen, K., & ben Zvi, T. (2015). Enhancing the measurement of information technology (IT) business alignment and its influence on company performance. *Journal of Information Technology.*

Mao, H., Liu, S., Zhang, J., & Deng, Z. (2016). Information technology resource, knowledge management capability, and competitive advantage: The moderating role of resource commitment. *International Journal of Information Management, 36*(6), 1062–1074. doi:10.1016/j.ijinfomgt.2016.07.001

Masli, A., Richardson, V. J., Watson, M. W., & Zmud, R. W. (2016). Senior executives' IT management responsibilities: serious it-related deficiencies and CEO/CFO turnover. *Management Information Systems Quarterly, 40*(3), 687–708. doi:10.25300/MISQ/2016/40.3.08

Melville, N., Kraemer, K., & Gurbaxani, V. (2004). Review: Information technology and organizational performance: An integrative model of IT business value. *Management Information Systems Quarterly, 28*(2), 283–322. doi:10.2307/25148636

Merhout, J. W., & Havelka, D. (2008). Information technology auditing: A value-added IT governance partnership between IT management and audit. *Communications of the Association for Information Systems, 23*(1), 26. doi:10.17705/1CAIS.02326

Mithas, S., & Rust, R. T. (2016). How information technology strategy and investments influence firm performance: Conjectures and empirical evidence. *Management Information Systems Quarterly, 40*(1), 223–245. doi:10.25300/MISQ/2016/40.1.10

Mithas, S., Tafti, A. R., Bardhan, I., & Goh, J. M. (2012). *Information technology and firm profitability: mechanisms and empirical evidence.* Academic Press.

Mittal, N., & Nault, B. R. (2009). Research Note-Investments in Information Technology: Indirect Effects and Information Technology Intensity. *Information Systems Research*, *20*(1), 140–154. doi:10.1287/isre.1080.0186

Mooney, J. G., Gurbaxani, V., & Kraemer, K. L. (1996). A process oriented framework for assessing the business value of information technology. *ACM SIGMIS Database*, *27*(2), 68–81. doi:10.1145/243350.243363

Nevo, S., & Wade, M. (2011). Firm-level benefits of IT-enabled resources: A conceptual extension and an empirical assessment. *The Journal of Strategic Information Systems*, *20*(4), 403–418. doi:10.1016/j.jsis.2011.08.001

Papp, R. (1999). Business-IT alignment: Productivity paradox payoff? *Industrial Management & Data Systems*, *99*(8), 367–373. doi:10.1108/02635579910301810

Parent, M., & Reich, B. H. (2009). Governing information technology risk. *California Management Review*, *51*(3), 134–152. doi:10.2307/41166497

Peng, J., Quan, J., Zhang, G., & Dubinsky, A. J. (2016). Mediation effect of business process and supply chain management capabilities on the impact of IT on firm performance: Evidence from Chinese firms. *International Journal of Information Management*, *36*(1), 89–96. doi:10.1016/j.ijinfomgt.2015.09.006

Peppard, J., Ward, J., & Daniel, E. (2007). Managing the Realization of Business Benefits from IT Investments. *MIS Quarterly Executive*, *6*(1).

Powell, T. C., & Dent-Micallef, A. (1997). Information technology as competitive advantage: The role of human, business, and technology resources. *Strategic Management Journal*, *18*(5), 375–405. doi:10.1002/(SICI)1097-0266(199705)18:5<375::AID-SMJ876>3.0.CO;2-7

Prasad, A., Heales, J., & Green, P. (2010). A capabilities-based approach to obtaining a deeper understanding of information technology governance effectiveness: Evidence from IT steering committees. *International Journal of Accounting Information Systems*, *11*(3), 214–232. doi:10.1016/j.accinf.2010.07.013

Preston, D. S., & Karahanna, E. (2009). Antecedents of IS strategic alignment: A nomological network. *Information Systems Research*, *20*(2), 159–179. doi:10.1287/isre.1070.0159

Ravichandran, T., Lertwongsatien, C., & Lertwongsatien, C. (2005). Effect of information systems resources and capabilities on firm performance: A resource-based perspective. *Journal of Management Information Systems*, *21*(4), 237–276. doi:10.1080/07421222.2005.11045820

Rivard, S., Raymond, L., & Verreault, D. (2006). Resource-based view and competitive strategy: An integrated model of the contribution of information technology to firm performance. *The Journal of Strategic Information Systems*, *15*(1), 29–50. doi:10.1016/j.jsis.2005.06.003

Sabherwal, R., & Chan, Y. E. (2001). Alignment between business and IS strategies: A study of prospectors, analyzers, and defenders. *Information Systems Research*, *12*(1), 11–33. doi:10.1287/isre.12.1.11.9714

Seddon, P. B. (2014). Implications for strategic IS research of the resource-based theory of the firm: A reflection. *The Journal of Strategic Information Systems*, *23*(4), 257–269. doi:10.1016/j.jsis.2014.11.001

Simonsson, M., Johnson, P., & Ekstedt, M. (2010). The effect of IT governance maturity on IT governance performance. *Information Systems Management*, *27*(1), 10–24. doi:10.1080/10580530903455106

Soh, C., & Markus, M. L. (1995). How IT creates business value: a process theory synthesis. *ICIS 1995 Proceedings*, 4.

Son, I., Lee, D., Lee, J.-N., & Chang, Y. B. (2014). Market perception on cloud computing initiatives in organizations: An extended resource-based view. *Information & Management*, *51*(6), 653–669. doi:10.1016/j.im.2014.05.006

Tallon, P. P. (2007). A process-oriented perspective on the alignment of information technology and business strategy. *Journal of Management Information Systems*, *24*(3), 227–268. doi:10.2753/MIS0742-1222240308

Tallon, P. P. (2008). Inside the adaptive enterprise: An information technology capabilities perspective on business process agility. *Information Technology Management*, *9*(1), 21–36. doi:10.100710799-007-0024-8

Tallon, P. P., Kraemer, K. L., & Gurbaxani, V. (2000). Executives' perceptions of the business value of information technology: A process-oriented approach. *Journal of Management Information Systems*, *16*(4), 145–173. doi:10.1080/07421222.2000.11518269

Tiwana, A., & Konsynski, B. (2010). Complementarities between organizational IT architecture and governance structure. *Information Systems Research*, *21*(2), 288–304. doi:10.1287/isre.1080.0206

Turel, O., Liu, P., & Bart, C. (2017). Board-Level Information Technology Governance Effects on Organizational Performance: The Roles of Strategic Alignment and Authoritarian Governance Style. *Information Systems Management*, *34*(2), 117–136. doi:10.1080/10580530.2017.1288523

Val, I. (2008). Enterprise Value: Governance of IT Investments. *The Val IT Framework, 2.*

Van Der Zee, J., & De Jong, B. (1999). Alignment is not enough: Integrating business and information technology management with the balanced business scorecard. *Journal of Management Information Systems*, *16*(2), 137–158. doi:10.1080/07421222.1999.11518249

Van Grembergen, W., & De Haes, S. (2009). *Enterprise governance of information technology: achieving strategic alignment and value*. Springer Science & Business Media.

Wade, M., & Hulland, J. (2004). Review: The resource-based view and information systems research: Review, extension, and suggestions for future research. *Management Information Systems Quarterly*, *28*(1), 107–142. doi:10.2307/25148626

Wang, N., Liang, H., Zhong, W., Xue, Y., & Xiao, J. (2012). Resource structuring or capability building? An empirical study of the business value of information technology. *Journal of Management Information Systems*, *29*(2), 325–367. doi:10.2753/MIS0742-1222290211

Wang, Y., Shi, S., Nevo, S., Li, S., & Chen, Y. (2015). The interaction effect of IT assets and IT management on firm performance: A systems perspective. *International Journal of Information Management*, *35*(5), 580–593. doi:10.1016/j.ijinfomgt.2015.06.006

Wang, Z., Huo, B., Qi, Y., & Zhao, X. (2016). A resource-based view on enablers of supplier integration: Evidence from China. *Industrial Management & Data Systems*, *116*(3), 416–444. doi:10.1108/IMDS-04-2015-0146

Wilkin, C., Campbell, J., Moore, S., & Van Grembergen, W. (2012). Co-creating value from IT in a contracted public sector service environment: Perspectives on COBIT and Val IT. *Journal of Information Systems*, *27*(1), 283–306. doi:10.2308/isys-50355

Wilkin, C. L., & Chenhall, R. H. (2010). A review of IT governance: A taxonomy to inform accounting information systems. *Journal of Information Systems*, *24*(2), 107–146. doi:10.2308/jis.2010.24.2.107

Wilkin, C. L., & Chenhall, R. H. (2019). Information Technology Governance: Reflections on the Past and Future Directions. *Journal of Information Systems*, 0000. doi:10.2308/isys-52632

Wilkin, C. L., Couchman, P. K., Sohal, A., & Zutshi, A. (2016). Exploring differences between smaller and large organizations' corporate governance of information technology. *International Journal of Accounting Information Systems*, *22*, 6–25. doi:10.1016/j.accinf.2016.07.002

Williams, P. (2012). *Optimising Value Creation From IT Investments.* Retrieved from overnance Institute: http://www. isaca. org/Knowledge-Center/Research/Documents/Outsourcing. pdf

Wu, F., Yeniyurt, S., Kim, D., & Cavusgil, S. T. (2006). The impact of information technology on supply chain capabilities and firm performance: A resource-based view. *Industrial Marketing Management*, *35*(4), 493–504. doi:10.1016/j.indmarman.2005.05.003

Wu, S. P.-J., Straub, D. W., & Liang, T.-P. (2015). How information technology governance mechanisms and strategic alignment influence organizational performance: Insights from a matched survey of business and IT managers. *Management Information Systems Quarterly*, *39*(2), 497–518. doi:10.25300/MISQ/2015/39.2.10

Xu, X., Zhang, W., & Li, L. (2016). The impact of technology type and life cycle on IT productivity variance: A contingency theoretical perspective. *International Journal of Information Management*, *36*(6), 1193–1204. doi:10.1016/j.ijinfomgt.2016.08.007

ENDNOTES

1. The Control Objectives for Information and related Technology (COBIT) is the most renowned framework for IT governance maturity assessments by the IT Governance Institute. The framework offers a definition of IT governance as consisting of four domains and 34 processes. Each process contains a number of IT governance maturity indicators, such as activities, documents, metrics, and support for role and responsibility assignment (Simonsson, Johnson, & Ekstedt, 2010; C. Wilkin et al., 2012).
2. Val IT views IT governance onto a higher level of abstraction by offering general directions on how to manage IT from a business point of view. Val IT clearly focuses on the interface between IT and the business. Val IT takes on where COBIT ends, and the two frameworks complement each other well (Simonsson et al., 2010).

[3] RBV limitations are described in Nevo and Wade (2011)) as:

1. It overlooks resources that are not strategic in and of themselves, like IT assets.
2. The theory is silent on the mechanisms through which organizational resources become strategic.
3. As IT assets often combined with firm resources, extant RBV logic cannot be used to theorize about the outcomes, thereby hiding their inner workings from view.

Chapter 6
Financial Performance Analysis of Companies Registered on BIST Corporate Governance Index:
An Empirical Analysis in the Istanbul Stock Exchange

Haşim Bağcı
https://orcid.org/0000-0002-5828-2050
Aksaray University, Turkey

Ceyda Yerdelen Kaygın
Kafkas University, Turkey

ABSTRACT

The aim of this study is to measure the 2018 financial performance of 49 businesses that are registered in the Istanbul Stock Exchange Corporate Governance Index. Therefore, the financial performances of 49 businesses were compared to the ROA, ROE, ROS, and MV performance indicators that were determined for the measurement of financial performance. For comparison, first, the significance levels of the indicators were determined by the AHP method, and MV was determined to be the most important indicator. The PROMETHEE method was used to be able to financially compare the businesses, and Tüpraş Türkiye Petrol Rafinerileri A.Ş. (Tüpraş Turkey Petroleum Refineries Inc.) was the most successful corporate governance business within the specified time period. The least successful business is Pınar Su ve İçecek Sanayi ve Ticaret A.Ş. (Pınar Water and Drink Industry and Trade Inc).

DOI: 10.4018/978-1-7998-4852-3.ch006

INTRODUCTION

Globalization and technological advancements created several concepts including computer, mobile phone, tablet, internet, internet banking, telephone banking and virtual money as an indispensable part of human life. Humankind makes an effort to meet its need since its inception. Globalization and technology turned trade into an activity that can be easily carried out from one end of the world to the other. The purchase and sale of local goods in international markets is the biggest evidence that all businesses operating in the world can be considered to be a global business. Rapid manufacture and easy transportation lead to changes in goods and services while companies found themselves in a challenging competition environment to adapt to this rapid change. Although the concept of globalization entered the literature in the second half of the twentieth century, the signs of the process we define as globalization go back much earlier. The importance and even distinctive feature of globalization for financial markets is that it increases financial integration (Bilir, 2018: 213).

As known, the economy of a country is affected by several negative factors including crises, war, political instability and natural disaster. Together with globalization, all countries in the world are integrated into each other. Economic problems taking place in a country have also negative effects on other countries what have trade connection in particular. It can be argued that the financial reporting scandals of some companies including Enron, World.com and Adelphia had an effect, even small, on the world economy in general. Therefore, the auditing of the financial reports of the companies is an issue that needs careful attention not only for that company but also for the world economy.

Measuring the financial performances of companies provides information about companies in various aspects including profitability, sustainability, audit and inspection. Contrary to the traditional understanding of investment, ethical, social, corporate governance and ecological investments have stood out in recent years. Corporate governance is very important to balance the interests of the internal and external stakeholders of companies, to ensure that companies obtain sustainable development and to provide the control of companies. Therefore, the issues of corporate governance and financial performance draw attention of various groups including company owners, investors, economists and academicians.

The objective of this company is to measure the financial performances of 49 companies operating in the corporate governance index of the Istanbul Stock Exchange. Therefore, the present study starts with the information about corporate governance and then explains financial performance and the variables used in the measurement of performance including a coverage of the relevant literature. The last part of the study includes the performance measured using 2 techniques with regards to the specified financial indicators to carry out the measurement of financial performance. The first technique was used to determine the significance level of the indicators while the second technique was used to compare the financial performances of 49 businesses.

Upon reviewing the literature, there are several studies on the measurement of financial performance, however, there are limited studies on the corporate governance index of the Istanbul Stock Exchange. In addition, the techniques that were used were suitable for the study and selected specifically for the subject. Therefore, it is expected that this study will contribute to the literature with regards to a different perspective on the measurement of financial performance as well as providing a methodological compliance.

CORPORATE GOVERNANCE

It is believed that corporate governance has a significant effect on the growth and development perspective of an economy. Solid corporate governance applications direct economy for higher performance and provide resource to capital investment by increasing the credibility of shareholders (Javaid, 2015, p.163). Corporate governance can be defined to be the financing and investment decisions taken by the management of companies in line with the corporate objectives. The basic goal of corporate financing is to increase the wealth of shareholders (Watson and Head, 2007, p.6).

In the environment of global competition, the corporate governance approach is considered to be a process of improvement in several issues of companies including knowledge, achievement, ethics, growth, energy, motivation, cooperation and labour force. Companies have to learn faster and adapt to innovations faster than their competitors to survive in the long term (Wiig, 2004, p.249). Corporate governance consists of four principles including justice/equality, responsibility, transparency and accountability (Sulaiman et al., 2018, p.731). Justice and equality refers to the protection of the interests of all shareholders and to the just and equal treatment to shareholders. Transparency in business management and justice in market operations are essential for a proper functioning of market economy. The market economy system relying on transparent work management and fair competition works is used to increase the corporate value in resource allocation, efficiency and growth potential in the market (Kang, 2005, p.3). Responsibility has become the most decisive instrument in the corporate governance understanding. For a company to be successful, it needs to be inspected in various aspects including the production of high quality goods and service, fair treatment to employees and all stakeholders, ethics, compliancy to legislation, compliance to contract and company's internal regulations, responsibility against environment and cooperation with local communities (Musa, Musová and Debnárová, 2015, p.1024). Transparency is an important principle for corporate governance that ensures the adoption of proper accountancy methods by a company, complete and rapid disclosure of company information and prevention of conflict of interests between managers or shareholders (Fung, 2014, p.73). Accountability refers to effective supervision of management by the board of management and the liability of the board of management before the company and the shareholders. Accountability enables companies to provide objectivity in issues like decision making processes and use of assets, to determine the quality of inspection and management, to provide strategic guidance and to have commitment and neutrality in monitoring performance for shareholders (Mohamad, 2014, p.8).

The corporate governance approach provides feedbacks reflecting the performances of businesses by an organizational point of view, taking into account the positions of institutions as whole in relation to the business world and reflecting the expectations of the shareholders of the businesses (Darabaris, 2019, p.197). The management of corporate performance is, however, a monitoring system related to processes, methodologies and technologies in order to determine and report the weaknesses of work processes for measuring, monitoring and managing the performance of companies (Scheer et al., 2005, p.11).

In Figure 1, it is possible to consider the concepts including indicator, trend analysis, allocation, incident and influence coefficients to be the basic performance indicators.

It is possible to divide corporate governance into two including traditional corporate governance and new corporate governance (Hilb, 2006, p.11).

Figure 1. Main Performance Indicators of Companies
Source: Scheer et al., 2005, p.11.

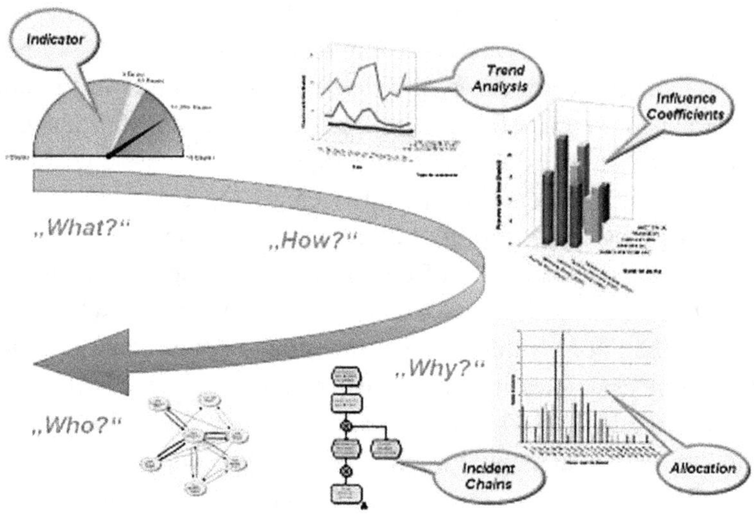

Figure 2. Classification of New Corporate Governance
Source: Hilb, 2006, p.11

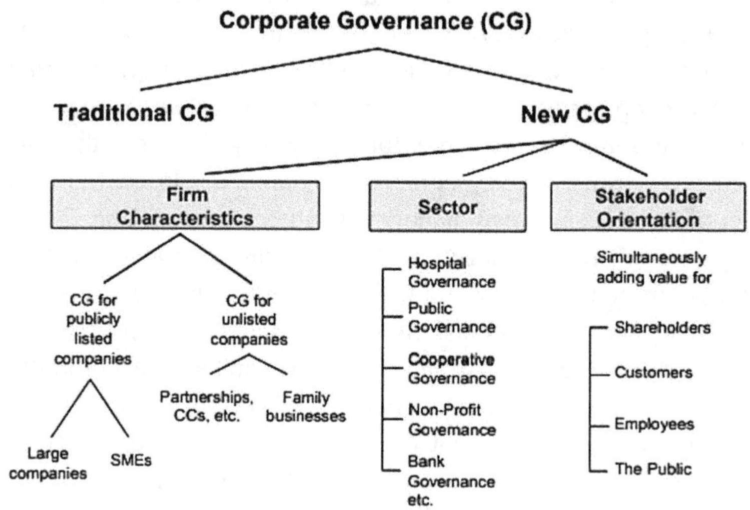

As seen in Figure 1, the new corporate governance divides public businesses into big, medium and small scale companies, and non-public companies into partnerships and family businesses. Upon sectoral classification, hospitals, public, cooperative, non-profit organizations and bank businesses should be evaluated. Upon classification with regards to shareholders in the sector, we have shareholders, customers, employees and public.

Companies can be defined to be the legal entities created by communities. In addition, companies are an effective way of organization contributing to economic growth and development, and ensuring improvement of living standards and reduction of poverty. It benefits from the assets of a society. A company with a good corporate governance understanding is expected to have increased efficiency in using its assets, higher ability to attract capital with low cost, higher ability to meet the expectations of society and increased achievement of general performance (Mohamad, 2014, p.3-4).

FINANCIAL PERFORMANCE

Financial performance allows the evaluation of a company from various aspects such as determining its past achievements and future expectations, revealing current financial status, determining the objectives of businesses, evaluating opportunities, analysing weak and strong sides, managing uncertainties and risks, growing and giving consistent and effective decisions. Financial performance analysis has a vital importance for companies and therefore companies need to follow a correct and fluent path when determining their financial performances. Financial performance has been and will continue to be the subject of several academic studies since companies are monitored carefully by both internal and external interest groups.

All performance management instruments can be used in the measurement of the performances of companies however they will not be used in analysing and reporting the underlying data of the performance problems (Sorensen and Peckham, 2002, p.19). For a manager to carry out a healthy analysis of the business performance (Prigent, 2007, p.128):

- Different risk groups should be taken into consideration and specific performance measures should be taken.
- Risks related to the business performance need to be evaluated and measures should be taken against various risks.
- Elements like investment decisions, manager skills and market should be associated with performance.
- Past performance and present performance of the business should be compared to examine the performance consistency of the business.

When talking about the determination of the performances of businesses, measurement of financial performance comes to mind first. Using financial ratios in measuring the performances of businesses are generally accepted in both national and international literature.

Financial ratios are defined to be the significant financial indicators that determine the relation between two logically connected quantitative financial values and that provide information on the financial status of a company. Financial ratios provide the possibility to compare, interpret and analyse the companies in the same sector with their current or past indicators. Financial ratios measure the earning capacity of companies and are considered to be an indicator for their growth, success and control (Kabajeh, Nuaimat and Dahmash, 2011, p.115-116). The ratios including return on equity (ROE), return on assets (ROA), return on sales (ROS) and market value/book value representing the market value (MV) of businesses, which are used for profitability, i.e. the basic gaol of businesses and for market value maximization, i.e. the basic goal of financial management provide us with information on the financial conditions of the companies in the financial performance measurement of the present study.

ROA is used as an instrument to measure the profit efficiency obtained by the use of assets of a company and the return rate of the total assets after deducting the interest expenses and taxes. Investors usually prefer to invest in the investment instruments that have high asset profitability to obtain higher return from their investments (Heikal, Khaddafi and Ummah, 2014, p.104).

$$ROA = \frac{Net\ Profits}{Total\ Assets}$$

ROE measures the rate of return that shareholders earn from their investments in the company. Return on equity indicates the relation between the net profit and equity of a company and refers to the return from each 1 lira invested by shareholders. The higher the return on equity the higher is expected the value of a company (Kamar, 2017, p.68).

$$ROE = \frac{Net\ Profit}{Equity}$$

The profitability of sales, also called as net profit margin, is obtained by dividing net profit to net sales. It is the ratio that measures the business performance of a company and profit ability form sales, i.e. the profitability of the sales of the company after deducting all expenses including tax and interest (Herciu, Ogrean and Belascu, 2011, p.45).

$$ROS = \frac{Net\ Profit}{Net\ Sales}$$

Market Value/Book Value is a ratio showing how many times is the market value of a company of its equity and it is effective in decision making of investors on shares. It is necessary to know the average of the sector which a company belongs to so that the ratio can be evaluated in a healthy manner. The increase of the ratio is generally interpreted as the increase in the value of the shares of the company (Ercan and Ban, 2005, p.50).

$$Market\ Value\ /\ Book\ Value = \frac{Market\ Value}{Book\ Value}$$

LITERATURE

In this section, information was given about the studies on the subject.

Silva and Leal (2005) examined with the panel data analysis the relation between the company valuation and performance with the corporate governance index applied by the companies operating in the Brazil Stock Market between 1998 and 2002. Upon the analysis, a positive significant relation was found between the Tobin Q ratio and better corporate governance applications while there was no statistically significant result between the company valuation and performance. Empirical results show that less than

4% of businesses in the corporate governance index, whose shares are traded on the Brazilian Stock Exchange, have good corporate governance practices and firms with better corporate governance have significantly higher performance (return on assets).

In the study of Chen et al. (2007), a correlation and regression analysis was conducted to test the relation between the ownership/leadership structures and share returns of the companies trading in the Taiwan Security Exchange between 1992 and 2001. Upon the analysis, a positive significant relation was found between the ownership/leadership structures and share returns of the companies. It was concluded that the corporate governance index was successful in evaluating the effectiveness of the management mechanisms of companies in Taiwan. The empirical results of the study show that companies with a good corporate governance understanding perform better, and there is a striking relationship between the management index and the stock performance of companies. Dinç and Abdioğlu (2009) conducted a survey to the managers of companies to statistically reveal and explain the relation between the accountancy information system and corporate governance understanding of the companies trading in the İMKB-100[1] index between 01.04.2008 and 31.07.2008. Upon the correlation analysis with the data obtained by the researchers, a statistically positive strong relation was found between the accountancy information system and the corporate governance understanding. In this context, it is necessary to attach importance to the accounting information system in order to ensure the successful implementation of corporate management in businesses and to provide solutions to the problems encountered. This is because the accounting information system and corporate governance approach create synergies for effective management. Dağlı, Ayaydın and Eyüpoğlu (2010) carried out a risk-return evaluation of the performance indice between September 2007 and November 2009 by using the Sharpe, Treynor and Jensen performance indice for each of the İMKB corporate governance index, İMKB national-100 index, İMKB national-50 index, İMKB national-30 index, İMKB national-all index, İMKB second national market index and İMKB new economy market index. The research reveals that the İMKB Corporate Governance Index is important for corporate compliance principles compliance score as a result of the evaluation made by the rating agencies and the stocks traded in markets other than watch list companies. Çonkar, Elitaş and Atar (2011) calculated financial ratios by using the financial data of 10 big-scale companies trading in the İMKB corporate governance index between 2007 and 2008. Financial ratios were analysed by the TOPSIS method and the financial achievements of companies were ranked. In the period under examination, the performance achievement points and corporate governance ranking points of companies were evaluated separately for each year. The empirical results of the research reveal the necessity to determine national and international standard criteria in order to eliminate the difference in rating by countries and sectors. Accordingly, domestic rating agencies should bring standard criteria in line with the rating criteria.

Lopes and Walker (2012) used the panel data analysis to find out whether there is any relation between the revaluation of the fixed assets of the companies in the Brazilian Corporate Governance Index between 1998 and 2004, and the future company performance, prices and revenues as well as the relation between the revaluation decision of the companies and the Brazil Corporate Management Index (BCGI) points. As a result of the analysis, they found a negative relation between the revaluation of the fixed assets of the companies and the future company performance, prices and revenues while there is also a negative relation between the revaluation decision of the companies and the Brazil Corporate Management Index (BCGI) points. It was also found that the possibility of companies adopting corporate governance arrangements to manipulate financial tables was lower. The research confirms the idea that firms that adopt voluntary management arrangements are less likely to take actions designed to manipulate their financial statements. Ege, Topaloğlu and Özyamanoğlu (2013) aimed to rank the financial performance points and corporate governance points of the 18 companies trading in the Istanbul Stock Exchange Corporate Governance Index in a comparative manner with the TOPSIS method. As a result of the analysis, they found out that the ranking of financial performance points and the ranking of corporate governance points of companies were different. The empirical result of the study shows that the quality of corporate governance of companies has no effect on financial performance.

Javaid (2015) studied the relation between the corporate governance index and the company performances by using the data obtained from the annual reports of 58 companies trading in the Karachi Stock Exchange textile sector between 2009 and 2013. As a result of the correlation and regression analysis, a positive significant relation was found between the corporate governance index and company performance. The study also concluded that the companies with a strong corporate governance mechanism had higher chances to find financing sources. The research also shows that companies with a strong corporate governance mechanism have a higher chance of obtaining financing. Acaravcı, Kandır and Zelka (2015) used the panel data analysis to examine whether there is any relation between the corporate governance applications and company performances of 126 companies trading in the Istanbul Stock Exchange and operating in the Production Industry Sector between 2005 and 2011. As a result of the analysis, they found a significant relation between the company performances and the corporate governance practices. In the research, it is expected that the increase in the asset sizes of the companies will increase the performance. Accordingly, it has been revealed that investing in companies with more board members and an asset size can be a positive investment decision for capital market investors. Akbar et al. (2016) studied the relation between the corporate governance compliance and company performance of 435 public companies in England between 1999 and 2009 by the generalized method of moments. As a result of the analysis, they found that compliance with the corporate governance arrangements was not a determinant of corporate governance in England. When the empirical results of the research are analyzed, it reveals that changes in the internal characteristics of companies may have the possibility of reverse causality as they may be responsible for corporate governance compatibility and performance relationship.

Ünlü, Yalçın and Yağlı (2017) attempted to associate the financial performance and value based performance criteria, results obtained with the TOPSIS and CRITIC method and their status in the corporate governance index of the companies included in the Istanbul Stock Exchange (BIST) 30 index in 2014 and trading or not trading in the Corporate Governance Index in 2014. As a result of the analysis, they found that there was no difference with respect to financial performance and shareholder value creation between the BIST 30 companies that were trading or not trading in the corporate governance index. As a result of the research, it contributes to the existing literature on the management compatibility and performance relationship of the companies. Arora and Bodhanwala (2018) used panel data analysis to study the relation between the corporate governance index and company performance of 407 companies indexed to BSE-500 trading in the Bombay Stock Exchange between 2009 and 2014. As a result of the analysis, they found a positive significant relation between the corporate governance and company performance. The empirical results of the research support that the corporate governance index is an important and causal factor in explaining firm performance. Güngör and Güney (2019) used the panel data analysis to study the relation between the corporate governance performance and stock returns of the companies trading in the BIST corporate governance index between 2010 and 2017. As a result of the analysis, they found a positive significant relation between the corporate governance performances and stock returns of companies. The research reveals that companies that are subject to the corporate governance index have the image of well-managed companies in the eyes of investors and funders because they are graded according to the criteria established in the light of corporate governance principles.

DATA SET

The study covers 49 businesses registered to the Istanbul Stock Exchange Corporate governance operating in Turkey. The financial performance of these businesses for the year 2018 was measured. The reason why the year 2018 was selected to be the time sample was that the 2019 data was not published yet and it was intended to help the companies see the current condition of the last year and take measures for the future. The data set used in the study includes 49 businesses recorded in the corporate governance index and 4 financial indicators. The criteria used in the financial performance measurement was selected according to the literature. The criteria included return on assets (ROA), return on equity (ROE), return on sales (ROS) and market value maximization (MV) which is the basic goal of financial management. ROA, ROE and ROS values consist of the profitability indicators expressed as Dupont rates developed by Pierre Dupont in 1920 and the main purpose of corporate governance enterprises is the market value maximization (Curtis et al. 2015: 1211). The study data was accessed through the Istanbul Stock Exchange and Public Disclosure Platform. This data set also constitutes the decision matrix to be used in the study. It includes the 49 businesses in the decision matrix and their codes. The corporate governance index businesses is registered to the Istanbul Stock Exchange. Table 1 shows the data set of these companies formed according to 4 financial indicators.

Table 1 shows the decision matrix consisting of the data of the companies. This decision matrix includes the ROA, ROE, ROS and MV values of the corporate governance companies for the year 2018.

Table 1. Data Set

Companies	ROA	ROE	ROS	MV
AGHOL	-0,02375	-0,05139	-0,04646	4627,972
AKSGY	0,183721	0,283651	2,749274	1211,027
AKMGY	0,333849	0,342138	0,7601	689,396
AKSA	0,053549	0,154956	0,063404	2200,111
ALBRK	0,003173	0,041076	0,005116	1277,678
ANSGR	0,038571	0,185196	0,60723	2095,297
AEFES	0,002489	0,004541	0,005184	13879,15
ARCLK	0,030025	0,103631	0,031659	10868,75
ASELS	0,119043	0,227787	0,257334	29227,42
AYGAZ	0,045556	0,091265	0,023903	3831,369
BTCIM	-0,00564	-0,01374	-0,01384	571,75
CCOLA	0,023307	0,050657	0,03076	8373,789
CRDFA	0,059294	0,181015	0,061484	100,892
DOHOL	0,331795	0,518874	0,299108	2700,71
DGGYO	0,002143	0,004447	0,039912	886,932

continues on following page

Table 1. Continued

Companies	ROA	ROE	ROS	MV
DOAS	0,027749	0,101812	0,012458	1452,619
ENJSA	0,032333	0,118703	0,040754	7015,817
ENKAI	0,038572	0,04865	0,113671	24163,35
EREGL	0,133981	0,191354	0,207216	35998,19
GARFA	0,016639	0,141653	0,025888	36893,83
GLYHO	-0,02357	-0,36887	-0,02457	191,686
HLGYO	-0,01591	-0,05362	-0,0832	1143,571
HURGZ	0,150293	0,173533	1,237004	646,464
IHEVA	0,006664	0,086896	0,010062	9770,92
IHLAS	0,308142	0,42078	0,638218	634,638
LIDFA	0,025026	0,035755	0,035411	75,928
LOGO	-0,01559	-0,04743	-0,0303	315,17
MGROS	0,019968	0,127454	0,025662	123,134
OTKAR	0,120221	0,21252	0,210853	1050,801
PRKME	-0,07676	-1,31565	-0,04464	3473,424
PGSUS	0,071365	0,421822	0,097897	2125,996
PETUN	0,07448	0,080963	88,97365	466,067
PINSU	0,03713	0,136559	0,061154	2895,067
PNSUT	0,084752	0,11219	0,088645	338,964
SKBNK	-0,07519	-0,3423	-0,09427	68,865
TATGD	0,035346	0,062982	0,033079	437,916
TAVHL	0,002757	0,036326	0,004199	1527,091
TOASO	0,044633	0,077019	0,033389	619,9
TRCAS	0,069925	0,233899	0,218332	8923,968
TUPRS	0,102326	0,358938	0,071515	12068,53
PRKAB	0,017257	0,140056	0,023846	2838,063
TTKOM	-0,0943	-0,22731	-2,74525	501,773
TTRAK	0,092737	0,373301	0,041928	29265,26
GARAN	0,042854	0,143139	0,028061	278,293
HALKB	-0,03843	-0,18666	-0,0681	17735
TSKB	0,077623	0,368342	0,061425	2964,384
SISE	0,083761	0,139049	0,149569	11174,54
VESTL	0,020665	0,111852	0,023413	2911,96
YKBNK	0,012501	0,119655	0,019864	17229,98

METHOD AND FINDINGS

Two methods were used in the study. The first method is the Analytic Hierarchy Process (AHP) method. The AHP method is a multicriteria decision making technique developed by Saaty (1977) including both objective and subjective judgements (Saaty, 1990, p.9-26). What is aimed with the AHP method is to determine how important the financial indicators are for businesses. AHP method provides subjective decision when making this determination. Therefore, this study reveals the decision matrix data by asking questions to the academicians specialized on finance about the significance levels of financial indicators as shown in Table 2.

Table 2. Decision Matrix

Criteria	ROA	ROE	ROS	MV
ROA	1	1/3	3	1/5
ROE	3	1	5	1/3
ROS	1/3	1/5	1	1/7
MV	5	3	7	1

Table 2 includes dual comparisons of the criteria of the study, i.e. the financial indicators and determines their superiority to each other. As stated above, specialist views are taken as basis when determining the decision matrix. This process is followed by standardization of data to collect in a certain range or by normalization of data.

Table 3 includes the column totals of the financial indicators from top to bottom and data were normalized by comparing each criteria to the total of column. This step is followed by finding the AHP scores, which is the last step of the method.

Table 3. Normalization Matrix

Criteria	ROA	ROE	ROS	MV
ROA	1	1/3	3	1/5
ROE	3	1	5	1/3
ROS	1/3	1/5	1	1/7
MV	5	3	7	1
TOTAL	9,333333333	4,533333333	16	1,676190476
ROA	0,107142857	0,073529412	0,1875	0,119318182
ROE	0,321428571	0,220588235	0,3125	0,198863636
ROS	0,035714286	0,044117647	0,0625	0,085227273
MV	0,535714286	0,661764706	0,4375	0,596590909

Table 4 includes the AHP scores where the arrhythmic averages of the normalized data were taken to determine those scores. As a result of the averages, the significance level of each variable was determined. According to the determination, the most important financial indicator is the market value while the least important one is the profitability of sales. The ranking for this study includes the indicators for MV, ROE, ROA and ROS. Therefore, the most important financial indicator for the companies registered to the corporate governance index is the market value. In addition, another point to take into consideration is that the total of both averages and percentages should be 1 or 100%. If the totals are not equal to 1 or 100%, the steps of the method have to be implemented again and the error should be corrected. Otherwise, the method will not provide a reliable result. When the equality is ensured, the AHP scores can be interpreted again.

Table 4. AHP Scores

	Criteria				Mean	Percent
ROA	0,107142857	0,073529412	0,1875	0,119318182	0,121872613	12%
ROE	0,321428571	0,220588235	0,3125	0,198863636	0,263345111	26%
ROS	0,035714286	0,044117647	0,0625	0,085227273	0,056889801	6%
MV	0,535714286	0,661764706	0,4375	0,596590909	0,557892475	56%
TOTAL	1	1	1	1	1	100%

After determining the significance levels of the financial indicators, the businesses with the best or the worst financial performance are determined. The second method for this determination is the Promethee method. The Promethee method was developed by Brans (1982) and had different versions by Brans and Vincke (1985) while it was updated by different versions including Promethee V and Promethee VI. The goal of these updates is to increase the usability and reliability of the method. In addition, this method has also a fuzzy version like the other methods (Macharis et al. 2004, p.307; Baki, 2017, p.184-185). The Promethee method was applied by using the Visual Promethee program however, it is necessary to correctly determine the preference functions in both program assisted analysis and manual analysis. Figure 3 shows the preference functions of the Promethee method.

Figure 3 shows the 6 types of preference functions. These preference functions vary according to the strategy determined by the decision maker (Durucasu et al. 2017, p.233):

- First type of preference function (Usual): it is used when the decision maker has no specific range or limitation with regards to the criteria.
- Second type of preference function (U-shape): It is the function where an individual chooses the alternative with higher values than the value determined while choosing.
- Third type of preference function (V-shape): It is the function where an individual takes into consideration the values that are lower than the determined value while preferring the alternatives that are higher than the determined value.
- Fourth type of preference function (Level): It is the preference function that gives value range to the criteria that were determined in the choice of alternatives.

- Fifth type of preference function (Linear): It is the preference function that determines a certain average for the criteria and selects the alternatives that are higher than this average.
- Sixth type of preference function (Gaussian): It is the function based on average deviation values of the criteria in the selection of alternatives.

Figure 3. Promethee Preference Functions
Source: Brans and Mareschal, 2005: 170

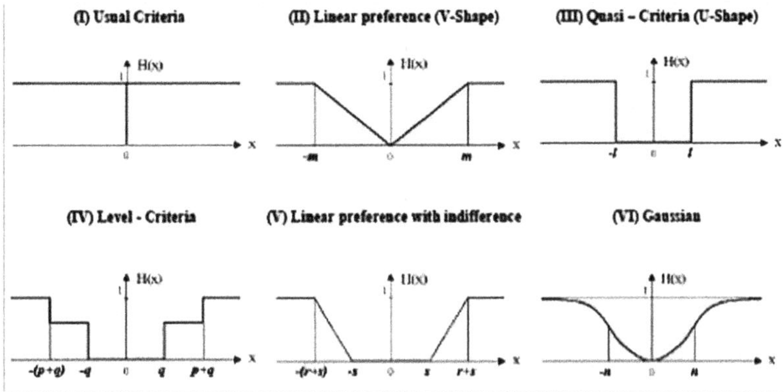

With regards to the preference functions mentioned in Figure 3 and explained above; the financial performance analysis was conducted with the Promethee program in 2018 for 49 companies and 4 financial indicator. In addition, the "Usual" first type preference function was used as there was no limitation or a special value range.

The data set created in first step of the Promethee method was entered to the program while the screen shot of the program is shown in Figure 4.

According to the interface of the Visual Promethee program shown in Figure 4, ROA, ROE, ROS and MV variables and 49 companies were entered in the program. In addition, the program preference choices included the maximum of the 4 variables, i.e. ROA, ROE, ROS and MV with the preference function being the first type (Usual). Analyses were conducted with the Promethee method after entering the data and information of the study.

The second stage includes the "Promethee Rankings", which is the first analysis of the method. According to the Promethee Rankings, there are 2 rankings including Promethee I Partial Ranking and Promethee II Complete Ranking. The results of the Promethee I Partial Ranking are shown in Figure 5.

According to Figure 5, the Promethee I partial ranking results are seen and the calculated values are between 0 and 1. The Promethee I method refers to partial ranking and there doesn't give definite result while it provides information about the positive and negative values. The left side of Figure 3 shows positive superiority while the right side shows the negative superiority. In both sides, the top companies are more dominant that the other companies. Since there are many companies, there is no clear information about all companies while it can be said that the companies Aselsan, Tofaş and Ereğli Demir Çelik display more dominant and higher financial performance than the other companies. "Promethee II Complete Ranking" needs to be checked to get information on clear superiority while the results are given in Figure 6.

Figure 4. Promethee Method Interface

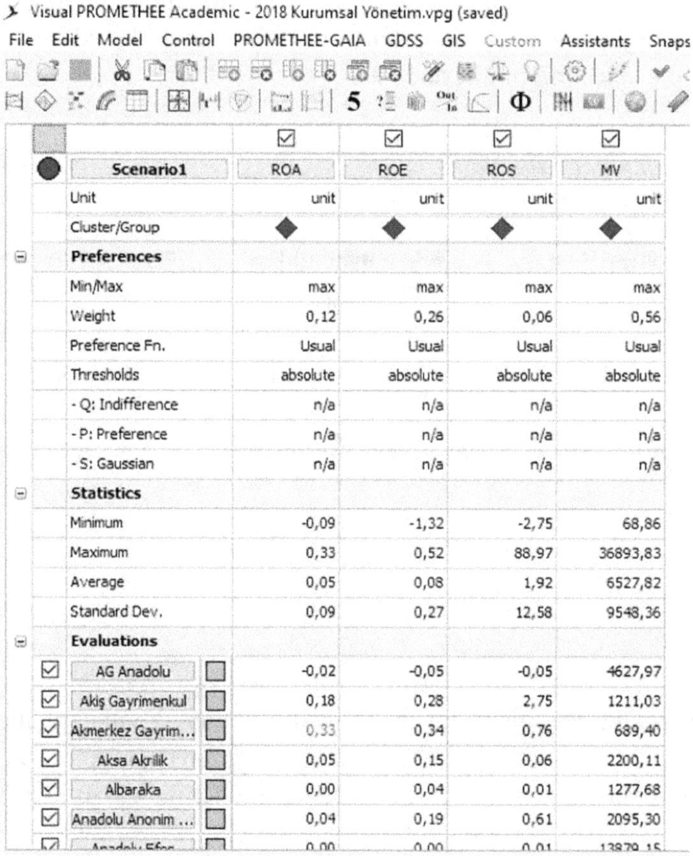

According to the Promethee II results in Figure 6, the positive and negative superiorities are individual and between 0 and 1. Therefore, the businesses between 0 and 1 have good financial performance. According to the results, all companies with a score above 0 and listed in the green section have good financial performance such as Tüpraş, Ereğli Demir Çelik, Aselsan and Tofaş. On the other hand, companies with a score below 0 and listed in the red section have insufficient and bad financial performance such as Tüpraş, Ereğli Demir Çelik, Aselsan and Tofaş. Another type of analysis to see the comparison between companies is "Promethee Diamond" as shown in Figure 7.

Each alternative shown in Figure 7 refers to a point in the "Promethee Diamond" analysis. There is a cone for each alternative. This cone is perpendicular to the axis shown in green and red. When the cones are intertwined, the alternative of the cone covering the other one is better. However, intersecting cones cannot be compared to each other. This way, the cones of the companies including Tüpraş, Aselsan and Ereğli Demir Çelik are listed on top and cover the others, which shows that these companies have the best financial performance. The positive and negative scores of these companies are shown in Figure 8 with the "Promethee Network" analysis.

Figure 5. Promethee I Partial Ranking

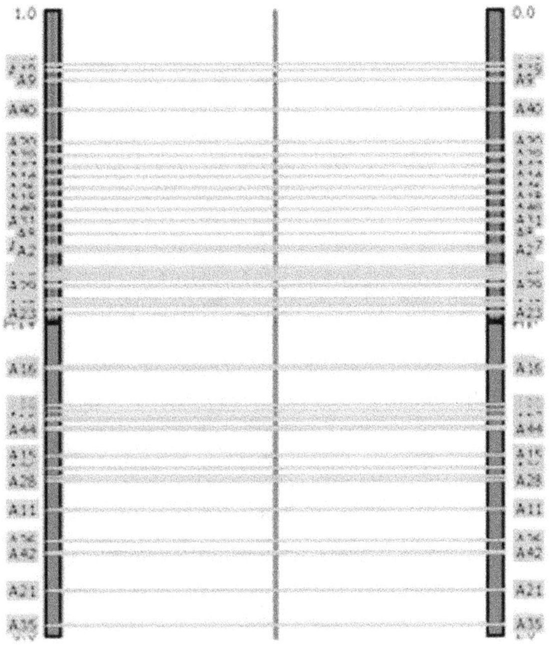

Figure 6. Promethee II Complete Ranking

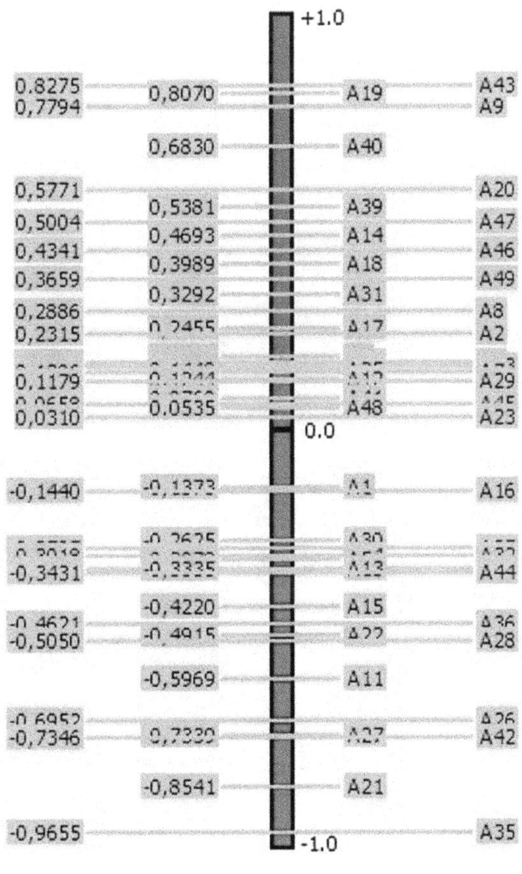

Figure 7. Promethee Diamond

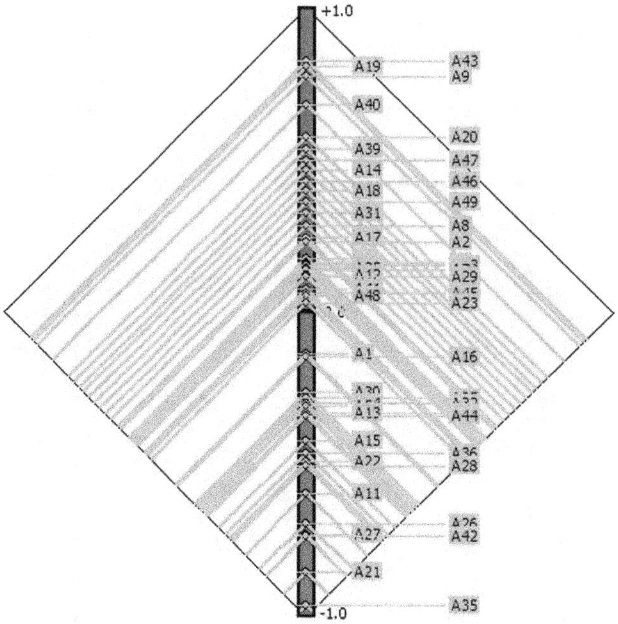

Figure 8. Promethee Network

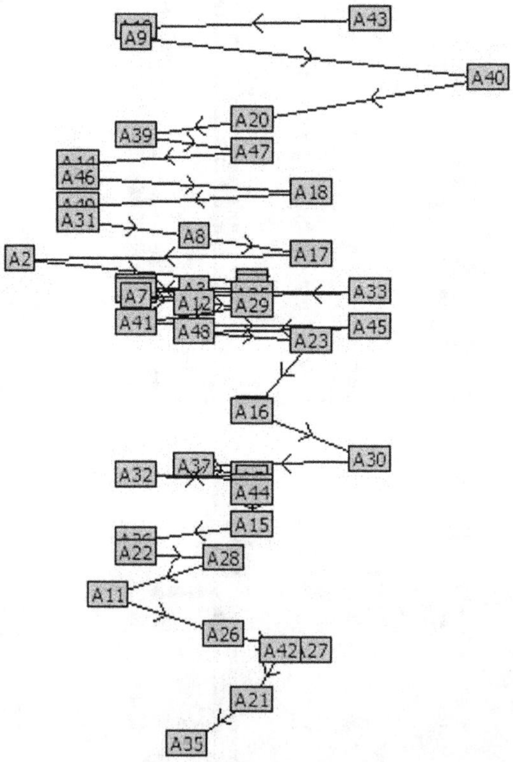

The "Promethee Network" analysis given in Figure 8 shows each alternative with the positive and negative scores in a rectangular. The preferences between alternatives are shown with arrows. There are arrows down from the business in the top box. Therefore, Tüpraş is the best company for this study followed by Ereğli Demir Çelik, Aselsan and Tofaş. Pınar Su company is at the bottom and has the lowest financial performance. Table 5 shows the "Promethee Flow Table" including the positive, negative and final scores of all businesses.

Table 5. Promethee Flow Table

Rank	Firms	Phi	Phi+	Phi-
1	Tüpraş	0,8275	0,9137	0,0863
2	Ereğli Demir Çelik	0,807	0,9035	0,0965
3	Aselsan	0,7794	0,8897	0,1103
4	Tofaş	0,683	0,8415	0,1585
5	Türkiye Garanti Bankası	0,5771	0,7886	0,2114
6	Tav Havalimanları Holding	0,5381	0,7691	0,2309
7	Türkiye Şişe ve Cam Fabrikaları	0,5004	0,7502	0,2498
8	Doğan Holding	0,4693	0,7346	0,2654
9	Türk Traktör	0,4341	0,717	0,283
10	Enka İnşaat	0,3989	0,6994	0,3006
11	Yapı ve Kredi Bankası	0,3659	0,6829	0,3171
12	Otokar Otomotiv	0,3292	0,6646	0,3354
13	Arçelik	0,2886	0,6443	0,3557
14	Enerjisa	0,2455	0,6227	0,3773
15	Akiş GYO	0,2315	0,6157	0,3843
16	Aksa Akrilik Kimya Sanayii	0,1765	0,5883	0,4117
17	Anadolu Anonim Türk Sigorta	0,1636	0,5818	0,4182
18	Türkiye Halk Bankası	0,163	0,5815	0,4185
19	Akmerkez GYO	0,16	0,58	0,42
20	Aygaz	0,1559	0,578	0,422
21	Pegasus	0,1538	0,5769	0,4231
22	Hürriyet	0,1448	0,5724	0,4276
23	Anadolu Efes	0,1396	0,5698	0,4302
24	Coca Cola	0,1244	0,5622	0,4378
25	Logo Yazılım	0,1179	0,5589	0,4411
26	TSKB	0,076	0,538	0,462
27	Türk Telekomünikasyon	0,0658	0,5329	0,4671
28	Vestel Elektronik	0,0535	0,5267	0,4733
29	Halk GYO	0,031	0,5155	0,4845
30	AG Anadolu Grubu Holding	-0,1373	0,4314	0,5686
31	Doğuş Otomotiv	-0,144	0,428	0,572

continues on following page

Table 5. Continued

Rank	Firms	Phi	Phi+	Phi-
32	Migros	-0,2625	0,3688	0,6312
33	Şekerbank	-0,2797	0,3601	0,6399
34	Pınar Et	-0,3004	0,3498	0,6502
35	Park Elektrik	-0,3018	0,3491	0,6509
36	Albaraka Türk Katılım Bankası	-0,3078	0,3461	0,6539
37	Tat Gıda	-0,3304	0,3348	0,6652
38	Credit West	-0,3335	0,3333	0,6667
39	Türk Prysmian	-0,3431	0,3285	0,6715
40	Doğuş GYO	-0,422	0,289	0,711
41	Pınar Süt	-0,4621	0,269	0,731
42	Global Yatırım Holding	-0,4915	0,2542	0,7458
43	Lider Faktoring	-0,505	0,2475	0,7525
44	Batıçim	-0,5969	0,2015	0,7985
45	İhlas Ev Aletleri	-0,6952	0,1524	0,8476
46	İhlas Holding	-0,7339	0,133	0,867
47	Turcas Petrol	-0,7346	0,1327	0,8673
48	Garanti Faktoring	-0,8541	0,073	0,927
49	Pınar Su	-0,9655	0,0172	0,9828

Figure 9. GAIA Visual Analysis

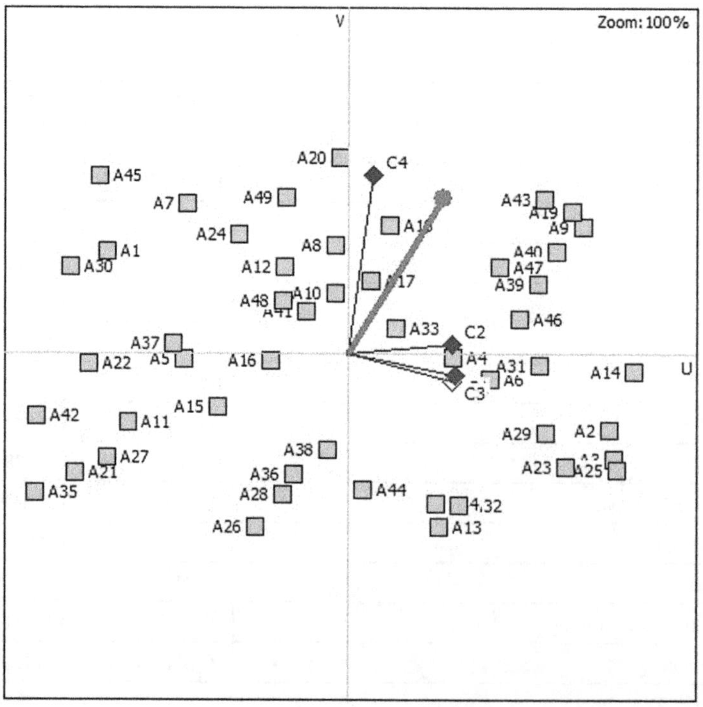

Table 5 includes the "Promethee Flow Table" with the net scores making the difference between the positive and negative points. Upon reviewing the table, Tüpraş is the business with the highest financial performance score. Tüpraş is followed by Ereğli Demir Çelik, Aselsan and Tofaş in performance ranking. The business performance scores of the top 29 businesses in the table are positive. However, the performance scores of 20 businesses in the ranks between 30 and 49 are negative. Therefore, the Promethee Flow Table reveals that the financial performances of the first 29 companies are good or sufficient, and the financial performances of the last 20 companies are insufficient, and the businesses are unsuccessful. Figure 9 shows the results of the GAIA analysis realizing the two-dimensional display of the results on a plane.

The thick linear in red in Figure 9 shows the optimal result and the businesses that are the closest to this linear have the highest financial performances. Accordingly, Tüpraş, Ereğli Demir Çelik, Aselsan and Tofaş are the businesses with the best financial performance. In addition, the thin line in blue shows the businesses with the best financial indicators. For instance, Otokar has the highest performance with regards to ROS and Pegasus has the highest performance with regards to ROE.

REFERENCES

Acaravcı, S. K., Kandır, S. Y., & Zelka, A. (2015). Investigating the Impact of Corporate Governance Over the Performance of BIST Companies. *Academic Review of Economics and Administrative Sciences*, *8*(1), 171–183.

Akbar, S., Hughes, J. P., Syed, R., & Shah, Z. A. (2016). More on the relationship between corporate governance and firm performance in the UK: Evidence from the aplication of generalized method of moments estimation. *Research in International Business and Finance*, *38*, 417–429. doi:10.1016/j.ribaf.2016.03.009

Arora, A., & Bodhanwala, S. (2018). Relationship between corporate governance index and firm performance: Indian evidence. *Global Business Review*, *19*(3), 675–689. doi:10.1177/0972150917713812

Baki, R. (2017). For supplier evaluation process through fuzzy Promethee method. *International Journal of Materials. Mechanics and Manufacturing*, *5*(3), 183–186.

Bilir, H. (2018). The distinctive features of contemporary era in the context of globalization. *2nd International Congress on Multidisciplinary Studies.*

Brans, J.-P. (1982). *L'ingenierie de la decision: elaboration d'instruments d'aide a la decision. la methode PROMETHEE*. Universite Laval, Colloque d'aide a la Decision, Quebec, Canada.

Brans, J.-P., & Mareschal, B. (2005). *PROMETHEE methods, Figueira vd* (C. D. A. MultipleState of the Art Survey, Ed.). Springer Science.

Brans, J.-P., & Vincke, P. (1985). A preference ranking organization method: The PROMETHEE method for MCDM. *Management Science*, *31*(6), 647–656. doi:10.1287/mnsc.31.6.647

Chen, A., Kao, L., Tsao, M., & Wu, C. (2007). Building a corporate governance index from the perspectives of ownership and leadership for firms in Taiwan. *Corporate Governance*, *15*(2), 251–261. doi:10.1111/j.1467-8683.2007.00572.x

Çonkar, K., Elitaş, C. & Atar, G. (2011). Measurement of financial management of firms taking place in ınstitutional ındex with Topsis method and its analysis with ınstitutional administration note. *İstanbul Üniversitesi İktisat Fakültesi Mecmuası*, *61*(1), 81-115.

Curtis, A., Lewis-Western, M.-F., & Toynbee, S. (2015). Historical cost measurement and the use of DuPont analysis by market participants. *Review of Accounting Studies*, *20*(3), 1210–1245. doi:10.100711142-015-9334-y

Dağlı, H., Ayaydın, H., & Eyüpoğlu, K. (2010). Corporate governance index performance evaluation: Case of Turkey. *The Journal of Accounting and Finance*, *48*(October), 18–31.

Darabaris, J. (2019). *Corporate environmental management*. CRC Press Taylor & Francis Group, Boca Raton, London. doi:10.1201/9780429029264

Dinç, E., & Abdioğlu, H. (2009). Relationships between corporate governance and accounting information systems on businesses: an empirical research on ISE–100 companies. Balıkesir University The Journal of Social Sciences Institute, 12(21), 157-184.

Durucasu, H., Aytekin, A., Saraç, B., & Orakçı, E. (2017). Current application fields of ELECTRE and PROMETHEE: A literature review. *Alphanumeric Journal*, *5*(2), 229–270. doi:10.17093/alphanumeric.320235

Ege, İ., Topaloğlu, E. E., & Özyamanoğlu, M. (2013). Relationship between financial performance and corporate governance scores: Application in BIST. *Journal of Academic Researches and Studies*, *5*(9), 100–117.

Ercan, M. K., & Ban, Ü. (2005). *Finansal yönetim: değere dayalı işletme finansmanı*. Gazi Publishing.

Fung, B. (2014). The demand and need for transparency and disclosure in corporate governance. *Universal Journal of Management*, *2*(2), 72–80.

Güngör, B., & Güney, G. (2019). Correlation with stock return of the corporate government performance. *Atatürk University The Journal of Social Sciences Institute*, *23*(1), 37–66.

Heikal, M., Khaddafi, M., & Ummah, A. (2014). Influence analysis of return on assets (ROA), return on equity (ROE), net profit margin (NPM), debt to equity ratio (DER), and current ratio (CR), against corporate profit growth in automotive in Indonesia stock exchange. *International Journal of Academic Research in Business and Social Sciences*, *4*(12), 102–114. doi:10.6007/IJARBSS/v4-i12/1331

Herciu, M., Ogrean, C., & Belascu, L. (2011). A Du Pont analysis of the 20 most profitable companies in the world. *2010 International Conference on Business and Economics Research*, 45-48.

Hilb, M. (2006). *New corporate governance, successful board management tools* (2nd ed.). Springer Berlin Heidelberg. doi:10.1007/3-540-28168-1

Javaid, F. (2015). Impact of corporate governance index on firm performance: Evidence from Pakistani manufacturing sector. *Journal of Governance and Regulation*, *4*(3), 163–174. doi:10.22495/jgr_v4_i3_c1_p6

Kabajeh, M. A. M., Nuaimat, S. M. A., & Dahmash, F. N. (2012). The relationship between the ROA, ROE and ROI ratios with Jordanian ınsurance public companies market share prices. *International Journal of Humanities and Social Science*, *2*(11), 115–120.

Kakilli Acaravcı, S., Kandır, S. Y., & Zelka, A. (2015). Investigating the ımpact of corporate governance over the performance of BIST companies. *Academic Review of Economic and Administrative Sciences*, *8*(1), 171–183.

Kamar, K. (2017). Analysis of the effect of return on equity (ROE) and debt to equity ratio (DER) on stock price on cement industry listed in Indonesia stock exchange (Idx) in the year of 2011-2015. *IOSR Journal of Business and Management*, *19*(5), 66–76. doi:10.9790/487X-1905036676

Kang, C. (2005). *Market economy and corporate governance – fairness and transparency for sustainable growth.* 6th Global Forum on Reinventing Government: Toward Participatory and Transparent Governance, Seoul, South Korea.

Lopes, A. B., & Walker, M. (2012). Asset revaluations, future firm performance and firm-level corporate governance arrangements: New evidence from Brazil. *The British Accounting Review*, *44*(2), 53–67. doi:10.1016/j.bar.2012.03.007

Macharis, C., Springael, J., De Brucker, K., & Verbeke, A. (2004). PROMETHEE and AHP: The design of operational synergies in multicriteria analysis. strengthening PROMETHEE with ideas of AHP. *European Journal of Operational Research*, *153*(2), 307–317. doi:10.1016/S0377-2217(03)00153-X

Mohamad, S. (2004). The importance of effective corporate governance. *SSRN Electronic Journal.* Retrieved from: SSRN: https://ssrn.com/abstract=617101

Musa, H., Musová, Z., & Debnárová, L. (2015). Responsibility in the corporate governance framework and financial decision making process. *Procedia Economics and Finance*, *23*, 1023–1029. doi:10.1016/S2212-5671(15)00371-8

Prigent, J. L. (2007). *Portfolio optimization and performance analysis.* Chapman & Hall/CRC. doi:10.1201/9781420010930

Saaty, T. L. (1977). A scaling method for priorities in a hierarchichal structure. *Journal of Mathematical Psychology*, *15*(3), 234–281. doi:10.1016/0022-2496(77)90033-5

Saaty, T. L. (1990). *Multicriteria decision making: Analytic Hierarchy Process* (2nd ed.). RWS Publications.

Scheer, A. W., Jost, W., Heß, H., & Kronz, A. (2005). Corporate performance management: ARIS in practice. Springer. doi:10.1007/b137635

Silva, A. L. C., & Leal, R. P. C. (2005). Corporate governance index, firm valuation and performance in Brazil. *Brazilian Review of Finance*, *3*(1), 1–18.

Sorensen, D., & Peckham, K. (2002). *Business performance ıntelligence software a market evaluation.* Financial Executives Research Foundation.

Sulaiman, A. N., Kesuma, F. T. M., Madjid, I., & Siregar, R. (2018). The role of good government governance principles in enhancing the performance of public organization in Aceh, Indonesia, Advances in Social Science, Education and Humanities Research. *1st Aceh Global Conference*, 292, 731-738.

Ünlü, U., Yalçın, N., & Yağlı, İ. (2017). Corporate governance and firm performance: An application on BIST 30 firms with Topsis method. *Dokuz Eylül University The Journal of Graduate School of Social Sciences*, *19*(1), 63–81.

Watson, D., & Head, A. (2007). *Corporate finance principles & practice* (4th ed.). Prentice Hall.

Wiig, K. M. (2004). People-Focused knowledge management: how effective decision making leads to corporate success. Elsevier Butterworth–Heinemann.

Chapter 7
Effect of Ownership Structure on Firm Performance Evidence From Non-Financial Listed Firms:
Ownership Structure and Performance

Muhammad Arslan
https://orcid.org/0000-0001-5046-7627
KIMEP University, Kazakhstan

ABSTRACT

In modern organizations, there is a separation between ownership and control of the firm. On the lenses of agency theory, this study statistically examines the relationship between ownership structure (i.e., ownership concentration and owner identity) and firm performance of non-financial listed firms of Pakistan by taking firm-level control variables of size, age, liquidity, financial leverage, and growth of the firm. Secondary data is collected from annual reports of 65 non-financial listed firms for the year 2008 to 2012. The least-square dummy variable model followed by the random effect model has been employed to statistically determining the impact of ownership structure on firm performance. The results of the least square dummy variable model reveal that the ownership concentration has a significant positive impact on firm performance. The owner identity (such as dispersed, family, institutional, and government ownership) has a significant causal effect on firm performance as indicated from t and p values.

INTRODUCTION

Among many others, poor corporate governance (CG) is also quoted as one of the main reasons that led to the global financial crisis. The nature of the relation between the ownership structure and corporate governance structure has been the core issue in the existing CG literature. Agency theory is the main fundamental concept in CG studies that focuses on the conflicts among principals (owners) and agents

DOI: 10.4018/978-1-7998-4852-3.ch007

(managers). Adam Smith (1776) contended that managers will not work with as much dedication as the owner. Since then, multiple dimensions of agency problems have been tinted in the existing literature. Existing literature suggests that ownership structure is one of the core corporate governance mechanisms influencing the scale and growth of a firm's agency costs (Alabdullah, 2018). Therefore, the effect of ownership structure and firm performance has been measured extensively both in empirical and theoretical literature(Alabdullah, 2018, Phung and Mishra, 2016, Ozili and Uadiale, 2017). However, prior studies have mainly focused on developed countries such as USA, UK, and other Western countries (Wintoki et al., 2012, Bhagat and Bolton, 2019) while few studies have focused on emerging economies especially in Asia (Arora and Sharma, 2016, Alabdullah, 2018, Shah et al., 2020). This provides us the opportunity to fill the gap in existing literature. Arslan and Alqatan (2020) argued that Asian firms operate in a distinctive legal and institutional framework and socioeconomic factors are quite different as compared to other developed countries that may have a material effect on ownership structure and firm performance relationship. In similar vein, Arslan et al. (2019) also found that developing countries have weak institutions and therefore, the CG practices are compromised. Researchers argued that ownership concentration positively affects the firm performance because it lessens the conflicts among the managers and owners of the firms (Jensen and Meckling, 1976, Ozili and Uadiale, 2017, Al-Matari et al., 2019). Recently, several studies have shifted the focus towards internal benefits that shareholders can experience inside a firm. Researchers (e.g. (Arslan and Abidin, 2019b, Arslan et al., 2019, La Porta et al., 2000, Arslan and Alqatan, 2020, Attiya et al., 2012) found the expropriation of minority shareholders by controlling shareholders. Expropriation exists in different forms such as the sale of assets and products to related parties at an unfair price, paying excessively to an executive, outright theft and giving lucrative positions to relatives. Expropriation can create inefficiency in the financial system in a sense that fund providers will be hesitant to surrender their wealth in the face of probable expropriation by the insider. The legal way to control expropriation is to develop laws and implement them effectively (La Porta et al, 1999, La Porta et al., 1998, Arslan and Abidin, 2019a, Arslan and Alqatan, 2020). In modern organizations, there is a separation between ownership and control of the firm. There is a lack of widely held corporations in Pakistan(Khan, 2017, Salman and Siddiqui, 2013, Samza, 2016). This ownership concentration is common in Pakistan and provides plenty of incentives to larger shareholders (Arslan and Abidin, 2019b, Arslan et al., 2019).

Pakistan is one such country where insiders block holdings are ubiquitous in the corporate sector but sufficient protection to minority shareholders is not available (Samza, 2016, Khan, 2014, Arslan and Abidin, 2019a). One evidence of low judicial efficiency in Pakistan comes from a report by the World Bank (Bank, 2010). According to this report of the World Bank, Pakistan ranks 158th among 183 countries on the overall contract agreement. Furthermore, this report shows that average costs are 23.8% of the claim and the average time taken in disposing of a judicial case is 978 days. From these statistics, it can be interpreted that the judicial process in Pakistan is costly and lengthy as compared to other countries. Several studies have been conducted in Pakistan to examine the relationship between ownership structure and firm performance while findings of these studies are inconclusive (Khan and Nouman, 2017, Anwar and Tabassum, 2011, Yasser and Al Mamun, 2015, Ullah et al., 2017). Hence, this provides us opportunity to examine the relationship between ownership structure and firm performance. In addition, there is a divergence between the interests of the owners and managers. To explore the link between ownership concentration and ownership identity concerning the performance of the firm seems more interested according to the context of Pakistan. The findings of some studies showed that the ownership identity has more impact on firm performance as compared to ownership concentration

(Attiya et al., 2012). Due to the non-availability of ownership structure data in an organized form, this area has attracted little attention to empirical researchers in Pakistan. This study empirically examines and analyses the relationship between ownership structure and performance of the firm by using the sample of non-financial listed firms of Pakistan that includes textile, beverages and oil and gas firms. Researchers also argued that ownership structure is pivotal in corporate governance, hence, it has important implications for firm performance (Luzhen and Morten, 2012, Vu et al., 2018). More specifically, the study determines whether the ownership concentration and owner identity have any impact on accounting measures of firm performance. At the end, this study also highlights the effect of the owner's identity in the reducing agency conflicts and increasing firm performance.

LITERATURE REVIEW

Ownership Structure and Firm Performance

In the absence of agency costs, it is considered that firm performance is independent of the ownership structure. In contrast, the agency problem is widely spread in modern organizations and researchers argued equity ownership as a driving factor in corporate governance (Denis and McConnell, 2003) which not only affects the CG quality but also reduces agency costs (Berk and DeMarzo, 2007). Previous studies revealed mix results in different contextual settings. Akimova and Schwodiauer (2004) conducted a study to investigate the impact of ownership structure on firm performance. Akimova & Schwodiauer (2004) used the regression analysis to test the hypotheses. The findings of the study showed that there was a significant effect of ownership on enterprise performance. There was a significant non- linear effect of insider ownership on the performance of enterprises. The results also showed that the outside owners have not a significant effect on performance in Ukraine (Akimova and Schwodiauer, 2004).

A study was conducted in Heilongjiang province by Jiang (2004). In his study, the researcher investigated the relationship between ownership structure and performance of the listed firms (Jiang, 2004). The researcher took the structure of ownership and ownership concentration as implications of ownership structure. The empirical findings of the study showed that the performance of firms controlled by legally or personally was not good (Jiang, 2004). The researcher recommended that diversification of ownership of state shares should be taken into the long run, not in short-run purposes (Jiang, 2004). Some researchers tried to examine that the variations in ownership structure yield the systematic deviation in observed performance of the firm (Kapopoulos and Lazaretou, 2006). In this study, the researchers used the data of 175 Greek firms to determine the impact of ownership structure on a firm performance that was measured by profitability (Kapopoulos and Lazaretou, 2006). The empirical results showed that concentrated ownership has positively related to the higher profitability of the firm (Kapopoulos and Lazaretou, 2006). A study was conducted by using the meta-analysis technique which was based on 33 firms, the findings of the study showed no substantive relationship between ownership structure and performance of the firms (Sanchez-Ballesta and Garcia-Meca, 2007). The results of the study also showed that measurement of performance, governance system and endogeneity control restraint the effect of ownership on firm performance (Sanchez-Ballesta and Garcia-Meca, 2007). In the year 2008, some researchers investigated the effect of insider ownership on firm performance (Kaserer and Moldenhauer, 2008). Researchers used the pooled data of 648 German firms for the year 1998 to 2003. The findings of the study have evidence of a significant positive relationship between insider ownership and firm performance (Kaserer and Moldenhauer, 2008). They used the stock price, return on assets and market to book value as a measure of performance. The researchers also argued that concentrated insider ownership and outsider block ownership both have a positive impact on performance (Kaserer and Moldenhauer, 2008). Results of previous studies showed that long term value creation in the corporate sector must include ownership structure as the explained variable (Kaserer and Moldenhauer, 2008). Lee (2008) used the panel data of South Korean firms for a period of 2000 to 2006 to examine the relationship between ownership structure and financial performance of firms. The researcher used the accounting measures and findings of the study showed that the accounting rate of return on assets improves with an increase in ownership concentration (Lee, 2008). Lee (2008) also found a hump-shaped relationship was at immediate levels of ownership concentration, firm performance peaks.

The previous studies showed that some researchers investigated the nonlinear relation between agency costs and managerial equity ownership (Jelinek and Stuerke, 2009). These researchers used two financial statement-based agency cost measure i.e. expense ratio and asset utilization and return on assets as a measure of profitability. They found that the relation of managerial equity ownership with asset utilization and return on assets is nonlinear and positive while the relation with expense ratio is nonlinear and negative (Jelinek and Stuerke, 2009). The impact of ownership structure and corporate governance on the capital structure of Pakistani listed companies was discussed by (Hasan and Butt, 2009). They took data of 58 non-financial listed companies for the years 2002 to 2005. The findings of the study showed that managerial shareholdings and board size have a significant negative correlation with the debt to equity ratio. The results also showed that there is no significant influence of non-executive directors and CEO duality on corporate financing behaviour (Hasan and Butt, 2009). The researchers also argued that variables of corporate governance like managerial shareholding, ownership structure and size play an important role in the fortitude of the financial mix of firms. In the year 2010, a study was conducted to determine the effect of managerial ownership and the board of directors on the financial performance of firms listed in Palestine securities exchange (Daraghma and Alsinawi, 2010). There were selected the firms and four years (i.e. 2005-2008) were used to find the results (Daraghma and Alsinawi, 2010). The findings of the study revealed that CEO duality has a significant impact on firm performance while the separation of the CEO has no significant impact. The results also revealed that there is a positive and significant impact of managerial ownership on firm performance while it was concluded that there is no effect of debt financing on the profitability of Palestinian firms (Daraghma and Alsinawi, 2010). There was found a strong positive relation between board size and firm performance of firms in Nigeria (Uadiale, 2010). Kumar and Singh (2013) found the significant positive relationship between managerial ownership and firm performance. Arora and Sharma (2016) found that increasing managerial ownership is an imperative element that decreases agency problems and fosters managers to enhance firm performance.

Ownership Concentration

The ownership concentration is a trade-off between risk and incentive efficiency (Atkinson and Stiglitz, 1980). An extensive body of literature examined the impact of ownership structure on firm performance, stock market reaction and earning management by taking ownership concentration and insider ownership as implications of ownership structure (Demsetz and Lehn, 1985, Claessens et.al.,, 2000, Himmelberg et.al.,, 1999, Kim and Yi, 2006, Arslan and Abidin, 2019b). There are few studies that examined the effect of ownership structure on R & D spending practices of companies (Parthiban et.al.,, 2001). The concentration of ownership might have two contrasting effects on management decisions about R & D spending i.e depending on incentive alignment effect or managerial entrenchment effect (Gul et.al.,, 2008). According to the incentive alignment perspective, it is argued that where there is a lack of controlling shareholders because the dispersed shareholders have little inducement to monitor the management. On the other hand, holding a large stake in the firm, ownership becomes more concentrated and it encourages and motivates owners to ensure that managers behave in ways that will benefit shareholders.

A larger shareholder might have stronger incentives to monitor and therefore, they should oblige managers to be aligned with their objective of increasing the value of their shares. Recent studies have emphasized another source of agency problems created by rising ownership concentration that gives more power to a circumscribed number of shareholders, which in turn might expropriate value from minority shareholders (Gedajlovic and Shapiro, 2002).

DISPERSED OWNERSHIP AND ITS IMPACT ON FIRM PERFORMANCE

The existing studies found the negative effect of ownership disbursement on firm performance (Alabdullah, 2018, Kumar and Singh, 2013). Family ownership is very common worldwide. The individuals and families play a double role by acting as owners and managers of the company. Anderson & Reeb (2003) found that more than one-third of the S&P 500 companies are family firms. Empirical findings of previous studies showed that there is a positive effect of family ownership on firm performance (Mishra et.el.,, 2001, McConaughy et.al.,, 1998, McConaughy et al.,, 2001). Morck et.al.,(2000) found the negative relationship between family ownership and the performance of the firm.

The financial institutions like banks, pension funds, insurance companies, and investment companies are supposed to be portfolio investors whose major purpose is to increase the shareholder value. There may be an exception to this rule (Monks and Minnow., 2001). Banks may give value to the security of their loans. Pension funds may have links with government and trade unions and they become more sensitive about job safety and public image of the company in which they invested (Woidtke, 2002). The extreme case of non-voting stock a higher ownership share can give more incentives and more power to monitor the management and thus implies a greater pressure to maximize the wealth of shareholders. Taylor (2003) finds that the percentage of US equity held by institutional owners has increased from 8% in 1950 to 45% in 1990. Institution ownership attracts much attention along with its increased importance in the equity markets. Although institutions can be divided into different types (financial and non-financial; domestic and foreign, etc.) in this review such distinctions are not made. Positive effects among institution ownership on firm performance are found by McConnell & Servaes (2003), Han & Suk (2008) and Tsai & Gu, who explain the positive effect of the active monitoring argument. The monitoring effect should be stronger for institutional investors than general shareholders. According to Hand (2006), institutional investors are more sophisticated than other shareholders because they are more professional regarding capital markets, industries and businesses and they are better informed. Studies also showed that the sensitivity to the news has influenced the institutional investors. According to previous studies, some researchers believed that the government may get benefit from entry barriers and by lowering the costs of capital (Hou and D.Robertson., 2000, Arslan and Abidin, 2019a). The determinants of government ownership should be in theory differ from determinants of private ownership.

This study used accounting-based measures for the robustness of results and these measures are well supported by prior studies (Chen and Cheung, 2000, Kaserer and Moldenhauer, 2008). Financial measures of firm performance like return on asset, return on equity and return on investment are used as dimensions of performance in this study. Return on asset means the net income/ total assets and return on equity means net income/ total equity. Return on investment measure is used to assess the efficacy of an investment and to compare the efficacy of the number of investments. These financial performance measures are frequently used in the prior literature and according to researchers, these financial measures signify the in-depth analysis of the firm (Arora and Bodhanwala, 2018, Dash and Raithatha, 2019, Arslan and Abidin, 2019b, Yeh, 2019).

THEORETICAL FRAMEWORK

In this study, the ownership structure is measured by taking the ownership concentration and owner identity as dimensions and performance of the firm will be measured by the accounting measure like return on assets, return on equity and return on investment to obtain the more reliable and authenticated findings. The dispersed, family, institutional and government ownership identities are used as dimensions of owner identity and to get more sophisticated results. The size, leverage, liquidity, firm age and growth rate are also taken as control variables in this study. The theoretical framework for this study is well supported by the existing literature and dimensions are chosen with the support of existing literature and previous studies (Luzhen and Morten, 2012, Villalonga and Amit, 2006, Welch, 2003, Attiya et al., 2012, Bahng, 2004, Blanca et al., 2009, Claessens et al., 2000). Figure 1 presents the theoretical framework of the study.

Figure 1. Theoretical Framework

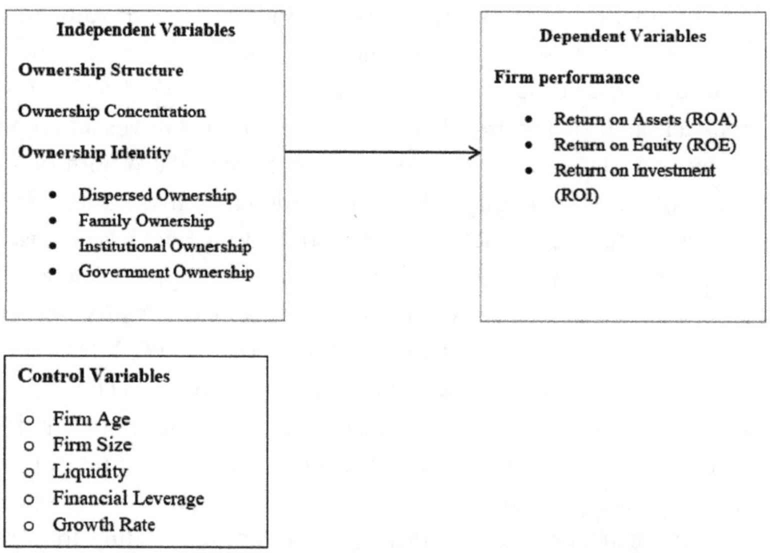

HYPOTHESIS DEVELOPMENT

Relationship Between Ownership Concentration and Firm Performance

A number of studies examined the relationship between ownership concentration and firm performance. The results of previous studies are mixed. Researchers also found no relationship between ownership concentration and firm performance (Thomsen and Pedersen, 2000). Some researchers examined that the variations in ownership structure yield the systematic deviations in performance (Kapopoulos and Lazaretou, 2006). Researchers used the data of 175 Greek firms and documented that concentrated ownership is positively related to the high performance of the firm (Kapopoulos and Lazaretou, 2006). The relationship between ownership concentration and firm performance is measured with the support of existing literature (Blanca et al., 2009, Attiya et al., 2012, King and Santor, 2008, Akimova and Schwodiauer, 2004, Gedajlovic and Shapiro, 2002, Han and Suk, 1998).

Hypothesis 1: Ownership Concentration has a positive effect on firm performance.
Hypothesis 1a: Ownership Concentration has a positive effect on Return on Assets.

The firm performance is measured by accounting measures. Return on assets is used as the measure of performance of the firm. Lee (2008) used the panel data of South Korean firms from the year 2000 to 2006 in order to examine the relationship between ownership structure and firm performance. He measured the performance by accounting measures. The researcher found that the accounting rate of return on assets increases by an increase in ownership concentration (Lee, 2008). A number of studies used Tobin's Q as a measure of firm performance (Attiya et al., 2012). In previous literature, many researchers documented the mixed results of the ownership structure and performance of the firm (Agrawal and Knoeber, 1996, Attiya et al., 2012, Gedajlovic and Shapiro, 2002).

Hypothesis 1b: Ownership Concentration has a positive effect on Return on Equity.

In many previous studies, the performance is measured by return on equity (Genc and Angelo, 2012). Some studies found the relationship as positive and some found it negative (Genc Alimehmeti and Angelo Paletta, Han and Suk, 1998). Some studies found mixed results (Leech and Leahy, 1991, Short, 1994). Return on Equity is a more sensitive measure in ownership structure.

Hypothesis 1c: Ownership Concentration has a positive effect on Return on Investment.

Return on investment is a good indicator of the performance of the firm (Leech and Leahy, 1991). It is used to evaluate the efficiency of the projects and the comparison of a number of projects. In literature, some researchers documented the positive relationship of return on investment with ownership concentration (Welch, 2003, Villalonga and Amit, 2006). In literature, few studies took a return on investment as a measure of performance. Most of the studies measured the performance of a firm by earning per share, return on asset and Tobin's Q (Attiya et al., 2012, Blanca et al., 2009, Gul et al., 2008, Kim and Yi, 2006).

Relationship Between Owner Identity and Firm Performance

A number of studies show the contradictory result for a consistent and strong relationship between owner identity and firm performance (Han and Suk, 1998, Hillier, 2004, Bahng, 2004). Some studies showed the positive effect of ownership identity with firm performance (McConaughy et al., 2001, Mishra et al., 2001). There were also found the negative significant impact of owner identity on firm performance (Bahng, 2004, Eckbo and Smith, 1998, Himmelberg et al., 1999).

Hypothesis 2: There is a positive relationship between owner identity and firm performance.
Hypothesis 2a: There is a positive relationship between owner identity and Return on Assets.
Hypothesis 2b: There is a positive relationship between owner identity and Return on Equity.
Hypothesis 2c: There is a positive relationship between owner identity and Return on Investment.

Owner identity has an impact on the performance of the firm because a different type of owners has different preferences. Due to the type of owners, the performance of the firm is affected due to the owners' own objectives. In previous literature, many researchers found different results due to different forms of owners (Short, 1994, Leech and Leahy, 1991, King and Santor, 2008).

RESEARCH DESIGN AND METHODOLOGY

The philosophy or research paradigm of this study reflects positivism. Consistent with the prior studies and study paradigm the approach of this study is deductive. The unit of analysis for the study is non-financial listed companies of Pakistan. Annual reports of only 65 non-financial listed companies were collected that includes non-financial sectors mainly textile, food and oil and gas for the year 2008 to 2012. The reason of choosing non-financial sector is their ownership structure which is different from other companies. Convenient sampling technique was incorporated for the selection of companies on the basis of the availability of annual reports. Secondary data was obtained from the published annual reports of companies operating in the non-financial sector of Pakistan. Least squares dummy variable model and random effect model were employed to estimate the impact of ownership structure on firm performance, to overcome the issues of endogenous explanatory as well as unobserved heteroscedasticity among variables. This method is well supported by prior literature (Genc and Angelo, 2012, Blanca et al., 2009, Attiya et al., 2012).

Econometric Techniques

The relationship and impact among variables incorporated in the study were estimated through GLS regression (Generalized least square method). The OLS assumption would not fulfil in the presence of heteroscedasticity as the GLS is applied when the variance of observations is unequal or when there are chances of a certain degree of correlation between the variables (Gujrati, 2004). The least-square dummy variable model (LSDV) which is also known as the fixed-effect model and panel data model was employed to conduct an in-depth analysis of variables. Panel data control for cross-sectional heterogeneity by observing individual firms and reduce the risk of biased and collinearity among variables (Rustam et al., 2013). After testing the general econometric model through the least square dummy variable and random effect models, Hausman (1978) specification test was applied to check statistically as to the selection of better model which explains the significance of the relationship between explanatory variables and dependent variable.

OPERATIONALISATION OF VARIABLES

In the absence of agency costs, firm performance is supposed to be independent of the ownership structure. A number of prior studies investigated the relationship between ownership structure and firm performance and found mixed results (Jayaraman et al., 2000, Kapopoulos and Lazaretou, 2006, Kim and Yi, 2006, Attiya et al., 2012, Blanca et al., 2009, Gross, 2007).

Ownership Structure

The Equity ownership structure as an important mechanism in corporate governance (Denis and McConnell, 2003), influence the quality of corporate governance and its ability to reduce agency costs (Berk and DeMarzo, 2007).

Ownership Concentration

Atkinson and Stiglitz (1980) defined ownership concentration as a trade-off between risk and incentive efficiency. Berle and Means (1932) discussed the separation of ownership and control in modern firms and argued that the separation of control and ownership leads to conflicts between managers and shareholders. In this study, the ownership concentration and owner identity were taken as dimensions of ownership structure. In the prior studies, different researchers used different measures for ownership structure according to the context of the study. Some researchers measured ownership concentration as a percentage of ownership in the hand of the largest shareholder (Thomsen and Pedersen, 2000). Some studies showed the threshold level at 15%. In some studies, the researchers used the top 10% as a threshold level, which means shareholders of the firm owned 10% or more than 10% of total shares (Larner, 1966). In some studies, the shares of a number of largest shareholders are combined to measure the ownership concentration (McConnell and Servaes, 1990, Gedajlovic and Shapiro, 2002). Some researchers used the proxy of the top five shareholders as a measure of ownership concentration (Attiya et al., 2012). In this study, owner concentration is measured by combining the top five numbers of the largest shareholders.

Owner Identity

A number of researchers used different measures for owner identity. Some researchers used owner identity as dummy variables and some used as an independent variable as different levels of shares (Luzhen and Morten, 2012, Tsai and Gu, 2007, Villalonga and Amit, 2006, Kole, 1996). The owner's identity is measured by using the dummies of dispersed, family, institutional and family ownership in this study. Dispersed ownership: value1 if the firm's largest owner owns less than 25% of shares, otherwise = 0. This threshold is supported by previous literature (Welch, 2003, Short et al., 2002). It is a dummy variable of dispersed owner identity. Family ownership: value 1 if the firm largest owner is family or foundation otherwise value 0. It is a dummy variable of family owner identity. Institutional ownership: value1 if the firm's largest ownership is an institution (financial or non-financial), otherwise 0. It is a dummy variable of institutional owner identity. Government institutions: value 1 if the firms' largest owner is a public authority, state or Government, otherwise value 0. It is a dummy variable of Government owner identity.

Firm Performance

In literature, the relationship between firm performance and ownership structure were investigated by a number of researchers (Chen and Cheung, 2000, Blanca et al., 2009, Barnhart and Rosenstein, 1988, Attiya et al., 2012, Akimova and Schwodiauer, 2004, Agrawal and Knoeber, 1996). Many researchers used accounting measures to measure the performance of firms (McConnell and Servaes, 1990, Kole, 1996, Himmelberg et al., 1999). A number of researchers used the return on assets (ROA) and return on equity (ROE) as a dimension of performance measure. In some studies, researchers applied both measures for examining the relationship between ownership structure and performance of firms (Welch, 2003, Denis and McConnell, 2003, Ødegaard and Bøhren, 2003). Return on investment and earnings per share were not frequently used as a measure in prior studies. Only a few researchers used these measures in their studies (Demsetz and Lehn, 1985, Leech and Leahy, 1991, Short, 1994). In this study, we used ROA, ROE, and ROI as a measure of performance. The Return on assets (ROA) is calculated with net income dividing by total assets, Return on Equity (ROE) is divided by net profit by total shareholder's equity. The Return on investment (ROI) is calculated by net profit divided by total long-term investment.

MODEL SPECIFICATION

In this study, the following least squares dummy variable model (LSDV) and panel data models are used to determine the impact of ownership structure on firm performance and the most appropriate model is selected. The Least square dummy variable model is also known as a fixed effect model (FEM) (Gujrati, 2004).

Least Square Dummy Variable Model

$$RoA_{it} = \beta_0 + \beta_1 OC_{1it} + \gamma_1 D_{1i} + \gamma_2 D_{2i} + \gamma_3 D_{3i} + \gamma_4 D_{4i}$$
$$+\beta_2 F\_LEV_{it} + \beta_3 FA_{it} + \beta_4 LIQ_{it} + \beta_5 SIZ_{it} + \beta_6 GRW_{it} + \mu_{it}$$

$$RoE_{it} = \beta_0 + \beta_1 OC_{1it} + \gamma_1 D_{1i} + \gamma_2 D_{2i} + \gamma_3 D_{3i} + \gamma_4 D_{4i}$$
$$+\beta_2 F\_LEV_{it} + \beta_3 FA_{it} + \beta_4 LIQ_{it} + \beta_5 SIZ_{it} + \beta_6 GRW_{it} + \mu_{it}$$

$$RoI_{it} = \beta_0 + \beta_1 OC_{1it} + \gamma_1 D_{1i} + \gamma_2 D_{2i} + \gamma_3 D_{3i} + \gamma_4 D_{4i}$$
$$+\beta_2 F\_LEV_{it} + \beta_3 FA_{it} + \beta_4 LIQ_{it} + \beta_5 SIZ_{it} + \beta_6 GRW_{it} + \mu_{it}$$

Random Effect Model

$$ROA_{it} = \beta 0_i + \beta_1 OC_{it} + \gamma_1 D_{1\,it} + \gamma_2 D_{2\,it} + \gamma_3 D_{3\,it} + \gamma_4 D_{4\,it} + \beta_2 F\_LEV_{it} + \beta_3 FA_{it} + \beta_4 LIQ_{it} + \beta_5 SIZ_{it} + \beta_6 GWR_{it} + \omega_{it}$$

$$ROE_{it} = \beta 0_i + \beta_1 OC_{it} + \gamma_1 D_{1\,it} + \gamma_2 D_{2\,it} + \gamma_3 D_{3\,it} + \gamma_4 D_{4\,it} + \beta_2 F\_LEV_{it} + \beta_3 FA_{it} + \beta_4 LIQ_{it} + \beta_5 SIZ_{it} + \beta_6 GWR_{it} + \omega_{it}$$

$$ROI_{it} = \beta 0_i + \beta_1 OC_{it} + \gamma_1 D_{1\,it} + \gamma_2 D_{2\,it} + \gamma_3 D_{3\,it} + \gamma_4 D_{4\,it} + \beta_2 F\_LEV_{it} + \beta_3 FA_{it} + \beta_4 LIQ_{it} + \beta_5 SIZ_{it} + \beta_6 GWR_{it} + \omega_{it}$$

Where

$$\omega_{it} = \varepsilon_I + \mu_{it}$$

The composite error term ω_{it} consists of two components i.e. ε_i, which is the cross section or individual specific and error component and μ_{it} which is the combined time series and cross- sectional error components. In the above model i stand for ith cross sectional unit and t stands for tth time period.

Where

Dependent Variables

ROA = Return on Assets (Net Income divided by Total Assets)
ROE = Return on Equity (Net Profit divided by Total Shareholder's Equity)
ROI = Return on Investment (Net income divided by Investment)

Independent Variables

OC = Ownership Concentration (Percentage of shares by proxy of top five shareholders)
D_1 = DISP = Dispersed Ownership or Insider Ownership (Dummy Variable)
$D_{2=}$ FAMI = Family Ownership (Dummy Variable)
D_3 = Institutional Ownership (Dummy Variable)
D_4 = Government Ownership (Dummy Variable)

Control Variables

F_LEV = Financial Leverage (Long Term Debt to Total Assets)
FA = Firm Age (logarithm of the number of years between founding and observed)
LIQ = Liquidity (Current Assets divided by Current Liabilities)
SIZ = Size (Logarithm of Total Assets of Firm)
GWR = Growth Rate (Growth Rate of Observed Year)

The fixed-effect model using the dummy variable is known as the least square dummy variable model (Gujrati, 2004). In the least square dummy variable model (LSDV), the intercept does not vary over time because it is time invariant. LSDV is appropriate where individual-specific intercepts may be correlated with one or more regressors (Gujrati, 2004). In random effect model or ECM (error components model, the intercept of an individual unit is randomly drawing from a much larger population with a constant mean value. The intercept varies over time because it is time-variant.

METHODOLOGY

Descriptive Statistics

Table 1 shows the summary statistics of the variables incorporated in the study. Descriptive statistics present simple summaries about the variables that have been incorporated in the study. There are selected 65 non-financial listed firms ranging from the year 2008 to 2012 and the total number of observations is 325. Moreover, Table 1 shows different statistical facts about data such as mean, medians, mode, standard deviation, skewness and Kurtosis of all explanatory, dependent and control variables. It also shows the minimum and maximum values of each variable. The mean value of ownership concentration (OC) is 57.43. The concentration of ownership is high in selected firms and these results are consistent with previous studies (La Porta et al., 1999, Luzhen and Morten, 2012). Table 1 also showed that the family firms are 24 firms from the 65 sampled firms and that is higher as compared to other owner identities (La Porta et al., 1999). Institutional ownership is the second highest with 22 firms. There are only 3 government firms included in the sampled firms. The number of dispersed or insider owner firms are 16 in number. According to prior studies, the family institutions were high in number (La Porta et al., 1999, Luzhen and Morten, 2012). The liquidity value is 61.48 from the sampled firms. The value of the firm age is 1.40. The average growth rate of firms is 5.37 percent per annum. The average size of the firms is 10.33.

Table 1. Descriptive Statistics of Variables used in Study

	ROE	*ROA*	*ROI*	*OC*	*Disp*	*Fami*	*Inst*	*Gov*	*Siz*	*FA*	*F_Lev*	*Liq*	*GWR*
Mean	9.12	4.13	14.38	57.43	0.25	0.37	0.34	0.05	10.33	1.40	11.63	61.48	5.37
Standard Error	1.26	0.60	2.16	0.66	0.02	0.03	0.03	0.01	0.05	0.01	0.94	4.44	0.13
Median	4.31	1.31	12.59	59.00	0.00	0.00	0.00	0.00	10.41	1.46	2.01	50.16	5.60
Mode	0.01	1.52	12.51	61.00	0.00	0.00	0.00	0.00	9.68	1.32	0.01	46.00	6.50
Standard Deviation	22.69	10.89	38.93	11.83	0.43	0.48	0.47	0.21	0.89	0.27	17.01	79.99	2.28
Kurtosis	2.34	7.60	2.91	0.63	-0.60	-1.71	-1.54	16.99	-0.52	1.32	2.87	47.23	-0.98
Skewness	-0.22	1.85	0.52	-0.63	1.18	0.54	0.69	4.35	-0.19	-1.11	1.77	5.97	0.05
Range	165.62	100.44	298.27	73.01	1.00	1.00	1.00	1.00	3.90	1.31	94.80	871.65	9.50
Minimum	-90.41	-38.44	-88.11	12.01	0.00	0.00	0.00	0.00	8.31	0.48	0.00	2.06	1.50
Maximum	75.21	62.00	210.16	85.02	1.00	1.00	1.00	1.00	12.21	1.79	94.80	873.71	11.00
Sum	2964.57	1343.21	4673.17	18663.50	80.00	120.00	110.00	15.00	3357.64	456.48	3778.24	19981.50	1745.50
Count	325	325	325	325	325	325	325	325	325	325	325	325	325

Least Square Dummy Variable Model Results of Ownership Structure and Firm Performance

Before proceeding to GLS (Generalized least square) regression, the study employed the common regression line equation. The results of the regression line show the insignificant causal relationship of ROA and ownership structure which includes ownership concentration and owner identity variables. The Durbin Watson value was 0.88 determining that there is a high autocorrelation among variables. Results also show that the t – values of family, institutional and government ownership are insignificant and the value of R^2 was 0.812 which is more than 0.80 and is on the higher side. According to Gujarati, (2004, pp 354), the insignificant t- values but higher overall R^2 is one of the root causes of multicollinearity in the data. Therefore, statistically, in the presence of these problems, the OLS assumption regarding BLUE is not fulfilled. The main reason behind these insignificant results may be the autocorrelation and heteroscedasticity problem (Gujarati, 2004). Due to these reasons in cross-section panel data, the regression line is to determine the insignificant relationship to the dependent variable of the study. The problem of heteroscedasticity may be due to the reason that cross-section weights are exceeding the number of periods included. To overcome this problem the cross-section weights are assigning to the data properties and the GLS method is employed to the data set (Gujrati, 2004).

Table 2. GLS results of Return on Assets and Ownership Structure

Dependent Variable: ROA				
Method: Panel EGLS (Cross-section Weights)				
Variable	**Coefficient**	**Std. Error**	**t-Statistic**	**Prob.**
C	22.17121	2.086212	10.62750	0.0000
DISP	-22.45085	1.797563	-12.48960*	0.0000
FAMI	-24.40773	1.723865	-14.15872*	0.0000
INST	-23.63149	1.766271	-13.37931*	0.0000
OC	0.059362	0.016711	3.552188*	0.0004
Weighted Statistics				
R-squared	0.423596	Mean dependent var		5.602179
Adjusted R-squared	0.416391	S.D. dependent var		11.86304
S.E. of regression	8.959031	Sum squared resid		25684.56
F-statistic	58.79162	Durbin-Watson stat		0.953162
Prob(F-statistic)	0.000000			
Unweighted Statistics				
R-squared	0.190711	Mean dependent var		4.132954
Sum squared resid	31121.42	Durbin-Watson stat		0.886691

Shows significance * at 1%, ** at 5%, and *** at 10% level of significance
Linear estimation after one-step weighting matrix

Table 2 shows the results of the least square dummy variable model GLS (cross-section weights) estimation. The statistical estimation of the least square dummy variable model shows that all explanatory variables have a highly significant result. Firstly, we run the regression with all the independent variables of the ownership structure. The regression could not be run due to the dummy variable trap. To cope with this issue, we remove one dummy variable of government ownership (Gujarati, 2004). According to p-values, the results showed the significance of all the explanatory variables. The negative t and p-value of ownership structure show a significant positive relationship. The t and p-value of dispersed, family and institutional ownership shows the significant inverse relationship with return on assets. The value of R^2 shows that 42.3596 percent variation in return on assets is due to these explanatory variables and remaining is due to unexplained variables.

Table 3 shows the results of the least square dummy variable model GLS (cross-section weights) estimation. The statistical estimation of the least square dummy variable model shows that explanatory variables have highly significant results except for the ownership concentration. Firstly, we run the regression with all the independent variables of the ownership structure. The regression could not be run due to the dummy variable trap. To overcome this issue, we remove one dummy variable of government ownership (Gujarati, 2004). According to p-values, the results showed the significance of all the explanatory variables. The t and p-value of ownership structure show a significant relationship with return on equity. The negative t and p-value of dispersed, family and institutional ownership show the significant inverse relationship with return on return. The value of R^2 shows that 34.85 percent variation in return on equity is due to these explanatory variables and remaining is due to unexplained variables that are not incorporated in this study.

Table 3. GLS results of Return on Equity and Ownership Structure

Dependent Variable: ROE				
Method: Panel EGLS (Cross-section weights)				
Variable	**Coefficient**	**Std. Error**	**t-Statistic**	**Prob.**
C	39.54584	4.904205	8.063660	0.0000
DISP	-30.31020	3.034051	-9.990010*	0.0000
FAMI	-32.11091	2.510730	-12.78947*	0.0000
INST	-29.15854	2.595826	-11.23286*	0.0000
OC	0.158377	0.059156	2.186835*	0.0045
Weighted Statistics				
R-squared	0.348538	Mean dependent var		15.13872
Adjusted R-squared	0.340395	S.D. dependent var		26.79948
S.E. of regression	21.45562	Sum squared resid		147309.9
F-statistic	42.80070	Durbin-Watson stat		1.149731
Prob(F-statistic)	0.000000			
Unweighted Statistics				
R-squared	0.037335	Mean dependent var		9.121754
Sum squared resid	160531.6	Durbin-Watson stat		1.327664

Shows significance * at 1%, ** at 5%, and *** at 10% level of significance
Linear estimation after one-step weighting matrix

Table 4. GLS results of Return on Investment and Ownership Structure

Dependent Variable: ROI				
Method: Panel EGLS (Cross-section weights)				
Variable	**Coefficient**	**Std. Error**	**t-Statistic**	**Prob.**
C	82.69816	12.11168	6.827966	0.0000
DISP	-52.95699	7.830760	-6.762689*	0.0000
FAMI	-61.62094	7.236323	-8.515505*	0.0000
INST	-57.29191	7.526381	-7.612146*	0.0000
OC	0.221853	0.132458	2.674888*	0.0509
Weighted Statistics				
R-squared	0.194494	Mean dependent var		20.81004
Adjusted R-squared	0.184425	S.D. dependent var		39.62703
S.E. of regression	34.90060	Sum squared resid		389776.7
F-statistic	19.31643	Durbin-Watson stat		1.094422
Prob(F-statistic)	0.000000			
Unweighted Statistics				
R-squared	0.170805	Mean dependent var		14.37898
Sum squared resid	407110.3	Durbin-Watson stat		1.047665

Shows significance * at 1%, ** at 5%, and *** at 10% level of significance
Linear estimation after one-step weighting matrix

Table 4 shows the results of the least square dummy variable model through GLS estimation. The statistical estimation of the least square dummy variable model shows that explanatory variables have a highly significant result except for the ownership concentration. Firstly, we run the regression with all the independent variables of the ownership structure. The regression could not be run due to the dummy variable trap. To overcome this issue, we remove one dummy variable of government ownership (Gujarati, 2004). According to the p-values, the empirical findings showed the significance of the explanatory variables. The t and p-value of ownership structure show a significant relationship with return on investment. The negative t and p-value of dispersed, family and institutional ownership show the significant inverse relationship with return on return. The value of R^2 shows that 19.44 percent variation in return on investment is due to these explanatory variables and remaining is due to unexplained variables.

HAUSMAN SPECIFICATION TEST

Table 5, Table 6 and Table 7 compares panel data models with dependent variables of ROA, ROE, and ROI. Hausman test empirically determines which model best explains the relationship among variables incorporated in the model. The hypotheses of the Hausman test are:

H_1 Random effects would be inconsistent (Fixed will be certainly consistent and efficient)
H_0 Random effect would be consistent and efficient

According to confidence the p values in Table 5, 6 and 7 are (0.424, 0.0541 and 0.0491) respectively which is less than 0.05 (level of significance), so the hypotheses H_1 is accepted that random effect model is inconsistent and least square dummy variable model which is also known as fixed effect model is certainly consistent and efficient. This study also incorporated a fixed effect (best alternative), model. The Hausman specification test statistically determines that the least square dummy variable model (cross-section weights) is best to explain the relationship of independent variables on firm performance.

Table 5. Results of Hausman Test

Correlated Random Effects - Hausman Test				
Test Cross-section Random Effects				
Test Summary		**Chi-Sq. Statistic**	**Chi-Sq. d.f.**	**Prob.**
Cross-section random		22.177323	4	0.0424
Cross-section Random Effects Test Comparisons				
Variable	**Fixed**	**Random**	**Var(Diff.)**	**Prob.**
OC	0.015215	0.016996	0.000002	0.2506
INST	0.003645	0.005346	0.000001	0.0996
FAMI	0.000742	0.000904	0.000000	0.5018
DISP	0.003151	0.002966	0.000000	0.4274
Cross-section Random Effects Test Equation				
Dependent Variable: ROA **Method: Panel Least Squares**				
Variable	**Coefficient**	**Std. Error**	**t-Statistic**	**Prob.**
C	44.74287	0.903751	49.50794	0.0000
OC	0.015215	0.015794	0.963354	0.3358
INST	0.003645	0.006760	0.539219	0.5900
FAMI	0.000742	0.000299	2.478789	0.0135
DISP	0.003151	0.001596	1.974841	0.0489
R-squared	0.503155	Mean dependent var		44.87900
Adjusted R-squared	0.492232	S.D. dependent var		8.956586
S.E. of regression	6.073660	Akaike info criterion		5.244425
Sum squared resid	4591.429	Schwarz criterion		6.029310
Log likelihood	-1446.350	Hannan-Quinn criter.		5.550148
F-statistic	43.16523	Durbin-Watson stat		1.499831
Prob(F-statistic)	0.000000			

Table 6. Results of Hausman Test

Correlated Random Effects - Hausman Test				
Test Cross-section Random Effects				
Test Summary		**Chi-Sq. Statistic**	**Chi-Sq. d.f.**	**Prob.**
Cross-section random		20.258745	4	0.05041
Cross-section Random Effects Test Comparisons				
Variable	**Fixed**	**Random**	**Var(Diff.)**	**Prob.**
OC	41.28597	0.012846	0.000012	0.3526
INST	0.013265	0.006316	0.000005	0.1098
FAMI	0.002649	0.001001	0.000000	0.4904
DISP	0.000841	0.002568	0.000000	0.4664
Cross-section Random Effects Test Equation				
Dependent Variable: ROE **Method: Panel Least Squares**				
Variable	**Coefficient**	**Std. Error**	**t-Statistic**	**Prob.**
C	41.28597	0.786930	58.58741	0.0000
OC	0.013265	0.014853	0.875421	0.3698
INST	0.002649	0.006081	0.596325	0.5140
FAMI	0.000541	0.004259	1.685412	0.0149
DISP	0.002141	0.001385	1.612538	0.0544
R-squared	0.428538	Mean dependent var		41.58900
Adjusted R-squared	0.413892	S.D. dependent var		9.154276
S.E. of regression	5.077460	Akaike info criterion		6.241421
Sum squared resid	6855.751	Schwarz criterion		5.023910
Log likelihood	-1866.520	Hannan-Quinn criter.		4.440138
F-statistic	50.12583	Durbin-Watson stat		1.348161
Prob(F-statistic)	0.000000			

Table 8 reports the GLS regression results of the least square dummy variable model by taking control variables and explanatory variables with return on assets. The results show in Table 8 are mixed. Some variables have significant results, and some have insignificant results. The ownership concentration has a significant impact on return on assets. The t value (3.40) and p-value (0.0008) shows a strong significant causal relationship with return on assets. According to t and p-value, liquidity, growth rate, and financial leverage have an insignificant relationship with return on assets. The t and p-value of these variables are greater than 0.05 (level of significance). The firm age and size have a significant relationship with return on assets because their t and p values are strongly significant. The p-value of size is 0.0000 which is less than 0.05 (level of significance) shows a very strong causal relationship with return on assets. The dummy variable of owner identity has also the significant causal relationship with return on assets in respect of their t stats and p values. The value of R^2 is 35.83; it means that the 35.83 percent variation in return on assets is due to these explanatory and control variables and the remaining 64.17 percent change is due to unexplained variables.

Table 7. Results of Hausman Test

Correlated Random Effects - Hausman Test				
Test Cross-section Random Effects				
Test Summary		**Chi-Sq. Statistic**	**Chi-Sq. d.f.**	**Prob.**
Cross-section random		19.547861	4	0.0491
Cross-section Random Effects Test Comparisons				
Variable	**Fixed**	**Random**	**Var(Diff.)**	**Prob.**
OC	0.018355	0.019856	0.000012	0.2984
INST	0.004125	0.006324	0.000015	0.0896
FAMI	0.000917	0.000802	0.000001	0.4987
DISP	0.004859	0.003857	0.000003	0.4958
Cross-section Random Effects Test Equation				
Dependent Variable: ROI **Method: Panel Least Squares**				
Variable	**Coefficient**	**Std. Error**	**t-Statistic**	**Prob.**
C	30.68527	0.805974	35.52844	0.0000
OC	0.018355	0.019561	0.874561	0.4851
INST	0.004125	0.007780	0.486985	0.7125
FAMI	0.000917	0.000498	1.274592	0.0279
DISP	0.004859	0.002586	1.773851	0.0407
R-squared	0.305285	Mean dependent var		34.52841
Adjusted R-squared	0.299232	S.D. dependent var		8.574115
S.E. of regression	7.075440	Akaike info criterion		6.485741
Sum squared resid	8580.914	Schwarz criterion		6.029310
Log likelihood	-1356.530	Hannan-Quinn criter.		6.054151
F-statistic	47.18965	Durbin-Watson stat		1.456351
Prob(F-statistic)	0.000000			

Table 9 reports the GLS regression results of the least square dummy variable model by taking control variables and explanatory variables with return on equity. The results show in Table 9 are mixed. Some variables have significant results, and some have insignificant results. The ownership concentration has significant casual relation with return on equity. The t value (1.32) and p-value (0.0446) shows the significant casual relation with return on equity. According to t and p-value, liquidity, growth rate, financial leverage, and firm age has an insignificant causal relationship with return on equity. The t and p-value of these variables are greater than 0.05 (level of significance). The size has a significant relationship with return on equity because their t and p values are strongly significant. The p-value of size is 0.05 which is equal to 0.05 (level of significance) shows the significant causal relationship with return on equity. The dummy variable of owner identity has also the significant causal relationship with return on equity with respect to their t stats and p values. The value of R^2 is 39.99; it means that the 39.99 percent variation in return on equity is due to these explanatory and control variables and the remaining 60.01 percent change is due to unexplained variables.

Table 8. GLS results of Control and Explanatory Variables on Return on Assets

Dependent Variable: ROA				
Method: Panel EGLS (Cross-section Weights)				
Variable	**Coefficient**	**Std. Error**	**t-Statistic**	**Prob.**
C	33.33963	4.938980	6.750307	0.0000
OC	0.072954	0.021443	3.402272*	0.0008
LIQ	0.011692	0.006434	1.817346*	0.0701
INST	-19.79470	2.840624	-6.968433*	0.0000
GWR	-0.124168	0.072073	-1.722802*	0.0859
FA	-4.583395	0.917028	-4.998099*	0.0000
F_LEV	-0.008396	0.016173	-0.519177*	0.6040
SIZ	-0.802778	0.300138	-2.674694*	0.0079
FAMI	-21.56812	2.818311	-7.652852*	0.0000
DISP	-19.88245	2.842210	-6.995421*	0.0000
Weighted Statistics				
R-squared	0.358341	Mean dependent var		5.154920
Adjusted R-squared	0.340008	S.D. dependent var		10.64768
S.E. of regression	8.867991	Sum squared resid		24772.00
F-statistic	19.54609	Durbin-Watson stat		0.815224
Prob(F-statistic)	0.000000			
Unweighted Statistics				
R-squared	0.247894	Mean dependent var		4.132954
Sum squared resid	28922.42	Durbin-Watson stat		0.706377

Shows significance * at 1%, ** at 5%, and *** at 10% level of significance
Linear estimation after one-step weighting matrix

Table 10 reports the GLS regression results of the least square dummy variable model by taking control variables and explanatory variables with return on investment. Table 10 shows mixed results. Some variables have significant results, and some have insignificant results. The ownership concentration has significant casual relation with return on equity. The t value (1.14) and p-value (0.04) shows the significant causal relationship with return on investment. According to t and p-value, liquidity, growth rate, financial leverage, and firm age has an insignificant relationship with return on investment. The t and p-value of these variables are greater than 0.05 (level of significance). The size has a significant relationship with return on investment because their t and p values are strongly significant. The p-value of size is 0.0000 which is less than 0.05 (level of significance) shows a significant causal relationship with return on investment. The dummy variable of owner identity has also the significant causal relationship with return on investment in respect of their t stats and p values. The value of R^2 is 24.97; it means that the 24.97 percent variation in return on investment is due to these explanatory and control variables and the remaining 75.03 percent change is due to unexplained variables.

Table 9. GLS results of Control and Explanatory Variables on Return on Equity

Dependent Variable: ROE				
Method: Panel EGLS (Cross-section Weights)				
Variable	**Coefficient**	**Std. Error**	**t-Statistic**	**Prob.**
C	51.22685	10.33242	4.957873	0.0000
FAMI	-26.52230	4.273757	-6.205851*	0.0000
DISP	-26.06285	4.547367	-5.731415*	0.0000
INST	-23.81148	4.255721	-5.595168*	0.0000
OC	-0.020514	0.062906	-1.326099*	0.0446
LIQ	0.015122	0.009394	1.609770*	0.1084
GWR	-0.279346	0.233164	-1.198067*	0.2318
FA	-2.635636	2.555247	-1.031460*	0.3031
F_LEV	0.067892	0.040015	1.696657*	0.0907
SIZ	-1.477731	0.764678	-1.932488*	0.0542
Weighted Statistics				
R-squared	0.399915	Mean dependent var		15.17810
Adjusted R-squared	0.382770	S.D. dependent var		27.22947
S.E. of regression	21.14030	Sum squared resid		140777.4
F-statistic	23.32509	Durbin-Watson stat		1.118947
Prob(F-statistic)	0.000000			
Unweighted Statistics				
R-squared	0.035621	Mean dependent var		9.121754
Sum squared resid	160817.3	Durbin-Watson stat		1.296922

Shows significance * at 1%, ** at 5%, and *** at 10% level of significance
Linear estimation after one-step weighting matrix

CONCLUSION

It is commonly accepted that the ownership structure is a significant component of corporate governance. The nature of the relationship between ownership structure and firm performance has been a core issue in corporate governance literature. As prior studies have given divergent theories and substantiation results on the relationship between ownership concentration and firm performance (Fama and Jensen, 1983, Demsetz and Lehn, 1985), there is always room for further evidence. Existing studies are divergent in terms of mixed findings (i.e. absent, linear and non-linear), time-period, contextual settings, and sample selection. This study has examined empirically the relationship between ownership structure and firm performance using a panel of listed firms of Pakistan from the year 2008 to the year 2012. The results of this study reveal that the Pakistani firms have more concentration of ownership which is the response of weak legal environment and these results are validated by the findings of La Porta et al. (1998, 1999, 2000). The findings of the study show that the results of the least square dummy variable model are more significant than the random effect model and the least square dummy variable model is more consistent and efficient because the Hausman test is significant. The results of the study show

Table 10. GLS results of Control and Explanatory Variables on Return on Investment

Dependent Variable: ROI				
Method: Panel EGLS (Cross-section Weights)				
Variable	**Coefficient**	**Std. Error**	**t-Statistic**	**Prob.**
C	-6.885661	27.37526	-0.251529	0.8016
FAMI	-49.67974	13.18339	-3.768358*	0.0002
DISP	-38.96528	14.09332	-2.764804*	0.0060
INST	-50.62574	13.49998	-3.750061*	0.0002
OC	-0.136305	0.143920	-1.147085*	0.0443
LIQ	0.006072	0.027938	0.217342*	0.8281
GWR	-0.171669	0.510210	-0.336468*	0.7367
FA	-1.645652	5.540288	-0.297034*	0.7666
F_LEV	-0.050762	0.073627	-0.689446*	0.4911
SIZ	7.541723	1.611889	4.678811*	0.0000
Weighted Statistics				
R-squared	0.249706	Mean dependent var		20.97364
Adjusted R-squared	0.228269	S.D. dependent var		39.63881
S.E. of regression	33.87718	Sum squared resid		361514.0
F-statistic	11.64836	Durbin-Watson stat		1.058683
Prob(F-statistic)	0.000000			
Unweighted Statistics				
R-squared	0.193533	Mean dependent var		14.37898
Sum squared resid	395951.7	Durbin-Watson stat		1.034325

Shows significance * at 1%, ** at 5%, and *** at 10% level of significance
Linear estimation after one-step weighting matrix

that the ownership structure has a significant effect on firm performance. Result reveals that there is a significant positive effect of ownership concentration on accounting measures of firm performance. These results are consistent with previous studies (Attiya et al., 2012, Genc and Angelo, 2012, Gedajlovic and Shapiro, 2002, Alabdullah, 2018). The results of this study reveal that there is a significant negative relationship between dispersed ownership and accounting measures of firm performance. These results are consistent with previous studies (Bahng, 2004, Eckbo and Smith, 1998, Himmelberg et al., 1999, Demsetz and Lehn, 1985). This study supports the argument that dispersed ownership leads to the creation of a hold-up problem. The findings of our study reveal that there is a significant negative impact of family ownership on accounting measure i.e. ROA, ROE, and ROI. These results are consistent with Villalonga and Amit, (2006), Hillier, (2004), Klein et al. (2005) and Oreland, (2006) findings. It supports the prior argument that conflict between the family owners and minority shareholders increases with the increased degree of family ownership. The findings of this study reveal that institutional ownership has a significant negative effect on ROA, ROE, and ROI. Prior studies also support this result. The studies of Pound (1988) and Hand (1990) also found a negative relationship between institutional ownership and firm performance of a firm. The results of the study reveal that government ownership has also a significant effect on the performance of a firm. The result of the study reveals that liquidity, growth rate, and financial leverage have an insignificant relationship with return on assets. The findings of the study show that control variables of firm liquidity, growth rate, financial leverage, and firm age have an insignificant relationship with return on equity and return on investment. Because the greater level of financial leverage is an alarming sign for the firm and it is also considered that there are poor management skills among the firm stakeholders (Holderness, 2003, La Porta et al., 2000). These results are consistent with the findings of prior studies (Agrawal and Mandelker, 1990).The result also reveals that size has a significant relationship with accounting measures of performance. These results are supported by the findings of Pedersen and Thomsen (1999).

Based on the findings, the study proposes some recommendations for non-financial firms, investors/shareholders and corporate governance setters. The findings of the study reveal that the percentage of ownership concentration is positively associated with financial performance in non-financial listed firms of Pakistan. The findings of the study also help policymakers to make such policies that can reduce the conflicts between owners and managers of non-financial listed firms of Pakistan. The study also recommends that there should be a need for interest alignment between shareholders and managers of the firms. The findings of the study also recommend that the high level of ownership concentrated has a positive effect on firm performance and increase the performance of firms. The findings of the study have some constraints. First, the study considers the ownership structure variables only in the non-financial sector of the economy, hence, the sample can be extended to other sectors of the economy like financial, automobile and parts, electricity and pharmaceutical for generalization of results. The second limitation of the study is about the measurement of ownership concentration, owner identity, and firm performance. Some other proxies can be taken for measuring ownership concentration.

REFERENCES

Agrawal, A., & Knoeber, C. R. (1996). Firm Performance and Mechanisms to Control Agency Problems between Managers and Shareholders. *Journal of Financial and Quantitative Analysis*, *31*(3), 377. doi:10.2307/2331397

Agrawal, A., & Mandelker, G. N. (1990). Large Shareholders and the Monitoring of Managers: The Case of Antitakeover Charter Amendments. *Journal of Financial and Quantitative Analysis*, *25*(2), 143. doi:10.2307/2330821

Akimova, I., & Schwodiauer, G. (2004). Ownership Structure, Corporate Governance, and Enterprise Performance: Empirical Results for Ukraine. *International Advances in Economic Research*, *10*(1), 28–42. doi:10.1007/BF02295575

Al-Matari, E. M., Al-Dhaafri, H. S., & Al-Swidi, A. K. (2019). The Effect of Government Ownership, Foreign Ownership, Institutional Ownership, and Audit Quality on Firm Performance of Listed Companies in Oman: A Conceptual Framework. *Proceedings of the Second International Conference on the Future of ASEAN (ICoFA) 2017, 1*, 585-595.

Alabdullah, T. T. Y. (2018). The relationship between ownership structure and firm financial performance. *Benchmarking*, *25*(1), 319–333. doi:10.1108/BIJ-04-2016-0051

Anderson, R. C., & Reeb, D. M. (2003). Founding-Family Ownership and Firm Performance: Evidence from the S&P 500. *The Journal of Finance*, *58*(3), 1301–1328. doi:10.1111/1540-6261.00567

Anwar, W., & Tabassum, N. (2011). Impact of ownership concentration on the operating performance of Pakistani firms. *Asian Economic and Financial Review*, *1*, 147–150.

Arora, A., & Bodhanwala, S. (2018). Relationship between corporate governance index and firm performance: Indian evidence. *Global Business Review*, *19*(3), 675–689. doi:10.1177/0972150917713812

Arora, A., & Sharma, C. (2016). Corporate governance and firm performance in developing countries: Evidence from India. *Corporate Governance*, *16*(2), 420–436. doi:10.1108/CG-01-2016-0018

Arslan, M., & Abidin, S. (2019). Institutional Determinants of Good Corporate Governance: Evidence from Emerging Economy. In *23rd New Zealand Finance Colloquium, 2019a Lincoln University*. Lincoln, New Zealand: NZFC.

Arslan, M., & Abidin, S. (2019b). Nexus between corporate governance practices and cost of capital in PSX listed firms. *Cogent Economics & Finance*, *7*(1), 1600222. doi:10.1080/23322039.2019.1600222

Arslan, M., Abidin, S., Alqatan, A. & Roudaki, J. (2019). Corporate Governance in Extreme Institutional Environment: Evidence From Emerging Economy. *Corporate Ownership & Control,* 17.

Arslan, M., & Alqatan, A. (2020). Role of institutions in shaping corporate governance system: Evidence from emerging economy. *Heliyon*, *6*(3), e03520. doi:10.1016/j.heliyon.2020.e03520 PMID:32181393

Atkinson, A. B., & Stiglitz, J. E. (1980). *Lectures on public economics*. McGraw-Hill.

Attiya, Javid, & Iqbal. (2012). Ownership Concentration, Corporate Governance and Firm Performance: Evidence from Pakistan. Pakistan Institute of Development Economics.

Bahng, J. S. (2004). *Nonlinear Effects of Insider Ownership on Corporate Value: Korean Evidence.* SSRN Working Paper Series.

Barnhart, S. W., & Rosenstein, S. (1988). Board Composition, Managerial Ownership and Firm Performance: An Empirical Analysis. *Financial Review*, *33*(4), 1–16. doi:10.1111/j.1540-6288.1998.tb01393.x

Berk, J., & Demarzo, P. (2007). *Corporate finance* (International ed.). Pearson Education.

Berle, A., & Means, G. (1932). *The Modern Corporation and Private Property*. Harcourt, Brace & World.

Bhagat, S., & Bolton, B. (2019). Corporate governance and firm performance: The sequel. *Journal of Corporate Finance*, *58*, 142–168. doi:10.1016/j.jcorpfin.2019.04.006

Blanca, A., Txomin, I., & Amaia, M. (2009). *Ownership Structure And Performance in Non-Listed Firms: Evidence From Spain. UPV/EHU*. University of the Basque Country.

Chen, Z., & Cheung, Y. L. (2000). *Corporate governance, firm performance and agency conflicts in closely-held firms: evidence from Hong Kong*. Working paper. University of Hong Kong.

Claessens, S., Djankov, S., & Lang, L. H. P. (2000). The separation of ownership and control in East Asian corporations. *Journal of Financial Economics*, *58*(1-2), 81–112. doi:10.1016/S0304-405X(00)00067-2

Daraghma, Z. M. A., & Alsinawi, A. A. (2010). Board of Directors, Management Ownership, and Capital Structure and Its Effect on Performance: The Case of Palestine Securities Exchange. *International Journal of Business and Management*, *5*(11), 118–125. doi:10.5539/ijbm.v5n11p118

Dash, S. R., & Raithatha, M. (2019). Corporate governance and firm performance relationship: Implications for risk-adjusted return behavior. *Managerial and Decision Economics*, *40*(8), 923–940. doi:10.1002/mde.3080

Demsetz, H., & Lehn, K. (1985). The Structure of Corporate Ownership: Causes and Consequences. *Journal of Political Economy*, *93*(6), 1155–1177. doi:10.1086/261354

Denis, D. K., & Mcconnell, J. J. (2003). International Corporate Governance. *Journal of Financial and Quantitative Analysis*, *38*(1), 1. doi:10.2307/4126762

Eckbo, B. E., & Smith, D. C. (1998). The Conditional Performance of Insider Trades. *The Journal of Finance*, *53*(2), 467–498. doi:10.1111/0022-1082.205263

Fama, E. F., & Jensen, M. C. (1983). Separation of Ownership and Control. *The Journal of Law & Economics*, *26*(2), 301–325. doi:10.1086/467037

Gedajlovic, E., & Shapiro, D. M. (2002). Ownership structure and firm profitability in Japan. *Academy of Management Journal*, *45*, 565–575.

Genc, A., & Angelo, P. (2012). Ownership Concentration and Effects over Firm Performance: Evidence From Italy. *European Scientific Journal*, 8.

Genc Alimehmeti, P. & Angelo Paletta, P. (n.d.). Ownership concentration and effects over firm performance: Evidences from Italy. *European Scientific Journal,* 8.

Gross, K. (2007). *Equity Ownership and Performance: An Empirical Study of German Traded Companies*. Physica Verlag.

Gujarati. (2004). *Basic Econometrics*. McGraw-Hill.

Gul, F., Kim, J., & Qiu, A. A. (2008). Ownership concentration, foreign shareholding, audit quality, and stock price synchronicity: Evidence from China. *Journal of Financial Economics*, 95.

Han, K. C., & Suk, D. Y. (1998). The Effect of Ownership Structure on Firm Performance: Additional Evidence. *Review of Financial Economics*, *7*(2), 143–155. doi:10.1016/S1058-3300(99)80150-5

Hand, J.R.M. (1990). A Test of the Extended Functional Fixation Hypothesis. *The Accounting Review*, *65*, 740.

Hasan, A., & Butt, S. A. (2009). Impact of Ownership Structure and Corporate Governance on Capital Structure of Pakistani Listed Companies. *International Journal of Business and Management*, *4*(2), 50–57. doi:10.5539/ijbm.v4n2p50

Hillier, D. (2004). *Firm Performance, Entrenchment and Managerial Succession in Family Firms.* SSRN eLibrary.

Himmelberg, C. P., Hubbard, R. G., & Palia, D. (1999). Understanding the determinants of managerial ownership and the link between ownership and performance. *Journal of Financial Economics*, *53*(3), 353–384. doi:10.1016/S0304-405X(99)00025-2

Holderness, C. (2003). A Survey of Blockholders and Corporate Control. *Economic Policy Review*, *9*, 51–63.

Hou, K., & Robertson, D. (2000). *Towards a Property Rights view of Ownership*. Working Paper.

Jayaraman, N., Khorana, A., Nelling, E., & Covin, J. (2000). CEO Founder Status and Firm Financial Performance; Narayanan. *Strategic Management Journal*, *21*(12), 1215–1224. doi:10.1002/1097-0266(200012)21:12<1215::AID-SMJ146>3.0.CO;2-0

Jelinek, K., & Stuerke, P. (2009). The Nonlinear Relation between Agency Costs and Managerial Equity Ownership: Evidence of Decreasing Benefits of Increasing Ownership. *International Journal of Managerial Finance*, *5*(2), 156–178. doi:10.1108/17439130910947886

Jensen, M. C., & Meckling, W. H. (1976). Theory of the Firm: Managerial Behavior, Agency Costs and Ownership Structure. *Journal of Financial Economics*, *3*(4), 305–360. doi:10.1016/0304-405X(76)90026-X

Jiang, P. (2004). The Relationship between Ownership Structure and Firm Performance: An Empirical Analysis over Heilongjiang Listed companies. *Journal of Nature and Science*, *2*, 87–91.

Kapopoulos, P., & Lazaretou, S. (2006). *Corporate Ownership Structure and Firm Performance: Evidence from Greek Firms*. Special Studies Division, Working Paper No.37. Bank of Greece: Economic Research Department.

Kaserer, C., & Moldenhauer, B. (2008). Insider Ownership and Corporate Performance: Evidence from Germany. *Academic Review of Managerial Science*, *2*(1), 1–35. doi:10.100711846-007-0009-3

Khan, F.,, & Nouman, M. (2017). Does Ownership Structure Affect Firm's Performance? Empirical Evidence from Pakistan. Empirical Evidence from Pakistan, 19.

Khan, I. A. (2014). Adaptation and convergence in corporate governance to international norms in Pakistan (PhD). University of Glasgow.

Khan, I. A. (2017). Enforcement of Corporate Laws and Stock Market Reforms in Pakistan. *Pakistan Journal of social Sciences,* 37.

Kim, J.-B., & Yi, C. H. (2006). Ownership structure, business group affiliation, listing status, and earning management: Evidence from Korea. *Contemporary Accounting Research*, *23*(2), 427–464. doi:10.1506/7T5B-72FV-MHJV-E697

King, M. R., & Santor, E. (2008). Family values: Ownership structure, performance and capital structure of Canadian firms. *Journal of Banking & Finance*, *32*(11), 2423–2432. doi:10.1016/j.jbankfin.2008.02.002

Klein, P., Shapiro, D., & Young, J. (2005). Corporate Governance, Family Ownership and Firm Value: The Canadian evidence. *Corporate Governance*, *13*(6), 769–784. doi:10.1111/j.1467-8683.2005.00469.x

Kole, S. (1996). Managerial ownership and firm performance: Incentives or rewards? *Advances in Financial Economics*, *2*, 119–149.

Kumar, N. & Singh, J. (2013). Effect of board size and promoter ownership on firm value: some empirical findings from India. *Corporate Governance: The International Journal of Business in Society*.

La Porta, R., Lopez-De-Silane, F., & Shleifer, A. (1999). Corporate Ownership around the World. *The Journal of Finance*, *54*(2), 471–517. doi:10.1111/0022-1082.00115

La Porta, R., Lopez-De-Silanes, F., Shleifer, A., & Vishny, R. W. (1998). Law and Finance. *Journal of Political Economy*, *106*(6), 1113–1155. doi:10.1086/250042

La Porta, R., Lopez-De-Silanes, F., Shleifer, A., & Vishny, R. W. (2000). Agency Problems and Dividend Policies around the World. *The Journal of Finance*, *55*(1), 1–33. doi:10.1111/0022-1082.00199

Larner, R. J. (1966). Ownership and Control in the 200 Largest Non-Financial Corporations. *The American Economic Review*, *56*, 777.

Lee, S. (2008). *Ownership Structure and Financial Performance: Evidence from Panel Data of South Korea.* Working Paper No.17. University of Utah, Department of Economics.

Leech, D., & Leahy, J. (1991). Ownership structure, control type classifications and the performance of large British companies. *Economic Journal (London)*, *101*(409), 1418–1437. doi:10.2307/2234893

Luzhen, C., & Morten, B. 2012. The effect of ownership structure on firm performance: Evidence from Non-Financial listed Companies in Scandinavia (MSc). Aarhus University.

Mcconaughy, D. L., Matthews, C. H., & Fialko, A. S. (2001). Founding Family Controlled Firms:Performance, Risk, and Value. *Journal of Small Business Management*, *39*(1), 31–49. doi:10.1111/0447-2778.00004

Mcconaughy, D. L. C. S., Mishra, M. C., Walker, G. V., & Henderson, J. (1998). Founding Family Controlled Firms: Efficiency and Value. *Review of Financial Economics*, *7*(1), 1–19. doi:10.1016/S1058-3300(99)80142-6

Mcconnell, J. J., & Servaes, H. (1990). Additional evidence on equity ownership and corporate value. *Journal of Financial Economics*, *27*(2), 595–612. doi:10.1016/0304-405X(90)90069-C

Mishra, C., Randoy, T., & Jenssen, J. I. (2001). The Effect of Founding Family Influence on Firm Value and Corporate Governance: A Study of Norwegian Firms. *Journal of International Financial Management & Accounting*, *12*(3), 235–259. doi:10.1111/1467-646X.00073

Monks, R. A. & Minnow., N. (2001). *Corporate Governance*. Oxford: Blackwell.

Morck, Strangeland, & Yeung. (2000). Inherited wealth, Corporate Control and Economic Growth? In *Concentrated Corporate Ownership*. Chicago: University of Chicago Press.

Ødegaard, B. A., & Bøhren, Ø. (2003). *Governance and Performance Revisited.* SSRN Working Paper Series.

Oreland, C. (2006). *Family Control, Firm Performance and Dividend Policy*. SSRN eLibrary.

Ozili, P. K., & Uadiale, O. (2017). Ownership concentration and bank profitability. *Future Business Journal*, *3*(2), 159–171. doi:10.1016/j.fbj.2017.07.001

Parthiban, D., Hitt, M. A., & Gimeno, J. (2001). The influence of activism by institutional investors on R&D. *Academy of Management Journal*, *44*, 144–157.

Pedersen, T., & Thomsen, S. (1999). Economic and Systemic Explanations of Ownership Concentration among Europe's Largest Companies. *International Journal of the Economics of Business*, *6*(3), 367–381. doi:10.1080/13571519984133

Phung, D. N., & Mishra, A. V. (2016). Ownership structure and firm performance: Evidence from Vietnamese listed firms. *Australian Economic Papers*, *55*(1), 63–98. doi:10.1111/1467-8454.12056

Pound, J. (1988). The information effects of takeover bids and resistance. *Journal of Financial Economics*, *22*(2), 207–227. doi:10.1016/0304-405X(88)90069-4

Rustam, S., Rashid, K., & Zaman, K. (2013). The relationship between audit committees, compensation incentives and corporate audit fees in Pakistan. *Economic Modelling*, *31*, 697–716. doi:10.1016/j.econmod.2013.01.008

Salman, F., & Siddiqui, K. (2013). Corporate Governance in Pakistan: From the Perspective of Securities and Exchange Commission of Pakistan. *IUP Journal of Corporate Governance*, *12*, 13.

Samza, F. (2016). Corporate governance in Pakistan: Beyond a minimalist approach (Doctor of Philosophy). University of Bedfordshire.

Sanchez-Ballesta, J., & Garcia-Meca, E. (2007). A Meta analytic Vision of the Effect of Ownership Structure on Firm Performance. *Journal of Corporate Governance,* 15.

Shah, M. H., Xiao, Z., Quresh, S., & Ahmad, M. (2020). Internal pyramid structure, contract enforcement, minority investor protection, and firms' performance: Evidence from emerging economies. *Research in International Business and Finance*, *52*, 101170. doi:10.1016/j.ribaf.2019.101170

Short, H. (1994). Ownership, Control, Financial Structure and The Performance of Firms. *Journal of Economic Surveys*, *8*(3), 203–249. doi:10.1111/j.1467-6419.1994.tb00102.x

Short, H., Keasey, K., & Duxbury, D. (2002). Capital Structure, Management Ownership and Large External Shareholders: A UK Analysis. *International Journal of the Economics of Business*, *9*(3), 375–399. doi:10.1080/13571510210000010382

Thomsen, S., & Pedersen, T. (2000). Ownership structure and economic performance in the largest European countries. *Strategic Management Journal*, *21*(6), 689–705. doi:10.1002/(SICI)1097-0266(200006)21:6<689::AID-SMJ115>3.0.CO;2-Y

Tsai, H., & Gu, Z. (2007). Institutional Ownership and Firm Performance: Empirical Evidence from U.S. Based Publicly Traded Restuarants Firms. *Journal of Hospitality & Tourism Research (Washington, D.C.)*, *31*(1), 91. doi:10.1177/1096348006296056

Uadiale, O. M. (2010). The Impact of Board Structure on Corporate Financial Performance in Nigeria. *International Journal of Business and Management*, *5*, 155–161.

Ullah, W., Ali, S., & Mehmood, S. (2017). Impact of excess control, ownership structure and corporate governance on firm performance of diversified group firms in Pakistan. *Business and Economic Review*, *9*(2), 49–72. doi:10.22547/BER/9.2.3

Villalonga, B., & Amit, R. (2006). How do family ownership, control and management affect firm value? *Journal of Financial Economics*, *80*(2), 385–417. doi:10.1016/j.jfineco.2004.12.005

Vu, M.-C., Phan, T. T., & Le, N. T. (2018). Relationship between board ownership structure and firm financial performance in transitional economy: The case of Vietnam. *Research in International Business and Finance*, *45*, 512–528. doi:10.1016/j.ribaf.2017.09.002

Welch, E. (2003). The Relationship Between Ownership Structure and Performance in Listed Australian Companies. *Australian Journal of Management*, *28*(3), 287–305. doi:10.1177/031289620302800304

Wintoki, M. B., Linck, J. S., & Netter, J. M. (2012). Endogeneity and the dynamics of internal corporate governance. *Journal of Financial Economics*, *105*(3), 581–606. doi:10.1016/j.jfineco.2012.03.005

Woidtke, T. (2002). Agents Watching agents? Evidence from Pension Fund Ownership and Firm Value. *Journal of Financial Economics*, *63*(1), 99–131. doi:10.1016/S0304-405X(01)00091-5

Yasser, Q. R., & Al Mamun, A. (2015). Effects of ownership concentration on firm performance: Pakistani evidence. *Journal of Asia Business Studies*, *9*(2), 162–176. doi:10.1108/JABS-07-2014-0047

Yeh, C. M. (2019). Ownership structure and firm performance of listed tourism firms. *International Journal of Tourism Research*, *21*(2), 165–179. doi:10.1002/jtr.2250

Chapter 8
The Effect of the Mandatory IFRS Adoption on Audit Fees in Malaysia

Yosra Makni Makni Fourati
Faculté des Sciences Economiques et de Gestion, Université de Sfax, Tunisia

Dorra Bougacha
Faculté des Sciences Economiques et de Gestion, Université de Sfax, Tunisia

ABSTRACT

This study examines the effect of the mandatory IFRS adoption on audit fees in an emergent context, such as the case of Malaysia. Using a comprehensive dataset of all publicly-traded Malaysians companies, the authors quantify an economy-wide increase in the mean level of audit costs after the IFRS transition. The final sample consists of 204 companies listed on the stock exchange of Malaysia, and publishes their information on audit fees in their annual reports allowed on the site of the Malaysian scholarship (Boursa Malaysia). Empirical results suggest that there has been some increase in audit fees in Malaysia after the mandatory adoption of IFRS in 2012. But this increase is considered more or less significant because Malaysia adopted the IFRS voluntarily in 2006. To discuss this meaning, the authors added an additional test that makes the results more robust.

I. INTRODUCTION

During recent decades, the world has experienced enormous trying to accelerate the internationalization of economies and thus the globalization of capital markets, which have placed the accounting at the heart of the functioning of financial markets.

These events marked the rise of stock markets, and foreign investment which makes investors have gradually emerged as the leading recipient of accounting information. It is therefore considered that the main purpose of accounting is to allow financial statement users to fully appreciate the situation of companies, and the situation of capital markets in general.

DOI: 10.4018/978-1-7998-4852-3.ch008

However the diversity of accounting systems worldwide, prevents the development of economic globalization, and after numerous financial scandals (Enron, Parmalat, Vivendi ...) caused by questionable accounting practices that have shaken the financial community, setting of a new accounting system seems to be necessary.

Hence the appearance of the great efforts towards the harmonization of accounting systems in the world, which began mainly in the European Union by the adoption of the Accounting Directives which are considered incomplete, then harmonization consists in reducing the differences between national accounting regulations, then standardization requires the establishment of common rules to standardize the presentation of accounting information, and ultimately the standardization of accounting standards by applying the same accounting rules by all countries, which translates into the emergence of international financial reporting standards IFRS[1] which are established by an international body, the IASB (International Accounting Standards Board), based on a conceptual framework with the primary purpose is to creating a unique language of financial reporting worldwide.

This led the European Union to impose IFRS for all listed European companies, from 2005 at the latest. And several countries have also certified the adoption of IFRS, since it is expected that these standards are in fact intended to enable investors to better understand the economic reality of companies. And hence adhesion or transition to IFRS has become a global phenomenon that affects more and more the developed countries like the European Union, Australia, Russia, developing countries such as China, New Zealand and several other countries in Africa, the Middle East and Asia as the case of Malaysia.

Malaysia can not afford to fall behind in the global movement towards the adoption of IFRS. The Malaysian companies must be in step with the evolution of these financial reporting practices worldwide to ensure that their financial statements presented are accepted around the world. Full convergence of international accounting standards will put Malaysia in a good position for the increased globalization of capital markets, provide financial statements comparable to promote investors' confidence. Malaysia has done well so far and continues to go to the front and so are the other countries in the region.

The objective of our study is to examine the impact of the mandatory adoption of IFRS by Malaysia on the audit engagement, specifically on audit fees.

The pertinence of this research lies in the fact that the adoption of IFRS is in propagation worldwide, this is because of the appropriateness of IFRS coming in order to harmonize the economies worldwide, facilitate comparison of financial statements produced internationally, and creates markets for foreign direct investment.

We view that the adoption of IFRS leads to various costs including those studied by previous research, and among these cost increases generated in the fees paid to auditors in return for their missions. Therefore we find several studies that have examined this topic in different contexts and specifically in the context of economically developed countries namely the European Union, other European countries and other research has studied this subject in the context of developing countries and emerging markets such as countries in Asia and Africa.

Hence compared to previous studies we choose to grasp the effect of the mandatory IFRS adoption on audit fees in an emergent context as Malaysia. Moreover, Malaysia is an emerging country, but it has experienced an economic boom during a short period. Boasting a location in the heart of Southeast Asia, it has become almost a modern country and relative to other emerging economies, it is the most developed. Thus Malaysia has voluntarily adopted the international accounting standards since 2006, and has deployed a lot of effort in this regard so that it can be fully converged with those standards in 2012.

Just as there are studies dealing with the impact of IFRS adoption on audit fees in Malaysia, however, these studies were done during the period of the voluntary adoption of IFRS before 2012, so we focus on the effect of the mandatory IFRS adoption on audit fees in Malaysia after 2012.

II. LITERATURE REVIEW AND HYPOTHESIS DEVELOPMENT

The audit engagement is based on four main factors namely: audit quality, audit complexity, audit risk, and audit fees. Hence we will divide previous studies according to these factors and in different contexts.

Audit Quality

A question to be addressed is whether IFRS adoption in Europe has led to an improvement in audit quality. The main variable that can explain the audit quality is the accounting quality (Francisco Rodriguez Galvez, 2012).

Starting with the European context, we find that Daske et al, (2008) who conducted a study of 3100 companies are charged to adopt IFRS in 26 countries in Europe, during the period 2001-2005 showed that there is an Improvement of the audit quality of financial statements caused by the use of higher quality standards in the formulation of financial statements.

Regarding the opinion on the IFRS' impact on accounting quality in Europe, it is necessary to identify two different strands of research. Authors who conclude that the IFRS adoption has brought a positive effect in accounting quality compose the first strand. The second strand concludes the opposite; IFRS has failed to increase the accounting quality.

Improvement of Accounting Quality After IFRS Adoption

Jiang Chen, Lin and Tang (2010), who studied this topic on listed companies in the European Union during the period 2000 -2007, have found that there is an improvement of accounting quality in listed companies in EU obtained by the mandatory IFRS adoption. They explained this result by the effect of IFRS adoption to: less earnings smoothing, more timely loss recognition, and lower magnitude of absolute discretionary accruals after mandatory IFRS adoption" (Chen et al. 2010).

Decrease in Accounting Quality After IFRS Adoption

Dumontier, Janin and Piot (2010) have stressed the importance of the concept "Conservatism" to explain the accounting quality. Using over 5,000 adopters of 22 EU countries during 2001-2008, they have found that the mandatory IFRS adoption in the EU has hampered accounting quality, and seems to be counter-productive for listed entities, despite the costs of such an accounting revolution (Dumontier et al.2011).

In the US, Beijerink (2008) conducted research on 22 companies listed on the US markets, and provided that the results under IFRS will be more relevant and timely than results by US GAAP.

A study by Barth et al (2008) on 327 companies that voluntarily adopt IFRS in different countries of the world, showed that IFRS adoption has provided a better financial information system, and the high level of interpretation of the principles, helps to manipulate the final results of an account or transaction (Barth et al.2008).

In Malaysia, Wan Adibah Wan Ismail et al, (2013) used a sample of 4010 Malaysian companies, three years before and three years after IFRS adoption, showed that IFRS adoption is associated with a better quality of reported results, and that there is a decrease in the earnings management level.

Audit Complexity

In Europe Kim et al, (2010), analyzed that there is an increase in audit complexity, when the management of enterprises use more complex estimates and "professional judgment" because of the characteristics of IFRS as the orientation of the fair value, based on principles, and thoroughness.

In the United States, Eickemeyer & Love (2009, found that the implementation of IFRS will force auditors to exercise more judgment.

In Australia, a study by Pawsey (2008) of 59 Australian listed companies in 2008, concluded that IFRS adoption led to "a continuous increase in the complexity of the company's financial reporting practices" (Pawsey 2008). This result is confirmed by Patel and Prasad (2010), who used a sample of 13 companies listed on the Stock Exchange of "South Pacific in Fiji" after IFRS adoption in 2007, which showed to their role that accounting standards have become more complex, leading to an increase in the complexity of the audit (Patel and Prasad, 2010).

In Malaysia, Najihah Marha Yaacob (2013), studied the effect on 1050 Malaysian companies during the period 2006-2008, and found that IFRS 139 is a complex standard forcing the auditor to spend more time in his mission.

Audit Risk

In Europe Schadewitz and Vieru (2010) studied this effect on listed Finnish companies that have adopted IFRS for the first time during 2004-2005, found that the change in accounting quality and complexity provided by IFRS adoption in Finland increased audit risk and more specifically the risk of material misstatement causing an increase in background procedures. Also they observed that the increase in audit risk is in parallel with the increase in audit fees.

In the US, Wittsiepe (2008), affirmed that IFRS introduce mandatory evaluation of some tangible and intangible assets using the method of fair value in contrast to US GAAP. Eickemeyer & Love (2009) were in agreement with them and confirmed that the judgment leads to more risk of errors by the auditors in the US.

For the other countries of the world, a study conducted by Lin and Yen (2010) on listed companies on the stock exchanges of Shanghai and Shenzhen during 2005-2008, demonstrated an increase of audit risk and the litigation risk level after IFRS adoption in China.

The two studies undertaken by Ayoib Che Ahmad (2012) and Najihah Marha Yaacob (2013) in Malaysia, have shown that there is an increase in audit risk with IFRS adoption and in particular the two IFRS 138 and IFRS 139 because of their complexity, and the need for professional judgments.

Audit Fees

In Europe Kim et al (2010) found a significant increase in audit fees after the mandatory IFRS adoption compared to the previous period of adoption. Their analysis was based on the idea that audit fees were "two opposite effects" (Kim et al, 2010). A positive effect is related to "the audit complexity" and a negative effect is related to "improving the quality of financial information" (Kim et al, 2010). Thus increasing the complexity and audit risk has increased audit fees in the European Union after the adoption of IFRS.

At the same time Kim et al (2010) found an improvement in the quality of financial information which generates a decrease in audit fees in the EU after IFRS adoption. This result confirms the idea that "the complexity of audit" is the "driving force" behind the increase in audit fees and not improving the quality of financial information (Kim et al, 2010).

In USA, Hobbs & Wright (2010) predicted that audit fees will increase at least during the first year after the mandatory IFRS adoption in the United States.

Lin and Yen (2010) conducted a study on listed companies on the stock exchanges in Shanghai and Shenzhen during the period 2005-2008 and found an increase in audit fees of listed companies in China significantly in the first two years of IFRS adoption.

In Malaysia Najihah Marha Yaacob (2011), studied this effect on 3050 Malaysian companies during the period 2004-2008, and confirmed that the companies that have adopted a higher number of IFRS are responsible for charging higher audit fees and it takes more time to complete the audit report. As the study of Najihah Marha Ayoib Yaacob and Che Ahmad (2012), on 2440 Malaysian companies during 2005-2008 approved that the new IFRS standards require detailed disclosure, which requires more effort and time to conduct an audit engagement which will increase audit fees. Also a research conducted by Wan Lokman Wan Abdul Wahid (2013), on 170 listed companies in 2006, found that there is a positive and significant association between IFRS adoption and audit fees increase.

Voluntary adoption of IFRS in Malaysia in 2006, introduced 21 Financial Reporting Standards by the MASB (Malaysian Accounting Standards Board), that are close to IFRS, but there are some differences that result in the fact that IFRS include IAS 38 and 39 which are not adopted by Malaysia in 2006 because of their complexity, while FRS contain four local standards, to follow the specification of Malaysia, local standards are FRS201 on the properties of development activities, FRS202 regarding general insurance business, FRS203 relating to the insurance business and FRS204 on accounting for aquaculture. From 1 January 2012, the total transition to IFRS has changed appointment of FRS to MFRS (Malaysian Financial Reporting Standard), so the period 2012-2013 marked a challenge for accountants and auditors in Malaysia, for account consolidation and implementation of the statement in fair value.

To highlight our hypothesis, it must be noted that the audit fees in Malaysia are regulated in the Recommended Practice Guide 7 which was established in 1994 by the Malaysian Institute of Accountants. This recommended practice guide sets out the basis for establishing a reasonable level of remuneration, commensurate with the provision of professional assurance services of an acceptable and recognized standard. Hence, it noted that audit fees are generally based on the degree of responsibility, risk, the skills involved and the time necessarily engaged on work. According to this revised guide, a professional fees of less than Ringgit Malaysia Eight Hundred (RM 800) for audit services shall be considered as an unrealistically low professional fees.

Thus according to the rules on professional ethics, conduct and practice of the Malaysian Institute of Accountants (MIA), Section 290 mentioned that companies have traditionally provided to their audit clients a range of services non- audit that are consistent with their skills and expertise. Provide non-audit services may, however, lead to threats to the independence of the company or members of the audit team. Also this section has shown that auditors may provide services other than auditing to their customers and named the content of these fees and prohibitions. (MIA).

Malaysia has ordered the obligation of the publication of audit fees and non-audit fees, where information on fees paid to auditors, is available in the annual reports of listed companies, published in the site of the stock exchange of Malaysia.

According to the factors discussed above, it is expected that audit pricing will be higher in the post-IFRS adoption period. Hence, our main hypothesis is as follows:

The IFRS adoption is significantly associated with an increase in audit fees.

III. RESEARCH DESIGN

Our sample includes 204 listed Malaysian companies on the stock exchange of Malaysia (Bursa Malaysia). In order to test our hypothesis, we collected the data from the annual reports of Malaysian companies published in the website of the Stock Exchange (Bursa Malaysia), and accounting data from the database In Financial for the period of the study covering the years 2010-2013.

We inspired our base model of traditional regression model of audit fees of Simunic 1980. Finally the results indicate that the mandatory adoption of IFRS in Malaysia in 2012, generating an increase in audit fees. These findings are considered robust after the addition of robustness test to test the significance of the results.

We consider the adoption of IFRS as expensive for companies because requiring great effort.

So we examine the hypothesis based on the costs of IFRS adoption focusing on audit fees at the moment of adoption. We saw that earlier studies that have examined the impact of changes prescribed in the accounting regulations and corporate governance of the audit function suggest that these costs are significant. These studies attribute these costs mainly to the increase in effort of auditors (Audit complexity) and audit risk.

We estimate a variant of the traditional audit fee regression model (Simunic 1980, Ferguson, Craswell, Francis, et Taylor 1995, Francis, et Stokes 2003).

We then include a number of experimental variables, including the dummy variable for the adoption of IFRS, to capture any increase in audit fees in the post-IFRS period compared to the pre-IFRS period as outlined below:

$$\begin{aligned} \text{LogAF}_{it} = {} & \beta 0 + \beta_1 \text{ IFRS\_ Var}_{it} + \beta_2 \text{ LogAsset}_{it} + \beta_3 \text{ LogNAS}_{it} + \beta_4 \text{ Rec}_{it} + \beta_5 \text{ Inv}_{it} \\ & + \beta_6 \text{ Accr}_{it} + \text{B}_7 \text{ Quick}_{it} + \beta_8 \text{ Debt}_{it} + \beta_9 \text{ ROA}_{it} + \beta_{10} \text{ LOSS}_{it} + \varepsilon_{it} \end{aligned}$$

Where subscripts refer to firm i in year t,

The variables are defined as shown in Box 1.

Our research aims to examine the effect of the mandatory IFRS adoption in Malaysia on the fees paid to external auditors. These amounts are available in the annual reports of Malaysian companies interviewed in our sample. Where the dependent variable of our model is that audit fees measured by Log AF.

IFRS_Var is an explanatory variable of interest which captures the effect of IFRS on audit fees in the period of IFRS adoption compared to the pre-IFRS period.

Box 1.

Variables	Definitions	Sign	Data
Dependent Variable			
LogAF	Natural log of total audit fees paid to external auditors.	?	Rapports annuels
Independent Variable			
IFRS_Var	Experimental variables capturing IFRS effect on mean audit fees in the period of IFRS adoption, relative to pre-IFRS period.	+	In Financial
Control Variables			
LogAsset	Natural log of total assets.	+	In Financial
LogNAS	Natural log of total non-audit service fees paid to external auditors.	+	Rapports annuels
Rec	Ratio of total receivables to ending total assets.	+/-	In Financial
Inv	Ratio of total inventory to ending total assets.	+	In Financial
Accr	Absolute value of accruals (computed as difference between net income and cashflow from operations) scaled by ending total assets.	+	In Financial
Quick	Ratio of current assets to current liabilities.	-	In Financial
Debt	Ratio of long-term debt to ending total assets.	+	In Financial
ROA	Ratio of net profit after tax to ending total assets.	-	In Financial
Loss	Indicator variable: equal to one if firm reported a loss in the current year, and a profit in the previous year, otherwise equal to zero.	+	In Financial

Log Asset is a dependent variable to control the size of the audited entity since the size of the audited entity has a positive impact on the audit engagement. This is confirmed in previous studies that showed significant empirical regularities in this direction, in different contexts. As well these studies namely (Simunic 1980 by George et al, 2012, Kim et al 2010, Chen et al 2014), approved that the size of the audited entity is a determinant key variable of audit fees, and found an association positive between size and fees. This positive association is no-linear, so researchers grow to a logarithmic transformation of the variable, and there is the log of the total assets as a measure of size.

Log NAS is a control variable explaining customer demand for additional audit services, which means that these customers have more problems, and the auditor will consider more risk, forcing it to charge a premium compensation as additional risk.

Rec INV and Accr: these variables control audit complexity that the most complex societies require more audit work which leads to a positive influence on the amount of fees.

Quick and Debt: These variables control the risk of loss measured by the level of debt, because the most leveraged companies are riskier because of their high dependence with external capital providers (shareholders, bank ...). Previous research expects that these determinants related to audit risk, are positively correlated with the level of audit fees. More specifically a negative association for the liquidity ratio (Quick), and a positive association for the ratio of long-term debt (Debt).

ROA and Loss: These variables are used increasingly in recent research, and measure the probability that losses from contentious are supported by the listener. In fact research exposes the level of the audit request by the business loss and are riskier, and therefore the increase in audit fees (De George et al, 2012). Previous studies expect a positive association between the variable Loss and audit fees after IFRS adoption against a negative association with ROA.

IV. RESULTS ANALYSIS

Table 1 presents the descriptive statistics for our sample of firms including the mean and standard deviation for all variables. According to this table, the results show that there is an increase in the value of the natural log of audit fees (Log AF) for the period post IFRS from an average (median) equal to 10.511 (10.622) in pre- convergence to IFRS at 10.732 (10.802) in the period post-convergence to IFRS. Hence an increase in audit fees can be seen in Malaysia after the total convergence to IFRS, based on the natural log of audit fees (Log AF).

Table 1. Descriptive Statistics of Study Variables

	Pre-IFRS Period (2010-2011)						Post-IFRS Period (2012-2013)					
Variables	**Obs**	**Mean**	**Median**	**σ**	**Min**	**Max**	**Obs**	**Moyenne**	**Médiane**	**σ**	**Min Max**	
The Dependent Variable												
LogAF	404	10.511	10.622	1.148	6.095	13.685	408	10.732	10.802	1.123	6.059	13.799
The Control Variables												
LogAsset	403	11.734	11.572	1.527	8.243	16.657	402	11.847	11.718	1.533	8.621	16.898
Log NAS	303	3.251	3.239	1.497	-2.303	6.774	296	3.317	3.247	1.442	-1.609	6.772
Rec	402	0.143	0.120	0.114	0.001	0.599	401	0.143	0.115	0.121	0.001	0.818
Inv	401	0.143	0.124	0.133	0	0.800	408	0.146	0.116	0.137	0	0.782
Accr	402	0.057	0.035	0.080	0	0.751	391	0.056	0.034	0.080	0	0.634
Quick	406	3.030	1.873	6.077	0.095	90.563	405	2.718	1.845	2.686	0.180	22.610
Debt	401	0.065	0.026	0.096	0	0.639	405	0.071	0.028	0.103	0	0.624
ROA	401	0.178	0.043	0.938	-0.934	10.586	385	0.168	0.037	0.992	-1.196	9.605
Loss	408	0.159	0	0.366	0	1	408	0.164	0	0.371	0	1

Notes: This table presents the descriptive statistics for the regression model variables for the pre-IFRS period (2010-2011) and the post-IFRS period (2012-2013). The sample consists of 204 Malaysian companies and the variables are defined previously.

Therefore descriptive statistics show that there is an increase in the size of the audited entity calculated by the natural logarithm of total assets (Log Asset) which passes an average (median) equal to 11.734 (11.572) in the pre-convergence to IFRS, to 11.847 (11.718) in the post-convergence to IFRS, thus confirming the results obtained in previous research that there is a positive association between the size of the audited entity, and audit fees.

An increase in non-audit fees based on the natural logarithm of these costs (Log NAS), which passes an average (median) equal to 3,251 (3,239) in the pre-convergence to IFRS, to 3,317 (3,247) in the post-convergence to IFRS, which explains the increased demand for customer additional auditing after the adoption of IFRS because of the problems brought by these standards, and increasing the risk to the auditor in the performance of his work.

Stability at the total debts of enterprises (Rec) which is a measurement indicator of the complexity of audit passing an average (median) equal to 0.143 (0.120) in the pre-convergence to IFRS, to 0.143 (0, 115) in the post-convergence to IFRS, a slight increase in the ration of the total stock (Inv) which is a measurement indicator of the complexity of audit, passing an average (median) equal to 0.143 (0.124) in the pre-convergence to IFRS at 0.146 (0, 116) in the post-convergence to IFRS, a decrease in the absolute value accruals (CAC), which is also an indicator for measuring the degree of complexity of the audit, which from an average (median) equal to 0.057 (0.035) in the pre-convergence to IFRS 0.056 (0.034) in the post-convergence to IFRS, which is reflected firstly by the decrease in management accounting income after the adoption of IFRS, and secondly by increasing the level of complexity of audit.

A decreased risk of loss calculated by (Quick), passing an average (median) equal to 3,030 (1,873) in the pre-convergence to IFRS, 2.718 (1.845) in the post-convergence to IFRS are explained by the assertion of earlier studies that there is a negative association between current ratio and audit risk, an increase in long-term debt (Debt), passing an average (median) equal to 0.065 (0.026) in the pre-convergence to IFRS, to 0.071 (0.028) in the post-convergence to IFRS, as explained by the assertion of previous studies on the existence of a positive association between the ratio of long-term debt and audit risk.

A decrease in the degree of risk sharing auditor / client, calculated by (ROA), passing an average (median) equal to 0.178 (0.043) in the pre-convergence to IFRS, to 0.168 (0.037) in the post-convergence to IFRS. And ultimately an increase in the variable (Loss), passing an average (median) equal to 0.159 (0) in the pre-convergence to IFRS, to 0.164 (0) in the post-convergence to IFRS meaning that businesses and risky loss require more auditing, and hence the increase in audit fees.

Table 2. Pearson Correlation

Variables	*IFRS*	*LogAF*	*LogAsset*	*Log NAS*	*Rec*	*Inv*	*Accr*	*Quick*	*Debt*	*ROA*	*Loss*
IFRS	1										
LogAF	**0.108**	1									
LogAsset	0.061*	0.073*	1								
Log NAS	0.010**	0.207	0.328	1							
Rec	-0.015***	-0.022***	-0.372***	-0.090***	1						
Inv	-0.012***	0.058*	-0.132***	-0.053***	0.070*	1					
Accr	-0.001***	-0.027***	-0.061***	-0.066***	0.022**	-0.122	1				
Quick	-0.044***	-0.064***	-0.179***	-0.095***	-0,085***	-0.049	0.131	1			
Debt	0.059*	-0.075***	0.447	0.218	-0.167***	-0.139***	0.016**	-0.179***	1		
ROA	0.004***	-0.051***	-0.168***	-0.122***	0.063*	-0.049***	-0.044***	0.105	-0.111***	1	
Loss	-0.000***	-0.104***	-0.188***	-0.089***	0.005***	-0.009***	0.184	0.071*	-0.034***	0.045**	1

Notes: This table of Pearson correlations for independent variables and control. ***, **, *: significant at the 1%, 5% and 10% respectively, the variables are defined previously.

The correlation matrix of our model shows both that IFRS are correlated positively and significantly with AF Log (0,108), Log Asset (0,061), Log Nas (0,010), Debt (0,059), ROA (0,004), secondly IFRS are negatively and significantly correlated with Rec (-0.015), Inv (-0.012) Accr (-0.001), Quick (-0.044) Loss (-0.000).

Thus the correlation table shows that audit fees brought by the natural log of audit fees Log AF are positively and significantly correlated with Log Asset (0.073), Log NAS (0.207), Inv (0.058) in against Log AF part is negatively and significantly correlated with Rec (-0.022) Accr (-0.027), Quick (-0.064) Debt (-0.075), ROA (-0.051) Loss (-0.104).

Also the correlation matrix shows that the size of the entity Log Asset is positively and significantly correlated with NAS Log (0,328) Debt (0.447) against Log Asset is negatively and significantly correlated with Rec (-0, 372), Inv (-0.132) Accr (-0.061), Quick (-0.179), ROA (-0.168) Loss (-0.188).

For the log NAS variable that expresses the natural logarithm of the non-audit fees, the correlation matrix shows that this variable is correlated positively and significantly with only Debt (0.218), for against this variable is correlated negatively and significantly with Rec (0.090), Inv (-0.053) Accr (-0.066), Quick (-0.095), ROA (-0.122) Loss (-0.089).

Relating to the REC variable (ratio of total debt / total assets), which can measure the level of complexity of audit, the correlation matrix shows that this variable is positively and significantly correlated with Inv (0.070) Accr (0,022) ROA (0,063) Loss (0.005), as it is correlated negatively and significantly with Quick (-0.085) Debt (-0.167).

In the following correlation matrix shows that the variable Inv (ratio of total stock / total assets), which can also measure the level of complexity audit is only correlated negatively and significantly with Accr (-0.122), Quick (- 0.049) Debt (-0.139), ROA (-0.049) Loss (-0.009).

Thus the correlation matrix shows that Accr variable is the absolute value of discretionary accruals, and can also measure the level of audit complexity is positively and significantly correlated with Quick (0,131) Debt (0,016) Loss (0.184) against Accr is negatively and significantly correlated with ROA (-0.044).

Subsequently the correlation matrix shows that Quick variable (current / current liabilities Assets), which can measure the level of potential loss is positively and significantly correlated with ROA (0,105) Loss (0.071), as it is correlated negatively and significantly with Debt (-0.179).

Also the correlation matrix shows that the variable Debt which is the ratio of long-term debt, and can also measure the level potential loss is negatively and significantly correlated with ROA (-0.111) Loss (- 0.034).

Finally the correlation matrix shows that the variable ROA (profit after tax / total assets), which can measure the level of auditor-client risk sharing, is positively and significantly correlated with Loss (0,045).

To investigate the hypothesis of our research on the effect of the mandatory IFRS adoption on audit fees in Malaysia, we presented our regression model based on panel data with the Stata software. The panel data has two dimensions: one for the space (audited entities), indicated by the index i, and for a time (4 years), indicated by the index t.

From Table 3, the results of the regression model show that IFRS variable has a positive coefficient $\beta 1 = 0.214$ and significant at the 1% ($Z = 0$), which explains the previous results suggesting the increase in audit fees after IFRS adoption.

Thus the Quick variable has a significant effect on audit fees, by a negative coefficient $\beta 7 = -0.013$, and significant at the 1% ($Z = 0$), which suggests a low level of potential loss resulting in the liquidity ratio, will increase audit fees in accordance with previous studies.

For the rest of variables in the regression, as the size of the audited company (Log Asset), fees on services other than auditing (Log NAS), the complexity of audit determined by (Rec), (Inv), and (Accr), the ratio of long-term debt (debt), there is a positive association but is not significant, as the level of auditor-client risk sharing measured by (ROA) and (Loss) we find that the regression is not significant and shows that there is a negative association.

Finally, and According to these results, we found that audit fees in Malaysia increased after the mandatory adoption of IFRS which confirm our hypothesis, however the significance of these findings remains to be discussed since it was found that only two variables have a significant effect on audit fees, which we will add model by a robust model, expecting to enhance the meaning of the variables.

Table 3. The impact of IFRS convergence on audit fees

Model: $LogAF_{it} = \beta_0 + \beta_1\, IFRS\_\, Var_{it} + \beta_2\, LogAsset_{it} + \beta_3\, LogNAS_{it} + \beta_4\, Rec_{it} + \beta_5\, Inv_{it} + \beta_6\, Accr_{it} + B_7\, Quick_{it} + \beta_8\, Debt_{it} + \beta_9\, ROA_{it} + \beta_{10}\, Loss_{it} + \varepsilon_{it}$		
	Log AF	
Variables	**Coefficients**	**Z (*P*>|z|)**
Ifrs	0.214	11.36 (0.000)***
Log Asset	0.016	0.37 (0.712)
Log NAS	0.001	0.27 (0.785)
Rec	0.055	0.22 (0.826)
Inv	0.280	0.92 (0.360)
Accr	0.037	0.17 (0.869)
Quick	-0.013	-4.30 (0.000)***
Debt	0.368	1.41 (0.158)
ROA	-0.028	-0.70 (0.485)
Loss	-0.015	-0.39 (0.699)

Wald chi 2(10)= 189.37 Prob > chi2 = 0.000***
Number of observations = 569
Notes: the impact of IFRS adoption on audit fees, ***, **, *: significant at the 1%, 5% and 10%.

V. ROBUSTNESS TEST

Order to better study our hypothesis, and to better achieve a result that confirms that the mandatory IFRS adoption in Malaysia generates an increase in audit fees, and to test the significance of that purpose we will support our model by test of robustness, by eliminating the variable Log NAS (natural logarithm of non-audit fees) from the basic regression. This elimination is explained by the fact that the Non Audit Fees are questionable costs that do not really belong to the audit engagement and usually include consulting costs. This growing demand from companies to obtain advice from specialists just in order to help them to achieve a business benefits in a market increasingly competitive. A big part of this advice is requested for audit firms, first because auditors are trained to understand the dynamics of a company from an external point of view and also because an independent view can often shed light on the problems that may appear intractable in an organization. It can constrain the independence of auditors and exploits their vulnerability to be honored by the remuneration on services other their missions.

Also because most previous studies have not introduced the Log NAS variable as a determinant of audit fees with the exception of DE George et al study in 2012, and since this variable was significantly correlated with most of the control variables, which created some noise in the matrix.

Table 4. The impact of IFRS convergence on audit fees by the robustness model

Model: $LogAF_{it} = \beta_0 + \beta_1$ IFRS_ $Var_{it} + \beta_2$ $LogAsset_{it} + \beta_3 Rec_{it} + \beta_4$ $Inv_{it} + \beta_5$ $Accr_{it}$ + B_6 $Quick_{it}$+ β_7 $Debt_{it} + \beta_8$ $ROA_{it} + \beta_9$ $Loss_{it} + \varepsilon_{it}$		
	Log AF	
Variables	**Coefficients**	**Z (P>|z|)**
Ifrs	0.203	11.36 (0.000)***
Log Asset	0.090	2.58 (0.010)**
Rec	0.179	0.92 (0.356)
Inv	0.139	0.59 (0.558)
Accr	-0.060	-0.40 (0.691)
Quick	-0.011	-4.01 (0.000)***
Debt	0.424	2.15 (0.032)**
ROA	-0.015	-0.49 (0.627)
Loss	-0.011	-0.39 (0.699)

Wald chi 2(10)= 189.37 Prob > chi2 = 0.000***

Number of observations = 569

Notes: This table shows the regression results of IFRS adoption effect on audit fees, ***, **, *: significant at the 1%, 5% and 10% respectively.

Hence, a new model is reproduced below:

$$LogAF_{it} = \beta0 + \beta_1\ IFRS\_\ Var_{it} + \beta_2\ LogAsset_{it} + \beta_3\ Rec_{it} + \beta_4\ Inv_{it}$$
$$+ \beta_5\ Accr_{it} + B_6\ Quick_{it} + \beta_7\ Debt_{it} + \beta_8\ ROA_{it} + \beta_9\ Loss_{it} + \varepsilon_{it}$$

And as we seek to improve the significance of the results obtained from the basic model, we will directly address reproduce the multivariate analysis for this additional model.

From Table 12, the results of the additional regression model show that IFRS parked his positive factor $\beta1 = 0.203$ and significant at the 1% (Z = 0), which explains the previous results suggesting the increase in audit fees after the adoption of IFRS by the positive and significant association between IFRS and audit fees.

The results of the additional regression of our model also shows that Quick parked his significant effect on audit fees, by a negative coefficient $\beta6 = -0.011$, and significant at the 1% (Z = 0), suggesting that a low level of potential loss will generate an increase in audit fees and confirms the previous results indicating the existence of a negative and significant association between liquidity ratio (Quick) and audit fees.

Furthermore according to the results of this additional regression, two other variables those are determined as significant, namely:

- Log Asset which measures the size of the audited entity, which has a significant effect on audit fees by a positive coefficient β2 = 0.090 and significant at the 5% (Z = 1), which explains the importance of company size in the pricing of audit fees, that is to say more the audited entity has an important size, more than there is an increase in audit fees, in accordance with the previous results, the association between the size of the audited entity and the audit fees is a significant positive association.
- Debt which is the long-term debt ratio, which measures the level of risk of loss, has a significant effect on audit fees by a positive coefficient β7 = 0, 424, and significant at the 5% (Z = 3.2), suggesting that a low level of potential loss will generate an increase in audit fees, and this also confirms the previous results that there is a positive and significant association between ratio of long-term debt and audit fees.

For the rest of variables of the additional regression, as the complexity of audit determined by (Rec), (Inv), and (Accr), and the level of auditor-client risk sharing measured by (ROA), and (loss), we find that the regression is not significant.

VI. SUMMARY AND CONCLUSION

The purpose of this research was to study the impact of mandatory IFRS adoption in Malaysia on audit fees. We selected a sample of 204 Malaysian listed companies on the stock exchange of Malaysia. Our data were collected from the database In Financial and the information on audit fees were assembled for the annual reports of these companies, located on the site of the stock exchange (Bursa Malaysia) for the period study covering the years 2010-2013.

To test our hypothesis, we inspired our methodology of traditional regression model of audit fees of (Sumunic 1980 Ferguson Craswel, Taylor and Francis, 1995, Francis and Stokes 2003). The results of the various tests affirm that there has been some increase in audit fees after the mandatory IFRS adoption in Malaysia. Let's focus on the significance of this increase; we confirmed our results by a robustness test which gave such improvements of the significance level of the increase in audit fees. The results are robust even by performing additional analysis to enhance the significance of the control variables by eliminating the variable Log NAS effectuating from noise.

The contribution of our research is conducted of made it a nuance dice the beginning of the effect of the mandatory IFRS adoption on audit fees due to the results previously found and which are mitigated, while our results highlight the relevance of the context studied since Malaysia has made great effort to the voluntary adoption of IFRS in 2006, which brought a level of expertise for accounting regulators and auditors vis- a-vis IFRS, and therefore the good mastery of these standards which become for them less complex and feature month risk.

As well the mandatory IFRS adoption in Malaysia in 2012, brought two standards that have been considered complex and tough for the voluntary adoption which are IFRS 138: Intangible assets and IFRS 139: Financial Instruments: Recognition and Measurement. So the application of these standards compulsory, increase audit fees, which explains the level of complexity of these standards.

Like most research, this study is subject to limitations which may be the choice of the sampling period that presents the transition and which includes in particular the transition year to the mandatory adoption of IFRS 2012- 2013. This requires studying this effect over a longer period. Based on these limits, we can open lines of research related to the study namely, for example using a larger sample and a longer period might better consider the significant effect of the mandatory IFRS adoption on the audit fees, and our hypothesis can be tested by the integration of other assumptions in testing the factors of the audit engagement as quality, complexity and audit risk, to finish with audit fees.

REFERENCES

Akerlof, G. (1970). *The Market for "Lemons"*. Quality Uncertainty and the Market Mechanism.

Al-Akra, M., Ali, M. J., & Marashdeh, O. (2009). Development of Accounting Regulation in Jordan. *The International Journal of Accounting*, *44*(2), 163–186. doi:10.1016/j.intacc.2009.03.003

Armstrong, C. S., Barth, M. E., Jagolinzer, A. D., & Riedl, E. J. (2009). Market Reaction to the Adoption of IFRS in Europe. *Accounting Review*. Available at SSRN: http://ssrn.com/abstract=903429

Barth, M. E., Landsman, W. R., & Lang, M. H. (2007). *International Accounting Standards and Accounting Quality*. Stanford University Graduate School of Business Research Paper No. 1976. Available at SSRN: http://ssrn.com/abstract=688041

Becker, C. P., Lawrence, H., & Sennetti, J. T. (2010). *The Effects of Type of Accounting Standard and Outcome Knowledge on Juror Evaluations of Auditor Responsibility* (Dissertation). Glenville State College, University of Mississippi, & Nova Southeastern University.

Beijerink, M. (2008). *Information quality of IFRS and US-GAAP: a comparison of multiple earnings attributes under IFRS and US-GAAP* (Dissertation). University of Twente.

Belkaoui. (1991). *Multinational Financial Accounting*. Academic Press.

Botica-Redmayne, N., & Laswad, F. (2010). *New Zealand Public sector audit fees and audit effort: the impact of IFRS adoption* (Dissertation). School of Accountancy, Massey University, New Zealand.

Brackney, K., & Marden, R. E. (2009). Audit risk and IFRS. Does increased flexibility increase audit risk? *The CPA Journal*, 32–36.

Chand & White. (2007). *A critique of the influence of globalization and convergence of accounting standards in Fiji*. https://www.researchgate.net/publication/222997248_A_critique_of_the_influence_of_globalization_and_convergence_of_accounting_standards_in_Fiji

Chen. (2014). *How does mandatory IFRS adoption affect the audit service market?* School of Accounting Seminar Series Semester 1.

Chen, H., Jiang, Y., Lin, Z., & Tang, Q. (2010). *Mandatory IFRS Adoption and Accounting Quality: Evidence from the European Union*. Dissertation.

Chen, H., Jiang, Y., Lin, Z., & Tang, Q. (2010). The Role of International Financial Reporting Standards in Accounting Quality: Evidence from the European Union (June 10, 2010). *Journal of International Financial Management & Accounting*, *21*(3), 220–278. doi:10.1111/j.1467-646X.2010.01041.x

Cohen, J. R., Krishnamoorthy, G., Peytcheva, M., & Wright, A. (2011). *Will Regulatory Enforcement and Principles-Based Accounting Influence Auditors' Ethical Judgments to Constrain Aggressive Reporting?* (Dissertation). Boston College, Northeastern University, Lehigh University & Northeastern University.

Craig & Diga. (1996). Financial reporting regulation in ASEAN: Features and prospects: The Australian National University, Australia. *The International Journal of Accounting, 2*. https://www.researchgate.net/publication/4739184_Financial_reporting_regulation_in_ASEAN_Features_and_prospects

Daske, H., Hail, L., Leuz, C., & Verdi, R. S. (2008). *Mandatory IFRS Reporting Around the World: Early Evidence on the Economic Consequences*. ECGI - Finance Working Paper No. 198/2008. Chicago GSB Research Paper No. 12.

Dumontier, P., Janin, R., & Piot, C. (2010). *IFRS Consequences on Accounting Conservatism Within Europe: The Role of Big 4 Auditors*. Academic Press.

Eickemeyer, J. H., & Love, V. J. (2009). IFRS and Accountants' Liability. *The CPA Journal*, 54–59.

Evolution de l'audit: Publié le 21 mars 2009 par KESSAB JAMAL. http://normes-ias-ifrs-au-maroc.over-blog.com/article-29313104.html

Francis, J. R., (2006). *Auditing Section Doctoral Consortium*. Presentation.

Friis, O., & Nielsen, M. (2010). *Audit fees and IFRS accounting. Is information costly? Discussion Papers on Business and Economics*. University of Southern Denmark.

Ghazali & Weetman. (2006). *Voluntary Disclosure in Malaysian Corporate Annual Reports*. Academic Press.

Godfrey & Chalmers. (2007). *Globalisation of accounting standards*. Monash Studies in Global Movements.

Griffin, P., Lont, D., & Sun, Y. (2008). *Governance Regulatory Changes, IFRS Adoption, and New Zealand Audit and Non-Audit Fees: Empirical Evidence.* University of California and University of Otago.

Gul. (2006). *Auditors' Response to Political Connections and Cronyism in Malaysia*. http://onlinelibrary.wiley.com/doi/10.1111/j.1475-679X.2006.00220.x/abstract

Haniffa & Cooke. (2002). *Culture, Corporate Governance and Disclosure in Malaysian Corporations*. https://papers.ssrn.com/sol3/papers.cfm?abstract_id=336822

Hobbs, C., & Wright, C. (2010). Impact and Implications of IFRS. Conversion or Convergence. *Journal of Bank Accounting & Finance*, 21-28.

International Standards on Auditing 400. (n.d.). *Risk Assessments and Internal Control.* Retrieved September 14, 2011 from http://www.icisa.cag.gov.in/Background% 20Material/ RISK%20ASSt%20AND%20INTNL%20CONTROL%20ISA_400.pdf/

International Standards on Auditing (ISA). (n.d.). *Financial Stability Board.* Retrieved April 29, 2012, from http://www.financialstabilityboard.org/cos/cos_021001b.htm

Ismail & Chandler. (2004). *The timeliness of quarterly financial reports of companies in Malaysia.* http://www.emeraldinsight.com/doi/abs/10.1108/eb060770

Jensen & Meckling. (1976). *Theory of the Firm: Managerial Behavior, Agency Costs and Ownership Structure*. Academic Press.

Jermakowicz, E., & Gornik-Tomaszewski, S. (2006). Implementing IFRS from the perspective of EU publicly traded companies. *Journal of International Accounting, Auditing & Taxation, 15*(2), 170–196. doi:10.1016/j.intaccaudtax.2006.08.003

Kim, J.-B., Liu, X., & Zheng, L. (2010). The impact of Mandatory IFRS Adoption on Audit Fee: Theory and Evidence. *CAAA Annual Conference 2010*. Available at SSRN: http://ssrn.com/abstract=1530776

Kohlberg. (1969). *Kohlberg's stages of moral development*. Academic Press.

Lee, P., Stokes, D., Taylor, S., & Walter, T. (2003). The association between audit quality, accounting disclosures and firm-specific risk: Evidence from initial public offerings. *Journal of Accounting and Public Policy, 22*(5), 377–400. doi:10.1016/j.jaccpubpol.2003.08.003

Lin, H.-L., & Yen, A.-R. (2010). *The Effects of IFRS Adoption on Audit Fees for Listed Companies in China* (Dissertation). National Chiao-Ton University. HsinChu, Taiwan & Northeastern Illinois University, Chicago, IL, US.

Lokman & Wahid. (2013). *The impact of IFRS adoption on audit fees: Evidence from Malaysian listed companies*. http://malrep.uum.edu.my/rep/Record/iium.eprints.35296/Description#tabnav

Loukil, L. (2010). Conséquences de l'adoption des normes internationales "IFRS" sur le coût d'audit financier. *Crises et nouvelles problématiques de la valeur*. https://halshs.archives-ouvertes.fr/hal-00481517/document

Mashayekhi & Mashayekh. (2008). *Developement of accounting in Iran*. https://www.researchgate.net/publication/222968551_Development_of_accounting_in_Iran

Muniandy & Ali. (2012). *Development of financial reporting environment in Malaysia*. Academic Press.

Nobes. (1983). *A judgemental international classification of financial reporting practices*. Academic Press.

Patel, A., & Prasad, A. (2010). Incentives and Preliminary Investigation of Incentives Facing Accounting Standard-Setters. *International Review of Business Research Papers*, 536-561.

Pawsey, N. (2008). *Australian Preparer Perceptions towards the Quality and Complexity of IFRS*. La Trobe University.

Rajan & Zingales. (1998). *Financial Dependence and Growth*. Academic Press.

Salleh. (2014). Convergence to IFRs and Audit Report Lag in Malaysia. *Research Journal of Finance and Accounting*. www.iistc.org

Schadewitz, H. J., & Vieru, M. J. (2008). *Impact of IFRS Transition Complexity on Audit Non- Audit Fees: Evidence from Small and Medium-Sized Listed Companies in Finland*. Available at SSRN: http://ssrn.com/abstract=967314

Sharma, S. (2010). The Impact of the Adoption of International Financial Reporting Standards on the Legal Profession. *Houston Business and Tax Journal*, 139-165.

Wan, A. W. I., Kamarudin, K. A., van Zijl, T., & Dunstan, K. (2013). Earnings quality and the adoption of IFRS based accounting standards: Evidence from an emerging market. *Asian Review of Accounting*, *21*(1), 53–73. doi:10.1108/13217341311316940

Wittsiepe, R. (2008). *IFRS for Small and Medium-Sized Enterprises: Structuring the Transition Process*. Gabler Verlag.

Yaacob & Che-Ahmad. (2012). Adoption of FRS 138 and Audit Delay in Malaysia. *International Journal of Economics and Finance, 4*(1)..

Yaacob. (2011). *The Effect of International Financial Reporting Standards (IFRS) Adoption on Audit Pricing and Audit Timeless: Evidence from Malaysia* (PhD thesis). Universiti Utara Malaysia. http://etd.uum.edu.my/3458/

Yaacob. (2013). The Relationship between Financial Reporting Standards (FRS) 139 and Audit Pricing: The Case of Malaysia. *Journal of Modern Accounting and Auditing, 9*(5), 641-649.

ENDNOTE

1 Accounting standards developed after 2001 are called the International Financial Reporting Standards (IFRS), while those developed before April 1, 2001 remains International Accounting Standards (IAS). For simplification purposes, we now use the term IFRS to refer to the two accounting standards: IAS and IFRS.

Chapter 9
The Audit Committee as Component of Corporate Governance:
The Case of the Netherlands

Sana Masmoudi Mardessi
Ecole Supérieure de Commerce, Université de Sfax, Tunisia

Yosra Makni Fourati
Faculté des Sciences Economiques et de Gestion, Université de Sfax, Tunisia

ABSTRACT

Recently, numerous financial scandals (WorldCom, Enron, Parmalat, eToys) have shown that plentiful companies produce manipulated financial information. Consequently, regulators have prescribed corporate governance structures to protect investors and to avoid fraudulent financial reporting which are likely to control managers and limit their opportunistic behavior. Thus, there has been much debate over the extent to which corporate governance is playing a crucial role in increasing financial reporting quality from the theoretical perspective of agency theory, signaling theory, and stakeholder theory. This chapter aims at scrutinizing the internal and external mechanisms of corporate governance mainly the audit committee in the Dutch context. Firstly, the authors expose the numerous corporate governance mechanisms. Secondly, they focus on the audit committee as the main component of corporate governance, and they present the theoretical background, the role, and the characteristics of audit committee. Eventually, they exhibit the regulatory background of the Dutch context of the audit committee.

INTRODUCTION

The recent invigorated debate over financial reporting quality has often made reference to corporate governance structure. To address the regulators' concerns and rebuild investors' confidence, corporate governance reformers have considered the audit committee as having a central role in ensuring improved

DOI: 10.4018/978-1-7998-4852-3.ch009

financial reporting quality as it is charged to oversee the financial reporting process. However, financial statements have raised the question on the effectiveness of Good Corporate Governance implementation in a company for minimizing earnings management. The conflict of interest between the management and the company owners can be minimized by a monitoring mechanism capable of balancing the interests between the management and shareholders. The level Good Corporate Governance users can be measured and it can be compared with each other. Nevertheless, the indicator of Good Corporate Governance mechanism used the mechanism of composition of Commissioners and Audit Committee. Overall, the composition of Commissioners is given the responsibilities to monitor the information quality contained in the financial statements. Regarding the Audit Committee, it consists to monitor and evaluate the planning and execution of the audit, as well as to monitor the follow-up of audit outcome for assessing the adequacy of the financial statement process (Muda et al.2018).

The present chapter is primarily motivated by the fact that, to the best of our knowledge, there has been no prior academic study dealing with the committee characteristics in the Netherlands. Given the uniqueness of the Dutch market, this chapter examines some audit committee characteristics in this context characterized by a small economic market that is quite different from that of the larger ones.

The remainder of this chapter is organized as follows. The next section presents the corporate governance definition and some governance mechanisms. In the second section, we accord more attention to the audit committee as the main component of corporate governance. Afterwards, we exhibit the regulatory background of the Dutch context in the third section. Eventually, we provide the conclusion.

1. CORPORATE GOVERNANCE: MAIN DEFINITIONS AND MECHANISMS

Corporate Governance is a concept which improve management performance in monitoring or supervising the management performance while guaranteeing the management accountability for the shareholders based on regulatory framework (Dalimunthe et al., 2016; Lubis et al., 2016). The concept of Corporate Governance is projected for achieving more transparent company management for all financial statements' users. If the concept is used properly, then the economic growth is expected to move forward in line with better transparent company management, which ultimately gives benefits to many parties.

In this section, we are going to define the main notions of corporate governance and mechanisms.

1.1. Corporate Governance: Main Definitions

Corporate governance has received increased attention and scrutiny over the last decades. In fact, corporate governance issues have became the most problematic one worldwide not only in the academic literature, but also in public policy debates.

The definition of this term is excessively "puzzling" (Aguilera et al., 2015)[1]. Actually, a great effort was made to give a universally accepted clarification. For instance, Corporate Governance was initially defined as "the total of operations and controls of an organization" (Fama and Jensen, 1983) or as "an overall structured system of principles according to which an enterprise operates and is organized, managed and controlled" (Dey, 1994).

The Cadbury Report (1992) also defined it[2] as "the systems and methods by which companies are controlled and managed". Another definition is granted by Parkinson (1994) which defines that Corporate

Governance is "the process of supervision and control intended to ensure that the company's management acts in accordance with the interests of shareholders."

According to Shleifer and Vishny (1997), "corporate governance deals with the ways in which suppliers of finance to corporations assure themselves of getting a return on their investment". This was confirmed by (Walker, 2009) who stated that "the ultimate reason for the existence of corporate governance is to protect and increase shareholders' value". All these definitions emphasize the narrow finance view of corporate governance.

John and Senbet (1998) proposed a more comprehensive definition, which is: "corporate governance deals with mechanisms by which stakeholders of a corporation exercise control over corporate insiders and management such that their interests are protected". They included then not only shareholders, but also several stakeholders like debt holders and even non-financial stakeholders such as employees, suppliers, customers, and other interested parties. In other words, a stakeholder approach was employed here in contrast to the previous one which was restricted to shareholder-value view.

In addition, various institutions have gradually paid attention to corporate governance and tried to define it such as the International Federation of Accountants (IFAC 2003) which proposed an expansive definition for governance, calling it "enterprise governance". "Enterprise governance covers both the corporate governance (legal compliance) and the business management governance (performance) aspects of organizations. It takes into consideration compliance of legal and ethical issues; it also covers strategic and tactical aspects of business performance and sustainability. The emerging term, "enterprise governance" applies itself not only to the private shareholder sector, but also the public taxpayer funded government sector. The emerging term is applicable also to strategic alliances, joint ventures, and generally any organization. Enterprise governance expands the definition of stakeholders beyond shareholders to cover employees, and society". The IFAC recognizes that governance of the whole organization can be better referred as enterprise governance. Enterprise governance is defined as" the organization's entire accountability framework".

The Organization for Economic Cooperation and Development (OECD 2004) provides a more conclusive definition of corporate governance, which is like, so: *"Corporate governance involves a set of relationships between a company's management, its board, its shareholders and other stakeholders. Corporate governance also provides the structure through which the objectives of the company are set, and the means of attaining those objectives and monitoring performances are determined. Good corporate governance should provide proper incentives for the board and management to pursue objectives that are in the interests of the company and its shareholders and should facilitate effective monitoring".*

Arguden (2010) advanced a current definition, which is like this: "Corporate governance refers to the quality, transparency and dependability of the relationships between the shareholders, board of directors, management, and employees. It defines the authority and responsibility of each in delivering sustainable value to all the stakeholders in order to attract financial and human capital to the corporation and to ensure sustainability of value creation; the governance mechanisms should ensure to gain the trust of all stakeholders".

The Information Systems Audit and Control Association (ISACA 2011) provided a more recent definition of corporate governance, which is as follows: *"The set of responsibilities and practices exercised by the board and executive management with the goal of providing strategic direction, ensuring that objectives are achieved, ascertaining that risks are managed appropriately and verifying that the organizations are used responsibly"* (ISACA 2011, p.35).

From the above-mentioned definitions, it seems clear that the regulation of corporate governance is the government's attempt to ensure that the company achieves its defined objectives and protects the interests of its owners and all stakeholders as well.

It is remarkable that over time, corporate governance has moved from shareholder value approach to stakeholder or partnership approach and that is extended to all types of organizations not only corporations.

To make sure that companies have a good and effective governance, corporate governance mechanisms are designed to attenuate agency problems and costs associated with separation of ownership and control as revealed by (Mora & Walker, 2015) who stated that "corporate governance mechanisms exist to overcome information asymmetry problems and reduce moral hazard problems". Consequently, it seems interesting to present some of these mechanisms.

1.2. Corporate Governance: Mechanisms Classification

Academic literature distinguishes several corporate governance mechanisms, which play a primary role in monitoring and controlling firm's management. Governance mechanisms can be split into two categories, external and internal. Among them, we can cite:

1.2.1. External Mechanisms

There is a wide range of external governance mechanisms but we will focus on the following ones:

1.2.1.1. Market for Corporate Control

The market for corporate control has historically received the greatest attention of the external mechanisms, especially in the finance and accounting literatures (Aguilera et al, 2015). It is commonly perceived as a key external mechanism. Indeed, Jensen (1986a) considered that it acts as "a mechanism of last resort". In fact, if a company's internal mechanisms fail, the market for corporate control is supposed to play a critical disciplinary role in solving this problem. In fact by definition, market of corporate control is a mechanism by which the risk that outside management teams gain the control of underperforming quoted companies increase. This occurs when managers make inappropriate decisions, whether that is because of incompetence, self-interest and shirking of responsibilities. Consequently, the firm's assets are undervalued in the equity market. As a result, the stock price declines. Other management teams will then target the firm and gain the control.

In sum, the market for corporate control disciplines underperforming managers. Particularly, "The threat of takeovers acts as a strong motivator for executives to manage the firm's assets in the interests of shareholders rather than in their own self-interest". This allows them to "avoid potential job loss and damage to their managerial reputation" (Cowen & Marcel, 2011). It is hard to evaluate the strength of this mechanism but "we can view the extent to which executives are exposed to the market for corporate control by looking at the firm's takeover defense provisions" (Humphery-Jenner, 2014). In fact, "Although takeover defenses are internal, researchers often use them as a means of examining the extent to which managers are subject to the external governance of the market for corporate control" (Humphery-Jenner, 2014; Kabir et al., 1997). Common takeover defenses include supermajorities, staggered board appointments, poison pills, and severance agreements. Kini et al. (2004) argued that the disciplinary function of the market for corporate control is largely ineffective when firms have takeover defenses such as these.

1.2.1.2. The External Labor Market

The labor market provides a measure of the returns earned by directors. The number of additional directorships held by a director is a common measure of these returns. So, the greater the number of additional boards a director is asked to serve on, the greater the reputation of this director. Additional directorships may therefore be regarded as a proxy for director quality. Assuming that the external labor market is efficient, higher quality directors should be closely associated with the promotion of shareholder interests and better company performance. Thus, the external labor market may be regarded an indirect external governance mechanism.

1.2.1.3. Rating Agencies

Recently, researchers have paid great attention to another form of external governance, which is rating agencies (Chen et al., 2015; Wiersema and Zhang, 2011). Scholars have begun to investigate how the expectations of external financial markets through rating agencies influence firm and managers behaviors (Benner and Ranganathan, 2012; Chen et al., 2015). Securities analysts predict the firm has expected future stock price. They are able then to give recommendations to investors about whether to 'buy,' 'hold,' or 'sell' the firm's stock. Thus, stock purchase behavior and then the value of a firm's stock will be affected by Positive or negative analysts' recommendations. As an illustration, sell recommendations reduce a firm's stock price and therefore impose external pressure on managers to take action. Buy recommendations over and above influence managers behavior as "they are likely to feel the burden of high earnings expectations when analysts are recommending their stock to capital markets" (Mishina et al., 2010). Collectively, analysts' forecasts and recommendations exert a pressure on managers who have become extremely attentive to analyst recommendations and the resultant changes in stock price (Rao and Sivakumar, 1999). In addition, "security analysts serve as legitimate external evaluators whose ratings (and forecasts) can be regarded as certifications of chief executive officer (CEO) ability and evaluations of their corporate strategies" (Wiersema & Zhang, 2011). Thus, managers will be motivated to have better information by acting in the interest of the whole company and avoiding earnings manipulation.

1.2.1.4. Institutional Investors

Institutional investors as well have the ability to control managers. They enjoy a wide range of tools to demand results, which "*makes them an unusually potent force of external governance*" (Goranova and Ryan, 2014). Dedicated institutional investors own significant portions of firms. Therefore, "they are endowed with immense power over top managers because their exit[3] would almost certainly be followed by a sizeable drop in the firm's stock price" (Bushee, 2004). Under the threat of exit, this class of investors can demand that managers offer consistently high performance maintained over time. Consequently, close oversight should constrain managerial discretion and manipulation of financial information by increasing the risk of detection (Hadani et al., 2011). The presence of sophisticated institutional investors as well as a higher analyst following may deter managers from engaging in real earnings management. Bushee (1998) and Roychowdhury (2006) provide empirical evidence suggesting that the presence of institutional investors creates disincentives for managers to engage in real earnings management".

1.2.1.5. Media

The word media involves many communication channels such as newspaper, magazines, radio television, and recently social media… With the technological evolution, the role of media is being more and more instrumental to societies. In particular, it can be considered as another external governance mechanism. In their review, Aguilera et al., (2015) claim that "much of the research on the influence of the media and in particular, its disciplining or governance role has come from accounting and finance scholars". For example, Bednar (2012) claim that it plays a governance role through its ability to exert influence and control on managers and firms to make decisions and adopt practices that are consistent with widely accepted principles of good governance. The Media may also serve as a watchdog by overseeing top management actions. Indeed, media and especially social media can broadly disseminate information. This phenomenon exerts a monitoring role in that" the threat of negative press can deter managers from acting in self-interested ways for fear of their reputational damage" (Dyck et al., 2008). Media is furthermore a powerful tool to reduce information asymmetry by shining light on events that stakeholders may not be aware of while reporting this issue. (Aguilera et al, 2015) declare that" good progress has been made in understanding the media's governance role, and that they have found evidence that media coverage can affect managerial decision-making in some circumstances". However, it is also clear that the media's governance role is somewhat limited and will not influence all firms in the same way.

1.2.2. Internal Mechanisms

Internal mechanisms include among others: ownership concentration, debt financing, board structure variables such as duality, the proportion of non-executive directors etc… We will present the following four mechanisms:

1.2.2.1. Ownership Concentration

Ownership structure is one of the key corporate governance mechanisms and is widely considered to interact with other corporate governance characteristics (La Porta et al., 1998). Ownership structure is a way to discipline managers in order to maximize shareholders-value and reduce agency costs. Property rights theory is the theoretical background of this mechanism. A corporation is defined as a nexus of contracting relationships where the managers are in charge of defining assignments and choosing competent persons who are able to execute them in this cooperative nexus. Agency theory stipulates that if the property is concentrated in the hands of internal shareholders, there will be an adjustment of the conflicting interests in the favor of the company's interest. However, entrenchment theory assumes that managers will act in their interest in expense of other stakeholders. The disagreement between these two theories persists even if major shareholders are external. In line with this, many researchers have found a positive relation between ownership structure and performance in the US and other markets like stipulated by agency theory. In contrast, entrenchment theory supposes that managers in order to take root and increase their opportunistic behavior may use ownership concentration (Shleifer& Vishny, 1989).

1.2.2.2. Debt Financing

Debt financing is another internal governance mechanism whereby "increased debt reduces free cash flow and so limits managerial discretion" (Jensen, 1986b). In fact, bankruptcy risk and periodic control by lenders reduce the opportunistic behavior of managers who will be under lenders pressure. Therefore, increased debt ameliorates managerial performance and investment choices efficiency. Indeed, rather than spending any excess funds on projects that have negative net values, debt requires managers to use these funds in the company's debt. Therefore, debt financing is a way to achieve economies of scale over agency costs and to limit damages caused by managers' manipulation and as a consequence to improve company performance. This mechanism may also be seen as an incentive for managers to perform well in order to limit their job loss and reduce insolvency risk.

1.2.2.3. Duality

It occurs when the same person undertakes the board's two most powerful posts, those of chief executive officer and chairman. "This gives one person too much power within the decision-making process" (Cadbury, 1992). The Code of Best Practice therefore recommended that there should be a clear division of responsibilities. Indeed, Jensen (1993) argued that it is difficult for a board to discipline a chief executive officer who is also the board chair (a situation often labeled as chief executive officer duality). Additionally, Loebbecke et al. (1989) declared that chief executive officer -duality firms are likely to exhibit poor financial reporting quality as the chief executive officer can manipulate financial reporting to achieve their own aims in detriment of shareholders.

1.2.2.4. Proportion of Non-executive Directors

The number of non-executive directors should be sufficient to have a significant impact on board decisions. In fact, the presence of non-executive directors represents a means of monitoring of the executive directors and ensuring that the executive directors are pursuing policies consistent with shareholders' interests (Fama, 1980). "Non-executive directors possess two characteristics that enable them to fulfill their monitoring function. First, their independence and second, they are concerned to maintain their reputation in the external labor market" (Fama and Jensen, 1983).

1.2.2.5. Audit Committee

With the increased public awareness on corporate governance issues, audit committee was included as an important component of a firm's overall corporate governance structure particularly with regard to audit quality and oversight of financial reporting. This independent governance body is an internal mechanism in charge with the oversight of the financial reporting and internal control process. Its formation may be perceived as part of the reaction to corporate collapses that happened over the last decades. Various researchers indicate that" the audit committee is one of the most influential parties in monitoring the accounting choices made by managers and in financial reporting" (Felo et al., 2003) and according to the US *Blue Ribbon Committee Report* (BRC Report), the audit committee is "the ultimate monitor" of the financial accounting reporting system (Klein, 2002b). In the light of its key role, researchers and institutions bestowed numerous definitions. It sounds that there is no universally accepted definition of ACs that could be found in regulations, surveys and research studies. Alternatively, some examples are quoted below:

"An Audit Committee is a committee of the board of the directors established to give additional assurance regarding the quality and reliability of financial information used by the board. An Audit Committee of

a company may be broadly defined as a committee of the board, composed wholly or predominantly of nonexecutive directors, set up to oversee, review and monitor the financial reporting process and the audit activities". (Marwick and Lintock, 1987).

In section 2 of the SOX[4] (Sarbanes-Oxley act, 2002), the audit committee is defined as "a committee established by and amongst the board of directors of an issuer for the purpose of overseeing the accounting and financial reporting processes of the issuer and audits of the financial statements of the issuer. DeZoort et al. (2002) added the concept of effectiveness to their definition, which stipulates that: "An effective audit committee has qualified members with the authority and resources to protect stakeholder interests by ensuring reliable financial reporting, internal controls and risk management through its diligent oversight efforts".

A more recent definition is as follows: *"An audit committee is a committee of the board of directors responsible for oversight of the financial reporting process, selection of the independent auditor, and receipt of audit results" (AICPA, USA; 2009).*

To sum up, the audit committee can be defined as a subcommittee of board of directors/ supervisory board that helps the board to monitor and oversee management to get a high quality financial reporting, which is useful to all stakeholders.

2. AUDIT COMMITTEE AS THE COMPONENT OF CORPORATE GOVERNANCE

The audit committee is additional organ required in the implementation of Good Corporate Governance principle, carrying out the directorial functions in the implementation of company management and managing important responsibilities related to the financial statement system. In fact, the audit committee is a committee set up by the board of commissioners for carrying out the monitoring mission over company management. The presence of the audit committee is highly crucial for the company management. The audit committee is considered as a connection between the management, the board of commissioners and the shareholders in handling control issues (Muda et al.2018).

This section is composed of three parts. The first provides the theoretical background of audit committee. Afterwards, we present the role of the audit committee, and eventually, we extant the audit committee characteristics. Before drawing on the literature review, we present the most important theories linked to our chapter, which are positive accounting theory, signaling theory, agency theory and stakeholders' theory.

2.1. Theoretical Background

Four theoretical perspectives can be used to explain the characteristics of Audit Committee. These include Positive accounting theory, Agency theory, Signaling theory and Stakeholder- theory.

2.1.1. Positive Accounting Theory

Positive accounting theory (PAT)[5] can be defined as a theory, which is able to explain the reasons of accounting choices, methods made by accountants, managers…and the impact of these phenomena on resource allocation and people. The logic of PAT is opposed to normative conception. In fact, the latter one describes what should be done while the PAT tends to explain what is done. PAT assumes that human behavior can be explained by individual wealth-maximizing behavior, implying that an actor will influence the choice of accounting policy to the extent that the choice influences the actor's wealth (Watts & Zimmerman, 1990). Particularly, the main objective of this theory is to explain managers accounting choices when preparing financial statements and especially earnings choices. This theory was established by Watts & Zimmerman (1978) and is based on agency theory and three main assumptions: The first hypothesis named as "bonus plan hypothesis" stipulates that managers choose accounting methods that ensure a higher income when their remuneration system is based on income (in particular variable remuneration part) in order to increase their own bonus. The second hypothesis "debt covenant hypothesis" supposes that when debt ratio is high, managers will adopt accounting choices, which enable them to overestimate the owner's equity in order to have access to more funds provided by financial institutions. The third assumption stipulates that the greater the size of the company, the greater the use of accounting choices that reduce income by managers. This choice is made to reduce taxes the firm is facing. This hypothesis is known as "political costs" assumption.

By investigating the audit committee's effectiveness, we attempt to build on the stream of PAT literature.

2.1.2. Signaling Theory

Signaling theory[6] suggests that managers make some decisions in order to show to investors and stakeholders that the company is in a good and competitive position. They may choose to be audited by a big 4 to announce to outsiders the consistency and reliability of their financial information. A company can also hire a manager with a good reputation in the labor market to send a signal that the management fulfills appropriately its duties. Managers may also announce good news and hide bad news to cover bad performance in order to maintain a good company's market value. This behavior may mislead external users. In this regard, having Audit Committee members with expertise, independence and diligence would give a signal about monitoring ability and would have a positive impact on stock returns and the market value of the company. For instance, (Fama, 1980) argued that: "independent directors have a stronger motivation to maintain the value of their reputational capital in the external labor market". Additionally, AC independence enhances the quality and credibility of information provided to the market (Smith, 2003). Furthermore, the focus on accounting expertise is supported by the results of early research: "accounting expertise is priced by capital markets (DeFond et al., 2005), and by market participants" (DeFond et al., 2005). Companies searching for audit committee members also value it (Beasley et al., 2009). In view of this, DeFond et al. (2005) found a more positive market reaction by the announcement of inclusion of financial experts in the AC of a firm when compared to that of a non-financial expert.

As a result of market information asymmetry, companies may use corporate financial reporting to signal to investors that they hold some favorable information. In fact, Arthur Levitt, former chairman of the United States Securities and Exchange Commission (SEC), says "high quality accounting standards"... improve liquidity [and] reduce capital costs" and claims that "quality information is the lifeblood of strong, vibrant markets. Without it, liquidity dries up. Fair and efficient markets cease to exist".

Given the importance of a quality financial reporting, corporations tend to set up audit committees as signal of good governance. Indeed, the formation of an audit committee in the governance structure of a firm has been signaled as a potential driver for quality and timely financial reporting (Bedard et al., 2004; Dellaportas et al., 2012).

The existence of such committee may exert a strong supervision of managers who always act in their own interest by manipulating financial information which may provide insurance to stakeholders that the economic firm's value is true by reducing information asymmetry between stakeholders and management and also between management and the external auditor. This reduction of information asymmetry could contribute to avoid mispricing of firm's shares and so lead to market efficiency as the efficient market hypothesis[7] supposes that "investors are rational and that prices efficiently incorporate all the available any given time". This Audit Committee effectiveness may give investors a better picture of company's financial performance and capacity. Indeed, the existence of such committee facilitates the building and maintaining of a satisfactory reputation and then strengthens the company's competitive advantage.

2.1.3. Agency Theory

According to agency theory, (Jensen and Meckling, 1976; Fama, 1980; Fama and Jensen, 1983), the most important relationship includes managers (agents) and shareholders (principles). There is a conflict of interest between shareholders who want to maximize their wealth and managers who seek to preserve their own self-interest rather than the firm's owners' interests. Opportunistic reporting of firm performance by manipulating financial numbers is detrimental to shareholders' value because shareholders will get misleading information which may result in higher information asymmetry and higher cost of capital.

In this regard, managers are well positioned to have internal information about facts that happen inside the firm. This information is not accessible to shareholders. So, they engage in manipulating earnings to mask the bad performance and to avoid being evocated. This behavior occurs when shareholders lack the necessary power to supervise managers' actions (Macey and O'Hara, 2003).

Thus, shareholders try to build a suitable governance structure in order to minimize earning management, which is seen as an agency cost as confirmed by (Xie et al., 2003). Among governance mechanisms, an effective Audit Committee may play this role when supervising financial reporting process. This committee will then increase reporting quality. Indeed, (Bedard and Gendron 2010) also claim that the audit committee acts as one such monitoring mechanism. In fact, "the role of the audit committee here is to ensure that the interests of shareholders are properly protected in relation to financial reporting".

This committee should include independent and financial experts' members to have an effective oversight. As argued by Fama and Jensen (1983), "independent directors are free from economic interests or personal links with the managers of the company and are therefore better suited to exercising the monitoring task". Thus, they are expected to have higher incentives to improve financial reporting quality when playing their role effectively. Moreover, financial experts are well positioned to understand and evaluate the quality of financial reports. Financial experts are thus important for the fulfilling of those duties and protecting shareholders' interests in relation to financial reporting quality (DeFond et al., 2005).

2.1.4. Stakeholder Theory

While audit committees are not subject to direct supervision by the Authority of Financial Market, they do have its particular attention because of the ever-increasing importance attached by capital providers to the proper functioning of audit committees in the internal governance of companies. In fact, capital providers are part of stakeholders who include" groups and individuals who, directly or indirectly, influence – or are influenced by – the attainment of the company's objectives: employees, shareholders and other lenders, suppliers, customers and other stakeholders" and Audit Committee should take into account their interests. DeZoort et al. (2002) claim that "the ultimate goal of audit committee is the protection of stakeholders' interests" and "Stakeholders expect audit committees to provide effective oversight that protects their varied interests".

According to the new Dutch corporate governance code, the Netherlands has traditionally followed the stakeholder model, under which management and supervisory board members are required to consider the interests of all stakeholders when making decisions and performing their duties. According to Paragraph 7 of its preamble, the Corporate Governance Code is based on the principle that "a company is a long-term alliance between the various parties involved in the company" which is rooted in the Stakeholders theory which explains the relationship between stakeholders and the information they receive. The management board and the supervisory board have responsibility for weighing up these interests to ensuring the continuity of the company and its affiliated enterprise, as the company seeks to create long-term value. If stakeholders are to cooperate within and with the company, they need to be confident that their interests are duly taken into consideration. Good entrepreneurship and effective supervision are essential conditions for stakeholder confidence in management and supervision. This includes integrity and transparency of the management board's actions and accountability for the supervision by the supervisory board. So, managers can be employed not only as the owner's agent but also as an agent of other stakeholders (Hill and Jones, 1992). However, they can take certain actions in an attempt to obtain personal gains at the expense of other stakeholders and to minimize threats of being dismissed.

2.2. Roles of the Audit Committee

From the above-mentioned definitions, it seems clear that ACs play an important role in ensuring faithful and reliable information and consequently an improved financial reporting quality. In point of fact, (Earnst and Young, 2013) assumed that "the increased importance of audit committees is caused by the increasing responsibilities in risk oversight and the increased scrutiny under which audit committees operate". Besides, Contessotto and Moroney (2014) affirmed that "audit committee enhances the integrity of financial statements and reduces the audit risk thereby enhancing the quality of reported figures". Therefore, it will be appealing to point out the main duties of this committee. In this regard, best practice guidelines suggest that the responsibilities of audit committees should include: considering the appropriateness of the entity's accounting policies and principles; assessing significant estimates and judgments in the financial reports; assessing information from internal and external auditors that affects the quality of financial reports; and asking the external auditor for an independent judgment about the appropriateness of the accounting principles used (AARF, IIAA and AICD 2001).

It is quite clear that in recent years the audit committee has become one of the main pillars of corporate governance system in companies around the world. An audit committee is prominent to the success of an organization, with the responsibilities to monitor the effectiveness of the internal audit function, and the internal control system, and review the financial statements and thereby have a more efficient vigilant internal control in the organization. The most salient roles from the above-mentioned ones involve overseeing financial reporting process, external auditing, and internal control.

After looking at some audit committee definitions and main duties, we will present a brief international regulatory background as well as an in-depth regulatory background in the Netherlands in the next section.

2.3. Audit Committee Characteristics

The audit committee is one of the most important board sub-committees and its main responsibility is to oversee then effectiveness of internal control and financial reporting quality (Albedal et al. 2020). In addition, the audit committee is a basic company's governance structure as the board to this committee delegates financial reporting oversight. The primary function of audit committees is to oversee the financial reporting quality (Abdul Rahman and Ali, 2006; Dellaportas et al., 2012). Mustafa et al. (2018) proposes that an audit committee can ensure high audit quality because of external monitoring mechanisms that can enhance the monitoring role of the audit committee to protect the minority shareholders from the effect of wedge. Some characteristics are critical to get a higher financial reporting quality. For instance, the NYSE rules[8] require that: "*Each issuer must have, and certify that it has and will continue to have, an Audit Committee of at least three members, each of whom must; (i) be independent as defined under Rule 4200(a)(15); (ii) meet the criteria for independent set forth in Rule 10A-3(b)(1) under the Act (subject to the exemptions provided in Rule 10A- 3(c); (iii) not have participated in the preparation of the financial statements of the company or any current subsidiary of the company at any time during the past three years...*".

The new Dutch corporate governance code as well, contains provisions that strengthen its role in corporate governance. First, the code requires independent directors on the audit committee. The audit committee should not be chaired by the chairman of the supervisory board or by a former member of the management board of the company. More than half of the members of the committees should be independent. Second, it indicates that it should include at least one member who has competence in accounting and/or auditing.

In the extant literature, the effectiveness of Audit committee could be explained by a range of variables such as: characteristics (e.g. composition and independence), diligence (e.g. meeting frequencies), and impact on aspects of corporate governance (e.g. financial reporting and audit quality) (Bedard and Gendron, 2010; Hassen et al. 2017; Mustafa et al. 2018).

In the Netherlands, regulators claim that the effectiveness of the Supervisory board is determined by its composition, with the size, expertise, diversity and independence of the supervisory board, as they are decisive characteristics. Given that the Audit committee is a part of the supervisory board, these characteristics also apply to it. So, we choose to focus on its composition in order to assess the audit committee. Therefore, this study investigates whether independent audit committees with financial knowledge, gender diversity and diligence are better positioned to oversee the financial reporting quality. We will start then with the first characteristic which is AC independence.

2.3.1. Audit Committee Independence

Audit committee independence has attracted significant interest. Academics and practitioners have stressed the importance of this feature on the effectiveness of the audit committee. For instance, Pomeroy and Thornton (2008) in a meta-analysis of 27 studies show that audit committee independence is the most chosen measure of audit committee quality and that the consensus shows that it increases financial reporting quality. Additionally, The BRC (1999) and the National Association of Corporate Directors (NACD, 1999) suggested that audit committees are likely to be more effective in assuring a truthful and correct financial reporting if committee members are independent of management.

Therefore, a growing strand of research has investigated the relationship between audit committee independence as a major feature and managerial financial reporting decisions. Nevertheless, there are competing arguments regarding the direction of this relationship in the extant literature: On the one hand, Carcello and Neal (2000) found that the higher the percentage of affiliated directors on the audit committee, the lower the likelihood of issuance of a going-concern report by the auditor for financially distressed firms during 1994. These results were supportive to regulators' concern about the importance of having independent audit committee members as key characteristic that could improve financial-reporting quality. In the U.S, some researchers found that there is a negative relationship between the proportion of audit committee members who are independent and earnings management such as Klein (2002) who hand-collected 692 firm-year observations with the data of composition of board from S&P 500 firms during the period 1992–1993. A negative relation is found between audit committee independence and abnormal accruals (which is a common measure of financial reporting quality). Davidson et al. (2005) also found that firms with most independent audit committee members have significantly smaller abnormal accruals, but this finding did not hold for completely independent audit committees. This was also confirmed by DeZoort et.al (2002) on its synthesis on Audit Committee Effectiveness who suggested that" Audit Committee independence is associated with a reduced incidence of financial reporting problems" as well as Bedard et al. (2004) and Dhaliwal et al. (2010). Moreover, Abbott et al. (2004) found a negative relationship between the presence of a very independent audit committee and the likelihood of restatements and financial fraud. In their meta-Analysis, Pomeroy and Thornton (2008) found that one of the unpublished papers reports statistically non-significant results and seven of the published papers report non-significant associations between AC independence and financial reporting quality. Yu-Hsuan Wu et al. (2015) documented that "their empirical findings indicate that failed firms with a higher proportion of independent non-executive directors on the audit committee are more likely to receive auditor going-concern modification". Therefore, the findings provide support for corporate governance regulators' concerns about the monitoring benefits of audit committee independence on the audit committee for auditors' reporting decisions.

On the other hand, in the UK, audit committee independence was not associated with the quality of intellectual capital disclosure according to the findings of Li et al. (2012). Ben Barka and Legendre (2017) find that when audit committee is fully independent, it is associated with lower firm performance using a cylindered panel data for French companies. However, the results of Kusnadi et al. (2016) cast doubt on the necessity of mandating all audit committee members. The sample firms have audit committees with many independent directors and any incremental independence of audit committees has no significant impact on firms' financial reporting quality.

Pomeroy and Thornton (2008) concluded that "the audit committee independence literature exhibits strikingly inconsistent conclusions. This inconsistency stems at least partly from the diverse financial reporting quality proxies used in the various studies". They declared that "this finding strongly suggests that extant proxies for financial reporting quality used in the audit committee independence literature are tapping into significantly different concepts. In particular, the impact of audit committee independence on high-quality proxies, such as cumulative abnormal returns and the cost of debt financing, is likely to differ from its impact on proxies for egregiously low financial reporting quality, such as fraud-related earnings".

Sun et.al (2014) examines the relationships between audit committee characteristics and real activities manipulation. They investigate the effectiveness of independent audit committees using US firms with stronger incentives to undertake real earnings as a sample. They found that audit committee members' additional directorships are positively associated with real earnings management measured by abnormal cash flows from operations, abnormal discretionary expenses and abnormal production costs, suggesting that audit committees with high additional directorships are less effective in constraining real earnings management. They explain that by the fact that audit committee members' busyness impairs their monitoring effectiveness.

Apart From academics, regulators were aware of the importance of this feature. In fact, SOX required that ACs should be solely formed by independent directors in the US. The UK Corporate Governance Code (2012) also recommended that an audit committee be composed of a minimum of three independent directors. For our context, The Dutch Code contains several provisions intended to safeguard the independence of supervisory board members, such as the absence of family ties and business interests. A best practice provision of the new corporate governance code stipulates that many of the supervisory board members should be independent and that more than half of the members of the committees should be independent.

2.3.2. Audit Committee Expertise

"In recent years, institutions and regulators emphasize the importance of integrating directors with financial and accounting expertise and new directors who are ''Fresh thinkers'' in the AC" (Afep-Medef, 2015; KPMG, 2015). In the USA, the Sarbanes–Oxley Act (U.S. Congress, 2002) mandates audit committees to include at least one financial expert and requires the rest of the members to be financially literate.

According to the EU Statutory Audits Directive[9], at least one member of the audit committee must have competence in the preparation and auditing of the financial statements. This article is implemented in Dutch legislation. Therefore, this characteristic is required in our context. However, the definition of Audit Committee expertise is different from code to code. Iyer et al. (2013) stated that: "A financial expert within the audit committee is defined as a director having accounting, auditing or finance background or relevant experience". Nevertheless, the most consensual dimension of financial expertise is financial-related expertise or experience. As the primary duty of audit committee is to oversee the financial process of the company, it is reasonable to believe that audit committee members with financial expertise have more effective means to monitor management's financial reporting practices to produce higher quality financial reporting.

Given the considerable attention drawn to this characteristic by regulators, researchers have investigated the impact of this individual aspect on financial reporting. DeZoort (1997) believe that audit committee members should have sufficient expertise in oversight areas related to accounting, auditing, and the law" in its survey study.

In addition, DeFond et al., (2005); Zaman et al., (2011) argue that financial expertise is deemed essential to an audit committee's effectiveness because the committee needs to perform a wide range of duties that require a high level of financial/accounting sophistication. According to Abbott et al. (2003), Bedard et al. (2004), having a greater proportion of financial experts on the audit committee increases the quality of earnings. Krishnan and Visvanathan (2008); Badolato et al. (2014); Abbolt et al. (2004); Cohen et al. (2004) and Chen et al. (2006) found that Audit Committee expertise improve the quality of financial reporting. Similarly, Basely et al. (2009) confirm these results. Abbott et al. (2004) found a negative relationship between the presence of financial experts on audit committees and the incidence of financial restatements as it reduces the probability of these restatements. Marciukaityte and Varma (2008) also found the same conclusion. Besides, in the UK, Mangena and Pike (2005) show that audit committee expertise enhances the quality of interim disclosure. However, Li et al. (2012) did not find a significant association between audit committee financial expertise and the quality of voluntary disclosure.

Furthermore, Dalhiwal et al. (2010) claim that expert ability increases earnings quality. In fact, they find that the presence of accounting and finance expert in audit Committee has a positive impact on financial quality as measured by accruals quality for US firms. Indeed, investment bankers as well as financial analysts who are finance experts complement accounting experts in order to have a higher reporting quality. Conversely, supervisors' experts like CEOs or company presidents cannot provide help to them to promote reporting quality. This finding is similar to the results of Krishnan and Visvanathan (2010) who report that audit committee financial expertise is positively associated with earnings quality and the results of Goh (2009) who find that Audit Committee financial expertise increases the probability of timelier remediation of internal control weaknesses.

Yu-Hsuan Wu et al. (2015) found that where the audit committee includes a greater proportion of financial experts, auditors providing the client with NAS are less likely to issue a standard unmodified going-concern report prior to failure. Kunsadi et al. (2015) document that mixed expertise with accounting, finance, and/or supervisory is better than a single expertise in the audit committee. They uncover that while financial reporting quality is positively and significantly associated with the presence of accounting expertise in audit committee, it is not associated with the presence of finance or supervisory expertise alone in audit committee. Additional findings reveal that audit committee with accounting expertise only have no significant impact on financial reporting quality. Instead, audit committees with mix of accounting, finance, and/or supervisory expertise enhances financial reporting quality.

In his AC effectiveness synthesis, DeZoort et al. (2002) raise the question about" whether audit committees should be composed primarily of accounting experts or of members with a mix of finance, accounting, and auditing competence". In this regard, the findings of Ghafran et al. (2017) highlight the usefulness of segregating financial expertise between specialists and non-specialists, something which regulators in the UK and in the US currently do not do. They also highlight the potential value of audit committee expertise in smaller as opposed to larger listed firms, suggesting that the value of expertise to audit quality depends on the specific financial reporting challenges firms face. In fact, the impact of expertise differs between FTSE100 and FTSE250 firms with the representation of non-accounting expertise being especially important in the case of smaller listed firms. There is a debate on whether a narrow or a broad definition of financial expertise should be adopted. A narrow definition refers to financial expertise with accounting knowledge and experience, whereas a broad definition also includes non-accounting financial expertise such as supervisory experience. The narrow view of financial expertise is adopted in this study given the importance of the audit committee oversight role. Dhaliwal et al. (2006) found that the firms with accounting financial experts are less likely to engage in earnings management, and that this is more pronounced for the firms with General Corporate Governance in practice.

Considering the association between audit committee financial expertise and real earnings management, Carcello et al. (2008) examine the effect of audit committee accounting financial expertise on abnormal production costs and abnormal discretionary expenses using a sample of 350 firms in 2003. They find that although audit committee accounting financial expertise has no association with abnormal production costs, it is positively related to abnormal discretionary expenditures for firms with weak corporate governance structures.

2.3.3. Gender Diversity

Another variable that is among the attributes of the Audit Committee and that can affect financial reporting quality is related to gender diversity.

"The term gender in psychology and sociology refers to feminists' efforts to distinguish between biological differences and those determined by social and cultural forces" (Welsh, 1992). Recently, there has been an increasing emphasis on the importance of gender representation on board and committees. As an illustration, evidence of the importance of the gender composition of teams on their performance has been reported in psychology contributions. These studies show that, on the one hand, teams can be more effective when women outnumber or equal men, particularly in complex managerial tasks that need relevant information management and processing, planning, and decision-making over long periods (Fenwick and Neal, 2001). On the other hand, the studies generally report that the proportion of women in teams is a significant predictor of team collective intelligence, intended as the general ability of a group to perform well across a wide range of different tasks (Woolley et al., 2015). In corporate governance and management literature, many empirical studies have been conducted with respect to female representation on boards (Mensi-Klarbach, 2014; Terjesen et al., 2009). In their review, Khlif and Achek (2017), show through a synthesis of empirical findings that female representation on boards, audit committees and top management leads to more conservative reporting through increased accounting conservatism, higher level of social and environmental disclosure, less tax aggressiveness and less intentions to commit frauds in financial statements; and higher audit fees. They also report that females are more cautious than males in the recognition and measurement of income and assets and exert higher control of good news than of bad news (Francis et al., 2015). Krishnan and Parsons (2008) posit that women are characterized by more ethical behavior compared to men in terms of accounting policy choices. This implies less aggressive earnings management to gain financial rewards. Gender diversity on boards and committees has also gained recognition as one of the factors that increase effectiveness. In fact, Adams and Ferreira (2009) claim that including female board members on the audit Committee not only adds diversity, but also strengthens the monitoring efforts of the board. Ittonen et al. (2010) indicate that female representation contributes to board effectiveness and improves the board's monitoring activities within the company. Besides, Thiruvadi (2012) found that" gender-diverse audit committees are more likely to display diligence by meeting more often. Attributes associated with women such as a questioning nature, communication skills, commitment to duty, and fair and morally consistent decision-making are essential to effective corporate governance and are likely to increase the effectiveness of an audit committee in implementing board policy and governance". Moreover, gender is a significant audit committee characteristic in predicting audit quality as the presence of women on the audit committee strengthens the positive relationship between firm size and audit fees, and between risk and audit Female members (Aldamena et al., 2016).

In our research, we consider the abovementioned feature as capable of improving the quality of supervision. The new Dutch corporate governance code stipulates that rules to promote gender diversity within the management boards and supervisory boards of large companies have been applied in the Netherlands since 1 January 2013, the target being a division within the board of at least 30 per cent females and 30 per cent males[10]. The rules are of a 'comply or explain' nature: if the target is not met this will not lead to the imposition of sanctions, but an explanation must be given in the management report as to why the target was not met and what steps will be taken towards meeting it. At the end of

2015, it was announced that these rules, which were originally meant to be abolished as of 1 January 2016, will be extended to 2019.

2.3.4. Audit Committee Meetings

Another strand of research has noted the positive effects of audit committee's diligence, measured by frequency of meetings[11].

As stated by DeZoort et al. (2002) "diligence is the process factor that is needed to achieve audit committee". Similarly, Kalbers and Fogarty (1993) highlight that the audit committee member's diligence is arguably the most important audit committee attribute. Diligence can be also defined as" the willingness of committee members to work together as needed to prepare, ask questions, and pursue answers when dealing with management, external auditors, internal auditors, and other relevant constituents". The NACD (2000) emphasize the importance of diligence when it suggested that audit committees should have four half-day meetings each year". The number of meetings provides a signal regarding effort. Greater meeting frequency is then associated with a reduced incidence of financial reporting problems and with greater external audit quality.

The accounting literature includes many calls for audit committee diligence (Beasley et al., 1999; BRC, 1999; Horton et al., 2000). For example, Beasley et al. (2000) find that "audit committees of fraudulent companies in the technology and healthcare industries met less often than did audit committees in comparable companies without reported fraud". The study indicate that fraud companies generally only met once per year while non-fraud companies met two or three times each year. DeZoort et al. (2002) claim that "Companies with reporting problems are less likely to have frequent audit committee meetings. Other studies find no association between audit committee meetings and financial reporting quality (Bedard et al., 2004). Other scholars find that a high frequency of such meetings minimizes opportunities for internal control and reporting problems (Abbott et al., 2004; DeFond and Francis, 2005). Visvanathan (2008) uses pre-SOX data to examine the association between real earnings management and three audit committee characteristics including audit committee independence, audit committee size and audit committee meeting frequency. He finds that audit committee meeting frequency is negatively associated with real earnings management through reduction of discretionary expenses, but not through sales manipulation or overproduction. Unlike Krishnan and Visvanathan (2008), our study addresses audit committees' characteristics in the post-SOX period.

Recently, in Australia, Bryce et al. (2015) find a negative and significant relationship between AC meetings and the level of discretionary accruals.

3. REGULATORY BACKGROUND OF THE DUTCH CONTEXT

During the past decades, there have been many significant reforms, which had as a purpose to develop and enhance corporate governance of publicly listed corporations in order to rebuild investor's confidence on financial information. An important focus was given to audit committees by several institutions all over the world such as the Financial Reporting Council in the UK, the International Organization of Security Commissions (IOSCO) and the International Forum of Independent Audit Regulators. In the US, in June 1978, audit committee became a listing requirement of the NYSE, and in 1987, the National Commission on Fraudulent Reporting recommended the establishment of audit committee by public companies (Treadway Commission 1987). In July 30, 2002, the Securities and Exchange Commission in the US amended the Securities Exchange Act of 1934 and introduced the Sarbanes-Oxley Act of 2002 (SOX), which has required, for the first time at a statutory level, all issuers in the USA to establish an audit committee as a subcommittee of the board of directors and has revised the requirements for the composition and responsibilities of the audit committees in order to protect the interests of shareholders and other stakeholders (SEC, 2002). For instance, Section 301(3) requires all audit committee members to be independent directors, and Section 202 (1) requires the audit committee to pre-approve all auditing services and non-audit services provided by the external auditor for ensuring the auditor's independence and the oversight of the financial reporting process and audits. Following SOX, corporate governance reforms have been undertaken in many countries across the world, with the key provisions of SOX for audit committees adopted at either a mandatory or a voluntary level (Pwc, 2003). These reforms include the UK, Corporate Governance Code, issued by the Financial Reporting Council (2012), the Principles of Good Corporate Governance and Best Practice Recommendations, issued by the Australian Securities Exchange Corporate Governance Council (ASX CGC) (2003), and the Malaysian Code on Corporate Governance, issued by the Securities Commission Malaysia (2012).

In the Dutch context, audit committee is still relatively new compared to other countries such as the United States of America, Britain, and Canada even though the existence of an audit committee is essential as one of the aspects of the implementation of good corporate governance. It seems important then to give a brief overview of the governance regime in this European country. The Netherlands is a civil law country[12], which has general rules of civil law relating to the governance of unquoted and listed companies. The general rules on financial reporting can be found in Book 2 of the Dutch Civil Code (DCC), which sets out the duties, and powers of the various corporate bodies, as well as rules on representation, conflicts of interest and the liability of management board members. The DCC also contains rules regarding financial reporting and disclosure. Compliance with the rules in the DCC can, if necessary, be forced through the court, while the FSA[13] contains additional rules applicable to listed companies regarding the supervision of business conduct.

A specially designated body, the Authority for the Financial Markets, carries out supervision of compliance with these rules. Alongside these statutory rules, there is a system of self-regulation consisting of codes of conduct containing principles and best-practice provisions drawn up by the sector itself. The first Dutch Corporate Governance Code (also known as the Tabaksblat Code (Witteloostuijn, 2007). Containing governance rules for listed companies, was adopted in 2003 and entered effect in 2004. It was amended in 2008 in order to get more transparency, accountability, fairness and responsibility, with more attention being paid to risk management, the supervisory duties of the supervisory board and the level and structure of remuneration. This code has become a model to many other civil law countries that have developing codes. Continuing developments, globalization and overlaps with legislation have pushed the issue of a new code in 2016 by the corporate governance monitoring committee at the request of the National Federation of Christian Trade Unions in the Netherlands (CNV), the Federation of Dutch Trade Unions (FNV), Euronext NV, the Association of Stockholders (VEB), the Association of Securities-Issuing Companies (VEUO) and the Confederation of Netherlands Industry and Employers (VNO-NCW). It is clear so that the subject of corporate governance remains high on the agenda of the Netherlands, especially with the issue of the new Corporate Governance Code (Calkoen, 2011). This Code provides guidance for effective cooperation and management (Calkoen, 2014). It was formed by self-regulation that means that parties draw up their own rules, without government intervention, to which they then commit themselves by following, enforcing and updating those rules. In fact, it was made by, and is intended for, the parties addressed by the Code. The merit of this Code as an instrument of self-regulation is that it focuses more on the behavior of management board members, supervisory board members and shareholders. The amendments in the Code are based on the applicable legislation and case law on the external and internal relations of companies and take into account relevant corporate governance trends. When formulating the principles and best practice provisions, overlaps with legislation have been avoided as much as possible. It applies to all companies whose registered offices are in the Netherlands and whose shares, or depositary receipts for shares, have been admitted to trading on a regulated market or a comparable system; and all large companies whose registered offices are in the Netherlands (balance sheet value > €500 million) and whose shares, or depositary receipts for shares, have been admitted to trading on a multilateral trading facility or a comparable system. It aims to facilitate – with or in relation to other laws and regulations – a sound and transparent system of checks and balances within Dutch listed companies and, to that end, to regulate relations between the management board, the supervisory board and the shareholders (including the general meeting of shareholders)" (Dutch corporate governance code, 2016). The principles and provisions are aimed at defining responsibilities for long-term value creation, risk control, effective management and supervision, remuneration and the relationship with shareholders and stakeholders. The principles reflect best practices and supplement the general principles of good corporate governance. Companies may deviate from these best practice provisions if they give reasons for doing so in accordance with "comply or explain" principle. This new Dutch corporate governance code contains a set of new amendments. Indeed, it expands upon the supervisory duties: if the supervisory board consists of more than four members, it must appoint from among its members an audit committee, a remuneration committee and a selection and appointment committee, whose duties are also specified. It includes stricter requirements regarding the independence of the audit committee members and an explicit role for the audit committee in the selection and nomination of the auditor. Besides, it contains provisions that aim to strengthen the position of the internal auditor and the role of the audit committee regarding staffing, work plan and functioning of the internal auditor. Furthermore, both the internal and the statutory auditor are now required to join the meetings of the audit committee to further strengthen risk management and disclosure related to risk.

Dutch corporate law has traditionally provided for a dualistic governance model (i.e. a two-tier governance structure), consisting of a management board and a separate supervisory board (each of is governed by different statutory provisions); however, the institution of a supervisory board is only mandatory for companies subject to the 'structure regime'[14]. "A company is subject to this regime if, for a period of three consecutive years:

- Its issued capital and reserves amount to not less than €16 million;
- It has a works council instituted pursuant to a statutory requirement; and
- It regularly employs at least 100 employees in the Netherlands".

Through the influence of international developments, the one-tier board structure (Calkoen, 2011), consisting of a single board comprising both executive and non-executive members, has also made its way into Dutch corporate practice. Chapter 5 pertains to companies with a one-tier governance structure. Companies with a one-tier governance structure have a single management board comprised of executive and non-executive directors. In this situation, the latter supervise the former, and there is no supervisory board. Given that the supervisory board establishes the audit committee, we will focus in our study on companies with two tier-structures.

Besides, the Netherlands provides an interesting context because its legal and institutional environment is different from that of larger markets such as the U.S., UK and Australia. His smaller size and reliance on the international economy and less regulated nature suggest that the findings based on larger markets may not be generalizable to this country. Further, the Netherlands market is characterized by large concentrated ownership and overlapping membership of directors. It is not clear how these unique characteristics affect the effectiveness of corporate governance.

This study fills an important void recognized by DeZoort et al. (2002) who call for governance research in smaller markets outside the U.S. to enhance our understanding of the legal and institutional impact on corporate governance. It provides, to the best of our knowledge, this study has potential implications for regulations and policy makers in this country. The findings of this research can also serve as a benchmark for studies in smaller countries with an institutional, economic, and legal environment like the Netherlands.

According to the new Dutch corporate governance code[15]: "the audit committee undertakes preparatory work for the Supervisory Board's decision-making regarding the supervision of the integrity and quality of the company's financial reporting and the effectiveness of the company's internal risk management and control systems. Among other things, it focuses on monitoring the Management Board regarding:

- Relations with, and compliance with recommendations and following up of comments by, the internal and external auditors;
- The funding of the company;
- The application of information and communication technology by the company, including risks relating to cyber security; and
- The company's tax policy".

Likewise, the audit committee should report to the supervisory board on its deliberations and findings. "This report must, at least, include the following information:

- The methods used to assess the effectiveness of the design and operation of the internal risk management and control systems referred to in best practice provisions 1.2.1 to 1.2.3, inclusive;
- The methods used to assess the effectiveness of the internal and external audit processes;
- Material considerations regarding financial reporting;
- The way material risks and uncertainties referred to in best practice provision 1.4.3 have been analyzed and discussed, along with a description of the most important findings of the audit committee".

The audit committee should also advise the supervisory board regarding the external auditor's nomination for appointment/reappointment or dismissal and should prepare the selection of the external auditor. The audit committee should give due consideration to the management board's observations during the abovementioned work.

CONCLUSION

With the ongoing worldwide development, numerous corporate governance mechanisms were produced which may be classified as internal and external. Among others, audit committee is one of the most important internal subcommittees, which has as a main duty to enhance information credibility and integrity.

This chapter highlights the role of Audit committee and its main characteristics in enhancing the quality of financial reporting, in the context of the Netherlands. Given the uniqueness of the Dutch market, this chapter contributes to the literature by investigating the relevance of audit committee as component of corporate governance. In fact, to the best of our knowledge, the Dutch context is not yet explored especially following the issue of the long-awaited new Dutch Corporate governance code in 2016 which has been updated since a long period in 2008. In addition, this chapter also has implications for managers, policy makers and regulators. Regarding managers, it emphasizes audit committee that has finance and accounting expertise may increase the information credibility. With respect to policy makers, this chapter highlights that effective audit committee help promote the disclosure of internal information. Hence, they should encourage corporate boards to insist on audit committees having people with finance and accounting qualification and meeting regularly with their external auditor. Moreover, regulators may consider making similar recommendations to companies to further enhance the effectiveness of audit committees in Netherlands and other economies. However, audit committees helps to mitigate the incidence of fraudulent financial reporting, which in turn decreases the likelihood of firms receiving unclean opinion from external auditors such as qualified opinion, no opinion, adverse opinion, or unqualified opinion with explanatory language. This implies that audit committees are performing their monitoring role of the financial reporting process more effectively, which subsequently leads to improved firm performance.

Future research could usefully explore this relevant topic in greater depth through examining other AC characteristics, such as the financial experience of its chair, director shareholding, etc. Therefore, AC effectiveness will be captured to a greater extent. This work might be also extended towards other countries besides the Netherlands.

REFERENCES

Abbott, L. J., Park, Y., & Parker, S. (2000). The effects of audit committee activity and independence on corporate fraud. *Managerial Finance*, *26*(11), 55–68. doi:10.1108/03074350010766990

Abbott, L. J., Parker, S., & Peters, G. F. (2004). Audit committee characteristics and restatements. *Auditing*, *23*(1), 69–87. doi:10.2308/aud.2004.23.1.69

Abdul Rahman, R., & Haneem Mohamed Ali, F. (2006). Board, audit committee, culture and earnings management: Malaysian evidence. *Managerial Auditing Journal*, *21*(7), 783–804. doi:10.1108/02686900610680549

Adams, R. B., & Ferreira, D. (2009). Women in the boardroom and their impact on governance and performance. *Journal of Financial Economics*, *94*(2), 291–309. doi:10.1016/j.jfineco.2008.10.007

Aguilera, R. V., Desender, K., Bednar, M. K., & Lee, J. H. (2015). Connecting the dots: Bringing external corporate governance into the corporate governance puzzle. *The Academy of Management Annals*, *9*(1), 483–573. doi:10.5465/19416520.2015.1024503

Aguilera, R. V., & Jackson, G. (2003). The cross-national diversity of corporate governance: Dimensions and determinants. *Academy of Management Review*, *28*(3), 447–465. doi:10.5465/amr.2003.10196772

Aguilera, R. V., Judge, W. Q., & Terjesen, S. A. (2018). Corporate governance deviance. *Academy of Management Review*, *43*(1), 87–109. doi:10.5465/amr.2014.0394

Albedal, F., Hamdan, A. M., & Zureigat, Q. (2020). Audit Committee Characteristics and Earnings Quality: Evidence From Bahrain Bourse. In *Corporate Governance Models and Applications in Developing Economies* (pp. 23–49). IGI Global. doi:10.4018/978-1-5225-9607-3.ch002

Argüden, R. Y. (2010). *A corporate governance model: building responsible boards and sustainable businesses*. International Finance Corporation.

Badolato, P. G., Donelson, D. C., & Ege, M. (2014). Audit committee financial expertise and earnings management: The role of status. *Journal of Accounting and Economics*, *58*(2-3), 208–230. doi:10.1016/j.jacceco.2014.08.006

Barka, H. B., & Legendre, F. (2017). Effect of the board of directors and the audit committee on firm performance: A panel data analysis. *The Journal of Management and Governance*, *21*(3), 737–755. doi:10.100710997-016-9356-2

Beasley, M. S., Carcello, J. V., Hermanson, D. R., & Neal, T. L. (2009). The audit committee oversight process. *Contemporary Accounting Research*, *26*(1), 65–122. doi:10.1506/car.26.1.3

Bédard, J., Chtourou, S. M., & Courteau, L. (2004). The effect of audit committee expertise, independence, and activity on aggressive earnings management. *Auditing*, *23*(2), 13–35. doi:10.2308/aud.2004.23.2.13

Bedard, J., & Gendron, Y. (2010). Strengthening the financial reporting system: Can audit committees deliver? *International Journal of Auditing*, *14*(2), 174–210. doi:10.1111/j.1099-1123.2009.00413.x

Bednar, M. K. (2012). Watchdog or lapdog? A behavioral view of the media as a corporate governance mechanism. *Academy of Management Journal*, *55*(1), 131–150. doi:10.5465/amj.2009.0862

Benner, M. J., & Ranganathan, R. (2012). Offsetting illegitimacy? How pressures from securities analysts influence incumbents in the face of new technologies. *Academy of Management Journal*, *55*(1), 213–233. doi:10.5465/amj.2009.0530

Blue Ribbon Committee (BRC). (1999). *Report and Recommendations of the Blue Ribbon*. BRC.

Board, F. A. S. (2010). *Statement of Financial Accounting Concepts No. 8, Conceptual Framework for Financial Reporting*. Financial Accounting Foundation.

Bozzolan, S., Fabrizi, M., Mallin, C. A., & Michelon, G. (2015). Corporate social responsibility and earnings quality: International evidence. *The International Journal of Accounting*, *50*(4), 361–396. doi:10.1016/j.intacc.2015.10.003

Bryce, M., Ali, M. J., & Mather, P. R. (2015). Accounting quality in the pre-/post-IFRS adoption periods and the impact on audit committee effectiveness—Evidence from Australia. *Pacific-Basin Finance Journal, 35*, 163–181. doi:10.1016/j.pacfin.2014.12.002

Bushee, B. J. (1998). The influence of institutional investors on myopic R&D investment behavior. *The Accounting Review*, 305–333.

Bushee, B. J. (2004). Discussion of disclosure practices of foreign companies interacting with US markets. *Journal of Accounting Research, 42*(2), 509–525. doi:10.1111/j.1475-679X.2004.00147.x

Calkoen, W. (2011). The One-Tier Board in the Changing and Converging World of Corporate Governance: A comparative study of boards in the UK. Academic Press.

Calkoen, W. J. (Ed.). (2014). The corporate governance review. Law Business Research, Limited.

Carcello, J. V., & Neal, T. L. (2000). Audit committee composition and auditor reporting. *The Accounting Review, 75*(4), 453–467. doi:10.2308/accr.2000.75.4.453

Chen, T., Harford, J., & Lin, C. (2015). Do analysts matter for governance? Evidence from natural experiments. *Journal of Financial Economics, 115*(2), 383–410. doi:10.1016/j.jfineco.2014.10.002

Cohen, J. R., Krishnamoorthy, G., & Wright, A. (2004). The corporate governance mosaic and financial reporting quality. *Journal of Accounting Literature*, 87–152.

Contessotto, C., & Moroney, R. (2014). The association between audit committee effectiveness and audit risk. *Accounting and Finance, 54*(2), 393–418. doi:10.1111/acfi.12010

Cowen, A. P., & Marcel, J. J. (2011). Damaged goods: Board decisions to dismiss reputationally compromised directors. *Academy of Management Journal, 54*(3), 509–527. doi:10.5465/amj.2011.61967992

Dalimunthe, D. M. J., Fadli, I. M., & Muda, I. (2016). The Application of Performance Measurement System Model Using Malcolm Baldrige Model (MBM) to Support Civil State Apparatus Law (ASN) Number 5 of 2014 in Indonesia. *International Journal of Applied Business and Economic Research, 14*(11), 7397–7407.

Davidson, R., Goodwin-Stewart, J., & Kent, P. (2005). Internal governance structures and earnings management. *Accounting and Finance, 45*(2), 241–267. doi:10.1111/j.1467-629x.2004.00132.x

DeFond, M. L., Hann, R. N., & Hu, X. (2005). Does the market value financial expertise on audit committees of boards of directors? *Journal of Accounting Research, 43*(2), 153–193. doi:10.1111/j.1475-679x.2005.00166.x

Dellaportas, S., Leung, P., Cooper, B. J., Ika, S. R., & Ghazali, N. A. M. (2012). Audit committee effectiveness and timeliness of reporting: Indonesian evidence. *Managerial Auditing Journal.*

DeZoort, F. (1997). An investigation of audit committees' oversight responsibilities. *Abacus, 33*(2), 208–227. doi:10.1111/1467-6281.00012

DeZoort, F. T., Hermanson, D. R., Archambeault, D. S., & Reed, S. A. (2002). Audit committee effectiveness: A synthesis of the empirical audit committee literature. *Audit Committee Effectiveness: A Synthesis of the Empirical Audit Committee Literature, 21*, 38.

Dhaliwal, G. S., Jindal, V., & Dhawan, A. K. (2010). Insect pest problems and crop losses: Changing trends. *Indian Journal of Ecology*, *37*(1), 1–7.

Dyck, A., Volchkova, N., & Zingales, L. (2008). The corporate governance role of the media: Evidence from Russia. *The Journal of Finance*, *63*(3), 1093–1135. doi:10.1111/j.1540-6261.2008.01353.x

Fama, E. F. (1980). Agency problems and the theory of the firm. *Journal of Political Economy*, *88*(2), 288–307. doi:10.1086/260866

Fama, E. F., & Jensen, M. C. (1983). Separation of ownership and control. *The Journal of Law & Economics*, *26*(2), 301–325. doi:10.1086/467037

Felo, A. J., Krishnamurthy, S., & Solieri, S. A. (2003). *Audit committee characteristics and the perceived quality of financial reporting: an empirical analysis.* Available at SSRN 401240

Francis, B., Hasan, I., Park, J. C., & Wu, Q. (2015). Gender differences in financial reporting decision-making: Evidence from accounting conservatism. *Contemporary Accounting Research*, *32*(3), 1285–1318. doi:10.1111/1911-3846.12098

Goranova, M., & Ryan, L. V. (2014). Shareholder activism: A multidisciplinary review. *Journal of Management*, *40*(5), 1230–1268. doi:10.1177/0149206313515519

Hadani, M., Goranova, M., & Khan, R. (2011). Institutional investors, shareholder activism, and earnings management. *Journal of Business Research*, *64*(12), 1352–1360. doi:10.1016/j.jbusres.2010.12.004

Hassan, Y., Hijazi, R., & Naser, K. (2017). Does audit committee substitute or complement other corporate governance mechanisms. *Managerial Auditing Journal*, *32*(7), 658–668. doi:10.1108/MAJ-08-2016-1423

He, X., Pittman, J. A., Rui, O. M., & Wu, D. (2017). Do social ties between external auditors and audit committee members affect audit quality? *The Accounting Review*, *92*(5), 61–87. doi:10.2308/accr-51696

Hill, C. W., & Jones, T. M. (1992). Stakeholder-agency theory. *Journal of Management Studies*, *29*(2), 131–154. doi:10.1111/j.1467-6486.1992.tb00657.x

Humphery-Jenner, M. (2014). Takeover defenses, innovation, and value creation: Evidence from acquisition decisions. *Strategic Management Journal*, *35*(5), 668–690. doi:10.1002mj.2121

Ittonen, K., Miettinen, J., & Vähämaa, S. (2010). Does female representation on audit committees affect audit fees? *Quarterly Journal of Finance and Accounting*, 113-139.

Iyer, V. M., Bamber, E. M., & Griffin, J. (2013). Characteristics of audit committee financial experts: An empirical study. *Managerial Auditing Journal*.

Jensen, M. C. (1986). Agency costs of free cash flow, corporate finance, and takeovers. *The American Economic Review*, *76*(2), 323–329.

Jensen, M. C. (1993). The modern industrial revolution, exit, and the failure of internal control systems. *The Journal of Finance, 48*(3), 831-880.

John, K., & Senbet, L. W. (1998). Corporate governance and board effectiveness. *Journal of Banking & Finance*, *22*(4), 371–403. doi:10.1016/S0378-4266(98)00005-3

Kabir, R., Cantrijn, D., & Jeunink, A. (1997). Takeover defenses, ownership structure and stock returns in the Netherlands: An empirical analysis. *Strategic Management Journal*, *18*(2), 97–109. doi:10.1002/(SICI)1097-0266(199702)18:2<97::AID-SMJ855>3.0.CO;2-2

Kalbers, L. P., & Fogarty, T. J. (1993). Audit committee effectiveness: An empirical investigation of the contribution of power. *Auditing*, *12*(1), 24.

Khlif, H., & Achek, I. (2017). Gender in accounting research: A review. *Managerial Auditing Journal*, *32*(6), 627–655. doi:10.1108/MAJ-02-2016-1319

Kim, H., Kwak, B., Lim, Y., & Yu, J. (2017). Audit committee accounting expertise, CEO power, and audit pricing. *Asia-Pacific Journal of Accounting & Economics*, *24*(3-4), 421–439. doi:10.1080/16081625.2015.1105753

Kini, O., Kracaw, W., & Mian, S. (2004). The nature of discipline by corporate takeovers. *The Journal of Finance*, *59*(4), 1511–1552. doi:10.1111/j.1540-6261.2004.00671.x

Klein, A. (2002). Economic determinants of audit committee independence. *The Accounting Review*, *77*(2), 435–452. doi:10.2308/accr.2002.77.2.435

Krishnan, G. V., & Parsons, L. M. (2008). Getting to the bottom line: An exploration of gender and earnings quality. *Journal of Business Ethics*, *78*(1-2), 65–76. doi:10.100710551-006-9314-z

Krishnan, G. V., & Visvanathan, G. (2008). Does the SOX definition of an accounting expert matter? The association between audit committee directors' accounting expertise and accounting conservatism. *Contemporary Accounting Research*, *25*(3), 827–858. doi:10.1506/car.25.3.7

Kusnadi, Y., Leong, K. S., Suwardy, T., & Wang, J. (2016). Audit committees and financial reporting quality in Singapore. *Journal of Business Ethics*, *139*(1), 197–214. doi:10.100710551-015-2679-0

Li, J., Mangena, M., & Pike, R. (2012). The effect of audit committee characteristics on intellectual capital disclosure. *The British Accounting Review*, *44*(2), 98–110. doi:10.1016/j.bar.2012.03.003

Loebbecke, J. K., Eining, M. M., & Willingham, J. J. (1989). Auditors experience with material irregularities-frequency, nature, and detectability. *Auditing*, *9*(1), 1–28.

Lubis, A., Torong, Z. B., & Muda, I. (2016a). The Urgency of Implementing Balanced Scorecard System on Local Government in North Sumatra – Indonesia. International. *Journal of Applied Business and Economic Research*, *14*(11), 7575–7590.

Mensi-Klarbach, H. (2014). Gender in top management research. *Management Research Review*, *37*(6), 538–552. doi:10.1108/MRR-03-2013-0066

Mishina, Y., Dykes, B. J., Block, E. S., & Pollock, T. G. (2010). Why "good" firms do bad things: The effects of high aspirations, high expectations, and prominence on the incidence of corporate illegality. *Academy of Management Journal*, *53*(4), 701–722. doi:10.5465/amj.2010.52814578

Mora, A., & Walker, M. (2015). The implications of research on accounting conservatism for accounting standard setting. *Accounting and Business Research*, *45*(5), 620–650. doi:10.1080/00014788.2015.1048770

Muda, I., Maulana, W., Sakti Siregar, H., & Indra, N. (2018). The Analysis of Effects of Good Corporate Governance on Earnings Management in Indonesia with Panel Data Approach. *Indian Economic Review*, *22*(2), 599–625.

Mustafa, A. S., Che-Ahmad, A., & Chandren, S. (2018). Board diversity, audit committee characteristics and audit quality: The moderating role of control-ownership wedge. *Business and Economic Horizons*, *14*, 587-614.

Parkinson, J. E. (1994). *Corporate Power and Responsibility: Issues in the Theory of Company Law*. Oxford Clarendon Press.

Pomeroy, B., & Thornton, D. B. (2008). Meta-analysis and the accounting literature: The case of audit committee independence and financial reporting quality. *European Accounting Review*, *17*(2), 305–330. doi:10.1080/09638180701819832

Rao, H., & Sivakumar, K. (1999). Institutional sources of boundary-spanning structures: The establishment of investor relations departments in the Fortune 500 industrials. *Organization Science*, *10*(1), 27–42. doi:10.1287/orsc.10.1.27

Roychowdhury, S. (2006). Earnings management through real activities manipulation. *Journal of Accounting and Economics*, *42*(3), 335–370. doi:10.1016/j.jacceco.2006.01.002

Shleifer, A., & Vishny, R. W. (1989). Management entrenchment: The case of manager-specific investments. *Journal of Financial Economics*, *25*(1), 123–139. doi:10.1016/0304-405X(89)90099-8

Shleifer, A., & Vishny, R. W. (1997). A survey of corporate governance. *The Journal of Finance*, *52*(2), 737–783. doi:10.1111/j.1540-6261.1997.tb04820.x

Sun, J., & Liu, G. (2014). Audit committees' oversight of bank risk-taking. *Journal of Banking & Finance*, *40*, 376–387. doi:10.1016/j.jbankfin.2013.12.015

Terjesen, S., Sealy, R., & Singh, V. (2009). Women directors on corporate boards: A review and research agenda. *Corporate Governance*, *17*(3), 320–337. doi:10.1111/j.1467-8683.2009.00742.x

Thiruvadi, S. (2012). Gender differences and audit committee diligence. *Gender in Management*, *27*(6), 366–379. doi:10.1108/17542411211269310

Walker, D. (2009). *A review of corporate governance in UK banks and other financial industry entities*. Academic Press.

Watts, R. L., & Zimmerman, J. L. (1978). Towards a positive theory of the determination of accounting standards. *The Accounting Review*, 112–134.

Watts, R. L., & Zimmerman, J. L. (1990). Positive accounting theory: A ten year perspective. *The Accounting Review*, 131–156.

Welsh, M. J. (1992). The construction of gender: some insights from feminist psychology. *Accounting, Auditing & Accountability Journal, 5*(3).

Wiersema, M. F., & Zhang, Y. (2011). CEO dismissal: The role of investment analysts. *Strategic Management Journal*, *32*(11), 1161–1182. doi:10.1002mj.932

Williams, P. F. (1989). The logic of positive accounting research. *Accounting, Organizations and Society*, *14*(5-6), 455–468. doi:10.1016/0361-3682(89)90011-1

Witteloostuijn, A. (2007). Corporate governance in the Netherlands: An overview of the application of the Tabaksblat Code in 2004. *Corporate Governance*, *15*(6), 1106–1118. doi:10.1111/j.1467-8683.2007.00634.x

Woolley, A. W., Aggarwal, I., & Malone, T. W. (2015). Collective Intelligence and Group Performance. *Current Directions in Psychological Science*, *24*(6), 420–424. doi:10.1177/0963721415599543

Wu, C. Y. H., Hsu, H. H., & Haslam, J. (2016). Audit committees, non-audit services, and auditor reporting decisions prior to failure. *The British Accounting Review*, *48*(2), 240–256. doi:10.1016/j.bar.2015.03.001

Xie, B., Davidson, W. N. III, & DaDalt, P. J. (2003). Earnings management and corporate governance: The role of the board and the audit committee. *Journal of Corporate Finance*, *9*(3), 295–316. doi:10.1016/S0929-1199(02)00006-8

Zaman, M., Hudaib, M., & Haniffa, R. (2011). Corporate governance quality, audit fees and non-audit services fees. *Journal of Business Finance & Accounting*, *38*(1-2), 165–197. doi:10.1111/j.1468-5957.2010.02224.x

ENDNOTES

1. Connecting the dots: Bringing external corporate governance into the corporate governance puzzle.
2. The report of the Cadbury Committee (1992) recommended that all public listed companies in U.K. should establish ACs within the two years following May 1992. It provided an outline of AC structure and membership, terms of reference, and a range of duties for the AC.
3. See Dou et al. (2018). Blockholder exit threats and financial reporting quality.
4. US Securities Exchange Act of 1934, SOX Section 404 (2002).
5. Watts and Zimmerman (1978, 1986), “the only accounting theory that will provide a set of predictions that are consistent with observed phenomena is one based on self-interest” (Watts & Zimmerman, 1979, p.300)”.
6. The idea that one party (termed the agent) credibly conveys some information about itself to another party (the principal).
7. Published in 1970, the definitive paper on the efficient markets hypothesis is Eugene. Fama’s first of three review papers: ‘Efficient capital markets: A review of theory and empirical work’ (Fama, 1970). He defines an efficient market thus: ‘A market in which prices always “fully reflect” available information is called “efficient”. He was also the first to consider the ‘joint hypothesis problem’.
8. See Final NYSE CG Rules, Section 303A (7) (a).
9. Directive 2006/43/EC.
10. Best practice provision 2.1.5 Diversity policy (Dutch Corporate Governance Code 2016, p 45).
11. For a summary, see DeZoort et al. (2002).
12. Book 2, Title 4, Part 6 of the DCC.
13. The Netherlands has rules on the supervision of the business conduct of listed companies, laid down in Chapter 5 of the Financial Supervision Act (FSA). The FSA contains rules on, *inter alia*,

the disclosure of major holdings, financial reporting, the prevention of market abuse and the obligations of institutional investors.

14 Book 2, Title 4, Part 6 of the Dutch Corporate Governance Code.

15 On 8 December 2016, the Dutch Corporate Governance Code Monitoring Committee published the revised Corporate Governance Code. The new Code is effective from 1 January 2017, so management reports for the year 2017 must comply with its provisions.

Chapter 10
Internal Audit and Fraud

Safa Chemingui
Higher Institue of Management of Tunis, Tunisia

ABSTRACT

The purpose of this chapter is to study the role of the internal audit function in detecting and preventing fraud. First, this chapter will determine the notion and types of fraud on the one hand and the fraud triangle that companies face and that internal auditors try to detect and address on the other hand. Second, a description of the notion of internal audit will be provided, along with the specificities of this function at the heart of companies. The procedure of internal control and the fundamental principles leading to its effectiveness will be identified. In this regard, the authors analysed the profile of internal auditor. Therefore, an internal audit function with competent staff would generate a good system of internal control and is able to maintain the internal audit's ability to detect fraud. Finally, the role of the internal auditor in preventing fraud is analysed with reference to three dimensions: The first dimension is preemptive. The second dimension is social and ethical. The third dimension is the practical dimension.

INTRODUCTION

No business is immune to the risks of fraud. It represents any act of deceit, and it can be found in all aspects of the economic sector. This criminal act seeks to destroy the social system of civil society and even undermine the sustainability of the enterprise. Fraud is best detected in details, a as it takes advantage of control gaps .Thus, the severe impact of fraud on ethics, on economic and financial profitability and on the company's reputation requires certain mechanisms to put an end to these practices. According to several KPMG investigations, internal auditors are more likely to uncover fraud than external auditors because of direct dealing with the activities of the company.

Detecting fraud is part of internal audits job (Brikett et al, 1999). An internal audit is essentially required to deal with these incidents and is well placed to identify certain anomalies that may be symptoms of fraud. He is, therefore, required to provide an independent evaluation of the information along with useful recommendations. For this reason, we present a challenge to be demonstrated by the function of the internal audit: how will this function guarantee the successful detection of and the fight against fraud. In other words, what role can the internal audit play in detecting and preventing fraud?

DOI: 10.4018/978-1-7998-4852-3.ch010

Enterprises are interested in establishing a self-control function that manages the situation of its internal control system in order to detect fraud in a timely manner. The primary responsibility for establishing and maintaining this control rests with management, and the role of the internal auditor is to assist this in order to prevent fraud.

The role of the internal auditor is to ensure that the policies of the appropriate authorization for transactions are established and maintained. Therefore, the prevention of fraud is the responsibility of management. This means that internal auditors guarantee the effectiveness of management, including its processes, which makes internal auditors responsible for assessing internal control and assessing fraud risks.

Seeking to minimise the risk of fraud, mechanisms for combating fraud are constantly increasing. One can distinguish between internal and external mechanisms. Internal mechanisms include internal control, inspection and internal audit while external mechanisms include external audit. Gramling et al (2004) state that «the internal audit function is one of the four cornerstones of corporate governance».

Our proportion in this chapter is to clarify the concept of fraud in its different aspects. First, we focus on the function of internal audit as the first line of defense against fraud so that most of the previous research focuses on other control mechanisms; second, we have clarified the role of the internal auditor in the prevention and detection of fraud. The focus of this chapter is centered around internal audit as a function developed by companies to take action against fraud. First, we tackle the different theoretical aspects of fraud (definition, types, models).Then, we highlight the role of the internal auditor in detecting fraud. Finally, we also demonstrate the role of the internal auditor in preventing fraud. The purpose of this chapter is to identify the different roles of the internal auditor in detecting and taking action against fraud.

1. NOTION, TYPES AND PATTERNS OF FRAUD THAT THE INTERNAL AUDITOR TRIES TO DETECT AND COMBAT

1.1. The Notion of Fraud

According to the report of the Association of Certified Fraud Examiners, « fraud within an enterprise is a particular form of economic and financial crime that refers to any form of misconduct that consequently leads to a financial loss to the enterprise». According to the ACFE, corporate fraud is « the benefit by a person of his or her professional activity to enrich himself or herself through the voluntary misappropriation of the resources or assets of his or her employer».

In the same regard, fraud is defined by KPMG (2004) as any dishonest activity involving the extraction of a company's value, whether directly or indirectly, regardless of personally benefiting the owner from these actions. Statements on Auditing Standards N°99 (now SAS) defines fraud as «an intentional act that results in notable inaccuracy in the audited financial statements».

According to the International Standard On Auditing N°240 (now ISA), what is termed as « the auditors' responsibilities for considering fraud in a (revised) financial audit» identify fraud as «an intentional act by one or more individuals between management, governance officials, employees or third parties, involving the use of deception in order to gain an unfair or illegal advantage».

1.2. Types of Fraud

According to SAS 82, fraud has two types: the misappropriation of assets and fraudulent financial statements. As for fraud that concerns financial statements, it has cost investors huge figures in recent years (Rezaee, 2005).

This type of fraud is considered as an attempt by which companies deliberately try to deceive users of financial statements such as by falsifying financial documents, intentionally providing inaccurate information, the voluntary misapplication of accounting standards, principles and methods used in the preparation of financial statements and the manipulation of accounting practices.

Misappropriation of assets is the most likely fraud that internal auditing uncovers within enterprises. We distinguish, therefore, between fraud committed against the company on the one hand, such as breach of trust, forgery, theft, abuse of social property and computer fraud.

On the other hand, we find fraud committed in favour of the company such as the publication of inaccurate balance sheets, tax fraud and money laundering.

1.3. Typology of Fraud According to ACFE

Albrecht et al. (1995) identified six types of fraud, namely: embezzlement of employees, management fraud, investment scams, supplier fraud, customer fraud and fraud of various cities Allyneet Howard, (2005). In addition, the SAS N ° 82 standard has granted two classifications for the fraud phenomenon, namely: management fraud and misappropriation of assets. Management fraud manifests itself either by the valuation of products and certain assets, or by the underestimation of expenses and liabilities in the but of fictitiously enriching the content of the financial statements communicated. Embezzlement, also known as employee fraud, involves the theft of money or other business assets and bribes. By browsing through previous work that has tried to explain corporate fraud or non-compliant presentation of financial statements, we find that fraud can be committed either for the benefit of a company or at the expense of the latter. Indeed, ACFE (2010) identifies three main categories of financial fraud, namely: forgery, embezzlement and corruption. Rezaee (2004) states that the three types of fraud are interdependent. As set misappropriation can also cause fraud. Falsification: the falsification of financial statements and reports through the manipulation of financial documents, accounting practices, vouchers and accounts with the objective, among other things, of increasing revenues and attracting investors or reducing profits for the purpose to pay less tax and to give users erroneous financial information which does not, in any case, reflect economic and financial reality.

Misappropriation of assets: The misappropriation of assets which corresponds to an illicit and prohibited transfer of property from the company's assets to that of an employee, third party or another company. This type of fraud is frequently detected by internal auditors during the performance of their mission to verify the effectiveness of the internal control system. From the studies carried out by ACFE (2010) and by PricewaterhouseCoopers (2009) (henceforth, PWC) on the phenomenon of fraud and its typology, we can conclude that the diversion of assets also called employee fraud is the type of fraud most prevalent within companies compared to management fraud or financial fraud resulting from fraudulent financial reports.

Corruption: corruption is generally characterized by the act of offering, giving, receiving or soliciting something of value to influence a decision or obtain a financial benefit. Thus, corruption has harmful consequences, not only for the entity, but also for the integral economic development of the country. In the same context, Klitgaard (1994) point out that the act of corruption hampers economic and political growth, encourages conspicuous consumption and accentuates ambiguity.

Likewise, the empirical work of Brempong (2002) definitively demonstrates that corruption degrades the economic growth of countries and contributes in full force to income inequality. Corruption also allows the transfer of public wealth to specific individuals or groups of people, through excessive use of public power (Bukovansky,2006) .This largely individualistic attitude undoubtedly deteriorates and weakens government capacities and considerably restricts public investment and the quality of the country's infrastructure.

1.4. The Models of Fraud

Committing fraud requires the presence of several factors facilitating this task. In fact, several studies have been done to point at these factors and propose a model of fraud that ensures the prevention and detection of fraud in a timely manner. Among the main models that have been developed throughout several years is «the triangle of fraud». In 1949, the criminologist Edwin H. Sutherland (1883-1950) at Indiana University coined the term «white-collar crime» to refer to the fraudulent acts of corporate executives. His student, Donald R Cressey, later in 1973 found a hypothesis based on the psychology of embezzlers known as the «fraud triangle». This concept is based on three variables: first, the perception of financial needs, second, opportunity or perceived opportunity, and, third, rationalization. According to Albrecht et al (1984), three elements must be present in order to commit fraud: the presence of incentives, rationalization to justify this fraudulent behaviour and the opportunity to produce fraud that refers to a weakness in the system. The combination of these three conditions, therefore, forms what is called «the fraud triangle».

Similarly, the 2002 SAS number 99, «Financial Statement Fraud Consideration» issued by AICPA (2002) was based on Albrecht's work on fraud review to conclude that fraud is associated with three factors: pressure, opportunity and rationalization. Consequently, researchers and practitioners commonly identify three key factors of fraud: Pressure or incitation to commit fraud, Possibility or opportunity, and rationalization.

Figure 1. The fraud triangle
(Donald Cressey, 1973 and Wells,1997)

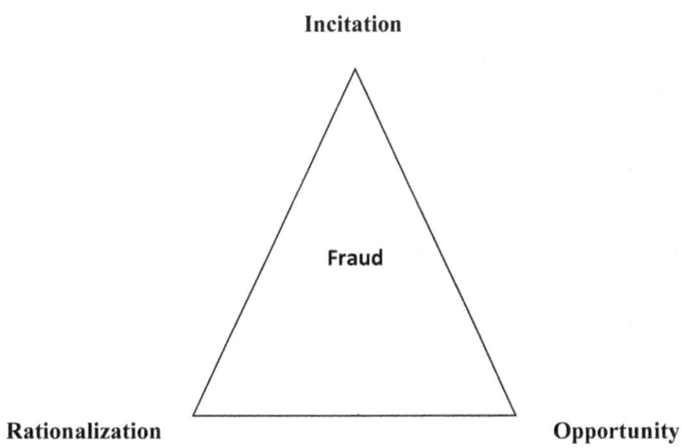

Factor 1. Pressure or Incitation to Commit Fraud

It refers to the fear of immediate need for assets caused by financial difficulties, and the risk of dealing with them is significant when fraudulent acts are committed (Albrecht et al, 1984). It is the reason that leads people to commit fraudulent acts that may have financial or non-financial origins: Financial pressure is a key element in evaluating fraud risk, Financial Market Pressures: the commitments of management to bankers, to the Financial Market Council and to the Stock Exchange must have a satisfactory explanation through reliable reports, Business Line: it provides information on the transparency of the various practices used in the assessment of fraud risk, the pressure of competition, Excessive pressure on management and staff.

Factor 2. Possibility or opportunity

The likelihood of committing fraud increases when an employee attains a high level of trust within the company or authority or weakness of internal control. Indeed, the quality of internal control facilitates the occurrence of fraud the same as other causes favour the commission of fraud.

Factor 3. Rationalization

The main preventative factor of fraud is personal integrity, even in the presence of opportunity and pressure. This entails that the responsibilities of managing and controlling assets must be given to trusted persons. Attitudes and justifications: the ethics of managers, the integrity of their behaviors, the reliability of management forecasts and the complexity of accounting operations.

2. THE ROLE OF THE INTERNAL AUDITOR IN FRAUD DETECTION

It is in the interest of the company to install fraud detection devices within its membership, since detecting fraud in a timely manner is the most urgent task. Fraud detection methods affect the specificities of fraud audits, the search for evidence and safeguard measures. The internal audit function is considered as the first measure of defense against fraud. According to Practice advisory 2130.1, «the active role of the internal auditor in a company's culture of ethics is to help detect misappropriation of a company's assets». (The Institute of Internal Auditors, 2004).

The internal auditor is responsible for detecting and preventing fraud, and this is notable within the various sections of the internal audit standards. Internal auditors are seen as a first measure of defense against fraud because of their knowledge and understanding of the organizational environment and the structure of internal control.

According to The Institute of Internal Auditors (2002), « internal auditors must identify the indexes and red flags that point at the presence of fraud and the circumstances conducive to the production of fraud such as weaknesses in internal control and the absence of the vigilant committee. Then, they must assess these indexes and the likelihood of their occurrence and determine the actions needed to reduce them».

Internal auditing is an analysis and evaluation function that is independent of the other functions of the company that are primarily responsible for the assessment of internal control. As a result, the internal auditor assists company staff in effectively fulfilling their tasks, evaluating the system of internal control, and proposing recommendations on the assessed activities.

The internal auditor, in fact, adopts three main phases in his/her mission within the enterprise: mission preparation, audit work and mission conclusions. In the first phase, the internal auditor studies all the elements involved in the mission such as the internal and external environment and the different working techniques. Then, the auditor begins to analyze the systems and procedures and assess the quality of internal control. Finally, the internal auditor synthesizes the work and develops the necessary recommendations. In order to detect fraud, the internal auditor must adopt working principles and features that ensure effectiveness, and here we mean the internal audit profile.

Internal audit is only a systematic and objective evaluation carried on by internal auditors of various activities and controls of an institution based on four principles which are independence, objectivity, periodicity and universality.

The auditor's ability to detect fraud depends on several factors such as the cleverness of the person who commits fraud, the frequency and extent of fraudulent acts and the degree of collusion surrounding the fraud. (ISA 610).

The effectiveness of the internal auditor is influenced by several factors of which one can cite education, the nature of his or her training and professional experience and skills. Professional skepticism is one of the competencies required by the internal auditor during an auditing mission. According to Fullerton and Durtschi (2004), the level of professional skepticism is a factor that influences internal auditors fraud detection ability.

Avram (2008) examines whether high levels of professional skepticism are correlated with behaviours that contribute to the internal auditors' fraud detection.

Results show that internal auditors with a high level of skepticism would likely increase the need to look for other facts and lead to improved fraud detection. Moreover, the internal auditor's experience improves his or her judgment, since the development of his or her knowledge ensures effective decision-making (Shelton, 1999). Another parameter, the source of the internal audit function, influences its effectiveness in fraud detection and prevention within the enterprise. There are three possibilities for this: the use of its own staff of internal audit, using an external firm or a combination of both possibilities. According to Avram (2008), outsourcing internal audit is the best method to guarantee its independence.

Coram et al (2006) affirm that the probability of fraud detection is greater within a company whose internal audit is partially subcontracted (co-sourcing). They find a positive relationship between an organization with its own internal auditing function and self-reported frauds.

Mihret and Yismaw (2007) propose a four-factor model influencing the effectiveness of the internal auditor. These factors are: the quality of the internal audit that is determined by the ability to provide useful conclusions and recommendations. This quality is undoubtedly based on the auditor's expertise, effective planning and executing skills, Management support is the commitment of management to implementing audit recommendations, the organizational framework is the context in which the internal auditor works. The latter must have a status providing the internal auditor better communication with management and ensuring the auditor's independence for purposes of objectivity and organization, the attributes of the activity include the competencies of the controlled entities and their attitudes toward internal auditing and the level of cooperation with the auditor.

Indeed, this model would only be effective thanks to the objectivity and independence of the internal audit function. We mean by the independence of the internal auditor its ability to carry out its responsibilities with integrity. By objectivity we mean the impartiality of the internal auditor to accomplish its tasks while making sure that the quality of the tasks is well maintained without any compromise.

The internal audit tends primarily to detect fraud, and since it is the assessment of the system of internal control at the heart of the enterprise, the detection mechanisms that are adopted must go through internal control where the internal control procedures as mechanisms for internal audit detection are developed.

The Procedure of Internal Control: Moyes and Baker (1995) notice that the increased use of appropriate audit techniques makes possible the identification of weaknesses in internal controls and the minimization of fraud. Thus, by better identifying weaknesses in internal control, appropriate corrective measures can then be taken, thereby leading to a better internal control quality. Consequently, having a good system of internal control remains an essential component of a company's quality measurement because weak internal control is cited as one of the major opportunities facilitating the occurrence of fraud. Internal control procedures are key elements in fraud detection.

Gibson (2003) considers «lack of separation of duties, poor documentation and internal control procedures» as factors contributing to the occurrence of fraud. In the absence of separation of duties, the same person can perform several functions at the same time, thereby weakening the likelihood of fraud detection, since the perpetrator will hide fraud and not disclose it.

Rae and Subramanian (2008) conclude that the quality of the procedures of internal control and the presence of computerized internal control are negatively correlated with the incident of fraud. Therefore, the quality of internal control procedures depends on three variables (Subramanian,2008): The ethics of the work environment within the company, Risk management training, Internal audit activities. The Ethics of the Work Environment within the Company: Even if the internal control procedures are well written in the form of the company's official policy, several factors may lead the agents to end up being distracted or to ignore the internal control procedures, thereby resulting in negligence and indiscipline.

In a more ethical environment, employees tend to abide by the company rules because it would be morally acceptable behavior. Acceptable ethical behaviour in the organization must be based on honesty, integrity and self-discipline. Risk Management Training: risk management within the enterprise is a process of identifying events affecting the entity and contributing to reasonable assurance of the achievement of the entity's goals (COSO 2004). Consequently, it is confirmed that well-trained employees better identify threats to organization due to weak internal control. Therefore, they can develop procedures that comply with the rules and even suggest changes, modifications and improvements ensuring the quality of internal control procedures, thereby guarantying a better understanding of their importance and benefits.

Internal Control Activities: According to ISA 610, «Use of Internal Auditors Work», the internal audit function is defined as "an evaluation activity designed or provided as a service to the enterprise. This mainly includes the review, evaluation and tracking of the adequacy and effectiveness of internal control". The internal audit function must deduce control weaknesses and reduce the occurrence of fraud.

According to Grambling and Myers (2003), the interest of internal auditors is centered around internal control and around features when assessing fraud risk. They evaluate internal control and its effectiveness in the context of understanding the company's control environment and suggest recommendations for reinforcing it.

As a result, a strong internal audit function with well-qualified staff creates a good system of internal control and is able to rely more on the ability of the internal audit to detect fraud.

Throughout the mission, the internal auditor uses various tools the most important of which are: surveys consist of statistically selecting one element of a set of elements and studying its characteristics. Then, results are extrapolated to the studied set while respecting the sample size and the selection method, Information flow diagrams are a technique for describing the procedures and movements of documents, the internal control questionnaire, rating internal control quality by summation of scores, direct confirmations ask third parties to confirm their transactions, analytical examination includes comparisons of homogeneous data over several periods, account justification means that every account must have a systematic justification for its existence, the IT tools.

3. THE ROLE OF THE INTERNAL AUDITOR IN FRAUD PREVENTION

All business lines are likely to be exposed to standard fraud risks such as corruption, misappropriation of assets and forgery of balance sheets. Taking action against fraud is undoubtedly a major issue for businesses today. Indeed, the economic and financial crisis seems to offer new opportunities for fraudsters to carry out their acts. Nevertheless, some internal or external factors may end up increasing the risk of exposure to fraud within companies. The risk of fraud is rising and could even damage a company's reputation and, above all, financial investors' confidence or any other interested party in the company. In fact, establishing a structured anti-fraud apparatus, in addition to the existing internal audit system, could promote better fraud prevention within companies.

Fraud prevention remains important and better than ex-post intervention because intervention prevents us from wasting time and facing financial deficits, thereby preserving the reputation of the company and the stability of its operations. Regulators insist on the importance of prevention, which is better than detection at all levels.

Internal audit has developed several mechanisms to help it prevent fraud, namely an assessment of fraud risks (preemptive dimension), the social dimension (organizational justice) and the practical dimension that encompasses the different fraud prevention techniques that the internal auditor has to reinforce.

- The Preemptive Dimension: The Assessment of Fraud Risks: for businesses, fraud is a particularly important risk to systematically take into account. After identifying the factors of fraud risks, the internal auditor must analyze these risk factors in order to identify, quantify and detect them. Internal auditors take into consideration the perspective of risk assessment and focus essentially on major corporate risks, risks related to operational systems and risks of control failures. The notion of risk has always been associated on the one hand with that of uncertainty and, on the other hand, with what one incurs if the event takes place.

The IIA and IFAC define risk as the possibility of an event that could have an impact on the achievement of objectives. The internal auditor must look for and demonstrate the risks, come up with solutions to convince managers, and then monitor the implementation of these plans.

The possibility of fraud within the enterprise is a risk which must be recognised by the managers because fraud is not inevitable.

Wilks and Zimbelman (2004) suggest that decomposing the assessment of fraud risk has more benefits than the general risk assessment . They also suggest a basis for this decomposition informed mainly by the factors in the fraud triangle. Thus, this detailed assessment allows auditors to deal with the risks of fraud independently of other parties. The documentation is considered as evidence of the fraud risk assessment. According to Agoglia et al (2003) «the format of supporting evidence can influence auditors' fraud risk assessments».

The IIA standards confirm the need to identify and assess the factors of fraud and the necessity of decisions and judgments related to fraud risks to reflect the assessments of these factors. The revised ISA 240 standard stresses the need to take into account the importance of fraud risk in the process of auditing and requires specific procedures for the detection of fraud. Grambling et al (2004) affirm that the auditor must reinforce and support an enterprise's governance mechanisms and evaluate the effectiveness of risk management and control. Recent regulations require relying on internal auditors' reports since they are well trained to identify and detect all Red flags that can lead to fraud.

Among the risks of fraud, one can find the strong turnover of staff, the demotivation of employees from late bank reconciliations of complex transactions. In fact, during an audit mission, managers are advised to: Have enough knowledge about the fraud to be identified and the indications that may have been committed, Be alert to opportunities like internal control weaknesses that contribute to the occurrence of fraud, Assess fraud indicators, Notify managers within the company when enough fraud indicators exist to recommend an investigation.

- The Social and Ethical Dimension: Perceptions of Organizational Justice: organizational justice concerns the rationalization of the individual and the motivation or incentive to commit fraud. This refers to the psychological concept that is based on theories of equity and justice. Perceptions of organizational justice are a strong influence on the motivation and rationalization of fraud and the quality of internal control procedures (Subramaniam, 2008). Justice is improved when there is open communication between employees and employers, as transparent and optimal communication can prevent fraud (Bostan and Grosu, 2010). The SOX 2002 Act requires companies to conduct an annual audit reporting the management of internal controls in order to ensure a fair and equitable working environment. Consequently, because of perceptions of low quality organizational justice, employees are more easily able to rationalize fraud. Salierno (2007) assumes that internal auditors are key actors in ensuring the integrity of the company and anti-fraud activities. That is why, internal auditors must be an element of governance.
- The Practical Dimension: the Different Techniques of Fraud Prevention: the main measures cited to act against fraud are rather preemptive: code of conduct: this contributes to establishing an ethical environment to explain and define, through a written document, the roles and responsibilities of each person in the context of his or her duties and commitment to the company to act against fraud. This also means anti-fraud training for employees and seeking legal advice.

Economic entities suffer from the costs and losses associated with all forms of fraud. Several prevention and detection techniques have been implemented in order to reduce these direct and indirect costs (Bierstaker et al, 2006). Well developed strategies to promote the quality, integrity and reliability of financial information and the effectiveness of audit functions include:

- Red flags are a method to act against fraud. It is based not only on the use of a list of fraud indicators, but also the conditions associated with fraud. Krambia-Kardis (2002) defines Red flags as an early warning of fraud.
- Maintaining a fraud policy: It means communicating clearly with employees through training seminars and annual performance assessments, securing an ethical work environment by promoting an ethical tone demonstrating zero tolerance for fraud, therefore, communicating the appropri-

ate policies and procedures that are monitored periodically and directed to all employees with no exceptions.

- Assist in the implementation and running of a fraud service: the most effective and profitable way is to set up a telephone line allowing employees to give anonymous advice on the occurrence of fraud.
- Employee reference checks: This refers to assessing the integrity of job applicants. Before recruitment, the honesty of new employees must be ensured through their references. The failure of this verification would likely lead to hiring dishonest people.
- A Fraud Vulnerability Test: it is an approach to the detection and prevention of fraud by exposing the enterprise to fraud and assessing the behaviors and actions of employees.
- Assessing the performance of companies contracts with suppliers: This is carried out by checking the company's contracts and its agreements in order to detect any likely sign of contract fraud.
- Analytical Assessment: fraud can affect financial statements and ratios. Different analytical techniques contribute to uncovering existing, but not presented, relationships or the absence of relationships that should be present. This assessment can also investigate unusual elements.
- Protect information systems: This refers to manipulating false data inputs or outputs that may damage the information system. This protects the system by using either passwords or other internal control devices.
- Discovery by Sampling: it refers to estimating the percentage of a population that has a particular characteristic or attribute and applying this method while considering fraud as an error message. Threat Analysis: it is carried out by adopting a proactive approach to fraud prevention.
- Enterprise Governance must be Vigilant and Effective: the governance of the enterprise aims to divide the responsibilities of the different enterprise participants and establish systems of internal control to protect the enterprise's assets from fraud and theft, Surprise Audit: It contributes to limiting fraudsters' time to react, modify or hide evidence of their fraud, Compulsory Holidays and Job Rotation, Separation of Duties, Tracking employees in sensitive positions, Creating a vigilant audit committee.

Figure 2. The role of internal audit on Fraud prevention[1]

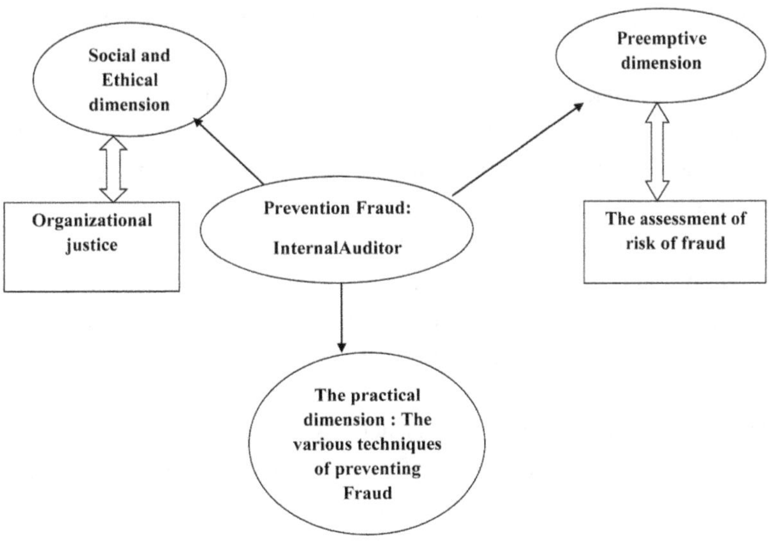

4. THE RELATIONSHIP BETWEEN INTERNAL AUDIT AND CORPORATE GOVERNANCE PRACTICES: THE INTERNAL AUDITOR: A KEY GOVERNANCE MECHANISM IN THE COMPANY

Internal audit is a very important mechanism in the corporate governance process. Thus, professionals consider that internal audit adds value to governance by providing useful and relevant information to the other pivots of governance (Burnaby and Hass, 2009). The internal audit function is performed by a department that reports to management but is independent of other departments. The hierarchical connection of the internal auditor to general management, the board of directors and / or the audit committee, gives him the possibility of participating in the reduction of asymmetry of information which persists between the various stakeholders of the company. Indeed, Piot (2005) stipulates that «a quality audit function should logically respond to a demand in the management of agency conflicts, a demand intended to minimize contractual costs and maintain the balance of the governance system».

IFACI defines internal auditing in the business as the function responsible for periodically reviewing the means available to management and managers at all levels to manage and control the business. The internal audit function was largely neglected by legal and financial regulators as well as by the company and its stakeholders. However, following the financial scandals in the United States, starting with the Enron affair, special attention was paid to strengthening the internal audit function. Consequently, internal audit is designed above all, by developed countries, as a key mechanism within companies. The internal audit function allows for an efficiency in the control process as well as a reduction in irregularities notably, embezzlement and corruption (Rahahleh, 2010). Consequently, an effective audit function allows, restore investor confidence in the quality of corporate financial reporting that has been seriously attacked. The IIA, in its position paper presented to the United States Congress, states that internal auditors, the board of directors, senior management and external auditors are the cornerstones of the foundation on which effective governance must be built (IIA, 2002).The IIA also admits that the internal auditor is both an active participant in the corporate governance process and an independent witness to this process. Internal audit is normally a function independent of management. This character of independence also gives the internal auditor the role of guardian of the trust of the agency relationship which unites shareholders and managers, even if this guardian is internal to the company.

IFACI defines internal auditing as «an independent and objective activity that gives an organization assurance on the degree of control of its operations, advises it to improve them, and contributes to creating added value. It helps this organization achieve its objectives by evaluating, through a systematic and methodical approach, its risk management, control, and corporate governance processes, and by making proposals to strengthen their effectiveness». The internal auditor allows for the integrity of the information disclosed, and therefore improves the quality of the financial reports disclosed, Abbott et al. (2012) illustrate the solemnity of the internal audit function in the prevention and detection of fraud, essentially involving the misappropriation of assets and corruption.

Therefore, it is the responsibility of the internal auditor to identify control activities that mitigate the risks of fraud that are likely to occur and could have significant consequences for the business. However, the IIA in its useful position paper on fraud in 2003 indicates that: «primary responsibility for the prevention, detection and investigation of fraud is the responsibility of management, which also has the responsibility of managing the risk of fraud». Thus, according to Rezaee (2005), the internal auditor faces certain responsibilities during the performance of his detection mission, drawing up a fraud report for the financial statements. These responsibilities are summarized by Rezaee in the following points: The identification of indices and red flags that spread the production of fraud on the financial statements; The declaration of dysfunctions, deficiencies in the internal control process, the absence of a concerned audit committee, which can give the chance to the creation of fraudulent financial statements; The assessment of the signals and circumstances identified, the estimation of the probability of their circumstances as well as the determination of the measures necessary to reduce or minimize their consequences; Warn the parties concerned within the organization such as senior executives not applied in the fraud, the board of directors and the audit committee for a more in-depth investigation of the possibility of fraud in the financial statements. The audit profession generally understates the importance of its role in detecting fraud and continues to emphasize the role of management. By contradicting responsibility for detecting fraud, auditors aim to avoid legal liability in order to protect oneself against claims (Cristina, 2009). Setting up an internal audit system within a firm is a costly measure taken by the firm. Nevertheless, in order to ensure the quality of internal control, while carrying out periodic and independent control of the processes and monitoring of internal control procedures, in order to prepare an audit report. This report can be considered as a robust means allowing the improvement of the internal control system as well as the reduction of the risks of fraud and corruption, insofar as the periodicity of such a report should allow the interested parties to put in place evidence of trends by comparing current results to those of previous periods.

CONCLUSION

This chapter explains the role of the internal auditor in fraud detection and Prevention. First, we have developed the notion of fraud within the company which is only a place favorable to an event. We have also tried to reveal the concept and types of fraud that the organization faces and that the internal auditor is trying to detect and combat. As we treated the triangle of fraud fixed according to Cressey (1973) and Wells (1997). Third, a description of the internal audit function and the profile of the internal auditor delineated by the various authors are provided. This profile requires several skills, a minimum of years of experience and professional skepticism in order to meet certain criteria ensuring its effectiveness. The internal auditor is mainly responsible for the assessment of internal control and its different mechanisms for detecting fraud. The internal control procedures are analyzed. Second, the role of the internal auditor in fraud prevention within the company is tackled. We need to act against fraud, thus, evaluate its risks, and then focus on the usual measures of prevention. It is noted that the prevention or fight against fraud is carried out through three dimensions: the first dimension is preemptive and concerns the assessment of the risk of fraud within the enterprise. The second is the social and ethical dimension that is raised in organizational justice, and the third is the practical dimension that brings together the different techniques of fraud prevention. Finally we have addressed The relationship between internal audit and corporate governance practices: the internal auditor: a key governance mechanism in the company.

REFERENCES

Abbott, L. J., Parker, S., & Peters, G. F. (2012). Internal audit assistance and external audit timeliness. *Auditing*, *31*(4), 3–20. doi:10.2308/ajpt-10296

Agoglia, C. P., Beaudoin, C., & Tsakumis, G. T. (2009). The effect of documentation structure and task-specific experience on auditors' ability to identify control weaknesses. *Behavioral Research in Accounting*, *21*(1), 1–17. doi:10.2308/bria.2009.21.1.1

Albrecht, W. S., Howe, K. R., & Romney, M. B. (1984). *Deterring fraud: the internal auditor's perspective*. Inst of Internal Auditors.

American Institute of Certified Public Accountants. Study Group on the Objectives of Financial Statements. (1973). Objectives of financial statements (Vol. 1). American Institute of Certified Public Accountants.

Bierstaker, J. L., Brody, R. G., & Pacini, C. (2006). Accountants' perceptions regarding fraud detection and prevention methods. *Managerial Auditing Journal*, *21*(5), 520–535. doi:10.1108/02686900610667283

Birkett, W. P., & Institute of Internal Auditors. (1999). *Internal auditing: the global landscape*. Academic Press.

Boţa-Avram, C. (2008). The approaches of fraud from internal audit's point of view. *International Journal of Business Research*, *8*(2), 83–187.

Bradbury, M. E., Mak, Y. T., & Tan, S. M. (2006). Board characteristics, audit committee characteristics and abnormal accruals. *Pacific Accounting Review*, *18*(2), 18. doi:10.1108/01140580610732813

Bukovansky, M. (2006). The hollowness of anti-corruption discourse. *Review of International Political Economy*, *13*(2), 181–209. doi:10.1080/09692290600625413

Cressey, D. R. (1950). The criminal violation of financial trust. *American Sociological Review*, *15*(6), 738–743. doi:10.2307/2086606

Cressey, D. R. (1967). Methodological problems in the study of organized crime as a social problem. *The Annals of the American Academy of Political and Social Science*, *374*(1), 101–112. doi:10.1177/000271626737400110

Cristina, B. A., & Cristina, P. (2009). Measuring and assessment of internal audit's effectiveness. *Annals of Faculty of Economics*, *3*(1), 784–790.

Fullerton, R., & Durtschi, C. (2004). *The effect of professional skepticism on the fraud detection skills of internal auditors*. Available at SSRN 617062

Gramling, A. A., & Myers, P. M. (2006). Internal auditing's role in ERM: As organizations lay their enterprise risk groundwork, many auditors are taking on management's oversight responsibilities, new research finds. *Internal Auditor*, *63*(2), 52–58.

Gyimah-Brempong, K. (2002). Corruption, economic growth, and income inequality in Africa. *Economics of Governance*, *3*(3), 183–209. doi:10.1007101010200045

Kassem, R., & Higson, A. (2012). The new fraud triangle model. *Journal of Emerging Trends in Economics and Management Sciences, 3*(3), 191-195.

Klitgaard, R. (1994). A framework for a country programme against corruption. *Accountability and Transparency in International Economic Development: The Launching of Transparency International, 55*.

Krambia-Kapardis, M. (2002). A fraud detection model: A must for auditors. *Journal of Financial Regulation and Compliance*, *10*(3), 266–278. doi:10.1108/13581980210810256

Mihret, D. G., & Yismaw, A. W. (2007). Internal audit effectiveness: An Ethiopian public sector case study. *Managerial Auditing Journal*.

Moyes, G. D., & Baker, C. R. (1995). How effective are audit techniques in detecting fraud? *Internal Auditing-Boston-Warren Gorham and Lamont Incorporated*, *10*, 32–32.

Piot, C. (2001). Agency costs and audit quality: Evidence from France. *European Accounting Review*, *10*(3), 461–499. doi:10.1080/713764630

Piot, C., & Janin, R. (2007). External auditors, audit committees and earnings management in France. *European Accounting Review*, *16*(2), 429–454. doi:10.1080/09638180701391030

PwC. (2010). *Future rich in opportunity: Internal audit must seize opportunities to enhance its relevancy. State of the internal profession study*. Author.

Rae, K., & Subramaniam, N. (2008). Quality of internal control procedures. *Managerial Auditing Journal*, *23*(2), 104–124. doi:10.1108/02686900810839820

Rahahleh, M. Y. (2010). Regulating the profession of internal auditing in Jordan. European Journal of Economics. *Finance and Administrative Sciences*, *20*, 162–180.

Reffett, A. B. (2010). Can identifying and investigating fraud risks increase auditors liability? *The Accounting Review*, *85*(6), 2145–2167. doi:10.2308/accr.2010.85.6.2145

Rezaee, Z. (2005). Causes, consequences, and deterence of financial statement fraud. *Critical Perspectives on Accounting*, *16*(3), 277–298. doi:10.1016/S1045-2354(03)00072-8

Sánchez-Ballesta, J. P., & García-Meca, E. (2007). Ownership structure, discretionary accruals and the informativeness of earnings. *Corporate Governance*, *15*(4), 677–691. doi:10.1111/j.1467-8683.2007.00596.x

Shelton, S. W. (1999). The effect of experience on the use of irrelevant evidence in auditor judgment. *The Accounting Review*, *74*(2), 217–224. doi:10.2308/accr.1999.74.2.217

Wells, J. T. (2002). Occupational fraud: The audit as deterrent. *Journal Of Accountancy-New York*, *193*(4), 24–29.

Wells, J. T. (2004). New approaches to fraud deterrence. *Journal Of Accountancy-New York*, *197*(2), 72–76.

ENDNOTE

1 This figure prepared by author.

Chapter 11
Succession Planning in Family-Owned Business Evidence From an Emerging Economy

Muhammad Arslan
https://orcid.org/0000-0001-5046-7627
KIMEP University, Kazakhstan

ABSTRACT

Family-owned businesses (FOBs) play an important role in the economy of a country through the creation of jobs. However, most FOBs lack strategies regarding succession planning in both developed and developing economies. This study explores the strategies that are used by FOBs to prepare future leaders. Drawing on qualitative research design, this study employed a multiple case study approach and selected 13 cases by employing a purposive sampling technique from the FOBs of Pakistan. Semi-structured interviews were conducted with the successors of FOBs. The findings reveal that succession planning is pivotal for the development of business and the successful transition of FOB from one generation to another. Most of the respondents fully understand the importance of succession planning for the sustainability of the business. However, in some cases, socioemotional aspects of generational succession planning require strategies that concurrently focus on successor suitability, the consensus of the family, mode of transition, leadership, and challenges faced by the FOBs.

INTRODUCTION

In the last decade, the phenomenon of the family owned businesses (FOBs) have received growing attention from academics and consultants. These FOBs are acknowledged as a fundamental and discrete organizational form. In many countries, FOBs are important for the creation of jobs and represent majority of companies (Aamir & Sohail, 2006). On the other side, the human resource management in any organization is struggling to maintain the workforce within the organization (Pandey & Sharma, 2014) . In addition, researchers also found that many FOBs fail due to lack of succession planning (Mehrabani & Mohamad, 2011) and human capital development. In similar vein, Pasban and Nojedeh (2016) argued

DOI: 10.4018/978-1-7998-4852-3.ch011

that human resources are pivotal in gaining sustainable competitive advantage and efficiency for any organization due to communication and knowledge with customers. Therefore, labor force is considered as productive asset rather costly assets (Hendricks, 2002). Succession planning has been acknowledged as one of most pivotal processes to increase the survival of FOBs from one generation to next generation. Griffeth, Allen, and Barrett (2006) documented that small FOBs play an intensifying part for the economic stability of any country. Williams, Zorn, Russell Crook and Combs (2013) argued that family businesses contribute 57% towards GDP and generates 75% of all new jobs in US. Therefore, the continuation of FOBs, generation after generation, is pivotal for businesses and economy as a whole and succession planning is the most important decision (Molly, Laveren, & Deloof, 2010). In contrast, the succession failures can cause conflicts among family relationships that lead to the destruction of businesses (Experts, 2012). Hall and Hagen (2014) argued that FOBs have an increased chance of failing without proper succession planning. Statistics reveal that 41% Canadian SMEs owners plan to exist their business within five years while only 35% of Canadian SMEs have informal and unwritten plan for their future succession (Checkley, 2010; Wang, Watkins, Harris, & Spicer, 2004). Lyon and Hollcroft (2012) and Hoch (2013) argued that many FOBs are vulnerable and in danger of failing due to lack of appropriate succession planning both in developed and developing countries.

According to a report of Small Medium Enterprise development authority, there are 3.2 million small FOBs in Pakistan that contributes 30% of its total GDP. Moreover, FOBs generate approximately 80 percent of employment within Pakistan, therefore, the well-being and continued growth of these FOBs is imperative for a developing country like Pakistan. According to tax ordinance of Pakistan, businesses having equity up to Rs. 25 million and turnover of Rs. 200 million are termed as small businesses. FOBs are those which are run or owned by a member/members of a single family. Ward (2016) documented that FOBs need assistance in development and implementation of succession planning. Sharma, Chrisman, Pablo and Chua (2001) documented that fewer than 30% successful FOBs make it to third generation while less than 15% of FOBs can make through third generation. Similarly, researchers found that, in case of retirement or death of owner of FOBs, less than one third of businesses sustained up to second generation (Lobley, Baker, & Whitehead, 2016) and less than 10% of FOBs sustain till third generation (Breton-Miller, Miller, & Steier, 2004). Though, researchers stressed the vitality of succession process to ensure the success of FOB (Brockhaus, 2004; Poza, 2013), but still, longevity of FOBs is alarmingly low despite substantial research (Abdille, 2013; Wang et al., 2004). These failures of FOBs can have severe implications for the developing countries whose economy is heavily dependent on these FOBs. The successor makes long term or short-term strategies and takes decisions that can lead business towards prosperity or decline. The longevity of FOBs depends on the strengths of the relationships which exist among members of families upon whose skills and experience the businesses depend. Whether they act as representatives, their dedication and motivation are essential for the accomplishing of congruity in privately owned businesses. In addition, the researchers found that succession planning is quite different in large firms as compared to small family owned businesses. The large firms have proper policies of succession planning and it is quite wider, however it is limited to only family members in case of FOBs (Tatoglu et al., 2008). As many researchers who have conducted studies of FOBs have pointed out, intergenerational mobility is a key factor for their prospects of survival. Consequently, responsibility among the members of the families establishes one of the important components which ensure viable and smooth succession in FOBs (Björnberg & Nicholson, 2012). Similarly, a survey conducted by PricewaterhouseCoopers (2007) revealed that 25% of the organizations which were included in the review were likely to change hands within the next five years. It was also found that 51% of the respondents who anticipated changes, in terms of responsibility for their organizations, believed that it would remain in their families and that approximately half of all the organizations which were reviewed had no formally articulated strategies for succession. Researchers argued that FOBs are usually systematized around a set of instigating emotional interpersonal relations that can have negative or positive consequences. Therefore, it is imperative for FOBs to improve the business practices while keeping the balanced association among business and family to achieve sustainability (Gomez, 2005; Wee & Ibrahim, 2012).

Sardeshmukh (2008) found less focus on preparation of heirs as a vital aspect of effective succession planning in FOBs. Similarly, Kaunda and Nkhoma (2013) found that notwithstanding of having the succession plans in place, successors or the heirs are ought to generate orderly career progression structures in the transition of FOBs. Existing studies only explored the factors affecting succession planning (Kaunda & Nkhoma, 2013; Magasi, 2016; Tatoglu et al., 2008) and reviewed the fundamental practices (Vassiliadis & Vassiliadis, 2014) but failed to explore the leadership strategies and challenges in succession planning in FOBs. This study explores the leadership strategies of succession planning in FOBs of Pakistan and determines how organizational leaders are prepared for succession planning. Moreover, the study also explores required skills and knowledge; and challenges faced to prepare future generations for leadership role in FOBs of Pakistan (Bennedsen, Fan, Jian, & Yeh, 2015).

LITERATURE REVIEW

Succession planning is considered as long-term process (Sharma, Chrisman, & Chua, 2003) which convoluted several activities and postulates sustainability and long-term continuity of an organization (Sharma et al., 2001). Therefore, effective succession planning can have positive effect on business practices and performance. Chrisman et al., (2009) documented that family business research literature revolves on exploration of problems, challenges and solutions associated with FOBs, however, some recent studies accentuated the need of succession planning in FOBs (Kim, 2012; Negrea, 2008; Rothwell, 2010) and focused on awareness (Arslan, Abidin, Alqatan, & Roudaki, 2019; Arslan & Alqatan, 2020). However, Santiago (2000) conducted a study in Philippine FOBs and found that succession process should be consistent with family values because persuasive succession is not wholly reliant on having succession planning. Distelberg and Blow (2010) found that integrated values perform an important role in the appropriate performance of the FOBs. Decker, Heinrichs, Jaskiewicz, and Rau (2016) documented that succession is over published, however, the literature on succession remains disjointed and non-cumulative in unique contextual factors. Researchers also argued that sustainable FOBs have some common succession practices (Cabrera-Suarez, 2005) and these FOBs leaders entrenched their personal skills in the business operations (Dana & Smyrnios, 2010). Giarmarco (2017) documented that leaders can use these three core problems to reduce family conflicts, transfer taxes and preparation for next generation. Moreover, financial service professionals should involve and play a pivotal role in developing succession planning for organization. Holistically, succession planning is a means of incorporating professional financial advisors who help organizational leaders to reduce tax burden and create most value of their business (Hall & Hagen, 2014). Elsaid and Ursel (2011) conducted a study of 679 CEOs in North American firms to investigate the gender of successors. They found that it is more likely for successors to be female if there are more percentage of female board members regardless of the characteristics of female board members. They also found that female CEOs use more measures to decrease the risks. Durst and Wilhelm (2012) conducted a study among German printing SMEs to investigate the risk of lack of knowledge and succession planning due to exit of key employees. They found that lack of knowledge and succession planning have negative effect on financial situation of organization. They also argued that knowledge training and succession planning is pivotal for organizations (Durst & Wilhelm, 2012). Filser, Kraus and Märk (2013) identified three crucial problems (i.e. organizational, interpersonal and individual) and leaders need to tackle these. Moreover, leaders should also handle the stage in which conflicts arise within the organization (Filser et al., 2013). Greenberg (2012) conducted a comparative study of FOBs and non-FOBs companies. The findings indicated not much difference in developing succession planning and innovativeness in FOBs and non-FOBs. In contrast, Grundström, Öberg and Rönnbäck (2011) documented that leaders can introduce radical changes and succession if leaders handle some contextual factors. Lussier and Sonfield (2012) conducted a cross country study of seven developed and developing countries to test FOBs for differences in succession planning and found that applied techniques affect FOBs and small businesses in the same way. Moreover, they also found considerable distinctions in some countries while no distinctions among others. Bjuggren and Sund (2014) conducted a Swedish FOBs and found that opinions of incumbent leaders and family members play pivotal role in organization's succession planning.

Consequently, the concept of social capital has great relevance to this study and latent role it performs in making the succession decision. Sirmon and Hitt (2003) argued that family firms can possess five different types of resources including social capital. This argument is also confirmed by studies of Pearson, Carr, & Shaw (2008) and Sharma (2008). Several other studies also emphasized the significance of social interactions and social capital (Chrisman, Chua, Pearson, & Barnett, 2012; Chrisman, Sharma, Steier, & Chua, 2013; R. G. Long, 2011). Moreover, family system, organizational and business development theories are also relevant to this study. Family systems theory implies that family is an emotional unit and comprises of interconnected and interdependent individuals and individuals cannot be understood in isolation from one another. Similarly, Rautiainen, Pihkala and Ikävalko (2012) argued that business growth has important implications for FOBs and can lead to organization strength. Therefore, it is pivotal to understand the knowledge of leadership and practices of family systems (Zepeda, Bengtson, & Parylo, 2012). Another theory is organization and business development theory that is relevant to this study. Succession planning provides long term sustainability for an organization. Jantti and Greenhalgh (2012) documented that succession management can be improved by increasing skill proficiency, improving goal clarity and developing source of information for succession planning. In addition, Baran, Shanock and Miller (2012) reported the importance of relationship among leaders and employers for growth of organization and performance (Arslan & Roudaki, 2019). Moreover, organizational theory developed four significant theoretical ideas: cross-cultural and international issues, workers considered nontraditional, the well- being of leaders and the enhancements that work together with multilevel modeling (Baran et al., 2012).

SUCCESSION PLANNING IN FAMILY BUSINESS

The successful succession planning processes drives strategic planning by preparing and recognizes future leaders of leadership positions. FOBs often exemplify a primogeniture culture in which one child such as the eldest child are expected to take more responsibility and take over the business while the other younger children enjoy freedom. Aligning strategic planning within organizations with succession planning is necessary for moving organizations toward effective leadership. Succession planning faces many challenges and it does not have an immediate effect; hence, many organizations do not recognize its potential. The presence of a well-planned succession, on the other hand, escalates the firm's growth by encouraging mutual collaboration among family members and reducing conflicts (Eddleston, Kellermanns, Floyd, Crittenden, & Crittenden, 2013). Distelberg and Sorenson (2009) developed a framework for interpreting family business holistically by viewing contemporary family businesses. They documented that it is more likely that a member of system will be recruited rather than a non-member. In contrast, Gilding, Gregory and Cosson (2015) found that family businesses have two main motives i.e. continuity and harmony and the cross–tabulation of these motives produces a typology, hence, there is need to have a closer inquiry into theses motives. Nonetheless, Stavrou (1999) documented that succession is dynamic process and it is imperative to understand family members intentions and choice of the most suitable successor before their joining. In similar vein, Vera and Dean (2005) highlighted the challenges faced by daughters in FOB succession. They found that daughters face fewer problems with their fathers and more with their mothers upon succession. They also found that daughters encounter work like balance difficulties and employee rivalry. On other perspective, stewardship theory highlights the behaviors of incumbents in selecting their successors. The non-opportunistic selection decision is entrenched within the incumbent's set of responsibilities as steward of the family business. The existing literature expounded a good steward as that who was philanthropically interested to perform organizational interests, and that leaders were persuaded to be good stewards if they belonged to a collectively oriented culture (Davis, Schoorman, & Donaldson, 1997). It is imperative to discuss it here because the current study is also conducted in Pakistani environment of collective orientation. Moreover, Solomon et al., (2011) unveiled four key effects (i.e. business internally, adult children, marriage, vision of retirement) that potentially constraint or facilitates the incumbent approach of succession. They also documented that stage in the individual's lifecycle has an overwhelming effect on his or her approach to succession. The next generation may not have required skills and capabilities to lead the business in absence of succession planning. In similar to this, Simoneaux and Stroud (2014) argued that active involvement of prospective competent leaders and staffs is pivotal in preparation and development of succession planning to ensure smooth transition of business leadership. Consequently, training and involvement of next generation will improve transparent succession plans in FOBs (Hagemann & Stroope, 2013). Hagemann and Stroope (2013) documented that it is pivotal for business leaders to maintain and develop the skills within the organization. They further documented that management skills, thinking skills and organization vision are essential tools for success of business. Besides these, ownership, management and transferring taxes are the main problems in implementing a succession plan. Darvish and Temelie (2014) documented that leaders of FOBs should look for competent candidates outside the organization and expand the number of qualified candidates. Fink (2011) documented that whilst internal grooming does not exclude hiring high quality applicants from outside, it has a potential of limiting recruitment faults because the inner aspirant strengths and weaknesses of the successor are known. He also documented that internal development also minimizes the costs of recruiting widely, time spent on learning about the organization and curbs employees' turnover that occurs when an outsider is brought into the organization (Fink, 2011). Promoting capable employees from inside is more motivating to other employees and paves a way for a seamless leadership transition (Pennell, 2010). In similar vein, Bunce (2013) argued that nurturing talent from within is strategic because candidates are already known with culture, history, values and background of an organization, even though it can be a disappointed for management when the selected candidates resign. In contrast, Miodonski and Hines (2013) argued that developing talent from within is more expensive than bringing in outside talent. However, Pollit (2009) documented that new brooms sweep clean and therefore bring in outside successors for purposes of restructuring within organization. Similarly, Garg and Van (2012) argued that external talent brings in new ideas and has high requirement to employ rapid and drastic changes. Zhang and Rajagopalan (2010) found that external talent does not hesitate to implement radical changes, as they have no prior relationship with the organization and employees. This type of talent is required for an organization that stems from rapidly technological or scientific developing sectors where inside grooming is not possible (Hills, 2009). In addition, researchers documented that outside blood comes along with fresh contacts and sources, which may be useful to the organization (McQuade, Sjoer, Fabian, Carlos Nascimento, & Schroeder, 2007). Rahman, Naqvi and Ramay (2008) also argued that an external successor is picked when there is a crisis and rapid changes need to be made in an organization.

Additionally, they are more preferable in small size organizations because they usually do not have sufficient internal talent (Lambertides, 2009). External successors are also opted for when the organizational performance is generally low and there are drastic strategic and operational changes that need to be implemented (Helfat & Bailey, 2005). In addition, Gandossy and Verma (2006) argued that opting for outsiders in succession does not only involve costs but also minimizes the prospects that the new incumbent will succeed. Altman (2009) further expounds that external successors are engaged when there are no obvious internal candidates. Cairns (2011) also documented that for organizations that do not have a strong knowledge bench, inner succession may promote favoritism, as choices are few and obvious. Virick and Greer (2012) argued that the evolution of economics and gender diversity affects leadership transition. Their study findings revealed that performance of incumbent managers influenced the nomination of women successors (Virick & Greer, 2012). In addition, Kippist (2013) argued that succession planning should involve all levels of organizations and management to lower cost and engage mentoring and development of possible candidates. Chung and Luo (2013) conducted a study in Taiwan and documented that rapid changes in emerging markets put outside successors in a position to surge organizations' profitability. Sinkin (2014) argued that future leaders' skills and developments develop on organizational leaders' ability to train and develop these leaders. Consequently, it is pivotal for organization leaders to meet the challenges convoluted in developing a succession plan. In addition, Contreras, Díaz, Tamez and Martínez (2015) conducted a study among 18 CEOs of FOBs and found that successors recognized that when organizations are antagonized with leadership, this creates a treacherous period. In addition, Schulaka (2015) argued that sometimes one leader may not be able to run the business effectively and needs more helping hands and skilled leaders to run the business. In similar vein, Viet (2015) found that family member successors can enhance the organizations value more than non-family member successors. He further documented that if right tools and training are provided, young CEOs can handle organization more effectively.

METHODOLOGY

This study explores the leadership strategies of succession planning in FOBs and also challenges faced by FOBs in development and implementation of succession planning. Cox (2012) argued that research problem, purpose and questions are kept into consideration while determining the research design. A qualitative method was more appropriate for collecting and analyzing of data regarding succession planning because it allows researchers to examine complex behavior in complex real environment (Yin, 2017). The study requires in depth examination for which case study method is more suitable because it provides more detailed investigation (Yin, 2017) and in-depth analysis in exploring the succession practices in different FOBs of Pakistan. Moreover, qualitative data measures the quality rather than quantity (Yin, 2013). The goal of multiple case study is to replicate the findings across selected cases (Yin, 2013), consequently, the findings of multiple case study method is considered more compelling and robust (Herriott & Firestone, 1983).

Population and Sample Size

The population of this study was family owned businesses (FOBs) and all FOBs examined in the study, hereafter referred as "cases" were purposively selected to mirror the business environment as regards to geographic dispersion, sector, and size. According to Eisenhardt, (1989), *"a number between four and ten cases usually works well and ensures sampling adequacy" (p. 545).* Hence, 13 cases were selected by employing purposive sampling technique. Purposive sampling is a process of selecting participants who have relevant knowledge, skills and experience (Truglio-Londrigan, 2013). According to objectives of the study, the criteria is determined to explore the leadership strategies of succession planning and challenges in FOBs. Only those respondents were selected who were at least in their 2nd generation to determine the leadership strategies and challenges of succession planning in FOBs. This helps in exploring the leadership strategies of succession planning, strategies and challenges in FOBs. Table 1 presents the interview protocol. It can be seen that 13 semi-structured interviews were conducted, and each interview was 32 to 45 minutes long. The mode of language was English and written consent was taken from the participants before conducting the interview. In addition, all the preliminary questions were addressed before conducting the interviews.

Table 1. Interview Protocol

Interview Type	Semi-structured interviews
Duration of Interview	32-45 minutes
Level of Interviewees	2nd generation successor or onward
No. of Semi-structured	13
Purpose and Style	Information extraction and exploration
Interview Place	Online or office
Language	English
Confidentiality	High
Morality and Ethics	Written consent is taken from participants
Recording Responses	At the start of interview, interviewee asked respondents that it will be recorded, and recording is started after their approval.
Information Exchange	Detailed information was provided about the project and process. Preliminary questions were addressed in advance.
Question Types	Open ended

The participants in each of 13 cases included the founder (or siblings if founder is deceased), key family members and designated successors. Interviewing members of different generations (2nd, 3rd and 4th generations of the FOBs) allowed for the collecting of data from several viewpoints to advance a well considerate of the succession planning. Most interviews were followed by telephone calls with interviewees for clarification or confirmation when needed. The interviewees were assured of absolute confidentiality.

Data

Semi structured interviews were conducted in early 2018 over a period of two months. An interview guide was prepared and followed to increase the consistency of collected data. The interviews were conducted in English, transcribed and only when permitted, they were recorded (see Table 1). As the reliability of qualitative data is considered to be only as good as the competency of interviewer, the researcher conducted four pilot interviews before the onset of study in order to hone his interviewing skills, thus trying to increase interviewer's and data reliability. The recorded interviews were transcribed and sent to participants for their review to ensure accuracy. This process is termed as " respondent validation" and thus leads to higher credibility (Long & Johnson, 2000). Additionally, the secondary data like company brochure, succession plan were also examined for triangulation. The multiplicity of sources of evidence helps in ensuring construct validity (Rowley, 2002), which involves establishing correct operational measure of underlying concepts (Yin, 2017). Table 2 presents the profile of the respondents. It can be seen that most of respondents were from 2nd or 3rd generation of FOB. In addition, Table 2 reveals that most of respondents have graduate degree while some of them have Master and Ph.D. degrees. Each participant has 2 or 3 interviews which includes the main interview and follow up interviews.

Table 2. Profile of Interviewees

Pseudonym	Generation	Education	Total Interviews	Interview Status
P1	2nd Generation	Ph.D./MPhil	2	Recorded and notes were taken
P2	3rd Generation	Graduate	2	Recorded and notes were taken
P3	3rd Generation	Graduate	3	Recorded and notes were taken
P4	2nd Generation	Ph.D./MPhil	2	Recorded and notes were taken
P5	3rd Generation	Master	2	Recorded and notes were taken
P6	4nd Generation	Graduate	3	Recorded and notes were taken
P7	3rd Generation	Ph.D./MPhil	2	Recorded and notes were taken
P8	2nd Generation	Master	2	Recorded and notes were taken
P9	4th Generation	Graduate	2	Recorded and notes were taken
P10	2nd Generation	Ph.D./MPhil	2	Recorded and notes were taken
P11	3rd Generation	Master	3	Recorded and notes were taken
P12	2nd Generation	Graduate	2	Recorded and notes were taken
P13	2nd Generation	Master	2	Recorded and notes were taken

The highly systematic approach is followed for data analysis. Initially, the researcher identified key words in each case liberally whether or not they matched the elements of theoretical framework of the study. These key words were instrumental in generating insights (Gersick, 1988) and allowed for emergence of unique keywords in each case before pushing them to make first order themes (Eisenhardt, 1989). After that, researcher conducted cross case comparison and ensure inter reliability with the help of another researcher by partial review of data. At the end, the aggregate themes were developed from these second order themes through discussion. Table 3 presents the aggregate themes of the study.

Table 3. Semi Structure Interviews - Aggregate Themes and Codes

Strategies of Succession Planning
1. Business Development Strategies
2. Management Strategies
3. Retention Strategies
4. Family Role Strategies
5. Future Strategies
6. Team Building Strategies
7. Training and Support Strategies
Challenges in Succession Planning
1. Difficult to identify potential successor
2. Ignore the need of succession planning
3. Conflict among family members

RESULTS

This section presents the results of qualitative data analysis. Seven themes arose concerning strategies linked to preparing future leaders of FOBs to assume leadership roles. In addition, challenges in implementing succession planning are also presented in this section. These seven themes help managers with useful strategies in developing a succession plan. Qualitative software like NVivo is useful tool and helps researchers who collects data from open ended questions in order to conduct in-depth analysis (Fielding, Fielding, & Hughes, 2013).

Strategies of Succession Planning

Theme 1 Business Development Strategies

The findings of qualitative data expound that succession planning helps in business development and sustainability of organization. Similarly, Kippist (2013) argued that succession plan has major contribution towards success of business. The participants also agreed that succession plan is pivotal for business. One participant informed that:

"Succession planning is important for business in future. It can help in sustainability of business. And there is less risk (participant- II)"

Moreover, the participants also recognized the need of succession planning and highlighted as major component of business development. Another participant informed that:

"Business needs succession planning. It is, it is a main part of business growth. It can save time to find right person for business (Participant -III)"

Similarly, Hall-Ellis (2015) documented that a well-designed and integrated succession plan can save time for company leaders to find a replacement in event of retirement, death or resignation of current leader of the company. It is revealed from the qualitative data that all the participants had official or unofficial succession plan and were well aware of it. Some of them already had meetings to highlight the importance and need of succession plan. In addition, managers were also well aware of succession plan in case of unforeseen event. One participant highlighted that:

"Our company has succession planning [but] that is unofficial. We are working to make it official and taking further necessary steps. We have meetings about it. Discuss it with managers to make it legal. My son will take over business if I die or retires. But if he do [es] not want, someone else will take over from company (Participant -I)"

In similar vein, Kirillova et al., (2015) argued that succession planning is essential for enhancing company future and sustainability and to define more flexible and efficient solutions. The findings reveal that leaders are well prepared for future of their company. However, Guillot (2013) documented that though, future plans of company are clear but there may be some apprehension, if leader unexpectedly leaves the company. In contrast, Boyd, Botero and Fediuk (2014) argued that incumbents in FOBs identify the strengths and weaknesses of their businesses and evaluate family members ability and related factors for long term sustainability of business. Consequently, owners consider these factors to take decision regarding succession planning (Boyd et al., 2014). Similarly, Cater and Young (2016) identified six family elements (i.e. Conflict management, succession planning, community involvement, leaders plan and vision, approach towards risk, family dynamics) that effect growth of FOBs.

Theme 2 Management Strategies

The findings reveal that individual characteristics greatly influence the success of family systems. Similarly, Whatley (2011) cultural views and opinions are considered at organizational level while interpersonal dynamics are affected at group level. In similar vein, García, Castejón and Pérez (2014) argued that disagreements are neither desirable nor encouraging but are natural phenomenon and part of human life. The participants pointed that management encourage staff to resolve the conflicts by themselves before taking it to notice of management. Consequently, mostly family systems are core of leaders and team management. One participant informed that:

"We discuss and plan a lot of strategies for the company. Being managers, we understand that ultimate decision will be made by leader of company. In future, another family member will be involved in decision making but we are still a team. We fully understand that leader of company has ultimate decision power (Participant-VI)".

It is evident from literature that family systems can create conflicts in FOBs, therefore, all the parties need to pick their battles and focus on goals of company (García et al., 2014). Another participant highlighted that:

"Being the managers, we did not see any conflict due to presence of another family members on board. There is open conversation about vision of company, and everyone works together to achieve it (Participant – VII)".

Another participant pointed that:

"Sometimes, outgoing leader train to incoming leader that helps in coping up the challenges (Participant – VIII)"

Similarly, Marcoux, Guihur and Koffi (2016) argued that success of FOBs depend on recommendations and ideas of successor and employees and successful transfer of leadership. Outgoing leader can provide valuable advice to incoming leader.

Theme 3 Retention Strategies

The retention of successors is pivotal for success of FOBs. Similarly, Gray (2014) argued that internal hiring lead towards better chance of retention. In addition, Avloniti, Iatridou, Kaloupsis and Vozikis (2014) argued that family members make unique decision to run FOBs as compared to professional managers. Moreover, they focus more on viewpoint of the business rather profitability of business (Avloniti et al., 2014). Sustainability is pivotal in FOBs and organizations ensure that their staffs are well acquainted with new and forthcoming processes. One participant informed that:

"We try to morale up and have an open-door policy. We conduct team building exercises, brown bad sessions, define road maps and provide feedback to retain the staff and successor (participant- V)"

In contrast, (Avloniti et al., 2014) argued that most of FOBs do not make it to second or third generation due to sibling rivalry. Another respondent highlighted that:

"I have two sons and I want them to join the business. My younger son has some other plans and is not interested in business; however, my elder son is business savvy. We will train him to take over the business and we are in process of succession planning (Participant -IX)"

It is evident that succession planning and retention are crucial elements in transferring business from one generation to another generation.

Theme 4 Family Role Strategies

The findings of qualitative data reveal that family members play a significant role in succession planning. Similarly, Appelbaum et al., (2012) argued that a succession plan is necessary which guides about step by step process and helps leaders in effectively managing the transition of new leaders and exist of baby boomers. The results reveal that some family members play an important role in company though, they do not hold any leadership positions. One participant informed that:

"My elder son is being groomed to take over the business while my younger daughter kept around to see if she would be interested in the business or could help in some matters (Participant -XI)"

Another participant pointed that:

" I have three sons. The younger son is not interested in business at all while other two are business savvy. I will train both of them and they will work together. But my younger son also comes to company to spend some time and see if he could help in anything. This is how family plays a role in business. Business belong to whole family, so I think everybody should play his/her role in business (Participant -IV)"

It is evident that leaders understand that dedication and significant commitment of time are required to managing business. Hence, they only give more focus on those family members who are really interested in business. Another participant highlighted that:

"My son is not really interested in business, but he gives some time to see if he could have some dedication to manage. Meanwhile, management is already in place and fully capable of running the business effectively. We have developed strategies to ensure that son or management in a position to take control of business (Participant – VII)"

It is evident that participants have applied practical elements to ensure the sustainability and performance of FOBs. Similarly, El-Chaarani (2014) found that practical elements such as succession planning significantly contributes to sustainability and performance of organizations in Lebanon and France. The findings also reveal some family members have provided the opportunity to take leadership role in business, but things did not work well for them. They may have opportunity again at later time. Moreover, the leaders are well aware of succession planning and give immense attention on transition within the company.

Theme 5 Future Strategies

It is evident that integration of succession plan with company strategic plan not only ensures success of both but also helps employees to understand the full picture. Similarly, Kumaran (2015) argued that integrating succession planning with strategic goals encompasses having the right people at right place and time. One participant pointed that:

"Sometimes, it gets very hard to find a dependable and trustworthy family member or individual. That's why we not only focus finding the replacement in our business but also try to prepare family members and trustworthy individuals who would be able to take over the business at any time. This is how we prepare for future (Participant -VIII)"

Another participant informed that:

"A lot of things are in place to train key people for execution of business plans (Participant -II)"

Researchers also argued that leaders should fulfill the key position with highly trained persons who fully understand the business and has capacity to run the business (Kumaran, 2015). One participant informed that:

"Succession planning is central part of future strategies. Our business is growing and there is need to equipped family members and key individuals with innovative opportunities. We have plans in place for next two year regarding strategic planning (participant – VI)"

The findings reveal that leaders are well prepared to tackle the turnover that will eventually happen by integration succession planning and strategic planning. Similarly, researchers argued that if organization doesn't plan for outgoing key personnel, it can create chaos within organization (Santora, Sarros, Bozer, Esposito, & Bassi, 2015).

Theme 6 Team Building Strategies

Team building is a way that can improve trust, support and interaction between team members. It can promote unified team and reduce stress at workplace (Karmakar, 2014). One participant informed that:

"I personally believe on team building and fully support it at workplace. It creates harmony at work. Employees need to support each other. It also provides opportunity to mentor future leaders and employees (Participant – IX)"

Similarly, another participant highlighted that:

"In team, the work can be done better. Senior staff should team up with newly joined staff to train them and provide them help and guidance in their weak areas. Team building is very good for every organization and it can create synergy (Participant -X)"

The findings reveal that FOBs focus on team building and provide them opportunity to work in team to create synergy. Similarly, researchers documented that leaders should understand competencies and qualities of each team member to build a successful team (Matthews & McLees, 2015). Moreover, team building also provides opportunity to leaders and organization to mentor future leaders and reiterate organization goals. Consequently, it also provides opportunity to future leaders to give their inputs on goals and participate at the same time.

Theme 7 Training and Support Strategies

Training and support are pivotal in sustainability of organization. The findings indicate that FOBs provide training and support to future leaders and key personnel to become successful leaders. One participant informed that:

"We (leader) provide training and support to our manger and key personnel. Sometimes, we organize the workshop at site. Otherwise, we support them to get professional courses and certification that are

necessary for our business. If we will focus on training, our employees will also show positive behavior towards training (Participant -VII)"

Another participant informed that:

"We encourage to share their knowledge and skills with other employee by conducting brown bag sessions (Participant – XII)"

Similarly, Towler, Watson and Surface (2014) also found that if leaders show support for training though their actions, trainees are more likely to perceive their leaders as placing a higher priority on training. In addition, Isbell, Seth, Atwood and Ray (2015) argued that training and support sessions allow everyone to learn from each other and maintains commitment to the company. It can be documented that training and support are pivotal to get up to data knowledge about technology and processes which ultimately helps in sustainability of company.

CHALLENGES IN SUCCESSION PLANNING

Difficult to Identify Potential Successor

The qualitative findings reveal that FOBs face difficulty in identifying and assessing the potential candidates. Moreover, it is also difficult for them to discuss about potential successors with their family members. One participant informed that:

"It is very hard to identify the potential successor from family members or key personnel. We are like a family here. My two family members are joining the business. Both are good in business. I do not know who will hold the leadership position. Maybe, they will decide by their own (participant – XIII)"

Another participant pointed that:

"It is hard to select a person outside the family. I need to discuss about potential successor with my family members to get their consensus. May be, they will not agree on it. It is hard, very hard (Participant – IV)"

Another participant highlighted that:

"You cannot make an easy comparison between two potential successors (Participant – VI)"

The tough decision for the small family-owned business owner is which relative- sibling, child, niece, nephew or combination thereof-will lead the business, and how will future decisions be made about the overall direction of the business. The business owner should identify one or more potential successors who have a demonstrated passion for the business and are interested in running the business. Business owners need to discuss this with their family members in an open discussion to avoid or reduce familial discord.

Ignore the Need of Succession Planning

The qualitative findings reveal that most of FOBs are unable to identify the need of succession planning. The awareness of succession planning is very limited. One participant informed that:

"Mostly FOBs are not aware of succession planning. I know one family; they do not have any formal or informal succession plan. The owner is not interested in it. I do not how they will survive if some contingency comes (Participant -XII)

Another participant highlighted that:

"We do not have any succession planning before. We just started last year and now it is in place. Too many FOBs could not survive due to lack of successor. I think this is biggest challenge in FOBs (Participant -VIII)"

Conflict Among Family Members

The qualitative findings reveal that participants agreed that wrangles within the family could adversely affect the survival of business. Ward and Aronoff (2011) explains that conflicts between the interests of the business and those of the family are very often compounded by emotional components which are not normally encountered in businesses which are not owned by a single family. Vries (1997) maintains that wrangling often becomes tremendously complex in FOBs (Bennedsen et al., 2015) which have lasted from one generation to the next. One participant informed that:

"We have conflict in our family about selection of successor. It is hard, always hard to convince everyone and make everyone happy (Participant – X)"

DISCUSSION

The study finds the leadership strategies of succession planning in FOBs. The findings of study are consistent with the prior literature. The study found that FOBs in Pakistan usually rely on natural succession planning i.e. unplanned and what Jaskiewicz et al (2014) termed as 'ordinary' succession. The study found seven different strategies of succession planning in FOBs in Pakistan such as business development, management, retention, family role, future, team building and training and support strategies of succession planning in FOBs. In addition, the study found the three main challenges that are faced by FOBs in development and implementation of succession planning. Findings reveal that some of FOBs have ordinary or unplanned succession planning and it varies from one firm to another. Similarly, Tatoglu et al., (2008) argued that large FOBs have proper and unique succession planning as compared to their smaller counterparts. The findings reveal that most of FOBs adopt different strategies of succession planning however, they still face many challenges due to lack of proper policies and guidelines. Kaunda and Nkhoma (2013) found that notwithstanding of having the succession plans in place, successors or the heirs are ought to generate orderly career progression structures in the transition of FOBs.

The study found that some FOBs have difficulty to identify the potential successor, need of succession planning and conflicts among family members also trigger this. Sardeshmukh (2008) found less focus on preparation of heirs as a vital aspect of effective succession planning in FOBs. Similarly, Dumas et al., (1995) argued that FOBs often exemplify a primogeniture culture in which one child such as the eldest child are expected to take more responsibility and take over the business while the other younger children enjoy freedom and choose their own career path. In addition, Solomon et al., (2011) also unveiled four key effects (i.e. business internally, adult children, marriage, vision of retirement) that potentially constraint or facilitates the incumbent approach of succession.

CONCLUSION AND RECOMMENDATIONS

The purpose of this study was to explore the leadership strategies of succession planning in FOBs. In addition, the study also explores the challenges in succession planning in FOBs. The findings reveal that succession planning is pivotal for development of business and successful transition of FOB from one generation to another. Most of respondents fully understand the importance of succession planning for sustainability of the business. The study finds that retention of successor is crucial for the FOBs and family plays an important role in sustainability of FOBs. However, in some cases, socioemotional aspects of generational succession planning require strategies that concurrently focus on successor suitability, consensus of the family, mode of transition, leadership and challenges faced by the FOBs. The qualitative findings also reveal that motivation, personal values, and enthusiasm of the potential successor are fundamental criteria in the succession planning and the selection of a suitable successor. FOB leaders do not only consider the costs and benefits of intrafamily and extra-family transitions but also reflect on socioemotional, nonfinancial aspects. Similarly, it is found that the incumbents of an FOB have a preference for intrafamily leadership succession rather than extra-family succession in order to preserve the family characteristics of the business. The findings also highlighted that if a suitable successor is not available within the owning family, a nonfamily executive would be a better solution. The findings reveal that successor needs to be dynamic, smart, communicative, and knowledgeable to assure leadership role in FOBs. Moreover, successor needs to keep good employee employer relationships, people-oriented attitude and engagement. At the end, the study finds that FOBs face many challenges in succession planning and implementation that include family conflicts, lack of potential successors and ignore the need of succession planning. FOBs face critical challenges when transferring business from one generation to other. FOBs represent 2/3 of all businesses around world, consequently, they can play critical role in domestic and global economy and are fundamental drivers of economic prosperity, growth and stability.

This study has several practical implications. First, policy makers, directors, corporate governance activists and shareholders need to understand the importance of succession planning in FOBs. It is recommended that Government of Pakistan and other organizations such as Security and Exchange Commission of Pakistan (SECP), Pakistan Institute of Corporate Governance (PICG) should provide support to these FOBs for their successful transition from one generation to other. It is also recommended that there is need to highlight the potential benefits of succession planning in FOBs. Findings may be used to increase FOB survival rates, provide new job opportunities, contribute to community growth, and enhance the well-being of stakeholder.

In addition, founder of FOBs should engage successors and board members in making policies of succession planning. Our research proposes that participation drives the development of formalized succession planning process that can provide systematic, rational and rigorous means to evaluate successor candidates. Second, the study finds that CEOs and boards are vulnerable to decision-making preconceptions. Hence, the introduction of formalised processes will surge the chances of overcoming the informational challenges and socio-political and socio-emotional dynamics. Board activities need management involvement, as well as fair assessments of candidates. It is also found that there is lack of collaboration in FOBs, hence boards and CEOs need to work together to implement the succession plan in more effective way. It will help in reducing the conflicts among board members and cope the informational challenge.

The study also has some limitations. First, the sample size may be small, and it can be questionable to generalize the findings of the study to the whole population. Second, the study used the qualitative methodology and conducted the interview with 13 participants in their 2nd generation to onward. Future studies may use quantitative method and/or survey to collect data from wider population and can consider the FOBs from transition to first generation. Third, the sample is drawn from FOBs of a developing economy (i.e. Pakistan), therefore the findings may not be applicable to the other developed and developing economies due to different socioeconomic environment. But it can still provide guidelines and recommendations.

REFERENCES

Aamir, A. C., & Sohail, Z. (2006). Antecedents and Consequences of Organizational Commitment Among Pakistani University Teachers. *Applied H.R.M. Research, 11*(1), 39–64.

Abdille, H. M. (2013). *The Effects Of Strategic Succession Planning On Family Owned Businesses In Kenya* (Unpublished dissertation). School of Business, University of Nairobi.

Altman, W. (2009). Who's next in line? *Engineering & Technology, 4*(15), 72–75. doi:10.1049/et.2009.1516

Appelbaum, S. H., Gunkel, H., Benyo, C., Ramadan, S., Sakkal, F., & Wolff, D. (2012). Transferring corporate knowledge via succession planning: Analysis and solutions–Part 1. *Industrial and Commercial Training, 44*(5), 281–289. doi:10.1108/00197851211245031

Arslan, M., Abidin, S., Alqatan, A., & Roudaki, J. (2019). Corporate Governance in Extreme Institutional Environment: Evidence From Emerging Economy. *Corporate Ownership & Control, 17*(1).

Arslan, M., & Alqatan, A. (2020). Role of institutions in shaping corporate governance system: Evidence from emerging economy. *Heliyon, 6*(3), e03520. doi:10.1016/j.heliyon.2020.e03520 PMID:32181393

Arslan, M., & Roudaki, J. (2019). Examining the role of employee engagement in the relationship between organisational cynicism and employee performance. *The International Journal of Sociology and Social Policy, 39*(1/2), 118–137. doi:10.1108/IJSSP-06-2018-0087

Avloniti, A., Iatridou, A., Kaloupsis, I., & Vozikis, G. S. (2014). Sibling rivalry: Implications for the family business succession process. *The International Entrepreneurship and Management Journal, 10*(4), 661–678. doi:10.100711365-013-0271-6

Baran, B. E., Shanock, L. R., & Miller, L. R. (2012). Advancing organizational support theory into the twenty-first century world of work. *Journal of Business and Psychology*, *27*(2), 123–147. doi:10.100710869-011-9236-3

Bennedsen, M., Fan, J. P., Jian, M., & Yeh, Y.-H. (2015). The family business map: Framework, selective survey, and evidence from Chinese family firm succession. *Journal of Corporate Finance*, *33*, 212–226. doi:10.1016/j.jcorpfin.2015.01.008

Björnberg, Å., & Nicholson, N. (2012). Emotional ownership: The next generation's relationship with the family firm. *Family Business Review*, *25*(4), 374–390. doi:10.1177/0894486511432471

Bjuggren, P.-O., & Sund, L.-G. (2014). A contractual perspective on succession in family firms: A stakeholder view. *European Journal of Law and Economics*, *38*(2), 211–225. doi:10.100710657-012-9331-6

Boyd, B., Botero, I. C., & Fediuk, T. A. (2014). Incumbent decisions about succession transitions in family firms: A conceptual model. *International Journal of Financial Studies*, *2*(4), 335–358. doi:10.3390/ijfs2040335

Breton-Miller, I. L., Miller, D., & Steier, L. P. (2004). Toward an integrative model of effective FOB succession. *Entrepreneurship Theory and Practice*, *28*(4), 305–328. doi:10.1111/j.1540-6520.2004.00047.x

Brockhaus, R. H. (2004). Family business succession: Suggestions for future research. *Family Business Review*, *17*(2), 165–177. doi:10.1111/j.1741-6248.2004.00011.x

Buhk, C., Sánchez Gómez, P., & Hensen, I. (2005). Plant regeneration mechanisms during early post-fire succession in south-eastern Spain. *Feddes Repertorium: Zeitschrift für botanische Taxonomie und Geobotanik, 116*(5-6), 392-404.

Bunce, L. (2013). Succession Planning and Its Impact on Organizational Performance. *American Journal of Behavioural Science and Psychology*, *3*(2), 86–96.

Cabrera-Suarez, K. (2005). Leadership transfer and the successor's development in the family firm. *The Leadership Quarterly*, *16*(1), 71–96. doi:10.1016/j.leaqua.2004.09.010

Cairns, T. D. (2011). Who's up next? Most companies fail to plan for leadership succession. *Employment Relations Today*, *38*(2), 27–34. doi:10.1002/ert.20341

Cater, J., & Young, M. (2016). Family factors in small family business growth. *The Journal of Applied Management and Entrepreneurship*, *21*(4), 56–86. doi:10.9774/GLEAF.3709.2016.oc.00005

Checkley, T. (2010). *Succession in small and family business*. Academic Press.

Chrisman, J. J., Chua, J. H., Pearson, A. W., & Barnett, T. (2012). Family involvement, family influence, and family-centered non-economic goals in small firms. *Entrepreneurship Theory and Practice*, *36*(2), 267–293. doi:10.1111/j.1540-6520.2010.00407.x

Chrisman, J. J., Chua, J. H., Sharma, P., & Yoder, T. R. (2009). Guiding family businesses through the succession process. *The CPA Journal*, *79*(6), 48.

Chrisman, J. J., Sharma, P., Steier, L. P., & Chua, J. H. (2013). The influence of family goals, governance, and resources on firm outcomes. *Entrepreneurship Theory and Practice*, *37*(6), 1249–1261. doi:10.1111/etap.12064

Chung, C. N., & Luo, X. R. (2013). Leadership succession and firm performance in an emerging economy: Successor origin, relational embeddedness, and legitimacy. *Strategic Management Journal*, *34*(3), 338–357. doi:10.1002mj.2011

Contreras, Y. S., Díaz, F. M. R., Tamez, L. L. G., & Martínez, D. G. J. (2015). *El liderazgo a partir del proceso de la sucesión en la empresa familiar mexicana/the leadership from the succession process in the mexican family enterprise.* Paper presented at the Global Conference on Business & Finance Proceedings.

Cox, R. D. (2012). Teaching qualitative research to practitioner–researchers. *Theory into Practice*, *51*(2), 129–136. doi:10.1080/00405841.2012.662868

Dana, L., & Smyrnios, K. (2010). *The MGI Australian Family and Private Business Survey*. RMIT University.

Darvish, H., & Temelie, Z. N. (2014). A Study on the Relationship between Succession Planning and Strategic Planning. Case Study: Payame Noor University of Aleshtar. *Economic Insights - Trends and Challenges*, *66*(1).

Davis, J. H., Schoorman, F. D., & Donaldson, L. (1997). Toward a stewardship theory of management. *Academy of Management Review*, *22*(1), 20–47. doi:10.5465/amr.1997.9707180258

De Vries, M. (1997). Family Business: Human Dilemmas in the Family Firm. *Organization Studies-Berlin-European Group for Organizational Studies*, *18*, 543–543.

Decker, C., Heinrichs, K., Jaskiewicz, P., & Rau, S. B. (2016). What do we know about succession in family businesses? Mapping current knowledge and unexplored territory. In *The Routledge Companion to Family Business* (pp. 45–74). Routledge.

Distelberg, B., & Blow, A. (2010). The role of values and unity in family businesses. *Journal of Family and Economic Issues*, *31*(4), 427–441. doi:10.100710834-010-9221-4

Distelberg, B., & Sorenson, R. L. (2009). Updating systems concepts in family businesses: A focus on values, resource flows, and adaptability. *Family Business Review*, *22*(1), 65–81. doi:10.1177/0894486508329115

Dumas, C., Dupuis, J. P., Richer, F., & St.-Cyr, L. (1995). Factors that influence the next generation's decision to take over the family farm. *Family Business Review*, *8*(2), 99–120. doi:10.1111/j.1741-6248.1995.00099.x

Durst, S., & Wilhelm, S. (2012). Knowledge management and succession planning in SMEs. *Journal of Knowledge Management*, *16*(4), 637–649. doi:10.1108/13673271211246194

Eisenhardt, K. M. (1989). Building theories from case study research. *Academy of Management Review*, *14*(4), 532–550. doi:10.5465/amr.1989.4308385

El-Chaarani, H. (2014). The success keys for family firms: Comparison between Lebanese and French systems. *Lebanese Science Journal*, *15*(2), 133–150.

Elsaid, E., & Ursel, N. D. (2011). CEO succession, gender and risk taking. *Gender in Management, 26*(7), 499–512. doi:10.1108/17542411111175478

Experts, F. B. (2012). *Want to fix or avoid problems in your family business*. Academic Press.

Fielding, J., Fielding, N., & Hughes, G. (2013). Opening up open-ended survey data using qualitative software. *Quality & Quantity, 47*(6), 3261–3276. doi:10.100711135-012-9716-1

Filser, M., Kraus, S., & Märk, S. (2013). Psychological aspects of succession in family business management. *Management Research Review, 36*(3), 256–277. doi:10.1108/01409171311306409

Fink, D. (2011). Pipelines, pools and reservoirs: Building leadership capacity for sustained improvement. *Journal of Educational Administration, 49*(6), 670–684. doi:10.1108/09578231111174811

Fürst, H. (2017). *Growing Up in a Business Family–An Analytic Autoethnography of 'Subtle Coerced Succession'* (Doctoral dissertation). University of Gloucestershire.

Gandossy, R. P., & Verma, N. (2006). Passing the torch of leadership. *Leader to Leader, 2006*(40), 37–44. doi:10.1002/ltl.176

García, J. O., Castejón, P. J. M., & Pérez, C. P. (2014). The culture of conflict in family business/La cultura del conflicto en la empresa familiar. *Revista de Empresa Familiar, 4*(2), 25.

Garg, A., & Van Weele, E. (2012). Succession planning and its impact on the performance of small micro medium enterprises within the manufacturing sector in Johannesburg. *International Journal of Business and Management, 7*(9), 96. doi:10.5539/ijbm.v7n9p96

Gersick, C. J. (1988). Time and transition in work teams: Toward a new model of group development. *Academy of Management Journal, 31*(1), 9–41.

Giarmarco, J. (2017). *The three levels of family business succession planning*. Academic Press.

Gilding, M., Gregory, S., & Cosson, B. (2015). Motives and outcomes in family business succession planning. *Entrepreneurship Theory and Practice, 39*(2), 299–312. doi:10.1111/etap.12040

Gray, D. (2014). Succession planning 101. *Professional Safety, 59*(3), 35.

Greenberg, H. (2012). Aligning future leaders today to take on the challenges of tomorrow. *Employment Relations Today, 38*(4), 55–60. doi:10.1002/ert.20365

Griffeth, R. W., Allen, D. G., & Barrett, R. (2006). Integration of family-owned business succession with turnover and life cycle models: Development of a successor retention process model. *Human Resource Management Review, 16*(4), 490–507. doi:10.1016/j.hrmr.2006.08.006

Grundström, C., Öberg, C., & Rönnbäck, A. Ö. (2011). View and management of innovativeness upon succession in family-owned SMEs. *International Journal of Innovation Management, 15*(03), 617–640. doi:10.1142/S136391961100326X

Guillot, C. (2013). Avoiding THE VOID. *Internal Auditor, 70*(6), 42-47. Retrieved from http://www.theiia.org/ecm/magazine.cfm?doc_id=540

Hagemann, B., & Stroope, S. (2013). Developing the next generation of leaders. *Industrial and Commercial Training*, *45*(2), 123–126. doi:10.1108/00197851311309570

Hall, L. O., & Hagen, C. D. (2014). Holistic Approach to Succession Planning Provides Added Value for Clients: Financial Service Professionals Play Key Role in Successful Plans. *Journal of Financial Service Professionals*, *68*(1).

Hall-Ellis, S. D. (2015). Succession planning and staff development–a winning combination. *The Bottom Line (New York, N.Y.)*, *28*(3), 95–98. doi:10.1108/BL-05-2015-0007

Helfat, C. E., & Bailey, E. E. (2005). External succession and disruptive change: Heirs-apparent, forced turnover and firm performance. *Strategic Organization*, *3*(1), 47–83. doi:10.1177/1476127005050031

Hendricks, L. (2002). How important is human capital for development? Evidence from immigrant earnings. *The American Economic Review*, *92*(1), 198–219. doi:10.1257/000282802760015676

Herriott, R. E., & Firestone, W. A. (1983). Multisite qualitative policy research: Optimizing description and generalizability. *Educational Researcher*, *12*(2), 14–19. doi:10.3102/0013189X012002014

Hills, A. (2009). Succession planning–or smart talent management? *Industrial and Commercial Training*, *41*(1), 3–8. doi:10.1108/00197850910927697

Hoch, H. (2013). Book review–Maggots for millions. *Deutsche Entomologische Zeitschrift*, *60*(2), 271–271.

Isbell, M. G., Seth, J. G., Atwood, R. D., & Ray, T. C. (2015). Development and implementation of client-centered nutrition education programs in a 4-stage framework. *American Journal of Public Health*, *105*(4), e65–e70. doi:10.2105/AJPH.2014.302512 PMID:25713950

Jantti, M., & Greenhalgh, N. (2012). Leadership competencies: A reference point for development and evaluation. *Library Management*, *33*(6/7), 421–428. doi:10.1108/01435121211266249

Jaskiewicz, P., Heinrichs, K., Rau, S. B., & Reay, T. (2016). To be or not to be: How family firms manage family and commercial logics in succession. *Entrepreneurship Theory and Practice*, *40*(4), 781–813. doi:10.1111/etap.12146

Karmakar, N. (2014). Tips of High-Performance Team Building for Organizational Effectiveness. *i-Manager's. Journal of Management*, *8*(4), 15.

Kaunda, S., & Nkhoma, A. (2013). Intergenerational survival of family businesses: Factors affecting the succession success of family owned businesses in Malawi. *European Journal of Business and Management*, *5*(7), 157–164.

Kim, T. H. (2012). Succession planning in hospitals and the association with organizational performance. *Nursing Economics*, *30*(1), 14. PMID:22479959

Kippist, L. (2013). Bridges or barriers? Succession planning for doctor managers. *International Employment Relations Review*, *19*(2), 24.

Kirillova, E. A., Pozdnyakova, E. V., Gorevoy, E. D., Ershova, I. V., & Nadezhin, N. N. (2015). Transboundary succession of business: Problems related to practice. *International Journal of Economics and Financial Issues*, *5*(3S), 125–130.

Kumaran, M. (2015). Succession planning process that includes visible minority librarians. *Library Management*, *36*(6/7), 434–447. doi:10.1108/LM-12-2014-0138

Lambertides, N. (2009). Sudden CEO vacancy and the long-run economic consequences. *Managerial Finance*, *35*(7), 645–661. doi:10.1108/03074350910960364

Lobley, M., Baker, J. R., & Whitehead, I. (2016). Farm succession and retirement: Some international comparisons. *Journal of Agriculture, Food Systems, and Community Development*, *1*(1), 49–64.

Long, R. G. (2011). Commentary: Social exchange in building, modeling, and managing family social capital. *Entrepreneurship Theory and Practice*, *35*(6), 1229–1234. doi:10.1111/j.1540-6520.2011.00500.x

Long, T., & Johnson, M. (2000). Rigour, reliability and validity in qualitative research. *Clinical Effectiveness in Nursing*, *4*(1), 30–37. doi:10.1054/cein.2000.0106

Lussier, R. N., & Sonfield, M. C. (2012). Family businesses' succession planning: A seven-country comparison. *Journal of Small Business and Enterprise Development*, *19*(1), 7–19. doi:10.1108/14626001211196370

Lyon, B. K., & Hollcroft, B. (2012). Risk assessments: Top 10 pitfalls & tips for improvement. *Professional Safety*, *57*(12), 28–34.

Magasi, C. (2016). *Factors influencing business succession planning among SMEs in Tanzania*. Working paper.

Marcoux, G., Guihur, I., & Koffi, V. (2016). Employees' contribution to the succession process of family small and medium-sized businesses: Conceptual model and research agenda. *Management Review: An International Journal*, *11*(1), 70.

Matthews, R., & McLees, J. (2015). Building effective projects teams and teamwork. *Journal of Information Technology and Economic Development*, *6*(2), 20.

McQuade, E., Sjoer, E., Fabian, P., Carlos Nascimento, J., & Schroeder, S. (2007). Will you miss me when I'm gone? A study of the potential loss of company knowledge and expertise as employees retire. *Journal of European Industrial Training*, *31*(9), 758–768. doi:10.1108/03090590710846701

Mehrabani, S. E., & Mohamad, N. A. (2011). Succession planning: A necessary process in today's organization. *International Journal of e-Education, e-Business, e- Management Learning*, *1*(5), 371.

Miodonski, K., & Hines, P. (2013). Leadership development and succession planning in case management. *Professional Case Management*, *18*(1), 5–12. doi:10.1097/NCM.0b013e31826b12a7 PMID:23211401

Molly, V., Laveren, E., & Deloof, M. (2010). Family business succession and its impact on financial structure and performance. *Family Business Review*, *23*(2), 131–147. doi:10.1177/0894486510023002003

Negrea, S. (2008). *Succession planning: A necessity for community colleges*. Institute for Community College Development.

Pandey, S., & Sharma, D. (2014). Succession planning practices and challenges: Study of Indian organisations. *Procedia Economics and Finance*, *11*, 152–165. doi:10.1016/S2212-5671(14)00185-3

Pasban, M., & Nojedeh, S. H. (2016). A Review of the Role of Human Capital in the Organization. *Procedia: Social and Behavioral Sciences*, *230*, 249–253. doi:10.1016/j.sbspro.2016.09.032

Pearson, A. W., Carr, J. C., & Shaw, J. C. (2008). Toward a theory of familiness: A social capital perspective. *Entrepreneurship Theory and Practice*, *32*(6), 949–969. doi:10.1111/j.1540-6520.2008.00265.x

Pennell, K. (2010). The role of flexible job descriptions in succession management. *Library Management*, *31*(4/5), 279–290. doi:10.1108/01435121011046344

Pollit, D. (2009). Success through succession at Hudson's Bay Company. *Human Resource Management International Digest*, *17*(5), 6–8. doi:10.1108/09670730910974260

Poza, E. J. (2013). *Family business*. Cengage Learning.

PricewaterhouseCoopers. (2007). *Making a difference: the pricewaterhousecoopers family business survey 2007/08*. PricewaterhouseCoopers.

Rahman, A., Naqvi, S., & Ramay, M. I. (2008). Measuring turnover intention: A study of it professionals in Pakistan. *International Review of Business Research Papers*, *4*(3), 45–55.

Rautiainen, M., Pihkala, T., & Ikävalko, M. (2012). Family business system models–a case study and some implications of open systems perspective. *Journal of Small Business and Entrepreneurship*, *25*(2), 155–168. doi:10.1080/08276331.2012.10593566

Rothwell, W. (2010). *Effective succession planning: Ensuring leadership continuity and building talent from within*. Amacom.

Rowley, J. (2002). Using case studies in research. *Management Research News*, *25*(1), 16–27. doi:10.1108/01409170210782990

Santiago, A. L. (2000). Succession experiences in Philippine family businesses. *Family Business Review*, *13*(1), 15–35. doi:10.1111/j.1741-6248.2000.00015.x

Santora, J. C., Sarros, J. C., Bozer, G., Esposito, M., & Bassi, A. (2015). Nonprofit executive succession planning and organizational sustainability. *The Journal of Applied Management and Entrepreneurship*, *20*(4), 66–83. doi:10.9774/GLEAF.3709.2015.oc.00006

Sardeshmukh, S. R., & Corbett, A. C. (2011). The duality of internal and external development of successors: Opportunity recognition in family firms. *Family Business Review*, *24*(2), 111–125. doi:10.1177/0894486510391783

Schulaka, C. (2015). Get creative. *Journal of Financial Planning*, *28*(2), 9.

Sharma, P. (2008). Commentary: Familiness: Capital stocks and flows between family and business. *Entrepreneurship Theory and Practice*, *32*(6), 971–977. doi:10.1111/j.1540-6520.2008.00266.x

Sharma, P., Chrisman, J. J., & Chua, J. H. (2003). Succession planning as planned behavior: Some empirical results. *Family Business Review*, *16*(1), 1–15. doi:10.1111/j.1741-6248.2003.00001.x

Sharma, P., Chrisman, J. J., Pablo, A. L., & Chua, J. H. (2001). Determinants of initial satisfaction with the succession process in family firms: A conceptual model. *Entrepreneurship Theory and Practice*, *25*(3), 17–36. doi:10.1177/104225870102500302

Simoneaux, S. L., & Stroud, C. L. (2014). Succession planning: Intentional and systematic preparation for the future. *Journal of Pension Benefits: Issues in Administration*, *21*(2), 62–63.

Sinkin, J. (2014). How to manage internal succession. *Journal of Accountancy*, *217*(2), 38.

Sirmon, D. G., & Hitt, M. A. (2003). Managing resources: Linking unique resources, management, and wealth creation in family firms. *Entrepreneurship Theory and Practice*, *27*(4), 339–358. doi:10.1111/1540-8520.t01-1-00013

Solomon, A., Breunlin, D., Panattoni, K., Gustafson, M., Ransburg, D., Ryan, C., Hammerman, T., & Terrien, J. (2011). "Don't Lock Me Out": Life-Story Interviews of Family Business Owners Facing Succession. *Family Process*, *50*(2), 149–166. doi:10.1111/j.1545-5300.2011.01352.x PMID:21564058

Stavrou, E. T. (1999). Succession in family businesses: Exploring the effects of demographic factors on offspring intentions to join and take over the business. *Journal of Small Business Management*, *37*(3), 43.

Tatoglu, E., Kula, V., & Glaister, K. W. (2008). Succession planning in family-owned businesses: Evidence from Turkey. *International Small Business Journal*, *26*(2), 155–180. doi:10.1177/0266242607086572

Towler, A., Watson, A., & Surface, A., E. (. (2014). Signaling the importance of training. *Journal of Managerial Psychology*, *29*(7), 829–849. doi:10.1108/JMP-03-2012-0092

Truglio-Londrigan, M. (2013). Shared decision-making in home-care from the nurse's perspective: Sitting at the kitchen table–a qualitative descriptive study. *Journal of Clinical Nursing*, *22*(19-20), 2883–2895. doi:10.1111/jocn.12075 PMID:23331469

Vassiliadis, S., & Vassiliadis, A. (2014). The Greek family businesses and the succession problem. *Procedia Economics and Finance*, *9*, 242–247. doi:10.1016/S2212-5671(14)00025-2

Vera, C. F., & Dean, M. A. (2005). An examination of the challenges daughters face in family business succession. *Family Business Review*, *18*(4), 321–345. doi:10.1111/j.1741-6248.2005.00051.x

Viet, H. N. (2015). Succession decision in Vietnamese family companies. *International Journal of Business and Management*, *10*(7), 208. doi:10.5539/ijbm.v10n7p208

Virick, M., & Greer, C. R. (2012). Gender diversity in leadership succession: Preparing for the future. *Human Resource Management*, *51*(4), 575–600. doi:10.1002/hrm.21487

Wang, Y., Watkins, D., Harris, N., & Spicer, K. (2004). The relationship between succession issues and business performance: Evidence from UK family SMEs. *International Journal of Entrepreneurial Behaviour & Research*, *10*(1/2), 59–84. doi:10.1108/13552550410521380

Ward, J. (2016). *Keeping the family business healthy: How to plan for continuing growth, profitability, and family leadership*. Springer.

Ward, J. L., & Aronoff, C. E. (2011). *Family meetings: How to build a stronger family and a stronger business*. Macmillan.

Wee, Y. G., & Ibrahim, M. D. (2012). Family business success factors: Management practices, relationship among members and succession experience. *International Journal of Arts and Commerce*, *1*(6), 262–274.

Whatley, L. (2011). A New Model for Family Owned Business Succession. *Organization Development Journal*, *29*(4).

Williams, D. W., Zorn, M. L., Russell Crook, T., & Combs, J. G. (2013). Passing the torch: Factors influencing transgenerational intent in family firms. *Family Relations*, *62*(3), 415–428. doi:10.1111/fare.12016

Yin, R. K. (2013). Validity and generalization in future case study evaluations. *Evaluation*, *19*(3), 321–332. doi:10.1177/1356389013497081

Yin, R. K. (2017). *Case study research and applications: Design and methods*. Sage publications.

Zepeda, S. J., Bengtson, E., & Parylo, O. (2012). Examining the planning and management of principal succession. *Journal of Educational Administration*, *50*(2), 136–158. doi:10.1108/09578231211210512

Zhang, Y., & Rajagopalan, N. (2010). CEO succession planning: Finally at the center stage of the boardroom. *Business Horizons*, *53*(5), 455–462. doi:10.1016/j.bushor.2010.05.003

Chapter 12
The Role of Governance Attributes in Corporate Social Responsibility (CSR) Practices Evidence From Jordan

Hamzeh Adel Al Amosh
https://orcid.org/0000-0002-6938-348X
Universiti Sultan Zainal Abidin, Malaysia

ABSTRACT

The importance of information disclosure is increasing for stakeholders, mainly the non-financial disclosure, and the primary objective of the current study is to investigate the impact of a set of governance attributes on the level of corporate social responsibility disclosure in the Jordanian context. The study sample consisted of 51 industrial companies listed during 2012 to 2017; a set of statistical analyzes were used, such as descriptive statistics and multiple regression. Empirical evidence shows that the board size and audit committee play a crucial role in the social responsibility disclosure, while other factors (board activity, board compensation, non-executive directors, and audit company type) have no effect on disclosure. The findings are expected to have potential effects on the capital market in Jordan in terms of focusing on the strengths that support the social responsibility disclosure and the development of guidelines that contribute to promoting a disclosure culture between the listed companies, which support government plans in achieving sustainability.

INTRODUCTION

Recently, Non-financial reporting and disclosures has received widespread attention from many stakeholders, mainly societies, government agencies, investors, and shareholders. Attention comes in light of increased international interest in issues related to sustainability, including corporate social responsibility. Sheehy (2015) defined corporate social responsibility as "a type of international private business self-regulation". In addition, Carrell (1979) defined CSR as "The social responsibility of business en-

DOI: 10.4018/978-1-7998-4852-3.ch012

compasses the economic, legal, ethical, and discretionary expectations that society has of organizations at any given point in time". In this context, Tilt (2009) provided a definition of social accounting as "the communication of social and environmental effects of a company's economic actions to particular interest groups within society and to society at large". It is noted from the previous definitions that social responsibility relates to two parties, the companies and the relevant stakeholders.

Companies should look more broadly outside the scope of the idea of achieving profits only, as they must engage more in activities related to social responsibility and disclose their contribution in order to improve their image in front of different stakeholders and meet their different demands and needs. On the other hand, stakeholders' awareness of their rights also contributed to pressuring companies to consider their information needs (Md Zaini, Samkin, Sharma, & Davey, 2018). On the other hand, many companies are trying to show their contribution through disclosure, either in their annual reports or in other available means of disclosure, which aim to being more involved in the social contract (ElHawary & Arafa, 2018). In this respect, companies began to deal with the social responsibility agenda as an obligation towards stakeholders and response to their expectations (Hamrouni et al. 2019).

Developing countries like Jordan need many of these initiatives related to social responsibility. Where that is known that the developing countries face great difficulties in sustainable development (Roseland, 2000), where Jordan is currently suffering from internal and external crises, such as the humanitarian asylum crisis which led to an increase in the population of the country, and the crises in the countries around Jordan, which affected the level of exports significantly. All of this led to major negative social and economic impacts. As for internal challenges, there are limited natural resources, the existence of financial and administrative corruption, high rates of tax evasion, in addition to unemployment and poverty rates that are increasing year after year. In 2015, the government launched an initiative called Jordan Vision 2025, which is related to achieving the goals of sustainable development and accelerating the pace of development in the economic, social and environmental fields in Jordan.

In the laws governing the capital markets in Jordan (Amman Stock Exchange and the Jordan Securities Commission) there is no clear obligation for companies to disclose information related to corporate social responsibility (CSR). As Article 5 of Chapter Five of the disclosure and transparency states: "The company shall disclose its policy regarding the local community and the environment" (Jordan Securities Commission, 2009). On the other hand, laws require companies to disclose their non-social contribution through an explicit text stating that there are no environmental or social contributions of the company.

The purpose of this chapter is to know the impact of factors related to corporate governance attributes as potential determinants of disclosure of social responsibility for Jordanian industrial companies listed on the Amman Stock Exchange during the period from 2012 to 2017. The study is primarily concerned with investigating a level of disclosure of social responsibility among the Jordanian industrial companies listed. Secondly, the main objective of this study is to investigate the impact of the factors related to governance. Corporate governance is likely to play a critical role in improving the quality of disclosures in corporate financial reporting (Basuony et al. 2018), which is (the audit committee, non-executive directors, board compensation, board size, board activity and audit company type) on the level of disclosure of social responsibility. Jordan is also seen as an important model for neighboring countries, as it shares many characteristics with these countries, such as religion, culture and economic conditions (Alshhadat, 2017), and the results of this study can be generalized to the countries surrounding Jordan.

Accordingly, the first research question will study the level of disclosure of social responsibility, while our second research question will study the governance attributes and its role of social responsibility disclosure. The results of the study will give an insight into the policy makers and relevant government destinations about the interaction extent of listed industrial companies with social responsibility in Jordan in light of the government's sustainable development plan, which aims to achieve social, economic and environmental goals by 2025.

LITERATURE REVIEW

Corporate governance has generated many changes in the business environment, in particular, the accounting and auditing professions and disclosure in corporate reports (Buallay & Al-Ajmi, 2019). In this regard, several literatures have reviewed the potential effects of governance attributes on the disclosure of corporate social responsibility.

In the context of the investigation on disclosure, Fallah & Mojarrad, (2019) presented evidence from 62 Iranian high pollution companies listed on the Tehran Stock Exchange, stating that the Audit Committee and the size of the Board of Directors play a positive role in environmental and social disclosure. Also, Hu & Loh, (2018) presented similar evidence, as their results indicated a positive effect of the Board activity and the Board size on sustainability reports, in a study that included 462 listed Singaporean companies. Allegrini & Greco (2013) supported these arguments in a previous study they conducted in Italy, where it was found through their study that tested several factors related to governance that the board size is a key player in voluntary disclosures, This suggestion was also supported by Abu Qa'dan & Suwaidan (2019).

Sadou et al. (2017), also studied disclosure of social responsibility in the Malaysian context, and the top 100 listed companies were chosen based on the market value of each company, the results showed that the board size and non-executive directors contribute positively to the disclosure of the corporate social responsibility.

Al-Janadi et al. (2016), reported a positive impact of factors of non-executive directors and the audit company type (the Big Four) on social disclosure in a study he conducted in Saudi Arabia. On the other hand, he objected to the idea that the board size has an impact on the level of social responsibility disclosure. In Egypt, Samaha & Dahawy (2011) tested a set of suggested factors that were identified as determinants of voluntary disclosure. The study sample included the 100 largest listed Egyptian companies. The experimental evidence concluded that the Audit Committee and non-executive directors affect voluntary disclosure, while the study did not provide any evidence that the type of the audit company affected the level of voluntary disclosure. Khan et al. (2013) also supported this evidence in a study he conducted in Bangladesh, where he argued that the existence of the audit committee supported the disclosure of corporate social responsibility. In another study, Akhtaruddin et al. (2009) examined the board size, non-executive directors, audit committee, the type of Audit Company, other factors, and the extent of their impact on the level of voluntary disclosure in Malaysia. Where a study sample included 110 industrial companies listed on the Malaysian Stock Exchange. The experimental results indicated that the board size, non-executive directors and auditing companies listed within the big four contribute significantly to the disclosure of voluntary information. As for the audit committee, the results did not provide evidence that it had any effect on the level of disclosure. In a comparative study between Nigeria and South Africa, Ofoegbu & Odoemelam (2018) investigated factors related to the board of directors' characteristics and their effect on environmental disclosure. The results showed that board meetings have a strong impact on environmental disclosure in Nigeria while the same factor has no effect in South

Africa. While the audit company type and the board size affected the level of environmental disclosure significantly in South Africa, their impact was less on disclosure in Nigeria.

In the context of the studies that dealt with the effect of the board's compensation on disclosure, Alhazaimeh et al. (2014) studied the effect of compensation on voluntary disclosure in the Jordanian industrial companies listed. The results were positive, as it showed a significant effect of compensation at the level of disclosure. As well as in the study of Albawwat &Basah (2015), where he tested the same previous factors but on a different sample of non-financial companies in Jordan, and the results showed that the board compensation has an important role in voluntary disclosure

Wuttichindanon, (2017) studied several factors, including the company of the type of audit company, at the level of social responsibility disclosure in Thailand, its results showed that there is a positive impact of the audit companies listed among the big 4 on the corporate social responsibility disclosure. Elfakey (2017) supports these results in a study conducted in the Egyptian context.

In the context of Western and developed countries studies, Basuony et al. (2017) studied a number of factors related to corporate governance and its impact on the voluntary disclosure in UK, and selected a sample consisting of 150 industrial companies from different sectors. The results showed positive indicators on the relationship between the board size, non-executive directors and the frequency of board meetings at the level of voluntary disclosure. In Australia, these results were supported by Rao & Tilt, (2016), as their study, which included 115 Australian companies revealed that board size and non-executives' directors have a large role in pushing Australian companies towards providing more information about social responsibility. On the other hand, Fuente et al. (2017) conducted a study on 98 Spanish companies listed on the Madrid Stock Exchange, examining several factors related to governance, including the board size and non-executives directors. The results did not conclude with conclusive evidence regarding the effect of the size of the plate on the level of sustainability disclosure, which includes social information, environmental and economic. In contrast, non-executives directors play a positive role in corporate disclosure.

THEORETICAL BACKGROUND

There is a fierce debate in the 21st century about balance in business economics (Harrison & Wicks, 2013). The corporate business environment witnesses major conflicts between shareholders and those who are the true owners of the company and the top management on the one hand. Which is one of the aspects of conflicts of interest and the shareholders' pursuit for governance to a balance in the distribution of rights in the company. The other side of the conflict puts another group of stakeholders in the front line with the departments of companies and shareholders, as they increase the demands to disclose the companies' contributions that they consider as rights. According to Brown & Deegan (1998), no single theory can provide an adequate explanation for corporate practices in disclosure. In this respect, to explain corporate practices in disclosing social responsibility, the study adopts a multiple theoretical framework, which includes the legitimacy theory and the stakeholder's theory.

In this regard, stakeholder theory has evolved over the past thirty years to address such problems (Harrison & Wicks,2013) through a perspective that places companies in a position of accountability to stakeholders (van der Laan, 2009). The Stakeholder's theory argues that corporate administrations must take into account all stakeholder interests because they are considered agents for all stakeholders and not for a group without others (Freeman & Reed, 1983). On the other hand, the stockholder theory theorists believe that stockholders have the right to consider their interests before the interests of another stakeholders' group (Clark et al. 2016). This controversy places management in front of difficult options to satisfy all stakeholders, including shareholders, who believe that their interests must be taken into account first, as they are the owners of the company.

The Stakeholder's theory assumes that companies must meet and satisfy the needs of information and interests of all stakeholders, not just shareholders. (Abed et al. 2014). As the Stakeholders are constantly demanding for companies to show their responsibility for society (Deegan & Blomquist, 2006) and this is done through many means, including the disclosure of information. According to Reverte (2016), the stakeholder theory assumes that companies must disclose information to meet the needs of different stakeholder groups (e.g. shareholders, investors, employees, and government agencies, etc.). Corporate social responsibility disclosure (CSRD) is one of the main demands of stakeholders (Malik & Kanwal, 2018). Corporate social responsibility contributes to enhancing transparency and improving the company's reputation among stakeholders (Benlemlih et al. 2018).

On the other hand, the legitimacy theory provides a broader view of the disclosure phenomenon, where the legitimacy theory argues that the disclosures that companies provide is a reaction to legitimizing their existence. Guthrie and Parker (1989) confirms that this theory is based on the principle of the social contract, that is, the company is working to provide what satisfies the surrounding community in exchange for a license to work in its environment. Also, the legitimacy theory insists on sticking to the disclosure of corporate social responsibility as one of the legitimacy requirements (Patten, 2019). Therefore, companies are required to defend their actions by providing more attention to social responsibility to appease local communities (Sadou et al. 2017). This gives the legitimacy theory preference in the disclosure literature because it provides a broad concept to explain the companies 'motives in disclosing their contributions to the society in which they operate (Tilling, 2004). Finally, it can be said that the legitimacy of the existence of companies is linked to the society's satisfaction with them, and this necessitates responding to their demands, especially the CSR disclosure.

Through reviewing the two theories, we find that the legitimacy theory puts the responsibility of the company in front of the entire society in order to meet their aspirations. While the theory of stakeholders gave a more specific picture of what stakeholders should companies meet their needs.

HYPOTHESES DEVELOPMENT

The hypotheses, related to the governance attributes variables, are developed as below:

Non-Executive Directors

The presence of non-executives in any facility is considered one of the indicators of corporate governance. The non-executive management represents the independent side of the board, according to the stakeholder's theory; non-executives play an important role in preserving the interests of the stakeholders in the company (Liu & Andersson, 2014). On the other hand, the presence of managers enhances non-executives in companies involved in social activities and they are considered as more in line with the aspirations of stakeholders (Alhazmi, 2017). Executive directors are full-time employees who run the company directly and daily (Mans-Kemp et al. 2018). While non-executives are not considered part of the executive team, so they are considered the essence of good governance (Alam, 2011). Therefore, non-executive directors can be considered as an important tool for achieving the aspirations of stakeholders.

Most literature gives important indications of the positive relationship of non-executive directors with disclosure (Sadou et al. 2017; Al-Janadi et al. 2016; Samaha & Dahawy 2011; Akhtaruddin et al. 2009). In line with the literature, the following hypothesis have been proposed:

Hypothesis One: H1: Non-Executive Directors has a significant positive effect on the level of corporate social responsibility disclosure in annual reporting.

Audit Committee

The audit committee is an Executive committee that is composed of members of the company's board of directors and it is considered one of the most important practices that fall within the framework of corporate governance (Buallay, & Al-Ajmi, 2019), where its work is directly related to assessing the adequacy and effectiveness of internal control systems. The audit committee plays a critical role in ensuring transparency for stakeholders and assisting shareholders by providing advice to them (Musallam, 2018). It also works to improve disclosures in corporate reports (Mangena & Pike, 2005). Consequently, the existence of committees related to institutional governance, such as the Audit Committee, this contributes to providing more guarantees to stakeholders that their demands will be taken into account.

Evidences from empirical studies that tested the impact of the audit committee on disclosure in company reports indicates a positive effect of this factor (e.g. Fallah & Mojarrad, 2019; Samaha et al. 2015; Khan et al. 2013; Samaha & Dahawy, 2011). This leads the current study to suggest the following hypothesis:

Hypothesis Tow: H2: Audit committee has a significant positive effect on the level of corporate social responsibility disclosure in annual reporting.

Board Compensation

Companies adopt the idea of board compensation to assess the performance of directors, especially in social areas (Baron, 2008). Shareholders provide compensation to the Board of Directors to meet their aspirations and interests (Baron, 2008). It is also seen as a one of solution to the agency's problems. Moreover, compensations are one of the most effective governance tools (Barontini & Bozzi, 2011). According to Coombs & Gilley (2005), the board of directors must be compensated in order to maximize the value of stakeholders. These propositions are consistent with the perspective of the stakeholder's theory, which argued that the compensation system is one of the governance mechanisms that are an incentive for management to act in accordance with the interests of stakeholders (Shao, 2009). Baron (2008) argues that the compensation awarded by companies to the Board of Directors must be positively reflected on corporate social responsibility. It is noticeable that the provision of compensation is directed broadly to the interest of stakeholders to implement their demands by management, in exchange for incentives offered to them.

Although the previous literature did not address the role of the Board compensation in the disclosure extensively, Albawwat & basah (2015) indicated that there is a significant impact of the compensation paid to the board on the voluntary disclosures, as his opinion was supported by Alhazaimeh et al. (2014) in a similar study. Thus, it is hypothesized that:

Hypothesis Three: H3: Board compensation has a significant positive effect on the level of corporate social responsibility disclosure in annual reporting.

Board Size

The board size is represented by the number of directors' present on the board. As it is considered one of the governance attributes and it is one of the important characteristics that play a crucial role in monitoring the Board of Directors (Liao et al. 2018). In terms of information disclosure, the persons assigned to manage the company are the ones who decide the company's policy to participate in social responsibility activities and disclose it in the annual reports (Matuszak et al. 2019). According to stakeholder theory, the board size contributes to enhancing transparency by giving greater representation to stakeholders in the board, which works to fulfill their aspirations in disclosing their information needs (Dias, Rodrigues & Craig. 2017). This is confirmed by Haji (2013), that the greater the board size, the more varied the experiences of its members and the variety of ideas presented in the board, including the proposals related to the agenda, among them are the proposals related to the CSR agenda.

Several previous literatures have argued that the relationship between board size and disclosure is a positive one (e.g. Liao et al. 2018; Sadou et al. 2017; Allegrini & Greco, 2013; Ofoegbu & Odoemelam, 2018). Based on the above discussion, the hypothesis is stated as follows:

Hypothesis Four: H4: Board size has a significant positive effect on the level of corporate social responsibility disclosure in annual reporting.

Board Activity

Board meetings is an important mechanism for corporate governance, as it is an effective tool for communication between the company's management, follow-up of its business, evaluation of its current status, and management decisions-making (Liao et al. 2018). According to the legitimacy theory, the frequency of board meetings is in the best interests of stakeholders, as it is considered an important indicator of the effectiveness of senior management and it provides greater transparency (Dienes & Velte, 2016). In addition, it expresses the management keenness on the company's various interests.

The evidence provided by the previous literature differed with regard to the impact of the Board activity on disclosure. As Alhazaimeh et al. (2014) argued that the frequency of Board meetings affects the disclosure, and Katmon et al. (2019) claimed that the Board's activity positively affects the disclosure of social responsibility, while Albawwat & Basah (2015) disagreed with them where they objected to the idea of the relationship between Board activity and disclosure. However, the current study assumes that the Board activity has a positive effect on the corporate social responsibility disclosure. Therefore, the following hypothesis has been suggested:

Hypothesis Five: H5: Board activity has a significant positive effect on the level of corporate social responsibility disclosure in annual reporting.

Audit Company Type

The audit is an important tool to urge companies to think seriously about their position on the issue of social responsibility and to disclose their contribution in this field (van der Wiele et al. 2001). The accreditation of one of the big four companies to carry out auditing tasks is an important indication that the company's management is working to enhance transparency and disclosure in the company (Elfeky, 2017). Palmer (2008) also argues that companies audited by high quality auditors (Big 4) have more disclosure of information. It is observed that the companies that adopt major auditing firms are at a high level of transparency and in addition to that, the large auditing companies have a reputation and certainly want to preserve it, this eliminates the idea of conflicts of interest between management and auditor. This is consistent with the perspective of stakeholder theory that the higher the levels of transparency in companies, the greater the amount of disclosures about information by corporate departments and the stakeholders' demands will be safeguarded.

While Ackers & Eccles (2015) claim that the role of auditing has become weaker with regard to corporate social responsibility, the empirical evidence provided by previous studies proves the opposite. Where Elfeky (2017) and Wuttichindanon (2017) argued that companies that accredit one of the big 4 auditing companies disclose information more than other companies. This study assumes that the external audit companies can have an effect on the companies in one way or another, including the impact of disclosure in annual reports, especially if it is one of the big 4 with a reputation and professional experience in auditing. According to the above, the following hypothesis has been developed:

Hypothesis Six: H6: Audit company type has a significant positive effect on the level of corporate social responsibility disclosure in annual reporting.

CONTROL VARIABLES

In line with the previous literature, the study proposed a set of control variables that may play a role in influencing the level of social disclosure, including the size of the company. Where studies presented a set of arguments that support the impact of the size of the company on corporate disclosure (Hu & Loh, 2018; Basuony et al. 2018; Alhazmi, 2017; Jizi, 2017). Thus, it is possible that larger companies are more concerned with social issues and their requirements. The company age is also a factor affecting the level of corporate disclosure of information according to a number of studies (Sri & Arief, 2018; Alhazmi, 2017; Bayoud et al. 2012; Thompson & Ke, 2012). Accordingly, companies of an older age may have greater experience and a broader social base, and this will place these companies in front of greater responsibility towards society and this may lead them to engage more in corporate social responsibility and disclosure of their related activities. Moreover, the literature suggested that the factor of the industrial sector as a control variable plays a crucial role in influencing the amount of information disclosed by companies (e.g., Sri & Arief, 2018: Haddad et al., 2015 and Ibrahim, 2014). It can be that companies with industries that are more dangerous or have more impact on society take into account these effects and make social contributions more than others make.

METHODOLOGY

Sample of the Study

The current study community consists of all 63 industrial companies listed on the Amman Stock Exchange, which operated during 2012 -2017. Data related to disclosure of social responsibility was obtained from 51 companies, this is due to the availability of its data during all the study years, and this sample represents 81% of the total study population. For this, 306 observations were chosen from companies' annual reports to be included in the analysis.

Data Collection

This study is based on the secondary data sources, where data was collected through the annual reports published of companies' profiles page on the Amman Stock Exchange website.

Variables Measurements

Dependent Variables

Previous studies generally go into two options, either to adopt ready-made or self-prepared checklists. The current study relied on the social disclosure index issued by the Global Reporting Initiative, where this organization provided the world with professional indicators to evaluate companies' disclosure of sustainability issues, including corporate social responsibility (Wang, 2017). The Global Initiative Reporting (GRI) was established in 1997, and its goal when establishing was to focus on companies' disclosure of environmental issues, later it developed to include many issues related to sustainability, namely economic, environmental and social, in 1998, and the first version of the guidelines framework for disclosure were issued in the same year (GRI, 2015). According to Fuente et al. (2017), GRI Indicators are used to measure social disclosure items and they are considered the most acceptable form for measuring corporate social responsibility. In this regard, the G3.1 version was adopted, which was released in March 2011, this is in line with the period in which the current study was conducted. The CSR Disclosure Index items in this version include 42 items, the corporate social responsibility disclosure will be investigated through content analysis, where score 1 is given if the item is disclosed in the annual report and a score of 0 if it is not disclosed, where the annual reports were completely read and the contents compatible with the disclosure index were identified and the mark was given accordingly. Several disclosure studies have adopted the GRI index as a checklist to test the extent to which sustainability issues disclosure, including social responsibility issues (e.g. Zhang, 2017: Sánchez, Bolívar & Hernández, 2017: Bhattacharyya, 2014: Grecco et al, 2013). Also, in the Jordanian context (e.g. Mazahrih, Katrib, & Rfaah, 2016: Alshannag, Basah, & Khairi 2016: Al-Hamadeen & Badran, 2014).

Independent Variables

Table 1 reviews the independent variables included in the study (Audit Committee, Board Compensation, Board Size, Board Activity, Non-Executive Directors, Audit Company Type). The table also contains a method for measuring control variables

Table 1. Independent variables Measurement

Independent Variables		Measurement
Audit Committee	AUCOM	Dummy = 1 in the case of an audit committee and 0 in the absence of it.
Board Compensation	BOCOM	The total annual compensation amount for the Board of Directors.
Board Size	BOSZE	The total number of members on the Board of Directors
Board Activity	BOMET	The total number of annual board meetings.
Non-Executive Directors	NEXDC	The ratio of the non-executive directors' number to the total number of directors on the board.
Audit Company Type	BIG4	Dummy = 1 if the audit company among the big 4 and 0 if otherwise.
Company Age	COAGE	The number of years of life of the company since its inception.
Company Size	CSIZE	The total assets.
Industry Sector	CSECT	The type of industry sector to which each company belongs.

The relationship between independent and dependent variables is illustrated in this study in the form of the following proposed mathematical model

$$\text{CSRD} = \beta_0 + \beta_1\,\text{AUCOM} + \beta_2\,\text{BOCOM} + \beta_3\,\text{BOSZE} + \beta_4\,\text{BOMET} \\ + \beta_5\,\text{NEXEC} + \beta_6\,\text{BIG4} + \beta_7\text{CAGE} + \beta_8\,\text{CSIZE} + \beta_9\,\text{CSECT} + \varepsilon$$

Where:

CSRD = Corporate Social Responsibility Disclosure
AUCOM = Audit Committee
BOCOM = Board Compensation
BOSZE = Board Size
BOMET = Board Activity
NEXDC = Non-Executive Directors
BIG4 = Audit Company Type
COAGE = Company Age
CSIZE = Company Size
CSECT= Industry sector
β_0 = Intercept
β_1 to β_9 = Coefficient of slope parameters
ε = Error term

First: Descriptive Analysis for Study Variables

1. Descriptive Analysis for Independent Variables

Table 2 show the level of study variables, where the data in the above table showed the mean and standard deviation for every independent variable. Also, the data showed that non-executive directors average is (90.65%) and this is an indication that industrial companies adhere to the governance instructions issued

Table 2. Descriptive Analysis for Independent Variables

	N	Minimum	Maximum	Mean	Std. Deviation
NEXDC	306	40.00	100.00	90.65	11.231
AUCOM	306	.00	1.00	.9085	.2888
BOCOM	306	.00	7.26E6	1.015	4.2628
BOSZE	306	4.00	23.00	8.219	2.759
BOMET	306	3.00	17.00	7.150	2.035
BIG4	306	.00	1.00	.3856	.4875

by Jordan Securities Commission, which states that one third of the board members of listed companies must be independent (non-executives). With regard to the audit committee, the results show that about 90.85% of the listed industrial companies have audit committees, and this indicator indicates that the largest percentage of companies follow the required governance rules. The results showed that board compensation mean is (1.015), this implies that the boards receives large amounts of compensation, the shareholders may have seen it as the most appropriate solution to the agency's problems, but at the same time companies' departments must consider all the stakeholders' demands without exception. The average number of boards member size is about 80.19%, meaning that companies adhere to the instructions issued by the Securities Commission, which requires companies to have the minimum number of members of the Board 5 and the upper limit of 13. This result indicates that most companies take the largest number of members i.e. with an average of 10 Members for each company. Board meetings range from 3 to 17, i.e., at a rate of 71.5%. According to the corporate Governance code, the required number of board meetings is not less than 6 during the year, at the rate of one meeting every two months. It seems that almost third of companies are not committed to the required number of annual meetings, i.e. by 29.5%, while the majority follow instructions accurately. The percentage of companies that contract with an auditing company ranges from the Big 4 to 38.56%. This indicates that there is no hegemony for the Big 4 on the industrial sector.

2. Descriptive Analysis for Dependent Variables

Table 3 indicates descriptive statistics for social responsibility (DV) disclosure, where the data in the above table showed the mean and standard deviation for every dependent variable. In addition, Table 2 showed that, the mean of social variable is (.3177).

Table 3. Descriptive Analysis for dependent Variables

	N	Minimum	Maximum	Mean	Std. Deviation
Social	306	.00	.60	.3177	.12735

Table 4 show the level of dimensions of the social variable, where the data in the above table showed the mean and standard deviation for each dimension. The data showed that, the (product responsibility) came at first rank with mean (.4040), while the (Labor Practices and Decent Work) impacts came at second rank with mean (.3521), then the (Society) came at third rank with mean (.3144), finally the (Human Rights) came at last rank with mean (.2032).

Table 4. Descriptive Analysis for social responsibility disclosure categories

	N	Minimum	Maximum	Mean	Std. Deviation
Product Responsibility	306	.00	.89	.4040	.19430
Labor Practices and Decent Work	306	.00	.73	.3521	.17634
Society	306	.00	.60	.3144	.15947
Human Rights	306	.00	.45	.2032	.12330
Total	306	.00	.60	.3177	.12735

The Table 5 indicates the level of disclosure for each item of the social disclosure index, where the table shows the percentages of repetition of the elements. In addition, the table show that the order of the disclosed elements is based on the percentage obtained by each element. In this regard, it is clear that the information that got the most disclosure is the (Total workforce by employment type, employment contract, and region, broken down by gender). This is followed by an item of (Percentage of employees covered by collective bargaining agreements). This indicates that companies are very interested in revealing information related to their employees. On the other hand, we find that the least disclosed elements by companies relate to (Programs for adherence to laws, standards, and voluntary codes related to marketing communications, including advertising, promotion, and sponsorship), followed by (Actions taken in response to incidents of corruption).

Table 5. Social Disclosure by Item

No.		Freq.	%	Rank
Labor Practices and Decent Work				
LA1	Total workforce by employment type, employment contract, and region, broken down by gender.	301	98.4	1
LA2	Total number and rate of new employee hires and employee turnover by age group, gender, and region.	67	21.9	22
LA3	Benefits provided to full-time employees that are not provided to temporary or part-time employees, by major operations.	96	31.4	20
LA15	Return to work and retention rates after parental leave, by gender.	8	2.6	31
LA4	Percentage of employees covered by collective bargaining agreements.	285	93.1	2
LA5	Minimum notice period(s) regarding significant operational changes, including whether it is specified in collective agreements.	0	0	37
LA6	Percentage of total workforce represented in formal joint management-worker health and safety committees that help monitor and advise on occupational health and safety programs.	57	18.6	23

continues on following page

Table 5. Continued

No.		Freq.	%	Rank
LA7	Rates of injury, occupational diseases, lost days, and absenteeism, and number of work-related fatalities by region and by gender.	18	5.9	27
LA8	Education, training, counseling, prevention, and risk-control programs in place to assist workforce members, their families, or community members regarding serious diseases.	247	80.7	4
LA9	Health and safety topics covered in formal agreements with trade unions.	158	51.6	16
LA10	Average hours of training per year per employee by gender, and by employee category.	108	35.3	19
LA11	Programs for skills management and lifelong learning that support the continued employability of employees and assist them in managing career endings.	75	24.5	21
LA12	Percentage of employees receiving regular performance and career development reviews, by gender.	8	2.6	32
LA13	Composition of governance bodies and breakdown of employees per employee category according to gender, age group, minority group membership, and other indicators of diversity.	182	59.5	13
LA14	Ratio of basic salary and remuneration of women to men by employee category, by significant locations of operation.	6	2	33
Human Rights				
HR1	Percentage and total number of significant investment agreements and contracts that include clauses incorporating human rights concerns, or that have undergone human rights screening.	0	0	38
HR2	Percentage of significant suppliers, contractors and other business partners that have undergone human rights screening, and actions taken.	0	0	39
HR3	Total hours of employee training on policies and procedures concerning aspects of human rights that are relevant to operations, including the percentage of employees trained.	19	6.2	26
HR4	Total number of incidents of discrimination and corrective actions taken.	192	62.7	12
HR5	Operations and significant suppliers identified in which the right to exercise freedom of association and collective bargaining may be violated or at significant risk, and actions taken to support these rights.	6	2	34
HR6	Operations and significant suppliers identified as having significant risk for incidents of child labor, and measures taken to contribute to the effective abolition of child labor.	0	0	40
HR7	Operations and significant suppliers identified as having significant risk for incidents of forced or compulsory labor, and measures to contribute to the elimination of all forms of forced or compulsory labor.	0	0	41
HR8	Percentage of security personnel trained in the organization's policies or procedures concerning aspects of human rights that are relevant to operations.	0	0	42
HR9	Total number of incidents of violations involving rights of indigenous people and actions taken.	240	78.4	6
HR10	Percentage and total number of operations that have been subject to human rights reviews and/or impact assessments.	14	4.6	28
HR11	Number of grievances related to human rights filed, addressed and resolved through formal grievance mechanisms.	213	69.6	9
Society				
SO1	Percentage of operations with implemented local community engagement, impact assessments, and development programs.	143	46.7	17
SO9	Operations with significant potential or actual negative impacts on local communities.	24	7.8	24
SO10	Prevention and mitigation measures implemented in operations with significant potential or actual negative impacts on local communities.	114	37.3	18
SO2	Percentage and total number of business units analyzed for risks related to corruption.	0	0	43
SO3	Percentage of employees trained in organization's anti-corruption policies and procedures.	6	2	35

continues on following page

Table 5. Continued

No.		Freq.	%	Rank
SO4	Actions taken in response to incidents of corruption.	0	0	44
SO5	Public policy positions and participation in public policy development and lobbying.	12	3.9	29
SO6	Total value of financial and in-kind contributions to political parties, politicians, and related institutions by country.	218	71.2	8
SO7	Total number of legal actions for anti-competitive behavior, anti-trust, and monopoly practices and their outcomes.	206	67.3	10
SO8	Monetary value of significant fines and total number of non-monetary sanctions for non-compliance with laws and regulations.	239	78.1	7
Product Responsibility				
PR1	Life cycle stages in which health and safety impacts of products and services are assessed for improvement, and percentage of significant products and services categories subject to such procedures.	12	3.9	30
PR2	Total number of incidents of non-compliance with regulations and voluntary codes concerning health and safety impacts of products and services during their life cycle, by type of outcomes.	197	64.4	11
PR3	Type of product and service information required by procedures and percentage of significant products and services subject to such information requirements.	23	7.5	25
PR4	Total number of incidents of non-compliance with regulations and voluntary codes concerning product and service information and labeling, by type of outcomes.	182	59.5	14
PR5	Practices related to customer satisfaction, including results of surveys measuring customer satisfaction.	6	2	36
PR6	Programs for adherence to laws, standards, and voluntary codes related to marketing communications, including advertising, promotion, and sponsorship.	0	0	45
PR7	Total number of incidents of non-compliance with regulations and voluntary codes concerning marketing communications, including advertising, promotion, and sponsorship by type of outcomes.	246	80.4	5
PR8	Total number of substantiated complaints regarding breaches of customer privacy and losses of customer data.	175	57.2	15
PR9	Monetary value of significant fines for non-compliance with laws and regulations concerning the provision and use of products and services.	269	87.9	3

Table 6 shows the trend in the total social practices over a 6 years period from 2012 to 2017. The total observations of the sample companies are similar throughout the study period with 51 annual reports for listed firms corresponding to the years 2012, 2013, 2014, 2015, 2016 and 2017. The Figure 1 shows the change in the level of social of the study sample during the period (2012-2017).

Table 6. Trend in the Total Social Variable

Variables	N	Minimum	Maximum	Mean	Std. Deviation	Variance
2012	51	.00	.60	.3027	.13203	.017
2013	51	.00	.60	.3096	.13167	.017
2014	51	.00	.60	.3176	.13079	.017
2015	51	.02	.60	.3200	.12479	.016
2016	51	.02	.60	.3225	.12647	.016
2017	51	.02	.60	.3294	.12305	.015

Figure 1 shows a slight increase in the level of corporate social responsibility disclosure (CSRD) with the passage of the years under study, this can be considered as an indication of a gradual increase in the company's awareness of social responsibility. On the other hand, it can also be a gradual reaction to the stakeholders' pressures and demands.

Figure 1. the level of social of the study sample during the period (2012-2017)

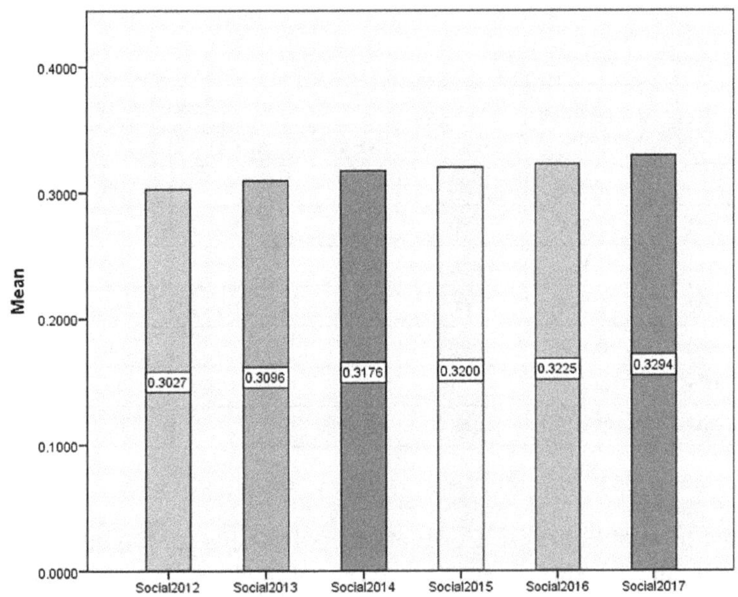

From the above table it can be noted that the VIF values for governance attributes dimensions are less than 10 and range from (1.023 to 1.526), and tolerance values ranged from (0.655 to 0.978), which is greater than 0.05. This is an indication that there is no high correlation between the independent variables (Multicollinearity). Therefore, it can be said that there is no real problem with the normal distribution of the study data (O'brien, 2007).

Table 7. Tolerance and VIF

Model		Collinearity Statistics	
		Tolerance	VIF
Corporate Social Responsibility Disclosure (CSRD)	NEXDC	.842	1.188
	AUCOM	.978	1.023
	BOCOM	.774	1.292
	BOSZE	.655	1.526
	BOMET	.887	1.128
	BIG4	.900	1.111

Testing Study Hypotheses

In addition to other statistical tests, the multiple linear regression was performed to test the effect of the independent variables (governance attributes) on the dependent variable (corporate social responsibility disclosure), taking into account the effect of control variables (company size, company age and industry type).

Table 8. Collinearity Diagnostics

Model	Dimension	Eigenvalue	Condition Index	Variance Proportions						
				(Constant)	NEXDC	AUCOM	BOCOM	BOSZE	BOMET	BIG4
1	1	5.309	1.000	.00	.00	.00	.00	.00	.00	.01
	2	.942	2.374	.00	.00	.00	.72	.00	.00	.01
	3	.544	3.124	.00	.00	.01	.06	.00	.00	.89
	4	.092	7.583	.00	.00	.06	.10	.43	.22	.05
	5	.080	8.167	.00	.00	.76	.00	.01	.23	.04
	6	.025	14.430	.12	.14	.10	.12	.56	.54	.00
	7	.007	27.617	.88	.85	.07	.00	.00	.00	.01

Table 9 present that tests of Pair-wise Correlation coefficients for the governance attributes dimensions (independent variables) of the current study, the table show that all results are less than 0.9. In this case, you do not have to worry about the problem of a possible correlation between the variables (Calkins, 2016).

Table 9. Pair-wise Correlation Matrix for Dependent Variables

Correlations										
		NEXDC	AUCOM	BOCOM	BOSZE	BOMET	BIG4	CSIZE	COAGE	CSECT
NEXDC	Pearson Corr.	1								
AUCOM	Pearson Corr.	-.074	1							
BOCOM	Pearson Corr.	.010	.034	1						
BOSZE	Pearson Corr.	.292**	-.036	.439**	1					
BOMET	Pearson Corr.	-.288**	.046	-.010	-.188**	1				
BIG4	Pearson Corr.	-.196**	-.121*	.150**	.268**	.027	1			
CSIZE	Pearson Corr.	-.040	.076	.353**	.537**	-.053	.337**	1		
COAGE	Pearson Corr.	-.129*	.004	.193**	.302**	-.054	.462**	.478**	1	
CSECT	Pearson Corr.	-.297**	.049	.136**	.194	-.076	.218**	.391**	.024	1

**. Correlation is significant at the 0.01 level (2-tailed).
*. Correlation is significant at the 0.05 level (2-tailed).
AUCOM = Audit Committee; BOCOM = Board Compensation; BOSZE = Board Size; BOMET = Board Activity; NEXDC = Non-Executive Directors; BIG4 = Audit company type; COAGE = Company Age; CSIZE = Company Size; CSECT=Type of Industry

The data in the above table showed that, F value is (13.632) and significant is (.000) which mean that governance attributes with control variables has significant effect on the level of social responsibility disclosure.

Table 10. Results of ANOVA for social responsibility disclosure by governance attributes with control variables

Model	Sum of Squares	Df	Mean Square	F	Sig.
Regression	1.450	9	.161	13.632	.000[a]
Residual	3.497	296	.012		
Total	4.947	305			

The above table showed that the R^2 is (.272), which mean that the governance attributes with control variables explain the amount of (27.2%) of variance in the dependent variable (corporate social responsibility disclosure).

Table 11. Results of multiple linear regressions for social responsibility disclosure by governance attributes with control variables

Model	R Square	Adjusted R Square	Std. Error of the Estimate
1	.293	.272	.10870

Table 12 showed the (T) and significant values for governance attributes dimensions, where the significant of non-executive directors is (.597); the significant of audit committee is (.029); the significant of board compensation is (.223); the significant of board size is (.001); the significant of board activity is (.238); the significant of audit company type is (.159); the significant of company size is (.062); the significant of company age is (.767); and the significant of type of industry is (.000); which mean that (audit committee, board size, and type of industry) have significant effect on the level of social responsibility disclosure, this evidence is consistent by (Fallah & Mojarrad, 2019; Abu Qa'dan & Suwaidan, 2019; Hu & Loh, 2018; Ofoegbu & Odoemelam, 2018; Sadou et al. 2017) regarding the effect of the board size, This can be explained by the fact that the larger board contain more diverse education and experiences than the smaller ones (Abu Qa'dan & Suwaidan, 2019), and this leads the board to give more attention to more issues including disclosure of social responsibility.. The results also supported allegations of (Fallah & Mojarrad, 2019; Samaha & Dahawy, 2011) concerning the audit committee factor and its impact on disclosure, as this could be due to the independent role played by the audit committee (Samaha & Dahawy, 2011), which promotes good governance. On the other hand, the results shown that (audit company type, non-executive directors, board compensation, and board activity) have no effect on the level of social responsibility disclosure. The results agreed with Samaha & Dahawy (2011) that the type of audit company had no effect on the disclosure, but Sadou et al. (2017) disagreed with them on the point regarding the influence of non-executives' directors. The results also oppose the tendencies of

Table 12. Results of multiple linear regressions for social responsibility disclosure by governance attributes with control variables

Variables	B	Std. Error	Beta	T	Sig.
(Constant)	.215	.061		3.504	.001
NEXDC	.000	.001	.029	.530	.597
AUCOM	.048	.022	.110	2.196	.029
BOCOM	2.051E-8	.000	.069	1.221	.223
BOSZE	.010	.003	.214	3.267	.001
BOMET	.004	.003	.061	1.183	.238
BIG4	.021	.015	.082	1.413	.159
CSIZE	5.429E-11	.000	.121	1.870	.062
COAGE	.000	.000	.018	.296	.767
CSECT	-.016-	.002	-.393-	-7.800-	.000

Albawwat &Basah (2015) and Alhazaimeh et al. (2014) in that the Board compensation has an impact on the information disclosure. The study evidences also did not support the allegations of Odoemelam (2018) and Hu & Loh, (2018) that the board activity affects disclosure.

CONCLUSION

This study examined the potential impact of a set of variables related to governance attributes, as the current study focused on 6 variables: audit committee, non-executive directors, board compensation, board size, board activity, audit company type and the extent of its impact on the corporate social responsibility disclosure. To achieve the objectives of the study, 51 samples from a Jordanian industrial company during the years (2012 - 2107) were selected to be included in the analysis. In addition to measuring the level of information disclosure related to social responsibility during the study period.

The results indicate that the level of disclosure of corporate social responsibility in its annual reports is relatively low, as the average level of disclosure of information during the six school years was equal to 33 percent of the disclosure index items. This indicates that the companies did not give some disclosure items the importance required in their reports, or that these items were not disclosed at all.

In the respect of the factors affecting the disclosure of social responsibility, the findings provides support for the stakeholder theory. In this regard, the stakeholders' drives are stronger in the larger boards -where the diversity of experience- by giving them greater representation within the board and this leads to strengthening the management of the relationship with them and meeting their demands, including the disclosure of the company's contribution in social responsibility agendas. Empirical evidence also provided support for the stakeholder perspective in relation to the relationship between the audit committee and corporate disclosure. As it was found that the audit committee has a critical role in implementing stakeholder demands in engaging in corporate social responsibility activities and disclosing it in their annual report. This is attributed to the fact that the audit committee represents one of the governance mechanism in the company and is therefore one of the guarantees of the interests of the stakeholders.

On the other hand, the results did not provide sufficient support for the theory of stakeholders regarding the effect of non-executive directors on the information disclosure, which is a basic requirement for them. Although non-executives' directors participate in the management of the company, they are not considered as the executive directors who participate daily in the management of the company and decision taking (Mans-Kemp et al.2018). This explains why they are not more informed of the company's activities, especially those related to social responsibility, as they may have busyness and other interests outside the board that may overwhelm their interests with topics of interest to different stakeholders. The experimental results do refute the stakeholder theory arguments regarding compensations granted to the board of directors as an important tool to guide management towards the aspirations of stakeholders, as the results indicate that compensation does not affect the corporate social responsibility disclosure. Therefore, stakeholders should work to link the size of boards' compensation to the goals achieved for them. This may contribute to motivating the management to meet more stakeholders' demands, in particular to disclose more information related to corporate social responsibility. This will give an indication that the company contribute in social responsibility activities. Also, the evidence did not provide sufficient support for the legitimacy theory, as the results show that the frequency of board meetings does not affect the corporate social responsibility disclosure. This can be attributed to the fact that board meetings discuss other agendas that are not related to social responsibility, which is one of the demands of stakeholders. This could lead in the future to a conflict of interests between management and stakeholders. As for the auditing company type that expresses the big four, it appears that it does not play an active role in disclosing social responsibility. These results are inconsistent with the perspective of stakeholders who are waiting for more transparency and disclosure, so it seems that stakeholders should seek other guarantees for their interests and aspirations outside the big audit companies to get more information and get companies to engage in social responsibility activities.

The present study contributes to the literature from several aspects. First, the study touched on the level of commitment to disclosing social responsibility, according to the indicator issued by the Global Reporting Initiative (GRI) G3.1 version in an emerging economic country as Jordan.

Second, the study tested a set of factors related to governance and its impact on the level of corporate social responsibility disclosure, where the results indicated a significant impact of the board size and the audit committee on the social responsibility disclosure. sw. In contrast, the evidence concluded that board activity, board compensation, non-executive directors, and the type of audit company do not affect the disclosure of corporate responsibility immunogenic in any way, these factors may have a greater role in disclosure in other economic contexts.

Third, the study tested the stakeholder's theory and legitimacy theory in the context of developing countries such as Jordan and provided adoption of some views on theories while other views were not adopted about what theories suggest. Some of the arguments of these theories may be partially suitable for developing countries; however, more tests of stakeholder theory and legitimacy theory in developing countries should be done to verify these claims.

Finally, evidences from the current study has important implications for policy makers, regulators and government agencies, as Jordan is working on a comprehensive plan to achieve sustainable development by 2025, which includes a set of economic, social and environmental goals. The current study gives an important indication on one of the mentioned aspects, which is the social indicator and the extent of compatibility of industrial companies, which are considered one of the representatives of the private sector with the government plan in sustainable development. Therefore, to reduce the current gap, government agencies, policy makers and regulators should issue a new set of agreed standards to guide

Jordanian industrial companies to participate more effectively in activities related to social responsibility and disclosure of its achievements in this area.

According to the results, the study recommends policy makers in Jordan and in the emerging and economically similar countries from neighboring countries and others to focus on supporting the strengths represented by focusing on enhancing the number of members of the council. In addition to obliging all companies to activate the role of the audit committee and set instructions for companies to commit them to accrediting audit committees from within the administrative structure of the institution

This study faces several limitations, where the current study focused on one source of disclosure, which is the annual reports of companies, there are more sources which can be taken, such as disclosure through the internet and various media. Including that, it focused on the industry sector exclusively, the other studies can be address other sectors such as financial companies for example. As well as examining the current study factors on other types of disclosure may be included in future studies, such as environmental disclosure or the disclosure of intellectual capital. Also, there are other factors that can tested as determinants of detection, such as duplication of the CEO or the presence of the women component on board.

REFERENCES

Abed, S., Roberts, C., & Hussainey, K. (2014). Managers' incentives for issuing cash flow forecasts. *International Journal of Accounting. Auditing and Performance Evaluation, 10*(2), 133–152.

Abu Qa'dan, M. B. A., & Suwaidan, M. S. (2019). Board composition, ownership structure and corporate social responsibility disclosure: The case of Jordan. *Social Responsibility Journal, 15*(1), 28–46.

Ackers, B., & Eccles, N. S. (2015). Mandatory corporate social responsibility assurance practices: The case of King III in South Africa. *Accounting, Auditing & Accountability Journal, 28*(4), 515–550.

Ahmed Haji, A. (2013). Corporate social responsibility disclosures over time: Evidence from Malaysia. *Managerial Auditing Journal, 28*(7), 647–676.

Akhtaruddin, M., Hossain, M. A., Hossain, M., & Yao, L. (2009). Corporate governance and voluntary disclosure in corporate annual reports of Malaysian listed firms. *Journal of Applied Management Accounting Research, 7*(1), 1.

Al-Hamadeen, R., & Badran, S. (2014). Nature and determinants of CSR disclosure: Experience of the Jordanian public shareholding companies. *European Journal of Business and Management, 6*(13).

Al-Janadi, Y., Abdul Rahman, R., & Alazzani, A. (2016). Does government ownership affect corporate governance and corporate disclosure? Evidence from Saudi Arabia. *Managerial Auditing Journal, 31*(8/9), 871–890.

Alam, F. (2011). *Corporate Governance: The Role of Non-Executive Directors and an International Perspective.* Available at SSRN 1894943

Albawwat, A., & Basah, M. (2015). Corporate governance and voluntary disclosure of interim financial reporting in Jordan. *Journal of Public Administration and Governance, 5*(2), 100–127.

Alhazaimeh, A., Palaniappan, R., & Almsafir, M. (2014). The impact of corporate governance and ownership structure on voluntary disclosure in annual reports among listed Jordanian companies. *Procedia: Social and Behavioral Sciences*, *129*, 341–348.

Allegrini, M., & Greco, G. (2013). Corporate boards, audit committees and voluntary disclosure: Evidence from Italian listed companies. *The Journal of Management and Governance*, *17*(1), 187–216.

Alshannag, F. M., Basah, M. Y. A., & Khairi, K. F. (2016). The Level of Corporate Social Responsibility Disclosure in Jordan. *International Journal of Accounting Research*, *42*(3968), 1–15.

Alshhadat, M. Q. A. (2017). *The Effect Of Corporate Governance On The Intellectual Capital Disclosure; Evidence From Jordan* (Doctoral dissertation). University of Reading.

Baron, D. P. (2008). Managerial contracting and corporate social responsibility. *Journal of Public Economics*, *92*(1-2), 268–288.

Barontini, R., & Bozzi, S. (2011). Board compensation and ownership structure: Empirical evidence for Italian listed companies. *The Journal of Management and Governance*, *15*(1), 59–89.

Basuony, M. A., Mohamed, E. K., & Samaha, K. (2018). Board structure and corporate disclosure via social media: An empirical study in the UK. *Online Information Review*.

Bayoud, N. S., Kavanagh, M., & Slaughter, G. (2012). Factors influencing levels of corporate social responsibility disclosure Libyan firms: A mixed study. *International Journal of Economics and Finance*, *4*(4), 13–29.

Benlemlih, M., Shaukat, A., Qiu, Y., & Trojanowski, G. (2018). Environmental and social disclosures and firm risk. *Journal of Business Ethics*, *152*(3), 613–626. PMID:30956372

Bhattacharyya, A. (2014). Factors Associated with the Social and Environmental Reporting of Australian Companies. Australasian Accounting. *Business and Finance Journal*, *8*(1), 25–50.

Brown, N., & Deegan, C. (1998). The public disclosure of environmental performance information—A dual test of media agenda setting theory and legitimacy theory. *Accounting and Business Research*, *29*(1), 21–41.

Buallay, A., & Al-Ajmi, J. (2019). The role of audit committee attributes in corporate sustainability reporting: Evidence from banks in the Gulf Cooperation Council. *Journal of Applied Accounting Research*.

Calkins, K. G. (2016). Andrews University. *Applied Statistics-Lesson, 5*.

Carrell, A. (1979). BA three-dimensional Conceptual Model of Corporate Social Performance. *Academy of Management Review*, *4*, 497–505.

Clark, C. E., Steckler, E. L., & Newell, S. (2016). Managing contradiction: Stockholder and stakeholder views of the firm as paradoxical opportunity. *Business and Society Review*, *121*(1), 123–159.

Coombs, J. E., & Gilley, K. M. (2005). Stakeholder management as a predictor of CEO compensation: Main effects and interactions with financial performance. *Strategic Management Journal*, *26*(9), 827–840.

Deegan, C., & Blomquist, C. (2006). Stakeholder influence on corporate reporting: An exploration of the interaction between WWF-Australia and the Australian minerals industry. *Accounting, Organizations and Society*, *31*(4-5), 343–372.

Dias, A., Rodrigues, L. L., & Craig, R. (2017). Corporate governance effects on social responsibility disclosures. *Australasian Accounting Business & Finance Journal, 11*(2).

Dienes, D., & Velte, P. (2016). The impact of supervisory board composition on CSR reporting. Evidence from the German two-tier system. *Sustainability*, *8*(1), 63.

Elfeky, M. I. (2017). The extent of voluntary disclosure and its determinants in emerging markets: Evidence from Egypt. *The Journal of Finance and Data Science, 3*(1-4), 45-59.

ElHawary, E., & Arafa, I. M. (2018). Studying the Effect of Stakeholders on the Disclosure of Corporate Social Responsibility by Banks: Evidence from Egypt. *Journal of Accounting and Finance Research, 7*(4), 200-226.

Fallah, M. A., & Mojarrad, F. (2019). Corporate governance effects on corporate social responsibility disclosure: Empirical evidence from heavy-pollution industries in Iran. *Social Responsibility Journal, 15*(2), 208–225.

Freeman, R. E., & Reed, D. L. (1983). Stockholders and stakeholders: A new perspective on corporate governance. *California Management Review*, *25*(3), 88–106.

Fuente, J. A., García-Sanchez, I. M., & Lozano, M. B. (2017). The role of the board of directors in the adoption of GRI guidelines for the disclosure of CSR information. *Journal of Cleaner Production, 141*, 737–750.

Grecco, M., Filho, M., Segura, L., Sanchez, I.-M., & Dominguez, L. (2013). The voluntary disclosure of sustainable information: A comparative analysis of spanish and brazilian companies. *Journal of Accounting and Organizations*, *17*, 45–55.

GRI. (2015). *Gri'S History. Global Reporting Initiative.* Retrieved from https://www.globalreporting.org/information/about-gri/gri-history/Pages/GRI's history.aspx

Guthrie, J., & Parker, L. D. (1989). Corporate social reporting: A rebuttal of legitimacy theory. *Accounting and Business Research*, *19*(76), 343–352.

Haddad, A. E., AlShattarat, W. K., AbuGhazaleh, N. M., & Nobanee, H. (2015). The impact of ownership structure and family board domination on voluntary disclosure for Jordanian listed companies. *Eurasian Business Review*, *5*(2), 203–234.

Hamrouni, A., Boussaada, R., & Ben Farhat Toumi, N. (2019). Corporate social responsibility disclosure and debt financing. *Journal of Applied Accounting Research.*

Harrison, J. S., & Wicks, A. C. (2013). Stakeholder theory, value, and firm performance. *Business Ethics Quarterly*, *23*(1), 97–124.

Hu, M., & Loh, L. (2018). Board governance and sustainability disclosure: A cross-sectional study of Singapore-listed companies. *Sustainability*, *10*(7), 2578.

Ibrahim, K. (2014). Firm Characteristics and Voluntary Segments Disclosure among the Largest Firms in Nigeria. International Journal of Trade. *Economics and Finance*, *5*(4), 327.

Jizi, M. (2017). The influence of board composition on sustainable development disclosure. *Business Strategy and the Environment*, *26*(5), 640–655.

Jordan Securities Commission. (2009). *Corporate governance code for publicly listed companies in Jordan*. Available at: www.jsc.gov.jo

Katmon, N., Mohamad, Z. Z., Norwani, N. M., & Al Farooque, O. (2019). Comprehensive board diversity and quality of corporate social responsibility disclosure: Evidence from an emerging market. *Journal of Business Ethics*, *157*(2), 447–481.

Khan, A., Muttakin, M. B., & Siddiqui, J. (2013). Corporate governance and corporate social responsibility disclosures: Evidence from an emerging economy. *Journal of Business Ethics*, *114*(2), 207–223.

Liao, L., Lin, T. P., & Zhang, Y. (2018). Corporate board and corporate social responsibility assurance: Evidence from China. *Journal of Business Ethics*, *150*(1), 211–225.

Liu, J., & Andersson, T. (2014). *Mind the Gap: Expectations on the Role of UK Non-Executive Directors* (RWPBM Working Paper No. 1402). Retrieved from Regent's Working Papers in Business & Management website: https://www.regents.ac.uk/media/975652/RWPBM1402-Liu-J-Andersson-T.pdf

Malik, M. S., & Kanwal, L. (2018). Impact of corporate social responsibility disclosure on financial performance: Case study of listed pharmaceutical firms of Pakistan. *Journal of Business Ethics*, *150*(1), 69–78.

Mangena, M., & Pike, R. (2005). The effect of audit committee shareholding, financial expertise and size on interim financial disclosures. *Accounting and Business Research*, *35*(4), 327–349.

Mans-Kemp, N., Viviers, S., & Collins, S. (2018). Exploring the causes and consequences of director overboardedness in an emerging market. *International Journal of Disclosure and Governance*, *15*(4), 210–220.

Matuszak, Ł., Różańska, E., & Macuda, M. (2019). The impact of corporate governance characteristics on banks' corporate social responsibility disclosure: Evidence from Poland. *Journal of Accounting in Emerging Economies*, *9*(1), 75–102.

Mazahrih, B. J., Katrib, D. I., & Rfaah, T. M. (2016). Environmental Disclosure: The Case of Jordanian Chemical Industry. *Journal of Accountancy*, *6*(1), 88–100.

Md Zaini, S., Samkin, G., Sharma, U., & Davey, H. (2018). Voluntary disclosure in emerging countries: A literature review. *Journal of Accounting in Emerging Economies*, *8*(1), 29–65.

Musallam, S. R. (2018). The direct and indirect effect of the existence of risk management on the relationship between audit committee and corporate social responsibility disclosure. *Benchmarking*, *25*(9), 4125–4138.

O'brien, R. M. (2007). A caution regarding rules of thumb for variance inflation factors. *Quality & Quantity*, *41*(5), 673–690.

Ofoegbu, N. G., & Odoemelam, N. (2018). *Corporate Board Characteristics and Environmental Disclosure Quantity: A comparative Analysis of Traditional and Integrated Reporting Evidence*. Academic Press.

Palmer, P. D. (2008). Audit quality and financial report disclosure. *Flinders Business School Research Paper Series, 1*, 1-29.

Patten, D. M. (2019). *Seeking legitimacy*. Sustainability Accounting, Management and Policy Journal.

Rao, K., & Tilt, C. (2016). *Board diversity and CSR reporting: an Australian study*. Meditari Accountancy Research.

Reverte, C. (2016). Corporate social responsibility disclosure and market valuation: Evidence from Spanish listed firms. *Review of Managerial Science, 10*(2), 411–435.

Roseland, M. (2000). Sustainable community development: Integrating environmental, economic, and social objectives. *Progress in Planning, 54*(2), 73–132.

Sadou, A., Alom, F., & Laluddin, H. (2017). Corporate social responsibility disclosures in Malaysia: Evidence from large companies. *Social Responsibility Journal, 13*(1), 177–202.

Samaha, K., & Dahawy, K. (2011). An empirical analysis of corporate governance structures and voluntary corporate disclosure in volatile capital markets: The Egyptian experience. International *Journal of Accounting. Auditing and Performance Evaluation, 7*(1-2), 61–93.

Sánchez, R. G., Bolívar, M. P. R., & Hernández, A. M. L. (2017). Corporate and managerial characteristics as drivers of social responsibility disclosure by state-owned enterprises. *Review of Managerial Science*, •••, 1–27.

Shao, G. (2009). *Toward a stakeholder model of corporate governance: Evidence from US media companies*. The University of Alabama.

Sheehy, B. (2015). Defining CSR: Problems and solutions. *Journal of Business Ethics, 131*(3), 625–648.

Sri, W. I. F., & Arief, B. M. (2018). Relationship between Company Financial Performance, Characteristic and Environmental Disclosure of ASX Listed Companies. In *E3S Web of Conferences* (Vol. 73, p. 10024). EDP Sciences.

Thompson, B., & Ke, Q. (2012). Whether environmental factors matter: Some evidence from UK property companies. *Journal of Corporate Real Estate, 14*(1), 7–20.

Tilling, M. V. (2004). *Refinements in Legitimacy Theory in Social and Environmental Accounting*. School of Commerce, Flinders University.

Tilt, C. A. (2009). Corporate responsibility, accounting and accountants. In *Professionals' perspectives of corporate social responsibility* (pp. 11–32). Springer.

Van der Laan, S. (2009). The role of theory in explaining motivation for corporate social disclosures: Voluntary disclosures vs' solicited'disclosures. *Australasian Accounting Business & Finance Journal, 3*(4), 15A.

van der Wiele, T., Kok, P., McKenna, R., & Brown, A. (2001). A corporate social responsibility audit within a quality management framework. *Journal of Business Ethics, 31*(4), 285–297.

Wang, M. C. (2017). The relationship between firm characteristics and the disclosure of sustainability reporting. *Sustainability*, *9*(4), 624.

Wuttichindanon, S. (2017). Corporate social responsibility disclosure—choices of report and its determinants: Empirical evidence from firms listed on the Stock Exchange of Thailand. *Kasetsart Journal of Social Sciences*, *38*(2), 156–162.

Zhang, J. (2017). *Users' perceptions of the drivers for corporate sustainability disclosures made by Chinese listed companies* (PhD thesis). Edith Cowan University. http://ro.ecu.edu.au/cgi/viewcontent.cgi?article=2954&context=theses

Chapter 13
Board Structure and Voluntary Disclosure:
Tunisian Evidence

Issal Haj-Salem
IHEC Carthage, University of Carthage, Tunisia

ABSTRACT

This chapter investigates the impact of board structure on the voluntary disclosure level in a Tunisian context. It aims to analyse the relationship between the different boards of directors characteristics of 51 companies listed on the Tunisian Stock Exchange for the year 2010. The empirical results affirm that the board independence and the presence of institutional shareholders in the board have a positive and significant influence on the voluntary disclosure in the Tunisian annual reports. However, the other characteristics presented in the chapter do not have significant impact on voluntary disclosure. This study could be considered as an important extension of prior research investigating the impact of governance mechanisms on voluntary disclosure, particularly those related to the impact of the board directors. It should be noted that, contrary to prior research, this chapter considers both financial and non-financial firms. Also, few studies examined the ownership structure within the board. The findings have potential implications for countries' regulators.

INTRODUCTION

The search for a sufficient level of transparency remains one of the primary interests of any organization since it guarantees not only short-term profit but also long-term progression and survival. Moreover, due to the contemporary context of globalization and market pressure on corporate management, demand has increased in terms of harmonization of corporate governance and disclosure to ensure a satisfactory level of transparency. Furthermore, firms worldwide are interested to penetrate international capital markets. Consequently, the disclosure of reliable and relevant information becomes necessary to stakeholders since it allows them to assess the management stewardship and to make adequate decisions (Albitar,

DOI: 10.4018/978-1-7998-4852-3.ch013

2015). In order to ensure a reasonable transparency, several legal frameworks have been implemented to regulate firm disclosure. A distinction was made between the mandatory disclosure and the voluntary one (Alnabsha, Abdou, Ntim, & Elamer, 2018; Bertomeu, Vaysman & Xue 2019; Noh & Weber, 2019). The latter has been defined as "disclosures in excess of requirements, represent free choices on the part of company management to provide accounting and other information deemed relevant to the decision needs of users of their annual reports" (Meek, Roberts, & Gray 1995, p. 555). Nevertheless, companies' behaviour regarding voluntary disclosure varies considerably as it is at the discretion of the managers. In some cases, the latter may judge the insufficiency of the mandatory information to reflect a faithful representation of the company, which leads them to go beyond the legal requirements and supplement it with further voluntary disclosure in order to enhance transparency. However, the problem arises when the manager abstains from the communication of such information. Gunawen (2019) believes that the neglect of voluntary disclosure such as business expansion may lead to an unsuitable judgement on the real firm performance and he cited the cases of Batavia Air and Citra Maharlika Nusantara Corpora Tbk in Indonesia who declared bankruptcy even though their performance were considered as "good".

As a result, and in a context of information asymmetry between managers and external investors, the company's communication policy is of paramount importance and represents a powerful tool for stakeholders. This need has become more and more essential in the business world to restore a confidence climate and avoid drifts, especially after many firm collapses. The corporate governance mechanisms are considered the control system for managers' behaviour. The interest on good corporate governance increased and many reforms took place around the world to enhance transparency, accountability and disclosure (Pillai & Al-Malkawi., 2018).

The concept of voluntary disclosure is one of the most discussed topics in financial accounting. Several researchers have focused on analysing the level of voluntary disclosure and identifying its determinants (Alfraih & Almutawa, 2017; Al-Janadi, Rahman, & Alazzani, 2016; El-Diftar, Jones, Ragheb, & Soliman 2017; Rouf & Akhtaruddin, 2018), while others have focused on its economic and financial implications (Cho & kim, 2020; Dawd & Charfeddine, 2019). Despite, the prior attention carried to the voluntary disclosure, it remains important to continue the investigation on it. Several researchers consider that, the voluntary disclosure is crucial to alleviate the information asymmetry which is greater nowadays compared to the past since that the current information needs are different and larger (Habbash, Hussainey, & Ibrahim, 2016).

It is in such context that appears the motivation for this chapter. It aims to find answers for the following questions: (1) what is the extent of voluntary disclosure in Tunisia? and (2) what are the board characteristics that influence the voluntary disclosure in Tunisian listed companies? Therefore, the objective of this chapter is to analyse the relationship between the directors' board characteristics of listed Tunisian companies and the recourse to voluntary disclosure. The investigation of this issue is essentially based on two theories namely agency theory and signalling theory which are both based on the assumption of information asymmetry between external investors and managers. Voluntary disclosure reduces agency costs arising from the divergence of interest between shareholders and managers, and between shareholders and creditors. As for the signalling theory, managers have benefits in reporting to the different stakeholders the company' profitability prospects in order to obtain new financing conditions and thus to reduce costs. This chapter examine five hypotheses related to the characteristics of the directors' board, namely the independence of its members, the duality of the Chief Executive Officer [CEO] and the chairman, board size, the presence of majority shareholders in the board and institutional shareholders.

For that this chapter has several contributions. Firstly, the author believes as other researchers (e.g, Alnabsha et al., 2018) that the relationship between corporate governance and voluntary disclosure have been mainly been examined in developed countries. Hence, this chapter aims to complement extant disclosure studies by investigating the voluntary disclosure practices with regard to the board in an emerging country, with specific focus on Tunisia. The choice of Tunisian context is motivated by a number of reasons. In fact, studies are scarce with this regard. In addition, Tunisia in line with global changes has pursued corporate governance reforms starting from 2008 and is continuing today. The Tunisian disclosure requirements explicitly ask firms to go beyond the legal framework. Furthermore, Tunisia has witnessed the last years the "Arab Spring" that influenced negatively the wealth of firms and consequently many companies' collapses. For that, it becomes crucial to reassure investors and restore their confidence by a satisfactory level of relevant disclosure. Moreover, this chapter examined the disclosure for both financial and non-financial firms

In this sense, the findings of this chapter have practical implications. They could be interesting for the policymakers and regulatory bodies, since they are helpful to recognize the main board characteristics that driver the voluntary disclosure in listed Tunisian companies. Hence, future regulatory initiatives have to take into account to set appropriate policies that improve the effectiveness of the board and hereby enhance the voluntary corporate disclosure.

CONCEPTS

Voluntary Disclosure

According to Leger (2003), voluntary disclosure borrows from marketing approaches, more specifically, it is for the company to "sell" its image on the market as much as to convey accounting and financial information. In addition, the voluntary disclosure has been defined by Meek et al. (1995) as publications that exceed the requirements of the law, thus representing free choices on the part of the company's management to provide accounting information and other information deemed relevant to users of the annual report. Indeed, mandatory disclosure remains indispensable but insufficient. Thus, the information voluntarily disclosed in annual reports should have crucial importance at the heart of the concerns of companies but also to investors and financial analysts. Indeed, the company opts for the communication of voluntary information, not under compulsory requirements such is the case of mandatory information, but relying on a specific communication policy to achieve several objectives such as investments, the prevention of market reactions, the sustainability and the company' reputation, etc.

Corporate Governance

Corporate governance is "the system of checks and balances of internal and external companies to ensure that companies should take responsibility for all stakeholders and to act in socially responsible manner in all areas of its business activities" (Solomon & Solomon, 2004). Many reforms took place, world-wide, after corporate collapses to implement good corporate governance. Tunisia, witnessed many reforms to strength corporate governance starting with the Law of the security of financial relations No. 2005-96 inspired from the American law Sarbanes (2002). In 2008, the Tunisian Center of Corporate Governance

[CTGE] with the support of the Center for International Private Enterprise [CIPE] and International Finance Corporation [IFC] elaborated the first code of good corporate governance practices.

However, in 2011 the Tunisian revolution make it essential to update this guide to enhance the corporate governance practices. In fact, political authorities make more attention to instore good governance practices who enhance transparency, restore investors' confidence and avoid corruptions (Haj-Salem, Damak, & Hussainey 2019).

Board of Directors: Tunisian Regulatory Framework

The board of directors is considered an internal mechanism to control managers. Tunisian companies have to comply with legal requirements:

Size and Composition of the Board

According to Articles 189 and 190 of the Commercial Companies Code [C.S.C], the number of directors has to be at least three members and at most twelve members. In addition, Article 11 of financial institutions' circular specifies that institution must ensure that the number of board members is suitable to the nature, complexity, diversity and volume of its activity and the risks inherent to this institution. It is important to point out that, unless contrary provision in status, shareholder is not required to be a member of the board of directors, while employees may be appointed members of the board of directors if they justify an effective employment and seniority equal to at least 5 years in the company.

Directors' Mandate and Age

Generally, the statutes set the mandate term of a director provided that does not exceed three years (Art.190 of the CSC). Indeed, the mandate renewal is possible at any time unless otherwise provided by statutes. Moreover, the assembly freely decides the non-renewal. Regarding the age of directors, Tunisian legislation does not set limits. However, in practice, the limit age can be indicated in the statutes regarding all the board members or some of them, in order to rejuvenate the board of directors and particularly to avoid any collusion of the latter with the company management.

Compensation

According to Articles 204 and 205 of the CSC, directors have a remuneration fixed annually as attendance fees. However, the board of directors may also allocate exceptional remuneration for missions or mandates done by its members. This compensation must be the counterpart of a special mandate, a mission that is not confused with the general mission of a director. Thus, it is important to note that according to Article 206 of the CSC, the members of the board of directors cannot receive from the company any remuneration other than those stated above.

Cross-Directorship

According to Article 192 CSC, a natural person cannot be simultaneously a member of the board of directors in more than eight public limited companies having their head office in Tunisia. However, according to Article 242 CSC, it is prohibited for a natural person to be simultaneously a member of the board of directors or supervisory board in at most eight public limited companies. It should also be noted that the legal limitation is only applied to natural persons and limited companies.

The Board of Directors' Functions

Directors do not have the power to exercise individually. Indeed, the board of directors is required to meet to make decisions. The members of the Board of directors must perform their duties with the diligence of a wise entrepreneur and a loyal agent.

GOVERNANCE AND VOLUNTARY DISCLOSURE: LITERATURE REVIEW AND HYPOTHESES DEVELOPMENT

Many researches have been taken to analyse the voluntary corporate reporting policy and identify its determinants. A major research area was investigated in developed countries (Arcay & Vasquez, 2005; Chen & Jaggi, 2000; Felo, 2010); others on emerging ones such as Samaha, Dahawy, Hussainey, & Stapleton (2012) in Egypt, Albitar (2015) in Jordan, Bueno, Marcon, Pruner-da-Silva, & Ribeirete (2018) in Brazil, Rouf (2017) in Bangladesh, Habbash et al., (2016) in Saudi Arabia and Sarhan & Ntim (2019) in five emerging Middle Eastern and North African [MENA] economies (Egypt, Jordan, Oman, Saudi Arabia, and United Arab of Emirates). Even that many researchers examined the voluntary disclosure within different contexts, others continue to believe that it crucial to continue investigating on it particularly in emerging markets.

Regarding the Tunisian context and according to a review of prior works, the researchers on corporate voluntary disclosure still need investigations. In the meta-analysis study of Samaha, Khlif, & Hussainey (2015) the authors after a sample selection process retained only the study of Juini (2013) for the Tunisian context. Juini (2013) examined the determinants of disclosure for non-financial listed Tunisian companies. The findings showed that the duality, concentration of ownership, size, leverage, profitability and control quality are determinant for the corporate disclosure policies. In addition, Kolsi (2012) found that Tunisian firm leverage, financial sector, audit quality and profitability have a significant effect on voluntary disclosure. However, the ownership structure and firm size have no impact on voluntary disclosure. Furthermore, Chakroun (2013) examined indirect effect of the board of directors' independence on the impact of family control with regard to the voluntary disclosure of non-financial Tunisian companies. Recently, Chakroun, Matoussi, & Mbirki (2017) was the first study to examine the voluntary disclosure in financial companies with a focus on Corporate social responsibility [CSR] disclosure. Although the investigation on corporate voluntary disclosure in the Tunisian context different interest have been identified and the empirical evidence is somewhat mixed.

This chapter, aims to examine the voluntary disclosure on both financial and non-financial companies with a focus on the board of directors. The board of directors is considered as the most important control mechanism in a company's internal governance structure and a central part of decision-making. It is responsible for setting objectives, monitoring and controlling activities of the company (Fama & Jensen, 1983). In addition, it is considered by the agency theory as one of the main ways to address deficiencies of managers. In fact, it is a body whose main objective is to minimize agency costs by managing, primarily, the conflicts between the managers and shareholders (Jensen & Meckling, 1976).

Thus, it is responsible for representing the interests of shareholders, to defend their wealth, fight against incompetent managers (Chau & Leung, 2006; Fama, 1980; Fama & Jensen, 1983) and agency problems between managers and stakeholders (Jensen, 1993).

According to the literature, the board of directors has four major functions: the agency/control function of supervising management, the strategic decision and policy support role, the resource acquirer role (Lasfer, 2006), and maintenance of firm legitimacy and reputation. In this context, Williamson (1988) considers the board of directors as a mechanism to ensure transaction security, firstly between the company and shareholders as providers of capital and secondly between company and managers as providers of human capital.

Subsequently, the review of studies was helpful to identify several characteristics of the board that may have an impact on the transparency of the company and especially on voluntary disclosure. Among these characteristics, the chapter focus on the board independence, the CEO Duality, the board size, the presence of large shareholders on the board and the presence of institutional shareholders on the board. Hence, the chapter examine them with regard to voluntary disclosure in different hypotheses.

The Board Independence

According to the Tunisian Guide of Good Corporate Governance Practices, "an independent director is any person free from any direct or indirect relationship with the company, the companies of its group or of its management". Tunisian law has not given a clear and concise definition of the concept of independent director. It was only in 2019 that the Law No. 2019-47 of May 29, 2019, relating to the improvement of the investment climate, explicitly defined the independence administrator by considering "independent member, any member having no relationship with companies, or with its shareholders or directors, which is likely to affect the independence of its decision or to render it in a situation of real or potential conflict of interest". Some researchers (e.g. Ibrahim & Hanefah, 2016) considered independent directors as providers of skills and insights to the firm and enhance in turn the effectiveness of the board. Based on agency theory, board independence can positively influence the level of voluntary disclosure. Indeed, if the directors are shareholders, they will have no interest to opt for a voluntary disclosure since they have a satisfactory view of the current firm situation. Hence, appears the information asymmetry. On the other hand, if the outside directors represent the majority of the board, they will tend to disseminate the information serving the interests of the different stakeholders in order to ensure the required level of transparency and fight against the managers' opportunism, and thus serve the overall interest of all parties. Moreover, they improve the financial accounting transparency and restrict likelihood of financial statement frauds (Sandhu & Singh, 2019).

The literature review showed mixed results. Some researchers found a non-significant association between the independent directors and the level of voluntary disclosure (Bueno et al., 2018; Habbash et al., 2016; Ho & Wong, 2001). However, several studies have affirmed a positive relationship between board independence and voluntary disclosure (Al-Janadi, Rahman, & Omar, 2013; Chen & Jaggi, 2000; Haniffa & Cooke, 2002) others showed a negative association between the two variables (Albitar, 2015; Gul & Leung, 2004).

Based on agency theory and prior studies the author set up the first research hypothesis as following:

H1: The board independence has a positive effect on the level of voluntary disclosure

The CEO Duality

The duality refers to the situation when the Chief Executive Officer is also the Chairman of the Board. Jensen & Meckling (1976) emphasized that the separation of management and control functions from decisions reduces agency costs and improves firm performance. Agency theory then considers the presence of the dual structure in a firm as an impediment to the effectiveness of the governance structure's control mechanisms and recommends the separation, since it is difficult and inappropriate to be at the same time judge and party. Thus, when two different individuals have the two positions separately, from CEO to chairman of the board, it can be expected that the chairman will be more diligent and have more equitable considerations. Consequently, he will respond to the interest of all the stakeholders and thus will decrease information asymmetry by opting for a higher level of voluntary disclosure. Duality is, therefore, expected to have a negative impact on corporate voluntary disclosure.

Through the literature there are conflicting results, most of them showed a negative impact of CEO duality on the voluntary disclosure (Eng & Mak, 2003; Samaha et al., 2012, Samaha et al., 2015, Sarhan, 2019). Other researches showed an insignificant impact (Alnabsha et al., 2018). Nevertheless, Al-Janadi et al. (2013) and Al-Janadi et al. (2016) found a positive impact of duality on the voluntary disclosure.

Hence the second hypothesis is the following:

H 2: The CEO duality negatively affects the voluntary disclosure

The Board Size

The board size refers to the number of directors in the board. The board size has, both, advantages and disadvantages. The results of previous research in this area are mixed. On the one hand, larger board could be considered more effective and, thus, leads to better voluntary disclosure since a significant size of the board enhances the members' expertise and makes it difficult to build a consensus between them and consequently avoid the entrenchment. On the other hand, other researchers have been able to contradict empirically these results, while having as theoretical support the agency theory. Indeed, the agency's theorists and particularly Jensen (1993), find that the high size of the board enhances the dominance of the manager by creating coalitions and group conflicts. As a result, directors' decisions will be easily manipulated and they will disseminate less information.

Nevertheless, others added that the role of the board of directors could be offset by the costs generated by a large board size. Indeed, these costs are all the more important as the number of directors is, this will lead to increased communication and coordination problems. Consequently, it will make it difficult for directors to perform their functions effectively, and therefore a decrease in their ability to control managers, which may negatively affect the level of voluntary disclosure.

The empirical evidence on the relationship between voluntary disclosure and board size is mixed. While Albitar (2015), Al-Janadi et al. (2013), Samaha et al. (2012), Samaha et al. (2015) and reported a significantly positive association between board size and voluntary disclosure; other studies reported an insignificant association (Cheng & Courtenay, 2006 ;Loukil & Triki, 2008).

In light of the divergence of the results thus presented, and relying on agency theory, it seems inter esting to test the following hypothesis:

H3: The board size negatively influences the level of voluntary disclosure of information.

The Presence of Large Shareholders in the Board

According to the agency theory, agency costs are high in companies characterized by a wide diffusion of capital. These costs can be controlled by the dissemination of information by the agent to mitigate information asymmetry. However, in companies where shareholding is not very diluted, information asymmetry will be high and the opportunism will not be only that of the manager, but rather that of the large shareholders. Because of their positions, these large shareholders have no interest to disclose additional information to the public since they have already access to all the information they need. Thereby, the quality and extent of their financial disclosure will be low. The findings of Loukil & Triki (2008) in the Tunisian context confirmed the existence of a negative relationship between the concentration ownership and the level of voluntary disclosure. In addition, Ho & Wong (2001) found that for companies characterized by a concentrated ownership, the level of disclosure is low, as the company will not have an incentive to disclose additional information since the main shareholders have direct access to private information. However, Hannifa & Cooke (2002) have found a positive relationship between the diffusion of capital and disclosure of voluntary information by Malaysian listed companies. Therefore, the next research hypothesis is:

H4: The presence of large shareholders in the board influences negatively the extent of voluntary disclosure

The Presence of Institutional Shareholders in the Board

The institutional investors, because of their professional experience as well as their power over the executives, ensure that the principles of corporate governance are respected in order to protect the rights and the wealth of shareholders. They require a more transparent disclosure of the risks incurred by the firm and its key factors of success in order to better evaluate it and estimate the distribution of future cash flow (Bushee & Noe, 2000). In addition, Bushee & Noe (2000) and Healy, Hutton, & Palepu (1999) argued that institutional investors are very demanding agents in terms of regular and timely information. The study of Healy et al. (1999) conducted on a sample of 97 firms from 1978 to 1991 shows a positive relationship between the institutional ownership and the quality of voluntary disclosure. The study of Haniffa & Cooke (2002) also showed the same results. In the Tunisian context, the results of the study of Omri & Turki (2008) showed that the presence of institutional shareholders improves the voluntary disclosure in the annual reports.

Referring to the agency theory, institutional directors with particular skills are likely to better appreciate the performance of the managerial team and therefore better control it. Their presence on the board of directors is supposed to have the same effects as their participation in the capital of the company. Moreover, they have notoriety and reputation that allows them to exercise their power over managers and compel them to follow their recommendations. In this context and in light of this review and the agency theory it seems appropriate to test the following hypothesis:

H5: The presence of institutional shareholders in the board has a positive impact on the level of voluntary disclosure.

DATA AND RESEARCH METHODOLOGY

Data: Sample Selection, Sources, and Description

A main sample of 51 listed companies on the Tunisian Stock Exchange was selected for the year 2010. The chapter retained only companies with available data. Both financial and non-financial companies were retained in contrast with prior studies in Tunisian context (Chakroun, 2013; Juini, 2013) who excluded the financial ones due to the specific financial reporting. However, the author believes that since the study consists on voluntary disclosure in annual reports rather than financial statements, and based on the Art 44 of Tunisian Financial Council Market [CMF] all information that companies may include in their annual reports have a voluntary nature whatever are financial or non-financial ones. Thus, the final sample was composed of 40 Tunisian companies listed on the Tunisian Stock Exchange. The data collection of annual reports was performed through the CMF, directly from the companies and few of them through Internet. Data related to the characteristics of the board of directors are collected either through the annual reports, company web sites or through questionnaire distributed to each company in order to collect the maximum amount of missing data. The distribution of the companies is displayed in Table 1.

Table 1. Firms' sample

Sector	Frequency
Financial firms Telecommunications	15 1
Consumer Services	3
Health	2
Consumer goods	9
Industrials	5
Basic Materials	4
Oil and Gas	1
Total	40

Research Methodology: Definition of Variables and Model Specification

Dependent Variable (DIV_VOL)

Several researchers measured voluntary disclosure using indexes (eg., Botosan, 1997). For instance, Eng & Mak developed their own disclosure index in 2001 and validated it in 2003 to analyze and measure disclosure in companies' annual reports. Eng & Mak (2003) relied on the index adopted by Lang & Lundholm (1996) and arranged by the International Federation of Financial Analysts to score companies according to their degree of disclosure. This chapter, adopted the same methodology of Eng & Mak (2003) because it turned out to be the most appropriate method in the Tunisian context. Indeed, this index is developed in a Singaporean context and considered more suitable for research conducted in developing countries; while the Botosan index (1997) is developed in an American context, a context different from the Tunisian one, and for the mechanical industry.

Moreover, Zéghal & Lahmar (2007), in their study of the impact of privatization on the level of voluntary disclosure in the annual reports of Tunisian private companies, adopted the index of Eng & Mak (2003) as it is considred more suitable for the Tunisian context, and this after making a comparison between the two indexes. The results of the descriptive analysis showed that the level of disclosure as measured by Eng & Mak (2003) index (Appendix) displays values close to those of the Botosan index (1997). Moreover, the Spearman test showed a positive and statistically significant correlation between the two measures. This confirms that both indexes, despite their differences, seem to yield comparable disclosure scores. The index of Eng & Mak (2003) is structured around three components:

- One component focuses on strategic information;
- Another is dedicated to non-financial information and;
- A third component focuses on the financial information of the company.

The procedure for measuring the disclosure index has been well defined by Eng & Mak (2003). Indeed, it is about performing a content analysis by reading the firm's annual reports and calculating an overall measure using the following quantification method:

- One point is given for general information;
- Two points are given if quantitative information is also provided;
- Three points are allocated if more detailed data are provided, whether quantitative or qualitative;
- For information on new achievements, a point is given for firms that simply provide such information. Three points are allocated for any quantitative information. Five points are awarded for more detailed information.

The chapter measures the voluntary disclosure score by calculating the total points given to the items for each company.

Hence the level of disclosure is calculated as follows:

$$DIV_j = \sum_{i=1}^{n} SCORE_{ij}$$

Where:

DIV_j: is the voluntary disclosure measure for firm j,
$SCORE_{ij}$: is the total points given to company j for categories of information i.
n: number of index items

It should be noted that the author has not removed from the index the items whose disclosure is mandatory in Tunisia, since no Tunisian company has been sanctioned because of non-compliance with the regulations and more specifically Article 44 of the CMF.

It is necessary to confirm the reliability and validity of voluntary disclosure score. For that, the author followed Haj-Salem et al. (2019) by checking the stability, reproducibility and accuracy of the content analysis. The stability (intra-rater reliability) is considered as the replication of the same results more than once by the same coder. Consequently, five annual reports were analysed at a very later date and the findings confirmed the stability of the findings since the differences are not significant. Then, a check of the reproducibility is conducted. This test consists on having the same findings by different coder. Consequently, another independent researcher read five annual reports following the voluntary disclosure index. The Scott's Pi test is used and calculated through the "ReCal" software following Haj-Salem et al. (2019). The Scott's Pi average is 0.83. Consequently, the author considers the voluntary disclosure score sufficiently reliable since a score of 0.75 was considered satisfactory to confirm the reproducibility of the results. Finally, regarding the accuracy is verified if there is "correspondence of the performance of a method with a given or known standard" Krippendorff (1980, p. 72). This is confirmed since the disclosure was inspired from earlier constructed index in the literature especially the index of Eng & Mak (2003) and the Article 44 of the CMF.

Regression Model

The impact of the board of directors on the corporate voluntary disclosure level on annual reports is tested empirically through a linear regression. The model is as following:

$$\begin{aligned} DIV\_VOL = {} & \beta 0 + \beta 1\ INDEP + \beta 2\ DUAL + \beta 3\ B\_SIZE \\ & + \beta 4\ INSTF + \beta 5\ CONC + \beta 6\ \mathit{F\_SIZE} + \beta 7\ SECT + \varepsilon \end{aligned}$$

Where:

α = the intercept.
$\beta_1, \ldots, \beta_{21}$= Regression coefficients.
ε = Error term

Table 2 presents the variables of the study.

RESULTS

Descriptive Statistics

Table 3 highlights that the voluntary disclosure score for listed Tunisian companies varies between a minimum value of 14 and a maximum value of 74. Moreover, the disclosure average score is 33.5. Accordingly, the voluntary disclosure for listed Tunisian companies is relatively low, moreover the variability is important given the considerable dispersion deduced through a high standard deviation. Similarly, the disclosure sub-scores are relatively low. Besides, the strategic and financial information are the most widely disclosed information. However, non-financial information is the least-reported information with an average of 3.425.

Table 2. Variables' description

Variable Name	Description	Measure	Studies
DIV_VOL	Level of voluntary disclosure	as described in Appendix	
INDEP	The board independence	The proportion of external directors relative to the Board size	Al-Janadi et al (2016)
DUAL	The CEO Duality	« 1 » if there is a duality, « 0 » otherwise	Bueno et al (2018)
B_SIZE	The board size	the total number of directors in the board.	Khlif and Samaha (2019)
CONC	Proportion of concentration shareholders in the board	1 if the shareholder owning more than 50 percent of the capital is a member of the board of directors, 0 otherwise.	Loukil et Triki (2008)
INSTF	The presence of institutional shareholders in the board	Proportion of institutional and financial directors divided by the total number of directors.	Al-Bassam et al., (2018)
F_Size	Firm size	Natural logarithm of total assets	Juini (2013)
SECT	Industry sector	1 if the firm belongs to financial firms, 2 if the firm belongs to industrials and 3 otherwise.	Cooke (1992)

Table 3. Descriptive statistics for dependent variables

Variable	Obs.	Min	Max	Mean	S.D
DIV_VOL	40	14	74	33.50	12.826
DIV_STG	40	1	36	15.350	6.754
DIV_NFN	40	0	18	3.425	3.782
DIV_FN	40	5	36	14.900	7.175

The Table 4 shows that the proportion of independent directors varies between 0 and 0.889 percent, and with a mean of 39.67 percent. Therefore, the majority of directors in listed Tunisian companies are not independent. Besides, the institutional directors mean is 22.40 percent. Indeed, their proportion varies between 0 percent and 91.7 percent of all directors. This implies that the institutional directors do not constitute the majority of directors. Regarding the size of the board, it has a mean of 8.6 and this considering a minimum value of 5 and a maximum value of 12. Similarly, the size of the company varies between 7.008 and 9.813 thousand of dinars with a mean of 8.198. This confirms that listed Tunisian companies are medium-sized companies.

Table 4. Descriptive statistics for continuous variables

Variable	Obs.	Min	Max	Mean	S.D
INDEP	40	.000	.889	.397	.240
B_SIZE	40	5	12	8.600	2.307
INSTF	40	.000	.917	.224	.242
F_SIZE	40	7.008	9.813	8.198	.690

The descriptive statistics of dichotomous variables in Table 5 show that 72.5 percent of the sampled companies have a dual leadership structure and that 40 percent are characterized by the presence of a director holding more than 50 percent of the capital in the board. Regarding the companies' distribution according to their industry sector, the financial companies represent 37.5 percent of the overall sample, 12.5 percent of industrial companies and the remainder are companies belonging to other sectors. In addition, the standard deviation is 0.939. Thus, author affirm the representativeness of the sample.

Table 5. Descriptive statistics for dichotomous variables

Variable	Obs.	Number	Proportion %
DUAL	0 1 Total	11 29 40	37.5 72.5 100
CONC	0 1 Total	24 16 40	60 40 100
SECT	1 2 3 Total	15 5 20 45	37.5 12.5 50 100

Multivariate Analysis

To check the non-multi-collinearity between explanatory variables the Pearson correlation matrix is used in Table 6, as well as the VIF multi-collinearity indicator in Table 7.

Table 6. Pearson Correlation Matrix

Variables	INDEP	DUAL	B_SIZE	CONC	INSTEF	F_SIZE	SECT
INDEP	1	.023	-.044	-.009	-.215	-.073	.404**
DUAL		1	.088	-.411**	.052	-.226	.083
B_SIZE			1	-.170	.298	.160	-.260
CONC				1	.030	-.085	.000
INSTF					1	.224	-.448**
F_SIZE						1	-.588**
SECT							1

From the Pearson correlation matrix, the author confirms that all correlation coefficients are less than "0.8", and this is the limit set by Kennedy (1985) to decide the non-multi-collinearity of variables. In addition, through Table 7, the author concludes the non multi-collinearity of the explanatory variables. Indeed, Myers (1990) predicted that the VIF should not exceed a value of 3 to assert the non- multi-collinearity between the variables.

Table 7. VIF

	1/VIF	VIF
INDEP	.788	1.270
DUAL	.742	1.348
B_SIZE	.854	1.171
CONC	.763	1.310
INSTF	.747	1.339
F_SIZE	.562	1.778
SECT	.446	2.243

Table 8 indicates that the model has relatively strong explanatory power. Indeed, the adjusted R2 is about 33.8 percent with a significance of 1 percent indicated through Fisher's statistics. In fact, the minimum required R2 to assert the quality of a model is 30 percent. Besides, the Durbin-Watson test is used to detect the presence of residual autocorrelation and its effect on the results. The value of this test must be between 1.5 and 2.5 to affirm that there is no auto-correlation of the errors. In this case, the author found a value of 1.796, which confirms the non-autocorrelation of residuals.

Table 8. Findings

Variable	R	R2	Adjusted R2	Variation de F	Prob>F	Durbin-Watson
DIV_VOL	.676[a]	.457	.338	3.847	.004	1.796

As for the normality of residuals, it is checked since the sample size is greater than 30. Moreover, the studied association is relatively linear and this is observed from the Figure 1, which shows that the histogram PP is similar to the straight line of identity (the diagonal).

After having reasonable assurance as to the quality of the model, the author proceeds to the regression analysis. As a result, the author relies on OLS regression coefficients presented in Table 9. Moreover, the author conducted an additional analysis by using a Poisson regression to check the robustness of the findings. The Poisson regression results as reported in Table 9 are similar to those of the OLS regression, which confirms the robustness of the results.

The findings reported in Table 9 show that among all independent variables introduced in the model, only the independence of the directors and the presence of institutional ownership in the board have a significant effect on the voluntary disclosure in Tunisian annual reports. On the other hand, the other variables namely, the duality, the board size, the presence of large ownership within the board, the company size and its industry sector, do not have a significant effect on the level of voluntary disclosure.

To deepen the analysis, the author tested three other models by considering the sub-scores of voluntary disclosure categories as dependent variables, to determine the factors that can influence each of these categories.

Figure 1. Linearity of the model

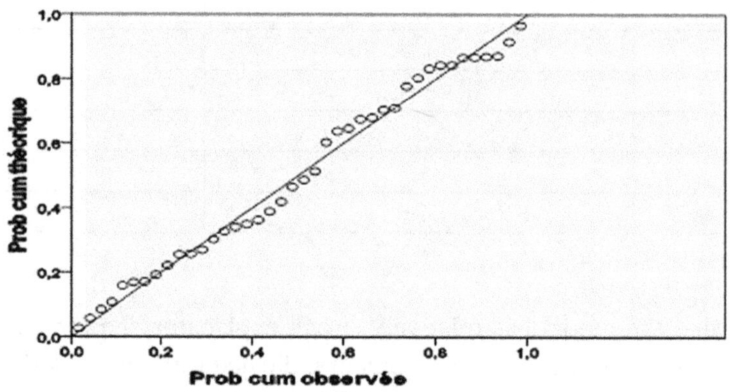

Table 9. Results

	OLS Regression			Poisson Regression		
	Coef.	t	P> |t|	Coef.	z	P> |z|
INDEP	.622	4.241	**.000*****	.9512077	7.65	**0.000*****
DUAL	.150	.990	.329	.1138634	1.63	0.102
B_SIZE	-.032	-.229	.821	-.0066832	-0.50	0.620
CONC	.154	1.031	.310	.0915946	1.48	0.140
INSTEF	.329	2.185	**.036****	.5422656	4.20	**0.000*****
F_SIZE	.151	.866	.393	.0846138	1.64	0.101
SECT	-.045	-.233	.817	-.0162327	-0.37	0.710
_Cons	—	-.262	.795	2.260514	4.41	0.000

The significance levels (two-tail test) are: *= 10%, ** =5% and *** = 1%.

According to Table 10, the Strategic Information Sub-score [DIV_STG], Non-financial Information Sub-score [DIV_NFN] and Financial Information Sub-score [DIV_FN] have an explanatory power respectively of 21.5 percent, 23.2 percent and 27 percent in addition to the significance of the three models at 5 percent. Thus, the author proceeds to the analysis of these models.

Table 10. Models about the sub-categories of voluntary disclosure

Dependent Variable	R	R2	Adjusted R2	Variation de F	Prob>F	Durbin-Watson
DIV_STG	.596[a]	.356	.215	2.525	.035	1.888
DIV_NFN	.608[a]	.370	.232	2.687	.026	1.802
DIV_FN	.634[a]	.401	.270	3.066	.014	2.286

First, with regard to the DIV_STG, a positive and significant relationship is revealed at 1 percent level between the independent directors and strategic voluntary disclosure. This confirms the hypothesis H1. This result is consistent with the result found in the DIV_VOL model. Besides, there is a positive but insignificant relationship between the presence of institutional directors and the voluntary disclosure of strategic information. While in the main model the findings show the same sense of relationship but with a significant effect. For the other variables, the findings show an insignificant relation like the results of the DIV_VOL model. Then, from the DIV_NFN model, the first hypothesis is accepted since there is a positive and significant relationship at the 1 percent level between the independence of directors and voluntary disclosure of non-financial information, which is consistent with the results of the main model. As for the presence of institutional directors, the author found a positive but insignificant relationship with the disclosure of non-financial information.

Finally, the findings of the DIV_FN model provide a positive and significant relationship between the independent directors and the voluntary disclosure of financial information. However, the impact of the presence of institutional directors is positive but insignificant. So according to the results related to the four models the author confirms the hypothesis H1 related to the independence of directors, whereas the hypothesis H5 regarding the presence of the institutional directors is confirmed partially. As for the other hypotheses, they are rejected. The findings of the models about the sub-categories of voluntary disclosure are presented in Table 11.

Table 11. Results of the models about the sub-categories of voluntary disclosure

	Dependent Variable								
	DIV_STG			DIV_NFN			DIV_FN		
	Coef.	t	P> |t|	Coef.	t	P> |t|	Coef.	t	P> |t|
INDEP	.449	2.808	**.008*** **	.554	3.503	**.001*** **	.380	2.463	**.019** **
DUAL	.074	.451	.655	.163	1.002	.324	.082	.518	.608
B_SIZE	.151	.981	.334	-.100	-.660	.514	-.099	-.671	.507
CONC	.111	.684	.499	-.010	-.064	.950	.202	1.293	.205
INSTEF	.236	1.436	.161	.323	1.992	**.055***	.163	1.029	.311
F_SIZE	-.169	-.892	.379	.113	.604	.550	.367	2.011	**.053***
SECT	.163	.766	.449	-.031	-.147	.884	-.242	-1.181	.246
_Cons	_	.806	.426		-.547	.588	_	-.934	.357

The significance levels (two-tail test) are: *= 10%, ** =5% and *** = 1%.

Discussion

The Board Independence

The empirical results of the DIV_VOL model show a positive and significant relationship between the presence of independent directors and the voluntary disclosure in Tunisian annual reports, which confirms H1. The same relationship was also confirmed with regard to the sub-categories of voluntary disclosure namely strategic, non-financial and financial. This result is consistent with the study of Arcay

& Vasquez (2005), Chen & Jaggi (2000), Cheng & Courtenay (2006), Haniffa & Cooke (2002), and Patelli & Prencipe (2007). However, it is not consistent with Habbash et al., (2016) who found a negative association and Bueno et al (2018) who did not find statistical significance in their findings.

This relationship could be explained through the information asymmetry between managers and stakeholders; indeed, independent directors are considered as guarantors of the latter interests by controlling the opportunistic behaviour of managers and enhancing the disclosure of useful information in annual reports. Hence, they tend to provide information going beyond the compulsory. This information is deemed relevant to decision-making and to a better understanding of the company's performance. As well, they will have a better reputation as independent experts.

Institutional Directors

The results reveal that the presence of institutional directors seems to affect positively and significantly the level of disclosure, which confirms H5. This is in accordance with several researches such as those of Bushee & Noe (2000), Haniffa & Cooke (2002), Healy et al. (1999), Lakhal (2005), and Omri & Turki (2008).

The sense of this relationship was confirmed for the sub-categories' disclosure; however, they do not have a significant effect. Thus, the presence of institutional shareholders on the board improves the dissemination of voluntary information. This could be explained by the fact that they are the most sensitive agents with regard to information and they exert pressure on managers to communicate the relevant information despite their non-compulsory nature.

The CEO Duality

The empirical findings show a positive effect of the CEO duality on voluntary disclosure with the different categories but without significant effect. Hence, H2 is rejected. This result seems surprising in terms of the expected sign, comparing it with the explanation provided by the agency theory, since the separation of management and control functions from decisions reduces agency costs. Indeed, through this theory the author has concluded that the separation of leadership function allows the CEO to be more diligent and consequently reduces the information asymmetry to respond to the interests of all stakeholders, this may be satisfied by opting to a higher voluntary disclosure. Moreover, Ashfaq & Rui (2019) explained that a positive sign of the association between CEO duality and disclosure can be interpreted through specific regulatory guidelines within the context. Several previous studies have confirmed the negative relationship between the dual leadership structure and voluntary disclosure such as Basset, Koh, & Tutticci (2007), Bueno et al., (2018), Gul & Leung (2004), Haniffa & Cooke (2002), Ho & Wong (2003), and Juini (2013). However, the result of this chapter coincides with the work of Alotaibi & Hussainey (2016), Arcay & Vasquez (2005), Cheng & Courtenay (2006), Loukil & Triki (2008).

The Board Size

The results showed a negative but insignificant effect. Consequently, H3 is rejected. This hypothesis was rejected in the additional models too. The hypothesis was based on the assumptions of the agency theory, which predicts that the larger the size of the board is, the more dominating is the manager. Besides, it is more likely to have coalitions and group conflicts. This leads to weak management control and informational opacity, which will reduce in turn the level of voluntary disclosure. Moreover, a large board size may lead to coordination and communication problems, which is an impediment for the effectiveness of the board. For this chapter, the sense of the relationship does not reject the explanation provided by agency theory. However, a problem is related to the significance of this relationship. The findings are consistent with Bradi (2003), Cheng & Courtenay (2006), Ebrahim & Fattah (2015), and Loukil & Triki (2008). However, they are not consistent with Al-Bassam et al., (2018) and Alotaibi & Hussainey (2016) who found a positive relationship.

The Large Shareholders in the Board

The empirical results showed a positive but insignificant relationship between voluntary disclosure and the presence of a large shareholder in the board, which contradicts the fourth hypothesis that was developed under the assumptions of agency theory. Indeed, according to the agency theory conflicts of interest can arise between the majority shareholders and the minority ones. This is due to the opportunistic behaviour of large shareholders who benefit of private information in the detriment of the latter; and thus, will mitigate the transparency of the company. Hence, their presence within the board constitutes an impediment to voluntary disclosure. Several researchers have empirically confirmed this relationship such as Ho & Wong (2001) and Loukil & Triki (2008). However, Arthur, Chen, & Tang (2019) argued that when the ownership concentration is over 51 percent, there will be increasing alignment between inside shareholders' interests and those of the firm. Indeed, the latter is virtually under their control and this leads to better financial reporting quality. Moreover, higher financial reporting quality leads to higher firm value and enhance the reputation of the firm and its management. Nevertheless, the results are in line with Eng & Mak (2003).

Finally, the chapter results are summarized in the Table 12.

Table 12. Summary of findings

Hypotheses	Expected Sign	Results	Validation/ Rejection
H1: The board independence	+	+***	**Validated**
H2: The CEO duality	-	+	Rejected
H3: The board size	-	-	Rejected
H4: The presence of large shareholders in the board	-	+	Rejected
H5: The presence of institutional shareholders in the board	+	+**	**Validated**

CONCLUSION

This chapter examined the relationship between voluntary disclosure and an internal governance mechanism that is the board of directors. Thus, the main objective was to analyze the influence of the board characteristics on the voluntary disclosure in Tunisian annual reports. The chapter, firstly defined several concepts. Then a literature review was necessary in order to identify the empirical findings in different contexts and to identify the attributes of the board that are most likely to influence the voluntary disclosure. Besides, the author used agency theory and signalling theory to develop the hypotheses. As a result, five hypotheses were developed regarding several characteristics of the board which are: the directors' independence, the board size, the duality of CEO, the presence of a large shareholder within the board and also the presence of institutional shareholder. A positive and significant relationship regarding the board independence and the presence of institutional shareholder have been expected. However, a negative and significant relationship is presumed regarding the other characteristics.

In this regard, a sample of 40 Tunisian listed companies was selected. The multivariate analysis showed that the independence of the directors and the presence of institutional shareholders in the board have a positive and significant influence on the voluntary disclosure. Moreover, the remainder characteristics do not have a significant impact on voluntary disclosure.

As for the board size, it is negatively associated with voluntary disclosure. However, this association remains insignificant. The findings of the OLS regressions confirmed that the independence of the directors has a positive and significant effect on the sub-scores of the voluntary disclosure, namely strategic information, non-financial information and financial information. Nevertheless, the presence of an institutional shareholder positively influences the disclosure of these sub-scores information, but the obtained effect was not significant. Regarding the remainder variables, the author found similar results compared to the main model.

However, like any research, the results obtained must be analysed in light of certain limitations. Thus, the first limitation, which the author can point out, is inherent to the relatively small size of the sample, knowing that it represents a significant proportion of the studied population: the listed Tunisian companies. The second limitation concerns the period of the study, year 2010, since the authors chose to exclude any potential effect of the revolution on the study in addition the author believes that is important for future researches to investigate this issue for a longer period before and after the revolution. The third limitation is about the measure of voluntary disclosure that was conducted using the Eng & Mak index (2003). Indeed, other indices could be used to measure voluntary disclosure such as the Botosan index (1997). Nonetheless, the index of Eng & Mak (2003) although is not far from all criticism, seems to be the most suitable to the chapter. Nevertheless, future researches may investigate better to develop an index specific to the Tunisian context.

Moreover, the author used one mean of voluntary information namely the annual report. Thus, other studies could investigate the voluntary disclosure with regard to other means of disclosure. Finally, the chapter focused on the relationship of voluntary disclosure and board characteristics. However, there are other governance mechanisms that can mitigate the opportunistic behaviour of managers and improve corporate transparency. Despite these limitations, the chapter includes contributions to the literature. Admittedly, it complements the studies that examined the influence of corporate governance mechanisms on voluntary disclosure, particularly those related to the influence of the board of directors. Nevertheless, it should be noted that the chapter considers all sectors compared to other studies that often eliminate the financial one. Moreover, few studies examined the ownership structure within the board.

Finally, the findings have potential implications for countries' reformers and regulators for whom the author confirms that the effectiveness of the board of directors in terms of voluntary disclosure of information in Tunisian listed companies depends on several characteristics. Hence, better reforms have to be taken in order to improve the effectiveness of the board and, thereby, the transparency.

REFERENCES

Al-Bassam, W. M., Ntim, C. G., Opong, K. K., & Downs, Y. (2018). Corporate boards and ownership structure as antecedents of corporate governance disclosure in Saudi Arabian publicly listed corporations. *Business & Society*, *57*(2), 335–377. doi:10.1177/0007650315610611

Al-Janadi, Y., Rahman, R. A., & Alazzani, A. (2016). Does government ownership affect corporate governance and corporate disclosure? *Managerial Auditing Journal*, *31*(8/9), 871–890. doi:10.1108/MAJ-12-2015-1287

Al-Janadi, Y., Rahman, R. A., & Omar, N. H. (2013). Corporate governance mechanisms and voluntary disclosure in Saudi Arabia. *Research Journal of Finance & Accounting*, *4*(4), 25–36.

Albitar, K. (2015). Firm characteristics, governance attributes and corporate voluntary disclosure: A study of Jordanian listed companies. *International Business Research*, *8*(3), 1–10. doi:10.5539/ibr.v8n3p1

Alfraih, M. M., & Almutawa, A. M. (2017). Voluntary disclosure and corporate governance: Empirical evidence from Kuwait. *International Journal of Law and Management*, *59*(2), 217–236. doi:10.1108/IJLMA-10-2015-0052

Alnabsha, A., Abdou, H., Ntim, C., & Elamer, A. (2018). Corporate boards, ownership structures and corporate disclosures: Evidence from a developing country. *Journal of Applied Accounting Research*, *19*(1), 20–41. doi:10.1108/JAAR-01-2016-0001

Alotaibi, K. O., & Hussainey, K. (2016). Determinants of CSR disclosure quantity and quality: Evidence from non-financial listed firms in Saudi Arabia. *International Journal of Disclosure and Governance*, *13*(4), 364–393. doi:10.1057/jdg.2016.2

Arcay, M. R. B., & Vasquez, M. F. M. (2005). Corporate Characteristics, governance rules and the extent of voluntary disclosure in Spain. *Advances in Accounting*, *21*, 299–331. doi:10.1016/S0882-6110(05)21013-1

Arthur, N., Chen, H., & Tang, Q. (2019). Corporate ownership concentration and financial reporting quality: International evidence. *Journal of Financial Reporting and Accounting*, *17*(1), 104–132. doi:10.1108/JFRA-07-2017-0051

Ashfaq, K., & Rui, Z. (2019). The effect of board & audit committee effectiveness on internal control disclosure under different regulatory environments in South Asia. *Journal of Financial Reporting and Accounting*, *17*(2), 170–200. doi:10.1108/JFRA-09-2017-0086

Basset, M., Koh, P. S., & Tutticci, I. (2007). The association between employee stock option disclosures and corporate governance. Evidence from enhanced disclosure regime. *The British Accounting Review*, *39*(4), 303–322. doi:10.1016/j.bar.2007.06.003

Bertomeu, J., Vaysman, I., & Xue, W. (2019). *Voluntary versus Mandatory Disclosure*. doi:10.2139srn.2872412

Botosan, C. A. (1997). Disclosure level and the cost of equity capital. *The Accounting Review*, *72*(3), 323–349.

Bueno, G., Marcon, R., Pruner-da-Silva, A. L., & Ribeirete, F. (2018). The role of the board in voluntary disclosure. *Corporate Governance, 18*(5), 886–910. doi:10.1108/CG-09-2017-0205

Bushee, B. J., & Noe, C. F. (2000). Corporate disclosure practices, institutional investors, and stock return volatility. *Journal of Accounting Research, 38*, 171–202. doi:10.2307/2672914

Chakroun, R. (2013). Family Control, Board of Directors' Independence and Extent of Voluntary Disclosure in the Annual Reports: Case of Tunisian Companies. *Journal of Business Studies Quarterly, 5*(1), 22.

Chakroun, R., & Matoussi, H. (2012). Determinants of the extent of voluntary disclosure in the annual reports of the Tunisian firms. *Accounting and Management Information Systems, 11*(3), 335.

Chakroun, R., Matoussi, H., & Mbirki, S. (2017). Determinants of CSR disclosure of Tunisian listed banks: A multi-support analysis. *Social Responsibility Journal, 13*(3), 552–584. doi:10.1108/SRJ-04-2016-0055

Chau, G. K., & Gray, D. J. (2002). Ownership structure and corporate voluntary disclosure in Hong Kong and Singapore. *The International Journal of Accounting, 37*(2), 247–265. doi:10.1016/S0020-7063(02)00153-X

Chen, J. P., & Jaggi, B. L. (2000). The association between Independent non-Executive Directors, Family Control and Financial Disclosures. *Journal of Accounting and Public Policy, 19*(4-5), 285–310. doi:10.1016/S0278-4254(00)00015-6

Cheng, E. C., & Courtenay, S. M. (2006). Board composition, regulatory regime and voluntary disclosure. *The International Journal of Accounting, 41*(3), 262–289. doi:10.1016/j.intacc.2006.07.001

Cho, H., & Kim, R. (2020). Asymmetric effects of voluntary disclosure on stock liquidity: Evidence from 8-K filings. *Accounting and Finance*, acfi.12594. Advance online publication. doi:10.1111/acfi.12594

Cooke, T. E. (1992). The impact of size, stock market listing and industry type on disclosure in the annual reports of Japanese listed corporations. *Accounting and Business Research, 22*(87), 229–237. doi: 10.1080/00014788.1992.9729440

Dawd, I., & Charfeddine, L. (2019). Effect of aggregate, mandatory and voluntary disclosure on firm performance in a developing market: The case of Kuwait. *International Journal of Accounting. Auditing and Performance Evaluation, 15*(1), 31–56. doi:10.1504/IJAAPE.2019.096735

El-Diftar, D., Jones, E., Ragheb, M., & Soliman, M. (2017). Institutional investors and voluntary disclosure and transparency: The case of Egypt. *Corporate Governance, 17*(1), 134–151. doi:10.1108/CG-05-2016-0112

Eng, L. L., & Mak, Y. T. (2003). Corporate governance and voluntary disclosure. *Journal of Accounting and Public Policy, 22*(4), 325–345. doi:10.1016/S0278-4254(03)00037-1

Felo, A. J. (2010). *Corporate reporting transparency, board independence and expertise, and CEO duality.* Available at SSRN: https://ssrn.com/abstract=1373942

Gul, F. A., & Leung, S. (2004). Board leadership, outside directors' expertise and voluntary corporate disclosure. *Journal of Accounting and Public Policy, 23*(5), 351–379. doi:10.1016/j.jaccpubpol.2004.07.001

Gunawan, A. (2019). The Role of Corporate Governance Mechanism On Voluntary Disclosure. *Jurnal Akuntansi*, *23*(1), 127–142. doi:10.24912/ja.v23i1.467

Habbash, M., Hussainey, K., & Ibrahim, A. (2016). The determinants of voluntary disclosure in Saudi Arabia: An empirical study. *International Journal of Accounting. Auditing and Performance Evaluation*, *12*(3), 213–236. doi:10.1504/IJAAPE.2016.077890

Haj-Salem, I., Damak, S., & Hussainey, K. (2019). Corporate governance and risk disclosure quality: Tunisian evidence. *Journal of Accounting in Emerging Economies*, *9*(4), 567–602. doi:10.1108/JAEE-01-2019-0005

Haniffa, R. M., & Cooke, T. E. (2002). Culture corporate governance and disclosure in Malysian corporations. *Abacus*, *38*(3), 317–349. doi:10.1111/1467-6281.00112

Healy, P. M., Hutton, A. P., & Palepu, K. G. (1999). Stock Performance and Intermediation Changes Surrounding Sustained Increases in Disclosure. *Contemporary Accounting Research*, *16*(3), 485–520. doi:10.1111/j.1911-3846.1999.tb00592.x

Ho, S. M., & Wong, K. S. (2003). Perception of Corporate Reporting and Disclosure. *International Journal of Disclosure and Governance*, *1*(1), 71–81. doi:10.1057/palgrave.jdg.2040014

Ho, S. S. M., & Wong, K. S. (2001). A study of the relationship between corporate governance structures and the extent of voluntary disclosure. *The International Journal of Accounting. Auditing and Taxation*, *10*(2), 139–156. doi:10.1016/S1061-9518(01)00041-6

Ibrahim, A. H., & Hanefah, M. M. (2016). Board diversity and corporate social responsibility in Jordan. *Journal of Financial Reporting and Accounting*, *14*(2), 279–298. doi:10.1108/JFRA-06-2015-0065

Jensen, M. C. (1993). The modern industrial revolution, exit, and the failure of internal control systems. *The Journal of Finance*, *48*(3), 831–880. doi:10.1111/j.1540-6261.1993.tb04022.x

Jensen, M. C., & Meckling, W. H. (1976). Theory of the firm: Managerial behaviour, agency costs and ownership structure. *Journal of Financial Economics*, *3*(4), 305–360. doi:10.1016/0304-405X(76)90026-X

Juini, F. (2013). Corporate governance and the level of financial disclosure by Tunisian firm. *Journal of Business Studies Quarterly*, *4*(3), 95–111.

Khlif, H., & Samaha, K. (2019). Board independence and internal control quality in Egypt: Does CEO duality matter? *International Journal of Law and Management*, *61*(2), 345–358. doi:10.1108/IJLMA-08-2017-0202

Krippendorff, K. (1980). *Content Analysis: An Introduction to its Methodology*. Sage Publications.

Lakhal, F. (2005). Voluntary earnings disclosures and corporate governance: Evidence from France. *Review of Accounting and Finance*, *4*(3), 64–85. doi:10.1108/eb043431

Lang, M. H., & Lundholm, R. J. (1996). Corporate Disclosure Policy and Analyst Behavior. *The Accounting Review*, *71*(4), 467–492.

Leger, J. Y. (2003). *La communication financière*. Dunod.

Loukil, L. & Triki, M. (2008). L'analyse De L'impact Des Mécanismes De Gouvernance Sur Le Niveau De Divulgation Volontaire: Cas Des Sociétés Tunisiennes Non Financières. *La Comptabilité, Le Contrôle et L'audit entre Changement et Stabilité*, France. CD Rom. halshs-00525414

Noh, S., So, E. C., & Weber, J. P. (2019). Voluntary and mandatory disclosures: Do managers view them as substitutes? *Journal of Accounting and Economics*, *68*(1), 101243. doi:10.1016/j.jacceco.2019.101243

Patelli, L., & Prencipe, A. (2007). The relationship between voluntary disclosure and independent directors in the presence of a dominant shareholders. *European Accounting Review*, *16*(1), 5–33. doi:10.1080/09638180701265820

Pillai, R., & Al-Malkawi, H. A. N. (2018). On the relationship between corporate governance and firm performance: Evidence from GCC countries. *Research in International Business and Finance*, *44*, 394–410. doi:10.1016/j.ribaf.2017.07.110

Rouf, M., & Akhtaruddin, M. (2018). Factors affecting the voluntary disclosure: A study by using smart PLS-SEM approach. *International Journal of Law and Management*, *60*(6), 1498–1508. doi:10.1108/IJLMA-01-2018-0011

Rouf, M. A. (2017). Firm-specific characteristics, corporate governance and voluntary disclosure in annual reports of listed companies in Bangladesh. *International Journal of Managerial and Financial Accounting*, *9*(3), 263–282. doi:10.1504/IJMFA.2017.086691

Samaha, K., Dahawy, K., Hussainey, K., & Stapleton, P. (2012). The extent of corporate governance disclosure and its determinants in a developing market: The case of Egypt. *Advances in Accounting*, *28*(1), 168–178. doi:10.1016/j.adiac.2011.12.001

Samaha, K., Khlif, H., & Hussainey, K. (2015). The impact of board and audit committee characteristics on voluntary disclosure: A meta-analysis. *Journal of International Accounting, Auditing & Taxation*, *24*, 13–28. doi:10.1016/j.intaccaudtax.2014.11.001

Sandhu, A., & Singh, B. (2019). Board composition and corporate reporting on internet: Indian evidence. *Journal of Financial Reporting and Accounting*, *17*(2), 292–319. doi:10.1108/JFRA-05-2017-0031

Sarhan, A. A., & Ntim, C. G. (2019). Corporate boards, shareholding structures and voluntary disclosure in emerging MENA economies. *Journal of Accounting in Emerging Economies*, *9*(1), 2–27. doi:10.1108/JAEE-03-2017-0033

Zéghal, D, & Lahmar, Z. (2007). Analyse de l'impact de la privatisation sur le niveau de divulgation volontaire dans les rapports annuels. *Revue Comptable et financière, 1*, 31-47.

APPENDIX: DISCLOSURE INDEX

Inspired from the research of Eng & Mak (2003)

A - Strategic Information

(A-1) General corporate information;

- Brief history of company
- Organizational structure/chart
- General description of business/activities
- Principal products
- Principal markets

(A-2) Corporate strategy:

- Statement of corporate goals or objectives
- Current strategy
- Impact of strategy on current results
- Future strategy
- Impact of strategy on future results

(A-3) Management discussion and analysis

- Review of operations
- Competitive environment
- Significant events of the year
- Change in sales/profits
- Change in cost of goods sold
- Change in expenses
- Change in inventory level
- Change in market share

(A-4) Future prospects:

- New developments
- Forecast of sales/profit
- Assumptions underlying the forecast
- Order book or backlog information

(A-5) Other useful strategic information:

- Sub-total (A)

B – Key Non-financial Information

(B-1) Employee information:

- Number of employees
- Compensation per employee
- Value-added per employee
- Productivity indicator

(B-2) Other useful non-financial disclosure:

- Sub-total (B)

C- Financial Information

(C-1) Performance indicators (not from financial Statements):

- Historical figures for last five years or more
- (or as long as company as formation)
- Turnover
- Profit
- Shareholders' funds
- Total assets
- Earnings per share

(C-2) Financial ratios:

- Return on shareholders' funds (ROE)
- Return on assets
- Gearing ratio
- Liquidity ratio
- Other useful ratios

(C-3) Projected information:

- Cash flow forecast
- Capital expenditures and/or R&D expenditures forecast
- Earnings forecast

(C-4) Foreign currency information:

- Impact of foreign exchange fluctuations on current results
- Foreign currency exposure management description
- Major exchange rates used in the accounts

(C-5) Other useful financial information:

- Sub-total (C)

Total (Company D Score)

Chapter 14
Corporate Governance and Cash Holdings

Ahmed Hassanein
Mansoura University, Egypt & Gulf University for Sceince and Technology (GUST), Kuwait

ABSTRACT

Corporate cash induces the opportunistic behavior of corporate managers that can create an agency problem. A corporate governance system controls the opportunistic behavior of managers and can affect the firm's policy on holding cash. This study explains how the aspects of corporate governance, country-level and firm-level governance, can affect the corporate policy on holding cash. First, the study provides the nature, definition, and importance of corporate cash holdings. Second, it outlines various motivations and theories behind holding corporate cash. Third, it explains the relation between firm-level governance and corporate cash holdings. Fourth, it focuses on the impact of firm-specific governance attributes on the level of corporate cash holdings. Fifth, it presents the relation between country-level governance and corporate cash holdings.

1. INTRODUCTION

Huang Weiming, the financial controller of Lenovo Group, states: "The fact that companies don't have cash is just like people who don't have blood. Even if they have strong capabilities, the company is also difficult to sustain." (Ye, 2018, PP. 1054). This statement points to the importance of cash for the survival of the firm. Cash enables firms to undertake their operating, investing, and financing activities and can be insurance against any unexpected future costs. It also gives firms the flexibility to seize immediate favorable investment opportunities. However, cash is a zero-return asset and holding excess cash can lead to losing different development opportunities in the market. Thus, the managerial decision on a corporate policy to hold cash is important.

Corporate cash is a vulnerable account that corporate managers can use to satisfy their opportunistic behavior. This behavior can easily decrease cash reserves. That is corporate managers can misappropriate part or all the excess cash. The agency theory argues that holding cash can create an agency problem between managers and shareholders if the incentives of corporate managers are not aligned with those

DOI: 10.4018/978-1-7998-4852-3.ch014

of the corporate shareholders. The availability of corporate cash induces the opportunistic behavior of corporate managers, and so they can use their discretion to waste cash in the form of rewards and compensation decisions at the expense of shareholders.

Some studies argue that the corporate governance system controls the opportunistic behavior of managers and so can affect the corporate policy on holding cash. Corporate governance can be divided into two factors: country-level and firm-level governance (Klapper & Love, 2004). The country-level governance is also called an *external governance mechanism* that includes the country's legal system (coded vs. common law systems), degree of investor protection, and market conditions. Firm-level governance is called an *internal governance mechanism* that includes all firm specific governance instruments such as the board of directors, structure of ownership, audit committee, and the external auditor. This study explains how country-level, and firm-level governances can effectively impact the corporate policy on cash holding to mitigate the conflict of interests between managers and shareholders and, consequently, reduce the agency problem.

First, this study presents the nature, definition, and importance of corporate cash holdings. Second, it outlines various motivations and theories of corporate cash holdings. Third, it explains the relation between firm-level governance and corporate cash holdings. Fourth, it focuses on the effect of firm-specific governance attributes on the level of corporate cash holdings. Fifth, it presents the relation between country-level governance and corporate cash holdings.

2. CASH HOLDING: DEFINITION

Cash is the first asset account listed on a statement of a firm's financial position. The amount of cash is of interest to different stakeholders, such as existing and potential investors, lenders, and creditors. Investors use cash as a proxy for liquidity. Cash holdings, also referred to as cash hoardings, are defined as the level of cash and cash equivalents that are highly liquid assets that a firm can convert into cash in a short period of time (Ferreira & Vilela, 2004). Cash equivalents include the firm's bank accounts, Treasury bills, and commercial paper as well as money market securities that have a maturity of 90 days. There are variations among countries in terms of the percentage of the level of cash. For instance, cash holdings can range from 8% to 12% in the UK, 8% to 17% in the US (Al-Najjar, 2013), and are 18.5% in Japan (Pinkowitz & Williamson, 2001). Also, the percentage ranges from 10% to15% in Switzerland (Drobetz & Grüninger, 2007), 7% to 9% in Spain (García-Teruel & Martínez-Solano, 2008), 9% to 10% in Italy (Bigelli & Sánchez-Vidal, 2012), and 10% to 13% in Turkey (Hassanein & Kokel, 2019). The variations in the levels of corporate cash holdings among countries may be due to differences in the corporate governance systems (Drobetz & Grüninger, 2007).

3. CASH HOLDINGS: MOTIVATIONS

This section has a discussion on the various motivations that encourage firms to hold cash. These motivations are: 1) transactional, 2) precautionary, 3) agency, 4) speculative, and 5) taxation. First, Beckhart and Keynes (1936) postulate that holding cash comes from transactional, precautionary, and speculative motives. Jensen (1986) adds the agency motive as a driver of corporate cash holdings. Further, some studies add the taxation motivation as a driver for holding cash (Fritz Foley, Hartzell, Titman, & Twite, 2007).

3.1 The Transaction Motivation

Holding cash helps different firms to undertake different operating activities and to satisfy their obligations. The transaction motivation argues that firms are more likely to hoard cash to be able to face higher transaction costs of raising funds externally and when they face difficulty in liquidating their assets (Beckhart & Keynes, 1936). Bates, Kahle, and Stulz (2009) argue that firms are likely to hold cash when the opportunity costs of hoarding are higher than the transaction costs. The level of corporate cash also depends on the industry within which the firm operates. For instance, assume that a firm operates in a retail sector (e.g., a fast food restaurant). Thus, we can expect a high inventory turnover; any reduction in inventory should be replaced quickly. Therefore, we can expect that this firm holds high levels of cash to satisfy its inventory needs. On the other hand, firms that do not face high transaction costs are likely to hold lower levels of cash, such as a software firms (Ferreira, Custodio, & Raposo, 2011).

3.2 The Precautionary Motivation

Holding cash can act as insurance for firms against any unexpected obligations and expenses in periods with shortfalls of liquidity (Bates et al., 2009). Also, firms can use cash to finance investment projects with positive net present values (NPVs) (Ozkan & Ozkan, 2004). In addition, cash can act as a guarantee against an adverse shock to cash inflows. Thus, firms are likely to hold more cash if there is volatility in cash inflows and limited access to the capital markets (Opler, 1999). Bates et al. (2009) advise firms to hold higher levels of cash when the economic conditions are unstable and when there is a possibility of an economic shock. This is because holding cash during an economic recession or a shock is less expensive than liquidating assets (Ferreira et al., 2011)

3.3 The Agency Motivation

Corporate managers consider the agency motivation when deciding on cash holdings. They can decide on dividend payments and cash distributions to maximize the wealth of shareholders. On the other hand, they can decide on holding cash for investment and corporate expansion reasons. The corporate management may benefit from holding cash rather than distributing it to shareholders. They may desire to reduce the risk associated with raising funds externally. This reduction may be because raising funds externally is more costly than internal financing. However, when managers hold cash rather than distributing it, they can create an agency conflict between them and shareholders. The research examines the effect of the agency problem on the level of corporate cash holdings. It finds that entrenched managers exist in countries with agency conflicts and that firms are likely to hold higher levels of cash in countries with more agency conflicts (e.g., Marwick, Hasan, & Luo, 2020; Dittmar & Mahrt-Smith, 2007; Harford, Mansi, & Maxwell, 2012).

3.4 The Speculative Motivation

Under the principle of speculative motivation, holding cash enables firms to avoid any cash shortfalls in case any investment opportunities arise in the market. Furthermore, the holding of cash gives some flexibility to firms in terms of the timing of undertaking investments. Assume that there is a good investment opportunity in the market; however, the firm has no cash. Thus, it will lose this opportunity that it could have gained if it had been holding cash. Thus, holding cash gives a firm the flexibility to avoid investing under conditions of uncertainty. Furthermore, it is difficult for firms to access financial markets and to raise funds externally to finance different investment opportunities. However, holding cash facilities the finance of different investment opportunities at any time. Thus, holding cash helps firms to seize profitable future investment opportunities (Hassanein & Kokel, 2019).

3.5 The Tax Motivation

Recently, Fritz Foley et al. (2007) have added the taxation motivation as a driver of corporate cash holdings. They argue that international firms that operate in countries with lower tax rates are likely to avoid repatriation of their earnings to reduce the negative consequences of higher tax rates in their home countries. Thus, international firms may hold their cash in foreign subsidiaries to gain benefits from lower tax rates. Sander, Teder, Viikmaa, and Kantšukov (2014) state that US international firms are likely to hold higher levels of cash abroad in their foreign subsidiaries because of the higher tax for repatriating foreign earnings. This, to some extent, is incorrect because international US firms can hold their cash in US banks. Thus, cash physically is not abroad. However, Sander et al. (2014) argue that many of the US firms are likely to hold higher levels of cash in their foreign subsidiaries to avoid the negative effects of tax when repatriating foreign income. Chen (2014) finds higher levels of foreign cash in US international firms due to the tax on repatriation. Furthermore, firms that apply different tax avoidance policies are likely to hold higher cash.

4. CASH HOLDING THEORIES

This section presents the three different theories commonly used in the literature on cash holdings. These theories are: 1) the trade-off theory that was developed by (Baumol, 1952; Tobin, 1956), 2) the pecking order theory that was proposed by (Myers & Majluf, 1984), and 3) the free cash-flow theory that was developed by (Jensen, 1986).

4.1 Trade-off Theory

Corporate cash holdings can create different benefits and costs for a firm. Thus, determining the amount of cash to be held is considered an important decision for firm management. Ferreira and Vilela (2004) identify different benefits from cash holding such as reducing the probability of suffering financial distress, reducing the costs of liquidating assets, and being a less expensive source of funds than external financing. On the other hand, the costs of cash holding include the opportunity costs of lost investments. This decision is the basis of the trade-off theory. This theory is further extended by Miller and Orr (1966) who consider the volatility of corporate cash flows. The theory argues that an optimal level of cash holding exists. At this optimal level the marginal costs of holding cash equals its marginal benefits (Opler, 1999). Furthermore, the trade-off between managers and shareholders is another cost of cash holding. For instance, there may be an agency conflict if managers hold cash instead of distributing it to shareholders (Han & Qiu, 2007). Thus, according to the trade-off theory, corporate managers should hold an optimal level of cash by balancing the marginal costs and benefits of cash hoarding.

4.2 Pecking Order/ Financial Hierarchy Theory

The pecking order theory, also referred to as the financial hierarchy theory explains the methods that firms use to finance their investments. In particular, firms use the following hierarchy to finance their different investments. First, they use internal funds that they have accumulated from retained earnings, then they use low risk debts, and third they use higher risk debts and equity (Myers & Majluf, 1984). The use of debts as a method of finance is costly for firms. However, holding cash is not expensive. Firms use equity as a last choice for financing to avoid any conflict of interest between managers and shareholders, that is, agency costs. The pecking order theory also aims to reduce the information asymmetry between the managers and shareholders of the firm by reducing the costs of financing (Ferreira & Vilela, 2004).

4.3 Free Cash-Flow Theory

The free cash-flow theory explains how managers can use cash to gain power over corporate investment decisions. The free cash flow is the value of cash that remains after subtracting the capital expenditures from the firm's operating cash flows. Jensen (1986) argues that managers should use the free cash flow to increase the sizes of their firms. This increased size helps corporate managers to gain sufficient power and control over their corporate investment decisions. The free cash flows help firms to make additional investments that may not be to the desire of shareholders. These investments may reduce the agency costs between managers and shareholders. The free cash flow helps firms to finance different investments internally rather than depending on costly external funds. The holding of free cash flows helps corporate managers to avoid pressures in terms of poor performance (Ferreira & Vilela, 2004).

5. FIRM-LEVEL GOVERNANCE AND CORPORATE CASH HOLDINGS

The agency theory, proposed by Jensen (1976), argues that in the case of a conflict of interest between the firm's managers and shareholders, it needs a mechanism to control the possible opportunistic actions of the corporate managers. The corporate governance instruments can fill this role and reduce the conflict of interests between managers and shareholders (Hassanein & Kokel, 2019). Corporate cash is a relatively vulnerable account that corporate managers can use to satisfy their opportunistic behavior (Dittmar & Mahrt-Smith, 2007) because the use of cash is discretionary. Therefore, mangers can waste it through rewards and compensation decisions that they make in the absence of a good control system.

The research and the agency theory indicate that the corporate governance system controls the opportunistic behavior of managers in relation to corporate cash (Akhtar, Tareq, Sakti, & Khan, 2018; Hassanein & Kokel, 2019). Firm-level corporate governance, also referred to as internal governance mechanisms, can enhance corporate value by optimizing the use of corporate cash (Dittmar & Mahrt-Smith, 2007). If the governance system of a firm is good, the amount of corporate cash is worth more than the same amount of corporate cash in a firm with a poor governance system. This is because a good governance system controls and invests the cash well by distributing it in an efficient manner. However, in a poor governance system, the corporate managers can use cash for their opportunistic behaviors to gain personal benefits at the expense of minority shareholders. Thus, in the absence of a good corporate governance system, corporate managers have no incentive to enhance the marginal value of cash in proper investment opportunities (Harford et al., 2012). Some studies find a higher marginal value of corporate cash in firms with good corporate governance mechanisms (Jain, Li, & Shao, 2013; Manoel, Moraes, Nagano, & Sobreiro, 2018). Furthermore, Kalcheva and Lins (2007) find a decrease in the value of a firm in the presence of managerial control over corporate cash. They further argue that the corporate cash is not invested in profitable projects, which causes a decrease in the corporate value.

Some studies investigate the impact of firm-level governance mechanisms on the agency costs and corporate cash holdings. For instance, Chen (2008) focuses on firms listed on the S&P index to explore how firm-level governance mechanisms can affect the corporate cash level. He divides the sample into two subsamples: firms operating in developing and developed economies. He finds that the effects of ownership by a CEO and the independence of the board of directors are different for firms in these economies. Particularly, a negative association exists between ownership by a CEO and the level of corporate cash holdings for firms in a developed economy. However, a positive association exists between the percent of independent directors and the level of corporate cash holdings for firms in a developing economy. Similarly, Chen and Chuang (2009) use a sample from high-tech firms to examine how corporate governance mechanisms affect the level of corporate cash holdings. They find that both the ownership by a CEO and the percent of independent directors affect the level of corporate cash holdings. Further, they report that the association between corporate governance mechanisms and corporate cash holdings is more observable in younger firms compared to older firms. Kuan, Li, and Chu (2011) focus on family-firms and find that the effect of corporate governance on the cash holding policy is significantly different between family and non-family-controlled firms. Moreover, Yu, Sopranzetti, and Lee (2013) use a sample from Taiwanese firms to examine how the level of governance can affect the level of its cash holdings. They find a positive (negative) relation between managerial ownership (bank relations) and the level of corporate cash holdings. In addition, Asante-Darko, Adu Bonsu, Famiyeh, Kwarteng, and Goka (2018) report a positive association between corporate cash holdings and the corporate value of firms with strong governance mechanisms. Furthermore, Dogru and Sirakaya-Turk (2018) find that the level of corporate cash holdings and the level of cash flows on investments are higher in firms with strong corporate governance mechanisms compared to firms with poor corporate governance mechanisms. Recently, Hassanein and Kokel, (2019) use a sample from firms listed in Bosra Istanbul to find that good firm-level governance reduces the level of corporate cash holdings. To conclude, the above research indicates the crucial effect of firm-level governance, internal governance mechanism, on the cash holding policy and consequently on the cash flow from investment and the value of a firm.

6. CORPORATE GOVERANCE ATTRIBUTES AND CORPORATE CASH HOLDINGS

In this section, we focus on firm-specific governance mechanisms that are commonly examined in prior studies and that influence the corporate policy on holding cash. Particularly, we explain how the following mechanisms could affect the policy: 1) size of the board of directors, 2) family control, 3) role duality of the CEO, 4) independence of board of directors, 5) frequency of board meetings, 6) audit committee, and 7) external auditor.

6.1 Size of Board of Directors and Cash Holdings

Jensen (1993) finds that corporate CEOs dominate the corporate decisions of larger boards of directors. This domination may occur because in larger boards, members are not likely to oppose the decisions of management. Thus, larger boards arguably are not effective in decision-making (Yermack, 1996). Thus, a negative relation exists between board size and the cooperation and communication of board members that reduces the quality and efficiency of the board of directors (Boubakri, Ghoul, & Saffar, 2013). Some studies find a positive effect of the size of the board of directors on the level of corporate cash holding (Bokpin, Isshaq, & Aboagye-Otchere, 2011; Gill & Shah, 2011; Hassanein & Kokel, 2019; Lee & Lee, 2010). That is, firms with a large (small) board of directors are likely to hold a high (low) level of cash. However, other studies find no effect from the size of the board of directors on the level of corporate cash holding (Boubakri et al., 2013).

6.2 Family-Control and Cash Holdings

The literature argues that in family-controlled firms, family members use cash to benefit their own interests at the expense of outside shareholders (La Porta, Lopez-de-Silanes, & Shleifer, 1999; Thanatawee, 2019). Kuan et al. (2011) find weak monitoring in family-controlled firms because they make their decisions after considering the requirements of family members. Thus, these firms should have higher levels of corporate cash. This high level satisfies the interest of family members at the expense of minority shareholders. Empirically, the research shows mixed results. For instance, Liu, Luo, and Tian (2015) and Hassanein and Kokel (2019) find that a positive association exists between family-controlled firms and their corporate cash holdings. However, Kuan, Li, and Liu (2012) report a non-monotonic level of corporate cash holdings in family-controlled films. Particularly, they find a higher level of corporate cash if the CEO of a firm is a member of the family than if the CEO is not a family member. Furthermore, Boubakri et al. (2013) examine how corporate governance could affect the level of corporate cash holdings in family-controlled firms; they find a negative effect. That is, a well-governed family-controlled firm is likely to hold a low level of corporate cash.

6.3 Duality of CEO and Cash Holdings

There is a negative association between the quality of a corporate board and the role duality of its CEO (Jensen, 1993). That is, if the roles of corporate CEO and its chairman are combined, the efficiency of the board of directors is likely to be negatively affected. The CEO is the most crucial position in the firm and allows the CEO to access all critical information (Manoel, Moraes, Nagano, & Sobreiro, 2018). Consequently, an entrenched CEO will share that critical information to gain personal benefits at the expense of shareholders (Brockmann, Hoffman, Dawley, & Fornaciari, 2004). Thus, the duality of the CEO can negatively affect the monitoring of the board of directors that reduces its effectiveness to detect undesirable actions by different board members (Goyal & Park, 2002). The research finds a negative impact of the role duality of the CEO on firm performance (Gul & Leung, 2004). Thus, there will be less control on the corporate cash level when role duality exists. Empirically, some studies find a positive impact of the role duality of the CEO on the level of corporate cash holding (Boubakri et al., 2013; Gill & Shah, 2011; Hassanein & Kokel, 2019). That is, the level is high in firms with the same person as both CEO and chairman.

6.4 Independence of Board of Directors and Cash Holdings

Lee and Lee (2010) argue that the independence of the board of directors is vital to a well-structured board. This is because independent directors are more likely, compared to executive directors, to reduce the desire of corporate managers to hold higher cash levels to pursue their own benefits. Adams, Hermalin, and Weisbach (2010) argue that non-executive and independent board members are likely to be more objective in decision-making. Thus, boards with more independent directors are likely to be more efficient in monitoring the actions of management (Yermack, 2004). This efficient monitoring enhances the corporate performance and reduces the managerial entrenchment (Lee & Lee, 2010). Some studies confirm that the monitoring duties of independent directors protect the rights of minority shareholders (Kim, Kitsabunnarat-Chatjuthamard, & Nofsinger, 2007). Based on the above discussion, we expect independent directors to play an active and effective role in controlling the actions of management and in preventing them from holding higher cash levels. Empirically, the research supports this argument and finds a negative association between the percent of independent board members and the corporate cash level (Boubakri et al., 2013; Hassanein & Kokel, 2019; Lee & Lee, 2010)

6.5 Frequency of Board Meetings and Cash Holdings

The main responsibility of the board of directors is oversight of the actions of corporate management. Studies have argued that the frequency of the board's meetings has a significant influence on board members effectively undertaking their monitoring duties (Jiraporn, Singh, & Lee, 2009). Furthermore, the research shows that the higher frequency of meetings enhances the effectiveness of the directors in undertaking their duties (García-Ramos & García-Olalla, 2011). The agency theory posits that corporate managers have the opposite tendency to shareholders in terms of holding cash (Jensen, 1986). That is, corporate managers tend to hold cash to gain benefits for their own interests; however, shareholders are likely to want a cash distribution in the form of dividends from their firms. The frequency of board meetings should enhance the effectiveness of the monitoring of the board of directors. This, in turn, leads to lower levels of corporate cash holdings. However, there is a noticeable lack of empirical research that explores how the frequency of board meetings could affect the corporate policy on holding cash. Recently, Hassanein and Kokel (2019) find an insignificant effect of the frequency of board meetings on the level of corporate cash holdings.

6.6 Size of Audit Committee and Cash Holdings

The agency theory posits that the conflict of interests between corporate managers and shareholders results in decisions that meet the interests of managers (Jensen, M. C., 1976). Further, the decisions against shareholders' interests are more common when the monitoring quality of a firm is low. The corporate audit committee plays a vital role in enhancing the monitoring quality of the board and in resolving the managers and shareholders' conflict of interests (Klein, 2002). That is, the main responsibility of audit committees is to monitor the corporate internal control system to enhance the reliability of financial reports. This role reduces the agency problem between managers and shareholders. In addition, Venkataraman, Weber, and Willenborg (2008) show that firms with audit committees are likely to face a lower number of lawsuits in terms of the conflicts between the firms' managers and their shareholders. A larger audit committee is better than a smaller one. This is because it is likely to have diversified skills and knowledge that enhances the monitoring quality. However, when it becomes too large its effectiveness decreases. Based on the above discussions, a firm with an audit committee is better monitored than a firm without one. This, in turn, controls the behavior of corporate managers in terms of corporate cash. There is a noticeable lack of studies that explore the effect of the audit committee on the corporate cash holding policy.

6.7 External Auditor and Cash Holdings

Studies have argued that high quality audits of financial reports reduce the information asymmetry and conflict of interest between managers and shareholders (Healy & Palepu, 2001). The external auditors play a significant role in providing assurance on the financial reports. This role can build trust between managers and shareholders. The big auditing firms provide higher quality audits compared to smaller auditing firms due to their expertise. Thus, we can argue that big auditing firms can detect managerial opportunism in terms of corporate cash holdings. The pecking order theory posits that information asymmetry influences the financing preferences of firms. High quality auditing reduces information asymmetry and, therefore, firms with a big auditor face less costs when raising funds externally. The trade-off theory argues that firms with big auditing firms should hold low levels of cash to mitigate the opportunity costs of holding higher levels of cash. There is a lack of research in terms of the association between auditor type and corporate cash holdings. Recently, Hassanein and Kokel (2019) find that firms audited by one of the big auditing firms hold low levels of cash compared to firms audited by a smaller auditor.

7. COUNTRY-LEVEL GOVERNANCE AND CORPORATE CASH HOLDINGS

The country-level governance refers to the external factors of the country within which the firm operates that may have an effect on the firm's performance and financial position. These external factors include the legal system of a country (coded vs. common law systems), degree of investor protection, and market conditions. Some studies report significant differences between common and coded law countries in terms of the strength of governance systems, degree of investor protection, and regulatory enforcement (La Porta et al., 1999).

The cross-country analyses report mixed findings regarding the effect of country-level governance instruments on the level of cash holdings, and most of the studies support the agency perspective of high cash reserves. The research focuses mainly on how the degree of investor protection could affect the level of cash holdings among different countries. For instance, La Porta, Lopez-De-Silanes, Shleifer, and Vishny (2000) find that firms working in countries with a low degree of investor protection are less likely to distribute dividends to shareholders. This lower distribution indicates a higher level of cash holdings for firms that operate in countries with weak country-level governance, that is, weak investor protection. Further, Dittmar, Mahrt-Smith, and Servaes (2003) examine how country-level governance mechanisms could directly affect the level of corporate cash holding. They use a sample of 11,000 firms that operate in 45 different countries. Their findings support the agency theory that firms in countries with poor investor protection are likely to hold higher liquid assets such as cash that leads to an agency conflict between managers and shareholders. However, firms operating in countries with strong investor protection are likely to hold low levels of cash. This low level indicates a reduction in the conflict of interest between managers and shareholders in countries with strong investor protection. Furthermore, they find that asymmetric information and investment opportunities do not influence the cash holding policy in countries with weak shareholder protections. They conclude that shareholders are likely to limit the level of cash holding available under the discretionary power of corporate managers, particularly when they have sufficient power.

Kalcheva and Lins (2007) focus on investor protection as a factor for country-level governance and examine how the degree of investor protection can affect the level of corporate cash holdings. Their results indicate that international firms that operate in countries with weak shareholder protection are likely to hold cash. In addition, they find that control of management over cash negatively affects the corporate value. Their results show that in countries with weak investor protection, firms do not invest excess cash in profitable projects. However, if corporate managers distribute cash in the form of dividend payments, they likely enhance the value of a firm, even in countries with weak investor protection. They conclude that holding cash does not influence the corporate value of the firms in countries with strong investor protection. Furthermore, Pinkowitz, Stulz, and Williamson (2006) use a large time series sample over 11 years from 1985 to 1994 with 35 countries to examine the impact of investor protection on the level of cash holdings. They, separately, examine two main factors related to investor protection: legal rights and enforcement. They apply the valuation regression model developed by Fama and French (1998). Their empirical analyses find a weak association between corporate cash holdings and corporate value in countries with poor investor protection. However, such an association is much stronger in countries with strong investor protection. They also find a weak impact from dividends on the value of a firm in countries with strong investor protection compared to countries with weak investor protection. Furthermore, their results support the agency theory that corporate management uses cash to benefit their own interests at the expense of minority shareholders in countries with weak investor protection. This usage in turn leads to an agency conflict between managers and minority shareholders. However, this situation does not exist in countries with strong investor protection. In addition, Dittmar and Mahrt-Smith (2007) focus on the US, which is a country with strong investor protection, and find results that support the findings of Pinkowitz et al. (2006). They find that corporate governance has a significant influence on the cash holding policy. That is, the level of cash is higher in firms with a strong corporate governance system compared to firms with poor corporate governance. This level indicates the significant influence of the system of corporate governance on reducing the agency conflicts between managers and shareholders. Further, they find a low level of cash in firms in countries with weak investor protection.

On the other hand, some studies find results that contradict the findings of the prior research. For instance, Harford, Mansi, and Maxwell (2012) use a sample of 1,872 firm-year observations to find that poorly governed firms are less likely to hold cash. This result is not consistent with the research that finds that firms with poor corporate governance tend to hold higher levels of cash (e.g., Dittmar & Mahrt-Smith, 2007; Pinkowitz et al., 2006). Harford et al. (2012) further argue that poorly governed firms are likely to spend cash on unnecessary capital expenditures rather than holding it. They explain that the increase in capital expenditure is due to their poor governance system that then leads to a decrease in corporate performance and financial position. Some studies support the findings of Harford et al. (2012). For instance, Caprio, Faccio, and McConnell (2013) find that in countries with strong investor rights, such as the UK, firms are likely to hold cash. This suggests that strong country-level governance instruments support holding of higher levels of cash that is not consistent with the findings of some other studies, such as Dittmar et al. (2003), Kalcheva and Lins (2007), and Pinkowitz et al. (2006).

Thus, there is no final conclusion in terms of the effect of country-level governance on the corporate policy on cash holding. On one hand, some studies find that firms in countries with strong country-level governance are less likely to hold cash and invest cash in proper projects to enhance the value of firms (e.g., Dittmar et al., 2003; Kalcheva & Lins, 2007; La Porta et al., 2000; Pinkowitz et al., 2006). However, other studies have contradictory results and find that strong country-level governance supports the holding of higher levels of cash (e.g., Caprio et al., 2013; Harford et al., 2012)

8. CONCLUSION

Cash holdings are the level of cash and cash equivalents that are highly liquid assets. Holding cash can help firms to overcome unexpected obligations in the case of shortages in cash inflows. Variations exist among countries in term of the percentage of the level of cash holding. Holding corporate cash is induced by different motivations such as transaction, precautionary, agency, speculative, and taxation motivations. Different theories are commonly used in the literature to explain a corporate policy on cash holding. These theories are the trade-off theory (Baumol, 1952; Tobin, 1956), pecking order theory (Myers & Majluf, 1984), and the free cash-flow theory (Jensen, 1986). The firm-level corporate governance can enhance the corporate value through optimizing the use of cash holding. In a firm with a good governance system, the cash is well-controlled and well-invested and distributed efficiently. However, in a poor governance system the corporate managers can use cash to gain personal benefits. The country-level governance has an effect on the corporate policy on holding cash. These external factors include the legal system of a country, degree of investor protection, and market conditions. The research focuses mainly on how the degree of investor protection of a country could affect the level of corporate cash holding. However, there is no final conclusion in terms of the effect of these instruments on the corporate policy on holding cash. Some studies find that firms with strong country-level governance are less likely to hold cash, and they invest cash in proper projects to enhance their value. However, other studies have contradictory results and find that strong country-level governance supports the holding of higher levels of cash.

This study provides important implications for investors and policymakers. First, there are several firm-level governance mechanisms that affect the corporate policy on holding cash. Thus, firms should choose the structures recommended by the capital market such as the appropriate size of a board of directors, the structure of ownership, role duality of the CEO, percent of independence of the board of directors, frequency of board meetings, size of audit committee, and type of external auditor. The literature reports mixed effects of different firm-level governance structures on corporate cash holdings. Given that there is no unified conclusion in terms of their effect on the corporate policy on holding cash, a firm should choose its appropriate governance structure. Second, the study provides important implications for policymakers to enhance the role of a the board of directors. To this end, firms are encouraged to increase the percent of independent directors on the board, avoid role duality, and to increase the frequency of board meetings. These recommendations can help to increase the monitoring duties of the board that in turn leads to effective decisions on the cash holding policy. Third, the review of related studies supports the association between the agency theory and cash holding motivations. Taking into account the different characteristics of firms, the impact of corporate governance on cash holdings verifies the ability of the agency theory to explain the corporate cash policy. In particular, good corporate governance structures mitigate the implicit agency costs of holding excess levels of corporate cash. Fourth, the study highlights the weak governance mechanisms (firm-level and/or country-level) in less developed countries. This provides an implication to firms that operate in developing countries to comply with some effective international governance standards. To this end, firms can adopt good international governance codes, enhance the reights of investors, and activate different laws and regulations that control their financial position. Fifth, the influence of corporate governance on the cash holding policy is not likely to be the same in different countries. This difference may be because firms in different countries experience different resources, business challenges, and opportunities. The firm governance system and the country-level governance, such as the degree of investor protection, can act to ensure a proper cash holding policy for corporate investors. Furthermore, firms in developing countries may be subject to more flexible governance codes that maintain freedom in decision-making. Thus, this flexibility may in turn effectively lead to making timely decisions on corporate cash holding.

The study highlights some limitations in other studies that could be conisdered as potential areas for future research. First, some studies focus on the impact of corprate governance mechanisms on the cash holding policy but ignore the demographic characteristics of the firms' managers (e.g., CEO). Given that managers' characteristics play a significant role in corporate-level decision-making, the consideration of the CEOs' demographic characteristics such as age, gender, education, functional track, tenure, and financial experience in this relation may be a potential avenue for future research. Second, some studies focus mainly on how the degree of investor protection could affect the level of cash holdings among different countries. Other country level governance such as the legal system, culture, and market conditions may be a potential area of interest for future research.

REFERENCES

Adams, R. B., Hermalin, B. E., & Weisbach, M. S. (2010). The role of boards of directors in corporate governance: A conceptual framework and survey. *Journal of Economic Literature*, *48*(1), 58–107. Advance online publication. doi:10.1257/jel.48.1.58

Akhtar, T., Tareq, M. A., Sakti, M. R. P., & Khan, A. A. (2018). Corporate governance and cash holdings: The way forward. *Qualitative Research in Financial Markets*, *10*(2), 152–170. doi:10.1108/QRFM-04-2017-0034

Al-Najjar, B. (2013). The financial determinants of corporate cash holdings: Evidence from some emerging markets. *International Business Review*, *22*(1), 77–88. Advance online publication. doi:10.1016/j.ibusrev.2012.02.004

Asante-Darko, D., Adu Bonsu, B., Famiyeh, S., Kwarteng, A., & Goka, Y. (2018). Governance structures, cash holdings and firm value on the Ghana Stock Exchange. *Corporate Governance (Bingley)*, *18*(4), 671–685. doi:10.1108/CG-07-2017-0148

Bates, T. W., Kahle, K. M., & Stulz, R. M. (2009). Why do U.S. firms hold so much more cash than they used to? *The Journal of Finance*, *64*(5), 1985–2021. Advance online publication. doi:10.1111/j.1540-6261.2009.01492.x

Baumol, W. J. (1952). The Transactions Demand for Cash: An Inventory Theoretic Approach. *The Quarterly Journal of Economics*, *66*(4), 545. Advance online publication. doi:10.2307/1882104

Beckhart, B. H., & Keynes, J. M. (1936). The General Theory of Employment, Interest and Money. *Political Science Quarterly*, *51*(4), 600. Advance online publication. doi:10.2307/2143949

Bigelli, M., & Sánchez-Vidal, J. (2012). Cash holdings in private firms. *Journal of Banking & Finance*, *36*(1), 26–35. Advance online publication. doi:10.1016/j.jbankfin.2011.06.004

Bokpin, G. a., Isshaq, Z., & Aboagye-Otchere, F. (2011). Ownership structure, corporate governance and corporate liquidity policy: Evidence from the Ghana Stock Exchange. *Journal of Financial Economic Policy*. doi:10.1108/17576381111152236

Boubakri, N., El Ghoul, S., & Saffar, W. (2013). Cash holdings of politically connected firms. *Journal of Multinational Financial Management*, *23*(4), 338–355. Advance online publication. doi:10.1016/j.mulfin.2013.06.002

Brockmann, E. N., Hoffman, J. J., Dawley, D. D., & Fornaciari, C. J. (2004). The Impact of CEO Duality and Prestige on a Bankrupt Organization. *Journal of Managerial Issues*. Advance online publication. doi:10.2307/40604453

Caprio, L., Faccio, M., & McConnell, J. J. (2013). Sheltering corporate assets from political extraction. *Journal of Law Economics and Organization*, *29*(2), 332–354. Advance online publication. doi:10.1093/jleo/ewr018

Chen, N. (Xi). (2014). Repatriation Taxes and the Value of Cash Holdings. *SSRN Electronic Journal*. doi:10.2139srn.2496756

Chen, Y. R. (2008). Corporate governance and cash holdings: Listed new economy versus old economy firms. *Corporate Governance*, *16*(5), 430–442. Advance online publication. doi:10.1111/j.1467-8683.2008.00701.x

Chen, Y. R., & Chuang, W. T. (2009). Alignment or entrenchment? Corporate governance and cash holdings in growing firms. *Journal of Business Research*, *62*(11), 1200–1206. Advance online publication. doi:10.1016/j.jbusres.2008.06.004

Dittmar, A., & Mahrt-Smith, J. (2007). Corporate governance and the value of cash holdings. *Journal of Financial Economics*, *83*(3), 599–634. Advance online publication. doi:10.1016/j.jfineco.2005.12.006

Dittmar, A., Mahrt-Smith, J., & Servaes, H. (2003). International Corporate Governance and Corporate Cash Holdings. *Journal of Financial and Quantitative Analysis*, *38*(1), 111. Advance online publication. doi:10.2307/4126766

Dogru, T., & Sirakaya-Turk, E. (2018). Cash holdings and corporate governance: Theory and contrary evidence from hotel firms. *International Journal of Contemporary Hospitality Management*, *30*(10), 3117–3134. Advance online publication. doi:10.1108/IJCHM-03-2017-0163

Drobetz, W., & Grüninger, M. C. (2007). Corporate cash holdings: Evidence from Switzerland. *Financial Markets and Portfolio Management*, *21*(3), 293–324. Advance online publication. doi:10.100711408-007-0052-8

Fama, E. F., & French, K. R. (1998). Taxes, financing decisions, and firm value. *The Journal of Finance*, *53*(3), 819–843. Advance online publication. doi:10.1111/0022-1082.00036

Ferreira, M. A., Custodio, C., & Raposo, C. C. (2011). *Cash Holdings and Business Conditions*. SSRN Electronic Journal., doi:10.2139srn.608664

Ferreira, M. A., & Vilela, A. S. (2004a). Why do firms hold cash? Evidence from EMU countries. *European Financial Management, 10*(2), 295–319. Advance online publication. doi:10.1111/j.1354-7798.2004.00251.x

Ferreira, M. A., & Vilela, A. S. (2004b). Why do firms hold cash? Evidence from EMU countries. *European Financial Management, 10*(2), 295–319. Advance online publication. doi:10.1111/j.1354-7798.2004.00251.x

Fritz Foley, C., Hartzell, J. C., Titman, S., & Twite, G. (2007). Why do firms hold so much cash? A tax-based explanation. *Journal of Financial Economics, 86*(3), 579–607. Advance online publication. doi:10.1016/j.jfineco.2006.11.006

García-Ramos, R., & García-Olalla, M. (2011). Board characteristics and firm performance in public founder- and nonfounder-led family businesses. *Journal of Family Business Strategy*. doi:10.1016/j.jfbs.2011.09.001

García-Teruel, P. J., & Martínez-Solano, P. (2008). On the determinants of SME cash holdings: Evidence from Spain. *Journal of Business Finance & Accounting, 35*(1-2), 127–149. Advance online publication. doi:10.1111/j.1468-5957.2007.02022.x

Gill, A., & Shah, C. (2011). Determinants of Corporate Cash Holdings: Evidence from Canada. *International Journal of Economics and Finance, 4*(1). Advance online publication. doi:10.5539/ijef.v4n1p70

Goyal, V. K., & Park, C. W. (2002). Board leadership structure and CEO turnover. *Journal of Corporate Finance, 8*(1), 49–66. Advance online publication. doi:10.1016/S0929-1199(01)00028-1

Gul, F. A., & Leung, S. (2004). Board leadership, outside directors' expertise and voluntary corporate disclosures. *Journal of Accounting and Public Policy, 23*(5), 351–379. Advance online publication. doi:10.1016/j.jaccpubpol.2004.07.001

Han, S., & Qiu, J. (2007). Corporate precautionary cash holdings. *Journal of Corporate Finance, 13*(1), 43–57. Advance online publication. doi:10.1016/j.jcorpfin.2006.05.002

Harford, J., Mansi, S. A., & Maxwell, W. F. (2012). Corporate governance and firm cash holdings in the U.S. In *Corporate Governance*. Recent Developments and New Trends., doi:10.1007/978-3-642-31579-4_5

Hassanein, A., & Kokel, A. (2019). Corporate cash hoarding and corporate governance mechanisms: Evidence from Borsa Istanbul. *Asia-Pacific Journal of Accounting & Economics*, 1–18. Advance online publication. doi:10.1080/16081625.2019.1617753

Healy, P. M., & Palepu, K. G. (2001). Information asymmetry, corporate disclosure, and the capital markets: A review of the empirical disclosure literature. *Journal of Accounting and Economics, 31*(1-3), 405–440. Advance online publication. doi:10.1016/S0165-4101(01)00018-0

Jain, B. A., Li, J., & Shao, Y. (2013). Governance, product market competition and cash management in IPO firms. *Journal of Banking & Finance, 37*(6), 2052–2068. Advance online publication. doi:10.1016/j.jbankfin.2013.01.032

JENSEN. M. C. (1993). The Modern Industrial Revolution, Exit, and the Failure of Internal Control Systems. *The Journal of Finance*. Advance online publication. doi:10.1111/j.1540-6261.1993.tb04022.x

Jensen, M. (1986). American Economic Association Agency Costs of Free Cash Flow, Corporate Finance, and Takeovers. *The American Economic Review*.

Jensen, M. C. W. H. M. (1976). Theory of the Firm : Managerial Behavior, Agency Costs and Ownership Structure. *Journal of Financial Economics*.

Jiraporn, P., Singh, M., & Lee, C. I. (2009). Ineffective corporate governance: Director busyness and board committee memberships. *Journal of Banking & Finance*, *33*(5), 819–828. Advance online publication. doi:10.1016/j.jbankfin.2008.09.020

Kalcheva, I., & Lins, K. V. (2007). International evidence on cash holdings and expected managerial agency problems. *Review of Financial Studies*, *20*(4), 1087–1112. Advance online publication. doi:10.1093/rfs/hhm023

Kim, K. A., Kitsabunnarat-Chatjuthamard, P., & Nofsinger, J. R. (2007). Large shareholders, board independence, and minority shareholder rights: Evidence from Europe. *Journal of Corporate Finance*, *13*(5), 859–880. Advance online publication. doi:10.1016/j.jcorpfin.2007.09.001

Klapper, L. F., & Love, I. (2004). Corporate governance, investor protection, and performance in emerging markets. *Journal of Corporate Finance*, *10*(5), 703–728. Advance online publication. doi:10.1016/S0929-1199(03)00046-4

Klein, A. (2002). Economic determinants of audit committee independence. *The Accounting Review*, *77*(2), 435–452. Advance online publication. doi:10.2308/accr.2002.77.2.435

Kuan, T. H., Li, C. S., & Chu, S. H. (2011). Cash holdings and corporate governance in family-controlled firms. *Journal of Business Research*, *64*(7), 757–764. Advance online publication. doi:10.1016/j.jbusres.2010.07.004

Kuan, T. H., Li, C. S., & Liu, C. C. (2012). Corporate governance and cash holdings: A quantile regression approach. *International Review of Economics & Finance*, *24*, 303–314. Advance online publication. doi:10.1016/j.iref.2012.04.006

La Porta, R., Lopez-de-Silanes, F., & Shleifer, A. (1999). Corporate ownership around the world. *The Journal of Finance*, *54*(2), 471–517. Advance online publication. doi:10.1111/0022-1082.00115

La Porta, R., Lopez-De-Silanes, F., Shleifer, A., & Vishny, R. (2000). Investor protection and corporate governance. *Journal of Financial Economics*, *58*(1-2), 3–27. Advance online publication. doi:10.1016/S0304-405X(00)00065-9

Lee, C.-F., & Lee, K. (2010). *Cash Holdings, Corporate Governance Structure and Firm Valuation*. doi:10.2139srn.1536481

Liu, Q., Luo, T., & Tian, G. G. (2015). Family control and corporate cash holdings: Evidence from China. *Journal of Corporate Finance*, *31*, 220–245. Advance online publication. doi:10.1016/j.jcorpfin.2015.02.007

Manoel, A. A. S., Moraes, M. B. C., Nagano, M. S., & Sobreiro, V. A. (2018a). Cash holdings and corporate governance: The effects of premium listing in Brazil. *Review of Development Finance*, *8*(2), 106–115. doi:10.1016/j.rdf.2018.11.002

Manoel, A. A. S., Moraes, M. B. C., Nagano, M. S., & Sobreiro, V. A. (2018b). Cash holdings and corporate governance: The effects of premium listing in Brazil. *Review of Development Finance*. doi:10.1016/j.rdf.2018.11.002

Marwick, A., Hasan, M. M., & Luo, T. (2020). Organization capital and corporate cash holdings. *International Review of Financial Analysis*, *68*, 101458. Advance online publication. doi:10.1016/j.irfa.2020.101458

Miller, M. H., & Orr, D. (1966). A Model of the Demand for Money by Firms. *The Quarterly Journal of Economics*, *80*(3), 413. Advance online publication. doi:10.2307/1880728

Myers, S. C., & Majluf, N. S. (1984). Corporate financing and investment decisions when firms have information that investors do not have. *Journal of Financial Economics*, *13*(2), 187–221. Advance online publication. doi:10.1016/0304-405X(84)90023-0

Opler, T. (1999). The determinants and implications of corporate cash holdings. *Journal of Financial Economics*, *52*(1), 3–46. Advance online publication. doi:10.1016/S0304-405X(99)00003-3

Ozkan, A., & Ozkan, N. (2004). Corporate cash holdings: An empirical investigation of UK companies. *Journal of Banking & Finance*, *28*(9), 2103–2134. Advance online publication. doi:10.1016/j.jbankfin.2003.08.003

Pinkowitz, L., Stulz, R., & Williamson, R. (2006). Does the contribution of corporate cash holdings and dividends to firm value depend on governance? A cross-country analysis. *The Journal of Finance*, *61*(6), 2725–2751. Advance online publication. doi:10.1111/j.1540-6261.2006.01003.x

Pinkowitz, L., & Williamson, R. (2001). Bank power and cash holdings: Evidence from Japan. *Review of Financial Studies*, *14*(4), 1059–1082. Advance online publication. doi:10.1093/rfs/14.4.1059

Sander, P., Teder, A., Viikmaa, K., & Kantšukov, M. (2014). The Distributed Profit Based Corporate Taxation, and the Valuation of Cash Holdings. *International Journal of Trade, Economics and Finance*. doi:10.7763/ijtef.2014.v5.373

Thanatawee, Y. (2019). *Alignment or entrenchment? Evidence from cash holdings in Thailand*. Afro-Asian Journal of Finance and Accounting. doi:10.1504/AAJFA.2019.100978

Tobin, J. (1956). The Interest-Elasticity of Transactions Demand For Cash. *The Review of Economics and Statistics*, *38*(3), 241. Advance online publication. doi:10.2307/1925776

Venkataraman, R., Weber, J. P., & Willenborg, M. (2008). Litigation risk, audit quality, and audit fees: Evidence from initial public offerings. *The Accounting Review*, *83*(5), 1315–1345. Advance online publication. doi:10.2308/accr.2008.83.5.1315

Ye, Y. (2018). *A Literature Review on the Cash Holding Issues*. Modern Economy., doi:10.4236/me.2018.96068

Yermack, D. (1996). Higher market valuation of companies with a small board of directors. *Journal of Financial Economics*, *40*(2), 185–211. Advance online publication. doi:10.1016/0304-405X(95)00844-5

Yermack, D. (2004). Remuneration, retention, and reputation incentives for outside directors. *The Journal of Finance*, *59*(5), 2281–2308. Advance online publication. doi:10.1111/j.1540-6261.2004.00699.x

Yu, H. C., Sopranzetti, B. J., & Lee, C. F. (2013). The impact of banking relationships, managerial incentives, and board monitoring on corporate cash holdings: An emerging market perspective. *Review of Quantitative Finance and Accounting*, *44*(2), 353–378. doi:10.100711156-013-0402-8

Chapter 15
Corporate Governance in Islamic Banks:
The Efficiency of the Shariah Supervisory Board

Sami Ben Mim
IHEC Sousse, Tunisia & University of Sousse, Tunisia

Yosra Mbarki
Institute of Advanced Business Studies of Sfax, Tunisia

ABSTRACT

This study investigates the efficiency of the Shariah supervisory board as a corporate governance mechanism in Islamic banks. The authors mainly seek to examine the effect of the Shariah board's composition (size and academic background of its members) on the performance of Islamic banks. They also try to highlight the transmission channels explaining this effect, and compare the efficiency of the Shariah board with that of traditional corporate governance mechanisms, namely the board of directors. The empirical investigation is based on a sample of 72 Islamic banks from 19 countries. Estimation results suggest that the Shariah board positively affects the Islamic banks performance through the number of Islamic Shariah scholars. This effect is mainly due to the size and cost transmission channels. These results are robust to different performance measures. On the other hand, results show that the board of directors' size produces a positive effect on a bank's performance, offering evidence for complementarity between traditional and Islamic governance mechanisms.

1. INTRODUCTION

Islamic banking assets have been growing faster than conventional banking assets in many Muslim countries during the past decades. There has also been a surge of interest in Islamic finance in non-Muslim countries. Islamic financial industry growth rate ranged regularly between 15 to 20% (The World Bank, 2015). Despite its rapid growth, Islamic finance is still in its early stages of development and needs to

DOI: 10.4018/978-1-7998-4852-3.ch015

address several challenges. To survive and persist, Islamic banks should mainly establish good and effective corporate governance mechanisms.

The Sharia supervisory board is one of the main corporate governance mechanisms in Islamic banks. It ensures that banking business operations adhere to the Islamic Sharia principles. According to the Accounting and Auditing Organization for Islamic Financial Institutions[1] (AAOIFI) standards, the Sharia Board is entrusted with the duty of directing, revising and monitoring the transactions of Islamic banks one by one to ensure that they are compliant with the rules and principles of Sharia. This board is not only independent of the Board of Directors, but it is also allowed to be present at the Board of Directors meetings to argue the religious aspects of their decisions (AAOIFI, 2005).

It is essential for Islamic banks to ensure the compatibility of their products and financial operations with the requirements of Sharia. There is an impending need for the Islamic banks to provide sufficient and reasonable assurance that they are strictly following the Sharia in their products, rules, procedures and contracts as most of their customers and investors are concerned about the respect of the Islamic laws. To ensure Sharia compliance of the banking operations and to inspire confidence to shareholders and stakeholders, each Islamic bank is required to establish a Sharia supervisory board.

During the review process, any revenue of the bank identified as resulting from activities considered as Sharia non-compliant have to be quoted in the Sharia report. The Sharia Board is then required to instruct the disposal of the profit, judged unlawful, for charity causes and to disclose this fact in the bank's Sharia report. Such oversights will generate, in addition to important financial losses, the loss of customers, stockholders and other stakeholders confidence and trust, which would ultimately lead to a loss of the bank's credibility. Such losses are specific to the Islamic banking industry and result from a specific category of risk known as the Sharia risk (Archer and Karim, 2007).

Efficient governance ensured by the Sharia Board may spur the Islamic banks performance through three different channels. First, it will limit the banks' exposure to the Sharia risk and hence reduce the potential financial losses. Second, it will preserve the banks' equity by dissipating the customers and stockholders doubts about the Sharia compliance of the banks activities. Finally, the Sharia Board members may contribute to the banks strategic decisions during their presence at the Board of Directors meetings.

This study investigates the efficiency of the Sharia supervisory board as a corporate governance mechanism in Islamic banks. We mainly seek to examine the effect of the Sharia Board's composition (size and academic background of its members) on the performance of Islamic banks. We also try to highlight the transmission channels explaining this effect, and compare the efficiency of the Sharia Board with that of traditional corporate governance mechanisms; namely the Board of Directors.

This paper is organized as follows. A literature review relative to the impact of the Sharia Board on Islamic banks performance is provided in Section 2. Section 3 describes the model and the sample, while Section 4 discusses the main results. Section 5 concludes.

2. THROUGH WHICH CHANNELS CAN THE SHARIA BOARD PROMOTE THE PERFORMANCE OF ISLAMIC BANKS?

Banks are exposed to specific risks inherent to their financial activities. Moral hazard and adverse selection risks, arising from the financial intermediation process, may significantly affect a bank's performance. In the case of Islamic banks such risks are exacerbated by the profit and loss sharing instruments. Islamic banks are also exposed to specific risks such as the risk of non-compliance with the Sharia (Archer and Karim, 2007) and the commercial displaced risk (Toumi and al., 2018). Effective monitoring is then crucial for the Islamic banking industry. In addition to the Board of Directors, Islamic banks are endowed with a specific governance body named the Sharia Supervisory Board. The primary mission of the Sharia Board is to ensure the compliance of the bank's financial transactions with the Islamic law. The Sharia Board may also play an important advisory role. Following the recommendations of the AAOIFI, the Sharia Board may include experts in law, economics and finance, in addition to Sharia scholars. The diversified academic background of the Sharia Board members should allow them to fulfill more effectively both their monitoring and advisory tasks.

Beck and al. (2013) argued that Islamic banks have strong incentives to implement effective monitoring in order to reduce their exposure to the moral hazard and adverse selection risks. For Pakistan, Baele et al. (2012) found that Islamic banks are exhibiting lower loan default rates than conventional banks. Beck and al. (2013) have drawn a similar conclusion from a sample of 510 conventional and Islamic banks belonging to 22 countries. According to their estimation results, non-performing loans are 2.1% lower for Islamic banks compared to their conventional peers. Ongena and Sendeniz-Yuncu (2011) found that Turkish Islamic banks mainly deal with transparent firms.

The Sharia Board members can also influence the bank's strategic decisions through their attendance at the Board of Directors meetings. Accordingly, Mollah et al. (2016) argued that the governance structure of Islamic banks enables them to adopt riskier strategies, thereby outperforming conventional banks. Similarly, Mollah and Zaman (2015) emphasized the importance of the Sharia Board's oversight and advisory roles and their positive impact on the performance of Islamic banks.

Finally, the Sharia Board may significantly contribute to reduce the costs incurred by Islamic banks. Such costs do not stem only from Sharia non-compliant financial transactions. Willison (2009) argued that Islamic banks are incurring higher costs then their conventional peers because of the complexity of the Islamic financial instruments. Beck and al. (2013) considered that the lower cost-efficiency of Islamic banks is mainly due to their young age. Following the same idea, Miah and Uddin (2017) and Johnes et al. (2018) found that Islamic banks are experiencing diseconomies of scale because of their small size.

Most of the studies interested in Sharia audit are theoretical. Few empirical studies have dealt with the impact of the Sharia Board on Islamic banks performance. Binti and al. (2009) compared the expected and actual practices of Sharia audit in the Malaysian Islamic financial institutions. They outlined four "desired" standards: (i) the theoretical framework of Sharia auditing should differ from conventional auditing framework, (ii) the scope of Sharia auditing should be broader than conventional auditing, (iii) Sharia auditors should be specialized in Sharia and accounting, (iv) finally, a Sharia auditor should be independent from the organization he/she is working for. They noticed that the actual practices do not coincide with the desired standards. They concluded that despite being a crucial monitoring tool, Sharia auditing is not taken seriously by Islamic financial institutions in Malaysia.

Alshehri (2015) empirically tested whether the existence and the size of a Sharia committee had a significant effect on the financial performance of Islamic banks. The estimation results revealed that neither the size nor the existence of a Sharia committee produced a significant effect on the return on assets and return on equity ratios. The author suggested further studies based on larger samples and different statistical methods.

Farook and Lanis (2007), Farook and al. (2011) and Abdul Rahman and Bukair (2013) found a positive and significant association between the Sharia supervisory board size and the academic qualification of its members on one hand, and Capital Social Responsibility disclosure index on the other hand. In particlaur, Farook and al. (2011) tested how effectively the Sharia Board characteristics enhanced the level of corporate social responsibility (CSR) information disclosure within Islamic banks. The following hypotheses were tested: (H1) the size of the Sharia Board should have a positive impact on CSR disclosure, (H2) Cross-memberships of Sharia Board members may also lead to a higher disclosure of CSR information, (H3) The qualifications and academic level of the Sharia Board members may influence the level of CSR disclosure, (H4) Reputable scholars are more likely to emphasize CSR activities and the subsequent disclosure of CSR information. Empirical results indicated that the above mentioned characteristics of the Sharia Board produced significant effects on CSR disclosure.

Abdul Rahman and Bukair (2013) examined the influence of the Sharia Board characteristics (the board size, cross memberships, reputable Sharia Board members, secular qualifications and the expertise of the SSB members) on the level of CSR disclosure for a sample of 53 Islamic banks. Their findings showed that the Islamic banks with larger Sharia Boards and board members who have additional experience in the banking industry, provided more information regarding CSR. Furthermore, based on the principles of accountability and full disclosure, the results indicated positive and significant correlation between the level of CSR disclosure and the bank's financial performance.

Nomran and al. (2017) distinguished six characteristics of the Sharia Supervisory Board and assessed their impact on Islamic banks performance, using a sample of 25 Malaysian and Indonesian banks. Estimations results revealed that four characteristics of the Sharia Board produced a significant effect on the performance of large banks, whereas only two characteristics influenced significantly the performance of small banks. Based on these results, the authors pointed out the lack of Sharia governance among small Islamic banks. In a more recent work, using a sample of 30 Islamic banks listed in Asian stock markets, Nomran and al. (2018) showed that the size of the Sharia Board and the independence of the audit committee enhanced Islamic banks efficiency. They concluded that both Corporate and Sharia governance are important for Islamic banks.

3. DATA AND METHODOLOGY

In order to assess the impact of the Sharia Board on the performance of Islamic banks, we estimate the following model:

$$Performance_i = \alpha_0 + \alpha I_i + \beta J_i + \varepsilon_i \quad (1)$$

where $Performance_i$ is a measure of the financial performance of bank i, I_i is a matrix of control variables and J_i a matrix of corporate governance variables. ε_i is the error term.

The dependent variable is proxied by two financial performance measures[2]: the Return On Assets (ROA) and the Return On Equity (ROE). The ROA is the most common bank performance indicator (Naushad and Abdul Malik, 2015). It indicates how effectively and efficiently a bank generates profits from its total resources. A higher ratio is therefore an indicator of better performance (Abdussamad and Kabir, 2000). Similarly, a higher ROE indicates a better use of shareholder's equity and is therefore a synonym of higher managerial performance (Siraj and Pillai, 2012).

The matrix of independent variables, J_i, is composed of six corporate governance indicators. First, we consider the size of the Sharia Supervisory Board measured by the number of members serving the Sharia Board. The larger the board size, the greater the monitoring effort, implying a greater level of compliance with Islamic laws and principles. Allocating functions across a large group of members allows the Sharia Board to review more aspects of the banks activities and hence ensure greater compliance (Farook, Hassan and Lanis, 2011). Abdul Rahman and Bukair (2013) consider that a greater number of members in a Sharia Board would provide more effective monitoring and higher consistency with the rules and principles of Sharia. The board size is likely to affect its ability to control and review all transactions of the Islamic banks in order to ensure their compliance with Sharia rules and principles. In addition, with more members, the collective knowledge and experience of the Sharia Board will increase, leading to better decisions and hence to greater performance within Islamic banks. Second, we control for the Sharia Board members academic background. The academic background is an important factor in the monitoring practice. With regards to the role that the Sharia Board members are expected to fulfill, they should have deep knowledge in Islamic law, economics, financial and accounting practice (Abdul Rahman and Bukair, 2013). In this study we distinguish three academic backgrounds: (i) the Sharia background, when the Sharia Board member possesses a Bachelor, Master or PhD degree in Islamic Sharia, Feqh, Hadith or Quran; (ii) the Law background when the Sharia Board member possesses a Bachelor, Master or PhD degree in law or legal studies; (iii) the Economics and finance background when the Sharia Board member possesses a Bachelor, Master or PhD degree in economics and finance.

The remaining governance proxies are relative to the Board of Directors. Firstly, we control for the board's size, measured by the number of directors on the board. The size of the board has been shown to influence its ability to oversee corporate governance (Ness, Miesing and Kang, 2012). Other studies suggested that large boards may increase the quality of decision-making since they offer a broader array of perspectives. Belkhir (2009) found that adding more directors to the board increases the return on assets of banks. Others believe that smaller boards are more effective in carrying out their governance oversight responsibilities. According to Jensen (1993), companies with oversized boards tend to become less effective. In fact, a high number of decision-makers in any committee may reduce their effort and give rise to some degree of free-riding. In addition, a larger size may hinder the ability to reach a consensus. Van Ness and Seifert (2007) added that expansive boards with large number of members may hit a critical mass and become bogged in bureaucracy thereby losing the ability to respond to issues surrounding corporate threats and/or opportunities. Secondly, we consider the Board of Directors' independent members, measured by the number of independent members on the Board of Directors. The main objective of appointing independent members is to avoid conflicts of interest among stakeholders and fulfill the functions of monitoring and advising in an efficient manner. The findings about the independent members' effect are inconclusive. Some studies sustained the hypothesis of a negative effect of independent directors on bank´s performance (Horváth and Spirollari, 2012). Other results indicated that the effect of board independence on a bank's performance is far from being robust (Peng, 2004). Finally, some studies found that the appointment of additional independent directors led to an increase in the firm´s value (Rosenstein and Wyatt, 1990).

Finally we retain three control variables which may influence significantly Islamic banks' performance (matrix I_i). We first introduce the bank's size, measured by the bank's total assets in US billion Dollars. Athanasoglou, Brissimis and Delis (2005) pointed out that a larger bank size leads to more profit. One explanation of the size's effect on profitability is the economies of scale theory. In fact many studies confirmed the existence of economies of scale in the banking industry (Stimper and Judith, 2011). Larger banks and financial institutions enjoy significant cost advantages, which lead to better profitability. At the same time, many studies concluded that expanding banks will eventually reach a point where diseconomies of scale will occur (Stimper and Judith, 2011). While increases in size are initially associated with lower costs and greater profitability, these advantages do not continue as the bank size continues to grow. Athanasoglou, Brissimis and Delis (2005) argued that if a bank has an extravagant size, this may produce a negative impact on its profitability. Hence, the size-profitability relationship may be expected to be non-linear. We included a quadratic size term in the model in order to control for a possible non-linear relationship. Secondly, we control for capital adequacy, measured by the shareholders' equity as a share of total assets of the bank. A higher capital adequacy ratio indicates less reliance on external funds and reflects the bank's ability to protect both depositors and lenders from bank failure (Siraj and Pillai, 2012). If the capital adequacy ratio is managed properly it may bring more stability and reduce the solvency risk of the bank. Other studies admit a negative relationship between profitability and the capital adequacy ratio. Mathuva (2009) found that a bank's profitability is negatively related to the equity to assets ratio. He explained this result by the fact that a higher adequacy ratio leads to higher claims for dividends. Thus, less retained funds are available to boost profits. The third and last control variable is the Operating Cost to Income ratio. This ratio gives a clear view of how efficiently the bank is run; the lower it is, the more profitable the bank will be. A lower operating cost ratio shows better control over operating expenses and highlights higher managerial skills. It should naturally lead to higher earnings (Siraj and Pillai, 2012). Table 1 summarizes the set of variables included in model (1).

Table 1. Definition of the model variables

Variable	Symbol	Definition
Return on assets	ROA	Net profit of the year divided by the total assets of the Islamic bank
Return on equity	ROE	Net profit of the year divided by the total shareholder's equity
Board of Directors size	BDSIZE	Number of directors serving the board
Board of Directors independent members	BDIM	Number of independent members on the Board of Directors
Sharia supervisory board size	SBSIZE	Number of supervisors serving the Sharia Board
Sharia supervisory board whose specialty is Sharia	SBSHARIA	Number of supervisor specialists in Islamic Sharia
Sharia supervisory board whose specialty is law	SBLAW	Number of supervisor specialists in law
Sharia supervisory board whose specialty is economics and finance	SBFIN	Number of supervisor specialists in economics and finance
The bank size	SIZE	Total assets of the Islamic bank
Capital adequacy ratio	EQUITY	Total shareholders' equity divided by the total assets of the Islamic bank
Operating cost to Income	COST	Total operating cost divided by the total operating income

The sample considered in this study is composed of Islamic banks operating in 19 countries from the Middle East, North Africa and Asia: Bahrain, Palestine, Tunisia, Egypt, Iraq, Jordan, Kuwait, Lebanon, Oman, Qatar, Saudi Arabia, Syria, United Arabs Emirates, Turkey, Pakistan, Malaysia, Sri Lanka, Brunei and Indonesia. There are about 102 Islamic banks operating in these countries[3]. Our final sample included 72 banks, for which data were available (see Table 2). It represents about 70% of the Islamic banks operating in these countries. The regression analysis was limited to 2014, due to constraints on data availability.

We used the annual report as a primary source of information. It is the most widely recognized internal document, as it includes information that has a high degree of precision and credibility. This document also contains detailed information about the Sharia Supervisory Board members and members of the Board of Directors, although the information provided varies from one bank to another. In addition to banks' annual reports, we sent questionnaires requesting for data from some banks which annual reports were not available or lacked some information. Five banks were cooperative and wrote back to provide the requested information.

Table 2. Sample composition by country, 2014

Country	Number of Banks
Bahrain	17
Palestine	1
Tunisia	2
Egypt	4
Iraq	1
Jordan	2
Kuwait	4
Lebanon	1
Oman	2
Qatar	4
Saudi Arabia	3
Syria	2
United Arab Emirates	5
Turkey	1
Pakistan	5
Malaysia	14
Sri Lanka	1
Brunei	1
Indonesia	2
Total	72

The descriptive statistics for the all the variables are reported in Table 3. The average ROA and ROE for 2014 are respectively about 0,71% and 7,40%. The banks considered in the sample show different characteristics. Their size varies from 38 million dollars for the smallest bank to more than 33 billion dollars for the largest one. They also differ by their ability to monitor their costs: the highest cost to income ratio is 216% while the least ratio is around 0,5%. Finally their capital adequacy ratios vary from 4,419% up to 97,779%.

Table 3. Descriptive Statistics, 2014

Variable	Mean	Minimum	Maximum	Std. Dev
ROA	0,717	-4,597	5,849	1,641
ROE	7,409	-9,821	25,932	7,755
SIZE	6,620	0,038	33,444	8,070
COST	56,426	0,559	216	34,32
EQUITY	20,425	4,419	97,779	22,078
BDSIZE	8,985	5	20	2,509
BDIM	4,046	3	11	2,399
SBSIZE	4,083	0	9	1,470
SBSHARIA	2,986	0	6	1,216
SBLAW	0,464	0	3	0,713
SBFIN	0,569	0	3	0, 765

Focusing on the Board of Directors, the average size of the board is about 9 directors, 4 of them are considered as independent members (BDIM). For the Sharia Supervisory Board, the average size (SBSIZE) is about 4 members, which is a relatively good average compared to the AAOIFI recommendations of at least 3 Sharia supervisors. The average composition of the Sharia Board indicates that it is highly dominated by the Sharia specialists (SBSHARIA). Law and economics specialists are still very weakly represented in the board.

The correlation matrix is represented in Table 4. High correlation coefficients may indicate a potential source of collinearity. In our case, all correlation coefficients are below the 0,7 limit. Results show a significant and negative correlation between Islamic banks performance measured by the ROA and the cost to income ratio (COST). We can also notice a significant and positive correlation between the ROA and the number of Sharia specialists in the Sharia Board (SBSHARIA).

Significant and positive correlations also exist between the return on equity ratio on one side, and the bank's size (SIZE), the size of the Sharia Board (SBSIZE) and the number of Sharia specialists in the Sharia Board (SBSHARIA) on the other side. We also note the significant and negative correlations between the ROE, the cost to income ratio (COST) and the equity to assets ratio (EQUITY). No significant correlation is detected between the two governance mechanisms' proxies; the Board of Directors and the Sharia Supervisory Board.

Finally, there exists a positive and significant correlation between the Sharia Board size (SBSIZE) and the academic background of its members. We note high positive and significant correlations between the board's size, law specialists (SBLAW) and economics and finance specialists (SBFIN) (0,568 and

Table 4. Correlation matrix

	ROA	ROE	SIZE	COST	EQUITY	BDSIZE	BDIM	SBSIZE	SBSHARIA	SBLAW	SBFIN
ROA	1.000										
ROE	0.682***	1.000									
SIZE	0.236	0.450***	1.000								
COST	-0.426**	-0.438***	-0.283*	1.000							
EQUITY	0.010	-0.347**	-0.271	0.207	1.000						
BDSIZE	0.236	0.111	0.280	0.107	-0.037	1.000					
BDIM	0.133	-0.108	0.141	0.261	0.375**	0.410**	1.000				
SBSIZE	0.190	0.423**	0.225	-0.059	-0.308*	-0.016	0.001	1.000			
SBSHARIA	0.348**	0.284*	0.178	0.082	-0.100	0.232	0.182	0.380**	1.000		
SBLAW	-0.090	0.115	0.044	-0.222	-0.232	-0.171	-0.129	0.568***	-0.406**	1.000	
SBFIN	-0.099	0.226	0.112	-0.037	-0.128	-0.242	-0.103	0.513***	-0.444***	0.555***	1.000

* Significance at the 10% level. ** Significance at the 5% level. *** Significance at the 1% level.

0,513 respectively). The correlation coefficient between the boards' size and the Islamic Sharia specialist (SBSHARIA) is about 0,38. These results suggest that the increase in the Sharia Board size should be in favor of law and economics specialists more than Sharia specialists. Thus, larger Sharia Boards allow Islamic banks to comply with AAOIFI recommendations, which required to include more experts in law, economics and finance.

4. RESULTS AND DISCUSSION

We estimated model (1) using cross sectional data relative to 72 Islamic banks observed during 2014. Ordinary Least Squares (OLS) regression results for the ROA are reported in Table 5. We ensured the robustness of the standard errors estimates by using the Heteroscedasticity and Autocorrelation Consistent (HAC) standard errors. The HAC estimator is used to overcome autocorrelation and heteroscedasticity in the error terms of the model.

The size of Islamic banks (SIZE) positively affects their performance (ROA). The regression coefficients are positive and significant in all the estimated equations. A larger bank size leads to a greater profit. This result is consistent with those indicating the existence of the economies of scale in the banking industry (Stimper and Judith, 2011). The regression coefficient of the squared size ($SIZE^2$) is significant and negative in all the estimated equations. As expected, the size-performance relationship is non-linear. The Islamic banking industry enjoys significant economies of scale up to a critical size, above which they begin to incur higher costs, which translate into lower levels of profitability.

As expected, performance (ROA) is negatively affected by the costs incurred by Islamic banks: the coefficient associated with operational costs (COST) is negative and significant for all the estimated equations. These findings are consistent with those of (Mathuva, 2009), who used the ROA and the ROE as commercial banks profitability proxies, and concluded that banks' profitability is negatively related to the cost to income ratio. The equity to assets ratio (EQUITY) does not produce any significant effect on a bank's profitability measured by ROA.

Table 5. Determinants of Islamic banks performance, Dependent variable ROA

	EQ 1	EQ 2	EQ 3	EQ 4	EQ 5	EQ 6	EQ 7
C	1.252** (0.494)	0.322 (0.621)	1.298 (0.806)	0.979** (0.467)	0.499 (0.384)	1.345** (0.531)	1.232** (0.490)
SIZE	0.096*** (0.030)	0.086*** (0.030)	0.129*** (0.039)	0.084** (0.033)	0.089** (0.036)	0.106*** (0.031)	0.109*** (0.034)
$SIZE^2$	-0.002** (0.001)	-0.002** (0.001)	-0.004*** (0.001)	-0.001* (0.001)	-0.002* (0.001)	-0.002*** (0.001)	-0.002** (0.001)
EQUITY	0.017 (0.016)	0.018 (0.015)	0.008 (0.023)	0.017 (0.016)	0.016 (0.015)	0.016 (0.017)	0.017 (0.016)
COST	-0.019*** (0.006)	-0.019*** (0.007)	-0.032** (0.013)	-0.019*** (0.006)	-0.019*** (0.006)	-0.019*** (0.006)	-0.018*** (0.005)
BDSIZE		0.114* (0.064)					
BDIM			0.217 (0.151)				
SBSIZE				0.088 (0.075)			
SBSHARIA					0.272* (0.144)		
SBLAW						-0.258 (0.169)	
SBFIN							-0.173 (0.151)
R-squared	0.221	0.258	0.286	0.230	0.280	0.238	0.230
Nb. of obs.	64	63	36	64	64	63	64

* Significance at the 10% level. ** Significance at the 5% level. *** Significance at the 1% level. Robust standard errors are between parentheses.

For the corporate governance proxies, estimation results reveal that the Board of Directors size (BDSIZE) positively and significantly affects the performance of Islamic banks. A larger Board of Directors allows for a broader range of opinions which improve decision-making and lead to better profitability. These results are in line with those of Belkhir (2009). On the other hand, the coefficient associated with the number of independent members (BDIM) is non-significant in all the regressions. Introducing independent members seems to have no effect on the Islamic banks performance.

Concerning the Sharia Supervisory Board, results show the effectiveness of the Sharia specialists (SBSHARIA) as a governance mechanism: the coefficient associated with this variable is positive and significant at the 10% level. A higher number of Sharia specialists within the Sharia Board spur the performance of Islamic banks (ROA). As for the Sharia Board size and the number of specialists in law and economics within the board, they do not produce any significant effect on the return on assets of Islamic banks.

Table 6 summarizes regression results when banking performance is measured by ROE. Estimation results confirm the non-linear relationship between the size and the banks financial performance. The size produces a positive and significant effect on profitability, whereas the quadratic term affects negatively the return on equity ratio. The cost to income ratio (COST) significantly deteriorates the Islamic banks performance measured by ROE. These results confirm those obtained with the return on assets ratio.

Table 6. Determinants of Islamic banks performance, Dependent variable ROE

	EQ 8	EQ 9	EQ 10	EQ 11	EQ 12	EQ 13	EQ 14
C	11.367*** (2.733)	8.153** (3.080)	9.366** (3.510)	9.776*** (2.603)	8.972*** (2.466)	11.651*** (2.842)	11.418*** (2.702)
SIZE	0.742*** (0.253)	0.712** (0.273)	0.851*** (0.278)	0.675** (0.273)	0.720** (0.273)	0.756*** (0.274)	0.708*** (0.263)
SIZE^2	-0.018** (0.007)	-0.018** (0.008)	-0.022** (0.008)	-0.017** (0.008)	-0.018** (0.008)	-0.019** (0.008)	-0.017*** (0.008)
EQUITY	-0.065* (0.036)	-0.060* (0.034)	-0.050 (0.036)	-0.065* (0.034)	-0.067** (0.033)	-0.067* (0.037)	-0.066* (0.036)
COST	-0.096*** (0.026)	-0.098*** (0.027)	-0.096** (0.042)	-0.100*** (0.026)	-0.906*** (0.025)	-0.096*** (0.026)	-0.098*** (0.026)
BDSIZE		0.391* (0.224)					
BDIM			0.171 (0.323)				
SBSIZE				0.512 (0.346)			
SBSHARIA					0.866* (0.444)		
SBLAW						-0.549 (0.714)	
SBECOFINANCE							0.434 (0.716)
R-squared	0.363	0.378	0.397	0.373	0.383	0.365	0.364
Nb. of obs.	64	63	36	64	64	63	64

* Significance at the 10% level. ** Significance at the 5% level. *** Significance at the 1% level. Robust standard errors are between parentheses.

The equity to assets ratio (EQUITY) produces a negative and significant effect on the ROE of Islamic banks. Mathuva (2009) explains this result by higher claims for dividends which lead to less retained funds available to boost profits.

Results relative to governance indicators are similar to those obtained for the ROA ratio. The Board of Directors size produces a positive effect on performance, while the number of independent members (BDIM) has no significant effect on the ROE of Islamic banks. The Sharia Board significantly and positively affects the performance of Islamic banks (ROE) through the number of Sharia specialists (SBSHARIA). The presence of law and economics specialists among the Sharia Board members does not produce any significant effect on the banks performance.

To get further explanations about these results we tried to investigate the channels through which Islamic Sharia specialists improve the profitability of Islamic banks. To achieve this objective we added interaction terms in the estimated models. The interaction terms are relative to the variables that may act as transmission channels through which Sharia specialists can influence performance. First, Sharia supervisors may prevent banks from reaching an excessive size. Regression results suggest a nonlinear relation between size and performance. Hence, reducing the size of large banks may contribute to enhance their performance. Secondly, improved Sharia control may reduce a bank's operational costs,

Table 7. Sharia specialists' transmission channels on ROA and ROE

	Dependent Variable: ROA			Dependent Variable: ROE		
	EQ 15	EQ 16	EQ17	EQ 18	EQ 19	EQ 20
C	-0.358 (0.579)	1.391 (1.005)	-0.150 (0.537)	6.040** (2.738)	5.231* (2.730)	5.171* (2.916)
SIZE	0.226*** (0.066)	0.090** (0.036)	0.154*** (0.044)	1.146*** (0.386)	0.717** (0.269)	1.103*** (0.314)
SIZE^2	-0.001** (0.001)	-0.002* (0.001)	-0.002*** (0.001)	-0.018** (0.007)	-0.018** (0.008)	-0.021*** (0.007)
EQUITY	0.015 (0.015)	0.016 (0.015)	0.015 (0.015)	-0.067** (0.031)	-0.069** (0.034)	-0.072** (0.031)
COST	-0.018*** (0.005)	-0.034 (0.021)	-0.014** (0.006)	-0.088*** (0.016)	-0.033 (0.036)	-0.070** (0.026)
SBSHARIA	0.543** (0.247)	-0.052 (0.270)	0.408** (0.183)	1.687** (0.741)	2.226** (0.955)	1.659*** (0.566)
SBSHARIA*SIZE	-0.044** (0.020)			-0.135* (0.080)		
SBSHARIA*COST		0.005 (0.006)			-0.023* (0.013)	
SBSHARIA*COST* SIZE			-0.0003** (0.0001)			-0.002** (0.0008)
R-squared	0.270	0.292	0.310	0.462	0.390	0.418
Nb. Of obs.	64	64	64	66	64	64

* Significance at the 10% level. ** Significance at the 5% level. *** Significance at the 1% level. Robust standard errors are between parentheses.

which leads to improved performance. These two channels may act simultaneously, as reducing the size should generally lower the bank's operating costs. Estimation results relative to these transmission channels are reported in Table 7.

Results show that Sharia specialists have, in addition to the direct impact on Islamic banks' performance[4], an indirect impact mainly through the size channel. Results reported in the first and fourth columns of Table 7 (EQ 15 and EQ18) show that the estimated coefficient of the interaction term between the boards members specialists in Sharia and the size of Islamic banks (SBSHARIA*SIZE) is negative and significant, which indicates that the Sharia specialist mitigates the negative effect of Islamic banks size on ROA and ROE.

We also noticed that when the interaction term includes Sharia specialists, the cost to income ratio and the size of Islamic banks (EQ17 and EQ20) the coefficient remains negative and significant. These results suggest that the Sharia specialists limit the negative effect of the size on profitability by reducing the cost supported by the banks. As mentioned above, both channels seem to act in a complementary way. Reducing the negative effect of the size on performance is fulfilled by reducing the costs supported by banks. Results reported in column 5 (EQ19) of table 7 offer further support for such a conclusion. The interaction term between Sharia specialists and the cost to income ratio (SBSHARIA*COST) is negative and significant, which suggests that an increase in Sharia specialists enables Islamic banks to reduce their cost to income ratios.

5. CONCLUSION

The Sharia Supervisory Board is a corporate governance mechanism specific to Islamic banks. Its task is to ensure adherence of the banking operations to the Islamic Sharia principles. The effectiveness of the Sharia Supervisory Board should be reflected on the performance of the Islamic bank through various channels. The main objective of this study is to examine the effect of the Sharia Board's composition (size and academic background of its members) on the performance of Islamic banks. We also try to highlight the transmission channels explaining this effect, and compare the efficiency of the Sharia Board with that of traditional corporate governance mechanisms; namely the Board of Directors.

An important finding of this study is that an increase in the number of Sharia specialists among the Sharia Board members leads to higher profitability in Islamic banks. However, no significant effect on performance can be associated with the size of the Sharia Board nor to the law and economics background of the its members. Estimation results also offer support for a positive effect of the Board of Directors size on banking performance. A larger Board of Directors appears to improve Islamic banks performance. However, the number of independent members in the Board of Directors produces no significant effect on a bank's profitability. Our results suggest that both Islamic and traditional governance mechanisms may spur banking performance simultaneously, which indicates that the Board of Directors and the Sharia Board may act in a complementary way.

As for control variables, estimation results show a non-linear relationship between the banks size and profitability. Such a result suggests that large banks endure diseconomies of scale. As expected, estimation results confirm that performance is negatively related to the cost to income ratio. We also note that equity to asset ratio significantly reduces the financial performance measured by the ROE ratio.

We also explored channels through which the Sharia scholars may enhance Islamic banks financial performance. Results suggest that both the size and the cost channels may explain such an effect. The Sharia Board may contribute to reduce operational costs, but may also prevent banks from reaching an excessive size and hence enduring diseconomies of scale.

We also note that Sharia Boards are still weakly diversified and are mainly composed of Sharia scholars. The non-significant impact of law and finance specialists can be attributed to their low representation in the Sharia Boards, which limits their influence on the decision-making process. Islamic banks need to make an extra effort to diversify the composition of their Sharia Boards in order to take full advantage of their advisory potential.

Finally, further investigations should be conducted to confirm the robustness of these results. Larger samples and different estimation techniques should be tested. Additional transmission channels need to be explored, namely those highlighting the impact of the Sharia Board on the customers' deposits and on the efficiency of specific Islamic financial products such as Moudharaba, Mourabaha...

REFERENCES

AAOIFI. (2005). Accounting, Auditing and Governance Standards (for Islamic Financial Institutions). Manama, Bahrain: AAOIFI.

Abdul Rahman, A., & Bukair, A. A. (2013). The Influence of the Sharia Supervision Board on Corporate Social Responsibility Disclosure by Islamic Banks of Gulf Co-Operation Council Countries. *Asian Journal of Business and Accounting*, *6*(2).

Abdussamad, M., & Kabir, H. (2000). The perfomance of Malaysian Islamic banks during 1984-1997: An exploratory study. *International Journal of Islamic Financial Services*, *1*(3).

Alshehri, A. (2015). *Corporate governance and the financial performance of Islamic banks: some new evidence. The World Finance Conference (WFC 2015)*, Buenos Aires, Argentina.

Archer, S., & Karim, R. A. (2007). *Islamic finance the regulatory challenge*. John Wiley & sons. doi:10.1002/9781118390443

Athanasoglou, P. P., Brissimis, S. N., & Delis, M. D. (2005). *Bank-specific, industry-specific and macroeconomics determinants of bank profitability*. Bank of Greece working paper n°25.

Baele, L., Farroq, M., & Ongena, S. (2012). *Of Religion and Redemption: Evidence from Default on Islamic Loans*. CentER Discussion Paper Series No. 2012-014. Tilburg University.

Beck, T., Demirguc-Kunt, A., & Merrouche, O. (2013). Islamic Vs. Conventional Banking: Business Model, Efficiency and Stability. *Journal of Banking & Finance*, *37*(2), 433–447. doi:10.1016/j.jbankfin.2012.09.016

Belkhir, M. (2009). Board of Directors' size and performance in the banking industry. *International Journal of Managerial Finance*, *5*(2), 201–221. doi:10.1108/17439130910947903

Binti Kasem, N., Mohamed Ibrahim, S. H., & Maliah, S. (2009). Sharia Auditing in Islamic Financial Institutions: Exploring the Gap Between the "Desired" and the "Actual". *Global Economy and Finance Journal*, *2*(2), 127–137.

Farook, S., Hassan, M. K., & Lanis, R. (2011). Determinants of corporate social responsibility disclosure:the case of Islamic banks. *Journal of Islamic Accounting and Business Research*, *2*(2), 114–141. doi:10.1108/17590811111170539

Farook, S., & Lanis, R. (2007). Banking on Islam? Determinants of Corporate Social Responsibility Disclosure. In *Islamic Economics and Finance, Proceedings of 6th International Conference on Islamic Economics and Finance*. Jeddah, Saudi Arabia: Islamic Research & Training Institute - Islamic Development Bank Group.

Horváth, R., & Spirollari, P. (2012). Do the Board of Directors' characteristics influence firm's performance? The U.S. evidence. *Prague Economic Papers*, *21*(4), 470–486. doi:10.18267/j.pep.435

Jensen, M. C. (1993). The modern industrial revolution, exit, and the failure of internal control systems. *The Journal of Finance*, *48*(3), 881–880. doi:10.1111/j.1540-6261.1993.tb04022.x

Johnes, J., Izzeldin, M., Pappas, V., & Alexakis, C. (2018). Performance and Productivity in Islamic and Conventional Banks: Evidence from the Global Financial Crisis. *Economic Modelling*, •••, 79.

Mathuva, D. M. (2009). capital adequacy, Cost Income ratio, and the performance of commercial banks; The Kenyan Scenario. *The International Journal of Applied Economics & Finance*, *3*(2), 35–47. doi:10.3923/ijaef.2009.35.47

Miah, D., & Uddin, H. (2017). Efficiency and stability: A comparative study between Islamic and conventional banks in GCC countries. *Future Business Journal.*, *3*(2), 172–185. doi:10.1016/j.fbj.2017.11.001

Mollah, S., Hassan, M. K., Farooque, O., & Mobarek, A. (2016). The Governance, Risk-taking, and Performance of Islamic Banks. *Journal of Financial Services Research*, *51*(2), 195–219. doi:10.100710693-016-0245-2

Mollah, S., & Zaman, M. (2015). Shari'ah Supervision, Corporate Governance and Performance: Conventional vs. Islamic Banks. *Journal of Banking & Finance*, *58*, 418–435. doi:10.1016/j.jbankfin.2015.04.030

Naushad, M., & Abdul Malik, S. (2015). Corporate Governance and Bank Performance: A Study of Selected Banks in GCC Region. *Asian Social Science*, *11*(9). Advance online publication. doi:10.5539/ass.v11n9p226

Ness, R. K., Miesing, P., & Kang, J. (2012). Board of Directors composition and financial performance in a Sarbanes-Oxley world. *Academy of Business and Economics Journal*, *10*(5), 56–74.

Nomran, N. M., Haron, R., & Hassan, R. (2017). Bank Performance and Shari'ah Supervisory Board Attributes on Islamic banks: Does Bank Size Matter? *Journal of Islamic Finance*, *6*(Special Issue), 174–187. doi:10.12816/0047348

Nomran, N. M., Haron, R., & Hassan, R. (2018). Shari'ah supervisory board characteristics effects on Islamic banks' performance: Evidence from Malaysia. *International Journal of Bank Marketing*, *36*(2), 290–304. doi:10.1108/IJBM-12-2016-0197

Ongena, S., & Sendeniz-Yuncu, I. (2011). Which firms engage small, foreign or state banks? And who goes Islamic? Evidence from Turkey. *Journal of Banking & Finance*, *35*(12), 3213–3224. doi:10.1016/j.jbankfin.2011.05.001

Peng, M. W. (2004). Outside directors and firm performnace during intitutional transitions. *Strategic Management Journal*, *25*(5), 453–471. doi:10.1002mj.390

Rosenstein, S., & Wyatt, J. G. (1990). Outside directors, board independence, and shareholder wealth. *Journal of Financial Economics*, *26*(2), 175–191. doi:10.1016/0304-405X(90)90002-H

Siraj, K., & Pillai, P. S. (2012). Comparative Study on Performance of Islamic Banks and Conventional Banks in GCC region. *Journal of Applied Finance & Banking*, *2*(3), 123–161.

Stimper, J. L., & Judith, A. L. (2011). Does Size Matter? Economies Of Scale In The Banking Industry. *Journal of Business & Economics Research*, *9*(3).

The World Bank. (2015). *Islamic Finance*. Author.

Toumi, K., Viviani, J. L., & Chayeh, Z. (2018). Measurement of the displaced commercial risk in Islamic Banks. *The Quarterly Review of Economics and Finance*. Advance online publication. doi:10.1016/j.qref.2018.03.001

Van Ness, R. K., & Seifert, C. F. (2007). Boards of directors and corporate performance: An analysis model. *Review of Business Research*, *7*(3), 11–21.

Willison, B. (2009). Technology trends in Islamic investment banking. *Islamic Finance News*, *6*(19), 22–23.

ENDNOTES

1 The Accounting and Auditing Organization for Islamic Financial Institutions (AAOIFI) is an Islamic international autonomous not-for-profit corporate body that prepares accounting, auditing, governance, ethics and Sharia standards for Islamic financial institutions and the industry. Professional qualification programs (notably CIPA, the Sharia Adviser and Auditor "CSAA", and the corporate compliance program) are presented now by AAOIFI in its efforts to enhance the industry's human resource base and governance structures.

2 The Tobin's q is frequently retained among the set of dependent variables in the empirical literature dealing with banking performance. However, the Tobin's q is a perceived performance indicator rather than a financial performance indicator. Consequently, it is not relevant to investigate the transmission channels through which the Sharia Board may affect banking performance.

3 The list of Islamic banks in these countries was taken from (http://lafinanceislamique.com/liste-banques-islamiques-france-monde/).

4 The coefficient of the variable "SBSHARIA" is significant and positive in all the estimated equations.

Chapter 16
An Overview of Corporate Governance and Innovation in Chinese IT and Manufacturing Listed Firms

Xihui Chen
Teesside University, UK

ABSTRACT

This study introduces the current structure of corporate governance (ownership and board structure) and innovation in Chinese IT and manufacturing listed firms. It highlights the unique features and potential issues of corporate governance and innovation in the Chinese institutional environment. This chapter helps advance the understanding of ownership and board structures, as well as innovation in Chinese IT and manufacturing industries. It is hoped that this study will encourage more research to pursue this interesting research field.

1. INTRODUCTION

China, the world's second-largest economy and one of the largest transition economies, has attracted many scholars in recent years, who have used Chinese financial data for their research and publications in top academic journals (e.g., Chen, 2014; Cheng et al., 2015; Qian & Yeung, 2015; Jiang & Kim, 2015; Hutson et al., 2019). This increase in scholarship is not surprising. Corporate governance (CG) is one of the most important topics in the research area since all firms, especially listed firms, require it. CG is central to how firms allocate resources and, therefore, it shapes the strategic choices that managers make in achieving the firm's objectives. Keasey and Wright (1993) viewed the role of CG from two broad perspectives. One emphasises the stewardship and accountability role, stressing the need for CG as a mechanism to monitor managers and enhance performance. The other emphasises the innovation role, considering innovation as providing the mechanisms that motivate management to optimise sharehold-

DOI: 10.4018/978-1-7998-4852-3.ch016

ers' wealth by sustaining corporate competitiveness. Thus, the two dimensions are highly relevant to each other, as they both aim to ensure that corporate resources are used to secure the firm's long-term performance, thus protecting and enhancing shareholders' wealth (O'Connor & Rafferty, 2012).

China has recently made huge strides in innovation and become a global force in the world's digital economy and cutting-edge technologies (Lo et al., 2019; Woetzel et al., 2019). China's continued innovation is at the heart of its economic development. For example, China's Medium to Long Term Science and Technology Development Plan 2016-2020 has two bold aims. The first is to raise R&D intensity to the current OECD (Organisation for Economic Cooperation and Development) average by 2020 (increasing spending as a share of GDP from 1.3% to 2.5%) and lift the country's comprehensive innovation capabilities into the world's top 15. The second is to reduce the reliance on imported technology sharply, obtain advanced core technologies in the equipment manufacturing, and the information industry (The National Development and Reform Commission of China, 2016). China's R&D investment is now 33 times what it was in 1995 and now accounts for more than 2% (2.08%) of the country's GDP for the first time in 2013, totalling RMB 1.18 trillion. This increase of 15% from 2012 shows that China is on track to achieve its target of R&D spending, accounting for 2.2% of GDP by 2015. In 2011, China surpassed Japan to become second in the world in total R&D investment. It is also the world's second-largest publisher of research (UK Science & Innovation Network, 2015).

As to how technological advancement occurs in the modern world, the literature stresses the significance of institutions involved in industrial innovation (Lo et al., 2019). These institutions include not only the regulations, policies, markets, and networks in a company's external environment, but also institutions within a firm, especially CG structure. This study argues that CG structures play a crucial role in innovation.

There are two shortcomings in the corporate governance literature. First, the theories (resources dependence, agency, upper echelon, and institutional theories) used in many papers that study China are developed in the West (e.g. the United States) (Hung et al., 2017; Lin et al., 2011; Shan & McIver, 2011). Second, using financial data without discussions on Chinese business customer and practices, financial, legal, and regulations might lead to a superficial understanding of Chinese institutional environment as a whole (Jiang & Kim, 2015; Jia et al., 2019). Jiang and Kim (2015) conducted an exceptional study, including an in-depth review of Chinese corporate governance using data from 1994 to 2012. Chinese economic growth has been explosive during the past two decades. Many changes have taken place, for example, the strategic direction of innovation and the introduction of new rules and regulations influencing the development of corporate governance in China (see Section 2.2 and 2.3). Given these two shortcomings, the primary purpose of this study is to use current financial data to discuss the corporate governance and innovation features unique to the Chinese institutional environment.

The study is organised as follows. Section 2 presents important institutional background information of China (e.g., regulations and innovation policy). Section 3 provides and discusses a summary of statistics of important variables related to corporate governance and innovation (e.g. ownership, board, R&D investment, patent counts, and firm-level factor-related variables). Section 4 discusses the unique features of corporate governance in China. Section 5 briefly discusses using the market for corporate control in China. Section 6 provides concluding remarks.

2. RESEARCH BACKGROUND

This section, on the institutional environment of China, provides broad and important institutional information relating to corporate governance and innovation. Specifically, three aspects are considered: 1) a brief background of the capital markets and capital structure in China; 2) a description of Chinese corporate governance regulation; and 3) the development of innovation in China.

2.1 Overview of Chinese Capital Markets

The Chinese current securities market began with the formation of the Shanghai Stock Exchange (SHSE) in December 1990 the and Shenzhen Stock Exchange (SZSE) in July 1991. Listing a firm in either the SHSE or SZSE is a way of raising new long-term equity finance for sellers, trading company securities, and allowing potential public and institutional investors to buy shares. The establishment of these exchanges represents one of the most critical steps toward market-based reform and decentralisation in China. There are three boards in the Shenzhen Stock Exchange, including a main board, a SMEs (small and medium-sized enterprises) board (opened on May 17, 2004), and a GEM (Growth Enterprise Market) board which is mainly for young firms (opened on October 30, 2009). Conversely, there is only one board in the Shanghai Stock Exchange, which is the main board. Generally speaking, firms listed on the SHSE are, on average, larger in terms of total assets than firms listed on the SZSE. Studies, for example, Jiang and Kim (2015), consider the SZSE and SHSE to be similar to NASDAQ and the New York Stock Exchanges, respectively. Based on the 2015 Yearbook of China Securities and Futures, at the 2015 year-end, there were 2,808 firms listed on the two stock exchanges. This was an increase in market capitalisation from US$3.8 trillion in 2012 to about US$6.271 trillion in 2015. In 2018, the SHSE was the fourth and the SZSE the eighth largest exchange in the world by market capitalization. If both the SHSE and SZSE were combined, they would come in third after the New York Stock Exchange and NASDAQ.

There are different types of Chinese share classes. For example, A-shares were originally for Chinese domestic investors only, and B-shares were for foreign investors. However, since 2001, the central government has gradually been opening both the SZSE and SHSE to a broader scope of potential public and investors to increase investment in Chinese businesses. Thus, Chinese investors could also own B-shares starting from 2001, and qualified foreign investors could own A-shares starting from 2003 (SSE, 2015). Other share classes, such as H-shares (China-based firms listed in Hong Kong), L-shares (London), N-shares (New York), and S-shares (Singapore) are known as cross-listed shares. A-shares are the most frequently used in trading compared to other share classes in China. Thus, in this study, all the reported summary statistics are based on A-shares information.

The main securities regulator in China is the China Securities Regulatory Commission (CSRC). Its main responsibility is to approve initial public offerings (IPOs). Originally, all IPO processes were tightly controlled by the central government (see Fan et al., 2012; Huyghebaert & Xu, 2013; Wu et al., 2013). According to Jiang and Kim (2015), the government would identify industrial sectors that allowed firms to go public, establish a quota system, and even determine the offer prices. However, things gradually changed in the late 1990s, as investment banks began to perform a more important role in the IPO process, with more responsibility for identifying and developing listing candidates. Nowadays, the responsibility of the CSRC is to ensure the IPO processes are in compliance with regulations and rules. However, in practice, according to Jiang and Kim (2015), it seems that the IPO process is still tightly controlled by the CSRC because the CSRC has the final say on which listing candidates can go public. For example, the CSRC put a freeze on all Chinese IPOs in 2012. At the close of 2013, 760 firms had applied to go public, but during that 14-month stretch, none of the firms was granted an IPO (Kreab, 2014). This example shows that unlike the registration system in western countries, the IPO process in China is based on an approval system. Nevertheless, the approval system may soon change, as the CSRC has begun speaking of moving away from its current approval-based system (seen as distorting the IPO market and encouraging official corruption) to fast-track the reform of a registration IPO system (Yu, 2017).

In addition, it is interesting to see the changes in investor composition in the Chinese stock market (see Jiang & Kim, 2015). For listed firms, there are two types of shares: tradable and non-tradable. When firms go public, the controlling shareholders normally hold non-tradable shares. Because all firms were originally state-owned, when SOEs go public, the controlling shareholders are either the central government, local authorities, government agencies, or other legal persons (Jia et al., 2019). The state-owned controlling shareholders can be the central government, local authorities, or government agencies. Legal persons can be domestic legal entities or institutional investors, for example, non-bank financial institutions, stock firms, or state-private mixed firms. The majority of legal persons are partially state-owned or purely state-owned (also known as state-owned legal persons), and some are private institutions (also known as social legal persons) (Liu et al., 2007). On the other hand, almost all the tradable shares are held by individual investors.

2.2 Corporate Governance Regulations

In China, the majority of company laws are imposed by the central government (e.g. the National People's Congress) and security regulations are imposed by the CSRC and the two stock exchanges (Shanghai and Shenzhen) (Hutson et al., et al., 2019; Saich, 2015).

There are many requirements a listed firm needs to fulfil, for example, at least one shareholder meeting per year. Additionally, large shareholders, boards of directors, or supervisory board members can require the firm to call interim shareholder meetings for extradentary discussions. Similar to Western countries, China uses a cumulative voting system for the board of directors' and supervisors' elections. A three-year term is offered once a director is elected, but they can serve consecutively. An interesting feature in China is that the government has significant influence on the selection of board members and management in the firms, in particular, in the SOEs (state-owned enterprises). For example, supervisory board members of large state-owned enterprises are designated by the State Council. This situation raises questions about board independence.

For the board of directors, it is required that they have a range of 5 to 19 board members (Company Law of the People's Republic of China, 2014. Hereafter Company Law, 2014). Some of the key responsibilities of directors are to make critical operational, investment (e.g., innovation-related projects), and financial decisions (e.g., raising capital and budgeting); to implement shareholder resolutions; and to evaluate the performance of top management teams (Tricker, 2012). Two board meetings must be held per year according to the Company Law 2014. Additionally, managers can be on the board of directors, and the firm is not allowed to lend money to managers and members sitting on the board of directors and supervisory board (Company Law, 2014).

In August 2001, the CSRC, authorised by the State Council, promulgated the Guidelines for Introducing Independent Directors to the Board of Directors of Listed Companies (hereafter, the Guidelines). According to the Guidelines, a Chinese listed firm was required to have at least two independent directors. To be independent, a director must not have a personal or business affiliation with the firm and the managers. Moreover, a director must not be one of the top 10 shareholders or hold more than 1% of the company shares (See Section I (1) in the Guidelines, 2001). Later, in June 2003 with the new amended version of Company Law, it was required that at least one-third of the members on a board be independent directors, and this remained the same in the 2014 Company Law.

In China, the 2014 Company Law requires limited-liability companies to have a two-tier system, consisting of a board of directors and a board of supervisors (Shapiro et al., 2015; Shan & McIver, 2011; Lin et al., 2009). A listed firm in China is required to have at least three supervisors. The supervisory board consists of shareholders' representatives and employees' representatives, and a third of members must be employees (see Article 117 in Company Law, 2014). However, senior managers or board of directors cannot concurrently be a supervisor. Like the directors, a supervisor is elected to a three-year term but can serve consecutively. The board of directors is responsible for the immediate governance of the firm. In contrast, the board of supervisors is supposed to monitor the board of directors and to protect the rights and interests of the firm and the stakeholders (Kim et al., 2007; Kim et al., 2010). In this capacity, supervisors can attend and observe the board of directors' meetings. However, in practice, the supervisors in Chinese listed firms often have low status and limited power because the supervisory board can only suggest sanctions on the board of directors and senior management or file lawsuits against them. They lack the legal authority to decide on and carry out such sanctions. Compared to Germany, where the supervisory board is the first-tier board (Tricker, 2012; Balsmeier et al., 2017), the supervisory board in China is considered a second-tier board with limited capacity (Lin et al., 2009). According to the Chinese Corporate Governance Code, supervisory board members must meet at least once every six months.

A particularly interesting board topic in China is the distinct role of the supervisory board. Tricker (2012) and Shan and McIver (2011) raised concerns about the usefulness of the supervisory board. They suggested that there is a further need to improve the level of independence of the supervisory board and enforce the board's function. Clarke (2006) also argued that the supervisory board in China is unable to actively perform the monitoring role due to its having no significant power to monitor financial activities or to appoint and evaluate senior management members (Company Law, 2014). Additionally, the supervisory board is composed of shareholder representatives and employee representatives. The shareholder representatives have a high probability of having connections with the controlling shareholder. Therefore, the employee representatives face more challenges in acting against the shareholder representatives, their superiors (Xing, 2003).

2.3 The Development of Innovation in China

Studies show that innovative capabilities are the key sources for growth and a competitive edge for firms and industries (Lo et al., 2019; Jia et al., 2019). In the last decades, the central government of China has been consistently emphasising the importance of technology development in the manufacturing sector. It views technology development as an engine for the process of catching up with the advanced industrial economies and industrialisation. It is believed that over the long-term, China's economic performance will ultimately depend upon its ability to acquire, adapt, and create new technologies (Tong et al., 2013). A goal of supporting domestic firms to build indigenous innovation capabilities has been emphasised in the Chinese national Plans.[1]

The Chinese government has long been aware of the weakness of its development strategy and has been trying to improve its own technological capacity through investments in basic research, innovation, and the application of new technologies (Woetzel et al., 2019; Lo et al., 2019). Many national initiatives, for instance, the Torch Programme, the 973 Programme and 985 Programme,[2] have been launched over the last decades. Large investments have been made in the Chinese Academy of Sciences (CAS) through the so-called Hundred, Thousand and Ten-Thousands Plan[3] to attract scientists from home and overseas to contribute their knowledge in China. In addition, the governments of China also issue regulations and policies to encourage R&D and technology investment.[4]

Table 1. Government Expenditures in Science and Technology (S&T) (100 million yuan)

Year	Total Government Expenditure	Expenditure in S&T	Share of Total Expenditure (%)
2007	49781.35	1783.04	3.58
2008	62592.66	2129.21	3.40
2009	76299.93	2744.52	3.60
2010	89874.16	3250.18	3.62
2011	109247.79	3828.02	3.50
2012	125952.97	4452.63	3.54
2013	140212.10	5084.30	3.63
2014	151785.56	5314.45	3.50
2015	175877.77	5862.57	3.33

Source: National Bureau of Statistics of China (2016)

Table 1 provides some basic information on government expenditure and particularly its expenditure on S&T in China between 2007 and 2015. The total sum of expenditure in S&T has increased significantly over time but, as a share of total government expenditure, it is actually quite stable. However, this does not mean that China's research capacity has not been improved. China's reform of S&T development was aimed at reducing the expenditure incurred by the central government and increasing the production efficiency of research institutes (Lo et al., 2019). Research expenses have been shifted from the central budget to regional governments and large and medium-sized enterprises.

Additionally, at the firm-level, over the nine-year period, the average R&D intensity is 4.83% of the annual revenue and reveals a significant increase since 2007 from 1.81% to 6.23% in 2015 (See Table 2). This means that firms in China value the importance of innovation and have increased investment in R&D to enhance their competitiveness.

3. CORPORATE GOVERNANCE STATISTICS IN CHINA

This section provides summary statistics on corporate governance in Chinese listed firms. First, this section provides descriptive statistics on ownership concentrations to demonstrate potential changes to the ownership structure in China. Second, a summary of statistics is provided on board structure, as the board is considered the key component of the internal corporate governance mechanism. Finally, a summary of statistics on debt ratios is also provided to demonstrate the capital structure of Chinese listed firms.

Table 2. R&D intensity

Year	Observations	Min	Max	25th Percentile	Mean	75th Percentile
R&D Intensity						
2015-2007	5118	.00	75.62	1.29	4.414	5.44
2015	706	.00	62.70	2.537	6.231	7.333
2014	683	.00	51.55	2.210	6.010	6.973
2013	661	.00	51.55	2.210	5.820	6.973
2012	669	.00	51.13	2.095	5.482	6.324
2011	616	.00	41.14	1.324	4.715	5.90
2010	537	.00	75.62	.773	4.077	4.963
2009	399	.00	32.57	.364	3.044	4.408
2008	339	.00	40.36	.121	2.536	3.691
2007	306	.00	40.23	.000	1.810	2.369

Note: This table shows the R&D intensity (the total R&D investment divided by the total operating income for IT and manufacturing firms listed on the SZSE and SHSE from 2007-2015. The data comes from the CSMAR database and firm annual reports.

3.1. Ownership Concentration in China

It is suggested that firms are monitored by their large shareholders if they have a concentrated ownership structure. This monitoring may result in a good or bad organisational outcome. For example, Minetti et al. (2012) found that the type of large shareholder affects innovation. For firms that were less innovative, the main shareholder of the firm was less often an individual person or a family, as opposed to a financial institution or a bank. Boubaker et al. (2017) showed that a higher degree of ownership concentration could contribute to higher accounting profitability instead of market valuation. This means a highly concentrated ownership structure that tends to improve the financial performance of Chinese firms may be due to a more unified strategy and consistent execution. On the other hand, Choi et al. (2011) and Wang and Shailer (2015) pointed out that Chinese listed firms are generally highly concentrated, and the market is not sensitive enough to distinguish amongst firms according to ownership features. They found no impact of ownership concentration on innovation. Similarly, Shan and McIver (2011) found that the non-financial sector firms with lower levels of state ownership concentration had higher market growth perspective levels than their counterparts when the study was controlled for firm age. Although various conclusions are found in the literature, ownership concentration is commonly used and considered one of the important corporate governance variables. Table 3 shows ownership concentrations of Chinese listed firms between 2007 to 2015.

According to Table 3 Panel A, in 2015, the largest shareholder holds, on average, 32.63% of shares of a listed firm, while the top five shareholders hold 49.8% of shares (see Panel B). Additionally, in the same year, the top 10 shareholders hold, on average, 54.8% of firm shares (see Panel C). The results in Table 3 also reveal that the main agency problem in China is between controlling shareholders and minority shareholders. Wang and Shailer (2015) stated that controlling shareholders might expropriate wealth and interest from minority shareholders. This agency problem is different from that found in developed countries, in which the main conflicts of interest are between shareholders and managers.

Table 3 also shows that the variations between 2007 and 2015 are relatively small throughout Panels A, B and C, which indicates that there are no major changes to the ownership concentration structure. Although China's government has been privatising and decentralising its SOEs gradually in the past decades, ownership is still highly concentrated among Chinese listed firms (Jiang & Kim, 2015; Jia et al., 2019). Especially in Panel C, a rise in the top 10 shareholders is observed from 2007 to 2012. This increased ownership concentration could be related to the economic recession recovery.

3.2. The Largest Shareholders in China

This section reviews the situation of the largest shareholders in Chinese IT and manufacturing industries. It is still uncertain whether firms with the largest amount of shareholder monitoring are more profitable (see Bertoni et al., 2014; Chen et al., 2014; Shan & McIver, 2011) or if they expropriate wealth from minority shareholders (Jiang & Kim, 2015; Zhu, 2019). Previous studies evaluating the relationship between large shareholders and firm performance have traditionally used various firm performance results including return on investment, ROE (Zhang et al., 2014), ROA (Price et al., 2013; Daily & Dalton, 1992), earnings per share (Zahra, 1992), Tobin's Q (Buallay et al., 2017; Bennouri et al., 2018), price earnings ratio, sales growth (Choi et al., 2011), and net profit margin. These firm performance measures can be grouped into those which are accounting-based and those which are market-based.

The market-based measure is characterised by its forward-looking aspect and its reflection of the expectations of the shareholders concerning the firm's future performance. The accounting-based measure presents past organisational performance (Al-Matari et al., 2014). This study uses Tobin's Q as a market-based measurement and ROA as an accounting-based measurement to measure firm performance, as they are the most commonly used in the literature. Table 5 illustrates the mean return on assets (ROA) and Tobin's Q based on three levels of top 10 shareholder ownership. The first level illustrates the situation where the top shareholder holds less than 30% of the sample firms, the second level, between 30% and 50%, and the third level, more than 50%. For each tercile of firms, Table 5 illustrates the mean ROA (Panel A) and median Q (Panel B) by year. Each panel also further divided firms into SOEs and non-SOEs. The table clearly presents that in most of the years (except for 2013 and 2014), SOEs with majority shareholders (i.e., where the largest shareholders hold more than 50%) have higher ROAs than other firms (i.e., where the largest shareholders hold less than 50%). Yet they also often have lower Q ratios than other firms. These relationships increase in non-SOEs. These results are consistent with Jiang and Kim (2015) when firm performance is measured as return on assets and Tobin's Q. The relationship between the top shareholder and ROA appears to be positively monotonic. That is, based on the results from Table 4, that the largest shareholders enhance a firm's ROA but harm the firm performance if it measured as Tobin's Q. However, it is still debated which firm performance measure, accounting-based versus market-based measures, is the appropriate or theoretically correct measure of firm performance (Jiang & Kim, 2015). There is no such thing as one measurement of firm performance that works better than the others. It depends on what the researcher would like to observe from the firm. Price et al. (2013) suggested that accounting-based measures (e.g., ROA, ROE, earnings per share, and earnings on invested capital) are a popular measure of organisational performance because unlike stock market return, they adjust for any divergences between the interests of shareholders and managers. Despite this argument, Tobin's Q is still the most frequently used measurement for firm performance in corporate governance literature (e.g., Bennouri et al., 2018; Bertoni et al., 2014; Mangena et al., 2012; Shan & McIver, 2011). There is no conclusion for why these conflicting firm performance results exist in the literature. However,

Table 3. Ownership Concentration

Year	Observations	Min	Max	25th Percentile	Mean	75th Percentile
Panel A: Proportion of Shares Held by the Largest Shareholder						
2015-2007	6615	1.46	75.14	22.62	35.00	46.48
2015	878	1.00	84.11	21.17	32.63	42.86
2014	859	3.62	87.5	21.90	33.90	44.79
2013	845	3.62	84.11	22.58	34.56	45.26
2012	839	3.62	84.11	22.72	35.18	46.48
2011	807	.36	81.5	23.02	35.04	46.80
2010	745	.27	81.5	22.94	35.56	47.87
2009	603	.43	93.61	23.02	36.17	48.78
2008	532	.17	78.94	23.13	36.14	48.35
2007	507	.09	83.83	23.12	35.83	47.11
Panel B: Proportion of Shares Held by the Five Largest Shareholders						
20015-2007	6615	14.55	96.57	40.71	52.00	63.52
2015	878	3.94	99.23	38.74	49.80	60.20
2014	859	10.76	97.50	39.73	50.54	61.27
2013	845	9.59	96.40	40.65	51.67	63.28
2012	839	9.92	96.72	41.93	53.07	65.11
2011	807	9.5	97.64	41.53	53.42	66.30
2010	745	10.19	97.15	41.79	54.00	66.51
2009	603	12.44	94.67	40.21	52.34	64.40
2008	532	12.43	94.95	40.71	51.63	62.90
2007	507	52.19	94.84	41.06	51.57	61.71
Panel C: Proportion of Shares Held by the Top 10 Largest Shareholders						
2015-2007	6615	15.87	98.23	45.42	56.55	68.55
2015	878	4.62	99.84	43.79	54.88	65.52
2014	859	12.72	99.00	44.45	55.28	65.92
2013	845	10.57	97.60	45.70	56.42	67.98
2012	839	10.91	97.12	46.88	57.78	70.98
2011	807	10.37	99.90	47.14	58.47	71.63
2010	745	10.85	99.90	46.4	58.33	71.58
2009	603	13.35	98.40	45.28	56.81	69.29
2008	532	13.03	95.24	44.31	55.38	67.00
2007	507	56.41	96.99	44.82	55.64	67.09

Note: This table presents the proportion of shares owned by the largest shareholder (Panel A), by the top 5 shareholders (Panel B), and by the top 10 shareholders (Panel C) for IT and manufacturing firms listed on both the SZSE and SHSE from 2007-2015. The data comes from the CSMAR and firm annual reports.

the results from Table 4 raise the point that when drawing conclusions on the research investigating the relationship between ownership structures and firm performance, authors should be careful about the interpretation of their analytical results based on firm performance measurements.

Table 4 Panel B also reveals why some previous studies find (inverse) U-shape relationships between firm performance and ownership concentration (e.g. Beyer et al., 2012; Francis & Smith, 1995). Sometimes the second level largest shareholder (i.e., between 30% and 50% ownership) appears to have the lowest firm value. For example, when compared to the first and third levels of the largest shareholder categories, the second-largest shareholder has the lowest Tobin's Q in 2007 (2.41%) and 2008 (1.05%) among the SOEs and 2014 (2.92%) and 2015 (4.54%) among the non-SOEs. Similar results are also found in Table 4, Panel A when the firm performance is measured as ROA. This finding is consistent with Jiang and Kim (2015). Most of the time, Tobin's Q is the highest when the large shareholder ownership is less than 30%, especially among the SOEs. Therefore, studies found a U-shape relationship might not indicate that ownership concentration is the optimal structure for the firm. Future studies might consider looking into the shareholding percentages of the top shareholders and doing a thorough study of the firm ownership structure before drawing conclusions. This will help understand better the relationship between ownership structure (large shareholders and ownership concentration) and firm performance. Interestingly, this study also found that the R&D investment is almost always the highest when the largest shareholder owns less than 20% of the shares (See Table 4 Panel C). The amount of R&D investment is higher in non-SOEs compared to SOEs throughout the sample period from 2007 to 2015. The result indicates in emerging economies, such as China, the government plays a critical role in influencing firm investment behaviour (Zhou et al., 2017). The Chinese government often directly aids firms in increasing their innovation capability via direct funding (for example, large-scale innovative projects for firms to enhance their competitive advantage) and developing targeted innovation areas through technology transfer efforts (Jia et al., 2019). This result also indicates that firms with more innovative effort are more often in non-SOEs than firms that are closely affiliated with the government.

3.3 Board Structure in China

Board structure in China is unique, bringing elements of both the insider and outsider systems of CG. In this case, listed firms in China operate both a single-tier and a two-tier board system composed of a board of directors and a supervisory board (Tong et al., 2013). The board of directors is structured like the outsider system and is composed of both executives and non-executive directors. The main duty for the directors is to oversee the firm on behalf of the shareholders. The Company Law 2014 requires that at least one-third of board members be independent directors. The introduction of a supervisory board is consistent with the insider model, for example, as practised in Germany. Many studies empirically examine the role of the board of directors on business-related research (Bertoni et al., 2014; Hillman et al., 2009). The efficacy of independent directors in the boardroom has been extensively studied as a prominent variable in board composition research (see Balsmeier et al., 2017; Coles et al., 2008; Tong et al., 2013). For example, studies such as Mangena et al. (2012) and Yu and Ashton (2015) argued that boards with a greater proportion of independent directors are better at monitoring and provide expertise and advice to the executive team. For this reason, several countries mandated specific board structures. For example, in UK listed firms, half of the board must be independent directors. Table 5 provides summary statistics on board size for both the board of directors and supervisory board, board composition and the CEO duality situation in Chinese listed firms.

Table 4. Firm Performance Based on Largest Shareholder Ownership

Year	SOEs						Non-SOEs					
	Topl < 30		30<=Topl<50		Topl>=50		Topl < 30		30<=Topl<50		Topl>=50	
	Observations	Mean	Observations	Mean	Observations	Mean	Observations	Mean	Observations	Mean	Observations	Mean
Panel A: Mean ROA Based on the Largest Shareholder Ownership												
2015	119	2.022	139	2.072	85	2.666	315	3.500	176	4.448	38	5.783
2014	113	1.475	139	2.756	93	1.898	286	4.094	175	5.136	51	7.228
2013	128	2.178	133	3.987	97	2.942	263	3.773	161	4.974	61	3.472
2012	123	3.259	133	3.352	101	3.301	254	4.482	161	5.753	64	5.608
2011	120	3.157	137	4.254	96	4.340	240	5.105	145	6.598	65	7.261
2010	126	4.074	137	4.443	97	5.220	196	5.644	125	6.802	59	8.286
2009	108	2.911	134	2.974	92	3.937	138	4.349	90	5.659	33	8.348
2008	107	3.285	134	1.828	90	3.981	98	4.528	77	4.263	23	8.962
2007	108	3.021	134	2.498	80	6.230	98	5.347	65	7.866	19	9.049
Panel B: Mean Tobin's Q Based on the Largest Shareholder Ownership												
2015	118	2.587	137	2.268	85	1.774	304	4.918	173	4.536	36	4.683
2014	113	1.824	139	1.699	92	1.292	281	3.120	173	2.923	50	3.375
2013	128	1.587	133	1.542	97	1.115	257	2.546	159	2.607	58	2.697
2012	123	1.327	132	1.393	100	1.161	251	1.904	161	2.072	64	2.059
2011	120	1.528	135	1.478	95	1.383	233	2.298	144	2.345	61	2.406
2010	125	2.781	136	2.650	96	2.407	182	3.777	116	3.837	51	4.348
2009	107	2.513	133	2.283	91	2.273	124	3.466	82	3.650	29	4.392
2008	105	1.254	134	1.053	90	1.286	93	1.646	77	1.699	22	2.409
2007	107	3.158	132	2.409	77	3.604	96	3.703	62	3.922	18	5.151
Panel C: Mean R&D Intensity Based on the Largest Shareholder Ownership												
2015	105	2.305	128	2.361	73	1.633	305	2.921	173	2.249	36	2.500
2014	98	2.307	131	2.115	84	1.472	275	2.955	165	2.498	49	2.688
2013	111	1.999	117	1.928	82	1.568	244	3.203	148	2.432	57	2.738
2012	106	2.426	110	2.067	88	1.567	233	2.842	153	2.465	60	2.475
2011	85	2.778	101	2.176	76	1.769	197	2.893	135	2.799	56	1.928
2010	83	2.969	87	1.892	62	1.489	148	2.425	101	2.245	42	1.751
2009	64	2.467	77	2.724	54	1.603	84	2.945	61	2.426	24	2.376
2008	50	2.319	64	3.846	45	1.612	53	3.018	49	2.672	15	3.191
2007	42	1.326	55	1.783	24	1.897	47	1.585	35	2.050	11	2.623

Note: This table presents mean return on assets (ROA in Panel A), mean Tobin's Q (in Panel B), and mean R&D intensity (in Panel C) based on the largest shareholder ownership of IT and manufacturing firms listed on both the SZSE and SHSE from 2007 to 2015. The data comes from the CSMAR database and firm annual reports. Top1<30 denotes firms where the largest shareholder owns less than 30% of the firm. Top1>=50 denotes firms where the largest shareholder owns between 30% and 50% of the firm. Top1>50 denotes firms where the largest shareholder owns more than 50% of the firm. ROA equals earnings before interest and tax divided by the total assets (Yu & Ashton, 2015). Tobin's Q is measured as the sum of the market value of equity and the book value of debt divided by the book value of total assets (Tong et al., 2013). The statistics are reported separately for SOEs and non-SOEs.

Panel A of Table 5 reports that Chinese listed firms in IT and manufacturing industries have, on average, nine board members throughout the sample period of 2007-2015. Panels B and C in Table 5 report the number and the proportion of independent directors, respectively. Panels B and C reveal that majority of the sample firms retain the same number (proportion) of independent directors throughout the sample period, for example, three independent directors out of nine board members on average. A similar situation appears in the statistics on supervisory boards (see Panel D). The number of supervisors remains relatively the same throughout the nine years in the sample firms. This study barely finds any increase or decrease in the sample period. Based on the statistics shown in Table 5, firms tend to follow the regulations strictly to reach the minimum requirement, such as having at least one-third independent directors in the boardroom. In other words, it can be argued that the board structure in China is not based on firm or sector-specific characteristics. It would be worth having an in-depth analysis of the characteristics of the board members, for example, their professional background, political connection or education level (Lee et al., 2020; Talavera et al., 2018).

Table 5. Board of Directors

Year	Observations	Min	Max	25th Percentile	Mean	75th Percentile
Panel A: Number of Directors						
2015-2007	5118	5	18	8	9	9
2015	706	4	17	7	9	9
2014	683	4	18	7	9	9
2013	667	5	18	7	9	9
2012	669	5	18	8	9	9
2011	633	5	18	5	9	9
2010	565	5	18	8	9	9
2009	431	5	18	8	9	9
2008	395	5	18	9	9	10
2007	369	3	18	9	9	10
Panel B: Number of Independent Directors						
2015-2007	5118	2	7	3	3	3
2015	706	1	8	3	3	3
2014	683	1	7	3	3	3
2013	667	2	6	3	3	3
2012	669	2	7	3	3	3
2011	633	2	6	3	3	3
2010	565	2	6	3	3	3
2009	431	2	6	3	3	4
2008	395	2	8	3	3	4
2007	369	1	7	3	3	4
Panel C: Proportion of Independent Directors						
2015-2007	5118	22.89	62.00	33.00	36.75	40.89

continues on following page

Table 5. Continued

Year	Observations	Min	Max	25th Percentile	Mean	75th Percentile
2015	706	14.00	67.00	33.00	37.58	43.00
2014	683	11.00	60.00	33.00	37.09	43.00
2013	667	25.00	63.00	33.00	37.15	43.00
2012	669	25.00	63.00	33.00	37.04	43.00
2011	633	25.00	60.00	33.00	36.72	40.00
2010	565	25.00	56.00	33.00	36.47	40.00
2009	431	27.00	57.00	33.00	36.50	40.00
2008	395	27.00	57.00	33.00	36.19	38.00
2007	369	27.00	75.00	33.00	36.00	38.00
Panel D: Number of Supervisors						
2015-2007	5118	2	11	3	4	5
2015	706	1	10	3	4	5
2014	683	2	11	3	4	5
2013	667	2	12	3	4	5
2012	669	2	12	3	4	5
2011	633	2	11	3	4	5
2010	565	3	11	3	4	5
2009	431	2	9	3	4	5
2008	395	2	10	3	4	5
2007	369	2	11	3	4	5
Panel E: CEO Duality						
Year	**SOEs**		**Non-SOEs**			
	Observations	**Combined**	**Observations**	**Combined**		
2015	243	7.41	463	35.21		
2014	242	8.26	441	37.64		
2013	252	6.35	415	37.83		
2012	253	8.30	416	38.94		
2011	251	8.76	382	39.01		
2010	256	7.42	309	38.51		
2009	234	7.27	197	31.47		
2008	234	9.70	161	28.57		
2007	226	9.73	143	26.57		

Note: This table presents the board size (Panel A), the number of independent directors (Panel B), the proportion of independent directors (Panel C), the number of supervisors (Panel D), and the proportion of firms where the CEO also serves as chairperson (Panel E) for IT and manufacturing firms listed on both the SZSE and SHSE from 2007-2015. For Panel E, the statistics are reported separately for SOEs and non-SOEs. The data comes from the CSMAR database and firm annual reports.

Panel E of Table 5 reports the proportion of CEOs who also serve as the chairperson. The role of the CEO is critical for the survival of any firm, as is that of the chairperson. However, whether the combination of CEO and chairperson should be allowed is a question for debate amongst researchers, regulators, and lawmakers internationally. The Chinese Corporate Governance Code suggests having separate individuals as CEO and chairperson, but differences exist between SOEs and non-SOEs in China. For example, since 2009, over one-third of non-SOEs in IT and manufacturing industries have CEO duality. An astute observer may notice that the number of non-SOEs having combined leadership structures increased from 26.57% in 2007 to 35.21% in 2015. For SOEs, throughout the sample period (2007 to 2015), the proportion of CEOs who also served as the chairperson is less than 10%. On the other hand, there is a dip in CEO duality in SOEs from 2007 (9.73%) to 2015 (7.41%). Therefore, it seems that non-SOEs are in favour of having a combined leadership structure, and the majority of SOEs follow the good practice of splitting the CEO and chairperson roles. Not surprisingly, Cao et al. (2017) found that politically connected CEOs have a lower probability of turnover for Chinese non-SOEs, especially when there is CEO duality. Bai et al. (2004) and Peng et al. (2007) found a significant and negative relationship between CEO duality and firm profitability. Similar results were also found in developed economies, for example, Australia (Kiel & Nicholson, 2003), Canada (Bozec, 2005), the US (Pi & Timme, 1993; Rechner & Dalton, 1991), and the UK (Dahya et al., 2003). In contrast, other studies found that CEO duality has a positive impact on firm performance, which supports the view of stewardship theory that CEO duality may be good for firm performance due to the unity of command. For example, the positive relationship is evident both in developed economies (e.g., Dey et al., 2011), and in developing economies (e.g., Azeez, 2015; Liu & Fong, 2010; Peng et al., 2007).

3.4 Capital Structure in China

Capital structure can influence both innovation and firm performance. Whereas innovation requires slack resources, firm performance may be affected by a change in the cost of capital (Chen et al., 2014). Different capital structures imply different levels of financial risk and prompt different levels of supervision from the creditors (usually banks), which consequently affects source allocation decisions (e.g., innovation investment). The higher risk arising from increases in the leverage ratio could lead risk-averse firms to expect more investment in CE. However, as debt increases, creditors may begin to exercise more supervision over the firm, making it difficult for management to entrench by spending money on risky projects (i.e., CE) (Tribo et al., 2007). In China, most banks are state-owned and play an important role in providing debt financing. Given the political and economic environment, banks are more likely to have strong incentives to monitor managers to ensure that they adhere to debt covenants, fulfil the communist agenda, and maximise a firm's profitability (Zhu et al., 2019).

Table 6 shows the leverage of listed IT and manufacturing firms in China. Overall, the sample firms maintain, on average, about a 42% debt ratio between 2007 and 2015. This ratio is slightly lower than the findings of Choi et al. (2011), who reported the average leverage of Chinese listed low-to-high-technology sectors in China to be 44.17%. Based on these highly leveraged figures, one could argue that firms in the IT and manufacturing industries may not be in a position to fund long-term projects (e.g., innovation projects). This could affect investment decisions on innovation resources and firm performance, due to the fact that it increases the likelihood of bankruptcy and the burden on innovation investment (Zhu et al., 2019).

Table 6. Leverage Ratios

Year	Observations	Min	Max	25th Percentile	Mean	75th Percentile
Panel A: Leverage						
2015-2007	5118	.0083	7.38	0.2388	0.4199	0.5628
2015	706	.0174	4.19	.2469	.4107	.5520
2014	683	.0131	46.16	.2376	.4730	.5665
2013	667	.0022	1.75	.2016	.3840	.5370
2012	669	.0027	2.66	.1874	.3912	.5437
2011	633	.0075	2.99	.1810	.3766	.5343
2010	565	.0127	2.53	.1935	.3858	.5443
2009	431	.0144	2.58	.2908	.4534	.5966
2008	391	.0022	1.66	.2956	.4452	.5883
2007	369	.0023	1.94	.3152	.4594	.6023

Note: This table presents the leverage ratios of IT and manufacturing firms listed on the SZSE and SHSE from 2007 to 2015. The data comes from the CSMAR database and firm annual reports. The leverage ratio is the ratio of total debt to total assets (Chen et al., 2014; Zhang et al., 2014).

4. CONCLUSION

This study introduces the current structure of corporate governance (ownership and board structure) and innovation in Chinese IT and manufacturing listed firms, and highlights and discusses the unique features of corporate governance in China. In particular, it discusses corporate governance regulations, ownership, and board structure governance mechanisms. Given that China, as the world's largest developing economy, is rapidly evolving, new regulations and rules for corporate governance and innovation are constantly being updated. This study tries to provide as recent an overview as possible. It is hoped that the breakdown of the statistical analyses for ownership, board structure, and innovation will encourage future studies to take care before adopting variable measurements, such as firm performance and different levels of large shareholders. It is also hoped that this study will inspire and motivate further research into this essential topic.

REFERENCES

Al-Matari, E. M., Al-Swidi, A. K., & Fadzil, F. H. B. (2014). The measurements of firm performance's dimensions. *Asian Journal of Finance & Accounting*, *6*(1), 24–49. doi:10.5296/ajfa.v6i1.4761

Azeez, A. (2015). Corporate governance and firm performance: Evidence from Sri Lanka. *The Journal of Finance*, *3*(1), 180–189.

Bai, C., Liu, Q., Lu, J., Song, F. M., & Zhang, J. (2004). Corporate governance and market valuation in China. *Journal of Comparative Economics*, *32*(4), 599–616. doi:10.1016/j.jce.2004.07.002

Balsmeier, B., Fleming, L., & Manso, G. (2017). Independent boards and innovation. *Journal of Financial Economics*, *123*(3), 536–557. doi:10.1016/j.jfineco.2016.12.005

Bennouri, M., Chtioui, T., Nagati, H., & Nekhili, M. (2018). Female board directorship and firm performance: What really matters? *Journal of Banking & Finance*, *88*, 267–291. doi:10.1016/j.jbankfin.2017.12.010

Bertoni, F., Meoli, M., & Vismara, S. (2014). Board independence, ownership structure and the valuation of IPOs in continental Europe. *Corporate Governance*, *22*(2), 116–131. doi:10.1111/corg.12051

Beyer, M., Czarnitzki, D., & Kraft, K. (2012). Managerial ownership, entrenchment and innovation. *Economics of Innovation and New Technology*, *21*(7), 679–699. doi:10.1080/10438599.2011.639978

Boubaker, S., Rouatbi, W., & Saffar, W. (2017). The role of multiple large shareholders in the choice of debt source. *Financial Management*, *46*(1), 241–274. doi:10.1111/fima.12148

Bozec, R. (2005). Boards of directors, market discipline and firm performance. *Journal of Business Finance & Accounting*, *32*(9-10), 1921–1960. doi:10.1111/j.0306-686X.2005.00652.x

Buallay, A., Hamdan, A., & Zureigat, Q. (2017). Corporate governance and firm performance: Evidence from Saudi Arabia. *Australasian Accounting. Business and Finance Journal*, *11*(1), 78–98.

Chen, V. Z., Li, J., Shapiro, D. M., & Zhang, X. (2014). Ownership structure and innovation: An emerging market perspective. *Asia Pacific Journal of Management*, *31*(1), 1–24. doi:10.100710490-013-9357-5

Cheng, M., Lin, B., & Wei, M. (2015). Executive compensation in family firms: The effect of multiple family members. *Journal of Corporate Finance*, *32*, 238–257. doi:10.1016/j.jcorpfin.2014.10.014

Choi, S. B., Lee, S. H., & Williams, C. (2011). Ownership and firm innovation in a transition economy: Evidence from China. *Research Policy*, *40*(3), 441–452. doi:10.1016/j.respol.2011.01.004

Clarke, D. C. (2006). The independent director in Chinese corporate governance. *Del. J. Corp. Law*, *31*, 125–228.

Coles, J. L., Daniel, N. D., & Naveen, L. (2008). Boards: Does one size fit all? *Journal of Financial Economics*, *87*(2), 329–356. doi:10.1016/j.jfineco.2006.08.008

Company Law of the People's Republic of China. (2014). *Standing Committee of the National People's Congress*. http://www.fdi.gov.cn/1800000121_39_4814_0_7.html

CSRC. (2001). *Guidelines for Introducing Independent Directors to the Board of Directors of Listed Companies*. China Securities Regulatory Commission. http://www.csrc.gov.cn/pub/csrc_en/newsfacts/release/200708/t20070810_69191.html

Dahya, J., Karbhari, Y., Xiao, J. Z., & Yang, M. (2003). The usefulness of the supervisory board report in China. *Corporate Governance*, *11*(4), 308–321. doi:10.1111/1467-8683.00329

Daily, C. M., & Dalton, D. R. (1992). The relationship between governance structure and corporate performance in entrepreneurial firms. *Journal of Business Venturing*, *7*(5), 375–386. doi:10.1016/0883-9026(92)90014-I

Dey, A., Engel, E., & Liu, X. (2011). CEO and board chair roles: To split or not to split? *Journal of Corporate Finance*, *17*(5), 1595–1618. doi:10.1016/j.jcorpfin.2011.09.001

Fan, J. P. H., Titman, S., & Twite, G. (2012). An international comparison of capital structure and debt maturity choices. *Journal of Financial and Quantitative Analysis*, *47*(1), 23–56. doi:10.1017/S0022109011000597

Francis, J., & Smith, A. (1995). Agency costs and innovation some empirical evidence. *Journal of Accounting and Economics*, *19*(2), 383–409. doi:10.1016/0165-4101(94)00389-M

Hillman, A. J., Withers, M. C., & Collins, B. J. (2009). Resource dependence theory: A review. *Journal of Management*, *35*(6), 1404–1427. doi:10.1177/0149206309343469

Hung, C. H. D., Jiang, Y., Liu, F. H., Tu, H., & Wang, S. (2017). Bank political connections and performance in China. *Journal of Financial Stability*, *32*, 57–69. doi:10.1016/j.jfs.2017.09.003

Hutson, E., Laing, E., & Ye, M. (2019). Mutual fund ownership and foreign exchange risk in Chinese firms. *Journal of International Financial Markets, Institutions and Money*, *60*, 169–192. doi:10.1016/j.intfin.2018.12.012

Huyghebaert, N., & Xu, W. (2015). What determines the market share of investment banks in Chinese domestic IPOs? *China Economic Review*, *34*, 150–168. doi:10.1016/j.chieco.2015.05.001

Jia, N., Huang, K. G., & Man Zhang, C. (2019). Public governance, corporate governance, and firm innovation: An examination of state-owned enterprises. *Academy of Management Journal*, *62*(1), 220–247. doi:10.5465/amj.2016.0543

Jiang, F., & Kim, A. K. (2015). Corporate governance in China: A modern perspective. *Journal of Corporate Finance*, *32*, 190–216. doi:10.1016/j.jcorpfin.2014.10.010

Keasey, K., & Wright, M. (1993). Issues in corporate accountability and governance: An editorial. *Accounting and Business Research, 23*(sup1), 291-303.

Kiel, G. C., & Nicholson, G. J. (2003). Board composition and corporate performance: How the Australian experience informs contrasting theories of corporate governance. *Corporate Governance*, *11*(3), 189–205. doi:10.1111/1467-8683.00318

Kreab, G. A. (2014). *China's IPO Reboot*. http://www.kreab.com/wp-content/uploads/2014/01/Kreab-Gavin-Anderson-Research-Asia-Report-on-IPO-Reform-in-China.pdf

Lee, J. M., Kim, J., & Bae, J. (2020). Founder CEOs and innovation: Evidence from CEO sudden deaths in public firms. *Research Policy*, *49*(1), 103862. doi:10.1016/j.respol.2019.103862

Lin, C., Lin, P., Song, F. M., & Li, C. (2011). Managerial incentives, CEO characteristics and corporate innovation in China's private sector. *Journal of Comparative Economics*, *39*(2), 176–190. doi:10.1016/j.jce.2009.12.001

Lin, C., Ma, Y., & Su, D. (2009). Corporate governance and firm efficiency: Evidence from China's publicly listed firms. *Managerial and Decision Economics*, *30*(3), 193–209. doi:10.1002/mde.1447

Liu, H., & Fong, M. W. (2010). Board characteristics of medium and large Chinese companies. *Corporate Governance: The International Journal of Business in Society*, *10*(2), 163–175. doi:10.1108/14720701011035684

Liu, Q., & Lu, Z. J. (2007). Corporate governance and earnings management in Chinese listed companies: A tunneling perspective. *Journal of Corporate Finance*, *13*(5), 881–906. doi:10.1016/j.jcorpfin.2007.07.003

Lo, Y. L., Li, Y., & Chan, K. C. (2019). Contemporary Innovation in China. *Chinese Economy*, *52*(5), 387–399. doi:10.1080/10971475.2019.1617925

Mangena, M., Tauringana, V., & Chamisa, E. (2012). Corporate boards, ownership structure and firm performance in an environment of severe political and economic crisis. *British Journal of Management*, *23*(S1), S23–S41. doi:10.1111/j.1467-8551.2011.00804.x

Minetti, R., Murro, P., & Paiella, M. (2012). *Ownership structure, governance, and innovation: Evidence from Italy*. Government of the Italian Republic (Italy), Ministry of Economy and Finance, Department of the Treasury Working Paper, Number 10.

O'Connor, M., & Rafferty, M. (2012). Corporate governance and innovation. *Journal of Financial and Quantitative Analysis*, *47*(02), 397–413. doi:10.1017/S002210901200004X

Peng, M. W., Zhang, S., & Li, X. (2007). CEO duality and firm performance during China's institutional transitions. *Management and Organization Review*, *3*(2), 205–225. doi:10.1111/j.1740-8784.2007.00069.x

Peng, W. Q., Wei, K. C. J., & Yang, Z. (2011). Tunneling or propping: Evidence from connected transactions in China. *Journal of Corporate Finance*, *17*(2), 306–325. doi:10.1016/j.jcorpfin.2010.08.002

Pi, L., & Timme, S. G. (1993). Corporate control and bank efficiency. *Journal of Banking & Finance*, *17*(2), 515–530. doi:10.1016/0378-4266(93)90050-N

Price, D. P., Stoica, M., & Boncella, R. J. (2013). The relationship between innovation, knowledge, and performance in family and non-family firms: An analysis of SMEs. *Journal of Innovation and Entrepreneurship*, *2*(1), 1–20. doi:10.1186/2192-5372-2-14

Qian, M., & Yeung, B. (2015). Bank financing and corporate governance. *Journal of Corporate Finance*, *32*, 258–270. doi:10.1016/j.jcorpfin.2014.10.006

Rechner, P. L., & Dalton, D. R. (1991). CEO duality and organizational performance: A longitudinal analysis. *Strategic Management Journal*, *12*(2), 155–160. doi:10.1002mj.4250120206

Saich, T. (2015). *The National People's Congress: Functions and Membership*. Ash Center for Democratic Governance and Innovation, Harvard Kennedy School.

Shan, Y. G., & McIver, R. P. (2011). Corporate governance mechanisms and financial performance in China: Panel data evidence on listed non-financial companies. *Asia Pacific Business Review*, *17*(3), 301–324. doi:10.1080/13602380903522325

Shapiro, D., Tang, Y., Wang, M., & Zhang, W. (2015). The effects of corporate governance and ownership on the innovation performance of Chinese SMEs. *Journal of Chinese Economic and Business Studies*, *1*(4), 311–335. doi:10.1080/14765284.2015.1090267

Talavera, O., Yin, S., & Zhang, M. (2018). Age diversity, directors' personal values, and bank performance. *International Review of Financial Analysis*, *55*, 60–79. doi:10.1016/j.irfa.2017.10.007

The National Development and Reform Commission of China. (2016). *The 13th five-year plan for economic and social development of the people's republic of China (2016-2020).* Central Compilation & Translation Press. https://en.ndrc.gov.cn/newsrelease/201612/P020161207645765233498.pdf

Tong, S., Junarsin, E., & Davidson, N. W., III. (2013). *A comparison of Chinese state-owned enterprise firm's boards and private firm's boards.* Paper presented at the 23rd International Business Research Conference, Melbourne, Australia.

Tribo, J. A., Berrone, P., & Surroca, J. (2007). Do the type and number of blockholders influence R&D investments? New evidence from Spain. *Corporate Governance, 15*(5), 828–842. doi:10.1111/j.1467-8683.2007.00622.x

Tricker, B. (2012). *Corporate governance: Principles, policies and practices* (2nd ed.). Oxford University Press.

UK Science & Innovation Network. (2015). *UK science & innovation network country snapshot: China.* UK Science & Innovation Network. https://www.gov.uk/government/uploads/system/uploads/attachment_data/file/471771/Science___Innovation_Country_Snapshot_-_China.pdf

Wang, K., & Shailer, G. (2015). Ownership concentration and firm performance in emerging markets: A meta-analysis. *Journal of Economic Surveys, 29*(2), 199–229. doi:10.1111/joes.12048

Woetzel, J., Seong, J., Leung, N., Ngai, J., Manyika, J., Madgvkar, A., Lund, S., & Mironenko, A. (2019). *China and the world: Inside the dynamics of a changing relationship.* McKinsey Global Institute. https://www.mckinsey.com/~/media/mckinsey/featured%20insights/china/china%20and%20the%20world%20inside%20the%20dynamics%20of%20a%20changing%20relationship/mgi-china-and-the-world-full-report-june-2019-vf.ashx

Wu, J., Li, S., & Li, Z. (2013). The contingent value of CEO political connections: A study on IPO performance in China. *Asia Pacific Journal of Management, 30*(4), 1087–1114. doi:10.100710490-012-9300-1

Xing, V. (2003). Corporate Governance in People's Republic of China: A new code for listed companies. *Bond Law Review, 15*(1), 376–397.

Yu, M., & Ashton, J. K. (2015). Board leadership structure for Chinese public listed companies. *China Economic Review, 34*, 236–248. doi:10.1016/j.chieco.2015.01.010

Yu, X. (2017). *Chinese regulator to fast-track reform of registration-based initial public offerings system.* Telegraph. https://www.telegraph.co.uk/news/world/china-watch/business/china-to-reform-ipo-system/

Zhang, Q., Chen, L., & Feng, T. (2014). Mediation or moderation? The role of R&D investment in the relationship between corporate governance and firm performance: Empirical evidence from the Chinese IT industry. *Corporate Governance, 22*(6), 501–517. doi:10.1111/corg.12073

Zhou, K. Z., Gao, G. Y., & Zhao, H. (2017). State ownership and firm innovation in China: An integrated view of institutional and efficiency logics. *Administrative Science Quarterly, 62*(2), 375–404. doi:10.1177/0001839216674457

Zhu, Y. (2019). Banks' governance and innovation: Evidence from the listed firms in China. *Emerging Markets Finance & Trade, 55*(11), 2409–2424. doi:10.1080/1540496X.2018.1483229

ENDNOTES

1 For example, in Chapter 10 of the 10th Five-Year (2001-2005) Plan of China, Chapters 3 and 7 of the 11th Five-Year (2006-2010) Plan of China, Chapters 3 and 7 of the 12th Five-Year (2011-2015) Plan of China, and Chapter 3 and 7 of the 13th Five-Year (2016-2020) Plan of China (The National Development and Reform Commission of China, 2016).

2 The Torch Programme was launched in the 1980s to boost the technological progress in small and medium-size enterprises (SMEs), especially the rural township and village enterprises (TVEs). The 973 and 985 Programmes were launched in the 1990s, and in recent years, to boost to the research capacities of universities through the establishment of national key laboratories and special support for key research scientists attracted from home and abroad. (http://www.most.gov.cn/eng/programmes1/200610/t20061009_36223.htm) (http://www.chinatorch.gov.cn/english/xhtml/Program.html).

3 The Hundred, Thousand and Ten Thousands Plan was launched for the Chinese Academy of Sciences in 1990 and has been ongoing until now. It aims to attract one hundred of the best scientists to lead the national key laboratories and institutes, one thousand top scientists to lead research programmes, and ten thousand high level researchers to work within the research network covered by the Chinese Academy of Sciences.

4 For example, the technology development expenditures of a company could be calculated as 150% of the real spending in tax deduction (Dong & Gou, 2010); high-technology start-ups in the national high-tech industrial development zones could enjoy 2-year tax-exemption and a 15% income tax rate from the third year (Ministry of Finance People's Republic of China, 2006).

Compilation of References

Aamir, A. C., & Sohail, Z. (2006). Antecedents and Consequences of Organizational Commitment Among Pakistani University Teachers. *Applied H.R.M. Research*, *11*(1), 39–64.

AAOIFI. (2005). Accounting, Auditing and Governance Standards (for Islamic Financial Institutions). Manama, Bahrain: AAOIFI.

Abbott, L. J., Parker, S., & Peters, G. F. (2004). Audit committee characteristics and restatements. *Auditing*, *23*(1), 69–87. doi:10.2308/aud.2004.23.1.69

Abbott, L. J., Parker, S., & Peters, G. F. (2012). Internal audit assistance and external audit timeliness. *Auditing*, *31*(4), 3–20. doi:10.2308/ajpt-10296

Abbott, L. J., Park, Y., & Parker, S. (2000). The effects of audit committee activity and independence on corporate fraud. *Managerial Finance*, *26*(11), 55–68. doi:10.1108/03074350010766990

Abdallah, A. A. N., & Ismail, A. K. (2017). Corporate governance practices, ownership structure, and corporate performance in the GCC countries. *Journal of International Financial Markets, Institutions and Money*, *46*, 98–115. doi:10.1016/j.intfin.2016.08.004

Abdille, H. M. (2013). *The Effects Of Strategic Succession Planning On Family Owned Businesses In Kenya* (Unpublished dissertation). School of Business, University of Nairobi.

Abdul Rahman, A., & Bukair, A. A. (2013). The Influence of the Sharia Supervision Board on Corporate Social Responsibility Disclosure by Islamic Banks of Gulf Co-Operation Council Countries. *Asian Journal of Business and Accounting*, *6*(2).

Abdul Rahman, R., & Ali, F. H. (2006). Board, Audit Committee, Culture and Earnings Management: Malaysian Evidence. *Managerial Auditing Journal*, *21*(7), 783–804. doi:10.1108/02686900610680549

Abdulrasool, F., & Turnbull, S. (2020). The Role of It Governance in Enhancing the Performance of Smart Universities. *Joint European-US Workshop on Applications of Invariance in Computer Vision*, 708-720. 10.1007/978-3-030-44289-7_66

Abdussamad, M., & Kabir, H. (2000). The perfomance of Malaysian Islamic banks during 1984-1997: An exploratory study. *International Journal of Islamic Financial Services*, *1*(3).

Abed, S., Roberts, C., & Hussainey, K. (2014). Managers' incentives for issuing cash flow forecasts. *International Journal of Accounting. Auditing and Performance Evaluation*, *10*(2), 133–152.

Abernathy, J. L., Beyer, B., Masli, A., & Stefaniak, C. M. (2015). How the source of audit committee accounting expertise influences financial reporting timeliness. *Current Issues in Auditing*, *9*(1), 1–P9. doi:10.2308/ciia-51030

Abu Jibril, A. Y., & Al-Thunaibat, A. (2016). The Effect of Internal Audit on Limiting Earnings Management for Industrial Companies Listed on The Oman Financial Market. *The Jordanian Journal of Business Administration*, *12*(4), 789–811.

Abu Qa'dan, M. B. A., & Suwaidan, M. S. (2019). Board composition, ownership structure and corporate social responsibility disclosure: The case of Jordan. *Social Responsibility Journal*, *15*(1), 28–46.

Acaravcı, S. K., Kandır, S. Y., & Zelka, A. (2015). Investigating the Impact of Corporate Governance Over the Performance of BIST Companies. *Academic Review of Economics and Administrative Sciences*, *8*(1), 171–183.

Ackers, B., & Eccles, N. S. (2015). Mandatory corporate social responsibility assurance practices: The case of King III in South Africa. *Accounting, Auditing & Accountability Journal*, *28*(4), 515–550.

Adams, R. B., & Ferreira, D. (2009). Women in the boardroom and their impact on governance and performance. *Journal of Financial Economics*, *94*(2), 291–309. doi:10.1016/j.jfineco.2008.10.007

Adams, R. B., Hermalin, B. E., & Weisbach, M. S. (2010). The role of boards of directors in corporate governance: A conceptual framework and survey. *Journal of Economic Literature*, *48*(1), 58–107. doi:10.1257/jel.48.1.58

Adegbie, F., Salawu, R. O., & Shiyanbola, A. (2019). Effect of Corporate Governance on Earnings Quality of Quoted Financial and Non-Financial Firms in Nigeria. *Journal of Research in Business and Management*, *7*(3), 40–51.

Afzal, M., & Habib, M. D. (2018). Corporate Governance and Earnings Management: A Model and Empirical Investigation from Karachi Stock Exchange. *Journal of Finance and Economics Research*, *3*(2), 51–67. doi:10.20547/jfer1803204

Agoglia, C. P., Beaudoin, C., & Tsakumis, G. T. (2009). The effect of documentation structure and task-specific experience on auditors' ability to identify control weaknesses. *Behavioral Research in Accounting*, *21*(1), 1–17. doi:10.2308/bria.2009.21.1.1

Agrawal, A., & Knoeber, C. R. (1996). Firm Performance and Mechanisms to Control Agency Problems between Managers and Shareholders. *Journal of Financial and Quantitative Analysis*, *31*(3), 377. doi:10.2307/2331397

Agrawal, A., & Mandelker, G. N. (1990). Large Shareholders and the Monitoring of Managers: The Case of Antitakeover Charter Amendments. *Journal of Financial and Quantitative Analysis*, *25*(2), 143. doi:10.2307/2330821

Aguilera, R. (2005). Corporate governance and director accountability: An institutional comparative perspective. *British Journal of Management*, *16*(s1), S39–S53. doi:10.1111/j.1467-8551.2005.00446.x

Aguilera, R. V., Desender, K., Bednar, M. K., & Lee, J. H. (2015). Connecting the dots: Bringing external corporate governance into the corporate governance puzzle. *The Academy of Management Annals*, *9*(1), 483–573. doi:10.5465/19416520.2015.1024503

Aguilera, R. V., & Jackson, G. (2003). The cross-national diversity of corporate governance: Dimensions and determinants. *Academy of Management Review*, *28*(3), 447–465. doi:10.5465/amr.2003.10196772

Aguilera, R. V., Judge, W. Q., & Terjesen, S. A. (2018). Corporate governance deviance. *Academy of Management Review*, *43*(1), 87–109. doi:10.5465/amr.2014.0394

Ahmed Haji, A. (2013). Corporate social responsibility disclosures over time: Evidence from Malaysia. *Managerial Auditing Journal*, *28*(7), 647–676.

Akbar, S., Hughes, J. P., Syed, R., & Shah, Z. A. (2016). More on the relationship between corporate governance and firm performance in the UK: Evidence from the aplication of generalized method of moments estimation. *Research in International Business and Finance*, *38*, 417–429. doi:10.1016/j.ribaf.2016.03.009

Akerlof, G. (1970). *The Market for "Lemons"*. Quality Uncertainty and the Market Mechanism.

Akhtar, T., Tareq, M. A., Sakti, M. R. P., & Khan, A. A. (2018). Corporate governance and cash holdings: The way forward. *Qualitative Research in Financial Markets*, *10*(2), 152–170. doi:10.1108/QRFM-04-2017-0034

Akhtaruddin, M., Hossain, M. A., Hossain, M., & Yao, L. (2009). Corporate governance and voluntary disclosure in corporate annual reports of Malaysian listed firms. *Journal of Applied Management Accounting Research*, *7*(1), 1.

Akimova, I., & Schwodiauer, G. (2004). Ownership Structure, Corporate Governance, and Enterprise Performance: Empirical Results for Ukraine. *International Advances in Economic Research*, *10*(1), 28–42. doi:10.1007/BF02295575

Alabdullah, T. T. Y. (2018). The relationship between ownership structure and firm financial performance. *Benchmarking*, *25*(1), 319–333. doi:10.1108/BIJ-04-2016-0051

Alagha, H. S. (2016). *Corporate governance practices and firm performance of listed companies including Islamic financial institutions in the United Arab Emirates* (Doctoral dissertation). Victoria University.

Al-Akra, M., Ali, M. J., & Marashdeh, O. (2009). Development of Accounting Regulation in Jordan. *The International Journal of Accounting*, *44*(2), 163–186. doi:10.1016/j.intacc.2009.03.003

Alam, F. (2011). *Corporate Governance: The Role of Non-Executive Directors and an International Perspective*. Available at SSRN 1894943

Alareeni, B. (2018). Does Corporate Governance Influence Earnings Management in Listed Companies in Bahrain Bourse? *Journal of Asia Business Studies*, *12*(4), 551–570. doi:10.1108/JABS-06-2017-0082

Al-Bassam, W. M., Ntim, C. G., Opong, K. K., & Downs, Y. (2018). Corporate boards and ownership structure as antecedents of corporate governance disclosure in Saudi Arabian publicly listed corporations. *Business & Society*, *57*(2), 335–377. doi:10.1177/0007650315610611

Albawwat, A., & Basah, M. (2015). Corporate governance and voluntary disclosure of interim financial reporting in Jordan. *Journal of Public Administration and Governance*, *5*(2), 100–127.

Albedal, F., Hamdan, A. M., & Zureigat, Q. (2020). Audit Committee Characteristics and Earnings Quality: Evidence From Bahrain Bourse. In *Corporate Governance Models and Applications in Developing Economies* (pp. 23–49). IGI Global. doi:10.4018/978-1-5225-9607-3.ch002

Albitar, K. (2015). Firm characteristics, governance attributes and corporate voluntary disclosure: A study of Jordanian listed companies. *International Business Research*, *8*(3), 1–10. doi:10.5539/ibr.v8n3p1

Albrecht, W. S., Howe, K. R., & Romney, M. B. (1984). *Deterring fraud: the internal auditor's perspective*. Inst of Internal Auditors.

Alesina, A., & Ferrara, E. L. (2005). Ethnic diversity and economic performance. *Journal of Economic Literature*, *43*(3), 762–800. doi:10.1257/002205105774431243

Al-Fad, M. A., & Hamad, M. A. (2015). Corporate Governance and its Role in Limiting Earnings Management A Test Study of the Iraq Case. Al-Qadisiyah. *Journal of Administrative and Economic Sciences*, *17*(3), 192–221.

Alfraih, M. M., & Almutawa, A. M. (2017). Voluntary disclosure and corporate governance: Empirical evidence from Kuwait. *International Journal of Law and Management*, *59*(2), 217–236. doi:10.1108/IJLMA-10-2015-0052

Alghamdi, S. A. (2012). *Investigation into Earnings Management Practices and the Role of Corporate Governance and External Audit in Emerging Markets!* Empirical Evidence from Saudi Listed Companies.

Algharaballi, E., & Albuloushi, S. (2008). Evaluating the specification and power of discretionary accruals models in Kuwait. *Journal of Derivatives & Hedge Funds*, *14*(3-4), 251–264. doi:10.1057/jdhf.2008.23

Al-Haddad, L., & Whittington, M. (2019). The impact of corporate governance mechanisms on real and accrual earnings management practices: evidence from Jordan. *Corporate Governance: The International Journal of Business in Society, 19*(6), 1167-1186.

Al-Hadi, A., Hasan, M. M., & Habib, A. (2016). Risk committee, firm life cycle, and market risk disclosures. *Corporate Governance, 24*(2), 145–170. doi:10.1111/corg.12115

Al-Hamadeen, R., & Badran, S. (2014). Nature and determinants of CSR disclosure: Experience of the Jordanian public shareholding companies. *European Journal of Business and Management, 6*(13).

Alhazaimeh, A., Palaniappan, R., & Almsafir, M. (2014). The impact of corporate governance and ownership structure on voluntary disclosure in annual reports among listed Jordanian companies. *Procedia: Social and Behavioral Sciences, 129*, 341–348.

Ali, K. E. (2019). *10 Principles of corporate governance*. Available at https://ethicalboardroom.com

Ali, M. (2013). *Corporate Governance and its Role in Reducing Earnings Practices - An Analytical Field Study on Khartoum Stock Exchange* (Master Thesis). Al-Neelain University, College of Graduate Studies, Sudan.

Ali, S., & Green, P. (2012). Effective Information Technology (It) Governance Mechanisms: An It Outsourcing Perspective. *Information Systems Frontiers, 14*(2), 179-193.

Ali, M., Ng, Y. L., & Kulik, C. T. (2014). Board age and gender diversity: A test of competing linear and curvilinear predictions. *Journal of Business Ethics, 125*(3), 497–512. doi:10.100710551-013-1930-9

Ali, S., Green, P., & Robb, A. (2015). Information technology investment governance: What is it and does it matter? *International Journal of Accounting Information Systems, 18*, 1–25. doi:10.1016/j.accinf.2015.04.002

Al-Janadi, Y., Al-Janadi, Y., Abdul Rahman, R., Abdul Rahman, R., Alazzani, A., & Alazzani, A. (2016). Does government ownership affect corporate governance and corporate disclosure? Evidence from Saudi Arabia. *Managerial Auditing Journal, 31*(8/9), 871–890. doi:10.1108/MAJ-12-2015-1287

Al-Janadi, Y., Rahman, R. A., & Omar, N. H. (2013). Corporate governance mechanisms and voluntary disclosure in Saudi Arabia. *Research Journal of Finance & Accounting, 4*(4), 25–36.

Aljifri, K., & Moustafa, M. (2007). The impact of corporate governance mechanisms on the performance of UAE firms: An empirical analysis. *Journal of Economic and Administrative Sciences, 23*(2), 71–93. doi:10.1108/10264116200700008

Alkababji, M. W. (2019). The Role of Corporate Governance in Controlling the Earnings Management Practices of Palestinian Shareholding Industrial Companies: A Field Study. *Arab Journal of Management, 39*, 99–124.

Al-Kabbaji, M. (2019). The Role of Corporate Governance in Controlling Earnings Management Practices in Palestinian Public Shareholding Industrial Companies - A Field Study. *The Arab Journal of Management, 39*(2), 99–124.

Allegrini, M., & Greco, G. (2013). Corporate boards, audit committees and voluntary disclosure: Evidence from Italian listed companies. *The Journal of Management and Governance, 17*(1), 187–216.

Al-Mamun, A., Yasser, Q. R., Entebang, H., & Nathan, T. M. (2013). Gender diversity and economic performance of firms: Evidences from emerging market. *Journal of Economic Development, Management, IT. Finance and Marketing, 5*(2), 100–110.

Al-Matari, E. M., Al-Dhaafri, H. S., & Al-Swidi, A. K. (2019). The Effect of Government Ownership, Foreign Ownership, Institutional Ownership, and Audit Quality on Firm Performance of Listed Companies in Oman: A Conceptual Framework. *Proceedings of the Second International Conference on the Future of ASEAN (ICoFA) 2017, 1*, 585-595.

Al-Matari, E. M., Al-Swidi, A. K., & Fadzil, F. H. B. (2014). The measurements of firm performance's dimensions. *Asian Journal of Finance & Accounting*, *6*(1), 24–49. doi:10.5296/ajfa.v6i1.4761

Alnabsha, A., Abdou, H., Ntim, C., & Elamer, A. (2018). Corporate boards, ownership structures and corporate disclosures: Evidence from a developing country. *Journal of Applied Accounting Research*, *19*(1), 20–41. doi:10.1108/JAAR-01-2016-0001

Al-Najjar, B. (2013). The financial determinants of corporate cash holdings: Evidence from some emerging markets. *International Business Review*, *22*(1), 77–88. Advance online publication. doi:10.1016/j.ibusrev.2012.02.004

AlNasser, Z. (2018). *The effect of internal corporate governance on earning quality in GCC country* (Unpublished thesis). Trinity College University.

Alonso, P., Palenzuela, V., & Iturriaga, F. (2000). *Managers' Discretionary Behavior, Earnings Management and Corporate Governance: An Empirical International Analysis*. Working Paper, Universidad de Valladolid.

Alotaibi, K. O., & Hussainey, K. (2016). Determinants of CSR disclosure quantity and quality: Evidence from non-financial listed firms in Saudi Arabia. *International Journal of Disclosure and Governance*, *13*(4), 364–393. doi:10.1057/jdg.2016.2

Alowaihan, A. K. (2004). Gender and business performance of Kuwait small firms: A comparative approach. *International Journal of Commerce and Management*, *14*(3/4), 69–82. doi:10.1108/10569210480000185

Alqatan, A., Chbib, I., & Hussainey, K. (2019). How does board structure impact on firm performance in the UK? *Corporate Board: Role, Duties and Composition, 15*(2).

Alsaeed, K. (2006). The association between firm-specific characteristics and disclosure: The case of Saudi Arabia. *Managerial Auditing Journal*, *21*(5), 476–496. doi:10.1108/02686900610667256

Al-Shammari, B., & Al-Saidi, M. (2014). Kuwaiti women and firm performance. *International Journal of Business and Management*, *9*(8), 51. doi:10.5539/ijbm.v9n8p51

Alshannag, F. M., Basah, M. Y. A., & Khairi, K. F. (2016). The Level of Corporate Social Responsibility Disclosure in Jordan. *International Journal of Accounting Research*, *42*(3968), 1–15.

Alshehri, A. (2015). *Corporate governance and the financial performance of Islamic banks: some new evidence. The World Finance Conference (WFC 2015)*, Buenos Aires, Argentina.

Alshhadat, M. Q. A. (2017). *The Effect Of Corporate Governance On The Intellectual Capital Disclosure; Evidence From Jordan* (Doctoral dissertation). University of Reading.

Altman, W. (2009). Who's next in line? *Engineering & Technology*, *4*(15), 72–75. doi:10.1049/et.2009.1516

Alvarado, N. R., Fuentes, P., & Laffarga, J. (2019). Do Auditors Mitigate Earnings Management During Economic Crisis? *Revista de Contabilidad*, *22*(1), 6–20.

Al-Wakeel, H. A. (2019). The effect of the mandatory periodic change of the external auditor on reducing earnings management practices in the Egyptian Business Environment - An Applied Study. *ATASU*, *23*(4), 1–48.

American Institute of Certified Public Accountants. Study Group on the Objectives of Financial Statements. (1973). Objectives of financial statements (Vol. 1). American Institute of Certified Public Accountants.

Anderson, R. C., Mansi, S., & Reeb, D. M. (2004). Board characteristics, accounting report integrity, and the cost of debt. *Journal of Accounting and Economics*, *37*(3), 315–342. doi:10.1016/j.jacceco.2004.01.004

Anderson, R. C., & Reeb, D. M. (2003). Founding-Family Ownership and Firm Performance: Evidence from the S&P 500. *The Journal of Finance*, *58*(3), 1301–1328. doi:10.1111/1540-6261.00567

Andrijasevic, M. (2018). *Theoretical Assumptions of Agency Problem*. https://www.researchgate.net

Anwar, H., & Buvanendra, S. (2019). *Earnings Management and Ownership Structure: Evidence from Sri Lanka*. Academic Press.

Anwar, W., & Tabassum, N. (2011). Impact of ownership concentration on the operating performance of Pakistani firms. *Asian Economic and Financial Review*, *1*, 147–150.

Appelbaum, S. H., Gunkel, H., Benyo, C., Ramadan, S., Sakkal, F., & Wolff, D. (2012). Transferring corporate knowledge via succession planning: Analysis and solutions–Part 1. *Industrial and Commercial Training*, *44*(5), 281–289. doi:10.1108/00197851211245031

Ararat, M., Aksu, M. H., & Tansel Cetin, A. (2010). *The impact of board diversity on boards' monitoring intensity and firm performance: evidence from the Istanbul Stock Exchange*. Working paper, 1-33.

Arcay, M. R. B., & Vasquez, M. F. M. (2005). Corporate Characteristics, governance rules and the extent of voluntary disclosure in Spain. *Advances in Accounting*, *21*, 299–331. doi:10.1016/S0882-6110(05)21013-1

Archer, S., & Karim, R. A. (2007). *Islamic finance the regulatory challenge*. John Wiley & sons. doi:10.1002/9781118390443

Argüden, R. Y. (2010). *A corporate governance model: building responsible boards and sustainable businesses*. International Finance Corporation.

Arıoglu, E. (2018). *Female Directors and Earnings Management: Director Characteristics*. Retractive from https://www.researchgate.net/publication/329443984_Female_Directors_and_Earnings_Management_Director_Characteristics/stats

Armstrong, C. S., Barth, M. E., Jagolinzer, A. D., & Riedl, E. J. (2009). Market Reaction to the Adoption of IFRS in Europe. *Accounting Review*. Available at SSRN: http://ssrn.com/abstract=903429

Arora, A., & Bodhanwala, S. (2018). Relationship between corporate governance index and firm performance: Indian evidence. *Global Business Review*, *19*(3), 675–689. doi:10.1177/0972150917713812

Arora, A., & Sharma, C. (2016). Corporate governance and firm performance in developing countries: Evidence from India. *Corporate Governance*, *16*(2), 420–436. doi:10.1108/CG-01-2016-0018

Arslan, M., & Abidin, S. (2019). Institutional Determinants of Good Corporate Governance: Evidence from Emerging Economy. In *23rd New Zealand Finance Colloquium, 2019a Lincoln University*. Lincoln, New Zealand: NZFC.

Arslan, M., Abidin, S., Alqatan, A. & Roudaki, J. (2019). Corporate Governance in Extreme Institutional Environment: Evidence From Emerging Economy. *Corporate Ownership & Control,* 17.

Arslan, M., Abidin, S., Alqatan, A., & Roudaki, J. (2019). Corporate Governance in Extreme Institutional Environment: Evidence From Emerging Economy. *Corporate Ownership & Control, 17*(1).

Arslan, M., & Abidin, S. (2019b). Nexus between corporate governance practices and cost of capital in PSX listed firms. *Cogent Economics & Finance*, *7*(1), 1600222. doi:10.1080/23322039.2019.1600222

Arslan, M., & Alqatan, A. (2020). Role of institutions in shaping corporate governance system: Evidence from emerging economy. *Heliyon*, *6*(3), e03520. doi:10.1016/j.heliyon.2020.e03520 PMID:32181393

Arslan, M., & Roudaki, J. (2019). Examining the role of employee engagement in the relationship between organisational cynicism and employee performance. *The International Journal of Sociology and Social Policy, 39*(1/2), 118–137. doi:10.1108/IJSSP-06-2018-0087

Arthur, N., Chen, H., & Tang, Q. (2019). Corporate ownership concentration and financial reporting quality: International evidence. *Journal of Financial Reporting and Accounting, 17*(1), 104–132. doi:10.1108/JFRA-07-2017-0051

Arun, T. G., Almahrog, Y. E., & Aribi, Z. A. (2015). Female directors and earnings management: Evidence from UK companies. *International Review of Financial Analysis, 39*, 137–146. doi:10.1016/j.irfa.2015.03.002

Asante-Darko, D., Adu Bonsu, B., Famiyeh, S., Kwarteng, A., & Goka, Y. (2018). Governance structures, cash holdings and firm value on the Ghana Stock Exchange. *Corporate Governance (Bingley), 18*(4), 671–685. doi:10.1108/CG-07-2017-0148

Ashbaugh, H., LaFond, R., & Mayhew, B. W. (2003). Do nonaudit services compromise auditor independence? Further evidence. *The Accounting Review, 78*(3), 611–639. doi:10.2308/accr.2003.78.3.611

Ashfaq, K., & Rui, Z. (2019). The effect of board & audit committee effectiveness on internal control disclosure under different regulatory environments in South Asia. *Journal of Financial Reporting and Accounting, 17*(2), 170–200. doi:10.1108/JFRA-09-2017-0086

Asogwa, C. I., Grace, N., Nnam, J. I., & Chukwunwike, O. D. (2019). Effect of Corporate Governance Board Leadership Models and Attributes on Earnings Quality of Quoted Nigerian Companies. *Cogent Business & Management, 6*(1), 2–24. doi:10.1080/23311975.2019.1683124

Athanasoglou, P. P., Brissimis, S. N., & Delis, M. D. (2005). *Bank-specific, industry-specific and macroeconomics determinants of bank profitability*. Bank of Greece working paper n°25.

Atkinson, A. B., & Stiglitz, J. E. (1980). *Lectures on public economics*. McGraw-Hill.

Attiya, Javid, & Iqbal. (2012). Ownership Concentration, Corporate Governance and Firm Performance: Evidence from Pakistan. Pakistan Institute of Development Economics.

Avloniti, A., Iatridou, A., Kaloupsis, I., & Vozikis, G. S. (2014). Sibling rivalry: Implications for the family business succession process. *The International Entrepreneurship and Management Journal, 10*(4), 661–678. doi:10.100711365-013-0271-6

Azeez, A. (2015). Corporate governance and firm performance: Evidence from Sri Lanka. *The Journal of Finance, 3*(1), 180–189.

Azzoz, A., & Khamees, B. (2016). The Impact of Corporate Governance Characteristics on Earnings Quality and Earnings Management: Evidence from Jordan. *Jordan Journal of Business Administration, 12*(1), 187–207. doi:10.12816/0030061

Badolato, P. G., Donelson, D. C., & Ege, M. (2014). Audit committee financial expertise and earnings management: The role of status. *Journal of Accounting and Economics, 58*(2-3), 208–230. doi:10.1016/j.jacceco.2014.08.006

Baele, L., Farroq, M., & Ongena, S. (2012). *Of Religion and Redemption: Evidence from Default on Islamic Loans.* CentER Discussion Paper Series No. 2012-014. Tilburg University.

Bahng, J. S. (2004). *Nonlinear Effects of Insider Ownership on Corporate Value: Korean Evidence.* SSRN Working Paper Series.

Bai, C., Liu, Q., Lu, J., Song, F. M., & Zhang, J. (2004). Corporate governance and market valuation in China. *Journal of Comparative Economics, 32*(4), 599–616. doi:10.1016/j.jce.2004.07.002

Baki, R. (2017). For supplier evaluation process through fuzzy Promethee method. *International Journal of Materials. Mechanics and Manufacturing*, *5*(3), 183–186.

Balsmeier, B., Fleming, L., & Manso, G. (2017). Independent boards and innovation. *Journal of Financial Economics*, *123*(3), 536–557. doi:10.1016/j.jfineco.2016.12.005

Baran, B. E., Shanock, L. R., & Miller, L. R. (2012). Advancing organizational support theory into the twenty-first century world of work. *Journal of Business and Psychology*, *27*(2), 123–147. doi:10.100710869-011-9236-3

Barka, H. B., & Legendre, F. (2017). Effect of the board of directors and the audit committee on firm performance: A panel data analysis. *The Journal of Management and Governance*, *21*(3), 737–755. doi:10.100710997-016-9356-2

Barney, J.B., & Clark, D.N. (2007). *Resource-based theory: Creating and sustaining competitive advantage*. Oxford University Press.

Barney, J. (1991). Firm resources and sustained competitive advantage. *Journal of Management*, *17*(1), 99–120. doi:10.1177/014920639101700108

Barney, J. B., Ketchen, D. J. Jr, & Wright, M. (2011). The future of resource-based theory revitalization or decline? *Journal of Management*, *37*(5), 1299–1315. doi:10.1177/0149206310391805

Barnhart, S. W., & Rosenstein, S. (1988). Board Composition, Managerial Ownership and Firm Performance: An Empirical Analysis. *Financial Review*, *33*(4), 1–16. doi:10.1111/j.1540-6288.1998.tb01393.x

Baron, D. P. (2008). Managerial contracting and corporate social responsibility. *Journal of Public Economics*, *92*(1-2), 268–288.

Barontini, R., & Bozzi, S. (2011). Board compensation and ownership structure: Empirical evidence for Italian listed companies. *The Journal of Management and Governance*, *15*(1), 59–89.

Barroso-Castro, C., Villegas-Periñan, M. D. M., & Casillas-Bueno, J. C. (2016). How boards' internal and external social capital interact to affect firm performance. *Strategic Organization*, *14*(1), 6–31. doi:10.1177/1476127015604799

Barth, M. E., Landsman, W. R., & Lang, M. H. (2007). *International Accounting Standards and Accounting Quality*. Stanford University Graduate School of Business Research Paper No. 1976. Available at SSRN: http://ssrn.com/abstract=688041

Bartov, E., Gul, F. A., & Tsui, J. S. L. (2001). Discretionary-accruals models and audit qualifications. *Journal of Accounting and Economics*, *30*(3), 421–452. doi:10.1016/S0165-4101(01)00015-5

Bar-Yosef, M. S., & Prencipe, A. (2013). The Impact of Corporate Governance and Earnings Management on Stock Market Liquidity in a Highly Concentrated Ownership Capital. *Journal of Accounting, Auditing & Finance*, *28*(3), 292–316. doi:10.1177/0148558X13492591

Basset, M., Koh, P. S., & Tutticci, I. (2007). The association between employee stock option disclosures and corporate governance. Evidence from enhanced disclosure regime. *The British Accounting Review*, *39*(4), 303–322. doi:10.1016/j.bar.2007.06.003

Basuony, M. A., Mohamed, E. K., & Samaha, K. (2018). Board structure and corporate disclosure via social media: An empirical study in the UK. *Online Information Review*.

Bates, T. W., Kahle, K. M., & Stulz, R. M. (2009). Why do U.S. firms hold so much more cash than they used to? *The Journal of Finance*, *64*(5), 1985–2021. Advance online publication. doi:10.1111/j.1540-6261.2009.01492.x

Batta, G., Sucre Heredia, R., & Weidenmier, M. (2014). Political connections and accounting quality under high expropriation risk. *European Accounting Review, 23*(4), 485–517. doi:10.1080/09638180.2014.906316

Baumol, W. J. (1952). The Transactions Demand for Cash: An Inventory Theoretic Approach. *The Quarterly Journal of Economics, 66*(4), 545. Advance online publication. doi:10.2307/1882104

Bayoud, N. S., Kavanagh, M., & Slaughter, G. (2012). Factors influencing levels of corporate social responsibility disclosure Libyan firms: A mixed study. *International Journal of Economics and Finance, 4*(4), 13–29.

Baysinger, B., & Hoskisson, R. E. (1990). The composition of boards of directors and strategic control: Effects on corporate strategy. *Academy of Management Review, 15*(1), 72–87. doi:10.5465/amr.1990.4308231

Beasley, M. S., Carcello, J. V., Hermanson, D. R., & Neal, T. L. (2009). The audit committee oversight process. *Contemporary Accounting Research, 26*(1), 65–122. doi:10.1506/car.26.1.3

Becker, C. P., Lawrence, H., & Sennetti, J. T. (2010). *The Effects of Type of Accounting Standard and Outcome Knowledge on Juror Evaluations of Auditor Responsibility* (Dissertation). Glenville State College, University of Mississippi, & Nova Southeastern University.

Becker, C., DeFond, M., Jiambalvo, J., & Subramanyan, K. R. (1998). The effect of audit quality on earnings management. *Contemporary Accounting Research, 15*(1), 1–24. doi:10.1111/j.1911-3846.1998.tb00547.x

Beckhart, B. H., & Keynes, J. M. (1936). The General Theory of Employment, Interest and Money. *Political Science Quarterly, 51*(4), 600. Advance online publication. doi:10.2307/2143949

Beck, T., Demirguc-Kunt, A., & Merrouche, O. (2013). Islamic Vs. Conventional Banking: Business Model, Efficiency and Stability. *Journal of Banking & Finance, 37*(2), 433–447. doi:10.1016/j.jbankfin.2012.09.016

Bédard, J., Chtourou, S. M., & Courteau, L. (2004). The effect of audit committee expertise, independence, and activity on aggressive earnings management. *Auditing, 23*(2), 13–35. doi:10.2308/aud.2004.23.2.13

Bedard, J., & Gendron, Y. (2010). Strengthening the financial reporting system: Can audit committees deliver? *International Journal of Auditing, 14*(2), 174–210. doi:10.1111/j.1099-1123.2009.00413.x

Bednar, M. K. (2012). Watchdog or lapdog? A behavioral view of the media as a corporate governance mechanism. *Academy of Management Journal, 55*(1), 131–150. doi:10.5465/amj.2009.0862

Beijerink, M. (2008). *Information quality of IFRS and US-GAAP: a comparison of multiple earnings attributes under IFRS and US-GAAP* (Dissertation). University of Twente.

Belkaoui. (1991). *Multinational Financial Accounting*. Academic Press.

Belkhir, M. (2009). Board of Directors' size and performance in the banking industry. *International Journal of Managerial Finance, 5*(2), 201–221. doi:10.1108/17439130910947903

Benlemlih, M., Shaukat, A., Qiu, Y., & Trojanowski, G. (2018). Environmental and social disclosures and firm risk. *Journal of Business Ethics, 152*(3), 613–626. PMID:30956372

Bennedsen, M., Fan, J. P., Jian, M., & Yeh, Y.-H. (2015). The family business map: Framework, selective survey, and evidence from Chinese family firm succession. *Journal of Corporate Finance, 33*, 212–226. doi:10.1016/j.jcorpfin.2015.01.008

Benner, M. J., & Ranganathan, R. (2012). Offsetting illegitimacy? How pressures from securities analysts influence incumbents in the face of new technologies. *Academy of Management Journal, 55*(1), 213–233. doi:10.5465/amj.2009.0530

Bennouri, M., Chtioui, T., Nagati, H., & Nekhili, M. (2018). Female board directorship and firm performance: What really matters? *Journal of Banking & Finance*, *88*, 267–291. doi:10.1016/j.jbankfin.2017.12.010

Bergeron, F., Croteau, A.-M., Uwizeyemungu, S., & Raymond, L. (2020). *A framework for research on information technology governance in SMEs. In Start-Ups and SMEs: Concepts, Methodologies, Tools, and Applications*. IGI Global.

Bergeron, F., Raymond, L., & Rivard, S. (2004). Ideal patterns of strategic alignment and business performance. *Information & Management*, *41*(8), 1003–1020. doi:10.1016/j.im.2003.10.004

Berk, J., & Demarzo, P. (2007). *Corporate finance* (International ed.). Pearson Education.

Berle, A. A. Jr, & Means, G. C. (1930). Corporations and the public investor. *The American Economic Review*, 54–71.

Berle, A., & Means, G. (1932). *The Modern Corporation and Private Property*. Harcourt, Brace & World.

Bernard, V. L., & Skinner, D. J. (1996). What motivates managers' choice of discretionary accruals? *Journal of Accounting and Economics*, *22*(1-3), 313–325. doi:10.1016/S0165-4101(96)00431-4

Bertomeu, J., Vaysman, I., & Xue, W. (2019). *Voluntary versus Mandatory Disclosure*. doi:10.2139srn.2872412

Bertoni, F., Meoli, M., & Vismara, S. (2014). Board independence, ownership structure and the valuation of IPOs in continental Europe. *Corporate Governance*, *22*(2), 116–131. doi:10.1111/corg.12051

Betz, M., O'Connell, L., & Shepard, J. M. (1989). Gender differences in proclivity for unethical behavior. *Journal of Business Ethics*, *8*(5), 321–324. doi:10.1007/BF00381722

Beyer, M., Czarnitzki, D., & Kraft, K. (2012). Managerial ownership, entrenchment and innovation. *Economics of Innovation and New Technology*, *21*(7), 679–699. doi:10.1080/10438599.2011.639978

Bhagat, S., & Black, B. S. (2002). *The Non-Correlation Between Board Independence*. Academic Press.

Bhagat, S., & Bolton, B. (2019). Corporate governance and firm performance: The sequel. *Journal of Corporate Finance*, *58*, 142–168. doi:10.1016/j.jcorpfin.2019.04.006

Bhattacharyya, A. (2014). Factors Associated with the Social and Environmental Reporting of Australian Companies. Australasian Accounting. *Business and Finance Journal*, *8*(1), 25–50.

Bierstaker, J. L., Brody, R. G., & Pacini, C. (2006). Accountants' perceptions regarding fraud detection and prevention methods. *Managerial Auditing Journal*, *21*(5), 520–535. doi:10.1108/02686900610667283

Bigelli, M., & Sánchez-Vidal, J. (2012). Cash holdings in private firms. *Journal of Banking & Finance*, *36*(1), 26–35. Advance online publication. doi:10.1016/j.jbankfin.2011.06.004

Bilir, H. (2018). The distinctive features of contemporary era in the context of globalization. *2nd International Congress on Multidisciplinary Studies*.

Binti Kasem, N., Mohamed Ibrahim, S. H., & Maliah, S. (2009). Sharia Auditing in Islamic Financial Institutions: Exploring the Gap Between the "Desired" and the "Actual". *Global Economy and Finance Journal*, *2*(2), 127–137.

Birkett, W. P., & Institute of Internal Auditors. (1999*). Internal auditing: the global landscape*. Academic Press.

Björnberg, Å., & Nicholson, N. (2012). Emotional ownership: The next generation's relationship with the family firm. *Family Business Review*, *25*(4), 374–390. doi:10.1177/0894486511432471

Bjuggren, P.-O., & Sund, L.-G. (2014). A contractual perspective on succession in family firms: A stakeholder view. *European Journal of Law and Economics*, *38*(2), 211–225. doi:10.100710657-012-9331-6

Blanca, A., Txomin, I., & Amaia, M. (2009). *Ownership Structure And Performance in Non-Listed Firms: Evidence From Spain. UPV/EHU*. University of the Basque Country.

Blue Ribbon Committee (BRC). (1999). *Report and Recommendations of the Blue Ribbon*. BRC.

Board, F. A. S. (2010). *Statement of Financial Accounting Concepts No. 8, Conceptual Framework for Financial Reporting*. Financial Accounting Foundation.

Boh, W. F., & Yellin, D. (2006). Using enterprise architecture standards in managing information technology. *Journal of Management Information Systems*, *23*(3), 163–207. doi:10.2753/MIS0742-1222230307

Bokpin, G. a., Isshaq, Z., & Aboagye-Otchere, F. (2011). Ownership structure, corporate governance and corporate liquidity policy: Evidence from the Ghana Stock Exchange. *Journal of Financial Economic Policy*. doi:10.1108/17576381111152236

Booth-Bell, D. (2018). Social capital as a new board diversity rationale for enhanced corporate governance. Corporate Governance. *The International Journal of Business in Society*, *18*(3), 425–439.

Boţa-Avram, C. (2008). The approaches of fraud from internal audit's point of view. *International Journal of Business Research*, *8*(2), 83–187.

Botica-Redmayne, N., & Laswad, F. (2010). *New Zealand Public sector audit fees and audit effort: the impact of IFRS adoption* (Dissertation). School of Accountancy, Massey University, New Zealand.

Botosan, C. A. (1997). Disclosure level and the cost of equity capital. *The Accounting Review*, *72*(3), 323–349.

Boubaker, S., Rouatbi, W., & Saffar, W. (2017). The role of multiple large shareholders in the choice of debt source. *Financial Management*, *46*(1), 241–274. doi:10.1111/fima.12148

Boubakri, N., El Ghoul, S., & Saffar, W. (2013). Cash holdings of politically connected firms. *Journal of Multinational Financial Management*, *23*(4), 338–355. Advance online publication. doi:10.1016/j.mulfin.2013.06.002

Bowen, P. L., Cheung, M.-Y. D., & Rohde, F. H. (2007). Enhancing It Governance Practices: A Model and Case Study of an Organization's Efforts. *International Journal of Accounting Information Systems*, *8*(3), 191-221.

Bowen, P. L., Cheung, M.-Y. D., & Rohde, F. H. (2007). Enhancing IT governance practices: A model and case study of an organization's efforts. *International Journal of Accounting Information Systems*, *8*(3), 191–221. doi:10.1016/j.accinf.2007.07.002

Bowerman, B. L., & O'Connell, R. T. (1990). *Linear statistical models: An applied approach*. Duxbury.

Boyd, B., Botero, I. C., & Fediuk, T. A. (2014). Incumbent decisions about succession transitions in family firms: A conceptual model. *International Journal of Financial Studies*, *2*(4), 335–358. doi:10.3390/ijfs2040335

Boynton, A. C., & Zmud, R. W. (1987). Information technology planning in the 1990's: Directions for practice and research. *Management Information Systems Quarterly*, *11*(1), 59–71. doi:10.2307/248826

Boynton, A. C., Zmud, R. W., & Jacobs, G. C. (1994). The influence of IT management practice on IT use in large organizations. *Management Information Systems Quarterly*, *18*(3), 299–318. doi:10.2307/249620

Bozec, R. (2005). Boards of directors, market discipline and firm performance. *Journal of Business Finance & Accounting*, *32*(9-10), 1921–1960. doi:10.1111/j.0306-686X.2005.00652.x

Bozzolan, S., Fabrizi, M., Mallin, C. A., & Michelon, G. (2015). Corporate social responsibility and earnings quality: International evidence. *The International Journal of Accounting*, *50*(4), 361–396. doi:10.1016/j.intacc.2015.10.003

Brackney, K., & Marden, R. E. (2009). Audit risk and IFRS. Does increased flexibility increase audit risk? *The CPA Journal*, 32–36.

Bradbury, M. E., Mak, Y. T., & Tan, S. M. (2006). Board characteristics, audit committee characteristics and abnormal accruals. *Pacific Accounting Review*, *18*(2), 18. doi:10.1108/01140580610732813

Brans, J.-P. (1982). *L'ingenierie de la decision: elaboration d'instruments d'aide a la decision. la methode PROMETHEE.* Universite Laval, Colloque d'aide a la Decision, Quebec, Canada.

Brans, J.-P., & Mareschal, B. (2005). *PROMETHEE methods, Figueira vd* (C. D. A. MultipleState of the Art Survey, Ed.). Springer Science.

Brans, J.-P., & Vincke, P. (1985). A preference ranking organization method: The PROMETHEE method for MCDM. *Management Science*, *31*(6), 647–656. doi:10.1287/mnsc.31.6.647

Breton-Miller, I. L., Miller, D., & Steier, L. P. (2004). Toward an integrative model of effective FOB succession. *Entrepreneurship Theory and Practice*, *28*(4), 305–328. doi:10.1111/j.1540-6520.2004.00047.x

Brickley, J. A., Coles, J. L., & Terry, R. L. (1994). Outside directors and the adoption of poison pills. *Journal of Financial Economics*, *35*(3), 371–390. doi:10.1016/0304-405X(94)90038-8

Brockhaus, R. H. (2004). Family business succession: Suggestions for future research. *Family Business Review*, *17*(2), 165–177. doi:10.1111/j.1741-6248.2004.00011.x

Brockmann, E. N., Hoffman, J. J., Dawley, D. D., & Fornaciari, C. J. (2004). The Impact of CEO Duality and Prestige on a Bankrupt Organization. *Journal of Managerial Issues*. Advance online publication. doi:10.2307/40604453

Brown, N., & Deegan, C. (1998). The public disclosure of environmental performance information—A dual test of media agenda setting theory and legitimacy theory. *Accounting and Business Research*, *29*(1), 21–41.

Bryce, M., Ali, M. J., & Mather, P. R. (2015). Accounting quality in the pre-/post-IFRS adoption periods and the impact on audit committee effectiveness—Evidence from Australia. *Pacific-Basin Finance Journal*, *35*, 163–181. doi:10.1016/j.pacfin.2014.12.002

Buallay, A., & Al-Ajmi, J. (2019). The role of audit committee attributes in corporate sustainability reporting: Evidence from banks in the Gulf Cooperation Council. *Journal of Applied Accounting Research*.

Buallay, A., Hamdan, A., & Zureigat, Q. (2017). Corporate governance and firm performance: Evidence from Saudi Arabia. *Australasian Accounting. Business and Finance Journal*, *11*(1), 78–98.

Bueno, G., Marcon, R., Pruner-da-Silva, A. L., & Ribeirete, F. (2018). The role of the board in voluntary disclosure. *Corporate Governance*, *18*(5), 886–910. doi:10.1108/CG-09-2017-0205

Buhk, C., Sánchez Gómez, P., & Hensen, I. (2005). Plant regeneration mechanisms during early post-fire succession in south-eastern Spain. *Feddes Repertorium: Zeitschrift für botanische Taxonomie und Geobotanik, 116*(5-6), 392-404.

Bukovansky, M. (2006). The hollowness of anti-corruption discourse. *Review of International Political Economy*, *13*(2), 181–209. doi:10.1080/09692290600625413

Bunce, L. (2013). Succession Planning and Its Impact on Organizational Performance. *American Journal of Behavioural Science and Psychology*, *3*(2), 86–96.

Bushee, B. J. (1998). The influence of institutional investors on myopic R&D investment behavior. *The Accounting Review*, 305–333.

Bushee, B. J. (2004). Discussion of disclosure practices of foreign companies interacting with US markets. *Journal of Accounting Research, 42*(2), 509–525. doi:10.1111/j.1475-679X.2004.00147.x

Bushee, B. J., & Noe, C. F. (2000). Corporate disclosure practices, institutional investors, and stock return volatility. *Journal of Accounting Research, 38*, 171–202. doi:10.2307/2672914

Byrd, J. W., & Hickman, K. A. (1992). Do outside directors monitor managers?: Evidence from tender offer bids. *Journal of Financial Economics, 32*(2), 195–221. doi:10.1016/0304-405X(92)90018-S

Byrd, T. A., Lewis, B. R., & Bryan, R. W. (2006). The leveraging influence of strategic alignment on IT investment: An empirical examination. *Information & Management, 43*(3), 308–321. doi:10.1016/j.im.2005.07.002

Cabrera-Suarez, K. (2005). Leadership transfer and the successor's development in the family firm. *The Leadership Quarterly, 16*(1), 71–96. doi:10.1016/j.leaqua.2004.09.010

Cadbury Committee. (1992). Report of the committee on the financial aspects of corporate governance. Gee.

Cairns, T. D. (2011). Who's up next? Most companies fail to plan for leadership succession. *Employment Relations Today, 38*(2), 27–34. doi:10.1002/ert.20341

Calkins, K. G. (2016). Andrews University. *Applied Statistics-Lesson, 5.*

Calkoen, W. (2011). The One-Tier Board in the Changing and Converging World of Corporate Governance: A comparative study of boards in the UK. Academic Press.

Calkoen, W. J. (Ed.). (2014). The corporate governance review. Law Business Research, Limited.

Cao, G., Wiengarten, F., & Humphreys, P. (2011). Towards a contingency resource-based view of IT business value. *Systemic Practice and Action Research, 24*(1), 85–106. doi:10.100711213-010-9178-0

Caprio, L., Faccio, M., & McConnell, J. J. (2013). Sheltering corporate assets from political extraction. *Journal of Law Economics and Organization, 29*(2), 332–354. Advance online publication. doi:10.1093/jleo/ewr018

Carcello, J. V., & Neal, T. L. (2000). Audit committee composition and auditor reporting. *The Accounting Review, 75*(4), 453–467. doi:10.2308/accr.2000.75.4.453

Carey, P., & Simnett, R. (2006). Audit partner tenure and audit quality. *The Accounting Review, 81*(3), 653–676. doi:10.2308/accr.2006.81.3.653

Carrell, A. (1979). BA three-dimensional Conceptual Model of Corporate Social Performance. *Academy of Management Review, 4*, 497–505.

Carroll, M. C., & Stanfield, J. R. (2003). Social capital, Karl Polanyi, and American social and institutional economics. *Journal of Economic Issues, 37*(2), 397–404. doi:10.1080/00213624.2003.11506587

Carter, D. A., Simkins, B. J., & Simpson, W. G. (2003). Corporate governance, board diversity, and firm value. *Financial Review, 38*(1), 33–53. doi:10.1111/1540-6288.00034

Carter, D., D'Souza, F., Simkins, B., & Simpson, W. (2010). The Gender and Ethnic Diversity of US Boards and Board Committees and Firm Financial Performance. *Corporate Governance, 18*(5), 396–414. doi:10.1111/j.1467-8683.2010.00809.x

Carter, S., Shaw, E., Lam, W., & Wilson, F. (2007). Gender, entrepreneurship, and bank lending: The criteria and processes used by bank loan officers in assessing applications. *Entrepreneurship Theory and Practice, 31*(3), 427–444. doi:10.1111/j.1540-6520.2007.00181.x

Cater, J., & Young, M. (2016). Family factors in small family business growth. *The Journal of Applied Management and Entrepreneurship*, *21*(4), 56–86. doi:10.9774/GLEAF.3709.2016.oc.00005

Centre, N. C. (2005). *IT Governance Developing a successful governance strategy. Oxford House, Manchester M1 7ED.* National Computing Centre.

Centre, N. C. (2005). *It Governance Developing a Successful Governance Strategy. Oxford House.*

Certo, S. T. (2003). Influencing initial public offering investors with prestige: Signaling with board structures. *Academy of Management Review*, *28*(3), 432–446. doi:10.5465/amr.2003.10196754

Chakroun, R. (2013). Family Control, Board of Directors' Independence and Extent of Voluntary Disclosure in the Annual Reports: Case of Tunisian Companies. *Journal of Business Studies Quarterly*, *5*(1), 22.

Chakroun, R., & Matoussi, H. (2012). Determinants of the extent of voluntary disclosure in the annual reports of the Tunisian firms. *Accounting and Management Information Systems*, *11*(3), 335.

Chakroun, R., Matoussi, H., & Mbirki, S. (2017). Determinants of CSR disclosure of Tunisian listed banks: A multi-support analysis. *Social Responsibility Journal*, *13*(3), 552–584. doi:10.1108/SRJ-04-2016-0055

Chand & White. (2007). *A critique of the influence of globalization and convergence of accounting standards in Fiji.* https://www.researchgate.net/publication/222997248_A_critique_of_the_influence_of_globalization_and_convergence_of_accounting_standards_in_Fiji

Chan, Y. E., Huff, S. L., Barclay, D. W., & Copeland, D. G. (1997). Business strategic orientation, information systems strategic orientation, and strategic alignment. *Information Systems Research*, *8*(2), 125–150. doi:10.1287/isre.8.2.125

Chau, G. K., & Gray, D. J. (2002). Ownership structure and corporate voluntary disclosure in Hong Kong and Singapore. *The International Journal of Accounting*, *37*(2), 247–265. doi:10.1016/S0020-7063(02)00153-X

Checkley, T. (2010). *Succession in small and family business.* Academic Press.

Chen, H., Jiang, Y., Lin, Z., & Tang, Q. (2010). *Mandatory IFRS Adoption and Accounting Quality: Evidence from the European Union.* Dissertation.

Chen, J. (2019). *Corporate Governance Definition.* Available at https://www.investopedia.com

Chen, N. (Xi). (2014). Repatriation Taxes and the Value of Cash Holdings. *SSRN Electronic Journal*. doi:10.2139srn.2496756

Chen, Z., & Cheung, Y. L. (2000). *Corporate governance, firm performance and agency conflicts in closely-held firms: evidence from Hong Kong.* Working paper. University of Hong Kong.

Chen. (2014). *How does mandatory IFRS adoption affect the audit service market?* School of Accounting Seminar Series Semester 1.

Chen, A., Kao, L., Tsao, M., & Wu, C. (2007). Building a corporate governance index from the perspectives of ownership and leadership for firms in Taiwan. *Corporate Governance*, *15*(2), 251–261. doi:10.1111/j.1467-8683.2007.00572.x

Cheng, E. C., & Courtenay, S. M. (2006). Board composition, regulatory regime and voluntary disclosure. *The International Journal of Accounting*, *41*(3), 262–289. doi:10.1016/j.intacc.2006.07.001

Cheng, M., Lin, B., & Wei, M. (2015). Executive compensation in family firms: The effect of multiple family members. *Journal of Corporate Finance*, *32*, 238–257. doi:10.1016/j.jcorpfin.2014.10.014

Chen, H., Jiang, Y., Lin, Z., & Tang, Q. (2010). The Role of International Financial Reporting Standards in Accounting Quality: Evidence from the European Union (June 10, 2010). *Journal of International Financial Management & Accounting*, *21*(3), 220–278. doi:10.1111/j.1467-646X.2010.01041.x

Chen, J. J., & Zhang, H. (2010). The impact of regulatory enforcement and audit upon IFRS compliance– Evidence from China. *European Accounting Review*, *19*(4), 665–692. doi:10.1080/09638180903384684

Chen, J. P., & Jaggi, B. L. (2000). The association between Independent non-Executive Directors, Family Control and Financial Disclosures. *Journal of Accounting and Public Policy*, *19*(4-5), 285–310. doi:10.1016/S0278-4254(00)00015-6

Chen, J., & Zhang, H. (2014). The Impact of the Corporate Governance Code on Earnings Management – Evidence from Chinese Listed Companies. *European Financial Management*, *20*(3), 596–632. doi:10.1111/j.1468-036X.2012.00648.x

Chen, L. (2010). Business–IT alignment maturity of companies in China. *Information & Management*, *47*(1), 9–16. doi:10.1016/j.im.2009.09.003

Chen, T., Harford, J., & Lin, C. (2015). Do analysts matter for governance? Evidence from natural experiments. *Journal of Financial Economics*, *115*(2), 383–410. doi:10.1016/j.jfineco.2014.10.002

Chen, V. Z., Li, J., Shapiro, D. M., & Zhang, X. (2014). Ownership structure and innovation: An emerging market perspective. *Asia Pacific Journal of Management*, *31*(1), 1–24. doi:10.100710490-013-9357-5

Chen, Y. R. (2008). Corporate governance and cash holdings: Listed new economy versus old economy firms. *Corporate Governance*, *16*(5), 430–442. Advance online publication. doi:10.1111/j.1467-8683.2008.00701.x

Chen, Y. R., & Chuang, W. T. (2009). Alignment or entrenchment? Corporate governance and cash holdings in growing firms. *Journal of Business Research*, *62*(11), 1200–1206. Advance online publication. doi:10.1016/j.jbusres.2008.06.004

Chen, Y., Wang, Y., Nevo, S., Benitez, J., & Kou, G. (2017). Improving strategic flexibility with information technologies: Insights for firm performance in an emerging economy. *Journal of Information Technology*, *32*(1), 10–25. doi:10.1057/jit.2015.26

Chen, Y., Wang, Y., Nevo, S., Jin, J., Wang, L., & Chow, W. S. (2014). IT capability and organizational performance: The roles of business process agility and environmental factors. *European Journal of Information Systems*, *23*(3), 326–342. doi:10.1057/ejis.2013.4

Chhaochharia, V., & Grinstein, Y. (2009). CEO Compensation and Board Structure. *The Journal of Finance*, *64*(1), 231–261. doi:10.1111/j.1540-6261.2008.01433.x

Chisholm, A., & Nielsen, K. (2010). Social Capital and the Resource Based View of the Firm. *International Studies of Management & Organization*, *39*(2), 7–32. doi:10.2753/IMO0020-8825390201

Cho, H., & Kim, R. (2020). Asymmetric effects of voluntary disclosure on stock liquidity: Evidence from 8-K filings. *Accounting and Finance*, acfi.12594. Advance online publication. doi:10.1111/acfi.12594

Choi, J. J., Park, S. W., & Yoo, S. S. (2007). The value of outside directors: Evidence from corporate governance reform in Korea. *Journal of Financial and Quantitative Analysis*, *42*(4), 941–962. doi:10.1017/S0022109000003458

Choi, S. B., Lee, S. H., & Williams, C. (2011). Ownership and firm innovation in a transition economy: Evidence from China. *Research Policy*, *40*(3), 441–452. doi:10.1016/j.respol.2011.01.004

Choi, S., & Rainey, H. G. (2010). Managing diversity in U.S. federal agencies: Effects of diversity and diversity management on employee perceptions of organizational performance. *Public Administration Review*, *70*(1), 109–121. doi:10.1111/j.1540-6210.2009.02115.x

Chrisman, J. J., Chua, J. H., Pearson, A. W., & Barnett, T. (2012). Family involvement, family influence, and family-centered non-economic goals in small firms. *Entrepreneurship Theory and Practice*, *36*(2), 267–293. doi:10.1111/j.1540-6520.2010.00407.x

Chrisman, J. J., Chua, J. H., Sharma, P., & Yoder, T. R. (2009). Guiding family businesses through the succession process. *The CPA Journal*, *79*(6), 48.

Chrisman, J. J., Sharma, P., Steier, L. P., & Chua, J. H. (2013). The influence of family goals, governance, and resources on firm outcomes. *Entrepreneurship Theory and Practice*, *37*(6), 1249–1261. doi:10.1111/etap.12064

Chung, C. N., & Luo, X. R. (2013). Leadership succession and firm performance in an emerging economy: Successor origin, relational embeddedness, and legitimacy. *Strategic Management Journal*, *34*(3), 338–357. doi:10.1002mj.2011

Claessens, S., Djankov, S., & Lang, L. H. P. (2000). The separation of ownership and control in East Asian corporations. *Journal of Financial Economics*, *58*(1-2), 81–112. doi:10.1016/S0304-405X(00)00067-2

Clark, C. E., Steckler, E. L., & Newell, S. (2016). Managing contradiction: Stockholder and stakeholder views of the firm as paradoxical opportunity. *Business and Society Review*, *121*(1), 123–159.

Clarke, D. C. (2006). The independent director in Chinese corporate governance. *Del. J. Corp. Law*, *31*, 125–228.

Clikeman, P. M., Geiger, M. A., & O'Connell, B. T. (2001). Student perceptions of earnings management: The effects of national origin and gender. *Teaching Business Ethics*, *5*(4), 389–410. doi:10.1023/A:1012252922571

Cohen, J. R., Krishnamoorthy, G., Peytcheva, M., & Wright, A. (2011). *Will Regulatory Enforcement and Principles-Based Accounting Influence Auditors' Ethical Judgments to Constrain Aggressive Reporting?* (Dissertation). Boston College, Northeastern University, Lehigh University & Northeastern University.

Cohen, J. R., Krishnamoorthy, G., & Wright, A. (2004). The corporate governance mosaic and financial reporting quality. *Journal of Accounting Literature*, 87–152.

Colbert, G., & Murray, D. (1999). The Association between Auditor Quality and Auditor Size: an Analysis of Small CPA Firms. *Journal of Accounting & Auditing &Finance-Control*, 976-983.

Coles, J. L., Daniel, N. D., & Naveen, L. (2008). Boards: Does one size fit all? *Journal of Financial Economics*, *87*(2), 329–356. doi:10.1016/j.jfineco.2006.08.008

Coltman, T., Tallon, P., Sharma, R., & Queiroz, M. (2015). Strategic IT alignment: Twenty-five years on. *Journal of Information Technology*, *30*(2), 91–100. doi:10.1057/jit.2014.35

Company Law of the People's Republic of China. (2014). *Standing Committee of the National People's Congress*. http://www.fdi.gov.cn/1800000121_39_4814_0_7.html

Çonkar, K., Elitaş, C. & Atar, G. (2011). Measurement of financial management of firms taking place in ınstitutional ındex with Topsis method and its analysis with ınstitutional administration note. *İstanbul Üniversitesi İktisat Fakültesi Mecmuası*, *61*(1), 81-115.

Contessotto, C., & Moroney, R. (2014). The association between audit committee effectiveness and audit risk. *Accounting and Finance*, *54*(2), 393–418. doi:10.1111/acfi.12010

Contreras, Y. S., Díaz, F. M. R., Tamez, L. L. G., & Martínez, D. G. J. (2015). *El liderazgo a partir del proceso de la sucesión en la empresa familiar mexicana/the leadership from the succession process in the mexican family enterprise.* Paper presented at the Global Conference on Business & Finance Proceedings.

Cooke, T. E. (1992). The impact of size, stock market listing and industry type on disclosure in the annual reports of Japanese listed corporations. *Accounting and Business Research*, *22*(87), 229–237. doi:10.1080/00014788.1992.9729440

Coombs, J. E., & Gilley, K. M. (2005). Stakeholder management as a predictor of CEO compensation: Main effects and interactions with financial performance. *Strategic Management Journal*, *26*(9), 827–840.

Cormier, D., Antunes, P., & Mc-Conomy, B. (2014). Forecasts in IPO Prospectuses: The Effect of Corporate Governance on Earnings Management. *Journal of Business Finance & Accounting*, *41*(1,2), 100–127.

Cowen, A. P., & Marcel, J. J. (2011). Damaged goods: Board decisions to dismiss reputationally compromised directors. *Academy of Management Journal*, *54*(3), 509–527. doi:10.5465/amj.2011.61967992

Cox, R. D. (2012). Teaching qualitative research to practitioner–researchers. *Theory into Practice*, *51*(2), 129–136. do i:10.1080/00405841.2012.662868

Cragg, P., King, M., & Hussin, H. (2002). IT alignment and firm performance in small manufacturing firms. *The Journal of Strategic Information Systems*, *11*(2), 109–132. doi:10.1016/S0963-8687(02)00007-0

Craig & Diga. (1996). Financial reporting regulation in ASEAN: Features and prospects: The Australian National University, Australia. *The International Journal of Accounting, 2*. https://www.researchgate.net/publication/4739184_Financial_reporting_regulation_in_ASEAN_Features_and_prospects

Cressey, D. R. (1950). The criminal violation of financial trust. *American Sociological Review*, *15*(6), 738–743. doi:10.2307/2086606

Cressey, D. R. (1967). Methodological problems in the study of organized crime as a social problem. *The Annals of the American Academy of Political and Social Science*, *374*(1), 101–112. doi:10.1177/000271626737400110

Cristina, B. A., & Cristina, P. (2009). Measuring and assessment of internal audit's effectiveness. *Annals of Faculty of Economics*, *3*(1), 784–790.

Croson, R., & Gneezy, U. (2009). Gender differences in preferences. *Journal of Economic Literature*, *47*(2), 448–474. doi:10.1257/jel.47.2.448

Cruz, M. E., & Vargas-Hernández, J. G. (2018). Corporate Governance and Agency Theory: Megacable Case. *Corporate Governance and Sustainability Review*, *2*(1), 59–70. doi:10.22495/cgsrv2i1p5

CSRC. (2001). *Guidelines for Introducing Independent Directors to the Board of Directors of Listed Companies*. China Securities Regulatory Commission. http://www.csrc.gov.cn/pub/csrc_en/newsfacts/release/200708/t20070810_69191.html

Curtis, A., Lewis-Western, M.-F., & Toynbee, S. (2015). Historical cost measurement and the use of DuPont analysis by market participants. *Review of Accounting Studies*, *20*(3), 1210–1245. doi:10.100711142-015-9334-y

Cyert, R. M., & March, J. G. (1963). A Behavioral Theory of the Firm (2nd ed.). Prentice Hall.

Dağlı, H., Ayaydın, H., & Eyüpoğlu, K. (2010). Corporate governance index performance evaluation: Case of Turkey. *The Journal of Accounting and Finance*, *48*(October), 18–31.

Dahya, J., Karbhari, Y., Xiao, J. Z., & Yang, M. (2003). The usefulness of the supervisory board report in China. *Corporate Governance*, *11*(4), 308–321. doi:10.1111/1467-8683.00329

Daily, C. M., & Dalton, D. R. (1992). The relationship between governance structure and corporate performance in entrepreneurial firms. *Journal of Business Venturing*, *7*(5), 375–386. doi:10.1016/0883-9026(92)90014-I

Dalimunthe, D. M. J., Fadli, I. M., & Muda, I. (2016). The Application of Performance Measurement System Model Using Malcolm Baldrige Model (MBM) to Support Civil State Apparatus Law (ASN) Number 5 of 2014 in Indonesia. *International Journal of Applied Business and Economic Research*, *14*(11), 7397–7407.

Dana, L., & Smyrnios, K. (2010). *The MGI Australian Family and Private Business Survey*. RMIT University.

Darabaris, J. (2019). *Corporate environmental management*. CRC Press Taylor & Francis Group, Boca Raton, London. doi:10.1201/9780429029264

Daraghma, Z. M. A., & Alsinawi, A. A. (2010). Board of Directors, Management Ownership, and Capital Structure and Its Effect on Performance: The Case of Palestine Securities Exchange. *International Journal of Business and Management*, *5*(11), 118–125. doi:10.5539/ijbm.v5n11p118

Darmadi, S. (2011). Board diversity and firm performance: The Indonesian evidence. *Corporate Ownership and Control.*, *9*(1), 524–539. doi:10.22495/cocv8i2c4p4

Darmadi, S. (2013). Board members' education and firm performance: Evidence from a developing economy. *International Journal of Commerce and Management*, *23*(2), 113–135. doi:10.1108/10569211311324911

Darvish, H., & Temelie, Z. N. (2014). A Study on the Relationship between Succession Planning and Strategic Planning. Case Study: Payame Noor University of Aleshtar. *Economic Insights - Trends and Challenges*, *66*(1).

Dash, S. R., & Raithatha, M. (2019). Corporate governance and firm performance relationship: Implications for risk-adjusted return behavior. *Managerial and Decision Economics*, *40*(8), 923–940. doi:10.1002/mde.3080

Daske, H., Hail, L., Leuz, C., & Verdi, R. S. (2008). *Mandatory IFRS Reporting Around the World: Early Evidence on the Economic Consequences*. ECGI - Finance Working Paper No. 198/2008. Chicago GSB Research Paper No. 12.

Das, P. K. (2019). Impact of Women Directors on Corporate Financial Performance- Indian Context. *American Journal of Humanities and Social Sciences Research*, *3*(2), 29–36. doi:10.22158/wjssr.v6n3p320

Davidson, R., Goodwin-Stewart, J., & Kent, P. (2005). Internal governance structures and earnings management. *Accounting and Finance*, *45*(2), 241–267. doi:10.1111/j.1467-629x.2004.00132.x

Davis, J. H., Schoorman, F. D., & Donaldson, L. (1997). *Davis, Schoorman, and Donaldson reply: The distinctiveness of agency theory and stewardship theory*. Academic Press.

Davis, J. H., Schoorman, F. D., & Donaldson, L. (1997). Toward a stewardship theory of management. *Academy of Management Review*, *22*(1), 20–47. doi:10.5465/amr.1997.9707180258

Dawd, I., & Charfeddine, L. (2019). Effect of aggregate, mandatory and voluntary disclosure on firm performance in a developing market: The case of Kuwait. *International Journal of Accounting. Auditing and Performance Evaluation*, *15*(1), 31–56. doi:10.1504/IJAAPE.2019.096735

De Haes, S., & Van Grembergen, W. (2009). An exploratory study into IT governance implementations and its impact on business/IT alignment. *Information Systems Management*, *26*(2), 123–137. doi:10.1080/10580530902794786

De Haes, S., & Van Grembergen, W. (2015). *Enterprise Governance of Information Technology*. Springer. doi:10.1007/978-3-319-14547-1

De Haes, S., Van Grembergen, W., Joshi, A., & Huygh, T. (2020). Enterprise Governance of It, Alignment, and Value. In *Enterprise Governance of Information Technology* (pp. 1–13). Springer. doi:10.1007/978-3-030-25918-1_1

De Vries, M. (1997). Family Business: Human Dilemmas in the Family Firm. *Organization Studies-Berlin-European Group for Organizational Studies*, *18*, 543–543.

Dechow, P. M., & Dichev, I. D. (2002). The quality of accruals and earnings: The role of accrual estimation errors. *The Accounting Review*, *77*(s-1), 35–59. doi:10.2308/accr.2002.77.s-1.35

Dechow, P. M., Sloan, R. G., & Sweeney, A. P. (1995). Detecting Earnings Management. *The Accounting Review*, *70*, 193–225.

Dechow, P. M., Sloan, R. G., & Sweeney, A. P. (1996). Causes and consequences of earnings manipulation: An analysis of firms subject to enforcement actions by the SEC. *Contemporary Accounting Research*, *13*(1), 1–36. doi:10.1111/j.1911-3846.1996.tb00489.x

Dechow, P., Ge, W., & Schrand, C. (2010). Understanding earnings quality: A review of the proxies, their determinants and their consequences. *Journal of Accounting and Economics*, *50*(2), 344–401. doi:10.1016/j.jacceco.2010.09.001

Decker, C., Heinrichs, K., Jaskiewicz, P., & Rau, S. B. (2016). What do we know about succession in family businesses? Mapping current knowledge and unexplored territory. In *The Routledge Companion to Family Business* (pp. 45–74). Routledge.

Deegan, C., & Blomquist, C. (2006). Stakeholder influence on corporate reporting: An exploration of the interaction between WWF-Australia and the Australian minerals industry. *Accounting, Organizations and Society*, *31*(4-5), 343–372.

DeFond, M. L., Hann, R. N., & Hu, X. (2005). Does the market value financial expertise on audit committees of boards of directors? *Journal of Accounting Research*, *43*(2), 153–193. doi:10.1111/j.1475-679x.2005.00166.x

DeFond, M. L., & Jiambalvo, J. (1994, January). Debt covenant violation and manipulation of accruals. Accounting choices in troubles companies. *Journal of Accounting and Economics*, *17*(1-2), 145–176. doi:10.1016/0165-4101(94)90008-6

DeFond, M. L., & Park, C. W. (2001). The reversal of abnormal accruals and the market valuation of earnings surprises. *The Accounting Review*, *76*(3), 375–404. doi:10.2308/accr.2001.76.3.375

Dellaportas, S., Leung, P., Cooper, B. J., Ika, S. R., & Ghazali, N. A. M. (2012). Audit committee effectiveness and timeliness of reporting: Indonesian evidence. *Managerial Auditing Journal*.

Demsetz, H., & Lehn, K. (1985). The Structure of Corporate Ownership: Causes and Consequences. *Journal of Political Economy*, *93*(6), 1155–1177. doi:10.1086/261354

Denis, D. K., & Mcconnell, J. J. (2003). International Corporate Governance. *Journal of Financial and Quantitative Analysis*, *38*(1), 1. doi:10.2307/4126762

Depken, C. A. II, & Sonora, R. J. (2005). Asymmetric effects of economic freedom on international trade flows. *International Journal of Business and Economics*, *4*(2), 141.

Dewey, K. (2019). *What are Four Characteristics of Good Corporate Governance?* Available at https://www.quora.com

Dey, A., Engel, E., & Liu, X. (2011). CEO and board chair roles: To split or not to split? *Journal of Corporate Finance*, *17*(5), 1595–1618. doi:10.1016/j.jcorpfin.2011.09.001

DeZoort, F. T., Hermanson, D. R., Archambeault, D. S., & Reed, S. A. (2002). Audit committee effectiveness: A synthesis of the empirical audit committee literature. *Audit Committee Effectiveness: A Synthesis of the Empirical Audit Committee Literature*, *21*, 38.

DeZoort, F. (1997). An investigation of audit committees' oversight responsibilities. *Abacus*, *33*(2), 208–227. doi:10.1111/1467-6281.00012

Dhaliwal, G. S., Jindal, V., & Dhawan, A. K. (2010). Insect pest problems and crop losses: Changing trends. *Indian Journal of Ecology*, *37*(1), 1–7.

Dias, A., Rodrigues, L. L., & Craig, R. (2017). Corporate governance effects on social responsibility disclosures. *Australasian Accounting Business & Finance Journal, 11*(2).

Dichev, I. D., Graham, J. R., Harvey, C. R., & Rajgopal, S. (2013). Earnings quality: Evidence from the field. *Journal of Accounting and Economics, 56*(2-3), 1–33. doi:10.1016/j.jacceco.2013.05.004

Dienes, D., & Velte, P. (2016). The impact of supervisory board composition on CSR reporting. Evidence from the German two-tier system. *Sustainability, 8*(1), 63.

Dimitropoulos, P. E., & Asteriou, D. (2010). The effect of board composition on the informativeness and quality of annual earnings: Empirical evidence from Greece. *Research in International Business and Finance, 24*(2), 190–205. doi:10.1016/j.ribaf.2009.12.001

Dinç, E., & Abdioğlu, H. (2009). Relationships between corporate governance and accounting information systems on businesses: an empirical research on ISE–100 companies. Balıkesir University The Journal of Social Sciences Institute, 12(21), 157-184.

Ding, Y., Zhang, H., & Zhang, J. (2007). Private versus state ownership and earnings management: Evidence from Chinese listed companies. *Corporate Governance, 15*(2), 223–238. doi:10.1111/j.1467-8683.2007.00556.x

Diria, M., Lambrinoudakis, C., & Alhadab, M. (2020). Corporate Governance and Earnings Management in Concentrated Markets. *Journal of Business Research, 108*, 291–306. doi:10.1016/j.jbusres.2019.11.013

Distelberg, B., & Blow, A. (2010). The role of values and unity in family businesses. *Journal of Family and Economic Issues, 31*(4), 427–441. doi:10.100710834-010-9221-4

Distelberg, B., & Sorenson, R. L. (2009). Updating systems concepts in family businesses: A focus on values, resource flows, and adaptability. *Family Business Review, 22*(1), 65–81. doi:10.1177/0894486508329115

Dittmar, A., & Mahrt-Smith, J. (2007). Corporate governance and the value of cash holdings. *Journal of Financial Economics, 83*(3), 599–634. Advance online publication. doi:10.1016/j.jfineco.2005.12.006

Dittmar, A., Mahrt-Smith, J., & Servaes, H. (2003). International Corporate Governance and Corporate Cash Holdings. *Journal of Financial and Quantitative Analysis, 38*(1), 111. Advance online publication. doi:10.2307/4126766

Dogru, T., & Sirakaya-Turk, E. (2018). Cash holdings and corporate governance: Theory and contrary evidence from hotel firms. *International Journal of Contemporary Hospitality Management, 30*(10), 3117–3134. Advance online publication. doi:10.1108/IJCHM-03-2017-0163

Donaldson, L., & Davis, J. H. (1990). *CEO governance and shareholder returns: Agency theory or stewardship theory.* Australian Graduate School of Management, University of New South Wales.

Donaldson, L., & Davis, J. H. (1991). Stewardship theory or agency theory: CEO governance and shareholder returns. *Australian Journal of Management, 16*(1), 49–64. doi:10.1177/031289629101600103

Dong, S. (2012). Decision Execution Mechanisms of It Governance: The Crm Case. *International Journal of Information Management, 32*(2), 147-157.

Dore, R. (1973). *British Factory–Japanese Factory: The Origins of National Diversity in Industrial Relations.* University of California Press.

Drees, J., & Heugens, P. (2013). Synthesizing and extending resource dependence theory: A meta-analysis. *Journal of Management, 39*(6), 1666–1698. doi:10.1177/0149206312471391

Drobetz, W., & Grüninger, M. C. (2007). Corporate cash holdings: Evidence from Switzerland. *Financial Markets and Portfolio Management*, *21*(3), 293–324. Advance online publication. doi:10.100711408-007-0052-8

Dumas, C., Dupuis, J. P., Richer, F., & St.-Cyr, L. (1995). Factors that influence the next generation's decision to take over the family farm. *Family Business Review*, *8*(2), 99–120. doi:10.1111/j.1741-6248.1995.00099.x

Dumontier, P., Janin, R., & Piot, C. (2010). *IFRS Consequences on Accounting Conservatism Within Europe: The Role of Big 4 Auditors*. Academic Press.

Durst, S., & Wilhelm, S. (2012). Knowledge management and succession planning in SMEs. *Journal of Knowledge Management*, *16*(4), 637–649. doi:10.1108/13673271211246194

Durucasu, H., Aytekin, A., Saraç, B., & Orakçı, E. (2017). Current application fields of ELECTRE and PROMETHEE: A literature review. *Alphanumeric Journal*, *5*(2), 229–270. doi:10.17093/alphanumeric.320235

Dwyer, S., Richard, O. C., & Chadwick, K. (2003). Gender diversity in management and firm performance: The influence of growth orientation and organizational culture. *Journal of Business Research*, *56*(12), 1009–1019. doi:10.1016/S0148-2963(01)00329-0

Dyck, A., Volchkova, N., & Zingales, L. (2008). The corporate governance role of the media: Evidence from Russia. *The Journal of Finance*, *63*(3), 1093–1135. doi:10.1111/j.1540-6261.2008.01353.x

Eckbo, B. E., & Smith, D. C. (1998). The Conditional Performance of Insider Trades. *The Journal of Finance*, *53*(2), 467–498. doi:10.1111/0022-1082.205263

Efendi, J., Srivastava, A., & Swanson, E. P. (2007). Why do corporate managers misstate financial statements? The role of option compensation and other factors. *Journal of Financial Economics*, *85*(3), 667–708. doi:10.1016/j.jfineco.2006.05.009

Ege, İ., Topaloğlu, E. E., & Özyamanoğlu, M. (2013). Relationship between financial performance and corporate governance scores: Application in BIST. *Journal of Academic Researches and Studies*, *5*(9), 100–117.

Ehsan, S., Abbas, Q., & Nawaz, A. (2018). An Inquiry into the Relationship between Earnings' Management. Corporate Social Responsibility and Corporate Governance. *Abasyn Journal of Social Sciences*, *11*(1), 104–116.

Eickemeyer, J. H., & Love, V. J. (2009). IFRS and Accountants' Liability. *The CPA Journal*, 54–59.

Eisenhardt, K. M. (1989). Building theories from case study research. *Academy of Management Review*, *14*(4), 532–550. doi:10.5465/amr.1989.4308385

Eisenhardt, M. (1986). Agency Theory! And Assessment Review. *Accounting Management Review*, *14*(1), 57–74.

El-Chaarani, H. (2014). The success keys for family firms: Comparison between Lebanese and French systems. *Lebanese Science Journal*, *15*(2), 133–150.

El-Diftar, D., Jones, E., Ragheb, M., & Soliman, M. (2017). Institutional investors and voluntary disclosure and transparency: The case of Egypt. *Corporate Governance*, *17*(1), 134–151. doi:10.1108/CG-05-2016-0112

Elfeky, M. I. (2017). The extent of voluntary disclosure and its determinants in emerging markets: Evidence from Egypt. *The Journal of Finance and Data Science, 3*(1-4), 45-59.

Elghuweel, M., Ntim, C., Opong, K., & Avison, L. (2017). Corporate Governance, Islamic Governance and Earnings Management in Oman: A new Empirical Insights from a Behavioral Theoretical Framework. *Journal of Accounting in Emerging Economies*, *7*(2), 190–224. doi:10.1108/JAEE-09-2015-0064

ElHawary, E., & Arafa, I. M. (2018). Studying the Effect of Stakeholders on the Disclosure of Corporate Social Responsibility by Banks: Evidence from Egypt. *Journal of Accounting and Finance Research, 7*(4), 200-226.

Eliwa, Y., Gregoriou, A., & Paterson, A. (2019). Accruals quality and the cost of debt: The European evidence. *International Journal of Accounting & Information Management, 27*(2), 333–351. doi:10.1108/IJAIM-01-2018-0008

Elsaid, E., & Ursel, N. D. (2011). CEO succession, gender and risk taking. *Gender in Management, 26*(7), 499–512. doi:10.1108/17542411111175478

Eng, L. L., & Mak, Y. T. (2003). Corporate governance and voluntary disclosure. *Journal of Accounting and Public Policy, 22*(4), 325–345. doi:10.1016/S0278-4254(03)00037-1

Enofe, A. O., Iyafekhe, C., & Eniola, J. O. (2017). Board ethnicity, gender diversity and earnings management: Evidence from quoted firms in Nigeria. *International Journal of Economics. Commerce and Management, 6*, 78–90.

Ercan, M. K., & Ban, Ü. (2005). *Finansal yönetim: değere dayalı işletme finansmanı.* Gazi Publishing.

Erhardt, N. L., Werbel, J. D., & Shrader, C. B. (2003). Board of director diversity and firm financial performance. *Corporate Governance, 11*(2), 102–111. doi:10.1111/1467-8683.00011

Estélyi, K. S., & Nisar, T. M. (2016). Diverse boards: Why do firms get foreign nationals on their boards? *Journal of Corporate Finance, 39*, 174–192. doi:10.1016/j.jcorpfin.2016.02.006

Eulaiwi, B., Al-Hadi, A., Taylor, G., Al-Yahyaee, K. H., & Evans, J. (2016). Multiple directorships, family ownership and the board nomination committee: International evidence from the GCC. *Emerging Markets Review, 28*, 61–88. doi:10.1016/j.ememar.2016.06.004

Eulerich, M., Velte, P., & van Uum, C. (2014). The impact of management board diversity on corporate performance. An empirical analysis for the German two-tier system. An Empirical Analysis for the German Two-Tier System (November 8, 2013). *Problems and Perspectives in Management, 12*, 25–39.

Evolution de l'audit: Publié le 21 mars 2009 par KESSAB JAMAL. http://normes-ias-ifrs-au-maroc.over-blog.com/article-29313104.html

Experts, F. B. (2012). *Want to fix or avoid problems in your family business.* Academic Press.

Fallah, M. A., & Mojarrad, F. (2019). Corporate governance effects on corporate social responsibility disclosure: Empirical evidence from heavy-pollution industries in Iran. *Social Responsibility Journal, 15*(2), 208–225.

Fama, E. F. (1980). Agency Problems and the Theory of the Firm. *Journal of Political Economy, 88*(2), 288–307. doi:10.1086/260866

Fama, E. F., & French, K. R. (1998). Taxes, financing decisions, and firm value. *The Journal of Finance, 53*(3), 819–843. Advance online publication. doi:10.1111/0022-1082.00036

Fama, E. F., & Jensen, M. C. (1983). Separation of Ownership and Control. *The Journal of Law & Economics, 26*(2), 301–325. doi:10.1086/467037

Fan, J. P. H., Titman, S., & Twite, G. (2012). An international comparison of capital structure and debt maturity choices. *Journal of Financial and Quantitative Analysis, 47*(1), 23–56. doi:10.1017/S0022109011000597

Farook, S., & Lanis, R. (2007). Banking on Islam? Determinants of Corporate Social Responsibility Disclosure. In *Islamic Economics and Finance, Proceedings of 6th International Conference on Islamic Economics and Finance.* Jeddah, Saudi Arabia: Islamic Research & Training Institute - Islamic Development Bank Group.

Farook, S., Hassan, M. K., & Lanis, R. (2011). Determinants of corporate social responsibility disclosure:the case of Islamic banks. *Journal of Islamic Accounting and Business Research*, *2*(2), 114–141. doi:10.1108/17590811111170539

Felo, A. J. (2010). *Corporate reporting transparency, board independence and expertise, and CEO duality.* Available at SSRN: https://ssrn.com/abstract=1373942

Felo, A. J., Krishnamurthy, S., & Solieri, S. A. (2003). *Audit committee characteristics and the perceived quality of financial reporting: an empirical analysis.* Available at SSRN 401240

Ferrarini, G., & Filippelli, M. (2014). *Independent directors and controlling shareholders around the world.* Academic Press.

Ferreira, D. (2015). Board diversity: Should we trust research to inform policy? *Corporate Governance*, *23*(2), 108–111. doi:10.1111/corg.12092

Ferreira, M. A., Custodio, C., & Raposo, C. C. (2011). *Cash Holdings and Business Conditions.* SSRN Electronic Journal., doi:10.2139srn.608664

Ferreira, M. A., & Vilela, A. S. (2004a). Why do firms hold cash? Evidence from EMU countries. *European Financial Management*, *10*(2), 295–319. Advance online publication. doi:10.1111/j.1354-7798.2004.00251.x

Ferrero-Ferrero, I., Fernández-Izquierdo, M. Á., & Muñoz-Torres, M. J. (2015). Age diversity: An empirical study in the board of directors. *Cybernetics and Systems*, *46*(3-4), 249–270. doi:10.1080/01969722.2015.1012894

Fielding, J., Fielding, N., & Hughes, G. (2013). Opening up open-ended survey data using qualitative software. *Quality & Quantity*, *47*(6), 3261–3276. doi:10.100711135-012-9716-1

Filser, M., Kraus, S., & Märk, S. (2013). Psychological aspects of succession in family business management. *Management Research Review*, *36*(3), 256–277. doi:10.1108/01409171311306409

Fink, D. (2011). Pipelines, pools and reservoirs: Building leadership capacity for sustained improvement. *Journal of Educational Administration*, *49*(6), 670–684. doi:10.1108/09578231111174811

Finkelstein, S., & D'aveni, R. A. (1994). CEO duality as a double-edged sword: How boards of directors balance entrenchment avoidance and unity of command. *Academy of Management Journal*, *37*(5), 1079–1108.

Fondas, N., & Sassalos, S. (2000). A different voice in the boardroom: How the presence of women directors affects board influence over management. *Global Focus*, *12*(1), 13–22.

Francis, J. R., (2006). *Auditing Section Doctoral Consortium.* Presentation.

Francis, B. B., Hasan, I., & Sun, X. (2009). Political connections and the process of going public: Evidence from China. *Journal of International Money and Finance*, *28*(4), 696–719. doi:10.1016/j.jimonfin.2009.01.002

Francis, B., Hasan, I., Park, J. C., & Wu, Q. (2015). Gender differences in financial reporting decision-making: Evidence from accounting conservatism. *Contemporary Accounting Research*, *32*(3), 1285–1318. doi:10.1111/1911-3846.12098

Francis, J. R., & Krishnan, J. (1999). Accounting accruals and auditor reporting conservatism. *Contemporary Accounting Research*, *16*(1), 135–165. doi:10.1111/j.1911-3846.1999.tb00577.x

Francis, J. R., & Krishnan, J. (2002). Evidence on auditor risk-management strategies before and after the Private Securities Litigation Reform Act of 1995. *Asia-Pacific Journal of Accounting & Economics*, *9*(2), 135–157. doi:10.1080/16081625.2002.10510607

Francis, J. R., & Wang, D. (2008). The joint effect of investor protection and Big-4 audits on earnings quality around the world. *Contemporary Accounting Research, 25*(1), 157–191. doi:10.1506/car.25.1.6

Francis, J., & Smith, A. (1995). Agency costs and innovation some empirical evidence. *Journal of Accounting and Economics, 19*(2), 383–409. doi:10.1016/0165-4101(94)00389-M

Freeman, R. E., & Reed, D. L. (1983). Stockholders and stakeholders: A new perspective on corporate governance. *California Management Review, 25*(3), 88–106.

Freihat, M. A. J. (2014). The Role of Disclosure of Other Elements of Comprehensive Income on the Practice of Earnings Management: A study Applied to the Saudi Banking and Financial Services Sector. *Journal of Scientific Research. Assiut University, 57*, 125–140.

Friis, O., & Nielsen, M. (2010). *Audit fees and IFRS accounting. Is information costly? Discussion Papers on Business and Economics*. University of Southern Denmark.

Fritz Foley, C., Hartzell, J. C., Titman, S., & Twite, G. (2007). Why do firms hold so much cash? A tax-based explanation. *Journal of Financial Economics, 86*(3), 579–607. Advance online publication. doi:10.1016/j.jfineco.2006.11.006

Fuente, J. A., García-Sanchez, I. M., & Lozano, M. B. (2017). The role of the board of directors in the adoption of GRI guidelines for the disclosure of CSR information. *Journal of Cleaner Production, 141*, 737–750.

Fullerton, R., & Durtschi, C. (2004). *The effect of professional skepticism on the fraud detection skills of internal auditors*. Available at SSRN 617062

Fung, B. (2014). The demand and need for transparency and disclosure in corporate governance. *Universal Journal of Management, 2*(2), 72–80.

Fürst, H. (2017). *Growing Up in a Business Family–An Analytic Autoethnography of 'Subtle Coerced Succession'* (Doctoral dissertation). University of Gloucestershire.

Gandossy, R. P., & Verma, N. (2006). Passing the torch of leadership. *Leader to Leader, 2006*(40), 37–44. doi:10.1002/ltl.176

García, J. O., Castejón, P. J. M., & Pérez, C. P. (2014). The culture of conflict in family business/La cultura del conflicto en la empresa familiar. *Revista de Empresa Familiar, 4*(2), 25.

García-Ramos, R., & García-Olalla, M. (2011). Board characteristics and firm performance in public founder- and nonfounder-led family businesses. *Journal of Family Business Strategy*. doi:10.1016/j.jfbs.2011.09.001

García-Teruel, P. J., & Martínez-Solano, P. (2008). On the determinants of SME cash holdings: Evidence from Spain. *Journal of Business Finance & Accounting, 35*(1-2), 127–149. Advance online publication. doi:10.1111/j.1468-5957.2007.02022.x

Garg, A., & Van Weele, E. (2012). Succession planning and its impact on the performance of small micro medium enterprises within the manufacturing sector in Johannesburg. *International Journal of Business and Management, 7*(9), 96. doi:10.5539/ijbm.v7n9p96

Gavious, I., Segev, E., & Yosef, R. (2012). Female directors and earnings management in high-technology firms. *Pacific Accounting Review, 24*(1), 4–32. doi:10.1108/01140581211221533

Gedajlovic, E., & Shapiro, D. M. (2002). Ownership structure and firm profitability in Japan. *Academy of Management Journal, 45*, 565–575.

Genc Alimehmeti, P. & Angelo Paletta, P. (n.d.). Ownership concentration and effects over firm performance: Evidences from Italy. *European Scientific Journal,* 8.

Genc, A., & Angelo, P. (2012). Ownership Concentration and Effects over Firm Performance: Evidence From Italy. *European Scientific Journal*, 8.

Gerow, J. E., Grover, V., & Thatcher, J. (2016). Alignment's nomological network: Theory and evaluation. *Information & Management*, *53*(5), 541–553. doi:10.1016/j.im.2015.12.006

Gerow, J. E., Grover, V., Thatcher, J. B., & Roth, P. L. (2014). Looking toward the future of IT-business strategic alignment through the past: A meta-analysis. *Management Information Systems Quarterly*, *38*(4), 1059–1085. doi:10.25300/MISQ/2014/38.4.10

Gersick, C. J. (1988). Time and transition in work teams: Toward a new model of group development. *Academy of Management Journal*, *31*(1), 9–41.

Ghazali & Weetman. (2006). *Voluntary Disclosure in Malaysian Corporate Annual Reports*. Academic Press.

Ghobakhloo, M., & Hong, T. S. (2014). IT investments and business performance improvement: The mediating role of lean manufacturing implementation. *International Journal of Production Research*, *52*(18), 5367–5384. doi:10.1080/00207543.2014.906761

Giannetti, M., Liao, G., & Yu, X. (2015). The Brain Gain of Corporate Boards: Evidence from China. *The Journal of Finance*, *70*(4), 1629–1682. doi:10.1111/jofi.12198

Giarmarco, J. (2017). *The three levels of family business succession planning*. Academic Press.

Gilding, M., Gregory, S., & Cosson, B. (2015). Motives and outcomes in family business succession planning. *Entrepreneurship Theory and Practice*, *39*(2), 299–312. doi:10.1111/etap.12040

Gill, A., & Shah, C. (2011). Determinants of Corporate Cash Holdings: Evidence from Canada. *International Journal of Economics and Finance*, *4*(1). Advance online publication. doi:10.5539/ijef.v4n1p70

Godfrey & Chalmers. (2007). *Globalisation of accounting standards*. Monash Studies in Global Movements.

Gomes, A. (2000). Going Public without Gover- nance: Managerial reputation effects. *The Journal of Finance*, *55*(2), 615–646. doi:10.1111/0022-1082.00221

Goncharov, I., & Hodgson, A. (2011). Measuring and Reporting Income in Europe. *Journal of International Accounting*, *10*(1), 30–31.

Gonzalez, J. S., & Garcia-Meca, E. (2014). Does corporate governance influence earnings management in Latin American markets? *Journal of Business Ethics*, *121*(3), 419–440.

Gonzalez, J., & Meca, E. (2014). Does Corporate Governance Influence Earnings Management in Latin American Markets? *Journal of Business Ethics*, *121*(3), 419–440. doi:10.100710551-013-1700-8

Goranova, M., & Ryan, L. V. (2014). Shareholder activism: A multidisciplinary review. *Journal of Management*, *40*(5), 1230–1268. doi:10.1177/0149206313515519

Gordini, N., & Rancati, E. (2017). Gender diversity in the Italian boardroom and firm financial performance. *Management Research Review*, *40*(1), 75–94. doi:10.1108/MRR-02-2016-0039

Gore, P., Pope, P., & Singh, A. (2001). *Non-audit services, auditor independence and earnings management*. Working Paper, Lancaster University.

Goyal, V. K., & Park, C. W. (2002). Board leadership structure and CEO turnover. *Journal of Corporate Finance*, *8*(1), 49–66. Advance online publication. doi:10.1016/S0929-1199(01)00028-1

Graham, J. R., Harvey, C. R., & Rajgopal, S. (2005). The economic implications of corporate financial reporting. *Journal of Accounting and Economics*, *40*(1-3), 3–73. doi:10.1016/j.jacceco.2005.01.002

Gramling, A. A., & Myers, P. M. (2006). Internal auditing's role in ERM: As organizations lay their enterprise risk groundwork, many auditors are taking on management's oversight responsibilities, new research finds. *Internal Auditor*, *63*(2), 52–58.

Gray, D. (2014). Succession planning 101. *Professional Safety*, *59*(3), 35.

Grecco, M., Filho, M., Segura, L., Sanchez, I.-M., & Dominguez, L. (2013). The voluntary disclosure of sustainable information: A comparative analysis of spanish and brazilian companies. *Journal of Accounting and Organizations*, *17*, 45–55.

Greenberg, H. (2012). Aligning future leaders today to take on the challenges of tomorrow. *Employment Relations Today*, *38*(4), 55–60. doi:10.1002/ert.20365

GRI. (2015). *Gri'S History. Global Reporting Initiative*. Retrieved from https://www.globalreporting.org/information/about-gri/gri-history/Pages/GRI's history.aspx

Griffeth, R. W., Allen, D. G., & Barrett, R. (2006). Integration of family-owned business succession with turnover and life cycle models: Development of a successor retention process model. *Human Resource Management Review*, *16*(4), 490–507. doi:10.1016/j.hrmr.2006.08.006

Griffin, P., Lont, D., & Sun, Y. (2008). *Governance Regulatory Changes, IFRS Adoption, and New Zealand Audit and Non-Audit Fees: Empirical Evidence*. University of California and University of Otago.

Gross, K. (2007). *Equity Ownership and Performance: An Empirical Study of German Traded Companies*. Physica Verlag.

Grundström, C., Öberg, C., & Rönnbäck, A. Ö. (2011). View and management of innovativeness upon succession in family-owned SMEs. *International Journal of Innovation Management*, *15*(03), 617–640. doi:10.1142/S136391961100326X

Guedes, M. J., Gaio, C., & Soares, N. (2018). Exploring the Relationship Between Gender Diversity and Earnings Management: Does Critical Mass Matter? In *International Conference on Gender Research*, (pp. 181-188). Academic Conferences and Publishing Limited.

Guest, P. M. (2019). Does Board Ethnic Diversity Impact Board Monitoring Outcomes? *British Journal of Management*, *30*(1), 53–74. doi:10.1111/1467-8551.12299

Guillot, C. (2013). Avoiding THE VOID. *Internal Auditor, 70*(6), 42-47. Retrieved from http://www.theiia.org/ecm/magazine.cfm?doc_id=540

Gujarati. (2004). *Basic Econometrics*. McGraw-Hill.

Gul. (2006). *Auditors' Response to Political Connections and Cronyism in Malaysia*. http://onlinelibrary.wiley.com/doi/10.1111/j.1475-679X.2006.00220.x/abstract

Gul, F. A., & Leung, S. (2004). Board leadership, outside directors' expertise and voluntary corporate disclosure. *Journal of Accounting and Public Policy*, *23*(5), 351–379. doi:10.1016/j.jaccpubpol.2004.07.001

Gul, F., Kim, J., & Qiu, A. A. (2008). Ownership concentration, foreign shareholding, audit quality, and stock price synchronicity: Evidence from China. *Journal of Financial Economics*, 95.

Gul, F., Srinidhi, B., & Ng, A. (2011). Does board gender diversity improve the in formativeness of stock prices? *Journal of Accounting and Economics*, *51*(3), 314–338. doi:10.1016/j.jacceco.2011.01.005

Gull, A. A., Nekhili, M., Nagati, H., & Chtioui, T. (2018). Beyond gender diversity: How specific attributes of female directors affect earnings management. *The British Accounting Review*, *50*(3), 255–274. doi:10.1016/j.bar.2017.09.001

Gunawan, A. (2019). The Role of Corporate Governance Mechanism On Voluntary Disclosure. *Jurnal Akuntansi*, *23*(1), 127–142. doi:10.24912/ja.v23i1.467

Güngör, B., & Güney, G. (2019). Correlation with stock return of the corporate government performance. *Atatürk University The Journal of Social Sciences Institute*, *23*(1), 37–66.

Guthrie, J., & Parker, L. D. (1989). Corporate social reporting: A rebuttal of legitimacy theory. *Accounting and Business Research*, *19*(76), 343–352.

Gyimah-Brempong, K. (2002). Corruption, economic growth, and income inequality in Africa. *Economics of Governance*, *3*(3), 183–209. doi:10.1007101010200045

Habbash, M., Hussainey, K., & Ibrahim, A. (2016). The determinants of voluntary disclosure in Saudi Arabia: An empirical study. *International Journal of Accounting. Auditing and Performance Evaluation*, *12*(3), 213–236. doi:10.1504/IJAAPE.2016.077890

Hadani, M., Goranova, M., & Khan, R. (2011). Institutional investors, shareholder activism, and earnings management. *Journal of Business Research*, *64*(12), 1352–1360. doi:10.1016/j.jbusres.2010.12.004

Haddad, A. E., AlShattarat, W. K., AbuGhazaleh, N. M., & Nobanee, H. (2015). The impact of ownership structure and family board domination on voluntary disclosure for Jordanian listed companies. *Eurasian Business Review*, *5*(2), 203–234.

Hagemann, B., & Stroope, S. (2013). Developing the next generation of leaders. *Industrial and Commercial Training*, *45*(2), 123–126. doi:10.1108/00197851311309570

Hail, L. (2002). *The Impact of Voluntary Corporate Disclosures on the Ex Ante Cost of Capital for Swiss Firms*. Working Paper, University of Zurich.

Hai, P., & Toan, L. D.c & Quy, N. (2019). Effect of Audit Rotation, Audit Fee and Auditor Competence to Motivation Auditor and Audit Quality: Empirical Evidence in Vietnam. *Academy of Accounting and Financial Studies Journal*, *23*(2), 1–14.

Haj-Salem, I., Damak, S., & Hussainey, K. (2019). Corporate governance and risk disclosure quality: Tunisian evidence. *Journal of Accounting in Emerging Economies*, *9*(4), 567–602. doi:10.1108/JAEE-01-2019-0005

Hall-Ellis, S. D. (2015). Succession planning and staff development–a winning combination. *The Bottom Line (New York, N.Y.)*, *28*(3), 95–98. doi:10.1108/BL-05-2015-0007

Hall, L. O., & Hagen, C. D. (2014). Holistic Approach to Succession Planning Provides Added Value for Clients: Financial Service Professionals Play Key Role in Successful Plans. *Journal of Financial Service Professionals*, *68*(1).

Hambrick, D. C., & Mason, P. A. (1984). Upper echelons: The organization as a reflection of its top managers. *Academy of Management Journal*, *9*(2), 193–206.

Hamidat, M., & Al-Rifai, K. (2019). Commitment to the Requirements of Corporate Governance and Its Impact on the Quality of Financial Reports (From the Point of View of the Internal Auditors in the Jordanian Public Shareholding Industrial Companies). *Ramah Research and Studies*, *31*, 12–44.

Hamrouni, A., Boussaada, R., & Ben Farhat Toumi, N. (2019). Corporate social responsibility disclosure and debt financing. *Journal of Applied Accounting Research*.

Hand, J.R.M. (1990). A Test of the Extended Functional Fixation Hypothesis. *The Accounting Review*, *65*, 740.

Haniffa & Cooke. (2002). *Culture, Corporate Governance and Disclosure in Malaysian Corporations.* https://papers.ssrn.com/sol3/papers.cfm?abstract_id=336822

Haniffa, R. M., & Cooke, T. E. (2002). Culture, corporate governance and disclosure in Malaysian corporations. *Abacus, 38*(3), 317-349. 10.1111/1467-6281.00112

Haniffa, R., & Hudaib, M. (2006). *Corporate Governance Structure and Performance of Malaysian Listed Companies.* Academic Press.

Han, K. C., & Suk, D. Y. (1998). The Effect of Ownership Structure on Firm Performance: Additional Evidence. *Review of Financial Economics*, *7*(2), 143–155. doi:10.1016/S1058-3300(99)80150-5

Han, S., & Qiu, J. (2007). Corporate precautionary cash holdings. *Journal of Corporate Finance*, *13*(1), 43–57. Advance online publication. doi:10.1016/j.jcorpfin.2006.05.002

Harford, J., Mansi, S. A., & Maxwell, W. F. (2012). Corporate governance and firm cash holdings in the U.S. In *Corporate Governance.* Recent Developments and New Trends., doi:10.1007/978-3-642-31579-4_5

Harjoto, M., Laksmana, I., & Lee, R. (2015). Board diversity and corporate social responsibility. *Journal of Business Ethics*, *132*(4), 641–660. doi:10.100710551-014-2343-0

Harrison, J. S., & Wicks, A. C. (2013). Stakeholder theory, value, and firm performance. *Business Ethics Quarterly*, *23*(1), 97–124.

Hart, D. M. (2014). Founder nativity, founding team formation, and firm performance in the U.S. high-tech sector. *The International Entrepreneurship and Management Journal*, *10*(1), 1–22. doi:10.100711365-011-0188-x

Hasan, S. (2020). Audit Committee Effectiveness towards Financial Reporting Quality in Malaysia. In *Postgraduate Research Symposium-January 2020* (*Vol. 1*, No. 1, pp. 1-1). Academic Press.

Hasan, A., & Butt, S. A. (2009). Impact of Ownership Structure and Corporate Governance on Capital Structure of Pakistani Listed Companies. *International Journal of Business and Management*, *4*(2), 50–57. doi:10.5539/ijbm.v4n2p50

Hassanein, A., & Kokel, A. (2019). Corporate cash hoarding and corporate governance mechanisms: Evidence from Borsa Istanbul. *Asia-Pacific Journal of Accounting & Economics*, 1–18. Advance online publication. doi:10.1080/16081625.2019.1617753

Hassan, Y., Hijazi, R., & Naser, K. (2017). Does audit committee substitute or complement other corporate governance mechanisms. *Managerial Auditing Journal*, *32*(7), 658–668. doi:10.1108/MAJ-08-2016-1423

Haynes, K. T., & Hillman, A. (2010). The effect of board capital and CEO power on strategic change. *Strategic Management Journal*, *31*(11), 1145–1163. doi:10.1002mj.859

Healy, P. M., Hutton, A. P., & Palepu, K. G. (1999). Stock Performance and Intermediation Changes Surrounding Sustained Increases in Disclosure. *Contemporary Accounting Research*, *16*(3), 485–520. doi:10.1111/j.1911-3846.1999.tb00592.x

Healy, P. M., & Palepu, K. G. (2001). Information asymmetry, corporate disclosure, and the capital markets: A review of the empirical disclosure literature. *Journal of Accounting and Economics*, *31*(1-3), 405–440. Advance online publication. doi:10.1016/S0165-4101(01)00018-0

Healy, P. M., & Wahlen, J. M. (1998). A review of the earnings management literature and its implications for standard setting. Boston. *Accounting Horizons*, 365–383.

Heikal, M., Khaddafi, M., & Ummah, A. (2014). Influence analysis of return on assets (ROA), return on equity (ROE), net profit margin (NPM), debt to equity ratio (DER), and current ratio (CR), against corporate profit growth in automotive in Indonesia stock exchange. *International Journal of Academic Research in Business and Social Sciences, 4*(12), 102–114. doi:10.6007/IJARBSS/v4-i12/1331

Held, D., & Ulrichsen, K. (Eds.). (2013). *The transformation of the Gulf: politics, economics and the global order.* Routledge. doi:10.4324/9780203813218

Helfat, C. E., & Bailey, E. E. (2005). External succession and disruptive change: Heirs-apparent, forced turnover and firm performance. *Strategic Organization, 3*(1), 47–83. doi:10.1177/1476127005050031

Henderson, J. C., & Venkatraman, N. (1993). Strategic Alignment: Leveraging Information Technology for Transforming Organizations. *IBM Systems Journal, 32*(1), 4-16.

Hendricks, L. (2002). How important is human capital for development? Evidence from immigrant earnings. *The American Economic Review, 92*(1), 198–219. doi:10.1257/000282802760015676

Henry, C. M., & Springborg, R. (2010). *Globalization and the Politics of Development in the Middle East* (Vol. 1). Cambridge University Press. doi:10.1017/CBO9780511778162

Herciu, M., Ogrean, C., & Belascu, L. (2011). A Du Pont analysis of the 20 most profitable companies in the world. *2010 International Conference on Business and Economics Research,* 45-48.

Hermalin, B. E., & Weisbach, M. S. (2003). Boards of directors as an endogenously determined institution: A survey of the economic literature. *FRBNY Economic Policy Review, 9,* 7–26.

Hernández-Carrión, C., Camarero-Izquierdo, C., & Gutiérrez-Cillán, J. (2020). The internal mechanisms of entrepreneurs' social capital: A multi-network analysis. *BRQ Business Research Quarterly, 23*(1), 1–19. doi:10.1177/2340944420901047

Herriott, R. E., & Firestone, W. A. (1983). Multisite qualitative policy research: Optimizing description and generalizability. *Educational Researcher, 12*(2), 14–19. doi:10.3102/0013189X012002014

Hessels, J., & Terjesen, S. (2010). Resource dependency and institutional theory perspectives on direct and indirect export choices. *Small Business Economics, 34*(2), 203–220. doi:10.100711187-008-9156-4

He, X., Pittman, J. A., Rui, O. M., & Wu, D. (2017). Do social ties between external auditors and audit committee members affect audit quality? *The Accounting Review, 92*(5), 61–87. doi:10.2308/accr-51696

Hilb, M. (2006). *New corporate governance, successful board management tools* (2nd ed.). Springer Berlin Heidelberg. doi:10.1007/3-540-28168-1

Hill, C. W., & Jones, T. M. (1992). Stakeholder-agency theory. *Journal of Management Studies, 29*(2), 131–154. doi:10.1111/j.1467-6486.1992.tb00657.x

Hillier, D. (2004). *Firm Performance, Entrenchment and Managerial Succession in Family Firms.* SSRN eLibrary.

Hillman, A. J., Shropshire, C., & Cannella, A. A. Jr. (2007). Organizational predictors of women on corporate boards. *Academy of Management Journal, 50*(4), 941–952. doi:10.5465/amj.2007.26279222

Hillman, A., Cannella, J., & Paetzold, R. (2000). The resource dependent role of corporate directors: Strategic adoption of board composition in response to environmental change. *Journal of Management Studies, 37*(2), 235–255. doi:10.1111/1467-6486.00179

Hillman, A., Withers, M., & Collins, B. (2009). Resource dependence theory: A review. *Journal of Management, 35*(6), 1404–1427. doi:10.1177/0149206309343469

Hills, A. (2009). Succession planning–or smart talent management? *Industrial and Commercial Training*, *41*(1), 3–8. doi:10.1108/00197850910927697

Himmelberg, C. P., Hubbard, R. G., & Palia, D. (1999). Understanding the determinants of managerial ownership and the link between ownership and performance. *Journal of Financial Economics*, *53*(3), 353–384. doi:10.1016/S0304-405X(99)00025-2

Hitt, L. M., Wu, D. J., & Zhou, X. G. (2002). Investment in enterprise resource planning: Business impact and productivity measures. *Journal of Management Information Systems*, *19*(1), 71–98. doi:10.1080/07421222.2002.11045716

Hobbs, C., & Wright, C. (2010). Impact and Implications of IFRS. Conversion or Convergence. *Journal of Bank Accounting & Finance*, 21-28.

Hoch, H. (2013). Book review–Maggots for millions. *Deutsche Entomologische Zeitschrift*, *60*(2), 271–271.

Hoffmann, S., & Rodrigo, P. (2018). *Board of Director Gender Diversity and Its Impact on Earnings Management: An Empirical Analysis for Selected European Firms*. Academic Press.

Holderness, C. (2003). A Survey of Blockholders and Corporate Control. *Economic Policy Review*, *9*, 51–63.

Horváth, R., & Spirollari, P. (2012). Do the Board of Directors' characteristics influence firm's performance? The U.S. evidence. *Prague Economic Papers*, *21*(4), 470–486. doi:10.18267/j.pep.435

Ho, S. M., & Wong, K. S. (2003). Perception of Corporate Reporting and Disclosure. *International Journal of Disclosure and Governance*, *1*(1), 71–81. doi:10.1057/palgrave.jdg.2040014

Ho, S. S. M., & Wong, K. S. (2001). A study of the relationship between corporate governance structures and the extent of voluntary disclosure. *The International Journal of Accounting. Auditing and Taxation*, *10*(2), 139–156. doi:10.1016/S1061-9518(01)00041-6

Hossain, K. K. (2017). *The primary drivers and mechanisms of corporate governance*. https://www.quora.com

Hossain, M., Mitra, S., Rezaee, Z., & Sarath, B. (2011). Corporate Governance and Earnings Management in the Pre– and Post–Sarbanes-Oxley Act Regimes: Evidence from Implicated Option Backdating Firms. *Journal of Accounting, Auditing & Finance*, *26*(2), 279–315. doi:10.1177/0148558X11401218

Hou, K., & Robertson, D. (2000). *Towards a Property Rights view of Ownership*. Working Paper.

Huang, P., Louwers, T., Moffitt, J., & Zhang, Y. (2008). Ethical Management, Corporate Governance, and Abnormal Accruals. *Journal of Business Ethics*, *83*(3), 469–487. doi:10.100710551-007-9632-9

Huang, S.-M., Ou, C.-S., Chen, C.-M., & Lin, B. (2006). An empirical study of relationship between IT investment and firm performance: A resource-based perspective. *European Journal of Operational Research*, *173*(3), 984–999. doi:10.1016/j.ejor.2005.06.013

Hu, M., & Loh, L. (2018). Board governance and sustainability disclosure: A cross-sectional study of Singapore-listed companies. *Sustainability*, *10*(7), 2578.

Humphery-Jenner, M. (2014). Takeover defenses, innovation, and value creation: Evidence from acquisition decisions. *Strategic Management Journal*, *35*(5), 668–690. doi:10.1002mj.2121

Hung, C. H. D., Jiang, Y., Liu, F. H., Tu, H., & Wang, S. (2017). Bank political connections and performance in China. *Journal of Financial Stability*, *32*, 57–69. doi:10.1016/j.jfs.2017.09.003

Hu, Q., & Quan, J. J. (2005). Evaluating the impact of IT investments on productivity: A causal analysis at industry level. *International Journal of Information Management*, *25*(1), 39–53. doi:10.1016/j.ijinfomgt.2004.10.006

Hutson, E., Laing, E., & Ye, M. (2019). Mutual fund ownership and foreign exchange risk in Chinese firms. *Journal of International Financial Markets, Institutions and Money*, *60*, 169–192. doi:10.1016/j.intfin.2018.12.012

Huyghebaert, N., & Xu, W. (2015). What determines the market share of investment banks in Chinese domestic IPOs? *China Economic Review*, *34*, 150–168. doi:10.1016/j.chieco.2015.05.001

Hwang, D., Yang, M. G. M., & Hong, P. (2015). Mediating effect of IT-enabled capabilities on competitive performance outcomes: An empirical investigation of ERP implementation. *Journal of Engineering and Technology Management*, *36*, 1–23. doi:10.1016/j.jengtecman.2015.03.001

Ibrahim, A. H., & Hanefah, M. M. (2016). Board diversity and corporate social responsibility in Jordan. *Journal of Financial Reporting and Accounting*, *14*(2), 279–298. doi:10.1108/JFRA-06-2015-0065

Ibrahim, K. (2014). Firm Characteristics and Voluntary Segments Disclosure among the Largest Firms in Nigeria. International Journal of Trade. *Economics and Finance*, *5*(4), 327.

Ilmudeen, A., Bao, Y., & Alharbi, I. M. (2019). How does business-IT strategic alignment dimension impact on organizational performance measures: Conjecture and empirical analysis. *Journal of Enterprise Information Management*, *32*(3), 457–476. doi:10.1108/JEIM-09-2018-0197

Ilmudeen, A., & Yukun, B. (2018). Mediating role of managing information technology and its impact on firm performance: Insight from China. *Industrial Management & Data Systems*, *118*(4), 912–929. doi:10.1108/IMDS-06-2017-0252

Institute on Governance (IOG). (2019). *What is Governance*. Available at https://iog.ca/what-is-governance

International Standards on Auditing (ISA). (n.d.). *Financial Stability Board.* Retrieved April 29, 2012, from http://www.financialstabilityboard.org/cos/cos_021001b.htm

International Standards on Auditing 400. (n.d.). *Risk Assessments and Internal Control.* Retrieved September 14, 2011 from http://www.icisa.cag.gov.in/Background% 20Material/ RISK%20ASSt%20AND%20INTNL%20CONTROL%20 ISA_400.pdf/

Isbell, M. G., Seth, J. G., Atwood, R. D., & Ray, T. C. (2015). Development and implementation of client-centered nutrition education programs in a 4-stage framework. *American Journal of Public Health*, *105*(4), e65–e70. doi:10.2105/AJPH.2014.302512 PMID:25713950

Ismail & Chandler. (2004). *The timeliness of quarterly financial reports of companies in Malaysia.* http://www.emeraldinsight.com/doi/abs/10.1108/eb060770

Ismail, W., Adibah, W., Van Zijl, T., & Dunstan, K. (2010). *Earnings quality and the adoption of IFRSbased accounting standards: Evidence from an emerging market.* Available at SSRN 1566634

Ittonen, K., Miettinen, J., & Vähämaa, S. (2010). Does female representation on audit committees affect audit fees? *Quarterly Journal of Finance and Accounting*, 113-139.

Iyer, V. M., Bamber, E. M., & Griffin, J. (2013). Characteristics of audit committee financial experts: An empirical study. *Managerial Auditing Journal.*

Jain, B. A., Li, J., & Shao, Y. (2013). Governance, product market competition and cash management in IPO firms. *Journal of Banking & Finance*, *37*(6), 2052–2068. Advance online publication. doi:10.1016/j.jbankfin.2013.01.032

Jantti, M., & Greenhalgh, N. (2012). Leadership competencies: A reference point for development and evaluation. *Library Management*, *33*(6/7), 421–428. doi:10.1108/01435121211266249

Jaskiewicz, P., Heinrichs, K., Rau, S. B., & Reay, T. (2016). To be or not to be: How family firms manage family and commercial logics in succession. *Entrepreneurship Theory and Practice*, *40*(4), 781–813. doi:10.1111/etap.12146

Javaid, F. (2015). Impact of corporate governance index on firm performance: Evidence from Pakistani manufacturing sector. *Journal of Governance and Regulation*, *4*(3), 163–174. doi:10.22495/jgr_v4_i3_c1_p6

Jayaraman, N., Khorana, A., Nelling, E., & Covin, J. (2000). CEO Founder Status and Firm Financial Performance; Narayanan. *Strategic Management Journal*, *21*(12), 1215–1224. doi:10.1002/1097-0266(200012)21:12<1215::AID-SMJ146>3.0.CO;2-0

Jebran, K., Chen, S., & Tauni, M. Z. (2019). Principal-principal conflicts and corporate cash holdings: Evidence from China. *Research in International Business and Finance*, *49*, 55–70. doi:10.1016/j.ribaf.2019.02.010

Jelinek, K. (2007). The effect of leverage increases on earnings management. Journal of Business and. *Economic Studies.*, *13*(2), 24–46.

Jelinek, K., & Stuerke, P. (2009). The Nonlinear Relation between Agency Costs and Managerial Equity Ownership: Evidence of Decreasing Benefits of Increasing Ownership. *International Journal of Managerial Finance*, *5*(2), 156–178. doi:10.1108/17439130910947886

Jensen & Meckling. (1976). *Theory of the Firm: Managerial Behavior, Agency Costs and Ownership Structure*. Academic Press.

Jensen, M. C. (1993). The modern industrial revolution, exit, and the failure of internal control systems. *The Journal of Finance, 48*(3), 831-880.

Jensen, M. C. W. H. M. (1976). Theory of the Firm : Managerial Behavior, Agency Costs and Ownership Structure. *Journal of Financial Economics.*

Jensen, M. (1986). American Economic Association Agency Costs of Free Cash Flow, Corporate Finance, and Takeovers. *The American Economic Review.*

Jensen, M. (1993). The modern industrial revolution, exit, and the failure of internal control systems. *The Journal of Finance*, *48*(3), 831–880. doi:10.1111/j.1540-6261.1993.tb04022.x

Jensen, M. C. (1986). Agency costs of free cash flow, corporate finance, and takeovers. *The American Economic Review*, *76*(2), 323–329.

Jensen, M. C., & Meckling, W. H. (1976). Agency Costs and the Theory of the Firm. *Journal of Financial Economics*, *3*(4), 305–360. doi:10.1016/0304-405X(76)90026-X

Jermakowicz, E., & Gornik-Tomaszewski, S. (2006). Implementing IFRS from the perspective of EU publicly traded companies. *Journal of International Accounting, Auditing & Taxation*, *15*(2), 170–196. doi:10.1016/j.intaccaudtax.2006.08.003

Jia, N., Huang, K. G., & Man Zhang, C. (2019). Public governance, corporate governance, and firm innovation: An examination of state-owned enterprises. *Academy of Management Journal*, *62*(1), 220–247. doi:10.5465/amj.2016.0543

Jiang, F., & Kim, A. K. (2015). Corporate governance in China: A modern perspective. *Journal of Corporate Finance*, *32*, 190–216. doi:10.1016/j.jcorpfin.2014.10.010

Jiang, P. (2004). The Relationship between Ownership Structure and Firm Performance: An Empirical Analysis over Heilongjiang Listed companies. *Journal of Nature and Science*, *2*, 87–91.

Jiang, W., Lee, P., & Anandarajan, A. (2008). The association between corporate governance and earnings quality: Further evidence using the GOV-score. *Advances in International Accounting, 24*(2), 191–201. doi:10.1016/j.adiac.2008.08.011

Jiraporn, P., Miller, G. A., Yoon, S. S., & Kim, Y. S. (2008). Is earnings management opportunistic or beneficial? An agency theory perspective. *International Review of Financial Analysis, 17*(3), 622–634. doi:10.1016/j.irfa.2006.10.005

Jiraporn, P., Singh, M., & Lee, C. I. (2009). Ineffective corporate governance: Director busyness and board committee memberships. *Journal of Banking & Finance, 33*(5), 819–828. Advance online publication. doi:10.1016/j.jbankfin.2008.09.020

Jiraporn, P., Singh, M., & Lee, C. I. (2009). Ineffective corporate governance: Director busyness. *Journal of Business Finance & Accounting, 26*, 797–805.

Jizi, M. (2017). The influence of board composition on sustainable development disclosure. *Business Strategy and the Environment, 26*(5), 640–655.

Joecks, J., Pull, K., & Vetter, K. (2013). Gender diversity in the boardroom and firm performance: What exactly constitutes a "critical mass?" *Journal of Business Ethics, 118*(1), 61–72. doi:10.100710551-012-1553-6

Johnes, J., Izzeldin, M., Pappas, V., & Alexakis, C. (2018). Performance and Productivity in Islamic and Conventional Banks: Evidence from the Global Financial Crisis. *Economic Modelling*, •••, 79.

John, K., & Senbet, L. W. (1998). Corporate governance and board effectiveness. *Journal of Banking & Finance, 22*(4), 371–403. doi:10.1016/S0378-4266(98)00005-3

Johnson, S. G., Schnatterly, K., & Hill, A. D. (2013). Board composition beyond independence: Social capital, human capital, and demographics. *Journal of Management, 39*(1), 232–262. doi:10.1177/0149206312463938

Jordan Securities Commission. (2009). *Corporate governance code for publicly listed companies in Jordan*. Available at: www.jsc.gov.jo

Juini, F. (2013). Corporate governance and the level of financial disclosure by Tunisian firm. *Journal of Business Studies Quarterly, 4*(3), 95–111.

Julizaerma, M. K., & Sori, Z. M. (2012). Gender diversity in the boardroom and firm performance of Malaysian public listed companies. *Procedia: Social and Behavioral Sciences, 65*, 1077–1085. doi:10.1016/j.sbspro.2012.11.374

Jurkus, A. F., Park, J. C., & Woodard, L. S. (2011). Women in top management and agency costs. *Journal of Business Research, 64*(2), 180–186. doi:10.1016/j.jbusres.2009.12.010

Kabajeh, M. A. M., Nuaimat, S. M. A., & Dahmash, F. N. (2012). The relationship between the ROA, ROE and ROI ratios with Jordanian ınsurance public companies market share prices. *International Journal of Humanities and Social Science, 2*(11), 115–120.

Kabir, R., Cantrijn, D., & Jeunink, A. (1997). Takeover defenses, ownership structure and stock returns in the Netherlands: An empirical analysis. *Strategic Management Journal, 18*(2), 97–109. doi:10.1002/(SICI)1097-0266(199702)18:2<97::AID-SMJ855>3.0.CO;2-2

Kakilli Acaravcı, S., Kandır, S. Y., & Zelka, A. (2015). Investigating the ımpact of corporate governance over the performance of BIST companies. *Academic Review of Economic and Administrative Sciences, 8*(1), 171–183.

Kalbers, L. P., & Fogarty, T. J. (1993). Audit committee effectiveness: An empirical investigation of the contribution of power. *Auditing, 12*(1), 24.

Kalcheva, I., & Lins, K. V. (2007). International evidence on cash holdings and expected managerial agency problems. *Review of Financial Studies, 20*(4), 1087–1112. Advance online publication. doi:10.1093/rfs/hhm023

Kamar, K. (2017). Analysis of the effect of return on equity (ROE) and debt to equity ratio (DER) on stock price on cement industry listed in Indonesia stock exchange (Idx) in the year of 2011-2015. *IOSR Journal of Business and Management, 19*(5), 66–76. doi:10.9790/487X-1905036676

Kang, C. (2005). *Market economy and corporate governance – fairness and transparency for sustainable growth.* 6th Global Forum on Reinventing Government: Toward Participatory and Transparent Governance, Seoul, South Korea.

Kaplan, S., Pany, K., Samuels, J., & Zhang, J. (2009). An examination of the association between gender and reporting intentions for fraudulent financial reporting. *Journal of Business Ethics, 87*(1), 15-30.

Kapopoulos, P., & Lazaretou, S. (2006). *Corporate Ownership Structure and Firm Performance: Evidence from Greek Firms.* Special Studies Division, Working Paper No.37. Bank of Greece: Economic Research Department.

Karamanou, I., & Vafeas, N. (2005). The Association between Corporate Boards, Audit Committees, and Management Earnings Forecasts: An Empirical Analysis. *Journal of Accounting Research, 43*(3), 453–486. doi:10.1111/j.1475-679X.2005.00177.x

Karmakar, N. (2014). Tips of High-Performance Team Building for Organizational Effectiveness. *i-Manager's. Journal of Management, 8*(4), 15.

Kaserer, C., & Moldenhauer, B. (2008). Insider Ownership and Corporate Performance: Evidence from Germany. *Academic Review of Managerial Science, 2*(1), 1–35. doi:10.100711846-007-0009-3

Kassar, F. M. (2018). The Impact of Compliance with Corporate Governance Rules in Reducing Earnings Management Practices -An Empirical Study on Private Banks and Insurance Companies Listed in Damascus Stock Exchange Market. *Al-Quds Open University Journal for Administrative and Economic Research, 3*(10), 97–122.

Kassem, R., & Higson, A. (2012). The new fraud triangle model. *Journal of Emerging Trends in Economics and Management Sciences, 3*(3), 191-195.

Katmon, N., Mohamad, Z. Z., Norwani, N. M., & Al Farooque, O. (2019). Comprehensive board diversity and quality of corporate social responsibility disclosure: Evidence from an emerging market. *Journal of Business Ethics, 157*(2), 447–481.

Kaunda, S., & Nkhoma, A. (2013). Intergenerational survival of family businesses: Factors affecting the succession success of family owned businesses in Malawi. *European Journal of Business and Management, 5*(7), 157–164.

Kearns, G. S., & Lederer, A. L. (2003). A resource-based view of strategic IT alignment: How knowledge sharing creates competitive advantage. *Decision Sciences, 34*(1), 1–29. doi:10.1111/1540-5915.02289

Keasey, K. & Wright, M. (1993) Issues in corporate accountability and governance: An editorial. *Accounting and Business Research, 23*(91A), 291-303.

Keasey, K., & Wright, M. (1993). Issues in corporate accountability and governance: An editorial. *Accounting and Business Research, 23*(sup1), 291-303.

Khan, I. A. (2014). Adaptation and convergence in corporate governance to international norms in Pakistan (PhD). University of Glasgow.

Khan, I. A. (2017). Enforcement of Corporate Laws and Stock Market Reforms in Pakistan. *Pakistan Journal of social Sciences,* 37.

Khan, A., Muttakin, M. B., & Siddiqui, J. (2013). Corporate governance and corporate social responsibility disclosures: Evidence from an emerging economy. *Journal of Business Ethics, 114*(2), 207–223.

Khan, F.,, & Nouman, M. (2017). Does Ownership Structure Affect Firm's Performance? Empirical Evidence from Pakistan. Empirical Evidence from Pakistan, 19.

Khan, M. A., Khidmat, W. B., Ullah, F., & Khan, N. U. (2019). Corporate governance and earnings management: The role of the board of director. *Sarhad Journal of Management Sciences*, *5*(2), 317–342.

Khlif, H., & Achek, I. (2017). Gender in accounting research: A review. *Managerial Auditing Journal*, *32*(6), 627–655. doi:10.1108/MAJ-02-2016-1319

Khlif, H., & Samaha, K. (2019). Board independence and internal control quality in Egypt: Does CEO duality matter? *International Journal of Law and Management*, *61*(2), 345–358. doi:10.1108/IJLMA-08-2017-0202

Khoury, T., Junkunc, M., & Deeds, D. (2013). The social construction of legitimacy through signaling social capital: Exploring the conditional value of alliances and underwriters at IPO. *Entrepreneurship Theory and Practice*, *37*(3), 569–601. doi:10.1111/etap.12030

Kiel, G. C., & Nicholson, G. J. (2003). Board Composition and Corporate Performance: How the Australian Experience Informs Contrasting Theories of Corporate Governance. *Corporate Governance*, *11*(3), 189–205. doi:10.1111/1467-8683.00318

Kim, J.-B., Liu, X., & Zheng, L. (2010). The impact of Mandatory IFRS Adoption on Audit Fee: Theory and Evidence. *CAAA Annual Conference 2010*. Available at SSRN: http://ssrn.com/abstract=1530776

Kim, H., Kwak, B., Lim, Y., & Yu, J. (2017). Audit committee accounting expertise, CEO power, and audit pricing. *Asia-Pacific Journal of Accounting & Economics*, *24*(3-4), 421–439. doi:10.1080/16081625.2015.1105753

Kim, H., & Lim, C. (2010). Diversity, outsider directors' and firm valuation: Korean evidence. *Journal of Business Research*, *63*(3), 284–291. doi:10.1016/j.jbusres.2009.01.013

Kim, J. K., Xiang, J. Y., & Lee, S. (2009). The impact of IT investment on firm performance in China: An empirical investigation of the Chinese electronics industry. *Technological Forecasting and Social Change*, *76*(5), 678–687. doi:10.1016/j.techfore.2008.03.008

Kim, K. A., Kitsabunnarat-Chatjuthamard, P., & Nofsinger, J. R. (2007). Large shareholders, board independence, and minority shareholder rights: Evidence from Europe. *Journal of Corporate Finance*, *13*(5), 859–880. Advance online publication. doi:10.1016/j.jcorpfin.2007.09.001

Kim, N. B., & Yi, C. H. (2006). Ownership structure, business group affiliation, listing status, and earnings management: Evidence from Korea. *Contemporary Accounting Research*, *23*(2), 427–464. doi:10.1506/7T5B-72FV-MHJV-E697

Kim, T. H. (2012). Succession planning in hospitals and the association with organizational performance. *Nursing Economics*, *30*(1), 14. PMID:22479959

Kim, Y. (2005). Board network characteristics and firm performance in Korea. *Corporate Governance*, *13*(6), 800–808. doi:10.1111/j.1467-8683.2005.00471.x

Kim, Y., & Cannella, A. A. Jr. (2008). Toward a social capital theory of director selection. *Corporate Governance*, *16*(4), 282–293. doi:10.1111/j.1467-8683.2008.00693.x

King, M. R., & Santor, E. (2008). Family values: Ownership structure, performance and capital structure of Canadian firms. *Journal of Banking & Finance*, *32*(11), 2423–2432. doi:10.1016/j.jbankfin.2008.02.002

Kini, O., Kracaw, W., & Mian, S. (2004). The nature of discipline by corporate takeovers. *The Journal of Finance*, *59*(4), 1511–1552. doi:10.1111/j.1540-6261.2004.00671.x

Kippist, L. (2013). Bridges or barriers? Succession planning for doctor managers. *International Employment Relations Review*, *19*(2), 24.

Kirillova, E. A., Pozdnyakova, E. V., Gorevoy, E. D., Ershova, I. V., & Nadezhin, N. N. (2015). Transboundary succession of business: Problems related to practice. *International Journal of Economics and Financial Issues*, *5*(3S), 125–130.

Klapper, L. F., & Love, I. (2004). Corporate governance, investor protection, and performance in emerging markets. *Journal of Corporate Finance*, *10*(5), 703–728. Advance online publication. doi:10.1016/S0929-1199(03)00046-4

Klein, A. (2002). Audit committee, board of director characteristics, and earnings management. *Journal of Accounting and Economics*, *33*(3), 375–400. doi:10.1016/S0165-4101(02)00059-9

Klein, A. (2002). Economic determinants of audit committee independence. *The Accounting Review*, *77*(2), 435–452. doi:10.2308/accr.2002.77.2.435

Klein, P., Shapiro, D., & Young, J. (2005). Corporate Governance, Family Ownership and Firm Value: The Canadian evidence. *Corporate Governance*, *13*(6), 769–784. doi:10.1111/j.1467-8683.2005.00469.x

Klitgaard, R. (1994). A framework for a country programme against corruption. *Accountability and Transparency in International Economic Development: The Launching of Transparency International, 55.*

Kohlberg. (1969). *Kohlberg's stages of moral development*. Academic Press.

Kolbjørnsrud, V. (2017). Agency problems and governance mechanisms in collaborative communities. *Strategic Organization*, *15*(2), 141–173. doi:10.1177/1476127016653727

Kole, S. (1996). Managerial ownership and firm performance: Incentives or rewards? *Advances in Financial Economics*, *2*, 119–149.

Kopp, M. (2019). *Agency Theory*. Available at https://www.investopedia.com

Kostopoulos, K. C., Spanos, Y. E., & Prastacos, G. P. (2002). The resource-based view of the firm and innovation: identification of critical linkages. *The 2nd European Academy of Management Conference*, 1-19.

Kostova, T., & Roth, K. (2003). Social capital in multinational corporations and a micro-macro model of its formation. *Academy of Management Review*, *28*(2), 297–317. doi:10.5465/amr.2003.9416356

Krambia-Kapardis, M. (2002). A fraud detection model: A must for auditors. *Journal of Financial Regulation and Compliance*, *10*(3), 266–278. doi:10.1108/13581980210810256

Kreab, G. A. (2014). *China's IPO Reboot*. http://www.kreab.com/wp-content/uploads/2014/01/Kreab-Gavin-Anderson-Research-Asia-Report-on-IPO-Reform-in-China.pdf

Krippendorff, K. (1980). *Content Analysis: An Introduction to its Methodology*. Sage Publications.

Krishnan, G. V., & Parsons, L. M. (2008). Getting to the bottom line: An exploration of gender and earnings quality. *Journal of Business Ethics*, *78*(1-2), 65–76. doi:10.100710551-006-9314-z

Krishnan, G. V., & Visvanathan, G. (2008). Does the SOX definition of an accounting expert matter? The association between audit committee directors' accounting expertise and accounting conservatism. *Contemporary Accounting Research*, *25*(3), 827–858. doi:10.1506/car.25.3.7

Kuan, T. H., Li, C. S., & Chu, S. H. (2011). Cash holdings and corporate governance in family-controlled firms. *Journal of Business Research*, *64*(7), 757–764. Advance online publication. doi:10.1016/j.jbusres.2010.07.004

Kuan, T. H., Li, C. S., & Liu, C. C. (2012). Corporate governance and cash holdings: A quantile regression approach. *International Review of Economics & Finance, 24*, 303–314. Advance online publication. doi:10.1016/j.iref.2012.04.006

Kumar, N. & Singh, J. (2013). Effect of board size and promoter ownership on firm value: some empirical findings from India. *Corporate Governance: The International Journal of Business in Society.*

Kumaran, M. (2015). Succession planning process that includes visible minority librarians. *Library Management, 36*(6/7), 434–447. doi:10.1108/LM-12-2014-0138

Kunze, F., Boehm, S. A., & Bruch, H. (2011). Age diversity, age discrimination climate and performance consequences—A cross organizational study. *Journal of Organizational Behavior, 32*(2), 264–290. doi:10.1002/job.698

Kunze, F., Boehm, S., & Bruch, H. (2013). Age, resistance to change, and job performance. *Journal of Managerial Psychology, 28*(7/8), 741–760. doi:10.1108/JMP-06-2013-0194

Kusnadi, Y., Leong, K. S., Suwardy, T., & Wang, J. (2016). Audit committees and financial reporting quality in Singapore. *Journal of Business Ethics, 139*(1), 197–214. doi:10.100710551-015-2679-0

Kyaw, K., Olugbode, M., & Petracci, B. (2015). Does gender diverse board mean less earnings management? *Finance Research Letters, 14*, 135–141. doi:10.1016/j.frl.2015.05.006

La Porta, R., Lopez-De-Silanes, F., & Shleifer, A. (1999). Corporate ownership around the world. *The Journal of Finance, 54*(2), 471–51. doi:10.1111/0022-1082.00115

La Porta, R., Lopez-De-Silanes, F., Shleifer, A., & Vishny, R. (2000). Investor protection and corporate governance. *Journal of Financial Economics, 58*(1-2), 3–27. Advance online publication. doi:10.1016/S0304-405X(00)00065-9

La Porta, R., Lopez-De-Silanes, F., Shleifer, A., & Vishny, R. W. (1998). Law and Finance. *Journal of Political Economy, 106*(6), 1113–1155. doi:10.1086/250042

La Porta, R., Lopez-De-Silanes, F., Shleifer, A., & Vishny, R. W. (2000). Agency Problems and Dividend Policies around the World. *The Journal of Finance, 55*(1), 1–33. doi:10.1111/0022-1082.00199

Labelle, R., Gargouri, R. M., & Francoeur, C. (2010). Ethics, diversity management, and financial reporting quality. *Journal of Business Ethics, 93*(2), 335–353. doi:10.100710551-009-0225-7

Lakhal, F. (2005). Voluntary earnings disclosures and corporate governance: Evidence from France. *Review of Accounting and Finance, 4*(3), 64–85. doi:10.1108/eb043431

Lakhal, F., Aguir, A., Lakhal, N., & Malek, A. (2015). Do women on boards and in top management reduce earnings management? Evidence in France. *Journal of Applied Business Research, 31*(3), 1107. doi:10.19030/jabr.v31i3.9236

Lambertides, N. (2009). Sudden CEO vacancy and the long-run economic consequences. *Managerial Finance, 35*(7), 645–661. doi:10.1108/03074350910960364

Lan, L. (2012). *Goals of Corporate Governance - A Singapore Perspective.* EU-Asia Corporate Governance Dialogue, Faculty of Law & NUS Business School, The National University of Singapore. Available at https://www.fsa.go.jp

Lang, M. H., & Lundholm, R. J. (1996). Corporate Disclosure Policy and Analyst Behavior. *The Accounting Review, 71*(4), 467–492.

Larner, R. J. (1966). Ownership and Control in the 200 Largest Non-Financial Corporations. *The American Economic Review, 56*, 777.

Lausten, M. (2002). CEO turnover, firm performance and corporate governance: Empirical evidence on Danish firms. *International Journal of Industrial Organization*, *20*(3), 391–414. doi:10.1016/S0167-7187(00)00083-7

Lee, S. (2008). *Ownership Structure and Financial Performance: Evidence from Panel Data of South Korea.* Working Paper No.17. University of Utah, Department of Economics.

Lee, C.-F., & Lee, K. (2010). *Cash Holdings, Corporate Governance Structure and Firm Valuation*. doi:10.2139srn.1536481

Leech, D., & Leahy, J. (1991). Ownership structure, control type classifications and the performance of large British companies. *Economic Journal (London)*, *101*(409), 1418–1437. doi:10.2307/2234893

Lee, J. M., Kim, J., & Bae, J. (2020). Founder CEOs and innovation: Evidence from CEO sudden deaths in public firms. *Research Policy*, *49*(1), 103862. doi:10.1016/j.respol.2019.103862

Lee, P., Stokes, D., Taylor, S., & Walter, T. (2003). The association between audit quality, accounting disclosures and firm-specific risk: Evidence from initial public offerings. *Journal of Accounting and Public Policy*, *22*(5), 377–400. doi:10.1016/j.jaccpubpol.2003.08.003

Leger, J. Y. (2003). *La communication financière*. Dunod.

Lennox, C., (1990). *Audit Quality and Auditor Size: an Evaluation of Reputation and Deep Pockets Hypotheses*. Academic Press.

Leonard, J. (2008). What Are We Aligning? Implications of a Dynamic Approach to Alignment. ACIS 2008 Proceedings, 76.

Liang, H., Wang, N., Xue, Y., & Ge, S. (2017). Unraveling the Alignment Paradox: How Does Business—IT Alignment Shape Organizational Agility? *Information Systems Research*, *28*(4), 863–879. doi:10.1287/isre.2017.0711

Liao, L., Lin, T. P., & Zhang, Y. (2018). Corporate board and corporate social responsibility assurance: Evidence from China. *Journal of Business Ethics*, *150*(1), 211–225.

Li, J., Mangena, M., & Pike, R. (2012). The effect of audit committee characteristics on intellectual capital disclosure. *The British Accounting Review*, *44*(2), 98–110. doi:10.1016/j.bar.2012.03.003

Lin, H.-L., & Yen, A.-R. (2010). *The Effects of IFRS Adoption on Audit Fees for Listed Companies in China* (Dissertation). National Chiao-Ton University. HsinChu, Taiwan & Northeastern Illinois University, Chicago, IL, US.

Lin, J., & Hwang, M. (2010). Audit Quality, Corporate Governance, and Earnings Management: A Meta-Analysis. *International Journal of Auditing, 10*, 1099-1123.

Lin, C., Lin, P., Song, F. M., & Li, C. (2011). Managerial incentives, CEO characteristics and corporate innovation in China's private sector. *Journal of Comparative Economics*, *39*(2), 176–190. doi:10.1016/j.jce.2009.12.001

Lin, C., Ma, Y., & Su, D. (2009). Corporate governance and firm efficiency: Evidence from China's publicly listed firms. *Managerial and Decision Economics*, *30*(3), 193–209. doi:10.1002/mde.1447

Linck, J. S., Netter, J. M., & Yang, T. (2009). The effects and unintended consequences of the Sarbanes-Oxley Act on the supply and demand for directors. *Review of Financial Studies*, *22*(8), 3287–3328. doi:10.1093/rfs/hhn084

Lin, J., & Hwang, M. (2010). Audit Quality, Corporate Governance, and Earnings Management: A Meta-Analysis. *International Journal of Auditing*, *14*(1), 57–77. doi:10.1111/j.1099-1123.2009.00403.x

Lin, N. (2002). *Social capital: A theory of social structure and action.* Cambridge university press.

Lin, N., Vaughn, J. C., & Ensel, W. (1981). Social resources and occupational status attainment. *Social Forces*, *59*(4), 1163–1181. doi:10.2307/2577987

Lipton, L., & Lorsch, J. (1992). A modest proposal for improved corporate governance. *Business Lawyer*, *48*(1), 59–77.

Liu, J., & Andersson, T. (2014). *Mind the Gap: Expectations on the Role of UK Non-Executive Directors* (RWPBM Working Paper No. 1402). Retrieved from Regent's Working Papers in Business & Management website: https://www.regents.ac.uk/media/975652/RWPBM1402-Liu-J-Andersson-T.pdf

Liu, H., & Fong, M. W. (2010). Board characteristics of medium and large Chinese companies. *Corporate Governance: The International Journal of Business in Society*, *10*(2), 163–175. doi:10.1108/14720701011035684

Liu, J., Shively, G. E., & Binkley, J. K. (2014). Access to variety contributes to dietary diversity in China. *Food Policy*, *49*, 323–331. doi:10.1016/j.foodpol.2014.09.007

Liu, Q., Luo, T., & Tian, G. G. (2015). Family control and corporate cash holdings: Evidence from China. *Journal of Corporate Finance*, *31*, 220–245. Advance online publication. doi:10.1016/j.jcorpfin.2015.02.007

Liu, Q., & Lu, Z. J. (2007). Corporate governance and earnings management in Chinese listed companies: A tunneling perspective. *Journal of Corporate Finance*, *13*(5), 881–906. doi:10.1016/j.jcorpfin.2007.07.003

Lobley, M., Baker, J. R., & Whitehead, I. (2016). Farm succession and retirement: Some international comparisons. *Journal of Agriculture, Food Systems, and Community Development*, *1*(1), 49–64.

Loebbecke, J. K., Eining, M. M., & Willingham, J. J. (1989). Auditors experience with material irregularities-frequency, nature, and detectability. *Auditing*, *9*(1), 1–28.

Lokman & Wahid. (2013). *The impact of IFRS adoption on audit fees: Evidence from Malaysian listed companies*. http://malrep.uum.edu.my/rep/Record/iium.eprints.35296/Description#tabnav

Lombardi, R., Del Giudice, M., Caputo, A., Evangelista, F., & Russo, G. (2016). Governance and Assessment Insights in Information Technology: The Val It Model. *Journal of the Knowledge Economy*, *7*(1), 292-308.

Lombardi, R., Del Giudice, M., Caputo, A., Evangelista, F., & Russo, G. (2016). Governance and assessment insights in information technology: The Val IT model. *Journal of the Knowledge Economy*, *7*(1), 292–308. doi:10.100713132-015-0328-6

Long, R. G. (2011). Commentary: Social exchange in building, modeling, and managing family social capital. *Entrepreneurship Theory and Practice*, *35*(6), 1229–1234. doi:10.1111/j.1540-6520.2011.00500.x

Long, T., & Johnson, M. (2000). Rigour, reliability and validity in qualitative research. *Clinical Effectiveness in Nursing*, *4*(1), 30–37. doi:10.1054/cein.2000.0106

Lopes, A. B., & Walker, M. (2012). Asset revaluations, future firm performance and firm-level corporate governance arrangements: New evidence from Brazil. *The British Accounting Review*, *44*(2), 53–67. doi:10.1016/j.bar.2012.03.007

Loukil, L. & Triki, M. (2008). L'analyse De L'impact Des Mécanismes De Gouvernance Sur Le Niveau De Divulgation Volontaire: Cas Des Sociétés Tunisiennes Non Financières. *La Comptabilité, Le Contrôle et L'audit entre Changement et Stabilité*, France. CD Rom. halshs-00525414

Loukil, L. (2010). Conséquences de l'adoption des normes internationales "IFRS" sur le coût d'audit financier. *Crises et nouvelles problématiques de la valeur*. https://halshs.archives-ouvertes.fr/hal-00481517/document

Low, D. C. M., Roberts, H., & Whiting, R. H. (2015). Board gender diversity and firm performance: Empirical evidence from Hong Kong, South Korea, Malaysia and Singapore. *Pacific-Basin Finance Journal, 35*, 381–401. doi:10.1016/j.pacfin.2015.02.008

Lowry, P. B., & Wilson, D. (2016). Creating agile organizations through IT: The influence of internal IT service perceptions on IT service quality and IT agility. *The Journal of Strategic Information Systems, 25*(3), 211–226. doi:10.1016/j.jsis.2016.05.002

Lo, Y. L., Li, Y., & Chan, K. C. (2019). Contemporary Innovation in China. *Chinese Economy, 52*(5), 387–399. doi:10.1080/10971475.2019.1617925

Lubis, A., Torong, Z. B., & Muda, I. (2016a). The Urgency of Implementing Balanced Scorecard System on Local Government in North Sumatra – Indonesia. International. *Journal of Applied Business and Economic Research, 14*(11), 7575–7590.

Lückerath-Rovers, M. (2013). Women on boards and firm performance. *The Journal of Management and Governance, 17*(2), 491–509. doi:10.100710997-011-9186-1

Luftman, J. (2000). Assessing Business-It Alignment Maturity. *Communications of the Association for Information Systems, 4*(1), 14.

Luftman, J. (2004). *Assessing Business-It Alignment Maturity*. Strategies for Information Technology Governance.

Luftman, J., & Lyytinen, K., & ben Zvi, T. (2015). Enhancing the measurement of information technology (IT) business alignment and its influence on company performance. *Journal of Information Technology*.

Lussier, R. N., & Sonfield, M. C. (2012). Family businesses' succession planning: A seven-country comparison. *Journal of Small Business and Enterprise Development, 19*(1), 7–19. doi:10.1108/14626001211196370

Luzhen, C., & Morten, B. 2012. The effect of ownership structure on firm performance: Evidence from Non-Financial listed Companies in Scandinavia (MSc). Aarhus University.

Lyon, B. K., & Hollcroft, B. (2012). Risk assessments: Top 10 pitfalls & tips for improvement. *Professional Safety, 57*(12), 28–34.

Mabogunje, A. L., & Kates, R. W. (2020). *Sustainable development in Ijebu-Ode, Nigeria: The role of social capital, participation, and science and technology*. CID Working Paper Series.

Macharis, C., Springael, J., De Brucker, K., & Verbeke, A. (2004). PROMETHEE and AHP: The design of operational synergies in multicriteria analysis. strengthening PROMETHEE with ideas of AHP. *European Journal of Operational Research, 153*(2), 307–317. doi:10.1016/S0377-2217(03)00153-X

Machuga, S. M., & Teitel, K. (2009). Board of director characteristics and earnings quality surrounding implementation of a corporate governance code in Mexico. *Journal of International Accounting, Auditing & Taxation, 18*(1), 1–13. doi:10.1016/j.intaccaudtax.2008.12.002

Mack, S. (2019). *Seven Characteristics of Good Corporate Governance*. Available at https://smallbusiness.chron.com

Magasi, C. (2016). *Factors influencing business succession planning among SMEs in Tanzania*. Working paper.

Mahadeo, J. D., Soobaroyen, T., & Hanuman, V. O. (2012). Board composition and financial performance:Uncovering the effects of diversity in an emerging economy. *Journal of Business Ethics, 105*(3), 375–388. doi:10.100710551-011-0973-z

Makhlouf, M. H., Laili, N. H. B., Basah, M. Y. A., & Siam, Y. I. S. A. (2015). *Board Members' age, Gender Diversity and Firm Performance, Proposing Conceptual Framework.* Kuala Lumpur International Business, Economics and Law Conference (KLIBEL6), Kuala Lumpur.

Malik, M. S., & Kanwal, L. (2018). Impact of corporate social responsibility disclosure on financial performance: Case study of listed pharmaceutical firms of Pakistan. *Journal of Business Ethics, 150*(1), 69–78.

Man, Y. (2018). *Earnings Management and Agency Costs: Evidence from China.* Available at https://www.researchgate.net/publication/323983941

Mangena, M., & Pike, R. (2005). The effect of audit committee shareholding, financial expertise and size on interim financial disclosures. *Accounting and Business Research, 35*(4), 327–349.

Mangena, M., Tauringana, V., & Chamisa, E. (2012). Corporate boards, ownership structure and firm performance in an environment of severe political and economic crisis. *British Journal of Management, 23*(S1), S23–S41. doi:10.1111/j.1467-8551.2011.00804.x

Manoel, A. A. S., Moraes, M. B. C., Nagano, M. S., & Sobreiro, V. A. (2018a). Cash holdings and corporate governance: The effects of premium listing in Brazil. *Review of Development Finance, 8*(2), 106–115. doi:10.1016/j.rdf.2018.11.002

Mans-Kemp, N., Viviers, S., & Collins, S. (2018). Exploring the causes and consequences of director overboardedness in an emerging market. *International Journal of Disclosure and Governance, 15*(4), 210–220.

Mao, H., Liu, S., Zhang, J., & Deng, Z. (2016). Information technology resource, knowledge management capability, and competitive advantage: The moderating role of resource commitment. *International Journal of Information Management, 36*(6), 1062–1074. doi:10.1016/j.ijinfomgt.2016.07.001

Marcoux, G., Guihur, I., & Koffi, V. (2016). Employees' contribution to the succession process of family small and medium-sized businesses: Conceptual model and research agenda. *Management Review: An International Journal, 11*(1), 70.

Martín-Ugedo, J. F., & Mínguez-Vera, A. (2014). Firm performance and women on the board: Evidence from Spanish small and medium-sized enterprises. *Feminist Economics, 20*(3), 136–162. doi:10.1080/13545701.2014.895404

Marwick, A., Hasan, M. M., & Luo, T. (2020). Organization capital and corporate cash holdings. *International Review of Financial Analysis, 68*, 101458. Advance online publication. doi:10.1016/j.irfa.2020.101458

Mashayekhi & Mashayekh. (2008). *Developement of accounting in Iran.* https://www.researchgate.net/publication/222968551_Development_of_accounting_in_Iran

Masli, A., Richardson, V. J., Watson, M. W., & Zmud, R. W. (2016). Senior executives' IT management responsibilities: serious it-related deficiencies and CEO/CFO turnover. *Management Information Systems Quarterly, 40*(3), 687–708. doi:10.25300/MISQ/2016/40.3.08

Masulis, R. W., & Mobbs, S. (2016). *Independent Director Reputation Incentives: CEO Compensation Contracting and Financial Accounting Quality.* Available at SSRN 2832549.

Masulis, R. W., & Mobbs, S. (2017). *Independent Director Reputation Incentives: The Supply of Monitoring Services.* ECGI-Finance Working Paper, (353).

Masulis, R. W., & Mobbs, S. (2014). Independent director incentives: Where do talented directors spend their limited time and energy? *Journal of Financial Economics, 111*(2), 406–429. doi:10.1016/j.jfineco.2013.10.011

Mathuva, D. M. (2009). capital adequacy, Cost Income ratio, and the performance of commercial banks; The Kenyan Scenario. *The International Journal of Applied Economics & Finance, 3*(2), 35–47. doi:10.3923/ijaef.2009.35.47

Matsumoto, D. (2002). Managements incentives to avoid negative earnings surprises. *The Accounting Review*, *77*(3), 483–514. doi:10.2308/accr.2002.77.3.483

Matteo, P., & Paolone, Fr. (2018). *The Case of Brazilian Real Estate Industry*. Available at https://www.abacademies.org

Matthews, R., & McLees, J. (2015). Building effective projects teams and teamwork. *Journal of Information Technology and Economic Development*, *6*(2), 20.

Matuszak, Ł., Różańska, E., & Macuda, M. (2019). The impact of corporate governance characteristics on banks' corporate social responsibility disclosure: Evidence from Poland. *Journal of Accounting in Emerging Economies*, *9*(1), 75–102.

Mazahrih, B. J., Katrib, D. I., & Rfaah, T. M. (2016). Environmental Disclosure: The Case of Jordanian Chemical Industry. *Journal of Accountancy*, *6*(1), 88–100.

Mcconaughy, D. L. C. S., Mishra, M. C., Walker, G. V., & Henderson, J. (1998). Founding Family Controlled Firms: Efficiency and Value. *Review of Financial Economics*, *7*(1), 1–19. doi:10.1016/S1058-3300(99)80142-6

Mcconaughy, D. L., Matthews, C. H., & Fialko, A. S. (2001). Founding Family Controlled Firms:Performance, Risk, and Value. *Journal of Small Business Management*, *39*(1), 31–49. doi:10.1111/0447-2778.00004

Mcconnell, J. J., & Servaes, H. (1990). Additional evidence on equity ownership and corporate value. *Journal of Financial Economics*, *27*(2), 595–612. doi:10.1016/0304-405X(90)90069-C

McNichols, M. F. (2000). Research design issues in earnings management studies. *Journal of Accounting and Public Policy*, *19*(4-5), 313–345. doi:10.1016/S0278-4254(00)00018-1

McQuade, E., Sjoer, E., Fabian, P., Carlos Nascimento, J., & Schroeder, S. (2007). Will you miss me when I'm gone? A study of the potential loss of company knowledge and expertise as employees retire. *Journal of European Industrial Training*, *31*(9), 758–768. doi:10.1108/03090590710846701

Md Zaini, S., Samkin, G., Sharma, U., & Davey, H. (2018). Voluntary disclosure in emerging countries: A literature review. *Journal of Accounting in Emerging Economies*, *8*(1), 29–65.

Meek, G. K., & Thomas, W. B. (2004). A review of markets-based international accounting research. *Journal of International Accounting Research*, *3*(1), 21–41. doi:10.2308/jiar.2004.3.1.21

Mehrabani, S. E., & Mohamad, N. A. (2011). Succession planning: A necessary process in today's organization. *International Journal of e-Education, e-Business, e- Management Learning*, *1*(5), 371.

Melville, N., Kraemer, K., & Gurbaxani, V. (2004). Review: Information technology and organizational performance: An integrative model of IT business value. *Management Information Systems Quarterly*, *28*(2), 283–322. doi:10.2307/25148636

Mensi-Klarbach, H. (2014). Gender in top management research. *Management Research Review*, *37*(6), 538–552. doi:10.1108/MRR-03-2013-0066

Merhout, J. W., & Havelka, D. (2008). Information Technology Auditing: A Value-Added It Governance Partnership between It Management and Audit. *Communications of the Association for Information Systems*, *23*(1), 26.

Merhout, J. W., & Havelka, D. (2008). Information technology auditing: A value-added IT governance partnership between IT management and audit. *Communications of the Association for Information Systems*, *23*(1), 26. doi:10.17705/1CAIS.02326

Mersni, H., & Othman, H. (2016). The impact of corporate governance mechanisms on earnings management in Islamic banks in the Middle East region. *Journal of Islamic Accounting and Business Research*, *7*(4), 318–348. doi:10.1108/JIABR-11-2014-0039

Miah, D., & Uddin, H. (2017). Efficiency and stability: A comparative study between Islamic and conventional banks in GCC countries. *Future Business Journal.*, *3*(2), 172–185. doi:10.1016/j.fbj.2017.11.001

Mihret, D. G., & Yismaw, A. W. (2007). Internal audit effectiveness: An Ethiopian public sector case study. *Managerial Auditing Journal.*

Miller, M. H., & Orr, D. (1966). A Model of the Demand for Money by Firms. *The Quarterly Journal of Economics*, *80*(3), 413. Advance online publication. doi:10.2307/1880728

Miller, T., & del Carmen Triana, M. (2009). Demographic diversity in the boardroom: Mediators of the board diversity–firm performance relationship. *Journal of Management Studies*, *46*(5), 755–786. doi:10.1111/j.1467-6486.2009.00839.x

Minetti, R., Murro, P., & Paiella, M. (2012). *Ownership structure, governance, and innovation: Evidence from Italy.* Government of the Italian Republic (Italy), Ministry of Economy and Finance, Department of the Treasury Working Paper, Number 10.

Miodonski, K., & Hines, P. (2013). Leadership development and succession planning in case management. *Professional Case Management*, *18*(1), 5–12. doi:10.1097/NCM.0b013e31826b12a7 PMID:23211401

Mishina, Y., Dykes, B. J., Block, E. S., & Pollock, T. G. (2010). Why "good" firms do bad things: The effects of high aspirations, high expectations, and prominence on the incidence of corporate illegality. *Academy of Management Journal*, *53*(4), 701–722. doi:10.5465/amj.2010.52814578

Mishra, C., Randoy, T., & Jenssen, J. I. (2001). The Effect of Founding Family Influence on Firm Value and Corporate Governance: A Study of Norwegian Firms. *Journal of International Financial Management & Accounting*, *12*(3), 235–259. doi:10.1111/1467-646X.00073

Mithas, S., Tafti, A. R., Bardhan, I., & Goh, J. M. (2012). *Information technology and firm profitability: mechanisms and empirical evidence*. Academic Press.

Mithas, S., & Rust, R. T. (2016). How information technology strategy and investments influence firm performance: Conjectures and empirical evidence. *Management Information Systems Quarterly*, *40*(1), 223–245. doi:10.25300/MISQ/2016/40.1.10

Mittal, N., & Nault, B. R. (2009). Research Note-Investments in Information Technology: Indirect Effects and Information Technology Intensity. *Information Systems Research*, *20*(1), 140–154. doi:10.1287/isre.1080.0186

Mohamad, S. (2004). The importance of effective corporate governance. *SSRN Electronic Journal*. Retrieved from: SSRN: https://ssrn.com/abstract=617101

Mollah, S., Hassan, M. K., Farooque, O., & Mobarek, A. (2016). The Governance, Risk-taking, and Performance of Islamic Banks. *Journal of Financial Services Research*, *51*(2), 195–219. doi:10.100710693-016-0245-2

Mollah, S., & Zaman, M. (2015). Shari'ah Supervision, Corporate Governance and Performance: Conventional vs. Islamic Banks. *Journal of Banking & Finance*, *58*, 418–435. doi:10.1016/j.jbankfin.2015.04.030

Molly, V., Laveren, E., & Deloof, M. (2010). Family business succession and its impact on financial structure and performance. *Family Business Review*, *23*(2), 131–147. doi:10.1177/089448651002300203

Monks, R. A. & Minnow., N. (2001). *Corporate Governance*. Oxford: Blackwell.

Monks, R. A. G., & Minow, N. (1995). *Corporate Governance*. Blackwell.

Mooney, J. G., Gurbaxani, V., & Kraemer, K. L. (1996). A process oriented framework for assessing the business value of information technology. *ACM SIGMIS Database*, *27*(2), 68–81. doi:10.1145/243350.243363

Mora, A., & Walker, M. (2015). The implications of research on accounting conservatism for accounting standard setting. *Accounting and Business Research*, *45*(5), 620–650. doi:10.1080/00014788.2015.1048770

Morck, Strangeland, & Yeung. (2000). Inherited wealth, Corporate Control and Economic Growth? In *Concentrated Corporate Ownership*. Chicago: University of Chicago Press.

Moss, S. (2016). The Impact of Corporate Governance and Earnings Management Practices on Cost of Equity Capital: Evidence from Thai Listed Companies. *ACRN Oxford Journal of Finance and Risk Perspectives*, *5*(1), 163–185.

Moyes, G. D., & Baker, C. R. (1995). How effective are audit techniques in detecting fraud? *Internal Auditing-Boston-Warren Gorham and Lamont Incorporated*, *10*, 32–32.

MSG. (2019). *Corporate Governance - Definition, Scope and Benefits*. Available at https://www.managementstudyguide.com

Muda, I., Maulana, W., Sakti Siregar, H., & Indra, N. (2018). The Analysis of Effects of Good Corporate Governance on Earnings Management in Indonesia with Panel Data Approach. *Indian Economic Review*, *22*(2), 599–625.

Muniandy & Ali. (2012). *Development of financial reporting environment in Malaysia*. Academic Press.

Musa, H., Musová, Z., & Debnárová, L. (2015). Responsibility in the corporate governance framework and financial decision making process. *Procedia Economics and Finance*, *23*, 1023–1029. doi:10.1016/S2212-5671(15)00371-8

Musallam, S. R. (2018). The direct and indirect effect of the existence of risk management on the relationship between audit committee and corporate social responsibility disclosure. *Benchmarking*, *25*(9), 4125–4138.

Mustafa, A. S., Che-Ahmad, A., & Chandren, S. (2018). Board diversity, audit committee characteristics and audit quality: The moderating role of control-ownership wedge. *Business and Economic Horizons*, *14*, 587-614.

Mustafa, M. B. (2010). *Impact of corporate governance on earnings management practices - An applied study on industrial companies listed on the Amman Financial Market* (Master Thesis). Faculty of Economics and Administrative Sciences, Al-Yarmouk University, Jordan.

Myers, S. C., & Majluf, N. S. (1984). Corporate financing and investment decisions when firms have information that investors do not have. *Journal of Financial Economics*, *13*(2), 187–221. Advance online publication. doi:10.1016/0304-405X(84)90023-0

Na, K., & Hong, J. (2017). CEO gender and earnings management. *Journal of Applied Business Research*, *33*(2), 297–308. doi:10.19030/jabr.v33i2.9902

Nakano, M., & Nguyen, P. (2011). *Do older boards affect firm performance? An empirical analysis based on Japanese firms*. Working paper. Retrieved from http://ssrn.com/abstract=1879825

Naushad, M., & Abdul Malik, S. (2015). Corporate Governance and Bank Performance: A Study of Selected Banks in GCC Region. *Asian Social Science*, *11*(9). Advance online publication. doi:10.5539/ass.v11n9p226

Negrea, S. (2008). *Succession planning: A necessity for community colleges*. Institute for Community College Development.

Nelson, M. W., & Skinner, D. J. (2013). How should we think about earnings quality? A discussion of "Earnings quality: Evidence from the field". *Journal of Accounting and Economics*, *56*(2-3), 34–41. doi:10.1016/j.jacceco.2013.10.003

Ness, R. K., Miesing, P., & Kang, J. (2012). Board of Directors composition and financial performance in a Sarbanes-Oxley world. *Academy of Business and Economics Journal*, *10*(5), 56–74.

Nevo, S., & Wade, M. (2011). Firm-level benefits of IT-enabled resources: A conceptual extension and an empirical assessment. *The Journal of Strategic Information Systems*, *20*(4), 403–418. doi:10.1016/j.jsis.2011.08.001

Nia, M. S., Huang, C. C., & Abidin, Z. (2015). A Review of Motives and Techniques and their Consequences in Earnings Management. *Malaysian Accounting Review, 14*(2), 1–28.

Niskanen, J., Karjalainen, J., Niskanen, M., & Karjalainen, J. (2011). Auditor gender and corporate earnings management behavior in private Finnish firms. *Managerial Auditing Journal, 26*(9), 778–793. doi:10.1108/02686901111171448

Nobes. (1983). *A judgemental international classification of financial reporting practices*. Academic Press.

Noh, S., So, E. C., & Weber, J. P. (2019). Voluntary and mandatory disclosures: Do managers view them as substitutes? *Journal of Accounting and Economics, 68*(1), 101243. doi:10.1016/j.jacceco.2019.101243

Nomran, N. M., Haron, R., & Hassan, R. (2017). Bank Performance and Shari'ah Supervisory Board Attributes on Islamic banks: Does Bank Size Matter? *Journal of Islamic Finance, 6*(Special Issue), 174–187. doi:10.12816/0047348

Nomran, N. M., Haron, R., & Hassan, R. (2018). Shari'ah supervisory board characteristics effects on Islamic banks' performance: Evidence from Malaysia. *International Journal of Bank Marketing, 36*(2), 290–304. doi:10.1108/IJBM-12-2016-0197

O'brien, R. M. (2007). A caution regarding rules of thumb for variance inflation factors. *Quality & Quantity, 41*(5), 673–690.

O'Connor, M., & Rafferty, M. (2012). Corporate governance and innovation. *Journal of Financial and Quantitative Analysis, 47*(02), 397–413. doi:10.1017/S002210901200004X

Ødegaard, B. A., & Bøhren, Ø. (2003). *Governance and Performance Revisited.* SSRN Working Paper Series.

OECD. (2015). *G20/OECD Principles of Corporate Governance*. OECD Publishing. doi:10.1787/9789264236882-

OECD. (2019). *OECD Corporate Governance Factbook 2019*. Available at www.oecd.org/corporate/corporate-governance-factbook.htm

OECD. (2019). *OECD Corporate Governance Factbook 2019*. OECD Publishing. Available at https://www.oecd.org/corporate/corporate-governance-factbook.htm

Ofoegbu, N. G., & Odoemelam, N. (2018). *Corporate Board Characteristics and Environmental Disclosure Quantity: A comparative Analysis of Traditional and Integrated Reporting Evidence*. Academic Press.

Omar, A., & Davidson, M. J. (2001). Women in management: A comparative cross-cultural overview. *Cross Cultural Management, 8*(3/4), 35–67. doi:10.1108/13527600110797272

Omoye, A. S., & Eriki, P. O. (2014). Corporate governance Determinants of earnings management: Evidence from Nigerian quoted companies. *Mediterranean Journal of Social Sciences, 5*(23), 553.

Ongena, S., & Sendeniz-Yuncu, I. (2011). Which firms engage small, foreign or state banks? And who goes Islamic? Evidence from Turkey. *Journal of Banking & Finance, 35*(12), 3213–3224. doi:10.1016/j.jbankfin.2011.05.001

Ooi, C. A., Hooy, C. W., & Mat Som, A. P. (2017). The influence of board diversity in human capital and social capital in crisis. *Managerial Finance, 43*(6), 700–719. doi:10.1108/MF-08-2016-0226

Opler, T. (1999). The determinants and implications of corporate cash holdings. *Journal of Financial Economics, 52*(1), 3–46. Advance online publication. doi:10.1016/S0304-405X(99)00003-3

Orcland, C. (2006). *Family Control, Firm Performance and Dividend Policy*. SSRN eLibrary.

Osma, B. G., & Noguer, B. G. D. A. (2007). The effect of the board composition and its monitoring committees on earnings management: Evidence from Spain. *Corporate Governance, 15*(6), 1413–1428. doi:10.1111/j.1467-8683.2007.00654.x

Oxelheim, L., & Randoy, T. (2003). The impact of foreign board membership on firm value. *Journal of Banking & Finance*, *27*(12), 2369–2392. doi:10.1016/S0378-4266(02)00395-3

Ozili, P. K., & Uadiale, O. (2017). Ownership concentration and bank profitability. *Future Business Journal*, *3*(2), 159–171. doi:10.1016/j.fbj.2017.07.001

Ozkan, A., & Ozkan, N. (2004). Corporate cash holdings: An empirical investigation of UK companies. *Journal of Banking & Finance*, *28*(9), 2103–2134. Advance online publication. doi:10.1016/j.jbankfin.2003.08.003

Paine, L. S., & Srinivasan, S. (2019). A Guide to the Big Ideas and Debates in Corporate Governance. *Harvard Business Review*, Available at https://hbr.org/2019

Palmer, P. D. (2008). Audit quality and financial report disclosure. *Flinders Business School Research Paper Series, 1*, 1-29.

Palmer, D., & Barber, B. M. (2001). Challengers, elites, and owning families: A social class theory of corporate acquisitions in the 1960s. *Administrative Science Quarterly*, *46*(87), 120. doi:10.2307/2667126

Palmer, J., Rae, C., & Sykes, G. (2019). *Corporate Governance: Chambers and Partners*. Available at racticeguides. chambers.com

Panda, B., & Leepsa, N. M. (2017). Agency theory: Review of Theory and Evidence on Problems and Perspectives. *Indian Journal of Corporate Governance*, *10*(1), 74–95. doi:10.1177/0974686217701467

Pandey, S., & Sharma, D. (2014). Succession planning practices and challenges: Study of Indian organisations. *Procedia Economics and Finance*, *11*, 152–165. doi:10.1016/S2212-5671(14)00185-3

Papp, R. (1999). Business-IT alignment: Productivity paradox payoff? *Industrial Management & Data Systems*, *99*(8), 367–373. doi:10.1108/02635579910301810

Parent, M., & Reich, B. H. (2009). Governing Information Technology Risk. *California Management Review*, *51*(3), 134-152.

Parent, M., & Reich, B. H. (2009). Governing information technology risk. *California Management Review*, *51*(3), 134–152. doi:10.2307/41166497

Parker, J. (2016). A Report into the Ethnic Diversity of UK Boards. The Parker Review Committee, 56.

Parkinson, J. E. (1994). *Corporate Power and Responsibility: Issues in the Theory of Company Law*. Oxford Clarendon Press.

Parthiban, D., Hitt, M. A., & Gimeno, J. (2001). The influence of activism by institutional investors on R&D. *Academy of Management Journal*, *44*, 144–157.

Pasban, M., & Nojedeh, S. H. (2016). A Review of the Role of Human Capital in the Organization. *Procedia: Social and Behavioral Sciences*, *230*, 249–253. doi:10.1016/j.sbspro.2016.09.032

Patel, A., & Prasad, A. (2010). Incentives and Preliminary Investigation of Incentives Facing Accounting Standard-Setters. *International Review of Business Research Papers*, 536-561.

Patelli, L., & Prencipe, A. (2007). The relationship between voluntary disclosure and independent directors in the presence of a dominant shareholders. *European Accounting Review*, *16*(1), 5–33. doi:10.1080/09638180701265820

Patten, D. M. (2019). *Seeking legitimacy*. Sustainability Accounting, Management and Policy Journal.

Pawsey, N. (2008). *Australian Preparer Perceptions towards the Quality and Complexity of IFRS*. La Trobe University.

Pearson, A. W., Carr, J. C., & Shaw, J. C. (2008). Toward a theory of familiness: A social capital perspective. *Entrepreneurship Theory and Practice*, *32*(6), 949–969. doi:10.1111/j.1540-6520.2008.00265.x

Peasnell, K. V., Pope, P. F., & Young, S. (2005). Board monitoring and earnings management: do outside directors influence abnormal accruals? *Journal of Business Finance & Accounting, 32*(7S8), 1311-1346.

Peck-Ling, T., Nai-Chiek, A., & Chee-Seong, L. (2016). Foreign ownership, foreign directors and profitability of Malaysian listed companies. *Procedia: Social and Behavioral Sciences*, *219*, 580–588. doi:10.1016/j.sbspro.2016.05.037

Pedersen, T., & Thomsen, S. (1999). Economic and Systemic Explanations of Ownership Concentration among Europe's Largest Companies. *International Journal of the Economics of Business*, *6*(3), 367–381. doi:10.1080/13571519984133

Peng, J., Quan, J., Zhang, G., & Dubinsky, A. J. (2016). Mediation effect of business process and supply chain management capabilities on the impact of IT on firm performance: Evidence from Chinese firms. *International Journal of Information Management*, *36*(1), 89–96. doi:10.1016/j.ijinfomgt.2015.09.006

Peng, M. W. (2004). Outside directors and firm performnace during intitutional transitions. *Strategic Management Journal*, *25*(5), 453–471. doi:10.1002mj.390

Peng, M. W., Zhang, S., & Li, X. (2007). CEO duality and firm performance during China's institutional transitions. *Management and Organization Review*, *3*(2), 205–225. doi:10.1111/j.1740-8784.2007.00069.x

Peng, W. Q., Wei, K. C. J., & Yang, Z. (2011). Tunneling or propping: Evidence from connected transactions in China. *Journal of Corporate Finance*, *17*(2), 306–325. doi:10.1016/j.jcorpfin.2010.08.002

Peni, E., & Vähämaa, S. (2010). Female executives and earnings management. *Managerial Finance*, *36*(7), 629–645. doi:10.1108/03074351011050343

Pennell, K. (2010). The role of flexible job descriptions in succession management. *Library Management*, *31*(4/5), 279–290. doi:10.1108/01435121011046344

Peppard, J., Ward, J., & Daniel, E. (2007). Managing the Realization of Business Benefits from IT Investments. *MIS Quarterly Executive*, *6*(1).

Petersson, C., & Wallin, F. (2017). *Three Types of Age Diversity in Boards of Directors and the Relationship to Firm Performance.* Uppsala University. Available at: https://uu.diva-portal.org/smash/get/diva2:1111350/FULLTEXT01.pdf

Pfeffer, J. (1982). *Organizations and organization theory*. Pitman.

Pfeffer, J., & Salancik, G. (1978). *The external control of organizations: A resource dependence perspective*. Herper & Row.

Phung, D. N., & Mishra, A. V. (2016). Ownership structure and firm performance: Evidence from Vietnamese listed firms. *Australian Economic Papers*, *55*(1), 63–98. doi:10.1111/1467-8454.12056

Pi, L., & Timme, S. G. (1993). Corporate control and bank efficiency. *Journal of Banking & Finance*, *17*(2), 515–530. doi:10.1016/0378-4266(93)90050-N

Pillai, R., & Al-Malkawi, H. A. N. (2018). On the relationship between corporate governance and firm performance: Evidence from GCC countries. *Research in International Business and Finance*, *44*, 394–410. doi:10.1016/j.ribaf.2017.07.110

Pinkowitz, L., Stulz, R., & Williamson, R. (2006). Does the contribution of corporate cash holdings and dividends to firm value depend on governance? A cross-country analysis. *The Journal of Finance*, *61*(6), 2725–2751. Advance online publication. doi:10.1111/j.1540-6261.2006.01003.x

Pinkowitz, L., & Williamson, R. (2001). Bank power and cash holdings: Evidence from Japan. *Review of Financial Studies, 14*(4), 1059–1082. Advance online publication. doi:10.1093/rfs/14.4.1059

Piot, C. (2001). Agency costs and audit quality: Evidence from France. *European Accounting Review, 10*(3), 461–499. doi:10.1080/713764630

Piot, C., & Janin, R. (2007). External auditors, audit committees and earnings management in France. *European Accounting Review, 16*(2), 429–454. doi:10.1080/09638180701391030

Pitts, D. W. (2005). Diversity, Representation, and Performance: Evidence about Race and Ethnicity in Public Organizations. *Journal of Public Administration: Research and Theory, 15*(4), 615–631. doi:10.1093/jopart/mui033

Pollit, D. (2009). Success through succession at Hudson's Bay Company. *Human Resource Management International Digest, 17*(5), 6–8. doi:10.1108/09670730910974260

Polovina, N., & Peasnell, K. (2015). The Effects of Foreign Management and Board Membership on the Performance of Foreign Acquired Turkish Banks. *International Journal of Managerial Finance, 17*(43), 32–40. doi:10.1108/IJMF-06-2014-0086

Pomeroy, B., & Thornton, D. B. (2008). Meta-analysis and the accounting literature: The case of audit committee independence and financial reporting quality. *European Accounting Review, 17*(2), 305–330. doi:10.1080/09638180701819832

Portes, A. (1998). Social capital: Its origins and applications in modern sociology. *Annual Review of Sociology, 24*(1), 1–24. doi:10.1146/annurev.soc.24.1.1

Portes, A., & Landolt, P. (2000). Social capital: Promise and pitfalls of its role in development. *Journal of Latin American Studies, 32*(2), 529–547. doi:10.1017/S0022216X00005836

Pound, J. (1988). The information effects of takeover bids and resistance. *Journal of Financial Economics, 22*(2), 207–227. doi:10.1016/0304-405X(88)90069-4

Powell, M., & Ansic, D. (1997). Gender differences in risk behaviour in financial decision-making: An experimental analysis. *Journal of Economic Psychology, 18*(6), 605-628.

Powell, T. C., & Dent-Micallef, A. (1997). Information technology as competitive advantage: The role of human, business, and technology resources. *Strategic Management Journal, 18*(5), 375–405. doi:10.1002/(SICI)1097-0266(199705)18:5<375::AID-SMJ876>3.0.CO;2-7

Poza, E. J. (2013). *Family business.* Cengage Learning.

Prasad, A., Heales, J., & Green, P. (2010). A capabilities-based approach to obtaining a deeper understanding of information technology governance effectiveness: Evidence from IT steering committees. *International Journal of Accounting Information Systems, 11*(3), 214–232. doi:10.1016/j.accinf.2010.07.013

Prencipe, A., & Bar-Yosef, S. (2011). Corporate Governance and Earnings Management in Family-Controlled Companies. *Journal of Accounting, Auditing & Finance, 26*(2), 199–227. doi:10.1177/0148558X11401212

Preston, D. S., & Karahanna, E. (2009). Antecedents of IS strategic alignment: A nomological network. *Information Systems Research, 20*(2), 159–179. doi:10.1287/isre.1070.0159

Price, D. P., Stoica, M., & Boncella, R. J. (2013). The relationship between innovation, knowledge, and performance in family and non-family firms: An analysis of SMEs. *Journal of Innovation and Entrepreneurship, 2*(1), 1–20. doi:10.1186/2192-5372-2-14

PricewaterhouseCoopers. (2007). *Making a difference: the pricewaterhousecoopers family business survey 2007/08.* PricewaterhouseCoopers.

Prigent, J. L. (2007). *Portfolio optimization and performance analysis*. Chapman & Hall/CRC. doi:10.1201/9781420010930

Pucheta-Martínez, M. C., & Gallego-Álvarez, I. (2019). Do board characteristics drive firm performance? An international perspective. *Review of Managerial Science*, 1–47. doi:10.100711846-019-00330-x

Pucheta-Martínez, M. C., & García-Meca, E. (2014). Institutional investors on boards and audit committees and their effects on financial reporting quality. *Corporate Governance*, *22*(4), 347–363. doi:10.1111/corg.12070

PwC. (2010). *Future rich in opportunity: Internal audit must seize opportunities to enhance its relevancy. State of the internal profession study*. Author.

Qian, M., & Yeung, B. (2015). Bank financing and corporate governance. *Journal of Corporate Finance*, *32*, 258–270. doi:10.1016/j.jcorpfin.2014.10.006

Rae, K., & Subramaniam, N. (2008). Quality of internal control procedures. *Managerial Auditing Journal*, *23*(2), 104–124. doi:10.1108/02686900810839820

Rahahleh, M. Y. (2010). Regulating the profession of internal auditing in Jordan. European Journal of Economics. *Finance and Administrative Sciences*, *20*, 162–180.

Rahman, A., Naqvi, S., & Ramay, M. I. (2008). Measuring turnover intention: A study of it professionals in Pakistan. *International Review of Business Research Papers*, *4*(3), 45–55.

Rahman, H. (2018). The Impact of Boardroom National Diversity on Firms Performance and Boards Monitoring in Emerging Markets: A Case of Malaysia. *International Journal of Managerial Science*, *8*(6), 13–18.

Rahman, H. U., Ibrahim, M. Y., & Ahmad, A. C. (2015). Corporate governance, firm financial performance, and shareholder's confidence: A proposed analysis of MCCG 2012. *Global Business and Management Research*, *7*(1), 139–147.

Rahman, M., Moniruzzaman, M., & Sharif, J. (2013). Techniques, Motives and Controls of Earnings Management. *International Journal of Information Technology and Business Management*, *11*(1), 22–34.

Rajan & Zingales. (1998). *Financial Dependence and Growth*. Academic Press.

Rajgopal, S., Venkatachalam, M., & Kotha, S. (2002). Managerial Actions, Stock Returns, and Earnings: The Case of Business-to-Business Internet Firms. *Journal of Accounting Research*, *40*(2), 529–556. doi:10.1111/1475-679X.00060

Ramachandran, J., Nget, Z. A., Subramanian, R., & Sambasivan, M. (2015). Does Corporate Governance Influence Earnings Management? Evidence from Singapore. *Journal of Developing Areas*, *49*(3), 264–274. doi:10.1353/jda.2015.0169

Ramaswamy, K., & Li, M. (2001). Foreign investors, foreign directors and corporate diversification: An empirical examination of large manufacturing companies in India. *Asia Pacific Journal of Management*, *18*(2), 207–222. doi:10.1023/A:1010620008101

Rao, H., & Sivakumar, K. (1999). Institutional sources of boundary-spanning structures: The establishment of investor relations departments in the Fortune 500 industrials. *Organization Science*, *10*(1), 27–42. doi:10.1287/orsc.10.1.27

Rao, K., & Tilt, C. (2016). *Board diversity and CSR reporting: an Australian study*. Meditari Accountancy Research.

Rathod, L. (2018). *Why Is Corporate Governance Important?* Available at https://diligent.com/en-gb

Rathod, L. (2019). *What Are the Principles of Good Corporate Governance?* Available at https://diligent.com/en-gb

Ratnawati, V., Abdul-Hamid, M. A., & Popoola, O. M. J. (2016). The Influence of Agency Conflict Types I and II on Earnings Management. *International Journal of Economics and Financial Issues*, *6*(S4), 126–131.

Rauf, F. H. A., Johari, N. H., Buniamin, S., & Rahman, N. R. A. (2012). The impact of company and board characteristics on earnings management: Evidence from Malaysia. *Global Review of Accounting and Finance*, *3*(2), 114–127.

Rautiainen, M., Pihkala, T., & Ikävalko, M. (2012). Family business system models–a case study and some implications of open systems perspective. *Journal of Small Business and Entrepreneurship*, *25*(2), 155–168. doi:10.1080/08276331.2012.10593566

Ravichandran, T., Lertwongsatien, C., & Lertwongsatien, C. (2005). Effect of information systems resources and capabilities on firm performance: A resource-based perspective. *Journal of Management Information Systems*, *21*(4), 237–276. doi:10.1080/07421222.2005.11045820

Rechner, P. L., & Dalton, D. R. (1991). CEO duality and organizational performance: A longitudinal analysis. *Strategic Management Journal*, *12*(2), 155–160. doi:10.1002mj.4250120206

Reffett, A. B. (2010). Can identifying and investigating fraud risks increase auditors liability? *The Accounting Review*, *85*(6), 2145–2167. doi:10.2308/accr.2010.85.6.2145

Reguera-Alvarado, N., de Fuentes, P., & Laffarga, J. (2017). Does Board Gender Diversity Influence Financial Performance? Evidence from Spain. *Journal of Business Ethics*, *141*(2), 337–350. doi:10.100710551-015-2735-9

Reverte, C. (2016). Corporate social responsibility disclosure and market valuation: Evidence from Spanish listed firms. *Review of Managerial Science*, *10*(2), 411–435.

Rezaee, Z. (2005). Causes, consequences, and deterence of financial statement fraud. *Critical Perspectives on Accounting*, *16*(3), 277–298. doi:10.1016/S1045-2354(03)00072-8

Rivard, S., Raymond, L., & Verreault, D. (2006). Resource-based view and competitive strategy: An integrated model of the contribution of information technology to firm performance. *The Journal of Strategic Information Systems*, *15*(1), 29–50. doi:10.1016/j.jsis.2005.06.003

Riyadh, S. M. R. (2012). The Role of Corporate Governance in Limiting Earnings Management: An Applied Study on Egyptian Pharmaceutical Companies. *The Arab Journal of Accounting*, *15*(8), 1–51.

Robbiano, M. (2019). *Different approaches toward gender diversity in European boards: a comparison between Germany, Italy and United Kingdom* (Doctoral dissertation).

Rodríguez, M. C., & Alegría, S. S. (2012). The value of audit quality in public and private companies: Evidence from Spain. *The Journal of Management and Governance*, *16*(4), 683–706. doi:10.100710997-011-9183-4

Rodriguez, R., Salter, S. B., & Smith, M. (2016). An Examination of the Agency Theory Problem of Earnings Management: Is it an Anglo-Saxon Cultural Phenomenon? *International Journal of Critical Accounting*, *7*(5/6), 487–511.

Rose, C. (2007). Does female board representation influence firm performance? The Danish evidence. *Corporate Governance*, *15*(2), 404–413. doi:10.1111/j.1467-8683.2007.00570.x

Roseland, M. (2000). Sustainable community development: Integrating environmental, economic, and social objectives. *Progress in Planning*, *54*(2), 73–132.

Rosenstein, S., & Wyatt, J. G. (1990). Outside directors, board independence, and shareholder wealth. *Journal of Financial Economics*, *26*(2), 175–191. doi:10.1016/0304-405X(90)90002-H

Rothwell, W. (2010). *Effective succession planning: Ensuring leadership continuity and building talent from within.* Amacom.

Rouf, M. A. (2017). Firm-specific characteristics, corporate governance and voluntary disclosure in annual reports of listed companies in Bangladesh. *International Journal of Managerial and Financial Accounting, 9*(3), 263–282. doi:10.1504/IJMFA.2017.086691

Rouf, M., & Akhtaruddin, M. (2018). Factors affecting the voluntary disclosure: A study by using smart PLS-SEM approach. *International Journal of Law and Management, 60*(6), 1498–1508. doi:10.1108/IJLMA-01-2018-0011

Rowley, J. (2002). Using case studies in research. *Management Research News, 25*(1), 16–27. doi:10.1108/01409170210782990

Rowley, T. J., Shipilov, A. V., & Greve, H. R. (2017). Board reform versus profits: The impact of ratings on the adoption of governance practices. *Strategic Management Journal, 38*(4), 815–833. doi:10.1002mj.2545

Roychowdhury, S. (2006). Earnings management through real activities manipulation. *Journal of Accounting and Economics, 42*(3), 335–370. doi:10.1016/j.jacceco.2006.01.002

Rustam, S., Rashid, K., & Zaman, K. (2013). The relationship between audit committees, compensation incentives and corporate audit fees in Pakistan. *Economic Modelling, 31*, 697–716. doi:10.1016/j.econmod.2013.01.008

Saaty, T. L. (1977). A scaling method for priorities in a hierarchichal structure. *Journal of Mathematical Psychology, 15*(3), 234–281. doi:10.1016/0022-2496(77)90033-5

Saaty, T. L. (1990). *Multicriteria decision making: Analytic Hierarchy Process* (2nd ed.). RWS Publications.

Sabherwal, R., & Chan, Y. E. (2001). Alignment between business and IS strategies: A study of prospectors, analyzers, and defenders. *Information Systems Research, 12*(1), 11–33. doi:10.1287/isre.12.1.11.9714

Sadou, A., Alom, F., & Laluddin, H. (2017). Corporate social responsibility disclosures in Malaysia: Evidence from large companies. *Social Responsibility Journal, 13*(1), 177–202.

Saich, T. (2015). *The National People's Congress: Functions and Membership.* Ash Center for Democratic Governance and Innovation, Harvard Kennedy School.

Salleh. (2014). Convergence to IFRs and Audit Report Lag in Malaysia. *Research Journal of Finance and Accounting.* www.iiste.org

Salman, A. (2016). Corporate Governance and Concentration of Property and Its Impact on Earnings Management in Emerging Markets: The Case of Saudi Joint Stock Companies. *Journal of Administrative and Economic Sciences, 10*(1), 1–48.

Salman, F., & Siddiqui, K. (2013). Corporate Governance in Pakistan: From the Perspective of Securities and Exchange Commission of Pakistan. *IUP Journal of Corporate Governance, 12*, 13.

Samaha, K., & Dahawy, K. (2011). An empirical analysis of corporate governance structures and voluntary corporate disclosure in volatile capital markets: The Egyptian experience. International *Journal of Accounting. Auditing and Performance Evaluation, 7*(1-2), 61–93.

Samaha, K., Dahawy, K., Hussainey, K., & Stapleton, P. (2012). The extent of corporate governance disclosure and its determinants in a developing market: The case of Egypt. *Advances in Accounting, 28*(1), 168–178. doi:10.1016/j.adiac.2011.12.001

Samaha, K., Khlif, H., & Hussainey, K. (2015). The impact of board and audit committee characteristics on voluntary disclosure: A meta-analysis. *Journal of International Accounting, Auditing & Taxation*, *24*, 13–28. doi:10.1016/j.intaccaudtax.2014.11.001

Samza, F. (2016). Corporate governance in Pakistan: Beyond a minimalist approach (Doctor of Philosophy). University of Bedfordshire.

Sanad, Z., Shiwakoti, R., & Kukreja, G. (2019). *The Role of Corporate Governance in Mitigating Real Earnings Management: Literature Review*. Conference Paper, PwR Symposium, Annual PwR Doctral Symposium.

Sanchez-Ballesta, J., & Garcia-Meca, E. (2007). A Meta analytic Vision of the Effect of Ownership Structure on Firm Performance. *Journal of Corporate Governance,* 15.

Sánchez-Ballesta, J. P., & García-Meca, E. (2007). Ownership structure, discretionary accruals and the informativeness of earnings. *Corporate Governance*, *15*(4), 677–691. doi:10.1111/j.1467-8683.2007.00596.x

Sánchez, R. G., Bolívar, M. P. R., & Hernández, A. M. L. (2017). Corporate and managerial characteristics as drivers of social responsibility disclosure by state-owned enterprises. *Review of Managerial Science*, ●●●, 1–27.

Sanda, A. U., Garba, T., & Mikailu, A. S. (2008). *Board independence and financial performance: evidence from Nigeria.* Paper presented at the Centre for the Study of African Economics at St Catherine's College, University of Oxford. Retrieved from https://www.africaportal.org/publications/board-independence-and-firm-financial-performance-evidence-from-nigeria

Sander, P., Teder, A., Viikmaa, K., & Kantšukov, M. (2014). The Distributed Profit Based Corporate Taxation, and the Valuation of Cash Holdings. *International Journal of Trade, Economics and Finance*. doi:10.7763/ijtef.2014.v5.373

Sandhu, A., & Singh, B. (2019). Board composition and corporate reporting on internet: Indian evidence. *Journal of Financial Reporting and Accounting*, *17*(2), 292–319. doi:10.1108/JFRA-05-2017-0031

Santiago, A. L. (2000). Succession experiences in Philippine family businesses. *Family Business Review*, *13*(1), 15–35. doi:10.1111/j.1741-6248.2000.00015.x

Santora, J. C., Sarros, J. C., Bozer, G., Esposito, M., & Bassi, A. (2015). Nonprofit executive succession planning and organizational sustainability. *The Journal of Applied Management and Entrepreneurship*, *20*(4), 66–83. doi:10.9774/GLEAF.3709.2015.oc.00006

Sardeshmukh, S. R., & Corbett, A. C. (2011). The duality of internal and external development of successors: Opportunity recognition in family firms. *Family Business Review*, *24*(2), 111–125. doi:10.1177/0894486510391783

Sarhan, A. A., & Ntim, C. G. (2019). Corporate boards, shareholding structures and voluntary disclosure in emerging MENA economies. *Journal of Accounting in Emerging Economies*, *9*(1), 2–27. doi:10.1108/JAEE-03-2017-0033

Schadewitz, H. J., & Vieru, M. J. (2008). *Impact of IFRS Transition Complexity on Audit Non-Audit Fees: Evidence from Small and Medium-Sized Listed Companies in Finland.* Available at SSRN: http://ssrn.com/abstract=967314

Scheer, A. W., Jost, W., Heß, H., & Kronz, A. (2005). Corporate performance management: ARIS in practice. Springer. doi:10.1007/b137635

Schulaka, C. (2015). Get creative. *Journal of Financial Planning*, *28*(2), 9.

Sealy, R. & Vinnicombe. (2007). *The female FTSE report 2007.* Cranfield University.

Seddon, P. B. (2014). Implications for strategic IS research of the resource-based theory of the firm: A reflection. *The Journal of Strategic Information Systems*, *23*(4), 257–269. doi:10.1016/j.jsis.2014.11.001

Seibert, S. E., Kraimer, M. L., & Liden, R. C. (2001). A social capital theory of career success. *Academy of Management Journal*, *44*(2), 219–237.

Selig, G. J. (2008). *Implementing It Governance-a Practical Guide to Global Best Practices in It Management*. Van Haren.

Sethibe, T., Campbell, J., & McDonald, C. (2007). It Governance in Public and Private Sector Organisations: Examining the Differences and Defining Future Research Directions. ACIS 2007 Proceedings, 118.

Shabbir, A., & Padgett, C. (2005). *The UK Code of Corporate Governance: Link between Compliance and Firm Performance*. Working Paper, ICMA Centre. Available at: http://ssrn.com/abstract=934313

Shahid, S. (2008). *A Business-Driven Evaluation of Distributed-Computing Models*. Academic Press.

Shah, M. H., Xiao, Z., Quresh, S., & Ahmad, M. (2020). Internal pyramid structure, contract enforcement, minority investor protection, and firms' performance: Evidence from emerging economies. *Research in International Business and Finance*, *52*, 101170. doi:10.1016/j.ribaf.2019.101170

Shan, Y. G., & McIver, R. P. (2011). Corporate governance mechanisms and financial performance in China: Panel data evidence on listed non-financial companies. *Asia Pacific Business Review*, *17*(3), 301–324. doi:10.1080/13602380903522325

Shao, G. (2009). *Toward a stakeholder model of corporate governance: Evidence from US media companies*. The University of Alabama.

Shapiro, D., Tang, Y., Wang, M., & Zhang, W. (2015). The effects of corporate governance and ownership on the innovation performance of Chinese SMEs. *Journal of Chinese Economic and Business Studies*, *1*(4), 311–335. doi:10.1080/14765284.2015.1090267

Sharma, S. (2010). The Impact of the Adoption of International Financial Reporting Standards on the Legal Profession. *Houston Business and Tax Journal*, 139-165.

Sharma, P. (2008). Commentary: Familiness: Capital stocks and flows between family and business. *Entrepreneurship Theory and Practice*, *32*(6), 971–977. doi:10.1111/j.1540-6520.2008.00266.x

Sharma, P., Chrisman, J. J., & Chua, J. H. (2003). Succession planning as planned behavior: Some empirical results. *Family Business Review*, *16*(1), 1–15. doi:10.1111/j.1741-6248.2003.00001.x

Sharma, P., Chrisman, J. J., Pablo, A. L., & Chua, J. H. (2001). Determinants of initial satisfaction with the succession process in family firms: A conceptual model. *Entrepreneurship Theory and Practice*, *25*(3), 17–36. doi:10.1177/104225870102500302

Sheehy, B. (2015). Defining CSR: Problems and solutions. *Journal of Business Ethics*, *131*(3), 625–648.

Shehata, N., Salhin, A., & El-Helaly, M. (2017). Board diversity and firm performance: Evidence from the UK SMEs. *Applied Economics*, *49*(48), 4817–4832. doi:10.1080/00036846.2017.1293796

Shelton, S. W. (1999). The effect of experience on the use of irrelevant evidence in auditor judgment. *The Accounting Review*, *74*(2), 217–224. doi:10.2308/accr.1999.74.2.217

Shen, C., & Chih, H. (2007). Earnings Management and Corporate Governance in Asia's Emerging Markets. *Corporate Governance*, *15*(5), 999–1021. doi:10.1111/j.1467-8683.2007.00624.x

Shleifer, A., & Vishny, R. W. (1989). Management entrenchment: The case of manager-specific investments. *Journal of Financial Economics*, *25*(1), 123–139. doi:10.1016/0304-405X(89)90099-8

Shleifer, A., & Vishny, R. W. (1997). A survey of corporate governance. *The Journal of Finance*, *52*(2), 737–783. doi:10.1111/j.1540-6261.1997.tb04820.x

Short, H. (1994). Ownership, Control, Financial Structure and The Performance of Firms. *Journal of Economic Surveys*, *8*(3), 203–249. doi:10.1111/j.1467-6419.1994.tb00102.x

Short, H., Keasey, K., & Duxbury, D. (2002). Capital Structure, Management Ownership and Large External Shareholders: A UK Analysis. *International Journal of the Economics of Business*, *9*(3), 375–399. doi:10.1080/13571510210000010382

Sila, V., Gonzalez, A., & Hagendorff, J. (2017). Independent director reputation incentives and stock price informativeness. *Journal of Corporate Finance*, *47*, 219–235. doi:10.1016/j.jcorpfin.2017.09.018

Silva, A. L. C., & Leal, R. P. C. (2005). Corporate governance index, firm valuation and performance in Brazil. *Brazilian Review of Finance*, *3*(1), 1–18.

Simoneaux, S. L., & Stroud, C. L. (2014). Succession planning: Intentional and systematic preparation for the future. *Journal of Pension Benefits: Issues in Administration*, *21*(2), 62–63.

Simonsson, M., Johnson, P., & Ekstedt, M. (2010). The Effect of It Governance Maturity on It Governance Performance. *Information Systems Management*, *27*(1), 10-24.

Simonsson, M., Johnson, P., & Ekstedt, M. (2010). The effect of IT governance maturity on IT governance performance. *Information Systems Management*, *27*(1), 10–24. doi:10.1080/10580530903455106

Singh, V. (2007). Ethnic diversity on top corporate boards: A resource dependency perspective. *International Journal of Human Resource Management*, *18*(12), 2128–2146. doi:10.1080/09585190701695275

Sinkin, J. (2014). How to manage internal succession. *Journal of Accountancy*, *217*(2), 38.

Siraj, K., & Pillai, P. S. (2012). Comparative Study on Performance of Islamic Banks and Conventional Banks in GCC region. *Journal of Applied Finance & Banking*, *2*(3), 123–161.

Sirmon, D. G., & Hitt, M. A. (2003). Managing resources: Linking unique resources, management, and wealth creation in family firms. *Entrepreneurship Theory and Practice*, *27*(4), 339–358. doi:10.1111/1540-8520.t01-1-00013

Slaheddine, T. (2015). Impact of New UK Corporate Governance Code on Earnings Quality- Evidences from UK FTSE 350 Companies. *Business and Economics Journal*, *6*(2), 1–5. doi:10.4172/2151-6219.1000142

Soh, C., & Markus, M. L. (1995). How IT creates business value: a process theory synthesis. *ICIS 1995 Proceedings*, 4.

Solomon, A., Breunlin, D., Panattoni, K., Gustafson, M., Ransburg, D., Ryan, C., Hammerman, T., & Terrien, J. (2011). "Don't Lock Me Out": Life-Story Interviews of Family Business Owners Facing Succession. *Family Process*, *50*(2), 149–166. doi:10.1111/j.1545-5300.2011.01352.x PMID:21564058

Son, I., Lee, D., Lee, J.-N., & Chang, Y. B. (2014). Market perception on cloud computing initiatives in organizations: An extended resource-based view. *Information & Management*, *51*(6), 653–669. doi:10.1016/j.im.2014.05.006

Sorensen, D., & Peckham, K. (2002). *Business performance ıntelligence software a market evaluation*. Financial Executives Research Foundation.

Srinidhi, B., Gul, F. A., & Tsui, J. (2011). Female directors and earnings quality. *Contemporary Accounting Research*, *28*(5), 1610–1644. doi:10.1111/j.1911-3846.2011.01071.x

Sri, W. I. F., & Arief, B. M. (2018). Relationship between Company Financial Performance, Characteristic and Environmental Disclosure of ASX Listed Companies. In *E3S Web of Conferences* (Vol. 73, p. 10024). EDP Sciences.

Stavrou, E. T. (1999). Succession in family businesses: Exploring the effects of demographic factors on offspring intentions to join and take over the business. *Journal of Small Business Management*, *37*(3), 43.

Stevenson, W. B., & Radin, R. F. (2009). Social capital and social influence on the board of directors. *Journal of Management Studies*, *46*(1), 16–44. doi:10.1111/j.1467-6486.2008.00800.x

Stimper, J. L., & Judith, A. L. (2011). Does Size Matter? Economies Of Scale In The Banking Industry. *Journal of Business & Economics Research*, *9*(3).

Strobl, S., Rama, D. V., & Mishra, S. (2016). Gender diversity in compensation committees. *Journal of Accounting, Auditing & Finance*, *31*(4), 415–427. doi:10.1177/0148558X16655704

Stulz, R. M., & Williamson, R. (2003). Culture, openness, and finance. *Journal of Financial Economics*, *70*(3), 313–349. doi:10.1016/S0304-405X(03)00173-9

Sulaiman, A. N., Kesuma, F. T. M., Madjid, I., & Siregar, R. (2018). The role of good government governance principles in enhancing the performance of public organization in Aceh, Indonesia, Advances in Social Science, Education and Humanities Research. *1st Aceh Global Conference*, 292, 731-738.

Sundaramurthy, C., Pukthuanthong, K., & Kor, Y. (2014). Positive and negative synergies between the CEO's and the corporate board's human and social capital: A study of biotechnology firms. *Strategic Management Journal*, *35*(6), 845–868. doi:10.1002mj.2137

Sun, J., & Liu, G. (2014). Audit committees' oversight of bank risk-taking. *Journal of Banking & Finance*, *40*, 376–387. doi:10.1016/j.jbankfin.2013.12.015

Susanto, Y. K. (2016). The effect of audit committees and corporate governance on earnings management: Evidence from Indonesia manufacturing industry. *International Journal of Business. Economics and Law*, *10*(1), 32–37.

Tabachnick, B., & Fidell, L. (2001). *Using Multivari- ate Statistics* (3rd ed.). Harper Collins College.

Talavera, O., Yin, S., & Zhang, M. (2018). Age diversity, directors' personal values, and bank performance. *International Review of Financial Analysis*, *55*, 60–79. doi:10.1016/j.irfa.2017.10.007

Tallon, P. P. (2007). A process-oriented perspective on the alignment of information technology and business strategy. *Journal of Management Information Systems*, *24*(3), 227–268. doi:10.2753/MIS0742-1222240308

Tallon, P. P. (2008). Inside the adaptive enterprise: An information technology capabilities perspective on business process agility. *Information Technology Management*, *9*(1), 21–36. doi:10.100710799-007-0024-8

Tallon, P. P., Kraemer, K. L., & Gurbaxani, V. (2000). Executives' perceptions of the business value of information technology: A process-oriented approach. *Journal of Management Information Systems*, *16*(4), 145–173. doi:10.1080/07421222.2000.11518269

Tanikawa, T., Kim, S., & Jung, Y. (2017). Top management team diversity and firm performance: Exploring a function of age. *Team Performance Management*, *23*(3/4), 156–170. doi:10.1108/TPM-06-2016-0027

Tasheva, S., & Hillman, J. (2019). Integrating Diversity at Different Levels: Multileval Human Capital, and Demographic Diversity and Their Implications for Team Effectivness. *Academy of Management Review*, *44*(4), 12–22. doi:10.5465/amr.2015.0396

Tatoglu, E., Kula, V., & Glaister, K. W. (2008). Succession planning in family-owned businesses: Evidence from Turkey. *International Small Business Journal*, *26*(2), 155–180. doi:10.1177/0266242607086572

Teoh, S. H., Welch, I., & Wong, T. J. (1998b). Earnings management and the underperformance of seasoned equity offerings. *Journal of Financial Economics*, *50*(1), 63–99. doi:10.1016/S0304-405X(98)00032-4

Teoh, S. H., Wong, T. J., & Rao, G. R. (1998a). Are accruals during initial public offerings opportunistic? *Review of Accounting Studies*, *3*(1/2), 175–208. doi:10.1023/A:1009688619882

Terjesen, S., Couto, E. B., & Francisco, P. M. (2016). Does the presence of independent and female directors impact firm performance? A multi-country study of board diversity. *The Journal of Management and Governance*, *20*(3), 447–483. doi:10.100710997-014-9307-8

Terjesen, S., Sealy, R., & Singh, V. (2009). Women directors on corporate boards: A review and research agenda. *Corporate Governance*, *17*(3), 320–337. doi:10.1111/j.1467-8683.2009.00742.x

Thanatawee, Y. (2019). *Alignment or entrenchment? Evidence from cash holdings in Thailand.* Afro-Asian Journal of Finance and Accounting. doi:10.1504/AAJFA.2019.100978

The National Development and Reform Commission of China. (2016). *The 13th five-year plan for economic and social development of the people's republic of China (2016-2020).* Central Compilation & Translation Press. https://en.ndrc.gov.cn/newsrelease/201612/P020161207645765233498.pdf

The World Bank. (2015). *Islamic Finance*. Author.

Thiruvadi, S. (2012). Gender differences and audit committee diligence. *Gender in Management*, *27*(6), 366–379. doi:10.1108/17542411211269310

Thiruvadi, S., & Huang, H. W. (2011). Audit committee gender differences and earnings management. *Gender in Management*, *26*(7), 483–498. doi:10.1108/17542411111175469

Thompson, B., & Ke, Q. (2012). Whether environmental factors matter: Some evidence from UK property companies. *Journal of Corporate Real Estate*, *14*(1), 7–20.

Thomsen, S., & Conyon, M. (2012). *Corporate governance: Mechanisms and systems*. McGraw-Hill.

Thomsen, S., & Pedersen, T. (2000). Ownership structure and economic performance in the largest European countries. *Strategic Management Journal*, *21*(6), 689–705. doi:10.1002/(SICI)1097-0266(200006)21:6<689::AID-SMJ115>3.0.CO;2-Y

Tilling, M. V. (2004). *Refinements in Legitimacy Theory in Social and Environmental Accounting*. School of Commerce, Flinders University.

Tilt, C. A. (2009). Corporate responsibility, accounting and accountants. In *Professionals' perspectives of corporate social responsibility* (pp. 11–32). Springer.

Tiwana, A., & Konsynski, B. (2010). Complementarities between organizational IT architecture and governance structure. *Information Systems Research*, *21*(2), 288–304. doi:10.1287/isre.1080.0206

Tobin, J. (1956). The Interest-Elasticity of Transactions Demand For Cash. *The Review of Economics and Statistics*, *38*(3), 241. Advance online publication. doi:10.2307/1925776

Tong, S., Junarsin, E., & Davidson, N. W., III. (2013). *A comparison of Chinese state-owned enterprise firm's boards and private firm's boards.* Paper presented at the 23rd International Business Research Conference, Melbourne, Australia.

Toumi, K., Viviani, J. L., & Chayeh, Z. (2018). Measurement of the displaced commercial risk in Islamic Banks. *The Quarterly Review of Economics and Finance*. Advance online publication. doi:10.1016/j.qref.2018.03.001

Towler, A., Watson, A., & Surface, A., E. (. (2014). Signaling the importance of training. *Journal of Managerial Psychology*, *29*(7), 829–849. doi:10.1108/JMP-03-2012-0092

Tribo, J. A., Berrone, P., & Surroca, J. (2007). Do the type and number of blockholders influence R&D investments? New evidence from Spain. *Corporate Governance*, *15*(5), 828–842. doi:10.1111/j.1467-8683.2007.00622.x

Tricker, B. (2012). *Corporate governance: Principles, policies and practices* (2nd ed.). Oxford University Press.

Triki Damak, S. (2018). Gender diverse board and earnings management: Evidence from French listed companies. *Sustainability Accounting. Management and Policy Journal*, *9*(3), 289–312.

Truglio-Londrigan, M. (2013). Shared decision-making in home-care from the nurse's perspective: Sitting at the kitchen table–a qualitative descriptive study. *Journal of Clinical Nursing*, *22*(19-20), 2883–2895. doi:10.1111/jocn.12075 PMID:23331469

Tsai, H., & Gu, Z. (2007). Institutional Ownership and Firm Performance: Empirical Evidence from U.S. Based Publicly Traded Restuarants Firms. *Journal of Hospitality & Tourism Research (Washington, D.C.)*, *31*(1), 91. doi:10.1177/1096348006296056

Tsoi, P. (2017). *The Importance of Corporate Governance*. Available at https://www.linkedin.com/pulse

Tuovila, A. (2019). *What is Earnings Management*. Available at https://www.investopedia.com

Turel, O., Liu, P., & Bart, C. (2017). Board-Level Information Technology Governance Effects on Organizational Performance: The Roles of Strategic Alignment and Authoritarian Governance Style. *Information Systems Management*, *34*(2), 117-136.

Turel, O., Liu, P., & Bart, C. (2017). Board-Level Information Technology Governance Effects on Organizational Performance: The Roles of Strategic Alignment and Authoritarian Governance Style. *Information Systems Management*, *34*(2), 117–136. doi:10.1080/10580530.2017.1288523

Uadiale, O. M. (2010). The Impact of Board Structure on Corporate Financial Performance in Nigeria. *International Journal of Business and Management*, *5*, 155–161.

UK Science & Innovation Network. (2015). *UK science & innovation network country snapshot: China*. UK Science & Innovation Network. https://www.gov.uk/government/uploads/system/uploads/attachment_data/file/471771/Science___Innovation_Country_Snapshot_-_China.pdf

Ullah, F., Jiang, P., Shahab, Y., Li, H. X., & Xu, L. (2019). Block ownership and CEO compensation: Does board gender diversity matter? *Applied Economics*, 1–15.

Ullah, W., Ali, S., & Mehmood, S. (2017). Impact of excess control, ownership structure and corporate governance on firm performance of diversified group firms in Pakistan. *Business and Economic Review*, *9*(2), 49–72. doi:10.22547/BER/9.2.3

Ünlü, U., Yalçın, N., & Yağlı, İ. (2017). Corporate governance and firm performance: An application on BIST 30 firms with Topsis method. *Dokuz Eylül University The Journal of Graduate School of Social Sciences*, *19*(1), 63–81.

Vafeas, N. (2000). Board structure and the informativeness of earnings. *Journal of Accounting and Public Policy*, *19*(2), 139–160. doi:10.1016/S0278-4254(00)00006-5

Val, I. (2008). Enterprise Value: Governance of IT Investments. *The Val IT Framework, 2*.

Val, I. (2008a). Enterprise Value: Governance of It Investments. *The Val IT Framework,* (2).

Val, I. (2008b). *Enterprise Value: Governance of It Investments. The Val It Framework 2.0*. IT Governance Institute.

Van der Laan, S. (2009). The role of theory in explaining motivation for corporate social disclosures: Voluntary disclosures vs' solicited'disclosures. *Australasian Accounting Business & Finance Journal*, *3*(4), 15A.

Van der Walt, N., & Ingley, C. (2003). Board dynamics and the influence of professional background, gender and ethnic diversity of directors. *Corporate Governance*, *1*(3), 218–234. doi:10.1111/1467-8683.00320

van der Wiele, T., Kok, P., McKenna, R., & Brown, A. (2001). A corporate social responsibility audit within a quality management framework. *Journal of Business Ethics*, *31*(4), 285–297.

Van Der Zee, J., & De Jong, B. (1999). Alignment is not enough: Integrating business and information technology management with the balanced business scorecard. *Journal of Management Information Systems*, *16*(2), 137–158. doi:10.1080/07421222.1999.11518249

van Diepen, N. (2015). *The effect of gender, age and nationality diversity on company performance – Evidence from the Netherlands Supervisors: Evidence From Indonesian Publicly- Listed Financial Firms* (PhD thesis). University of Canberra.

Van Grembergen, W., De Haes, S., & Guldentops, E. (2004). Structures, Processes and Relational Mechanisms for It Governance. *Strategies for Information Technology Governance*, *2*(4), 1-36.

Van Grembergen, W. (2000). The Balanced Scorecard and It Governance. *IRMA Conference*, 1123-1124.

Van Grembergen, W., & De Haes, S. (2009). *Enterprise governance of information technology: achieving strategic alignment and value*. Springer Science & Business Media.

Van Grembergen, W., & De Haes, S. (2009). *Enterprise Governance of Information Technology: Achieving Strategic Alignment and Value*. Springer Science & Business Media.

Van Ness, R. K., & Seifert, C. F. (2007). Boards of directors and corporate performance: An analysis model. *Review of Business Research*, *7*(3), 11–21.

Vann, C. (2018). Big 4 Auditors, Corporate Governance, and Earnings Management under Principles- and Rules-Based Reporting Regimes: Cross-Country Empirical Evidence. *Journal of Managerial Issues*, *3*(3), 279–302.

Vassiliadis, S., & Vassiliadis, A. (2014). The Greek family businesses and the succession problem. *Procedia Economics and Finance*, *9*, 242–247. doi:10.1016/S2212-5671(14)00025-2

VComply. (2018). *9 characteristics to look out for, for good corporate governance*. Available at https://blog.v-comply.com/good-cg

Venkataraman, R., Weber, J. P., & Willenborg, M. (2008). Litigation risk, audit quality, and audit fees: Evidence from initial public offerings. *The Accounting Review*, *83*(5), 1315–1345. Advance online publication. doi:10.2308/accr.2008.83.5.1315

Vera, C. F., & Dean, M. A. (2005). An examination of the challenges daughters face in family business succession. *Family Business Review*, *18*(4), 321–345. doi:10.1111/j.1741-6248.2005.00051.x

Viet, H. N. (2015). Succession decision in Vietnamese family companies. *International Journal of Business and Management*, *10*(7), 208. doi:10.5539/ijbm.v10n7p208

Villalonga, B., & Amit, R. (2006). How do family ownership, control and management affect firm value? *Journal of Financial Economics*, *80*(2), 385–417. doi:10.1016/j.jfineco.2004.12.005

Virick, M., & Greer, C. R. (2012). Gender diversity in leadership succession: Preparing for the future. *Human Resource Management*, *51*(4), 575–600. doi:10.1002/hrm.21487

Vitez, O. (2017). *Three Types of Corporate Governance Mechanisms*. Available at https://bizfluent.com/

Vu, M.-C., Phan, T. T., & Le, N. T. (2018). Relationship between board ownership structure and firm financial performance in transitional economy: The case of Vietnam. *Research in International Business and Finance*, *45*, 512–528. doi:10.1016/j.ribaf.2017.09.002

Wade, M., & Hulland, J. (2004). Review: The resource-based view and information systems research: Review, extension, and suggestions for future research. *Management Information Systems Quarterly*, *28*(1), 107–142. doi:10.2307/25148626

Wahid, A. (2018). The Effects and the Mechanisms of Board Gender Diversity: Evidence from Financial Manipulation. *Journal of Business Ethics*, 1–21. doi:10.100710551-018-3785-6

Wahlen, J. M., Jones, J. P., & Pagach, D. P. (2012). *Intermediate Accounting: Reporting and Analysis*. South-Western Pub.

Walker, D. (2009). *A review of corporate governance in UK banks and other financial industry entities*. Academic Press.

Wan, A. W. I., Kamarudin, K. A., van Zijl, T., & Dunstan, K. (2013). Earnings quality and the adoption of IFRS based accounting standards: Evidence from an emerging market. *Asian Review of Accounting*, *21*(1), 53–73. doi:10.1108/13217341311316940

Wang, K., & Shailer, G. (2015). Ownership concentration and firm performance in emerging markets: A meta-analysis. *Journal of Economic Surveys*, *29*(2), 199–229. doi:10.1111/joes.12048

Wang, L., & Men, R. (2012). Impacts of other comprehensive income disclosure on earnings management. *Business Review International*, *3*(1), 93–101.

Wang, L., & Yung, K. (2011). Do State Enterprises Manage Earnings More than Privately Owned Firms? The Case of China. *Journal of Business Finance & Accounting*, *38*(7–8), 794–812. doi:10.1111/j.1468-5957.2011.02254.x

Wang, M. C. (2017). The relationship between firm characteristics and the disclosure of sustainability reporting. *Sustainability*, *9*(4), 624.

Wang, N., Liang, H., Zhong, W., Xue, Y., & Xiao, J. (2012). Resource structuring or capability building? An empirical study of the business value of information technology. *Journal of Management Information Systems*, *29*(2), 325–367. doi:10.2753/MIS0742-1222290211

Wang, Y., Shi, S., Nevo, S., Li, S., & Chen, Y. (2015). The interaction effect of IT assets and IT management on firm performance: A systems perspective. *International Journal of Information Management*, *35*(5), 580–593. doi:10.1016/j.ijinfomgt.2015.06.006

Wang, Y., Watkins, D., Harris, N., & Spicer, K. (2004). The relationship between succession issues and business performance: Evidence from UK family SMEs. *International Journal of Entrepreneurial Behaviour & Research*, *10*(1/2), 59–84. doi:10.1108/13552550410521380

Wang, Z., Huo, B., Qi, Y., & Zhao, X. (2016). A resource-based view on enablers of supplier integration: Evidence from China. *Industrial Management & Data Systems*, *116*(3), 416–444. doi:10.1108/IMDS-04-2015-0146

Ward, J. (2016). *Keeping the family business healthy: How to plan for continuing growth, profitability, and family leadership*. Springer.

Ward, J. L., & Aronoff, C. E. (2011). *Family meetings: How to build a stronger family and a stronger business*. Macmillan.

Watson, D., & Head, A. (2007). *Corporate finance principles & practice* (4th ed.). Prentice Hall.

Watts, R. L., & Zimmerman, J. L. (1978). Towards a positive theory of the determination of accounting standards. *The Accounting Review*, 112–134.

Watts, R., & Zimmerman, J. (1990). Positive accounting theory: A ten year perspective. *The Accounting Review*, *65*, 131–156.

Wee, Y. G., & Ibrahim, M. D. (2012). Family business success factors: Management practices, relationship among members and succession experience. *International Journal of Arts and Commerce*, *1*(6), 262–274.

Wegge, J., Roth, C., Neubach, B., Schmidt, K. H., & Kanfer, R. (2008). Age and gender diversity as determinants of performance and health in a public organization: The role of task complexity and group size. *The Journal of Applied Psychology*, *93*(6), 1301–1313. doi:10.1037/a0012680 PMID:19025249

Weir, C., & Laing, D. (2000). The performance-governance relationship: The effects of Cadbury compliance on UK quoted companies. *The Journal of Management and Governance*, *4*(4), 265–281. doi:10.1023/A:1009950903720

Weir, C., Laing, D., & McKnight, P. J. (2002). Internal and External Governance Mechanisms: Their Impact on the Performance of Large UK Public Companies. *Journal of Business Finance & Accounting*, *29*(5), 579–611. doi:10.1111/1468-5957.00444

Welch, E. (2003). The Relationship Between Ownership Structure and Performance in Listed Australian Companies. *Australian Journal of Management*, *28*(3), 287–305. doi:10.1177/031289620302800304

Wells, J. T. (2002). Occupational fraud: The audit as deterrent. *Journal Of Accountancy-New York*, *193*(4), 24–29.

Wells, J. T. (2004). New approaches to fraud deterrence. *Journal Of Accountancy-New York*, *197*(2), 72–76.

Welsh, M. J. (1992). The construction of gender: some insights from feminist psychology. *Accounting, Auditing & Accountability Journal, 5*(3).

Whatley, L. (2011). A New Model for Family Owned Business Succession. *Organization Development Journal*, *29*(4).

Wiersema, M. F., & Zhang, Y. (2011). CEO dismissal: The role of investment analysts. *Strategic Management Journal*, *32*(11), 1161–1182. doi:10.1002mj.932

Wiig, K. M. (2004). People-Focused knowledge management: how effective decision making leads to corporate success. Elsevier Butterworth–Heinemann.

Wikipedia. (2019). *Earnings management*. Available at https://en.wikipedia.org

Wilkin, C., Campbell, J., Moore, S., & Van Grembergen, W. (2012). Co-Creating Value from It in a Contracted Public Sector Service Environment: Perspectives on Cobit and Val It. *Journal of Information Systems*, *27*(1), 283-306.

Wilkin, C. L., & Chenhall, R. H. (2010). A review of IT governance: A taxonomy to inform accounting information systems. *Journal of Information Systems*, *24*(2), 107–146. doi:10.2308/jis.2010.24.2.107

Wilkin, C. L., & Chenhall, R. H. (2019). Information Technology Governance: Reflections on the Past and Future Directions. *Journal of Information Systems*, 0000. doi:10.2308/isys-52632

Wilkin, C. L., Couchman, P. K., Sohal, A., & Zutshi, A. (2016). Exploring Differences between Smaller and Large Organizations' Corporate Governance of Information Technology. *International Journal of Accounting Information Systems*, *22*, 6–25. doi:10.1016/j.accinf.2016.07.002

Wilkin, C., Campbell, J., Moore, S., & Van Grembergen, W. (2012). Co-creating value from IT in a contracted public sector service environment: Perspectives on COBIT and Val IT. *Journal of Information Systems*, *27*(1), 283–306. doi:10.2308/isys-50355

Williams, P. (2012). *Optimising Value Creation From IT Investments.* Retrieved from overnance Institute: http://www.isaca. org/Knowledge-Center/Research/Documents/Outsourcing. pdf

Williams, D. W., Zorn, M. L., Russell Crook, T., & Combs, J. G. (2013). Passing the torch: Factors influencing trans-generational intent in family firms. *Family Relations*, *62*(3), 415–428. doi:10.1111/fare.12016

Williams, P. F. (1989). The logic of positive accounting research. *Accounting, Organizations and Society*, *14*(5-6), 455–468. doi:10.1016/0361-3682(89)90011-1

Willison, B. (2009). Technology trends in Islamic investment banking. *Islamic Finance News*, *6*(19), 22–23.

Wimelda & Chandra, A. (2018). Opportunistic Behavior, External Monitoring Mechanisms, Corporate Governance, and Earnings Management. *Accounting Financial Review*, *3*(1), 49–57.

Wintoki, M. B., Linck, J. S., & Netter, J. M. (2012). Endogeneity and the dynamics of internal corporate governance. *Journal of Financial Economics*, *105*(3), 581–606. doi:10.1016/j.jfineco.2012.03.005

Witteloostuijn, A. (2007). Corporate governance in the Netherlands: An overview of the application of the Tabaksblat Code in 2004. *Corporate Governance*, *15*(6), 1106–1118. doi:10.1111/j.1467-8683.2007.00634.x

Wittsiepe, R. (2008). *IFRS for Small and Medium-Sized Enterprises: Structuring the Transition Process.* Gabler Verlag.

Woetzel, J., Seong, J., Leung, N., Ngai, J., Manyika, J., Madgvkar, A., Lund, S., & Mironenko, A. (2019). *China and the world: Inside the dynamics of a changing relationship.* McKinsey Global Institute. https://www.mckinsey.com/~/media/mckinsey/featured%20insights/china/china%20and%20the%20world%20inside%20the%20dynamics%20of%20a%20changing%20relationship/mgi-china-and-the-world-full-report-june-2019-vf.ashx

Woidtke, T. (2002). Agents Watching agents? Evidence from Pension Fund Ownership and Firm Value. *Journal of Financial Economics*, *63*(1), 99–131. doi:10.1016/S0304-405X(01)00091-5

Woolley, A. W., Aggarwal, I., & Malone, T. W. (2015). Collective Intelligence and Group Performance. *Current Directions in Psychological Science*, *24*(6), 420–424. doi:10.1177/0963721415599543

Wu, S. P.-J., Straub, D. W., & Liang, T.-P. (2015). How Information Technology Governance Mechanisms and Strategic Alignment Influence Organizational Performance: Insights from a Matched Survey of Business and It Managers. *MIS Quarterly*, *39*(2), 497-518.

Wu, C. Y. H., Hsu, H. H., & Haslam, J. (2016). Audit committees, non-audit services, and auditor reporting decisions prior to failure. *The British Accounting Review*, *48*(2), 240–256. doi:10.1016/j.bar.2015.03.001

Wu, F., Yeniyurt, S., Kim, D., & Cavusgil, S. T. (2006). The impact of information technology on supply chain capabilities and firm performance: A resource-based view. *Industrial Marketing Management*, *35*(4), 493–504. doi:10.1016/j.indmarman.2005.05.003

Wu, J., Li, S., & Li, Z. (2013). The contingent value of CEO political connections: A study on IPO performance in China. *Asia Pacific Journal of Management*, *30*(4), 1087–1114. doi:10.100710490-012-9300-1

Wu, S. P.-J., Straub, D. W., & Liang, T.-P. (2015). How information technology governance mechanisms and strategic alignment influence organizational performance: Insights from a matched survey of business and IT managers. *Management Information Systems Quarterly*, *39*(2), 497–518. doi:10.25300/MISQ/2015/39.2.10

Wuttichindanon, S. (2017). Corporate social responsibility disclosure—choices of report and its determinants: Empirical evidence from firms listed on the Stock Exchange of Thailand. *Kasetsart Journal of Social Sciences*, *38*(2), 156–162.

Xie, B., Davidson, W. III, & DaDalt, P. (2003). Earning management and corporate governance: The role of the board and the audit committee. *Journal of Corporate Finance*, *9*(3), 295–316. doi:10.1016/S0929-1199(02)00006-8

Xing, V. (2003). Corporate Governance in People's Republic of China: A new code for listed companies. *Bond Law Review*, *15*(1), 376–397.

Xu, X., Zhang, W., & Li, L. (2016). The impact of technology type and life cycle on IT productivity variance: A contingency theoretical perspective. *International Journal of Information Management*, *36*(6), 1193–1204. doi:10.1016/j.ijinfomgt.2016.08.007

Yaacob & Che-Ahmad. (2012). Adoption of FRS 138 and Audit Delay in Malaysia. *International Journal of Economics and Finance, 4*(1)..

Yaacob. (2011). *The Effect of International Financial Reporting Standards (IFRS) Adoption on Audit Pricing and Audit Timeless: Evidence from Malaysia* (PhD thesis). Universiti Utara Malaysia. http://etd.uum.edu.my/3458/

Yaacob. (2013). The Relationship between Financial Reporting Standards (FRS) 139 and Audit Pricing: The Case of Malaysia. *Journal of Modern Accounting and Auditing, 9*(5), 641-649.

Yaseen, A. T., Adam, A. K., & Fashakh, M. J. (2018). Creative Accounting Standards and its Techniques. *Opción*, *34*(86), 1611–1642. https://www.researchgate.net/publication/331687350

Yasser, Q. R., & Al Mamun, A. (2015). Effects of ownership concentration on firm performance: Pakistani evidence. *Journal of Asia Business Studies*, *9*(2), 162–176. doi:10.1108/JABS-07-2014-0047

Yeh, C. M. (2019). Ownership structure and firm performance of listed tourism firms. *International Journal of Tourism Research*, *21*(2), 165–179. doi:10.1002/jtr.2250

Yermack, D. (1996). Higher market valuation of companies with a small board of directors. *Journal of Financial Economics*, *40*(2), 185–211. Advance online publication. doi:10.1016/0304-405X(95)00844-5

Yermack, D. (2004). Remuneration, retention, and reputation incentives for outside directors. *The Journal of Finance*, *59*(5), 2281–2308. Advance online publication. doi:10.1111/j.1540-6261.2004.00699.x

Yeung, W. H., & Lento, C. (2018). Ownership structure, audit quality, board structure, and stock price crash risk: Evidence from China. *Global Finance Journal*, *37*, 1–24. doi:10.1016/j.gfj.2018.04.002

Ye, Y. (2018). *A Literature Review on the Cash Holding Issues*. Modern Economy., doi:10.4236/me.2018.96068

Yin, R. K. (2013). Validity and generalization in future case study evaluations. *Evaluation*, *19*(3), 321–332. doi:10.1177/1356389013497081

Yin, R. K. (2017). *Case study research and applications: Design and methods*. Sage publications.

Younis, N. M. (2019). The Impact of Disclosure of Other Comprehensive Income on Earnings Management: An Applied Study on the Banking Sector in the Egyptian Stock Exchange. *Scientific Journal Economics and Commerce*, Faculty of Commerce. *Ain Shams University*, *49*(1), 169–214.

Yu, X. (2017). *Chinese regulator to fast-track reform of registration-based initial public offerings system.* Telegraph. https://www.telegraph.co.uk/news/world/china-watch/business/china-to-reform-ipo-system/

Yu, F. (2008). Corporate Governance and Earnings Management. *Journal of Financial Economics*, *88*(2), 245–271. doi:10.1016/j.jfineco.2007.05.008

Yu, H. C., Sopranzetti, B. J., & Lee, C. F. (2013). The impact of banking relationships, managerial incentives, and board monitoring on corporate cash holdings: An emerging market perspective. *Review of Quantitative Finance and Accounting, 44*(2), 353–378. doi:10.100711156-013-0402-8

Yu, M., & Ashton, J. K. (2015). Board leadership structure for Chinese public listed companies. *China Economic Review, 34*, 236–248. doi:10.1016/j.chieco.2015.01.010

Zalata, A. M., Tauringana, V., & Tingbani, I. (2018). Audit committee financial expertise, gender, and earnings management: Does gender of the financial expert matter? *International Review of Financial Analysis, 55*, 170–183. doi:10.1016/j.irfa.2017.11.002

Zaman, M., Hudaib, M., & Haniffa, R. (2011). Corporate governance quality, audit fees and non-audit services fees. *Journal of Business Finance & Accounting, 38*(1-2), 165–197. doi:10.1111/j.1468-5957.2010.02224.x

Zéghal, D, & Lahmar, Z. (2007). Analyse de l'impact de la privatisation sur le niveau de divulgation volontaire dans les rapports annuels. *Revue Comptable et financière, 1*, 31-47.

Zepeda, S. J., Bengtson, E., & Parylo, O. (2012). Examining the planning and management of principal succession. *Journal of Educational Administration, 50*(2), 136–158. doi:10.1108/09578231211210512

Zhang, J. (2017). *Users' perceptions of the drivers for corporate sustainability disclosures made by Chinese listed companies* (PhD thesis). Edith Cowan University. http://ro.ecu.edu.au/cgi/viewcontent.cgi?article=2954&context=theses

Zhang, Q., Chen, L., & Feng, T. (2014). Mediation or moderation? The role of R&D investment in the relationship between corporate governance and firm performance: Empirical evidence from the Chinese IT industry. *Corporate Governance, 22*(6), 501–517. doi:10.1111/corg.12073

Zhang, Y., & Rajagopalan, N. (2010). CEO succession planning: Finally at the center stage of the boardroom. *Business Horizons, 53*(5), 455–462. doi:10.1016/j.bushor.2010.05.003

Zhou, K. Z., Gao, G. Y., & Zhao, H. (2017). State ownership and firm innovation in China: An integrated view of institutional and efficiency logics. *Administrative Science Quarterly, 62*(2), 375–404. doi:10.1177/0001839216674457

Zhu, Y. (2019). Banks' governance and innovation: Evidence from the listed firms in China. *Emerging Markets Finance & Trade, 55*(11), 2409–2424. doi:10.1080/1540496X.2018.1483229

About the Contributors

Ahmad Alqatan has published nine refereed papers in academic journals, one chapter and one book. He organised, member of committees, discussant, and presenter in more than 30 international conferences. His principal research area concerned with corporate governance, diversity earnings management, firm performance. He has awarded several times such as the prestigious 2019 Best Paper Award of the honor issuer Financial Economics Meeting: Post-crisis challenge conference and the prestigious 2019 Best poster Award of the 15th Research and Innovation Conference. He is a Co-Editor-in-Chief in eight journals.

* * *

Muhammad Arslan is currently working as Assistant Professor in Accounting and Finance at KIMEP University, Kazakhstan. He obtained his Ph.D. degree in accounting and finance from Lincoln University, New Zealand. His doctoral thesis explored the institutional determinants of good corporate governance (CG) practices in an emerging market and investigated their link with CG compliance and firm performance by using exploratory sequential research design. Dr. Arslan received Dean's Award for his exceptional Ph.D. thesis. Before joining KIMEP, he worked at Lincoln University and New Zealand tertiary institute(s) where he taught accounting and finance courses. Dr. Arslan has presented his research work at both national and international conferences such as New Zealand Finance Colloquium (NZFC), International Conference of the Journal of International Accounting Research (JIAR), International Corporate Governance Society (ICGS), AOM specialized conference, and International Conference of Corporate Governance, Ownership and Control and has published several articles in international peer-reviewed journals.

Sami Ben Mim is a Professor of economics in the High institute of Commercial Studies of Sousse, PhD in economics from Paris-Est Créteil University, Statistics engineer from INSEA Rabat Morocco.

Xihui Chen is a Lecturer in Accounting and Finance at Teesside University Business School. She joined Teesside in 2019 after completing her PhD in Corporate Governance from Nottingham Trent University. Her PhD research looks at the relationship between corporate governance, corporate entrepreneurship, and firm performance amongst Chinese listed firms. Xihui was awarded the Nottingham Trent University Vice-Chancellor Scholarship for her PhD. She was awarded the Highly Commended International Student of the Year in 2013 by the UK Council for International Students, and the National Union of Students (NUS) for outstanding performance in extracurricular activities as well as contributions at the University of Northampton and the local community. She was the 2013-2014 President of Students' Union at the University of Northampton and the Internationalisation Ambassador for Shaoguan University, P.R. China.

Yosra Makni Fourati, PhD, is an Associate Professor of Accounting at Faculté des Sciences Economiques et de Gestion at the University of Sfax, Tunisia. Her main research interests include corporate governance, international accounting, financial reporting, audit quality and taxation. She is a member of the research laboratory: Governance, Finance and Accounting.

Ahmed Hassanein is an Assistant Professor of accounting at Gulf University for Science and Technology, Kuwait, and Lecturer of accounting at Mansoura University, Egypt. He holds a PhD in Accounting from the University of Plymouth School of Management (October 2015) and an MSc in International Accounting and Finance (with distinction) from the University of Stirling (November 2011). Past academic positions held include a Lecturer (Salford University, UK), Research fellow (University of Plymouth, UK), Lecturer (Plymouth University International College, UK), and Teaching Assistant (Stirling University, UK). Dr. Hassanein has a record of publications in international peer-reviewed journals. His current research areas include: Narrative Reporting, Risk Governance, IFRS, Corporate Governance, Financial Markets, and Econometric Models.

Aboobucker Ilmudeen completed his Ph.D. at Huazhong University of Science and Technology. Currently, he is working as a Senior Lecturer in management and IT at South Eastern University of Sri Lanka. His research interests are IT governance, business IT alignment, big data, social media, and IT-enabled capabilities and innovation. He has published many research articles in peer-reviewed academic journals some of them appeared in Industrial management and data systems, European Journal of Innovation Management, Journal of Enterprise Information Management, The journal of high technology management research, etc. In addition, he has participated in local and international research conferences and fellowship programs.

Sana Masmoudi Mardassi, PhD, is an Associate Professor of Accounting at Ecole Supérieure de Commerce at the University of Sfax Tunisia. Her main research interests include internal audit and control, corporate governance, audit quality, taxation, enterprise risk management and involvement organizational.

Yosra Mbarki is a Quality Assurance Engineer at Talan Tunisie.

Nagat Mohamed Marie Younis is Assistant Professor and Supervisor of Accounting, Finance and Insurance, College of Business, Jeddah University, Al-Kamil Governorate, Saudi Arabia. She obtained his Ph.D. degree in accounting, Faculty of Commerce, Ain Shams University, Egypt. she has published several articles in international peer-reviewed journals.she has presented and published many papers in regional and international conferences and journals. she is an Associate Editor in many academic journals. And also the Supervisor of the Community Service Unit at the University of Jeddah. Founder and supervisor of the Entrepreneur Club in the College of Business. Supervisor of the Scientific Research Unit at the College of Business.

Index

F

G

I

J

K

L

M

N

O

P

Q

R

S

T

V

www.ingramcontent.com/pod-product-compliance
Lightning Source LLC
LaVergne TN
LVHW060359300926
849162LV00006B/1301